The Bill of Rights

YALE UNIVERSITY PRESS
NEW HAVEN & LONDON

The Bill

Creation and

AKHIL REED AMAR

of Rights

Reconstruction

Copyright © 1998 by Yale University. All rights reserved. This book may not be reproduced, in whole or in part, including illustrations, in any form (beyond that copying permitted by Sections 107 and 108 of the U.S. Copyright Law and except by reviewers for the public press), without written permission from the publishers.

Printed in the United States of America by R.R. Donnelley & Sons Company, Harrisonburg, Virginia

Library of Congress Cataloging-in-Publication Data

Amar, Akhil Reed.
The Bill of Rights : creation and reconstruction / Akhil Reed Amar.
p.   cm.
Includes bibliographical references and index.
ISBN 0-300-07379-8 (cloth : alk. paper)
ISBN 0-300-08277-0 (pbk. : alk. paper)
1. United States. Constitution. 1st–10th Amendments. 2. Constitutional amendments—United States. 3. Civil rights—United States. I. Title.
KF4750.A436 1998
342.73'085—dc21   97-38370

A catalogue record for this book is available from the British Library.

The paper in this book meets the guidelines for permanence and durability of the Committee on Production Guidelines for Book Longevity of the Council on Library Resources.

For Vinita

Contents

Acknowledgments   ix

Introduction   xi

PART I CREATION

One • First Things First   3

Two • *Our* First Amendment   20

Three • The Military Amendments   46

Four • Searches, Seizures, and Takings   64

Five • Juries   81

Six • The Popular-Sovereignty Amendments   119

PART II RECONSTRUCTION

Seven • Antebellum Ideas   137

Eight • The Reconstruction Amendment: Text   163

Nine • The Reconstruction Amendment: History   181

Ten • Refining Incorporation   215

Eleven • Reconstructing Rights   231

Twelve • A New Birth of Freedom   284

Afterword   295

Appendix: Amendments I–X and XIV   309

Notes   313

Index   397

Acknowledgments

I am reminded of the exasperated barber who, after an hour's hard work, sighed that no matter how much he tried, the cut was still too short. My personal and intellectual debts are such that, no matter how much I work on my thank-you list, it will always be too short. To those whom I cannot name here, I say, you know who you are, and so do I. Bless you.

Now, for my short list. Among my colleagues at Yale, I owe a special measure of gratitude to Bruce Ackerman, Jack Balkin, Guido Calabresi, Owen Fiss, Joe Goldstein, Tony Kronman, Burke Marshall, Jed Rubenfeld, and Reva Siegel for the countless hours they have spent nourishing me and nudging me forward. Among my students—who collectively inspired this book—I have particularly benefited from the assistance and insights of Ryan Bounds, Shawn Chen, Jacob Cogan, Brannon Denning, Emmet Flood, Leslie Hakala, Hannah Horsley, Erez Kalir, Brian Kalt, Neal Katyal, Kurt Lash, Renée Lettow, Doug Lichtman, Sandra Rierson, Jeff Rosen, Amit Saluja, Teena-Ann Sankoorikal, Cynthia Ward, and John Yoo. I am also most grateful for the warm support of

Vik Amar, Dick Aynes, Les Benedict, Jon Blue, Michael Kent Curtis, Roger Newman, Paul Schwartz, and Ron Wright, each of whom read the entire manuscript and offered detailed suggestions and wise counsel. My deepest debt of all is to my wife, Vinita. This book is for her.

I have been pondering the ideas in this book for almost a decade, and early versions of some of these ideas have appeared in articles published in volumes 100 and 101 of the *Yale Law Journal* and volume 2 of the *Roger Williams University Law Review*. Portions of this book derive from these articles and appear here with the permission of the Yale Law Journal Company and Fred B. Rothman and Company.

Introduction

The Bill of Rights stands as the high temple of our constitutional order—America's Parthenon—and yet we lack a clear view of it. Instead of being studied holistically, the Bill has been broken up into discrete blocks of text, with each segment examined in isolation. In a typical law school curriculum, for example, the First, Ninth, and Tenth Amendments are integrated into an introductory survey course on Constitutional Law; the Sixth, Eighth, and much of the Fifth are taught in Criminal Procedure; the Seventh is covered in Civil Procedure; the Fifth Amendment takings clause is featured in Property; the Fourth Amendment becomes a course unto itself, or is perhaps pushed into Criminal Procedure or Evidence (because of the judicially created exclusionary rule); and the Second and Third are ignored.[1]

When we move beyond law school classrooms to legal scholarship, a similar pattern emerges. Each clause is typically considered separately, and some amendments—again, the Second and Third—are generally ignored by mainstream constitutional theorists.[2] Indeed, no legal academic in the twentieth century has attempted to write in a truly comprehensive way about the Bill of Rights as a whole.[3] So too, today's scholars rarely consider the rich interplay between the original Constitution and the Bill of Rights. Leading constitutional casebooks treat "the structure of government" and "individual rights" as separate blocks[4] (facilitating curricular bifurcation of these subjects into different semesters), and the conventional wisdom seems to be that the original Constitution was concerned with the former, the Bill of Rights with the latter.

In Part One I challenge the prevailing practice by offering an integrated overview of the Bill of Rights as originally conceived, an overview that illustrates how its provisions related to each other and to those of the original Constitution. In the process I hope to refute the prevailing notion that the Bill of Rights and the original Constitution represented two very different types of regulatory strategies.

Conventional wisdom acknowledges that the original Constitution proposed by the Philadelphia convention focused primarily on issues of organizational structure and democratic self-governance: federalism, separation of powers, bicameralism, representation, republican government, and constitutional amendment. By contrast, the Bill of Rights proposed by the first Congress is generally thought to have little to say about such issues. Its dominant approach, according to conventional wisdom, was rather different: to vest individuals and minorities with substantive rights against popular majorities.[5] I disagree.

Individual and minority rights did constitute a motif of the Bill of Rights—but not the sole, or even the dominant, motif. A close look at the Bill reveals structural ideas tightly interconnected with language of rights; states' rights and majority rights alongside individual and minority rights; and protection of various intermediate associations—church, militia, and jury—designed to create an educated and virtuous electorate. The genius of the Bill was not to downplay organizational structure but to deploy it, not to impede popular majorities but to empower them.

Consider, in this regard, Madison's famous assertion in *The Federalist* No. 51 that "[i]t is of great importance in a republic not only to guard the society against the oppression of its rulers, but to guard one part of the society against the injustice of the other part."[6] The conventional understanding of the Bill seems to focus almost exclusively on the second issue (protection of minority against majority) while ignoring the first (protection of the people against self-interested government). Yet as I shall show, this first issue was indeed first in the minds of those who framed the Bill of Rights. To borrow from the language of economics, the Bill of Rights was centrally concerned with controlling the "agency costs" created by the specialization of labor inherent in a representative government. In such a government, the people (the "principals") delegate power to run day-to-day affairs to a small set of specialized government officials (the "agents") who might try to rule in their own self-interest, contrary to the interests and expressed wishes of the people. To minimize such self-dealing ("agency costs"), the Bill of Rights protected the ability of local governments to monitor and deter federal abuse, ensured that ordinary citizens would participate in the federal administration of justice through various jury provisions, and preserved the transcendent sovereign right of a majority of the people themselves to alter or abolish government and thereby pronounce the last word on constitutional questions. The essence of the Bill of Rights was more structural than not, and more majoritarian than counter.

But if all this is so, how can we account for the conventional wisdom that the Bill of Rights is overwhelmingly about rights rather than structure—and individual, countermajoritarian rights at that? The answer, I believe, lies not in the 1780s and 1790s but in the 1860s—in particular in the letter and spirit of the Fourteenth Amendment. In Part Two I try to show how the Reconstruction Amendment transformed the nature of the original Bill of Rights, leaving us with something much closer to the Bill as conventionally understood today.

The relationship between the original Bill of Rights and the Fourteenth Amendment has typically been framed by the question of whether the latter "incorporates" the former against states, and if so, how. Although this is one of the most important questions in all of constitutional law, no dominant answer has emerged, and with good reason.

Each of the three main approaches—Hugo Black's "total incorporation" theory, William Brennan's "selective incorporation" model, and Felix Frankfurter's "fundamental fairness" doctrine—contains both a deep insight and a fatal flaw. I shall therefore propose a synthesis of their three divergent approaches to break the current stalemate.

This synthesis, which I shall call "refined incorporation," begins with Black's insight that *all* of the privileges and immunities of citizens recognized in the Bill of Rights became "incorporated" against states by dint of the Fourteenth Amendment. But not all of the provisions of the original Bill of Rights were indeed rights of citizens. Some instead were at least in part rights of states, and as such, awkward to fully incorporate *against* states. Most obvious, of course, is the Tenth Amendment, but other provisions of the first eight amendments resembled the Tenth much more than Justice Black admitted. Thus there is deep wisdom in Justice Brennan's invitation to consider incorporation clause by clause— or more precisely still, right by right—rather than wholesale. But having identified the right unit of analysis, Brennan posed the wrong question: Is a given provision of the original Bill a *fundamental* right? The right question is whether the provision guarantees a privilege or immunity of *individual citizens* rather than a right of *states* or the *public* at large. And when we ask this question, clause by clause and right by right, we must be attentive to the possibility, flagged by Frankfurter, that a particular principle in the Bill of Rights may change its shape in the process of absorption into the Fourteenth Amendment. This change can occur for reasons rather different from those that Frankfurter offered. (He, more than Black and Brennan, diverted attention from the right question by his insistence on abstract conceptions of "fundamental fairness" and "ordered liberty" as the sole Fourteenth Amendment litmus tests, and by his disregard of the language and history of the privileges-or-immunities clause.) Certain alloyed provisions of the original Bill—part citizen right, part state right—may need to undergo refinement and filtration before their citizen-right elements can be absorbed by the Fourteenth Amendment. And other provisions may become less majoritarian and populist, and more libertarian, as they are repackaged in the Fourteenth Amendment as liberal civil rights—"privileges or immunities" of individuals—rather than republican political "right[s] of the people," as in the original Bill.

With the new analytic framework of refined incorporation in place, we can trace the ways in which various provisions of the original Bill are transformed when they come into contact with the Fourteenth Amendment. In area after area—freedom of speech and of the press, the right to keep and bear arms, the right of jury trial, the unenumerated rights retained, and so on—we shall chart how the gravitational pull of the Fourteenth Amendment has altered the trajectory of the original Bill. The point is true even more broadly; the general concept of a "Bill of Rights"—indeed, the very phrase itself—has been reshaped by the Fourteenth Amendment. Nowhere is this more obvious than in the writings of Hugo Black, whose Fourteenth Amendment theory of total incorporation required him to redefine the Bill of Rights as comprising only the first eight amendments, rather than the first ten.

In short: in Part One I contest conventional wisdom about the Bill of Rights by exploring its Creation, and in Part Two I confirm conventional wisdom about the Bill by explicating its Reconstruction.*

---

*A topic as vast as the Bill of Rights has obviously forced me to make hard choices to omit or downplay certain issues, themes, and approaches while emphasizing others. A few words about my criteria of selection are in order at the outset. (A more comprehensive and theoretical discussion of methodology appears in my Afterword.) This book aims to offer a general theory of the Bill of Rights—that is, an account that seeks to illuminate not simply individual clauses of the Bill but their relation to each other and to other constitutional provisions. Thus in Part One I pay special attention to questions obscured by the clausebound approach that now dominates constitutional discourse: Why are various clauses lumped together in a single amendment, and how do they interrelate? What themes connect amendments? What words, phrases, and ideas link the original Constitution and the Bill? How do structural ideas and rights fit together? And so on. In Part Two I examine the intricate interplay between the Bill and the later Fourteenth Amendment. This, too, is a topic obscured by dominant constitutional discourse. Frankfurter's followers deny that there is any logical link between the Fourteenth Amendment and the Bill of Rights as such, whereas incorporationists posit an essentially mechanical relationship that begs many of the most interesting questions.

Part I

Creation

Overleaf, John Trumbull, *The Death of General Warren at the Battle of Bunker's Hill, 17 June 1775* (1786) Yale University Art Gallery, Trumbull Collection

First Things First

The 1789 Bill of Rights was, unsurprisingly, a creature of its time. Yet because these eighteenth-century words play such an active role in twentieth-century legal discourse, we may at times forget that more than two centuries separate us from the world that birthed the Bill. Before we fix our gaze on this eighteenth-century document, let us briefly consider how nineteenth- and twentieth-century events and ideas have organized our legal thinking, predisposing us to see certain features of the Bill of Rights and to overlook others. And before we rush to examine the words that are first in our modern Bill of Rights, let us briefly consider the words that were first in the original Bill of Rights.

Modern Blinders

The Ideology of Nationalism We inhabit a world whose constitutional terrain is dominated by landmark Supreme Court cases that invalidated state laws and administrative practices in the name of individual constitutional rights. Living in the shadow of *Brown v. Board of Education*[1] and the second Reconstruction of the 1960s, many lawyers embrace a tradition that views state governments as the quintessential threat to individual and minority rights, and federal officials—especially federal courts—as the special guardians of those rights.[2]

This nationalist tradition has deep roots. Over the course of two centuries, the Supreme Court has struck down state and local action with far more regularity than it has invalidated acts of coordinate national branches.[3] Early in this century, Justice Holmes declared, "I do not think the United States would come to an end if we lost our power to declare an Act of Congress void. I do think the Union would be imperiled if we could not make that declaration as to the laws of the several States."[4] Professor Thayer's famous 1893 essay on judicial review also embraced an expansive role for federal courts in reviewing state legislation, even as Thayer preached judicial deference to congressional acts of doubtful constitutionality.[5] Holmes and Thayer had reached maturity during the Civil War era, and they understood from firsthand experience that the constitutional amendments adopted following the war—particularly the Fourteenth Amendment—evinced a similar suspicion of state governments.

In fact, the nationalist tradition is far older than Reconstruction; its deepest roots lie in Philadelphia, not Appomattox. One of the Federalists' most important goals was to forge a strong set of federally enforceable rights against abusive state governments, a goal dramatized by the catalogue of rights in Article I, section 10—the Federalist forebear of the Fourteenth Amendment.[6] Indeed, the very effort to create a strong central government drew much of its life from the Federalists' dissatisfaction with small-scale politics and their belief that an "enlargement" of the government's geographic "sphere" would improve the caliber of public decision-making.[7] The classic statement of this view is Madison's *Federalist* No. 10.

Alongside this nationalist tradition, however, lay a states'-rights tradition—also championed by Madison—that extolled the ability of local governments to protect citizens against abuses by central authorities. Classic statements of this view include Madison's *Federalist* No. 46, his *Virginia Resolutions of 1798,* and his *Report of 1800.* Heavy traces of these ideas appear even in the work of the strong centralizer Alexander Hamilton.[8]

The foundations of this states'-rights tradition are even older than those of the nationalist tradition—indeed, older than the Union itself. In the seventeenth century, British North America began not as a single continentwide juridical entity but as a series of different and distinct colonies, each founded at a different moment with a distinct charter, a distinct history, a distinct immigration pattern, a distinct set of laws and legal institutions, and so on. In 1760, "Virginia" was, legally speaking, an obvious fait accompli—its House of Burgesses had been meeting since the 1620s—but "America," as a legal entity, was still waiting to be born. During the fateful years between the end of the French and Indian War and the beginning of the Revolutionary one, colonial governments took the lead in protecting their citizens from perceived Parliamentary abuses. Colonial legislatures kept a close eye on the central government; sounded public alarms whenever they saw oppression in the works; and organized political, economic, and (ultimately) military opposition to perceived British evils.[9] The rallying cry of the Revolution nicely illustrates how states' rights and citizens' rights were seen as complementary rather than conflicting: "No taxation without representation" sounds in terms of both federalism and the rights of Englishmen.[10]

The complementary character of states' rights and personal rights was dramatized yet again by the Virginia and Kentucky Resolutions of 1798–1800. Self-consciously echoing their colonial forebears, legislators in these two states sounded the alarm when they saw the central government taking actions that they deemed dangerous and unconstitutional.* Like its 1776 predecessor, the "Revolution of 1800" fused rhetoric

---

*Eight years earlier, the Virginia legislature had adopted resolutions denouncing as unconstitutional the federal government's assumption of state war debts. *Virginia Resolutions on the Assumption of State Debts, in* DOCUMENTS OF AMERICAN HISTORY 155–56 (Henry Steele Commager ed., 9th ed. 1973) (describing state legislators as "guardians . . . of the rights and interests of their constituents" and "sentinels placed by them over the ministers of the federal government, to shield it from their encroachments, or at least to sound an alarm when it is threatened with invasion"). This 1790 declaration is an important link in the historical chain connecting the anti-Parliamentary activity of colonial legislatures before 1776 with the resolutions of 1798. Note especially the use of the revealing word *ministers* to describe federal officers.

of federalism and freedom: the Alien and Sedition Acts were seen as violating both the First and the Tenth Amendments.[11] Although many other state legislatures rejected Kentucky's open-ended claims that a state could nullify a federal law, state legislatures as a whole played a central role in the denouement of the new nation's first constitutional crisis. Through their power to select senators and presidential electors, state lawmakers helped sweep the high-Federalist friends of the Alien and Sedition Acts out of national office in the election of 1800, replacing them with Jeffersonians who allowed the repressive acts to expire.

Madison was quite careful to identify the limits, as well as the affirmative scope, of states' rights. State governments could monitor the federal one and mobilize political opposition to federal laws seen as oppressive, but no state entity could unilaterally nullify those laws or secede from the Union.[12] Moreover, Madison's scheme gave the federal government a crucial role in protecting citizens from abusive state governments. Later spokesmen for the states'-rights position, like John C. Calhoun, Jefferson Davis, and Alexander Stephens, disregarded these vital limits. Not only did their arguments on behalf of nullification and secession misread the Constitution's federal structure,[13] but these arguments were deployed on behalf of slavery, the ultimate violation of human dignity. Once again, a war was fought on American soil over intertwined issues of states' rights and human rights, but this time with a critical difference. In sharp contrast to the Revolutionaries' rhetoric of the 1770s, the Rebels' rhetoric of federalism in the 1860s came to be seen as conflicting with, rather than supportive of, true freedom.

Twentieth-century Americans are still living with the legacy of the Civil War, with modern rhetorical battle lines tracking those laid down more than a century ago. Thus, in the tradition of Thaddeus Stevens, twentieth-century nationalists recognize the need for a strong national government to protect individuals against abusive state governments, but often ignore the threat posed by a monstrous central regime unchecked by competing power centers. Conversely, in the tradition of Jefferson Davis, twentieth-century states' rightists wax eloquent about the dangers of a national government run rampant, but regularly deploy the rhetoric of states' rights to defend states' wrongs. Sadly, *states' rights* and *federalism* have often served as code words for racial injustice and disregard for the rights of local minorities[14]—code words for a worldview far closer to Jefferson Davis's than James Madison's.

What has been lost in this twentieth-century debate is the crucial Madisonian insight that localism and liberty can sometimes work together rather than at cross-purposes. This is one of the themes that I hope will emerge from a fresh look at Madison's Bill of Rights.

The Logistics of Incorporation Through the Fourteenth Amendment, almost all the provisions of the Bill of Rights have come to be "incorporated" against the states. Although generally sound, the process of incorporation has had the unfortunate effect of blinding us to the ways in which the Bill has thereby been transformed. Originally a set of largely structural guarantees applying only against the federal government, the Bill has become a bulwark of rights against all government conduct. Originally drafted to protect the general citizenry from a possibly unrepresentative government, the Bill has been pressed into the service of protecting vulnerable minorities from dominant social majorities. Given the core concerns of the Fourteenth Amendment, all this is fitting, but because of the peculiar logistics of incorporation, the Fourteenth Amendment itself often seems to drop out of the analysis. We *appear* to be applying the Bill of Rights directly; the Reconstruction Amendment is mentioned only in passing if at all.[15] Like people with spectacles who often forget that they are wearing them, most lawyers read the Bill of Rights through the lens of the Fourteenth Amendment without realizing how powerfully that lens has refracted what they see.

It is time, then, to take off these spectacles and try to see how the Bill of Rights looked *before* Reconstruction. Only then can we fully appreciate some of its most important features, as originally conceived. As we shall see, when we remove modern spectacles and blinders, a rather different Bill of Rights comes into view; what follows in this chapter and the next five chapters may sometimes startle modern readers. But upon reflection, we should not be surprised to learn that those present at the Creation inhabited a world very different from our own. And only after we understand their world and their original vision can we begin to assess, in a self-conscious and systematic way, how much of this vision, if any, has survived—or should survive—subsequent constitutional developments.*

Let us begin by considering two provisions that are not part of our Bill of Rights, but were part of Madison's.

Size and Representation

The First Congress proposed a Bill of Rights that contained twelve amendments, but only the last ten were ratified by the requisite three-fourths of state legislatures in 1791, thereby becoming "valid to all Intents and Purposes, as Part of [the] Constitution."[16] Thus the words that we refer to as the First Amendment really weren't "first" in the minds of the First Congress. Hear, then, the words that began *their* Bill of Rights:

> Article the first. . . . After the first enumeration required by the first Article of the Constitution, there shall be one Representative for every thirty thousand, until the number shall amount to one hundred, after which, the proportion shall be so regulated by Congress, that there shall be not less than one hundred Representatives, nor less than one Representative for every forty thousand persons, until the number of Representatives shall amount to two hundred, after which the proportion shall be so regulated by Congress, that there shall not be less than two hundred Representatives, nor more than one Representative for every fifty thousand persons.[17]

This would-be First Amendment obviously sounds primarily in structure; it is an explicit modification of the structural rule set out in Article I, section 2, which mandates that the "Number of Representatives shall not exceed one for every thirty Thousand" constituents.[18] Had this original First Amendment prevailed in the state-ratification process rather than suffering a narrow defeat in the 1790s—it fell one state short of the requisite three-fourths—it would no doubt be much harder for twentieth-century citizens and scholars to ignore the Bill of Rights' emphasis on structure, for the Bill would begin and end with structural pro-

*This assessment lies at the heart of Part Two.

visions. As it stands instead, the fact that the most evident structural provision (our Tenth Amendment, their Twelfth) sits at the end of the decalogue may mislead us into viewing it as an afterthought, discontinuous
with the perceived individual-rights theme of the earlier provisions. The
original First Amendment suggests otherwise. It is poetic that *this*
amendment was first, for it responded to perhaps the single most important concern of the Anti-Federalists.*

Part of this concern focused on demography and geography—on the
numerical size of the polity and the spatial size of the nation. Classical
political theory had suggested that republics could thrive only in geographically and demographically small societies, where citizens would
be shaped by a common climate and culture, would hold homogeneous
worldviews, would know each other, and could meet face-to-face to deliberate on public issues. Models of such republics included the Greek
city-states and pre-Imperial Rome.[19]

The Federalists' Contribution The Federalists stood this orthodoxy on its
head by claiming that a large and modestly heterogeneous society could
actually produce a more stable republic than could a small city or state.
Madison's *Federalist* No. 10 is today recognized as the most elegant and
incisive presentation of this revolutionary idea, but in fact the entire
introductory section of *The Federalist* sought to confront squarely the
Anti-Federalist concern about size. In *The Federalist* No. 2, John Jay
noted the many ways in which (white) Americans shared a basic homo-
geneity that constituted them as one people, ethnically, culturally, lin-
guistically, historically, commercially, and geographically. Over the next
seven papers, Jay and Hamilton sketched the inability of small republics
to defend themselves against external threats while maintaining internal democracy. This was primarily a geopolitical and military argument
for an extended nation.[20] Finally, Madison took the stage in Nos. 10 and
14, stressing the purely domestic reasons for preferring a large state. The
last sentence of No. 14 marked the end of the first section of *The Feder-*

---

*For a less poetic and more prosaic reason for the "firstness" of the original First
Amendment, see Chapter 2.

alist, rhetorically signaling closure by its echo (". . . you are now to deliberate . . . ") of the first sentence of No. 1 (". . . you are called upon to deliberate . . . ").

Madison's first two *Federalist* papers demonstrate the rich interplay among the issues of national size, legislative size, and representation. (The last issue, of course, had played a central role in the debates leading up to and growing out of the American Revolution; anyone claiming that the new Constitution vindicated rather than betrayed that Revolution had to address the subject of representation head on.) Direct democracy, Madison argued, was impossible in any society more expansive than a small city-state.[21] Even in tiny Rhode Island, the mass of citizens could not assemble regularly to decide matters of state; instead, citizens had to rely on a smaller body of government agents to represent them.[22] Rather than cause for alarm, representation was a great blessing in Madison's eyes. A small, select group of representatives could "refine"[23] public opinion and produce more virtuous, wise, and stable decisions. The image here is akin to skimming a small amount of cream (the representatives) off the top of a bucket of milk (the polity).[24] Just as representative systems were better (creamier) than direct democracies, so a large society was preferable to a small one. In order to get the same absolute amount of cream, we need skim an even thinner (and thus richer) layer off the top of a bigger bucket. This last argument, of course, presupposes an absolute numerical limit on the size of the legislature: no matter how large the polity, the legislature could not expand beyond a certain number (just as direct democracy could not expand beyond a certain size), after which deliberation and discussion would be impossible.[25]

Yet even Madison noted that the skimming principle should not be carried to extremes: "By enlarging too much the number of electors [per representative], you render the representative too little acquainted with all their local circumstances and lesser interests . . . . "[26]

The Anti-Federalists' Critique   Probably the deepest Anti-Federalist objection to the Constitution was that the document took the skimming principle too far: Congress was too small, too rich, too "refined." Indeed, this *structural* concern underlay most of the Anti-Federalists' other arguments. Because the legislature was so small, the Anti-Federalists feared that only great men with reputations spanning wide geographic areas could secure election.[27] Thus for Anti-Federalists the Constitution was at heart an aristocratic document, notwithstanding both its ringing populist proclamations ("We the People . . . ") and the process of ratification itself, which was far more democratic than the process by which the Articles of Confederation and most state constitutions had been adopted.[28] Anti-Federalists feared that the aristocrats who would control Congress would have an insufficient sense of sympathy with, and connectedness to, ordinary people. Unlike state legislators, lordly men in Congress would disdain their lowly constituents, who would in turn lose faith in the national government. In the end, the new government would be obliged to rule through corruption, force, and fear—with monopolies and standing armies—rather than through mutual confidence.[29]

Thus Anti-Federalists rejected the novel logic of *The Federalist* No. 10 in favor of more orthodox political science: because of the attenuated chain of representation, Congress would be far *less* trustworthy than state legislatures.

The Anti-Federalists' lack of confidence in the federal legislature's ability to truly represent the people made them insist all the more on popular representation in the judicial branch. Precisely because ordinary citizens could not aspire to serve as national legislators, there was a vital need to guarantee their role as jurors. This was especially true because national laws, adopted by distant men unfamiliar with local circumstances, would need to be modified in their application by representatives better acquainted with local needs and customs.[30]

The Anti-Federalists were not simply concerned that Congress was too small relatively—too small to be truly representative of the great diversity of the nation. Congress was also too small absolutely—too small to be immune from cabal and intrigue. As Gilbert Livingston pointed out during the New York ratifying convention, the extraordinary powers of the Senate were vested in twenty-six men, fourteen of whom would constitute a quorum, of which eight would make up a majority.[31]

Although the House of Representatives looked much better, with its initial allocation of sixty-five members, it could conceivably end up even worse, as Patrick Henry noted in the Virginia ratifying convention: "In the clause under consideration, there is the strangest language that I can conceive. . . . 'The number shall not exceed one for every thirty thousand.' This may be satisfied by one representative from each state. Let our numbers be ever so great, this immense continent may, by this artful expression, be reduced to have but thirteen representatives."[32] And of course, by logic similar to Livingston's, seven representatives could conceivably form a House quorum, four of whom would constitute a majority.

Friends of the Constitution were not oblivious to these concerns, as Madison's own language in *The Federalist* shows.[33] In fact, at the Philadelphia convention Madison had championed a motion to double the initial size of the House of Representatives from 65 to 130 members: "A *majority* of a *Quorum* of 65 members, was too small a number to represent the whole inhabitants of the U. States; They would not possess enough of the confidence of the people, and wd. be too sparsely taken from the people, to bring with them all the local information which would be frequently wanted."[34] Though Madison's motion went down to defeat in July, another proposal to increase the initial House size resurfaced in early September. Madison seconded the motion, and even the high-toned Hamilton supported it: "Col: Hamilton expressed himself with great earnestness and anxiety in favor of the motion. He avowed himself a friend to a vigorous Government, but would declare at the same time, that he held it essential that the popular branch of it should be on a broad foundation. He was seriously of the opinion that the House of Representatives was on so narrow a scale as to be really dangerous, and to warrant a jealousy in the people for their liberties."[35] Though this measure, too, was voted down by the delegates, the issue of House size would not die. Indeed, the thirty-thousand clause set the scene for a dramatic finale to the Philadelphia convention in which George Washington, for the first and last time, took center stage to address his fellow delegates on a substantive issue.

The date was September 17, 1787—the final day of the convention.

Two days earlier the convention had unanimously agreed to a final text and had authorized the engrossment of the parchment for signing.[36] This final version provided that the number of Representatives not exceed "one for every *forty* thousand." Moments before the copy was finally voted upon and signed, Nathaniel Gorham of Massachusetts "said if it was not too late he could wish, for the purpose of lessening objections to the Constitution, that the clause . . . might be yet reconsidered, in order to strike out 40,000 & insert 'thirty thousand.'"[37] The irregularity of this eleventh-hour motion only underscored the importance of the issue. Equally irregular was the response of presiding officer Washington, who had until then officially maintained a scrupulous silence on all substantive issues:

> When the President rose, for the purpose of putting the question, he said that although his situation had hitherto restrained him from offering his sentiments on questions depending in the House, and it might be thought, ought now to impose silence on him, yet he could not forbear expressing his wish that the alteration proposed might take place. It was much to be desired that the objections to the plan recommended might be made as few as possible—The smallness of the proportion of Representatives had been considered by many members of the Convention, an insufficient security for the rights & interests of the people. He acknowledged that it had always appeared to himself among the exceptionable parts of the plan; and late as the present moment was for admitting amendments, he thought this of so much consequence that it would give much satisfaction to see it adopted.[38]

With the weight of its president behind the measure, the convention unanimously adopted the amendment. An erasure was made in the parchment, the word *thirty* was inserted where *forty* had been, and the document was then finally approved and signed. Thus, even before the ratification struggle took shape, Federalist supporters of the Constitution showed themselves sensitive to the structural issue of congressional size.

During the ratification debates Anti-Federalists seized upon the issue, taking up Publius's challenge to frame their opposition in structural terms. In *The Federalist* No. 23, Hamilton laid down the gauntlet—"the adversaries of the plan promulgated by the convention would have given a better impression of their candor if they had confined themselves to showing that the internal structure of the proposed government was such as to render it unworthy of the confidence of the people"[39]—and in No. 32 he double-dared the doubters: "[A]ll observations founded upon the danger of usurpation ought to be referred to the composition and structure of the government, not to the nature or extent of its powers."[40]

Nowhere was Anti-Federalist concern with size more evident than in the ratification conventions themselves. Of the six states where conventions endorsed various amendments before the First Congress met—Massachusetts, South Carolina, New Hampshire, Virginia, New York, and North Carolina—all but South Carolina proposed a secure minimum size for the House of Representatives.[41] This proposal was never placed lower than second on an ordinarily long list of desired amendments. Only one principle ever ranked higher—the idea of limited federal power that eventually made its way into our Tenth (their Twelfth) Amendment.[42] In the words of Melancton Smith, a leading Anti-Federalist, at the New York ratifying convention, "We certainly ought to fix, in the Constitution, those things which are essential to liberty. *If any thing falls under this description, it is the number of the legislature.*"[43]

*The First Amendment Compromise** Given all this, it is not surprising that the First Congress's First Amendment attempted further fine tuning of the structure of representation in the lower house. Nor is it surprising that Virginia, the home state of both Madison and Henry, ratified this

---

*As will be evident throughout Part One, much of the original Bill of Rights can be seen as a compromise between Federalists and Anti-Federalists, epitomized by Federalist James Madison's efforts to find common ground with, and to ease the fears of, Anti-Federalist critics of the Philadelphia Constitution.

amendment separately, weeks before approving the rest of the Bill of Rights.[44] What remains to be explained is why the amendment failed, even by a single vote.[45] Although the legislative history on this point is sparse, a close analysis of the text itself yields a couple of possible explanations.

First, the amendment's intricate mathematical formula made little sense. If the population rose from eight to nine million in a decade, the requirement that there be at least two hundred representatives would be inconsistent with the requirement that there be not more than one representative for every fifty thousand people. In effect, the amendment required the population to jump from eight to at least ten million in a single decade. The mathematical oddness of the text is confirmed by the lean legislative history that does exist. When initially passed by the House of Representatives, the amendment was worded identically to its final version with one exception: its last clause provided for "not . . . less than one Representative for every fifty thousand persons."[46] So worded, the proposal was sent to the Senate, along with all the other amendments proposed by the House. When the Senate adopted a Bill of Rights whose wording and substance diverged from the House version, the two chambers convened a joint committee to harmonize the proposed bills.[47] At this conference, the word *more* was inexplicably substituted for *less*, and the conference paste job was hurriedly adopted by both houses under the shadow of imminent adjournment, apparently without deep deliberation about the substitution's (poor) fit with the rest of the clause.[48] Thus it is quite possible that the technical glitches in the First Amendment's formula became evident only during the later process of ratifying Congress's proposed amendments.

Second, what the First Amendment promised in the short term— increased congressional size—it took back in the long run. Its final clause established a maximum, not a minimum, on congressional size. Even worse, this maximum was more stringent than that in the existing Constitution. In effect, the amendment dangled the bait of more "democracy" now in exchange for more "aristocracy" in the future. Some committed democrats may have been wary of snatching that bait. Tellingly, not a single state ratifying convention had proposed a stricter constitutional maximum on the size of the House.[49]

Why, then, did the joint House-Senate committee insert a maximum? The lack of extant records of the committee's deliberations requires us to speculate, but the most plausible culprit is James Madison, one of three representatives (the other two being John Vining and Roger Sherman) appointed by the House. As noted earlier,[50] Madison's *Federalist* presupposed an absolute maximum on the size of the legislature:

> Sixty or seventy men may be more properly trusted with a given degree of power than six or seven. But it does not follow that six or seven hundred would be proportionably a better depository. And if we carry on the supposition to six or seven thousand, the whole reasoning ought to be reversed. . . . In all very numerous assemblies, of whatever characters composed, passion never fails to wrest the scepter from reason. Had every Athenian citizen been a Socrates, every Athenian assembly would still have been a mob.[51]

Thus when Madison initially offered up to the First Congress his proposed amendments to the Constitution, he integrated both minimum and maximum, without specifying the numbers: "the number shall never be less than ____, nor more than ____."[52] Although the full House eventually rejected the idea of a maximum,[53] Madison may well have seen his appointment to the joint committee as a chance to slip his idea back in—especially given that fellow committee member Sherman had earlier voiced doubts about very large assemblies.[54]

A final, more obvious explanation for the failure of the First Amendment focuses on Delaware, the only state that ratified the last ten amendments while rejecting the first.[55] The Constitution guaranteed each state at least one seat in the House of Representatives, and Delaware in 1789 had only that one seat. With its tiny population and limited room for growth, the state had selfish reasons to favor as small a House as possible—indeed to endorse the hypothetical congressional bill that Patrick Henry had conjured up in the Virginia ratifying debates *decreasing* the size of the House from sixty-five members to thirteen.[56]

Under Henry's nightmare bill, Delaware could achieve equality of representation in both legislative branches, as its delegates had strenuously urged in the Philadelphia convention during the summer of 1787.[57] Prior to the convention, the Delaware legislature had in fact issued binding instructions to its delegates to oppose all attempts to modify the one-state, one-vote rule of the Articles of Confederation.[58] This political explanation for Delaware's vote against the original First Amendment gains added support from the conduct of Delaware Representative Vining. When an early version of Madison's First Amendment initially came up for debate on the floor of the House of Representatives, Vining unsuccessfully sought to amend it in a way that would assure small states more than proportional representation in an expanded House.[59]

Whatever Delaware's reasons for ultimately rejecting Madison's First Amendment, we do well to remember that only a single state—and a tiny one at that—stood between the ten success stories of Amendments III–XII and the failure of Amendment I.

Economic Self-Dealing

The Second Amendment proposed by the First Congress also went down to defeat in the 1790s but apparently lived to fight another day: after lying dormant—and presumed dead—for nearly two centuries, the Rip Van Winkle Amendment reawoke to a burst of attention and a flurry of ratifications in the 1980s and 1990s. Indeed, in 1992, more than two hundred years after being proposed, the amendment was officially proclaimed valid—as the Twenty-seventh rather than the Second Amendment to the United States Constitution.*

*Whether this official proclamation was in fact correct turns on whether Article V contains an implicit requirement that proposal and ratification of an amendment occur roughly contemporaneously and on whether the First Congress implicitly intended that its proposals "sunset" at some point. This is not the place for detailed analysis of that issue; a fun and informative account appears in Michael Stokes Paulsen, *A General Theory of Article V: The Constitutional Lessons of the Twenty-Seventh Amendment*, 103 YALE L.J. 677 (1993), and a vigorous presentation of the opposing view may be found in 2 BRUCE ACKERMAN, WE THE PEOPLE: TRANSFORMATIONS (forthcoming 1998) (chapter 13, n.1).

But its fate in the 1790s was far less auspicious—only six state legisla-tures[60] ratified its words: "Article the second. . . . No law, varying the compensation for the services of the Senators and Representatives, shall take effect, until an election of Representatives shall have intervened."[61]

As with the original First Amendment, the original Second dealt centrally with an issue of governmental structure rather than substan-tive individual right. The First tried to reduce the general danger that federal lawmakers would lack knowledge of and sympathy with their constituents, whereas the Second tried to limit the ability of Congress-men to line their own pockets at public expense, a concern also evident in the emolument clause of the original Constitution's Article I, section 6. At base, both amendments shared a fundamentally similar outlook; both addressed the "agency cost" problem of government—possible self-dealing among government "servants" who may be tempted to plunder their "masters," the people—rather than the analytically dis-tinct problem of protecting minorities of ordinary citizens from tyran-nical majorities. If anything, both amendments were attempts to strengthen majoritarianism rather than check it, for both sought to tighten the link between representatives and their constituents—the First by democratizing representation, and the Second by stressing elections.[62]

Of the three states whose ratifying conventions had suggested a con-gressional salary amendment in 1787–88—Virginia, New York, and North Carolina[63]—only the two southern states voted to ratify the idea when it formally came before their legislatures. Perhaps this was an is-sue about which New York state legislators felt more natural sympathy with future congressmen than had the specially called, ad hoc conven-tion of the people of New York in 1788. Because the First Congress's First Amendment had focused on a key difference between an "aristocratic" Congress and more "democratic" state legislatures, the latter bodies could cheerfully support that amendment without calling into question their own legitimacy. But the issue of legislative salaries hit closer to home—close to their own pocketbooks. How could state legislators vote for Congress's Second Amendment without also triggering public demand for similar amendments to their respective state constitutions regulating their own salaries?* Thus the lukewarm reaction of state leg-islatures to the original Second Amendment is itself mildly suggestive of a possible agency cost gap between the interests of constituents and legislators.

The events of 1816 are also suggestive. When Congress enacted the first increase in congressional pay since 1789 and refused to defer the in-crease until after the next election, an outraged electorate responded by voting congressional incumbents out of office in record numbers. Op-position to the act found voice not simply in newspapers but in grand-jury presentments from Vermont to Georgia and in petitions and local resolutions from ordinary citizens across the continent.[64]

These anticongressional articles, presentments, and petitions should remind us of the need to prevent Congress from silencing its critics. This is of course a key concern of *our* First Amendment, to which we now turn.

*On the other hand, consider the argument of the Anti-Federalist essayist "Cor-nelius," who trusted state legislators to set their own pay, but distrusted congressmen. State lawmakers, he argued, were elected annually, chosen in small districts, easily moni-tored by constituents, and "sent but a small distance from their respective homes," to which they quickly returned to "mix with their neighbours of the lowest rank." Con-gressmen, by contrast, would emerge from large districts and sit for long terms, "far re-moved, and long detained, from the view of their constituents." Living in an imperial capital city, they would daily mix with foreign "Ambassadors," other "Ministers," and men "bred in affluence" and "luxury." *Essay by Cornelius, reprinted in* 4 THE COMPLETE ANTI-FEDERALIST 141 (Herbert J. Storing ed., 1981). Perhaps reflecting the vision of men like Cornelius, the original Second Amendment sounded not just in populism but also in localism, insofar as it limited congressmen but not state legislators.

Two

Our First Amendment

The First Congress's first two proposed amendments offer an illuminating perspective on its Third (our First) Amendment. From this perspective, we can see features of that amendment that tend to be obscured by conventional wisdom. The amendment affirms vital rights of religion and expression, but it does so with a distinctly (majoritarian) and (localist accent.

Expression

Let us begin by considering the second half of the amendment: "Congress shall make no law . . . abridging the freedom of speech, or of the press; or the right of the people peaceably to assemble, and to petition the Government for a redress of grievances."

Speech and Press Like the two preceding amendments, this declaration sounds in structure and focuses (at least in part) on the representational linkage between Congress and its constituents. On this account, the

First Amendment reaffirms the structural role of free speech and a free press in a working democracy.[1] Yet many scholars tend to view these rights as fundamentally minority rights—rights of paradigmatically unpopular individuals or groups to speak out against a hostile and repressive majority.[2] Even here, a weak brand of majoritarianism is often at work. Political action by today's minority may eventually persuade some members of today's majority or members of the next generation, thus enabling a new majority to emerge in the future. Fittingly, the classic First Amendment dissents of Holmes and Brandeis[3] were themselves exercises of free speech by a minority inspired by the hope of persuading a future majority (of the Court, of course).

The perspective furnished by the first two proposed amendments suggests that an even stronger kind of majoritarianism underlies our First Amendment. The body that is restrained is not a hostile majority of the people, but rather Congress; and the earlier two amendments remind us that congressional majorities may in fact have "aristocratical" and self-interested views in opposition to views held by a majority of the people. Thus, although the First Amendment's text is broad enough to protect the rights of unpopular minorities (like Jehovah's Witnesses and Communists),[4] the Amendment's historical and structural core was to safeguard the rights of popular majorities (like the Republicans of the late 1790s) against a possibly unrepresentative and self-interested Congress.

Recall Madison's distinction in *The Federalist* No. 51 between the two main problems of republican government—first, protecting citizens generally from government officials pursuing their own self-interested agendas at the expense of their constituents; and second, protecting individuals and minorities from tyrannical majority factions of fellow citizens.[5] As did the First Congress's first two amendments, its next amendment betrayed more concern about the first issue than the second. To begin to see this, we need only reflect on the amendment's first word. *Congress* was restrained, but not state legislatures. Yet as Madison's *Federalist* No. 10 reminds us, the danger of majority oppression of minorities (the second issue) was far greater at the state than at the national level. Of course, this was largely because state legislative representation was much less attenuated than congressional representation, making

state legislative majorities far more likely to reflect the unrefined sentiments of popular majorities. Our First Amendment's focus on Congress
suggests that its primary target was attenuated representation, not overweening majoritarianism.[6] Congress was singled out precisely because
it was *less* likely to reflect majority will.

Madison himself had a rather different goal. As part of his initial proposed Bill of Rights, he included an amendment proscribing states from
violating "freedom of the press"[7] and went on to declare:

> But I confess that I do conceive, that in a Government modified like
> this of the United States, the great danger lies rather in the abuse of
> the community than in the legislative body. The prescriptions in fa-
> vor of liberty ought to be levelled against that quarter where the great-
> est danger lies, namely, that which possesses the highest prerogative
> of power. But this is not found in either the executive or the legisla-
> tive departments of Government, but in the body of the people, op-
> erating by the majority against the minority.[8]

Madison's proposed amendment also obliged state governments to protect "equal rights of conscience" and "trial by jury in criminal cases," and
it was soon reworded to protect "speech" as well as "press" from state interference.[9] When the package came up for discussion on the floor of
the House, Madison described it as "the most valuable amendment in
the whole list. If there was any reason to restrain the Government of the
United States from infringing upon these essential rights, it was equally
necessary that they should be secured against the State Governments."[10]

Madison's proposal passed the House of Representatives (as its
prophetically numbered Fourteenth Amendment)[11] but died in the
Senate.[12] To the extent that principles of free political expression were
implicit in the republican structure of the original Constitution,[13] state
legislatures were already bound to observe those principles; indeed, the
Article IV republican-government clause gave Congress an explicit role
in protecting these principles. And where citizens sought to speak out
about issues of national concern, any state effort to stifle this debate would
also seem vulnerable on more general supremacy clause grounds.[14] But
full vindication of the Madisonian vision did not occur until the adop-

tion of *our* Fourteenth Amendment after the Civil War. The equal-protection clause of that amendment, directed at state governments, obviously focuses more on overweening majoritarianism than attenuated representation. And, as shall become clear in Part Two, strong arguments support a reading of the "privileges or immunities" clause as incorporating most of the provisions of the Bill of Rights, most definitely including the speech and press clauses, against the states.

Although many modern speech theorists echo Madison's 1789 fear of popular majorities, we must remember that the First Amendment tradition of "uninhibited, robust, and wide-open" criticism of government celebrated by *New York Times v. Sullivan*[15] took root when Madison and Jefferson successfully appealed to a popular majority during 1798–1800. No court invalidated the Alien and Sedition Acts (unless one cheats by counting the *Sullivan* court itself, 150-odd years later, or the "court of history"[16] that it invoked). Rather, a popular majority adjudicated the First Amendment question in the election of 1800, by throwing out the haughty and aristocratic rascals who had tried to shield themselves from popular criticism. (The Sedition Act itself was a textbook example of attempted self-dealing among the people's agents; it criminalized libel of incumbents, but not of challengers. Yet another dead giveaway: the act conveniently provided for its own expiration after the next election.)[17] If we see the First Amendment as primarily about minority rights, Jefferson's strategy of appealing to a popular majority seems odd indeed. But once we see the amendment's populist roots, its vindication by the election of 1800 borders on the poetic. The election of 1816 was less dramatic, but it, too, spotlighted the role of the press in alerting popular majorities to the dangers of congressional self-dealing.[18]

It becomes even more clear that popular speech was the paradigm of our First Amendment when we recall its historic connection to jury trial: popular bodies outside regular government would protect popular speech criticizing government. The historic common-law rule against "prior restraint"[19]—courts could not enjoin a publisher from printing offensive material but could entertain civil and criminal prosecutions for libel and sedition afterward—had bite largely because of the structural differences between the two proceedings. The former could occur in equity courts, presided over by permanent government officials on the government payroll (chancellors),[20] but the latter required the intervention of ordinary citizens (jurors) free to vote for the publisher without fear of reprisal. In the colonies, the celebrated 1730s trial of the New York publisher John Peter Zenger had placed the jury at center stage in libel cases—and it remained there even after the Revolution and Constitution.[21] As we shall see in more detail in Chapter 5, publishers prosecuted under the Alien and Sedition Acts in the late 1790s tried to plead their First Amendment defense directly to jurors. The judges, after all, had been appointed by the very same (increasingly unpopular) Federalist administration that the defendants had attacked in the press.

This episode contrasts sharply with modern First Amendment discourse, in which friends of the amendment often seek to limit the power of juries on speech questions by appealing to federal judges. As the First Amendment's center of gravity has (appropriately, in light of the later Fourteenth Amendment) shifted to protection of unpopular, minority speech, its natural institutional guardian has become an insulated judiciary rather than the popular jury.[22]

Today's First Amendment champions tend to see state and local "community standards" of discourse as the paradigmatic threat to free speech; but the amendment's defenders in the 1790s turned to local juries and state legislatures for refuge. Once Congress enacted the Sedition Act, where could opponents vigorously voice their criticism without fear of prosecution under the act itself?[23] In state legislatures, of course. Even if, as the high Federalists claimed, freedom for partisan publishers was not absolute but limited to freedom from prior restraint,* who would dare claim that absolute "freedom of speech" did not obtain within constitutionally recognized legislative bodies?[24] Indeed, the very notion of free speech for citizens had grown out of a much older tradition, enshrined in the celebrated English Bill of Rights of 1689, establishing immunity from prosecution for *legislative* discourse: "the freedom of speech, and debates or proceedings in parliament, ought not to be impeached or questioned in any court or place

---

But see infra Chapter 10.

out of parliament."[25] The very word *parliament* emphasized the centrality of legislative speech and debate—a parliament (from the French *parler*) is a speaking spot, a place where people parley. In Article I, section 6, the federal Constitution likewise shielded congressmen from various reprisals "for any Speech or Debate in either House." The earlier Articles of Confederation had explicitly used the phrase "freedom of speech" to immunize members of the federal Congress from state libel law,[26] and the Virginia and Kentucky legislatures in 1798 were simply returning the compliment: they, too, were constitutionally ordained speaking spots and parley places.* Thus even as the Virginia and Kentucky legislators themselves invoked both First and Tenth Amendment protections in arguing that the Alien and Sedition Acts were unconstitutional,[27] their own speech was specially protected by a states'-rights gloss on the free-speech clause.

In the end, the individual-rights vision of the speech and press clauses powerfully illuminates a vital part of our constitutional tradition, but only by obscuring other parts. The special structural role of freedom of speech in a representative democracy; the localist and majoritarian accent of the First Amendment circa 1800; the massive transformation brought about by the Fourteenth Amendment; the competing claims of judge, jury, and electorate to define the boundaries of free speech; the obvious agency problem of incumbent self-dealing at the heart of the Sedition Act; the special role of free speech in state legislatures; the link-

---

*For an especially vivid illustration of the connection between American freedom of speech for the people and the earlier model of freedom of speech for legislators, see VT. CONST. OF 1786, ch. I, §§ XV, XVI (declaring, in back-to-back passages, that "the people have a right of freedom of speech and of writing and publishing their sentiments, concerning the transactions of government" and that "freedom of deliberation, speech, and debate, in the legislature, is . . . essential to the rights of the people"). As we shall see in more detail in Chapter 10, the First Amendment took the British idea of Parliamentary "freedom of speech and debate" and ultimately extended that freedom to all Americans. Here, the people, not Parliament, stand as the ultimate sovereign, and the eventual wording of the First Amendment's speech clause is a textual exemplification of this structural truth of American popular sovereignty. (And so, yet again, we see populist and structural themes at work in the original Bill of Rights, upon close inspection.)

ages between the original Constitution's "speech" clause and the First Amendment's "speech" clause; and the deep popular-sovereignty logic underlying America's extension of freedom of speech from Parliament to the people—all this and much more is simply bleached out of the standard sketch drawn from the individual-rights perspective.

Assembly and Petition When we turn our attention to the assembly and petition clauses, a similar pattern emerges. Both clauses plainly protect individuals and minority groups, but the clauses contain a majoritarian core that many contemporary scholars have overlooked. The right *of the people* to assemble does not simply protect the ability of self-selected clusters of individuals to meet together; it is also an express reservation of the *collective* right of We the People to assemble in a future convention and exercise our sovereign right to alter or abolish our government. In the words of Rousseau's 1762 treatise on the social contract, "the sovereign can act only when *the people are assembled.*"[28]

Listen carefully to the remarks of President Edmund Pendleton at the Virginia ratifying convention of 1788:

> *We, the people,* possessing all power, form a government, such as we think will secure happiness: and suppose, in adopting this plan, we should be mistaken in the end; where is the cause of alarm on that quarter? In the same plan we point out an easy and quiet method of reforming what may be found amiss. No, but, say gentlemen, we have put the introduction of that method in the hands of our servants, who will interrupt it from motives of self-interest. What then? . . . Who shall dare to resist *the people?* No, *we* will *assemble in Convention;* wholly recall our delegated powers, or reform them so as to prevent such abuse. . . . [29]

This rich paragraph has it all: primary attention to the agency problem of government self-dealing, dogged unwillingness to equate Congress with a majority of the people, and keen appreciation of the collective right of the people to bring wayward government to heel by *assembling* in convention. Pendleton saw that the agency problem of government meant that future amendments might be necessary to bring government under control. Obviously, ordinary government officials—Congress, state legislatures, and so on—could not be given a monopoly over the amendment process, for that would enable them to thwart desperately needed change by self-interested inaction. Hence the need to keep open the special channel of the popular convention acting outside of all ordinary government, convenable, if necessary, by popular petition.[30] (Indeed, it was the very threat of a second constitutional convention that induced many Federalists in the First Congress to support a Bill of Rights limiting their own powers, lest a new convention propose even more stringent amendments.)[31]

Pendleton's language illuminates the textual and conceptual bridge between the Preamble's invocation of "the People" and the reemergence of that phrase in our First Amendment. The Preamble's dramatic opening words, quoted by Pendleton, trumpeted the Constitution's underlying theory of popular sovereignty.[32] Those words and that theory implied a right of "the People" (acting by majority vote in special conventions) to alter or abolish their government whenever they deemed proper: what "the People" had "ordain[ed] and establish[ed]" (by majority vote in special conventions), they or their "posterity" could disestablish at will (by a similar mode).[33] To good lawyers of the late 1780s, Pendleton was merely restating first principles—words made flesh by the Constitution itself. The Constitution, after all, was not just a text, but an act—a doing, a constitut*ing*. In the Preamble's performative utterance, "We the people . . . *do*" alter the old and ordain and establish the new.

Madison's very first proposed amendment was a prefix to the Preamble that similarly declared: "*[T]he people* have an indubitable, unalienable, and indefeasible right to reform or change their Government. . . ."[34] Not a single representative quarreled with Madison on the substance of this claim, although some considered any prefix superfluous. James Jackson of Georgia declared that the Preamble's "words, as they now stand, speak as much as it is possible to speak; it is a practical recognition of the right of the people to ordain and establish Governments, and is more expressive than any other mere paper declaration."[35] Similarly, Roger Sherman argued that "[t]he people of the United States have [in the Preamble] given their reasons for doing a certain act. . . . Now, if this right is indefeasible, and the people have recognized it in practice, the truth is better asserted than it can be by any words whatever. The words 'We the people' in the original constitution, are as copious and expressive as possible; any addition will only drag out and lengthen the sentence without illuminating it . . . . "[36]

When Congress eventually decided to add amendments to the end of the document rather than interweave them into the original text, the prefix was abandoned; but the underlying idea survived, repackaged as a guarantee of the right of "*the people* to assemble." Members of the First Congress shared Pendleton's understanding that constitutional conventions were paradigmatic exercises of this right.[37] As Gordon Wood has observed, "conventions . . . of the people . . . were closely allied in English thought with the people's right to assemble."[38] For example, we find Blackstone describing how, in 1688, the British people, through Parliament, "assemble[d]" in "convention."[39] And in Revolutionary America, we almost invariably find the words *people, assemble,* and *convention* tightly clustered in discussions of popular sovereignty and the right to alter or abolish government—in state constitutions and bills of rights,[40] in early state and federal case law,[41] in the wording of the Philadelphia convention's initial version of Article VII,[42] and throughout the ratification debates.[43] Thus our First Amendment's language of "the right of the people to assemble" simply made explicit at the end of the Constitution what Pendleton and others already saw as implicit in its opening. (Many other provisions of the Bill of Rights were also understood as declaratory, inserted simply out of an abundance of caution to clarify pre-existing constitutional understandings.)[44]

Pendleton's language about the people's right to assemble was echoed by the Declaration of Rights proclaimed by the Virginia convention: "the people have a right peaceably to assemble together to consult for the common good, or to instruct their representatives."[45] This was neither the first nor the last time that the people's asserted rights of assembly and instruction were yoked together. The same pairing had already appeared in the Pennsylvania and North Carolina Constitutions of 1776, the Vermont Constitutions of 1777 and 1786, the Massachusetts Constitution of 1780, and the New Hampshire Constitution of 1784,* and would later appear in the Declarations of Rights of the New York, North Carolina, and Rhode Island ratifying conventions.[46] When Madison proposed the assembly clause to the First Congress, Thomas Tucker of South Carolina quickly moved to add to it an express right of the people "to instruct their Representatives."[47]

The juxtaposition of assembly and instruction is illuminating. Both clauses have strong majoritarian components and reflect the recurring Anti-Federalist concern with attenuated representation in Congress. And the right of instruction helps confirm that, at its core, the related right of the people to assemble referred to formal gatherings of voters— who else could presume to instruct lawmakers?—rather than mere informal clumps of self-selected persons seeking to associate. Yet there is a vital difference between the two rights—a difference that led Madison and his fellow Federalists to embrace assembly while successfully opposing instruction. Instruction would have completely undermined the Madisonian system of deliberation among refined representatives. All the advantages of skimming would be lost if each representative could be bound by his relatively uninformed and parochial constituents rather than his conscience, enlightened by full discussions with his fellow representatives bringing information and ideas from other parts of the country.[48] As Garry Wills has pointed out, all of Madison's central arguments in *The Federalist* No. 10 are premised on a repudiation of the idea of instruction.[49]

---

*Throughout this book, I shall use state constitutional antecedents and descendants of the federal Bill of Rights to shed light on the federal Bill itself. The American constitutional experience encompasses state constitutions, too—indeed, these constitutions came first—and thus these documents can provide rich insights into the federal document. Gordon Wood's pathbreaking book, THE CREATION OF THE AMERICAN REPUBLIC, 1776–1787 (1969), began as a dissertation on state as well as federal constitution-making; and as Donald Lutz has shown, no account of the federal Bill can ignore its state constitutional antecedents. *See* Donald S. Lutz, *The States and the U.S. Bill of Rights*, 16 S. ILL. U. L.J. 251 (1992). As will become clear, however, some of the most interesting insights about the federal Bill appear when we note the ways in which it subtly or not so subtly diverged from its state constitutional counterparts.

By contrast, Madison and his fellow Federalists could embrace the idea of a popular right to assemble in convention. Unlike instruction, such a right would not continually undermine ordinary congressional deliberation on day-to-day affairs but would reserve to the people the right to meet in future conventions to consider amending the Constitution—just as the people had assembled in convention in the previous months to ratify the Constitution proposed by Madison and company. Under the Federalists' two-track scheme, ordinary legislation during periods of "normal politics" should be reserved to the legislature, but We the People could take center stage during "constitutional moments."[50] Thus, like the rights *of the people* explicitly reserved in the Ninth and Tenth Amendments, the assembly clause has important implications for the structural process of constitutional amendment.

So too with the petition clause. I have argued elsewhere that whenever a majority of voters so petitioned, Congress would be obliged to convene a constitutional convention, just as it would be when presented with "Application of the Legislatures of two thirds of the several States" under Article V.[51] The key textual point here is that the amendment explicitly guarantees "the right of *the people*" to petition—a formulation that decisively signals its connection to popular-sovereignty theory and underscores Gordon Wood's observation that the ideas of petition, assembly, and convention tightly intertwined in eighteenth-century America.[52] In the Continental Congress's 1774 Declaration of Rights and in all six of the Revolutionary-era state constitutions affirming a right of the people to assemble, the right was explicitly yoked to the right of petition.[53] The precursors of the petition clause suggested in state ratifying conventions had obscured these connections. The conventions spoke of the "people's" right to "assemble" or to alter or abolish government, yet each convention described the right of petition in purely individualistic language—a right of "every freeman," "every person," or "every man."[54] Under these formulations, petition appeared less a political than a civil right, akin to the right to sue in court and receive due process.[55] The language and structure of our First Amendment suggest otherwise. As with assembly, the core petition right is collective and popular—it, too, is a right of *the people*.

To be sure, like its companion assembly clause, the petition clause also protects individuals and minority groups. Stephen Higginson has persuasively shown that the clause was originally understood as giving extraordinary power to even a single individual, for the right to petition implied a corresponding congressional duty to respond, at least with some kind of hearing.[56]

But to focus only on minority invocations of the right to petition is to miss at least half of the clause's meaning, even if we put to one side its momentous implications for constitutional amendment. Like the other provisions of the First Amendment, the clause is not primarily concerned with the problem of overweening majoritarianism; it is at least equally concerned with the danger of attenuated representation. Higginson shows that part of the purpose and effect of petitions was to help inform representatives about local conditions and popular sentiments.[57] In eighteenth-century Virginia, for example, more than half of the statutes ultimately enacted by the legislature originated in the form of popular petitions.[58] Thus, James Madison's famous 1785 *Memorial and Remonstrance Against Religious Assessments* was circulated as one of several petitions that collectively gained more than ten thousand signatures; this "graphic expression of popular opinion proved decisive" in the Virginia legislature's eventual decision to adopt its famous Bill for Establishing Religious Freedom.[59] If anything, the need for populist petitions was even greater at the federal level; as we have seen, Congress's small size and elite status gave rise to special concern about whether representatives would have adequate knowledge of their constituents' wants and needs. If we seek historical examples illustrating this point, we need look no further than the 1816 election, when citizens used petitions to Congress as one of several devices to educate their agents and each other.

Indeed, the populist possibilities implicit in the petition clause should be evident from a simple side-by-side comparison of the First Amendment's language with Blackstone's account of English law. The landmark English Bill of Rights of 1689 had explicitly and sweepingly affirmed Englishmen's right of petition, but according to Blackstone's *Commentaries,* this ringing proclamation merely codified earlier Stuart statutes regulating petitions as follows: *"[N]o petition to the king, or either house of parliament, for any alterations in church or state, shall be signed by above twenty persons,* unless the matter thereof be approved by three justices of the peace or the major part of the grand jury, in the country; and in London by the lord mayor, alderman, and common council; *nor shall any petition be presented by more than [ten] persons at a time."*[60] In his American edition of Blackstone, St. George Tucker took obvious satisfaction in reminding his readers that, "In America, there is no such restraint."[61]

Like their speech and press clause counterparts, the rights of assembly and petition became applicable against state governments after the adoption of the Fourteenth Amendment. As we shall see in Part Two, incorporation of these guarantees against state governments makes a good deal of sense in light of the text of the amendment's privileges-or-immunities clause, its historical purpose of safeguarding vulnerable minorities against majority oppression, and the overall structure of federalism implied by that amendment—namely, that those citizen rights formerly protected against the national government should also be protected against state governments. Nor should we forget the central role the right of petition played in abolitionist thought and practice in the antebellum era. What may make less sense, however, is the Supreme Court's attempt to fully "incorporate" against states the First Amendment's establishment clause. To that clause, and its free-exercise counterpart, we now turn.

Religion

Congress shall make no law respecting an establishment of religion, or prohibiting the free exercise thereof. . . .

Religion and Federalism　The establishment clause did more than prohibit Congress from establishing a national church. Its mandate that Congress shall make no law *"respecting* an establishment of religion" also prohibited the national legislature from interfering with, or trying to *dis*establish, churches established by state and local governments.[62] In 1789, at least six states had government-supported churches—Congregationalism held sway in New Hampshire, Massachusetts, and Connecticut under local-rule establishment schemes, while Maryland, South Carolina, and Georgia each featured a more general form of establishment in its state constitution.[63] Even in the arguably "nonestablishment" states, church and state were hardly separate; at least four of these states, for example—in their constitutions, no less—barred non-Christians or non-Protestants from holding government office.[64] According to one tally, eleven of the thirteen states had religious qualifications for officeholding.[65] Interestingly, the federal establishment clause as finally worded most closely tracked the proposal from the ratifying convention of one of the staunchest establishment states, New Hampshire, that "Congress shall make no laws *touching* religion"; this proposal, if adopted, would obviously have immunized New Hampshire from any attempted federal disestablishment.[66] In the First Congress, Representative Samuel Livermore from New Hampshire initially won the assent of the House for this wording, only to lose in turn to another formulation.[67] But when all the dust had settled, the final version of the clause returned to its states'-rights roots. In the words of Joseph Story's celebrated *Commentaries on the Constitution*, "the whole power over the subject of religion is left exclusively to the state governments."[68]

The key point is not simply that, as with the rest of the First Amendment, the establishment clause limited only Congress and not the states; that point is obvious on the face of the amendment and is confirmed by its legislative history. (It also has the imprimatur of Chief Justice Marshall's opinion in *Barron v. Baltimore*.)[69] Nor is the main point exhausted once we recognize that state governments are in part the special beneficiaries of, and rights holders under, the clause; indeed, the same thing could be said, to some degree, about the free-speech clause.[70] The special pinprick of the point is this: the nature of the states' establishment-clause right against federal disestablishment makes it quite awkward to mechanically "incorporate" the clause against the states via the Fourteenth Amendment. Incorporation of the free-speech clause against states does not negate state legislators' own First Amendment rights to freedom of speech in the legislative assembly. But incorporation of the establishment clause has precisely this kind of paradoxical effect; to apply the clause against a state government is precisely to eliminate its right to choose whether to establish a religion—a right clearly confirmed by the establishment clause itself.

To put the point a slightly different way, the structural reasons that counsel caution in attempting to incorporate the Tenth Amendment against the states seem valid here, too. The original establishment clause, on a close reading, is not antiestablishment but pro–states' rights; it is agnostic on the substantive issue of establishment versus nonestablishment and simply calls for the issue to be decided locally. (In this respect it is the American equivalent of the European Peace of Augsburg in 1555 and Treaty of Westphalia in 1648, which decreed that religious policy would be set locally rather than imperially.)* But how can such a local option clause be mechanically incorporated *against* localities, requiring them to pass no laws (either way) on the issue of—"respecting"—establishment?[71]

To my knowledge no scholar or judge has argued for incorporating the Tenth Amendment, but few seem critical of, or even concerned about, the blithe manner in which the establishment clause has come to apply against the states. The apparent reason for this lack of concern, and for the Supreme Court's initial decision to incorporate the clause, is the conventional assumption that virtually all the provisions of the Bill of Rights, except the Tenth Amendment, were essentially designed to protect individual rights. On this assumption, total incorporation of the first nine amendments seems eminently sensible, and wonderfully clean to boot. Unfortunately, this assumption is false.

Thomas Jefferson, often invoked today as a strong opponent of religious establishment, appears to have understood the states'-rights aspects of the original establishment clause. Although he argued for an

---

*A related aspect of imperial neutrality—somewhat akin to the Article I, section 9 clause forbidding congressional favoritism toward any state's port—was the Article VI clause barring any federal religious test for federal officials. Otherwise, Congress could have favored New England by requiring federal officers to be Congregationalists, or Pennsylvania by barring non-Quakers, and so on. In the section of his treatise offering a states'-rights reading of the establishment clause, Joseph Story also invoked the religious-test clause. Yet again we see important connections between the original Constitution and the Bill of Rights.

absolutist interpretation of the First Amendment—the federal government should have *nothing* to do with religion in the states, control of which was beyond Congress's limited delegated powers—he was more willing to flirt with governmental endorsements of religion at the state level, especially where no state coercion would impinge on dissenters' freedom of conscience. The two ideas were logically connected; it was especially easy to be an absolutist about the federal government's involvement in religion if one understood that the respective states had broad authority over their citizens' education and morals. Thus, President Jefferson in 1802 refused to proclaim a day of religious Thanksgiving, but Governor Jefferson had agreed to do so some twenty years before.[72] In defending his practice to the Reverend Samuel Miller in 1808, Jefferson quoted both the First and Tenth Amendments and explained: "I am aware that the practice of my [presidential] predecessors may be quoted. But I have ever believed that the example of state executives led to the assumption of that authority by the general government, without due examination, which would have discovered that what might be a right in a state government, was a violation of that right when assumed by another."[73] Interestingly, a virtually identical view was voiced in the First Congress on September 25, 1789—the very day the Bill of Rights cleared both houses. When New Jersey Representative Elias Boudinot introduced a bill recommending "a day of public thanksgiving and prayer," South Carolina's Thomas Tucker rose up in opposition: "[I]t is a religious matter, and as such, is proscribed to us. If a day of thanksgiving must take place, let it be done by the authority of the several States . . . ."[74]

This states'-rights understanding helps to explain why the religion clauses and the rights of speech, press, and the like were lumped together into a single amendment. To be sure, there is much truth in a libertarian reading, rooted in conventional wisdom: the free-exercise clause flanks the free-speech clause to remind us of the importance of protecting not only political speech (as emphasized by the adjoining assembly and petition clauses) but religious speech, too.[75] As I hope to show in Part Two, this libertarian reading draws strong support from the history of the antebellum and Reconstruction eras. But once again, the conventional account tends to miss an important federalism dynamic at work in the 1780s.

Like the general topic of state religious policy, restrictions on speech and press were seen by many as beyond Congress's enumerated powers in Article I.[76] During the closing days of the Philadelphia convention a proposal to explicitly guarantee "liberty of the Press" quickly went down to defeat after Roger Sherman shrugged it off as "unnecessary—The power of Congress does not extend to the Press."[77] During the ratification debates, Sherman's one-liner became the Federalist party line on press freedom, affirmed over and over, not just by Sherman and fellow moderates like Oliver Ellsworth, Hugh Williamson, Richard Dobbs Spaight, and Edmund Randolph, but also by strong nationalists like Alexander Hamilton, James Iredell, Charles Pinckney, Charles Cotesworth Pinckney, Noah Webster, and James Wilson.[78] Likewise, Federalists of all stripes—Madison, Wilson, Iredell, Randolph, Spaight, Ellsworth, and Sherman, for example— declared that the federal government simply had no jurisdiction over religion in the several states.[79] Thus our First Amendment opened with words suggesting an utter lack of enumerated power to regulate religion in the states or restrict speech—"Congress shall make *no* law"—in sharp contrast to the language of later amendments dealing with areas where Congress clearly did enjoy enumerated Article I power to "make . . . law." (The militia and war power clauses of Article I gave Congress broad power over military matters addressed by the Second and Third Amendments; federal searches and seizures—the subject of the Fourth Amendment—clearly fell within Congress's explicit power to regulate customs and captures, among other things; and Article I expressly authorized Congress to "constitute tribunals," whose procedures were the main subject of Fifth, Sixth, Seventh, and Eighth Amendments.)[80]

The "Congress shall make no law" amendment's precise location in the original Bill is also quite illuminating. The original First Amendment on congressional size modified Article I, section 2; and the original Second amended Article I, section 6, dealing with congressional salary. Then came our "no law" amendment, glossing the Article I, section 8 catalogue of enumerated congressional powers by suggesting that Congress lacked enumerated power to censor expression or regulate state religious policy—a kind of reverse "necessary and proper" clause. Only after this gloss on section 8–enumerated powers was it appropriate to add later amendments expanding the catalogue of Congress-limiting clauses set out in Article I, section 9, many of whose provisions cut across powers that were indeed conferred in section 8. Seen from this angle, the order of amendments precisely tracks the order of the original Constitution itself—first section 2, then section 6, then section 8, and only then section 9 and so on. (Later amendments governing the judicial process can also be seen as modifying Article III rules for federal courts; and the last two amendments laid down global rules of construction aimed at all federal powers, not just those of Congress.) When we remember that Madison originally proposed to interweave his amendments into the original Constitution rather than tack them on at the end, it makes sense that the order of amendments would track the order of the Constitution itself.

Of course, the idea that Congress simply lacked Article I–enumerated power over various First Amendment domains may seem wholly fanciful today, given the widespread acceptance of expansive twentieth-century commerce clause cases, themselves inspired by a broad reading of the nineteenth-century classic, *McCulloch v. Maryland*.[81] Reading the Constitution through twentieth-century eyes, we must squint quite hard to see the First Amendment as any different from the seven amendments that follow it, so far as enumerated powers are concerned. But to avoid anachronism we must ask why so many Federalists cheerfully conceded a lack of congressional power over press and religion in the states but failed to make similar concessions in response to other Anti-Federalist objections. Is there not a kernel of truth in the widespread eighteenth-century notion that, say, searches and seizures were naturally incidental to—"necessary and proper" for—the power to collect revenue in a way that press censorship and religious regulations were generally not? Vestiges of this eighteenth-century notion can be found even in *McCulloch*, where Chief Justice Marshall warned that Congress could not "under the pretext of executing its power, pass laws for the accomplishment of objects not entrusted to the government."[82] Though this language has lain dormant in recent years, it hints at a stricter reading of enumerated powers in terms of their natural "objects" or "purposes."* Under this stricter view, each of the next seven amendments seems to track the natural object of specific enumerated powers much more closely than does our First.

The Senate, at least, appears to have thought so, for there seems to be no other good explanation for its conscious decision to fold certain prohibitions, but not others, into the "Congress shall make no law" category. The subjects covered by our First Amendment had initially been dealt with by the House of Representatives in two separate amendments. The first addressed religion and opened with the formulation "Congress shall make no law"; the second encompassed the rights of speech, press, petition, and assembly but omitted the "no law" formulation in favor of language more like that of subsequent amendments (which eventually became our Amendments II–VIII).[83] Although the Senate merged the two amendments behind closed doors, leaving us with no transcript of its oral deliberations, it is plausible to presume that states'-rights sentiment motivated the merger. After all, the Constitution had structured the upper house to safeguard the interests of state governments—whose legislatures, of course, directly elected senators. In responding to other aspects of the Bill of Rights proposed by the lower house, the Senate acted true to its states'-rights form: as we noted earlier, the upper house killed "the most valuable" amendment on Madison's list, the lower house's presciently numbered Fourteenth, which would have imposed various restrictions on state government.

---

*Marshall's approach resembles the colonists' arguments before 1776 that Parliament could enact bills to regulate trade for the overall benefit of the empire but could not use this power pretextually to raise revenues. *See* EDMUND S. MORGAN, THE CHALLENGE OF THE AMERICAN REVOLUTION 3–42 (1976). The resemblance is unsurprising because the debates before 1776 involved, in effect, an early attempt to "constitutionalize" federalism by marking the respective boundaries of the central and local governments within an extended empire. *See* Akhil Reed Amar, *Of Sovereignty and Federalism*, 96 YALE L.J. 1425, 1445 (1987); Andrew C. McLaughlin, *The Background of American Federalism*, 12 AM. POL. SCI. REV. 215 (1918).

Also suggestive is the extensive consideration that the Senate gave to various ideas that originated in the Virginia ratifying convention but that Madison had chosen to omit from his proposed package of amendments.[84] In its formal instrument of ratification the Virginia convention had expressly listed two (and only two) "essential rights" that the convention suggested were beyond the enumerated powers "granted" to the federal government: "liberty of conscience, and of the press."[85] In keeping with Virginia's view, the Senate first reworded the House's press amendment so that it, too, began with the clause "Congress shall make no law," and then folded this amendment into the only other one that shared this opening formulation.[86]

Most important, we must recall that the exact wording of the First Amendment—*"Congress shall make no law"*—precisely tracked and inverted the exact wording of the Article I, section 8 necessary-and-proper clause: "*Congress shall* have power . . . to *make all laws* which shall be necessary and proper . . . . " We should also note that no state constitution placed press freedoms alongside religion clauses, a fact that suggests a federalism-based logic for their conjunction in the First Amendment.

Unsurprisingly, Jefferson's absolutist reading of the First Amendment extended beyond the religion clauses to encompass speech and press— yet once again it was an absolutism rooted in federalism and the idea of enumerated powers. Thus his Kentucky Resolutions of 1798 self-consciously read the First Amendment with a Tenth Amendment gloss:

[I]t is true as a general principle, and is also expressly declared by one of the amendments to the Constitution that "the powers not delegated to the United States by the Constitution, nor prohibited by it to the states, are reserved to the states respectively or to the people;" and that no power over the freedom of religion, freedom of speech, or freedom of the press [was] delegated to the United States by the Constitution . . . . And that in addition to this general principle and express declaration, another and more special provision has been made by one of the amendments to the Constitution which expressly declares, that "Congress shall make no law respecting an Establishment of religion, or prohibiting the free exercise thereof, or abridging the freedom of speech, or of the press," . . . . [87]*

Although this passage could be read to imply that speech and press rights were reserved to "the people" rather than "the states," and thus limited state governments as well, Jefferson thought otherwise. As he explained to Abigail Adams in 1804: "While we deny that Congress have a right to control the freedom of the press, we have ever asserted the right of the States, and their exclusive right, to do so."[88]

Similarly, Madison's famous *Report of 1800* on the Virginia Resolutions declared that "the power . . . over the press . . . was neither among the enumerated powers, nor incident to any of them" and that the First Amendment simply reaffirmed "a positive denial to Congress of any power whatever on the subject."[89] Madison then proceeded to quote the language of the Virginia convention's formal instrument of ratification linking press and religion to states' rights, and he concluded that "liberty of conscience and freedom of the press were *equally* and *completely* exempted from all authority whatever of the United States."[90] The italics were Madison's. Madison's words in 1800 mesh well with his earlier words in the First Congress. In embracing an early version of the establishment clause, Madison wondered aloud whether it was, strictly speaking, "necessary"—because in Madison's view, Congress lacked enumerated power here—but noted that an amendment would resolve any possible ambiguity.[91] Note how he explicitly linked the establishment issue to the necessary-and-proper clause: "[S]ome of the State Conventions . . . seemed to entertain an opinion that . . . the clause of the constitution, which gave power to Congress to make all laws necessary and proper to carry into execution the constitution, and the laws made under it, enabled them to make such laws of such a nature as might infringe the rights of conscience, and establish a national religion; to prevent these effects he presumed the amendment was intended. . . . "[92] And in the 1791 debates over the first national bank, Madison yoked to-

---

*In his canonical 1830s reprint, Jonathan Elliot misquoted this resolution—substituting "laws" for "law" in the First Amendment—thus rendering that amendment's language even closer to that of the necessary-and-proper clause.

gether religion and press as examples of domains beyond Congress's Article I jurisdiction: "The defence against the charge founded on the want of a bill of rights pre-supposed . . . that the powers not given were retained; and that those given were not to be extended by remote implications. On any other supposition, the power of Congress to abridge the freedom of the press, or the rights of conscience, &c. could not have been disproved."[93]

Yet we must not let the similarities between the First Amendment's expressive rights and its establishment clause obscure a difference that may well have profound implications for the relative ease with which they can be incorporated against states by the Fourteenth Amendment. The expressive-rights clauses sound in more than federalism pure and simple. They speak of personal "freedoms" (as does the *free*-exercise clause) and "right[s] of the people." The establishment clause's bland language of laws "respecting . . . establishment" does not. Put another way, even nationalists in the 1780s may have been willing to concede that Congress lacked power to restrict speech and press, but none of them claimed that Congress lacked power to protect a vigorous debate about national issues against states that might seek to censor such speech. Nor is there anything in the First Amendment that limits congressional power to *promote* speech, press, petition, and assembly against state repression.[94] (And let us not forget that the Article IV republican-government clause plausibly *obliges* Congress to protect political expression from state censorship.)[95] The First Amendment, then, was not agnostic on whether speech, press, petition, assembly, and free exercise were liberties of citizens and good things. By contrast, the amendment was indeed agnostic on the issue of establishment. Congress had no more authority in the states to disestablish than to establish. Both actions were equally beyond Congress's delegated powers; and the unfettered choice between establishment and dis- was given to the states. As a more pure federalism provision, then, the establishment clause seems considerably more difficult to incorporate against states.

In the end, of course, the incorporation question will ultimately depend on a careful examination of the Fourteenth Amendment itself; regardless of its status in 1789, perhaps by 1866 the establishment clause had come to be viewed as affirming an individual right against establishments rather than an agnostic federalism rule. We shall revisit this issue in Part Two. For present purposes, it is enough to note that, given its special logic and language, the establishment clause has less in common with its fellow First Amendment clauses, and more with the Tenth Amendment, than conventional wisdom admits.

Religion and Liberty A federalism-inspired reading of the First Amendment also has profound implications for the original meaning of the free-exercise clause. If the phrase "Congress shall make no law" really meant that Congress simply lacked enumerated power to intrude into religious freedom in the several states, the kind of intrusion prohibited must have been a congressional law that sought to abridge religious exercise *as such*—a congressional law *targeted at* the free exercise of religion. These laws simply lay outside of Congress's legitimate province—they were not necessary-and-proper exercises of its secular enumerated powers—and thus they could be flatly barred: "*no law* . . . prohibiting the free exercise*" of religion means no law designed to prohibit religious freedom. A law that regulated worship qua worship would be unconstitutional from the very moment of its enactment—its *"mak[ing]"*—and so would an artful sham framed in seemingly secular terms but motivated by an attempt to target a given religion. (This sham would offend the *McCulloch* "pretext" test.) Though enforceable in courts after the fact, the First Amendment's first addressee—its first word—was Congress, and it commanded conscientious congressmen to vote against offending bills, to "*make* no law."

On this analysis, general laws designed to serve secular purposes enumerated in Article I would be a very different matter, even if, in operation, they had the effect of impairing some particular group's religious practices. Imagine, say, a congressional ban on the importation of some drug that a particular religion deemed central to its worship practice. The Congress that made the law might not even know that such a practice existed; indeed, the practice may well have arisen only after the law was passed. And surely some religious practices, even if bona fide, must yield to neutral congressional laws—consider, for example, human sacrifice of nonbelievers seeking to vote in federal elections. But once some neutral laws trump contrary religious practice, why not all neutral laws? The apparent grammar and logic of the clause do not seem to invite a balancing of the federal interest against the religious interest; rather, the clause seems to invite careful attention to the purpose of a law, and its nexus to legitimate, secular, enumerated powers in Article I.[96]

On this reading, the controversial Supreme Court decision in the 1990 case *Employment Division v. Smith*[97] might appear to have even more textual, structural, and historical support than its author, Justice Scalia, claimed for it. In limiting the protection of the free-exercise clause to laws targeting religion, the Court said only that "[a]s a textual matter, we do not think the words [of the First Amendment] must be given [a broader] meaning" that would enable some religious practices to trump neutral, general, secular laws.[98]

But *Smith* involved a state law, not a federal one. The true constitutional provision at issue was the Fourteenth Amendment, not the First. And perhaps a sensitive reading of the text, history, and structure of the Reconstruction Amendment calls for a broader protection of some forms of religious worship, even against neutral, secular laws. As we shall see in Part Two, the federalism-based reading of the First Amendment may not have been foremost in the minds of the Reconstruction Congress as it reglossed the federal Bill of Rights and made its freedoms, and other rights and privileges, applicable against states. Though the language of the Fourteenth Amendment at first seems to track that of the First Amendment—"*No* state *shall make* or enforce *any law* which *shall* abridge the privileges or immunities of citizens"—in fact, subtle differences exist that might support critics of *Smith*. To begin with, the Fourteenth focuses not just on making laws but on enforcing them, which may suggest that we should look at the clash between church and state not just at the time of enactment but at the moment of application, too. And perhaps some religious practices that affect only the religious community itself (with no externalities imposed on religious nonbelievers) might be deemed "privileges" and "immunities"—islands of institutional privacy and communal autonomy against general laws. Under this approach, the precise text of the Fourteenth Amendment might enable us

to distinguish among different types of free religious exercise in a principled and textually defensible way.

Once again, a proper resolution of this issue will require close attention to the Reconstruction experience and not just the Founding. And
so here, too, we must defer further analysis to Part Two.

Religion and Education It is apt that the incorporation of the establishment clause first arose in a school case, *Everson v. Board of Education*,[99]
and has had its most visible—if problematic—impact in public schools.
From one perspective, the twentieth-century state school is designed to
serve a function very similar to that of the eighteenth-century state
church: imparting community values and promoting moral conduct
among ordinary citizens, upon whose virtue republican government ultimately rests.[100] The Pennsylvania Constitution of 1776, for example,
dealt with public schools and religious organizations in back-to-back
sections, and treated "religious societies" as entities designed for the "encouragement of virtue" and "for the advancement of religion *or learning*."[101] The Massachusetts Constitution of 1780 likewise spoke of
"public instructions" and "public teachers" in its provisions for establishing churches, and declared that "the happiness of a people, and the good
order" of society "depend upon piety, religion, and morality."[102] The
language of Article III of the Northwest Ordinance of 1787, adopted by
the Confederation Congress during the very summer that the Philadelphia convention met, was to similar effect: "Religion, morality, and
knowledge being necessary to good government and the happiness of
mankind, schools and the means of education shall forever be encouraged." Consider also the Massachusetts Constitution's language concerning Harvard College: "[O]ur wise and pious ancestors . . . laid the
foundation of Harvard College . . . . [E]ncouragement of arts and sci-
ences, and all good literature, tends to the honor of God, the advantage
of the Christian religion, and the great benefit of this and the other United States of America . . . . "[103] Harvard, of course, was hardly unique;
most of the leading centers of learning in eighteenth-century America
had religious roots.[104]

But to see the analogy between today's public schools and yesterday's state churches is to see once again the federalism dimension of the original establishment clause. The possibility of national control over a powerful intermediate association self-consciously trying to influence citizens' worldviews, shape their behavior, and cultivate their habits obviously struck fear in the hearts of Anti-Federalists. Yet local control over such intermediate organizations seemed far less threatening, less distant, less aristocratic, less monopolistic—just as local banks were far less threatening than a national one, and local militias far less dangerous than a national standing army. Given the religious diversity of the continent—with Congregationalists dominating New England, Anglicans down south, Quakers in Pennsylvania, Catholics huddling together in Maryland, Baptists seeking refuge in Rhode Island, and so on—a single national religious regime would have been horribly oppressive to many men and women of faith; local control, by contrast, would allow dissenters in any place to vote with their feet and find a community with the right religious tone.[105] On a more positive note, allowing state and local establishments to exist would encourage participation and community spirit among ordinary citizens at the grass roots—a vision not too different from that underlying parent-teacher associations or local school boards of our own era. (The Massachusetts Constitution of 1780, it should be noted, devolved the designation of established churches upon "the several towns, parishes, precincts, and other bodies politic" within the state.)[106]

The educational importance of religious intermediate associations resurfaces in the free-exercise clause. For if state-established churches in the eighteenth century were in some ways like today's public schools, other churches also played the role of educators, as Tocqueville stressed: "Almost all education is entrusted to the clergy."[107] Thus the free-exercise clause protected not simply the "private" worship of an individual, but also the nongovernmental yet "public" (Tocqueville's word)[108] education of citizens—the very foundation of democracy.

As we shall see, the next two amendments in the Bill also sought to safeguard the foundations of democracy, albeit in a different way.

Three

The Military Amendments

Immediately after the "Congress shall make no law" amendment, we find the following words: "A well regulated Militia, being necessary to the security of a free State, the right of the people to keep and bear Arms, shall not be infringed." As with our First Amendment, the text of the Second is broad enough to protect rights of private individuals and discrete minorities; but, as with the First, the Second's core concerns are populism and federalism. At heart, the amendment reflects a deep anxiety about a potentially abusive federal military, an anxiety also reflected in the Third Amendment.

The Militia Amendment

Populism We have already noted the populist and collective connotations of the rights of the people to petition and assemble in conventions, rights intimately bound up with the people's transcendent right to alter or abolish their government. Whenever self-interested government actors abused their powers or shirked their duties, "the people" could "assemble" in convention and reassert their sovereignty. "Who shall dare to resist the people?" asked Edmund Pendleton with flourish in the Virginia ratifying convention.[1]

To many Anti-Federalists, the answer seemed both obvious and ominous. An aristocratic central government, lacking sympathy with and confidence from ordinary constituents, might dare to resist—especially if that government were propped up by a standing army of mercenaries, vagrants, convicts, aliens, and the like. Only an armed populace could deter such an awful spectacle. Hence the need to bar Congress from disarming freemen. Thus the Second Amendment was closely linked to the textually adjoining First Amendment's guarantees of assembly and petition. One textual tip-off is the use of the magisterial Preamble phrase "the people" in both contexts, thereby conjuring up the Constitution's grand principle of popular sovereignty and its concomitant popular right to alter or abolish the national government. More obvious is the preamble to the Second Amendment itself, and its structural concern with democratic self-government in a "free State." Compare this language with a proposed amendment favored by some Pennsylvania Anti-Federalists: "[T]he people have a right to bear arms for the defence of themselves and their own State, or the United States, *or for the purpose of killing game* . . . ."[2] Unlike our Second Amendment, this text puts individual and collective rights on equal footing.

History also connected the right to keep and bear arms with the idea of popular sovereignty. In Locke's influential *Second Treatise of Government*, the people's right to alter or abolish tyrannous government invariably required a popular appeal to arms.[3] To Americans in 1789, this was not merely speculative theory. It was the lived experience of their age. Beginning with the shot heard round the world, when British soldiers met armed Massachusetts minutemen at Lexington and Concord, Americans had seen the Lockean words of the Declaration of Independence—affirming "the Right of the People to alter or to abolish" oppressive government—made flesh (and blood) in a Revolution wrought by arms. Thus when Pendleton trumpeted the right of the people to assemble in convention as the answer to any federal misbehavior, Patrick Henry rose up to offer a more bleak assessment: "O sir, we should have fine times, indeed, if, to punish tyrants, it were only sufficient to assemble the people! Your arms, wherewith you could defend yourselves, are gone . . . ."[4]

To see the connection between arms and populism from another angle, consider the key nineteenth-century distinction between political rights and civil rights. The former were rights of members of the polity—call them First-Class Citizens—whereas the latter belonged to all (free) members of the larger society. Alien men and single white women circa 1800 typically could speak, print, worship, enter into contracts, hold personal property in their own name, sue and be sued, and exercise sundry other civil rights, but typically could not vote, hold public office, or serve on juries. These last three were political rights, reserved for First-Class Citizens. So too, the right to bear arms had long been viewed as a political right, a right of First-Class Citizens.* Thus the "people" at the core

---

*There is some fuzziness at the edges, but arms bearing and suffrage were intimately linked two hundred years ago and have remained so. *See generally* Akhil Reed Amar, *The Central Meaning of Republican Government: Popular Sovereignty, Majority Rule, and the Denominator Problem*, 65 U. COLO. L. REV. 749, 771–73 (1994). During the Founding era, various militiamen who had borne arms for America were allowed to vote on the federal Constitution regardless of whether they met ordinary property qualifications. *See id.* at 772; *cf.* 2 THE RECORDS OF THE FEDERAL CONVENTION OF 1787, at 210 (Max Farrand rev. ed., 1937) (remarks of Benjamin Franklin). Years later, aliens who had already voted in various elections (as some states allowed) were subject to the military draft in the Civil War, *see* Jamin B. Raskin, *Legal Aliens, Local Citizens: The Historical, Constitutional, and Theoretical Meanings of Alien Suffrage*, 141 U. PA. L. REV. 1391, 1412–13 (1993). Lincoln's initial decision to propose the Thirteenth Amendment, and the Republicans' eventual decision to endorse the black franchise in the Fifteenth Amendment, were substantially influenced by the fact that black soldiers had served the Union during the Civil War. Derrick A. Bell, Jr., *Racial Remediation: An Historical Perspective on Current Conditions*, 52 NOTRE DAME LAW. 5, 9–11 (1976). Indeed, section 2 of the Fourteenth Amendment defined a state's presumptive electorate as all males over age twenty-one. This was rather close to the definition of the general militia, which encompassed all adult males capable of bearing arms. *See infra* page 218, note. In our own century, Woodrow Wilson and other national politicians explicitly endorsed women's suffrage in recognition of women's roles as "partners" in the war effort against Germany. 1 WOODROW WILSON, WAR AND PEACE 263, 265 (Ray Stannard Baker and William E. Dodd eds., 1927);

of the Second Amendment were the same "We the People" who in conventions had "ordain[ed] and establish[ed]" the Constitution and whose right to reassemble in convention was at the core of the First Amendment. Apart from the Preamble, the words "the People" appeared only once in the original Constitution, just a single sentence removed from the Preamble and in a context where "the People" unambiguously connoted voters: "The House of Representatives shall be . . . chosen every second Year by the People of the several States."

In emphasizing the structural and populist core of the Second Amendment, I do not deny that the phrase *the people* can be read broadly, beyond what I have called the core. As with the language of petition and assembly, other concerns can be placed under the language's spacious canopy.[5] But to see the un-Reconstructed amendment as primarily concerned with an individual right to hunt or to protect one's home is like viewing the heart of the speech and assembly clauses as the right of persons to meet to play bridge or to have sex.[6]

And if we seek more expansive modern-day readings of the amendment's broad language, attention to the amendment's first clause—focusing on the necessary preconditions for democratic self-government by the people of a "free state"—suggests a broad understanding of *arms*. The amendment is about empowering the people so that they may rule, and today that empowerment may call for much more than guns (a word that, in fact, nowhere appears in the amendment). To preserve a free state today, perhaps the people must be "armed" with modems more than muskets, with access to the Internet more than to the shooting range.

AILEEN S. KRADITOR, THE IDEAS OF THE WOMAN SUFFRAGE MOVEMENT, 1890–1920, at 166 (1965); ALAN P. GRIMES, DEMOCRACY AND THE AMENDMENTS TO THE CONSTITUTION 92 (1978). Even more recently, the Twenty-sixth Amendment extending the franchise to eighteen-year-olds grew out of the perceived unfairness of any gap between the Vietnam draft age and the voting age. *Id.* at 141–47. For an extraordinarily rich discussion of the political connotations of arms bearing, see Elaine Scarry, *War and the Social Contract: Nuclear Policy, Distribution, and the Right to Bear Arms,* 139 U. PA. L. REV. 1257 (1991).

As recent events in Russia and China have shown, fax machines are perhaps the most powerful weapons of all.

Federalism Even if heavily armed, citizens acting individually would face an uphill struggle when confronting a disciplined and professional standing army. In *The Federalist* No. 28, Alexander Hamilton described a typical nonfederal regime: "[I]f the persons intrusted with supreme power become usurpers, the different parcels, subdivisions, or districts of which [the nation] consists, having no distinct government in each, can take no regular measures for defense. The citizens must rush tumultuously to arms, without concert, without system, without resource . . . ."[7] In the federal system of America, however, Article I, section 8, clause 16 of the Constitution explicitly devolved upon state governments the power of "Appointment of the Officers, and the Authority of training the Militia according to the discipline prescribed by Congress." In the event of central tyranny, state governments could do precisely what colonial governments had done beginning at Lexington and Concord and Bunker Hill: organize and mobilize their citizens into an effective fighting force capable of besting even a large standing army. Wrote Madison in *The Federalist* No. 46: "[T]he State governments with the people on their side would be able to repel the danger. . . . [A standing army] would be opposed [by] a militia amounting to near half a million of citizens with arms in their hands, officered by men chosen from among themselves, fighting for their common liberties and united and conducted by governments possessing their affections and confidence."[8]

Yet the "military check of federalism"[9] built into the original Constitution did not quiet Anti-Federalist fears. Many pointed a suspicious finger at earlier language in clause 16 empowering Congress "to provide for organizing, arming, and disciplining, the Militia." Might Congress try to use the power granted by these words, they asked darkly, to *dis*arm the militia?[10] The Second Amendment was designed to make clear that any such congressional action was off-limits.

The obvious importance of federalism to the Constitution's original allocation of military power prompts key questions about federalism's role in the Second Amendment's clarifying gloss. Several modern scholars have read the amendment as protecting only arms bearing in organized "state militias," like SWAT teams and National Guard units.[11] If this reading were accepted, the Second Amendment would be at base a right of state governments rather than citizens. If so, the amendment would be analogous to the establishment clause, and similarly resistant to incorporation against state governments via the Fourteenth Amendment.[12]

Though in some ways congenial to my overall thesis about the original Bill of Rights, this reading doesn't quite work. The states'-rights reading puts great weight on the word *militia,* but this word appears only in the amendment's subordinate clause. The ultimate right to keep and bear arms belongs to "the people," not the states. As the language of the Tenth Amendment shows, these two are of course not identical: when the Constitution means "states," it says so.[13] Thus, as noted above, "the people" at the core of the Second Amendment are the same people at the heart of the Preamble and the First Amendment. Elbridge Gerry put the point nicely in the First Congress, in language that closely tracked the populist concern about governmental self-dealing at the root of earlier amendments: "This declaration of rights, I take it, is intended to secure *the people* against the mal-administration of the *Government.*"[14]

What's more, the "militia," as used in the amendment and in clause 16, had a very different meaning two hundred years ago than in ordinary conversation today. Nowadays, it is quite common to speak loosely of the National Guard as "the state militia," but two hundred years ago, any band of paid, semiprofessional, part-time volunteers, like today's Guard, would have been called "a *select* corps" or "*select* militia"—and viewed in many quarters as little better than a standing army.[15] In 1789, when used without any qualifying adjective, "the militia" referred to all citizens capable of bearing arms.[16] The seeming tension between the dependent and the main clauses of the Second Amendment thus evaporates on closer inspection—the "militia" is identical to "the people" in the core sense described above. Indeed, the version of the amendment that initially passed in the House, only to be stylistically shortened in the

Senate, explicitly defined the militia as "composed of the body of the People."[17] This is clearly the sense in which "*the* militia" is used in clause 16 and throughout *The Federalist*,[18] in keeping with standard usage[19] confirmed by contemporaneous dictionaries, legal and otherwise. As Tench Coxe wrote in a 1788 Pennsylvania essay, "Who are the militia? Are they not ourselves?"[20]

A more plausible bit of text to stress on behalf of a states'-rights reading is "well regulated."[21] It might be asked, who, if not state governments, would regulate the militia and organize them into an effective fighting force capable of deterring would-be tyrants in the federal government? And does not the right to "regulate" subsume the right to prohibit, as the Supreme Court has explicitly recognized in such commerce-clause cases as *Champion v. Ames*?[22] And if so, how can a provision designed to give state governments broad regulatory power over their citizens' arms bearing be incorporated against states to limit that very power?

Though much stronger than the standard states'-rights reading, this chain of argument has some weak links of its own. First, it appears that the adjective "well regulated" did not imply broad state authority to disarm the general militia; indeed, its use in various state constitutional antecedents of the Second Amendment suggests just the opposite.[23] Second, and connected, the notion that congressional power in clause 16 to "organiz[e]" and "disciplin[e]" the general militia logically implied congressional power to disarm the militia entirely is the very heresy that the Second Amendment was designed to deny. How, then, can we use the amendment's language to embrace the same heresy vis-à-vis state regulation?[24] What's more, as shall become evident in Part Two, the right to keep and bear arms was plainly viewed by the framers of the Fourteenth Amendment as a "privilege of national citizenship" that henceforth would apply, and perhaps should always have applied, against states.[25] A final puzzle: if the Second Amendment is purely a states'-rights provision, does this mean that it has no bite outside of states—say, in the federal territories? The Republican Party obviously thought otherwise when it drafted its national platform in 1856, declaring that residents of the Kansas Territory had the right "to keep and bear arms."[26]

But there is another area in which the Second Amendment can be seen as analogous to the establishment clause, imposing federalism limits on the central government in favor of state governmental regulation: the draft. Under this reading, the federal government cannot directly draft ordinary Americans into its army, but state governments can conscript, organize, and train their respective citizens—the militia—who can in times of emergency be called into national service. Consider first the key texts in Article I, section 8:

The Congress shall have Power . . .

To raise and support Armies . . .

To provide for calling forth the Militia to execute the Laws of the Union, suppress Insurrections and repel Invasions;

To provide for organizing, arming, and disciplining, the Militia, . . . reserving to the States respectively, the Appointment of the Officers, and the Authority of training the Militia according to the discipline prescribed by Congress.

By itself, the authority to "raise" armies no more naturally subsumed a power to conscript soldiers than the authority to "lay and collect Taxes [and] Duties" and to "constitute Tribunals inferior to the supreme Court" naturally subsumed power to draft tax collectors, customs officers, judges, and bailiffs.[27] (Similarly, more than mere implication from the naked text authorizing a navy would seem necessary to allow the Congress to engage in the historically odious practice of impressment.)[28] In 1789, the word *army*—in contradistinction to *militia*—connoted a mercenary force, as even a casual glance at contemporaneous dictionaries reveals.[29] This was largely why an "army" was feared. It was not composed of a randomly conscripted cross-section of the general militia (all citizens capable of bearing arms), but was instead filled with hired guns. These men, full-time soldiers who had sold themselves into virtual bondage to the government, were typically considered the dregs of society—men without land, homes, families, or principles. Full-time service in the army further weakened their ties to civil(ized/ian) society, and harsh army "discipline" increased their servility to the government.

Small wonder, then, that many traditional republicans opposed standing armies, at least in peacetime. (Perhaps in war, with the very survival of the nation at stake, an army was the lesser of two evils—a nominally American army might be marginally less threatening to domestic liberty than the enemy's army.) Thus, mainstream republican thought in the late eighteenth century saw a "well regulated *Militia*" as the best "security of a free State." Article I clearly gave Congress authority in actual emergencies to federalize the militia instead of raising an army—but only under a system of cooperative federalism designed to maintain the integrity of the militia. Clause 16 painstakingly prescribed the precise role that state governments had to play in training and organizing the militia and in appointing its officers. These carefully wrought limitations in clause 16 were widely seen in 1789 as indispensable bulwarks against any congressional attempt to misuse its power over citizen militiamen. Yet these bulwarks would become trivial—a constitutional Maginot Line—if Congress could outflank them by relabeling militiamen as army "soldiers" conscriptable at will, in time of war or peace, under the plenary power of the army clause.[30] Seen from another angle, the Constitution's explicit invocation of "the Militia" in clause 16, in contradistinction to its use of "Armies" in clause 12, makes clear that each word is used in its ordinary-language sense: *army* means enlisted soldiers, and *militia* means citizen conscripts.[31]

Structure confirms this technical parsing of text. Wretches miserable enough to volunteer as hired guns might deserve whatever treatment that they got at the hands of army officers, but citizens wrenched by conscription from their land, their homes, and their families deserved better. They were entitled to be placed in units with fellow citizens from their own locality, and officered by local leaders—men chosen by state governments closest to them and most representative of them, men who were likely to be persons of standing in their communities (indeed, likely to be elected civilian officials), men whom they were likely to know directly or indirectly from civilian society and who were likely to know them.[32] The ordinary harshness of military discipline would be tempered by the many social, economic, and political linkages that predated military service and that would be renewed thereafter.* Officers would know that, in a variety of ways, they could be called to account back home after the fighting was over.

Nor should we forget the relationship among militiamen at the bottom ranks. Men serving alongside their families, friends, neighbors, classmates, and fellow parishioners—in short, their community—would be constantly reminded of civil(ian/ized) norms of conduct. They were less likely to become uncivilized marauders or servile brutes. Thus the transcendent constitutional principle of civilian control over the military[33] would be internalized in the everyday mind-set of each militiaman. Adam Smith put the point as follows, in words later quoted by the most important Second Amendment case decided by the Supreme Court this century: "In a militia, the character of the labourer, artificer, or tradesman, predominates over that of the soldier: in a standing army, that of the soldier predominates over every other character; and in this distinction seems to consist the essential difference between those two different species of military force."[34]

In the end, the militia system was carefully designed to protect lib-

---

*"The [militia] muster was almost a family reunion. Fathers and sons, uncles and nephews, brothers, cousins and in-laws often enlisted in the same units." ROBERT A. GROSS, THE MINUTEMEN AND THEIR WORLD 71 (1976). "The Minutemen of the towns were held together less by chains of command than by familial loyalties. . . . Over one-quarter of the Lexington militiamen mustered by Captain John Parker on April 19, 1775, were related to him by blood or marriage." GORDON S. WOOD, THE RADICALISM OF THE AMERICAN REVOLUTION 45 (1992).

The social aspects of militias are nicely captured in the following account of a typical militia muster in late-seventeenth-century Massachusetts: "On the training days, a town's militia company generally assembled on public grounds, held roll call and prayer, practiced the manual of arms and close order drill, and passed under review and inspection by the militia officers and other public officials. There might also be target practice and sham battles followed in the afternoon—when times were not too perilous—by refreshments, games, and socializing." RUSSELL F. WEIGLEY, HISTORY OF THE UNITED STATES ARMY 6 (1967). Note how the reference to prayer fits well with the role of local religious establishments in Massachusetts, see supra Chapter 2. See also DANIEL J. BOORSTIN, THE AMERICANS: THE COLONIAL EXPERIENCE 354–56 (1958).

erty through localism. Here, as with the Virginia and Kentucky Resolutions, freedom and federalism pulled together. Just as the establishment clause saw a national establishment as far more likely to oppress than state and local establishments—and in the worst case scenario, it was always easier to flee an oppressive locality or state than the nation as a whole—so here, national conscription was far more dangerous than the state and local militia system. Like the jury of the vicinage, which we shall examine shortly, the militia was a local institution, bringing together representative citizens to preserve popular values of their society.

Thus far my federalism argument has stressed the language and structure of Article I. Why have I advertised this as a *Second Amendment* argument? Because for me, it is the Second Amendment's gloss on Article I—a synthesis of original Constitution and Bill of Rights, if you will—that is decisive. For the stylized portrait of "army" and "militia" I have just presented was not universally subscribed to in 1789. Hamilton, for example, painted a less affectionate picture of the militia[35] and might well have pointed to the expansive language of the "necessary and proper" clause to support a national army draft. In contrast, I have up to now omitted all reference to that clause and have read federal power strictly, emphasizing structural arguments that resonate best with Anti-Federalist and republican ideology. My warrant for this interpretive posture is the Second Amendment. I have read clause 16 jealously and have been especially vigilant about congressional circumvention of its terms, because jealousy and vigilance are at the heart of the amendment's gloss on clause 16.[36] I have emphasized republican ideology about militias and armies because that ideology was expressly written into the amendment's preamble.[37] Truly, no other clause in the Constitution is so self-consciously didactic and ideological, save perhaps the (other) Preamble. If the amendment is not about the critical difference between the vaunted "well regulated Militia" of "the people" and the disfavored standing army, it is about nothing. And to ask what *makes* this militia "well regulated"—a protector of, rather than a threat to, civilian society—is to confront the social and structural vision outlined above. To put the point yet another way, the Second Amendment takes the expansive word *necessary*—originally a word on the congressional-power side of the ledger, as Chief Justice Marshall stressed in *McCulloch v. Maryland*[38]—and puts that word to work as a restriction on Congress. It is a well-regulated militia, and not an army of conscripts, that is "*necessary* to the security of a free State"; the Second Amendment estops Congress from claiming otherwise.

Postconstitutional history supports the foregoing analysis. During the War of 1812, various sorts of federal draft bills were introduced, setting the scene for an important congressional debate over the army and militia clauses of Article I and their Second Amendment gloss. Opposition to these bills in the House of Representatives was led by none other than Daniel Webster, who argued that any federal draft under the army clause impermissibly evaded the constitutional limitations on federal use of the militia. The plan was an illegitimate attempt to raise "a standing army out of the militia by draft."[39] Webster's vivid image of the evils of such an evasion of clause 16 should by now be familiar:

> Where is it written in the Constitution, . . . that you may take children from their parents, and parents from their children . . . [?]
>
> . . . .
>
> But this father or this son . . . goes to the camp. With whom do you associate him? With those only who are sober and virtuous and respectable like himself? No, sir. But you propose to find him companions in the worst men of the worst sort. Another bill lies on your table offering a bounty to deserters from your enemy. Whatever is most infamous in his ranks you propose to make your own . . . . In the line of your army, with the true levelling of [Napoleonic] despotism, you propose a promiscuous mixture of the worthy and the worthless, the virtuous and the profligate; the husbandman, the merchant, the mechanic of your own country, with [the dregs of Europe] who possess neither interest, feeling, nor character in common with your own people, and who have no other recommendation . . . than their propensity to crimes.[40]

Webster closed with an invocation of the libertarian localism of the Virginia and Kentucky Resolutions, and a quotation of the "Right of Revolution" clause of the New Hampshire Constitution:

> It will be the solemn duty of the State Governments to protect their own authority over their own militia, and to interpose between their citizens and arbitrary power. These are among the objects for which the State Governments exist; and their highest obligations bind them to the preservation of their own rights and the liberties of their people . . . . [My constituents and I] live under a constitution which teaches us that "the doctrine of non-resistance against arbitrary power and oppression is absurd, slavish, and destructive of the good and happiness of mankind."[41]

In the tradition of the Virginia and Kentucky Resolutions, representatives of various New England states met in the Hartford convention of 1814–15 to denounce as unconstitutional any national attempt to "subject[] the militia . . . to forcible drafts, conscriptions, or impressments."[42] The eventual republican triumph on this issue—none of the proposed draft bills passed[43]—should be as central a precedent for our Second Amendment as the 1800 triumph over the Sedition Act is for our First.

Only in the twentieth century did the Supreme Court uphold a federal draft, in the *Selective Draft Law Cases*[44] decided during World War I.* The arguments of the Court can be charitably described as unper-

---

*During the Civil War, the federal government adopted a draft bill of sorts, although many of its supporters conceded that the army clause might not allow direct conscription. These supporters tried to characterize the bill as akin to a tax and denied that it established illegitimate conscription, pointing to its provisions allowing money payment in lieu of personal military service, 1 FRED A. SHANNON, THE ORGANIZATION AND ADMINISTRATION OF THE UNION ARMY, 1861–1865, at 308 (1928). In the end, fewer than one-fifth of the men "drafted" personally served, *see* Harrop A. Freeman, *The Constitutionality of Peacetime Conscription*, 31 VA. L. REV. 40, 72 n.102 (1944). In an unpublished sketch in preparation for a proper judicial case that never materialized, Chief Justice Taney nevertheless declared the act unconstitutional as an impermissible circumvention of the militia clause. Roger B. Taney, *Thoughts on the Conscription Law of the United States, reprinted in* THE MILITARY DRAFT 207–18 (Martin Anderson ed., 1982).

suasive. Less charitably, the Court's opinion can be said to resemble its contemporaneous First Amendment jurisprudence, epitomized by such now malodorous cases as *Debs*[45] and *Abrams;*[46] none of these cases presented a sympathetic account of the worldview that gave rise to our First and Second Amendments. The "Revolution of 1800" had been all but forgotten in the Court's controlling opinions until *New York Times v. Sullivan*[47] made it a polestar of the First Amendment; so today, the central lessons of 1812–15 lie dormant, waiting to be rediscovered by students of the Second Amendment.

A case can be right for the wrong reasons, of course, and perhaps a national draft can be defended in the twentieth century for reasons rather different from those offered by the *Selective Draft Law Cases.* Circumstances have changed—the Founders' militia does not really exist today—and as will be evident in Part Two, the Fourteenth Amendment reflected a much more sympathetic view of a national army and a much more skeptical view of state-organized militias. Thus it is possible that modern judges must Reconstruct the Creation vision here. But the first step of proper analysis is to get that vision right.

The Quartering Amendment

Consider next the Third Amendment: "No Soldier shall, in time of peace be quartered in any house, without the consent of the Owner, nor in time of war, but in a manner to be prescribed by law."

Like the Second, the Third centrally focuses on the structural issue of protecting civilian values against the threat of an overbearing military. No standing army in peacetime can be allowed to dominate civilian society, either openly or by subtle insinuation. The Second Amendment's militia could thwart any open military usurpation—say, a siege—but what about more insidious forms of military occupation, featuring federal soldiers cowing civilians by psychological guerrilla warfare, day by day and house by house? Bostonians who had lived under the hated Quartering Act of 1774 knew that this was no wild hypothetical. Hence the Third Amendment was needed to deal with military threats too subtle and stealthy for the Second's "well regulated Militia."

It is no accident that the Second and Third Amendments stand back-to-back, for these siblings spring from the same stock: at heart they are military amendments. In the English Bill of Rights of 1689, the quartering question locked arms with the more general military issue of standing armies. In the words of the Bill's preamble, James II had subverted the liberties of his subjects by "raising and keeping a standing army within this kingdom in time of peace, without consent of parliament, and quartering soldiers contrary to law."[48] Americans learned these lines well and reenacted them in staging their own Glorious Revolution a century later. In the Declaration of Independence, the colonists scolded King George for keeping "among us, in times of peace, Standing Armies without the Consent of our legislatures"; and in the very next clause for affecting "to render the Military independent of and superior to the Civil power"; and in the next clause for approving Parliamentary laws "quartering large bodies of armed troops among us."[49] Most Revolutionary state constitutions that addressed quartering followed a rather similar pattern, treating various military issues in an integrated package. In the Delaware Constitution of 1776, the Maryland Constitution of 1776, and the New Hampshire Constitution of 1784, successive provisions: (1) praised a "well regulated militia" as the "proper" and "natural" defense of a free state; (2) condemned standing armies as "dangerous to liberty" and unconstitutional without legislative consent; (3) declared that the military power must at all times yield to civilian supremacy; and (4) forbade all peacetime quartering of troops and wartime quartering without legislative authorization.[50] In the Maryland Constitution, the antiquartering clause was further flanked by sharp restrictions on martial law, a formation also featured in the Massachusetts Constitution of 1780.[51] Similar military linkages appeared in the proposals floated in each of the six state ratifying conventions that addressed the quartering question: Maryland, New Hampshire, Virginia, New York, North Carolina, and Rhode Island.[52] These linkages are nicely visible in the remarks of Patrick Henry in Virginia:

> [T]he clause which gives Congress the power of raising armies . . . appears a very alarming power, when unlimited. [Congress] are not only

to raise, but to support, armies; and this support is to go to the utmost abilities of the United States. If Congress shall say that the general welfare requires it, they may keep armies continually on foot. There is no control on Congress in raising or stationing them. They may billet them on the people at pleasure. This unlimited authority is a most dangerous power: its principles are despotic. If it be unbounded, it must lead to despotism; for the power of a people in a free government is supposed to be paramount to the existing power.

. . . Here we may have troops in times of peace. They may be billeted in any manner—to tyrannize, oppress, and crush us.[53]

Note also how the Third Amendment reinforces the federalism argument against the draft inspired by the Second. Given that the Third flatly forbids Congress to conscript civilians as involuntary innkeepers and roommates of soldiers in peacetime, what sense does it make to read the army clause as giving Congress peacetime power to exercise even more drastic coercion by conscripting civilians into the army itself? It would be odd to say that Congress has absolutely no peacetime power to force soldiers upon civilians, but virtually total peacetime power to force civilians into soldiers. I stress peacetime, because the army clause makes no distinction between war and peace. If its text allows a wartime draft, peacetime conscription must likewise be deemed necessary and proper. The militia clause, by contrast, limits Congress's conscription power to specified national emergencies[54]—just as the Third Amendment limits Congress's quartering power to wartime. (Note also that the English Bill of Rights, the Declaration of Independence, each state constitution and convention canvassed above, and Patrick Henry's above-quoted speech all sharply distinguished between peacetime and wartime.)[55]

The strict limits in both the militia clause and the Third Amendment derive from the awesome nature of the conscription power. Like a criminal sanction, conscription of a person's body or his place of abode can take over much of his life. This leads to my final structural point about the Third Amendment. Just as criminal law requires special legislative and judicial safeguards to protect against possible executive overreaching, the Third Amendment requires a special legislative finding before a civilian's house can be conscripted. Military use must be prescribed by national law, and as the *Youngstown* Court pointedly observed in an analogous context, only Congress can pass such a law.[56] Thus the amendment stands as an important reaffirmation of separation of powers, and limited executive authority. Surprisingly, only one of the seven opinions in *Youngstown* even mentioned the Third Amendment;[57] as with federalism, the separation-of-powers implications of the Bill of Rights often go unnoticed because of our modern-day fixation on individual rights. To put the point a different way, the deep spirit of the Third Amendment cautions skepticism about unilateral executive assertions of military necessity; and yet six of the seven *Youngstown* opinions utterly ignored that amendment in a case that genuinely implicated the amendment's spirit, if not its letter.

To the extent that modern lawyers think about the Third Amendment at all, they are likely to see it as an affirmation of the general right of individual privacy thought to pervade the penumbras and inhabit the interstices of the Bill of Rights. The most notable Supreme Court mention of the amendment in the modern era, Justice Douglas's opinion of the Court in *Griswold v. Connecticut*,[58] epitomizes this perspective. In today's world, lawyers, scholars, and judges are wont to link the Third Amendment to the Fourth rather than to the Second, despite the fact that no state constitution or convention paired antiquartering and antisearch clauses. A computer check of Supreme Court citations to the Third Amendment since *Youngstown* reveals seven attempts to associate the amendment with privacy and only one case invoking the amendment in a context involving alleged military overreaching.[59] But as we have seen, privacy is not the whole story—indeed perhaps not even the headline. To be sure, there *is* an important connection between the Third and Fourth Amendments. Both explicitly protect "houses"— above and beyond all other buildings—from needless and dangerous intrusions by governmental officials. And as we shall see in Part Two, the Fourteenth Amendment highlighted this Third-Fourth nexus, with an explicit accent on the privacy-sounding word *privileges*, even as Reconstructors simultaneously downplayed antiarmy ideology (for obvious reasons). But the privacy connections between the Third Amendment and the Fourth must not be allowed to obscure the originally more significant but typically unmentioned military linkages between the Third Amendment and the Second. With this in mind, let us now turn to the Fourth in its own right.

Four

Searches, Seizures,
and Takings

The right of the people to be secure in their persons, houses, papers, and effects, against unreasonable searches and seizures, shall not be violated, and no Warrants shall issue, but upon probable cause, supported by Oath or affirmation, and particularly describing the place to be searched, and the persons or things to be seized.

So reads our Fourth Amendment. How do its words and spirit fit with the rest of the Bill?

A Right of the People?

We have already noted that the First and Second Amendments' references to "the people" implied a core collective right, echoing the Preamble's commitment to the ultimate sovereignty of "We the People of the United States." So too with the Ninth and Tenth Amendments' use of that phrase, as will become clear in Chapter 6. Indeed, the historian Lawrence Cress has argued that in constitutions in "state after state, [the phrases] 'the people' or 'the militia' [were used to connote] the sovereign citizenry, described collectively." In contrast, "the expression, 'man' or 'person' [was typically] used to describe individual rights such as freedom of conscience."[1] The Virginia ratifying convention's declaration of rights followed a similar pattern, invoking "the people's" rights to assembly, instruction, speech, and arms bearing but using "every freeman" and "man" in connection with a variety of civil rights involving due-process and criminal-procedure safeguards.[2] The Virginia prototype of the Fourth Amendment fell in the latter category—"every *freeman* has a right to be secure from all unreasonable searches and siezures [*sic*] of his *person* . . . . "[3] This formulation followed the general outlines of the search-and-seizure clause of the highly influential Massachusetts Constitution of 1780 and its New Hampshire look-alike and was in turn echoed by ratifying conventions in New York and North Carolina.[4] Madison was surely aware of these formulations, given his leading role in the Virginia convention, but his initial proposal instead invoked "the people"[5]—language that survived all subsequent congressional modifications. Of the original thirteen colonies, only one had featured this search-and-seizure phrasing in its state constitution—the rather atypical Pennsylvania Constitution of 1776, penned before the American reconceptualization of English popular-sovereignty theory reached full flower.[6]

Was Madison's use of the phrase "the people" simply sloppy draftsmanship, or is there a way of understanding the phrase as a collective noun even in the Fourth Amendment? On one reading, the amendment's language of "the people" could be read as reminding us that we must be especially watchful of government efforts to use search-and-seizure powers to interfere with the people's political activities—circulating petitions (literally *the people's papers*), attending political meetings (with their literal *persons*), assembling in a constitutional convention (which might be seen as a *house* of the *people*), and so on. But without more, this reading seems a bit too cute; surely, the main "houses" to be protected here are private abodes, not public assemblies.[7]

Madison's choice of language here may well have been influenced by the celebrated 1763 English case of *Wilkes v. Wood*,[8] one of the two or

three most important search-and-seizure cases on the books in 1789.*
Wood involved a famous cast of characters—both the target of the gov-
ernment search, John Wilkes, and the author of the opinion, Lord Chief
Justice Charles Pratt (soon to become Lord Camden), became folk he-
roes in the colonies. (Pennsylvania residents named the town of Wilkes-
Barre after the plaintiff; North Carolina and Georgia each created a

---

*The other leading case here was *Entick v. Carrington*, 95 Eng. Rep. 807 (C.P. 1765),
19 Howell's State Trials 1029. The Boston writs of assistance case appears to have played
very little role in the discussion leading up to the Fourth Amendment. Thus far, historians of the amendment have uncovered only one reference to the writs of assistance, *see*
NELSON B. LASSON, THE HISTORY AND DEVELOPMENT OF THE FOURTH AMENDMENT
TO THE UNITED STATES CONSTITUTION 89 n.40 (1937). Lasson attributed the pseudo-
nymous pamphlet containing this reference to Elbridge Gerry. In fact, Charles Warren
has shown that this pamphlet was written by Mercy Otis Warren, the sister of the colonial lawyer James Otis, who argued the writs of assistance case. Charles Warren, *Elbridge
Gerry, James Warren, Mercy Warren, and the Ratification of the Federal Constitution in
Massachusetts, in* 64 MASSACHUSETTS HISTORICAL SOCIETY PROCEEDINGS 143 (1931).
Further evidence casting doubt on the importance of the Boston case in the framing of
the Fourth Amendment is textual: the amendment speaks of warrants, not writs. It also
focuses on persons, papers, and houses. All three were centrally implicated by the *Wilkes*
case, but the Boston case turned only on houses. We should also note that the Declaration of Independence made no mention of the writs-of-assistance affair. This fact is hard
to explain if the affair was widely seen at the time as the epochal event that John
Adams—writing fifty years after the fact—claimed it was: "Then and there was the first
scene of the first Act of Opposition to the arbitrary claims of Great Britain. Then and
there the child Independence was born." 2 LEGAL PAPERS OF JOHN ADAMS 107 (L. Kinvin Wroth and Hiller B. Zobel eds., 1965) (letter to William Tudor, March 29, 1817). Although this passage has been very widely cited by modern judges and law professors, the
best historical scholarship now suggests that Adams was engaging in a bit of historical
revisionism, to convince Americans that Boston, not Virginia, had truly been the cradle
of the Revolution, and that James Otis had preceded Patrick Henry as the first great orator of American liberty. *See* M. H. SMITH, THE WRITS OF ASSISTANCE CASE 250–54,
380, 384, 466, 508, 518 (1978). For more discussion and analysis of these points, see Akhil
Reed Amar, *The Fourth Amendment, Boston, and the Writs of Assistance*, 30 SUFFOLK L.
REV. 53 (1996). And for a more detailed overall account of the Fourth Amendment than
is possible here, see Akhil Reed Amar, *Fourth Amendment First Principles*, 107 HARV. L.
REV. 757 (1994); AKHIL REED AMAR, THE CONSTITUTION AND CRIMINAL PROCEDURE:
FIRST PRINCIPLES 1–45 (1997).

Wilkes County; New Jersey, South Carolina, and Maine each dedicated a city in Camden's honor; and Baltimore, Maryland, named two
streets—and later, Camden Yards, home of today's Baltimore Orioles—
after the great chief justice.)[9] No less famous were the facts of the case.
Wilkes, a champion of the people and a member of Commons, had used
the press to communicate with his constituents and criticize George III's
ministry and majesty. When the government reacted by trying to use
general warrants to suppress his political activity, breaking into his house
and rummaging through his personal papers, Wilkes brought suit in
Wood and successfully challenged the legality of those warrants. Wilkes
also brought suit to challenge the "seizure" of his "person." (The government had imprisoned him in the Tower of London.) In a companion case to *Wood,* the lord chief justice ordered Wilkes released on habeas
corpus on the ground of his Parliamentary privilege from arrest.[10]

In the Fourth Amendment, as elsewhere, we need not view the phrase
the people as sounding solely in collective, political terms; once again, the
language is broad enough to radiate beyond its core. Indeed, it is far from
clear that populism is the core here. For in the Fourth Amendment, as
nowhere else in the Constitution, the collective-sounding phrase *the people*
is immediately qualified by the use—twice—of the more individualistic
language of *persons.* The amendment's text seems to move quickly from
the public to the private, from the political to the personal, from "the
people" out-of-doors in conventions and suchlike to "persons" very
much indoors in their private homes. Again, we must note that the
amendment singles out "houses" for special mention above and beyond
other buildings subsumed within the catchall word *effects. Houses* first
appeared alongside a ban on "unreasonable" searches and seizures in the
famous Article XIV of the Massachusetts Constitution of 1780, and here
it clearly referred to a right of "[e]very subject" to be "secure from all
unreasonable searches, and seizures, of *his* person, *his* houses, *his* papers,
and all *his* possessions."[11]

Yet even here, in talking the familiar talk of individual rights, we must
be wary of anachronism and must not automatically assume that the
right was essentially countermajoritarian. As with virtually every Bill of
Rights provision thus far examined, the Fourth Amendment evinces at

least as much concern with the agency problem of protecting the people generally from self-interested government policy as with protecting minorities against majorities of fellow citizens. A self-dealing and oligarchic government, after all, could threaten rights of the people collectively by singling out certain persons—opposition leaders like John Wilkes, for example—for special abuse. To counter this and other threats, the Fourth and Seventh Amendments armed civil juries, drawn from "the people," with special weapons to protect both individual persons and the collective people against a possibly unrepresentative and self-serving officialdom.

Reflect, for a moment, on the fact that the Fourth Amendment actually contains two different commands. First, all government searches and seizures must be reasonable. Second, no warrants shall issue without probable cause. The modern Supreme Court has intentionally collapsed the two requirements, treating all unwarranted searches and seizures—with various exceptions, such as exigent circumstances—as per se unreasonable.[12] Otherwise, the Court has reasoned, the requirement that a neutral magistrate verify probable cause ex ante would be obviously frustrated—the special safeguards of the warrant clause would be all but meaningless.

If we assume that the amendment is primarily about protecting minority rights and further assume that judges and magistrates are the best institutional guardians of those rights, this reading might seem to make sense. Why should government officials be allowed greater latitude (general reasonableness rather than the stricter probable cause) when they intentionally avoid the courtroom and intrude on individuals in a judicially unwarranted manner? Hence the seeming need, under these assumptions, to engraft a constructive second sentence onto the amendment: "Absent special circumstances, no search or seizure shall occur without a warrant."

But the fact that the amendment does not contain such a sentence should invite us to rethink our assumptions. (So should the combination of the silliness of the engrafted sentence without the "special circumstances" escape hatch, and the extraordinary difficulty of specifying the appropriate size and shape of the hatch. Indeed, reading a warrant requirement into the amendment, and then reading an elaborate set of exceptions into that warrant requirement, seems more like rewriting the amendment than reading it as written.) To begin rethinking, consider the paradigmatic way in which Fourth Amendment rights were to be enforced at the Founding. Virtually any search or seizure by a federal officer would involve a physical trespass under common-law principles. An aggrieved target could use the common law of trespass to bring suit for damages against the official—just as Wilkes brought a trespass action in *Wood*. If the search or seizure were deemed lawful in court, the defendant would prevail; but if, as in *Wood*, the search were found unlawful, the defendant government official would be held strictly liable. There was no such thing as "good faith" immunity.[13]

Given this risk, many officials would obviously prefer to litigate the lawfulness of a contemplated search or seizure before it occurred—to seek a judicial warrant authorizing the intrusion. Such a warrant, if strictly complied with, would act as a sort of declaratory judgment whose preclusive effect could be subsequently pled in any later damage action. A lawful warrant, in effect, would compel a sort of directed verdict for the defendant government official in any subsequent lawsuit for damages.[14]

But note what has happened. A warrant issued by a judge or magistrate—a permanent government official, on the government payroll—has had the effect of taking a later trespass action away from a jury of ordinary citizens. Because juries could often be trusted more than judges to protect against government overreaching (the agency problem), warrants were generally *dis*favored: "*No* warrants shall issue, but . . . ." And warrants had other flaws. First, they issued from a single person (as opposed to a judge sitting alongside a jury, twelve good men and true). Next, that single decisionmaker was an officer of the central government (unlike jurors of the community). Also, the decision occurred ex parte, with no notice or opportunity to be heard given to the target of a search. Moreover, the warrant proceeding was a secret affair, unlike a tort suit open to the watchful eye of a public able to monitor its judicial agents. (We shall return to the issue of public trials in Chapter 5.) Thus even when issued by a judge—and in some places executive magistrates also claimed authority to issue warrants—warrants lacked many traditional safeguards of judicial process: notice, adversarial presentation of issues, publicity, and so on. To make matters even worse, the government could forum shop; if only a single magistrate were lazy or abusive, cynical officers would know where to go to get an easy warrant. Judges and warrants are the heavies, not the heroes, of our story.

We can now see the Fourth Amendment with fresh eyes. Searches without warrants are not presumptively illegitimate; nor does every warrantless search or seizure require probable cause. Rather, whenever such a search or seizure occurred, a jury, guided by a judge in a public trial and able to hear arguments from both sides of the case, could typically assess the reasonableness of government action in an after-the-fact tort suit. If the properly instructed jury deemed the search unreasonable, the plain words of the Fourth Amendment would render the search unlawful. The defendant official could thus be held strictly liable and made to pay compensatory and (in egregious cases) punitive damages (though he might well in turn be indemnified by the government). The ultimate issue—were the defendant's actions reasonable or unreasonable—was often a classic question of fact for the jury;[15] and the Seventh Amendment, in combination with the Fourth, would require the federal government to furnish a jury to any plaintiff-victim who demanded one and to protect that jury's finding of fact from being overturned by any judge or other government official. The prospect of jury oversight and jury-awarded punitive damages would powerfully deter government officials contemplating unreasonable conduct. (In England, the government ended up paying out a king's ransom in damages and court expenses in the Wilkes affair.)* Judicial warrants, though, were another matter. Pre-

---

*See NELSON B. LASSON, THE HISTORY AND DEVELOPMENT OF THE FOURTH AMENDMENT TO THE UNITED STATES CONSTITUTION 45 (1937) ("The expenses incurred were said to total £100,000."). In *Wilkes v. Wood* itself, Wilkes's lawyers went out of their way to stress the rights and duties of the civil jury:

> That the constitution of our country had been so fatally wounded, that it called aloud for the redress of a jury of Englishmen. . . . He then congratulated the jury, that they now had in their power, the present cause . . . . [T]he jury would effectually prevent the question from being ever revived again. He therefore recommends it to them to

cisely because they were granted by government officials in closed ex parte proceedings—and had the effect of taking the reasonableness issue away from the jury altogether—they had to be strictly limited. Such warrants needed to meet stricter requirements (probable cause, and so on) than mere reasonableness.

Thus, contrary to the modern Court's approach, the words of the Fourth Amendment mean what they say: warrantless searches are not always unconstitutional, and the probable-cause requirement applies only if and when a warrant issues.[16] Put another way, the Court has simply misread the original linkage between the Fourth Amendment's two different commands. It is not that a search or seizure without a warrant was presumptively unreasonable, as the Court has assumed; rather, an overbroad warrant lacking probable cause or specificity—in other words, a general warrant—was per se unreasonable, in part because it unjustifiably displaced the proper role of the jury.

There is an obvious connection here to the common-law rule against prior restraint, which we noted in the First Amendment context.[17] Just as judges were barred ex ante from restraining the press while civil and

---

embrace this opportunity . . . of instructing those great officers in their duty, and that they (the jury) would now erect a great sea mark, by which our State pilots might avoid, for the future, those rocks upon which they now lay shipwrecked.

Wilkes v. Wood, 98 Eng. Rep. 489, 490 (C.P. 1763), 19 Howell's State Trials 1153, 1154–55. In a companion case to *Wilkes,* even Lord Mansfield spotlighted the jury's role in judging the reasonableness of the government's search and seizure. Money v. Leach, 97 Eng. Rep. 1075, 1087 (K.B. 1765), 19 Howell's State Trials 1001, 1026; 96 Eng. Rep. 320, 323 (same case) ("What is a probable cause of suspicion, and what is a reasonable time of detainer, are matters of fact to be determined by a jury."). And in *Wilkes* and two other companion cases, Pratt/Camden made clear that juries, not judges, should play the lead role in assessing punitive damages in these officer trespass suits. *Wilkes,* 98 Eng. Rep. at 498–99, 19 Howell's State Trials at 1167 ("a jury have it in their power to give damages for more than the injury received . . . to deter from any such proceeding for the future, and as proof of the detestation of the jury to the action itself"); Huckle v. Money, 95 Eng. Rep. 768, 768–69 (C.P. 1763) ("it is very dangerous for the Judges to intermeddle in damages for torts"; to grant new trials for excessive damages "would be laying aside juries"); Beardmore v. Carrington, 95 Eng. Rep. 790, 792–93 (C.P. 1764) (similar).

criminal juries ex post could impose sanctions on publishers, so here judges and magistrates acting before a search were much more strictly limited than juries acting afterward. This connection would hardly have been lost on the Fourth Amendment framers. In sixteenth- and seventeenth-century England, general warrants were the very devices by which various schemes of prior restraint and printer licensing were enforced.[18] Indeed, in *Wood* itself the secretary of state, Lord Halifax, had issued a general warrant against Wilkes in an attempt to enforce the seditious libel laws, an area of law where the proper role of the jury was a hot topic.*

If warrants were in some ways like prior restraints, why, it might be asked, didn't the framers of the Fourth Amendment simply ban all warrants? A good modern-day analogy is the temporary restraining order. Sometimes, emergency action must be taken to freeze the status quo and prevent future harm, and so judges may act ex parte, without the traditional safeguards of adversarial adjudication. But precisely because of the due-process dangers it poses, an ex parte temporary restraining order is strictly limited to situations where there is a risk of "irreparable injury" and a high likelihood of "success on the merits." At common law, a warrant could likewise issue when there was a high likelihood—"probable cause"—that a particular place contained stolen goods. The whole point of the ex parte warrant was to authorize a search that would bring the stolen goods before the magistrate. To give the owner of the hideaway a heads-up in advance of the surprise search might enable him to whisk the goods away—a kind of irreparable injury to the truth, to the justice system, and to the victim of the theft seeking to recover his goods. The need for a surprise search on these facts is obviously strong, but without

---

*Lord Mansfield favored a narrow role for criminal juries in libel cases; a jury, he thought, should decide only whether a defendant published a particular pamphlet, and a judge should decide whether the pamphlet was libelous. Lord Camden and others favored a broader role for juries, and the issue was sharply contested on the eve of the American Revolution. (In 1792, the broader view on this issue prevailed in Fox's Libel Act, and truth was recognized as a defense in England in 1843.) For discussion, see generally LEONARD W. LEVY, EMERGENCE OF A FREE PRESS 24–25, 37–45, 128–29, 156–58, 169, 212, 285 (1985).

the absolute guarantee of immunity provided by a warrant, an officer might hesitate to perform the surprise search for fear of a future lawsuit. Once extended beyond the limited context of the common-law warrant for stolen goods, though, warrants had the potential for great evil. If general warrants were authorized on less than probable cause, they would give government henchmen absolute power to "round up the usual suspects," rousting political enemies (like Wilkes). In the end, the Fourth Amendment framers accepted some warrants as necessary but imposed strict limits on these dangerous devices. Warrantless searches did not pose the same threat because those searches would be subject to full and open after-the-fact review in civil-trespass cases featuring civil juries.

As with the First Amendment, the central role of the jury in the Fourth Amendment should remind us that the core rights of "the people" were popular and populist rights—rights that the popular body of the jury was well suited to vindicate. And here, in focusing on a role for this popular branch in helping to determine the reasonableness of official action and to levy punitive damages to deter official misconduct, we have a more satisfying account than our earlier too-cute story of the deep meaning of the inclusion of the words *the right of the people* in an otherwise individualistic and "person[al]" Fourth Amendment. Our more satisfying account also fits snugly with another amendment that Madison put forth contemporaneously with his proto–Fourth Amendment, proclaiming the common-law civil jury to be "one of the best securities to the rights of the people" and something that "ought to remain inviolate."[19] Note the obvious harmony between this language ("securities," "rights of the people," and "inviolate") and the wording of the Fourth Amendment ("secure," "the right of the people," and "shall not be violated"). We shall consider the more general role of civil juries in much greater detail in Chapter 5, but these harmonies suggest a more populist Fourth Amendment—with juries playing a more important enforcement role—than is generally acknowledged by today's conventional wisdom. To see the original Fourth Amendment as mainly concerned with countermajoritarian rights is to miss the later transformation brought about by the Fourteenth Amendment, with its core concerns about minority rights and its heavy reliance on federal judges.

The founding generation well understood the deep connections between the Fourth and Seventh Amendments—connections modern scholars miss when these amendments are taught in different parts of the curriculum and studied by different groups of academics. Here, for example, are the words of a Pennsylvania Anti-Federalist in a 1787 essay: "[If a federal constable searching] for stolen goods, pulled down the clothes of a bed in which there was a woman, and searched under her shift . . . a trial by jury would be our safest resource, heavy damage would at once punish the offender, and deter others from committing the same: but what satisfaction can we expect from a lordly [judge] always ready to protect the officers of government against the weak and helpless citizens . . . ?"[20]

In the Pennsylvania ratifying convention, Robert Whitehill made a similar point, though less colorfully, by invoking "the case of Mr. Wilkes"—a trespass action that had been tried to a jury—and reminding his audience that "the doctrine of general warrants show[s] that judges may be corrupted."[21] More vivid was the Anti-Federalist essayist Hampden, who declared that "[w]ithout [a jury] in civil actions, no relief can be had against the High Officers of State, for abuse of private citizens."[22] Government officials shared Hampden's sense of the importance of the civil jury in proto–Fourth Amendment cases, as shown by a mournful 1761 comment of Massachusetts royal Governor Bernard in response to a citizen trespass suit: "A Custom house officer has no chance with a jury."[23]

The Fourth-Seventh Amendment linkage was especially visible in the Maryland ratification debates. (And we should recall here Lord Camden's conspicuous popularity among the people of Baltimore.) The prominent Anti-Federalist essayist Maryland Farmer set the tone:

[S]uppose for instance, that an officer of the United States should force the house, the asylum of a citizen, by virtue of a general warrant, I would ask, are general warrants illegal by the [C]onstitution of the United States? . . . [N]o remedy has yet been found equal to the task of deterring and curbing the insolence of office, but a jury—[i]t has become an invariable maxim of English juries, to give ruinous damages whenever an officer had deviated from the rigid letter of the law, or been guilty of any unnecessary act of insolence or oppression. [By contrast,] an American judge, who will be judge and jury too [would probably] spare the public purse, if not favour a brother officer.[24]

Luther Martin also clearly had in mind what we now call Fourth Amendment cases in emphasizing the importance of juries in "every case, whether civil or criminal, between government and its officers on the one part, and the subject or citizen on the other. . . . [Without civil juries] every arbitrary act of the general government, and every oppression of [its officers] for the collection of taxes, duties, imports, excise, and other purposes must be submitted to by the individual . . . . "[25*] Notes from a speech delivered by Marylander Samuel Chase suggest that this future justice likewise saw juries and warrants as linked; and he, too, stressed the need for civil juries in trespass suits against government "officers."[26] In response, a Maryland ratifying convention committee recommended a federal constitutional amendment requiring civil-jury trial in "all cases of trespasses"—plainly contemplating trespasses by *government officers*—and prohibiting appellate relitigation of the jury's factual findings.[27] Committee members went on to warn that loose warrants should be "forbidden to those magistrates who are to administer the general government."[28]

We are now positioned to see a subtle triangular interrelation among the First, Fourth, and Seventh Amendments. We have already observed how Seventh Amendment civil juries could safeguard First and Fourth Amendment values in civil libel and civil trespass cases, respectively. It remains to sketch with more precision the third leg of our triangle, linking the First and Fourth Amendments. The Fourth singles out "papers" for special mention and protection above and beyond all other "effects." In England, Lord Camden's famous decision in *Entick v. Carrington* had suggested that "paper-search[es]" were specially disfavored.[29] As Professors Stuntz and Schnapper have pointed out, Camden's direct limita-

---

*Publius's discussion of the civil jury directly responds to this passage. *See* THE FEDERALIST No. 83, at 499–500 (Alexander Hamilton) (Clinton Rossiter ed., 1961).

tions on paper searches indirectly protected values of free religious and political expression.[30] As Stuntz puts it, *Entick* and *Wilkes* were "classic First Amendment cases in a system with no First Amendment, no vehicle for direct substantive judicial review. Restricting paper searches had the effect of limiting government power" over opposition speakers and expressive activity.[31] Although the Fourth Amendment does not, in so many words, demand special solicitude for expressive "papers," it surely invites it, just as it invites a special sensitivity to searches and seizures of "persons" and "houses" above and beyond all other "effects." Under this amendment, American judges and juries were invited to carry on Camden's tradition by requiring heightened justification and special procedures before deeming searches of expressive "papers" constitutionally "reasonable." The modern Supreme Court has in theory (but not always in practice) embraced just such an approach: "Where the materials sought to be seized may be protected by the First Amendment, the requirements of the Fourth Amendment must be applied with 'scrupulous exactitude.' 'A seizure reasonable as to one type of material in one setting may be unreasonable in a different setting or with respect to another kind of material.'"[32]

Nor should we ignore the Fourth Amendment's image of federalism. The reasonableness requirement limited all federal officers, and the warrant clause imposed special restrictions on federal judges and magistrates, but vindication of these restrictions would largely come from state bodies. State statutes and state common law, after all, would typically define and protect ordinary individuals' property rights to their "persons, houses, papers, and effects." Thus state law would initially create the trespass cause of action that would enable ordinary men and women to challenge unconstitutional intrusions by federal officials.[33] Even if these actions were tried in federal court (because they raised federal questions arising under the Fourth Amendment),[34] a Seventh Amendment jury composed of local citizens, rather than a judge appointed in Washington, D.C., would often decide the general question of reasonableness. Here, as elsewhere, localism would protect liberty.

With this picture of the Fourth Amendment in mind, let us now peek at the next block of amendments—Five through Eight. Each of the clauses in this block can be understood as regulating the structure and procedure of federal courts—each, that is, except for the takings clause of the Fifth Amendment. In a number of ways, this clause doesn't quite fit with its companion clauses in the Fifth Amendment, but it does mesh in interesting ways with the principles of the Fourth Amendment.

Takings

. . . [N]or shall private property be taken for public use without just compensation.

This prohibition seems primarily designed to protect individuals and minority groups. After all, any government action imposing a financial burden on a majority of the populace would look more like a legitimate tax than an unconstitutional taking. In this respect, the provision might seem to run counter to the dominant majoritarian thrust of other provisions that we have encountered thus far. The clause also seems distinctly modern in proclaiming that limits should be imposed on government action, even when government agents are acting on behalf of their constituents rather than pursuing their own self-interest. Thus the clause requires private compensation even if property is taken for genuinely "public" use. In his chapter on the "absolute rights of individuals"—a chapter that loomed large in antebellum America, as we shall see in Part Two—Blackstone described the right to just compensation as follows: "So great moreover is the regard of the law for private property, that it will not authorize the least violation of it; no, not even for the general good of the whole community."[35]

The concerns underlying the takings clause were deeply felt by James Madison, who, we should recall, was ahead of his time in arguing that the dominant danger in America came from a possibly overweening majority rather than from self-interested government agents. But as we noted in considering Madison's failed Fourteenth Amendment—a precursor of our own—he was unsuccessful in bringing the needed majorities in Congress around to his way of thinking.[36] How, then, did he manage to slip the takings clause through?

In part by clever bundling, tying the clause to a variety of other provisions that commanded more enthusiasm. One key bit of evidence in support of the clever-bundling hypothesis has already been noted: the subject of the clause seems to fit akwardly with the other clauses of the Fifth Amendment, each of which deals centrally with criminal procedure. Granted, unlike the grand-jury, double-jeopardy, and self-incrimination clauses that precede it, the due-process clause does apply outside of criminal suits; and unless the just-compensation rule were to be drafted as a stand-alone amendment, like the Fourth, it did make some analytic sense to yoke it to due process. Both Fifth Amendment clauses, after all, imposed limits on government's ability to "take" away, or "deprive" persons of, "property." Madison no doubt knew that Article II of the then-recent Northwest Ordinance of 1787 had featured prototypes of the due-process and just-compensation clauses side-by-side. Yet camouflage is not quite compatibility, and on close inspection the takings clause is the odd man out in the Fifth Amendment—an openly substantive requirement following a string of procedural rules. (Of course, subsequent generations of lawyers and judges would deploy the "due process" norm as a substantive limitation on certain forms of legislative redistribution of property, a deployment in tension with the clause's emphasis on "process," not "substance," but very much in keeping with the substantive accent of the companion takings clause.)

Far more dramatic support for the clever-bundling hypothesis comes from the fact that unlike every other clause in the First Congress's proposed Bill, the just-compensation restriction was not put forth in any form by any of the state ratifying conventions.[37] So too with Madison's failed Fourteenth Amendment,[38] which was more vulnerable to attack precisely because it was not as cleverly bundled as the takings clause. With these two provisions, then, Madison was putting forth his own somewhat prophetic ideas rather than distilling the Zeitgeist.

Following in the tradition of Charles Beard, many modern scholars have stressed the importance of property protection in Federalist thought. Both the Article I, section 10 contracts clause and Madison's now-canonical *Federalist* No. 10 do indeed evince hostility to redistributive legislation.* But we must remember that the Bill of Rights grew out of a marriage between Madisonian Federalism and un-Madisonian Anti-Federalism, and many Anti-Federalists were suspicious of the "aristocratical" tendencies of Federalists. Of the original thirteen colonies, only Massachusetts had a just-compensation clause in its state constitution in 1789;[39] and Jefferson's famous Declaration of 1776 had spoken of "life, liberty, and the pursuit of happiness" rather than "life, liberty, and property." Property protection, it seems, was more central to Madison than to some of his contemporaries.

Yet the success of the takings clause was not solely the result of one man's clever bundling. Though less populist than many of the provisions that preceded it, the takings clause did harmonize with the original Bill of Rights' underlying vision of federalism. Like all the rest of the Bill, and unlike his abortive Fourteenth Amendment, Madison's takings clause applied only against the federal government. This is especially noteworthy given that the clause of the original Constitution that most closely foreshadowed the substance of the takings clause—the Article I, section 10 contracts clause—did apply against state government. Indeed, in exact contrast to the takings clause, the contracts clause applied only against state, and not federal, officials. Professor McConnell has flagged this contrast to argue that the takings clause may have been primarily motivated by agency cost concerns about remote and self-interested federal officials, especially military officers.[40] McConnell's explanation, which self-consciously tracks the analytic framework of Madison's *Federalist* No. 51, derives support from St. George Tucker's 1803 writings that the just-compensation clause "was probably intended to restrain the arbitrary and oppressive mode of obtaining supplies for the army, and other public uses, by impressment."[41] In his pathbreaking work on the

---

*I say "now-canonical" because, as Douglass Adair brilliantly demonstrated, *The Federalist* No. 10 was utterly ignored before Beard rediscovered it and made it famous in the early twentieth century. *See* DOUGLASS ADAIR, FAME AND THE FOUNDING FATHERS 75–76 (Trevor Colbourn ed., 1974). Adair's insight about No. 10 fits snugly with my overall theme in this book: only after the Fourteenth Amendment did Madison's vision of strong national protection of minorities against majoritarian oppression become the dominant strand of American constitutionalism.

takings clause, Professor Rubenfeld has likewise linked its origins to the issue of military impressment, and has emphasized, alongside Tucker, a 1778 tract authored by John Jay condemning "the Practice of impressing Horses, Teems [*sic*], and Carriages by the military, without the Intervention of a civil Magistrate, and without any Authority from the Law of the Land."[42] These sentiments, of course, resonate with the special fears of an overweening and unaccountable federal military audible in the Second and Third Amendments.

There is also a conspicuous connection between the Fourth Amendment's limitations on "seizures" of "houses" and "effects" and the Fifth's restrictions on "takings" of "private property." In both cases, state law typically defines the property rights given constitutional protection against federal officials. (The same holds true for the Fifth Amendment's ban on federal deprivation of property without due process.) And let us also note the ways in which liberal-ish individual rights of "persons" and "private property" were to be enforced by republican-ish institutions. In both the Fourth Amendment and the takings clause, civil juries of ordinary people loomed large in providing justice to citizens aggrieved by governmental grabbing—by helping decide which searches were "reasonable," whether punitive damages should be awarded to deter outrageous governmental misconduct, and what kind of compensation would be "just."

As it turns out, juries loomed large in other contexts as well, as a close look at the other clauses of Amendments Five to Eight will make clear.

Five

Juries

V.

No person shall be held to answer for a capital, or otherwise infamous crime, unless on a presentment or indictment of a Grand Jury, except in cases arising in the land or naval forces, or in the Militia, when in actual service in time of War or public danger; nor shall any person be subject for the same offence to be twice put in jeopardy of life or limb, nor shall be compelled in any criminal case to be a witness against himself, nor be deprived of life, liberty, or property, without due process of law; nor shall private property be taken for public use without just compensation.

VI.

In all criminal prosecutions, the accused shall enjoy the right to a speedy and public trial, by an impartial jury of the State and district wherein the crime shall have been committed, which district shall have been previously ascertained by law, and to be informed of the nature and cause of the accusation; to be confronted with the witnesses against him; to have compulsory process for obtaining witnesses in his favor, and to have the assistance of counsel for his defence.

VII.
In Suits at common law, where the value in controversy shall exceed twenty dollars, the right of trial by jury shall be preserved, and no fact tried by a jury shall be otherwise re-examined in any Court of the United States, than according to the rules of the common law.

VIII.
Excessive bail shall not be required, nor excessive fines imposed, nor cruel and unusual punishments inflicted.

More so than the takings clause, most other provisions of Amendments V–VIII were centrally concerned with the agency problem—the danger that government officials might attempt to rule in their own self-interest at the expense of their constituents' sentiments and liberty. For example, a special historical tie linked the First and Eighth Amendments. The most grisly punishments in England had typically been inflicted on those who spoke out against the government. Justice Hugo Black noted one example in his James Madison Lecture on the Bill of Rights: the case of the English lawyer William Prynne, who was tried in the 1630s by judges of the infamous Star Chamber (which sat without a jury). For the crimes of "writing books and pamphlets," Prynne's "ears were first cut off by court order and . . . subsequently, by another court order, . . . his remaining ear stumps [were] gouged out while he was on a pillory."[1] Even more gruesome was the typical sentence heaped upon a political dissenter in a treason trial:

> You are to be drawn upon a hurdle to the place of execution, and there you are to be hanged by the neck, and being alive cut down, and your privy-members to be cut off, and your bowels to be taken out of your belly and there burned, you being alive; and your head to be cut off, and your body to be divided into four quarters, and that your head and quarters be disposed of where his majesty shall think fit.[2]

Likewise, the English origins of the right against compelled self-incrimination, according to a leading scholar on the topic, were "most closely linked to freedom of religion and speech"—that is, freedom to challenge the official government ideology and the official government hierarchy, political or religious.[3] (In a country like England with an officially established church, criticism of religious orthodoxy was not simply religious speech but inescapably political speech as well.)[4]

The dominant strategy to keep agents of the central government under control was to use the populist and local institution of the jury.

Jurors as Populist Protectors

Juries, guaranteed in no fewer than three amendments, were at the heart of the Bill of Rights. The Fifth Amendment safeguarded the role of the grand jury; the Sixth, the criminal petit jury; and the Seventh, the civil jury. (In addition, Madison's unsuccessful Fourteenth Amendment would have explicitly guaranteed jury trial against state governments.) What's more, trial by jury in all federal criminal cases had earlier been mandated by the clear words of Article III: "The Trial of all Crimes, except in Cases of Impeachment, shall be by Jury." Indeed, the entire debate at the Philadelphia convention over whether to add a Bill of Rights was triggered when George Mason picked up on a casual comment from another delegate that "no provision was yet made for juries in civil cases."[5] Between the close of the Philadelphia convention and the opening of the First Congress, five of the six state ratifying conventions that advanced amendments put forth two or more jury-related proposals.[6] State constitutions further confirm the centrality of the jury. According to Leonard Levy's tally, the only right secured in all state constitutions penned between 1776 and 1787 was the right of jury trial in criminal cases.[7] We should also note the emphatic words of the Declaration of Independence, condemning George III and Parliament "[f]or depriving us, in many cases, of the benefits of trial by jury"; these words, in turn, built on the 1774 Declaration of Rights of the First Continental Congress—"the respective colonies are entitled to . . . the great and inestimable privilege of being tried by their peers of the vicinage"—and the 1775 Declaration of the Causes and Necessity of Taking Up Arms affirming the "inestimable privilege of trial by jury."[8]

Spanning both civil and criminal proceedings, the jury played a leading role in protecting ordinary individuals against governmental overreaching. Jurors would be drawn from the community; like the militia they were ordinary citizens, not permanent government officials on the government payroll. Just as the militia could check a paid professional standing army, the jury could thwart overreaching by powerful and ambitious prosecutors and judges. In the words of one Anti-Federalist pamphlet, "Judges, unincumbered by juries, have been ever found much better friends to government than to the people. Such judges will always be more desireable than juries to [would-be tyrants,] upon the same principle that a large standing army . . . is ever desireable to those who wish to enslave the people."[9] Thus Madison proposed a jury amendment in language reminiscent of the Second Amendment's ode to the militia—"the trial by jury, as one of the best securities to the rights of the people, ought to remain inviolate"*—and a leading Anti-Federalist described jurors as "centinels and guardians" of "the people."[10]

The grand jury, for example, could thwart any prosecution that it deemed unfounded or malicious, especially if it suspected that the executive was trying to use the powers of incumbency illegitimately to entrench itself in office by prosecuting its political critics. Note how the Fifth Amendment differs from the Fourth. In contrast to the Fourth's warrant clause, the decision whether sufficient cause exists to prosecute a felony can never under the Fifth be made solely by permanent government officials. Before officials can force a defendant to suffer the physical and financial ordeal of a serious criminal prosecution, they must first win the consent of a large panel of ordinary Americans—twenty-three citizens, good and true, acting by majority rule.

Colonial grand juries flexed their muscles to resist unpopular prosecutions. In the 1730s, two successive New York grand juries had refused to indict the popular publisher John Peter Zenger—and when the gov-

---

*As we saw in Chapter 4, this language also stands as a bridge between Fourth Amendment and Seventh Amendment ideology.

ernment instead proceeded by information, the petit jury famously acquitted.[11] (One of the articles for which Zenger was prosecuted had featured an attack on New York Governor Cosby for having engaged in personal litigation tactics that sought to evade the right to jury trial in civil cases.)[12] Similarly, in the 1760s and 1770s various grand juries refused to indict leaders of the Stamp Act protests and other patriot publishers and speakers.[13]

More broadly, the grand jury had sweeping proactive and inquisitorial powers to investigate suspected wrongdoing or cover-ups by government officials and to make its findings known through the legal device of "presentment"—a public document stating its accusations. The grand jury's role thus went far beyond oversight of a prosecutor's proposed indictments. Through presentments and other customary reports, the American grand jury in effect enjoyed a roving commission to ferret out official malfeasance or self-dealing of any sort and bring it to the attention of the public at large. In the words of James Wilson: "The grand jury are a great channel of communication, between those who make and administer the laws, and those for whom the laws are made and administered. All the operations of government, and of its ministers and officers, are within the compass of their view and research. They may suggest publick improvements, and the modes of removing publick inconveniences: they may expose to publick inspection, or to publick punishment, publick bad men, and publick bad measures."[14] This vision of the grand jury was nicely illustrated by the events of 1816: the congressional pay increase mentioned in Chapter 1 was the target of several grand-jury proceedings that helped inform and mobilize the electorate about "publick bad men, and publick bad measures."[15]

In cases where an indictable criminal offense had occurred, the grand jury could not compel prosecution on its own initiative without the concurrence of the executive but could nonetheless use presentments and other reports to publicize to the people at large any suspicious executive decisions to decline prosecution.[16] The image here is akin to that of modern-day blue-ribbon commissions and special prosecutors called to investigate in areas where regular government officials may have conflicts of interest. By focusing public attention on otherwise low-visibility executive decisions, the grand jury could deter executive self-dealing and enhance executive accountability.

Granted, the Fifth Amendment does not specifically refer to grand-jury reports—but it does refer to a "Grand Jury," and in America that very phrase conjured up a body with traditional watchdog and reporting powers. As Wilson's comments and early practice make clear, a body without these powers was no more a grand jury than was, say, a group of ten men on the government payroll.* And let us not overlook the key connections between the First and Fifth Amendments implicated by grand-jury reports and presentments. Like legislators who claimed a special level of freedom of speech in a deliberative assembly, grand jurors enjoyed special immunity from libel laws and the like when they issued reports and presentments: the grand jury, too, was a special speaking spot.[17] On occasion, grand jurors themselves explicitly invoked these connections by styling their presentments as First Amendment petitions for redress of "grievances." Here, for example, are excerpts from a Georgia federal grand-jury presentment in 1791:

> We the Grand federal Inquest for the district of Georgia do make the following presentments . . . .
> 2. We present the want of a Bill of rights clearly defining the reserved rights of the several States, comprehended in the Guarantee of a Republican form of Government to each state by the constitution of the United States . . . .
> 5. We present as a greivance [sic], every measure of the general gov-

---

*What's more, some authorities seem to view presentments—which *are* explicitly mentioned by the Fifth Amendment—as encompassing noncriminal accusations of public wrongdoing. *Compare* STEPHEN A. SALTZBURG AND DANIEL J. CAPRA, AMERICAN CRIMINAL PROCEDURE 673 (4th ed. 1992) (reprinting Model Grand Jury Charge) *and* Renée B. Lettow, Note, *Reviving Federal Grand Jury Presentments*, 103 YALE L.J. 1333, 1336–39 and n.25, 1354–55 (1994) *with* 4 WILLIAM BLACKSTONE, COMMENTARIES ON THE LAWS OF ENGLAND 298–99 (Oxford: Clarendon, 1765) *and* Kate Stith, *The Role of the Government Under the Bill of Rights*, 15 HARV. J. L. & PUB. POL'Y 129, 135–36 (1992).

ernment by which the territorial rights of this state are or may be in-fringed.[18]

Though not as proactive as its "grand" counterpart, the criminal petit jury could interpose itself on behalf of the people's rights by refusing to convict when the executive sought to trump up charges against its po-litical critics (as in the Zenger case). Once again, more than a perma-nent government official—even an independent Article III judge—was required to safeguard liberty. In England, judges had at times abetted government tyranny, as the case of Prynne and the infamous "Bloody Assizes" of Judge George Jeffreys in the 1680s graphically illustrated.[19] Even in America, federal judges would be appointed by the central gov-ernment and might prove reluctant to rein in their former benefactors and current paymasters—as illustrated by the brazenly partisan conduct of some Federalist judges during the Sedition Act controversy.[20] Thus in those aspects of a criminal case that might involve a judge acting with-out a jury—issuing arrest warrants, setting bail, and sentencing—addi-tional restrictions came into play via the Fourth Amendment warrant clause and the Eighth Amendment. The language of both the Massa-chusetts and New Hampshire state constitutions is revealing here: "No *magistrate* or court of law shall demand excessive bail or sureties, impose excessive fines, or inflict cruel or unusual punishments."[21] Indeed, in the late eighteenth century, every schoolboy in America knew that the En-glish Bill of Rights' 1689 ban on excessive bail, excessive fines, and cruel and unusual punishments—a ban repeated virtually verbatim in the Eighth Amendment—arose as a response to the gross misbehavior of the infamous Judge Jeffreys.[22]

The petit jury's power would be especially great if it could lawfully refuse to convict a defendant charged under any federal law it deemed unconstitutional. As we shall see, this right of "jury review" was advo-cated by many constitutional theorists in the late eighteenth and early nineteenth centuries and was invoked by publishers accused of violating the 1798 Sedition Act.

A Sixth Amendment right of jury review gains added plausibility when we remember the central role of the Seventh Amendment civil jury in adjudicating the Fourth Amendment issue of "reasonableness." Here the order of the parties was typically reversed—the target of government harassment would be the plaintiff, and a government official the defendant—but the basic idea was the same. Ordinary citizens would check executive overreaching and monitor the professional judiciary. Similarly, Seventh Amendment civil juries could help decide the Fifth Amendment constitutional issue of how much "just compensation" to award when government took private property for public use, and the First Amendment constitutional issue of how much (if any) money a publisher should be obliged to pay in a civil libel suit brought by an aggrieved government officer.

As Tocqueville observed, the overall jury system was fundamentally populist and majoritarian: "The institution of the jury . . . places the real direction of society in the hands of the governed, . . . and not in that of the government. . . . [It] invests the people, or that class of citizens, with the direction of society. . . . The jury system as it is understood in America appears to me to be as direct and as extreme a consequence of the sovereignty of the people as universal suffrage. They are two instruments of equal power, which contribute to the supremacy of the majority."[23]

Jurors as Provincials

The jury was not simply a popular body but a local one as well. Indeed, the Sixth Amendment explicitly guaranteed a jury "of the State and district wherein the crime shall have been committed," going a step beyond the language of Article III, which required only that jury trials be held somewhere within the state where the crime occurred. Early in the Philadelphia convention, Madison captured an important truth in a telling analogy, arguing for the need to "preserve the State rights, as carefully as the trials by jury."[24] Just as state legislators could in various ways protect their constituents against national oppression, grand and petit jurors could interpose themselves against central tyranny through the devices of presentments, nonindictments, and general verdicts. As with the militia, the jury would be composed of citizens from the same community, and its actions were expected to be informed by community values.

The Seventh Amendment linked juries and federalism in a related way. What did it mean to "preserve" a jury-trial right in suits at common law, given that the right to a civil jury in the late eighteenth century was widely understood as defined only by state-law rules—judicial, legislative, and constitutional—that varied considerably from state to state and were evolving over time?[25] Though not free from doubt, the best reading of the amendment is probably as follows: if a state court entertaining a given common-law case would use a civil jury, a federal court hearing the same case (because, say, it involves diverse citizens or raises a federal question) must follow—must "preserve"—that state-law jury right. Like the establishment clause, the Seventh Amendment thus resembles the Tenth in requiring that certain matters be governed by state law. To put the point another way, the Seventh Amendment parallels the famous Rules of Decision Act. That act, passed as Section 34 of the First Judiciary Act, cleared the First Congress the same week as the Bill of Rights. It provided that in trials "at common law" federal courts must follow "the laws of the several states" on issues of substantive right not governed by federal law.[26] What the act did for substantive law the Seventh Amendment did for the procedural issue of jury trial, with one difference: the amendment established only a state-law floor and not a ceiling. Congress would remain free to provide civil juries above and beyond what state law required.

This reading of the Seventh Amendment differs substantially from current Supreme Court case law but enjoys considerable historical support. In responding to various prototypes of the Seventh Amendment proposed in state ratifying conventions, for example, Alexander Hamilton in *The Federalist* No. 83 described their intent as follows: "[Cases] in the federal courts should be tried by jury, if, in the State where the courts sat, that mode of trial would obtain in a similar case in the State courts . . . ."[27] Note the precision of this formulation: state law sets a floor, not a ceiling, and a dynamic one at that—that is, one that shifts as state law shifts. Though Hamilton was critical of these prototypes, many other commentators in 1788, both Federalist and Anti-, suggested that dynamic conformity with state jury rules would make good sense.* The Supreme Court has instead adopted a static, historical test, looking to "preserve" the brooding omnipresence of English common-law jury rules circa 1791.[28] This is surely one way to understand the right that is to be preserved, but another is to focus on current state law. Doctrinally, the Supreme Court's reading has generated many knotty questions that might be avoided by the state-law approach. Textually, it is hard to see why the word *preserved* in the Seventh Amendment requires a radically different approach from the one given its etymological cousin, *reserved,* in the Tenth Amendment.[29]

---

*See, e.g., 2 THE RECORDS OF THE FEDERAL CONVENTION OF 1787, at 588 (Max Farrand rev. ed., 1937) (remarks of Roger Sherman implying that federal courts would follow state constitutional rules regarding civil juries); Charles W. Wolfram, *The Constitutional History of the Seventh Amendment,* 57 MINN. L. REV. 639, 662 (1973) (similar reading of Sherman); Oliver Ellsworth, *The Landholder* (VI), *reprinted in* ESSAYS ON THE CONSTITUTION OF THE UNITED STATES 161, 165 (Paul Leicester Ford ed., New York: Burt Franklin, 1892) (arguing that trials will "be by jury also in most or all of the causes which were wont to be tried by them"); 3 DEBATES ON THE ADOPTION OF THE FEDERAL CONSTITUTION 68 (Jonathan Elliot ed., AYER Co. reprint ed., 1987) (1836) (remarks of Edmund Randolph in Virginia ratifying convention) ("Congress must regulate [civil juries] so as to suit every state"); 2 *id.* at 112 (remarks of Christopher Gore in Massachusetts ratifying convention) ("The [civil jury] laws of Congress may and will be conformable to the local laws in this particular"); 4 *id.* at 150 (remarks of Governor Samuel Johnston in North Carolina ratifying convention) (federal jury system "will probably be, in each state, as it has hitherto been used in such state"); *id.* at 155 (remarks of Samuel Spencer in North Carolina ratifying convention) (framers should "have provided that all those cases which are now triable by a jury should be tried in each state by a jury, according to the mode usually practiced in such state"); *Essay by One of the Common People, reprinted in* 4 THE COMPLETE ANTI-FEDERALIST 120, 122 (Herbert J. Storing ed., 1981) (proposing language that "the citizens of each state shall enjoy [the privilege of civil juries] conformably to the usage in the state where the tribunal shall be established"). For the (too quick) Federalist claim that dynamic conformity would be unworkable, *see, e.g.,* 4 DEBATES ON THE ADOPTION OF THE FEDERAL CONSTITUTION 165 (remarks of James Iredell at North Carolina ratifying convention); PAMPHLETS ON THE CONSTITUTION OF THE UNITED STATES 157 (Paul Leicester Ford ed., New York: Burt Franklin, 1888) (remarks of James Wilson on October 6, 1787).

The leading scholarly work on the Seventh Amendment concedes that the state-law-incorporation approach is the reading that is "best supported by the historical materials" but ultimately dismisses it on the ground that the amendment's bite would vary from state to state and year to year: "Neither result seems consistent with the notion of a nationally applicable Bill of Rights."[30] Yet dismissal on this ground alone seems sensible only if we insist on a conventional wisdom that blinds us to the fact that states' rights were indeed part of the original Bill. Under the state-law-incorporation reading, the Seventh Amendment would require federal respect for state law, as did the establishment clause and the Tenth Amendment. Were these provisions also inconsistent with the notion of a nationally applicable Bill of Rights? And what about the Fourth Amendment, the takings clause, and the due-process clause, all of which linked constitutional rights to property interests typically created by state law (and thus capable of varying from time to time and state to state)?*

The Fourth Amendment is especially suggestive here given the historical and logical connections between it and the Seventh Amendment jury. Once we recall that current state law would provide the substantive cause of action in trespass suits against overreaching federal officials, it seems more plausible that current state law should also be able to guarantee a civil jury, regardless of whether such a guarantee precisely tracked the one established by English common law circa 1791. (In the converse situation, the modern Supreme Court has held that in certain federal lawsuits in state court, civil-jury trials are part and parcel of the cause of action and therefore obligatory.)[31] State-law causes of action defined the core of the Seventh Amendment; the two paradigmatic Seventh Amendment cases were state-law trespass suits against federal officers, and diversity cases pitting creditor-state plaintiffs against debtor-state defendants.[32] Molded around these two foci, the amendment had less

---

*The same Congress that proposed the Bill of Rights also adopted various statutes that tied the procedure of federal courts to the rules followed in the respective states. *See* Judiciary Act of 1789, §29, 1 Stat. 73, 88 (regulating federal jury selection); Process Act of 1789, 1 Stat. 93 (regulating process more generally).

bite in suits based on federal statutes; a Congress bent on evading civil juries could draft statutes sounding in equity, not law. The centrality of state-law cases to the Seventh Amendment also explains why its jury rules were keyed to state practice whereas the jury rules of the Fifth and Sixth Amendments—dealing overwhelmingly with suits under federal law—were not.

By enabling states to adapt the civil jury to changing times, the state-law-incorporation approach would free state governments either to restrict or extend civil juries as circumstances warranted. A dynamic floor can shift in either direction. Yet this prospect probably did not bother the Anti-Federalists who were the biggest proponents of civil juries, for these men were generally willing to place their bets on states: unlike distant aristocratic congressmen, local democratic legislators would have strong incentives to protect, and perhaps expand, the role of local democratic juries. High Federalists like Hamilton, less enamored of civil juries, had their own reasons for preferring dynamic conformity to a hidebound historical test. We must also note here that in almost every state, a constitution or bill of rights safeguarded the role of civil juries.[33] Most of these documents used language suggesting a static historical floor for civil juries. Yet unlike many other portions of the federal Bill, which borrowed language verbatim from state documents, the Seventh Amendment used language different from every state counterpart. The state-law-incorporation reading provides a nice explanation: like the establishment clause and the Tenth Amendment, the Seventh had a federalism dimension that made the language of state counterparts ill suited for imitation. This reading might also explain why the amendment avoided the backward-looking language proposed by the Virginia and North Carolina ratifying conventions to safeguard "the ancient trial by jury."[34]

If the Seventh Amendment is read in the most sensible way, it, too, becomes somewhat awkward to incorporate against states. What would incorporation mean? That state courts must follow current state-law rules providing for jury trial in state courts? Why wouldn't they do so even without incorporation? We shall examine the incorporation issue more carefully in Part Two, but for now it suffices to say that, however we read the Seventh Amendment, the local character of civil and criminal juries under the original Bill of Rights must not be missed.

Jurors as Pupils

The jury was to be informed by community values, but also by judges—most obviously in the judges' instructions. As Ralph Lerner has shown in his essay on "Republican Schoolmasters," judges often seized the occasion to educate the jurors about legal and political values ranging well beyond the narrow issues before them.[35] Like the church and the militia, the jury was in part an intermediate association designed to educate and socialize its members into virtuous thinking and conduct. Churches stressed religious and moral virtues; militias struck a proper balance between civilian and martial virtues; and juries instilled republican legal and political virtues. In the words of the Federal Farmer, the leading Anti-Federalist essayist of the ratification period, "jury trial brings with it an open and public discussion of all causes . . . [and this is] the means by which the people are let into the knowledge of public affairs."[36]

No one understood all this better than Tocqueville, a keen student of American constitutional law and the leading theorist on the importance of intermediate associations:

> The jury, and more especially the civil jury, serves to communicate the spirit of the judges to the minds of all the citizens; and this spirit, with the habits which attend it, is the soundest preparation for free institutions. It imbues all classes with a respect for the thing judged and with the notion of right. . . . It teaches men to practice equity; every man learns to judge his neighbor as he would himself be judged. . . .
>
> . . . *It may be regarded as a gratuitous public school,* ever open, in which every juror learns his rights, enters into daily communication with the most learned and enlightened members of the upper classes, and becomes practically acquainted with the laws, which are brought within the reach of his capacity by the efforts of the bar, the advice of the judge, and even the passions of the parties. . . .
>
> . . . I look upon [the jury] as one of the most efficacious means for the education of the people which society can employ.[37]

Through the jury, citizens would learn self-government by doing self-government. In Tocqueville's memorable phrase, "the jury, which is the most energetic means of making the people rule, is also the most efficacious means of teaching it how to rule well."[38] In 1788, the Anti-Federalist Maryland Farmer noted that although ordinary folk were "much degraded in the powers of the mind," jury service would uplift them. *Give them power and they will find understanding to use it.*[39]

Jurors as Political Participants

Unable to harbor any realistic expectations of serving in the small House of Representatives or the even more aristocratic Senate, ordinary citizens could nevertheless participate in the application of national law through their service on juries.[40] In the words of the Federal Farmer, through juries "frequently drawn from the body of the people . . . we secure to the people at large, their just and rightful controul in the judicial department."[41] Juries, wrote another republican in 1791, give the people "a share of Judicature which they have reserved for themselves."[42] As the most prominent historian of Anti-Federalist thought, Herbert J. Storing, has observed, "The question was not fundamentally whether the lack of adequate provision for jury trial would weaken a traditional bulwark of individual rights (although that was also involved) but whether it would fatally weaken the role of the people in the *administration* of government."[43]

Analogies between legislatures and juries abounded. Wrote the Federal Farmer:

> It is essential in every free country, that common people should have a part and share of influence, in the judicial as well as in the legislative department.
>
> . . . The trial by jury in the judicial department, and the collection of the people by their representatives in the legislature . . . have procured for them, in this country, their true proportion of influence, and the wisest and most fit means of protecting themselves in the community. Their situation, as jurors and representatives, enables them to acquire information and knowledge in the affairs and government of

the society; and to come forward, in turn, as the centinels and guardians of each other.[44]

Similarly, Jefferson declared in 1789 that "it is necessary to introduce the people into every department of government . . . . Were I called upon to decide whether the people had best be omitted in the Legislative or Judicial department, I would say it is better to leave them out of the Legislative."[45] Tocqueville later made much the same point: "The jury is, above all, a political [and not a mere judicial] institution . . . . The jury is that portion of the nation to which the execution of the laws is entrusted, as the legislature is that part of the nation which makes the laws; and in order that society may be governed in a fixed and uniform manner, the list of citizens qualified to serve on juries must increase and diminish with the list of electors."[46]

Even more elaborate was the vision of the jury conjured up by John Taylor of Caroline, one of the early republic's leading constitutional theorists. The jury, wrote Taylor, was the "lower judicial bench" in a bicameral judiciary.[47] The judicial structure mirrored that of the legislature, with an upper house of greater stability and experience and a lower house to represent popular sentiment more directly. Thus the Maryland Farmer defined the jury as *"the democratic branch of the judiciary power*—more necessary than representatives in the legislature."[48] So too, the Anti-Federalist Hamden described "trial by jury" as "the democratical balance in the Judiciary power," tracking Publius's description of House-Senate bicameralism as a "legislative balance[]" (as in "checks and balances") in *The Federalist* No. 9.[49]

Tocqueville explicitly defined the jury as "a certain number of citizens chosen by lot and invested with a temporary" commission[50]—the analogy to militias suggests itself once again—and the Federal Farmer also seemed to stress the rotating quality of jury service, as evidenced by his reference to citizens coming forward "in turn."[51] The idea of mandatory rotation also illustrates the connections between juries and legislators, for many Anti-Federalists wanted compulsory rotation in the legislature as well.[52] Indeed, Thomas Jefferson's two biggest objections to the original Constitution were its lack of a bill of rights and its abandonment of

the republican principle of mandatory rotation.[53] At the New York ratifying convention Gilbert Livingston criticized the lack of mandatory
rotation in the legislature, but his comments fit the jury context as well:
"[Rotation] will afford opportunity to bring forward the genius and information of the states, and will be a stimulus to acquire political abilities. It will be the means of diffusing a more general knowledge of the
measures and spirit of the administration. These things will confirm the
people's confidence in government."[54] Like so many other Creation-era
ideas that we have encountered, the mandatory rotation principle drew
its strength from structural concerns about attenuated representation
rather than elaborate ideas about minority rights.

The Centrality of the Jury

If we seek a paradigmatic image underlying the original Bill of Rights,
we cannot go far wrong in picking the jury. Not only was it featured in
three separate amendments (the Fifth, Sixth, and Seventh), but its absence strongly influenced the judge-restricting doctrines underlying
three other amendments (the First, Fourth, and Eighth).

Likewise the double-jeopardy clause, which makes no explicit mention of juries, dovetails with the Sixth Amendment jury right. Together
these clauses safeguard not simply the individual defendant's interest in
avoiding vexation but also the integrity of the initial petit jury's judgment (somewhat like the Seventh Amendment's rule against "reexam-
in[ation]" of the civil jury's fact finding). At common law, jeopardy attached
upon a jury's fact finding; as Blackstone put the point in a section discussing jury trial, "[i]f the jury therefore find the prisoner not guilty, he
is then for ever quit and discharged of the accusation." [55] Modern American courts have deviated from this common-law rule and have said that
jeopardy "attaches" when the jury is impaneled or when it is charged—
but here, too, the linkage between double jeopardy and jury trial is
clear.[56] And under all three attachment schemes, the hard core of the
double-jeopardy clause is the absolute, unquestionable finality of a properly instructed jury's verdict of acquittal, even if this verdict is egregiously
erroneous in the eyes of judges. In this sense, all three formulations respect the de facto power—indeed the right—of the petit jury to do jus-

tice by acquitting against the evidence.[57] We should thus not be surprised to learn that the only state constitutional precursor of the double-jeopardy clause conjoined this provision to its criminal jury–trial guarantee;[58] or that the Maryland state ratifying convention—one of only two that raised the double-jeopardy issue—made this linkage even more explicit: "That there shall be a trial by jury in all criminal cases . . . and that there be no appeal from matter of fact, or second trial after acquittal . . . ."[59] This clause was immediately followed by a proto–Seventh Amendment bar on appellate relitigation of facts found by a civil jury.[60] To be sure, we must not miss a key difference between civil and criminal juries: the criminal reexamination ban was asymmetric, offering special protection to the defendant. If a properly instructed jury voted to convict, a judge could set aside the conviction, but if that jury voted to acquit, reexamination was barred.

In Joseph Story's celebrated *Commentaries on the Constitution*, various nonjury clauses of the Sixth Amendment—speedy trial, public trial, confrontation, and so on—were treated in a section captioned "Trial by Jury" and described as "valuable appendage[s] of the trial by jury."[61] The Fifth Amendment due-process clause implicated the jury even more directly, for its core meaning was to require lawful indictment or presentment by a grand jury.[62] (We shall return to this clause, and ponder its Fourteenth Amendment cousin, in Part Two.) Even those amendments that at first seem rather far afield appear on closer inspection to link up with the values underlying the jury. We have glimpsed important parallels between the jury and the Second Amendment's vaunted "well regulated Militia." The vision underlying the jury also harmonizes well with Congress's first two proposed amendments, which went down to defeat in 1791; these amendments, too, reflected suspicion of government agents on the permanent payroll and far removed from the people. The jury summed up—indeed embodied—the ideals of populism, federalism, and civic virtue that were the essence of the original Bill of Rights.

If the foregoing picture of the jury seems somewhat unconventional, perhaps the reason is that the present-day jury is only a shadow of its former self. First Amendment doctrine has evolved beyond the prohibition against prior restraint,* while the judge-created and judge-enforced exclusionary rule has displaced the jury trial for damages as the central enforcement mechanism of the Fourth Amendment—in part because of judge-created doctrines of government officials' immunity from damages.[63] As we shall now see, even the core role of the jury in criminal trials has seriously eroded over the past two centuries.

Jury Review

Consider first the issue of jury review. Let us begin by defining the question with precision. First, the issue is not the general one of jury nullification (can a jury disregard a law it thinks unjust?), but the narrower question of whether a jury can refuse to follow a law if and only if it deems that law unconstitutional.[64] The concept is exactly analogous to the idea of judicial review, as traditionally understood. Judges may not ignore a law simply because they think it wrong, or unjust, or silly; but they may—indeed must—do so if they deem it unconstitutional. Second, the question is not whether a jury has the raw power of review by entering a general verdict and "getting away with it"—that is, escaping sanctions that would affect the Holmesian "bad man." Rather, the question is whether and to what extent a jury has the legal right—perhaps even the duty—to refuse to follow a law it deems unconstitutional. As a practical matter, the issue often boils down to whether an attorney should be allowed to argue unconstitutionality, typically as a defense, to a jury.[65]

This is exactly how the issue arose in perhaps the most famous of all federal Sedition Act prosecutions, *United States v. Callender*,[66] tried in 1800 in a federal Circuit Court. When the publisher James Callender's attorney, William Wirt, tried to argue the statute's unconstitutionality to the jury, he was cut off by presiding Circuit Justice Samuel Chase. Chase was later impeached for his overall handling of *Callender* and for refusing to allow defense counsel in another criminal case to argue law to the jury. About half of the Senate voted to convict, several votes short of the two-thirds required by the Constitution.[67] Wirt, by contrast, went on to become "one of the greatest Supreme Court advocates of all time

---

*And rightly so. *See* Chapter 10.

and the man who holds the record for years of service as Attorney General."[68] Here is an edited transcript of the Chase-Wirt exchange:

> Here CHASE, Circuit Justice—Take your seat, sir, if you please. If I understand you rightly, you offer an argument to the petit jury, to convince them that the . . . Sedition Law[] is contrary to the constitution of the United States and, therefore, void. Now I tell you that this is irregular and inadmissible; it is not competent to the jury to decide on this point . . . .
>
> . . . [W]e all know that juries have the right to decide the law, as well as the fact—and the constitution is the supreme law of the land, which controls all laws which are repugnant to it.
>
> Mr. Wirt.—Since, then, the jury have a right to consider the law, and since the constitution is law, the conclusion is certainly syllogistic, that the jury have a right to consider the constitution.
>
> CHASE, Circuit Justice.—A non sequitur, sir.
>
> Here Mr. Wirt sat down.[69]

Chase went on to try to explain his ruling, but if anything, it is his arguments that border on non sequitur. At times he seemed to say that if the jury could consider constitutionality, it would necessarily follow that judges could not. But nothing in the idea of judicial review, or in the subsequent *Marbury* case, requires that only judges consider constitutionality.[70] Surely, for example, President Jefferson was within his constitutional rights—perhaps duties—when he pardoned those convicted under the Sedition Act because he deemed the act unconstitutional, notwithstanding that Article III Circuit Courts had held to the contrary in cases involving the very convicts in question. Judges took oaths to uphold the Constitution, as *Marbury* emphasized, but so did presidents and so could jurors. In his celebrated 1791 lectures on law, James Wilson, who had been second (if that) only to Madison in his contributions to the Constitution, declared: "[W]hoever would be obliged to obey a constitutional law, is justified in refusing to obey an unconstitutional act of the legislature . . . . [W]hen a question, even of this delicate nature, occurs, every one who is called to act, has a right to judge . . . . "[71] Though Wilson did not single out juries by name, surely they were "called to act" when requested to send James Callender to jail. Theophilus Parsons, who would one day sit as chief justice of his state supreme court, was even more explicit in the Massachusetts ratifying convention: "[T]he people themselves have it in their power effectually to resist usurpation, without being driven to an appeal to arms. An act of usurpation is not obligatory; it is not law; and any man may be justified in his resistance. Let him be considered as a criminal by the general government, yet only his own fellow-citizens can convict him; they are his jury, and if they pronounce him innocent, not all the powers of Congress can hurt him; and innocent they certainly will pronounce him, if the supposed law he resisted was an act of usurpation."[72]

Likewise, *Marbury's* sonorous claim that "it is emphatically the province and duty of the judicial department to say what the law is"[73] does not necessarily support Chase. As John Taylor's and the Maryland Farmer's bicameral image illustrates, juries can be seen as part of the judicial department—the lower (and if anything, presumptively more legitimate, because more popular) house.[74] Just as both House and Senate had to agree the Sedition Bill was constitutional before it became law, why shouldn't both judge and jury be required to agree on its constitutionality before Callender was sent to jail?* In language borrowing from vocabulary about legislative checks and balances, the Federal Farmer had declared that if judges tried to "subvert the laws, and change the forms of government," jurors would "check them, by deciding against their opinions and determinations."[75]

Nor was today's strict law/fact distinction between the roles of upper and lower judicial houses so clear in 1800. On the contrary, it was widely believed in late-eighteenth-century America that the jury, when rendering a general verdict, could take upon itself the right to decide both

*Cf. 2 THE WORKS OF JOHN ADAMS 253 (Charles Francis Adams ed., Boston: Little, Brown, 1850) (diary entry Feb. 12, 1771) ("As the constitution requires that the popular branch of the legislature should have an absolute check, so as to put a peremptory negative upon every act of the government, it requires that the common people, should have as complete a control, as decisive a negative, in every judgment of a court of judicature.").

law and fact.[76]* So said a unanimous Supreme Court in one of its earliest cases (decided before *Callender*),[77] in language that resonates with the writings of some of the most eminent American lawyers of the age— Jefferson, Adams, Wilson, Iredell, and Kent, to mention just a few.[78] Indeed, Chase himself went out of his way to concede that juries were judges of law as well as of fact.[79] Perhaps, however, this concession had to do with the peculiarities of sedition law and its somewhat unusual procedures—driven, it should be recalled, by the struggle between judge and jury. In any event, the line between constitutional law and constitutional fact is often hazy, as illustrated by the "reasonableness" issue in Fourth Amendment jurisprudence.[80]

Chase also suggested that decentralized jury review would undermine the idea of uniform national law—one jury might acquit on constitutional grounds, another might not—but the same thing could, in 1800, be said of Article III judicial review.[81] Through its power to make exceptions to the Supreme Court's appellate jurisdiction, Congress could vest the last word in constitutional cases in lower federal courts who, like juries, might disagree among themselves.[82] The *Callender* case was itself a remarkable example of this truth, for under the Judiciary Act of 1789 the Supreme Court lacked jurisdiction to hear this or any other criminal appeal from circuit courts.[83] (Thus the most important constitutional issue of the Federalist era never reached the Supreme Court.) Truly, the situation in 1800 was even more decentralized than this. Trials in circuit court, such as Callender's, were presided over by two or even three judges. In the event that these judges disagreed among themselves, whose instructions must the jury follow? If anything, the very structure of the judges' hierarchy implied a radical decentralization and nonuniformity rather consistent with jury review.[84] Consider, in this regard, the language of Article XLI of the Georgia Constitution of 1777:

---

*The general verdict limitation is an important one; in civil trials, judges have a variety of devices to prevent general verdicts: demurrers, directed verdicts, special verdicts, and so on. In criminal trials, by contrast, a judge may never take away a defendant's right to a general jury verdict, in which law and fact are decided "complicately," to use an eighteenth-century expression. Note also that the Seventh Amendment explicitly highlights the civil jury's fact-finding role, whereas the Sixth does not.

"The jury shall be judges of law, as well as of fact . . . but if all or any of the jury have any doubts concerning points of law, they shall apply to the bench, who shall *each* of them in rotation give their opinion."

But would not such a decentralized system lead to confusion and anarchy? Not in any single case, given the Constitution's rather clear procedural structure for aggregating substantive disagreement. In general, these rules work in a systematically antigovernmental way. In the event that any major institutional actor at the federal level deems a federal law unconstitutional, that institution is typically able to make its constitutional objection stick—at least in criminal law, where persons' lives, liberties, and property are most vulnerable. If either House or Senate deems a criminal bill unconstitutional, it cannot become law; and no person can be convicted in the absence of such a law, because there is no such thing as a federal common law of crimes.[85] If the president deems the bill unconstitutional, he may veto or pardon (even before indictment). If judges deem the law unconstitutional, they may order the defendant released and make their decision stick through the Great Writ of habeas corpus. By symmetric logic, juries should be allowed to use their power to issue a general verdict for defendant to achieve the same result.

Chase's final argument simply asserted the jury's lack of "competence" to decide the Sedition Act's (un)constitutionality. Judges were learned in law, and juries were not. Though this may seem quite obvious today, perhaps the reason is that we have lost the powerful and prevailing sense of two hundred years ago that the Constitution was *the people's* law. Even if juries generally lacked competence to adjudicate intricate and technical "lawyer's law," the Constitution was not supposed to be a prolix code. It had been made, and could be unmade at will, by We the People of the United States—citizens acting in special single-issue assemblies (ratifying conventions), asked to listen, deliberate, and then vote yea or nay. How, it might be asked, were juries different from conventions in this regard? If ordinary citizens were competent to make constitutional judgments when signing petitions or assembling in conventions, why not in juries, too? Is there not an important truth in Jefferson's exuberant 1789 definition of jury trials as "trials by the people themselves" or in rival John Adams's equally gushing 1771 description of the jury as "the voice of the people"?[86] In a similar vein the great popular-sovereignty theorist James Wilson, in his famous 1791 *Lectures on Law,* described jurors as "the ultimate interpreters of the law."[87] In the words of the Federal Farmer, "the freemen of a country are not always minutely skilled in the laws, but they have common sense in its purity, which seldom or never errs in making and applying laws to the condition of the people, or in determining judicial causes."[88] Or as John Adams wrote in 1771, "The great principles of the constitution are intimately known; they are sensibly felt by every Briton; it is scarcely extravagant to say they are drawn in and imbibed with the nurse's milk and first air."[89]

In setting forth the strong arguments for jury review, I do not mean to suggest that I am wholly convinced. But the mere fact of their strong plausibility shows how strikingly powerful the jury might have become had post-1800 history unfolded differently. The Supreme Court never heard *Callender* or any other Sedition Act case, and indeed did not definitively address the issue of jury review until the 1895 case of *Sparf and Hansen v. United States.*[90] In upholding Chase's approach, the *Sparf* Court added no real arguments beyond those canvassed above. The strongest defense of its holding comes from provisions never cited by the Court, namely the Civil War Amendments. These amendments did not repeal the fundamentally populist philosophy of the original Constitution and Bill of Rights, but they did radically transform the nature of American federalism. As Jefferson and Taylor understood all too well, acceptance of Wirt's argument for jury review would have vested in fundamentally local bodies a power that approached de facto nullification in a wide range of situations. Existence of such a power in local bodies to nullify Congress's Reconstruction statutes might have rendered the Civil War Amendments a virtual dead letter. Thus it is plausible to think that these amendments implicitly qualified the (equally implicit) power of local juries to thwart national laws. This, however, was hardly an argument that lay in the mouth of the *Sparf* Court. In the previous two decades, the Supreme Court had itself systematically destroyed congressional Reconstruction with the scalpel of stingy statutory construction and the sledgehammer of judicial review.[91]

But even today remnants of the Founders' vision remain, in doctrinal rules preventing judges from directing verdicts of guilt or requiring special verdicts in criminal cases; barring trial judges from reversing, and appellate courts from reviewing, criminal jury acquittals; allowing criminal defendants to escape government efforts to use collateral estoppel offensively; and preventing challenges to inconsistent criminal jury verdicts. In logic, each of these doctrines seems to bow to the criminal jury's right to go beyond merely deciding the facts.[92]

Waivability of Jury Trial

For whose benefit did the right to criminal jury trial exist? To Tocqueville, the answer was easy—the core interest was that of the citizen jurors, rather than the parties: "I do not know whether the jury is useful to those who have lawsuits, but I am certain it is highly beneficial to those who judge them . . . ."[93] Similarly, Justice Blackmun has written that the public has interests, independent of a criminal defendant, in monitoring judges, police, and prosecutors—and in being "educat[ed]" about "the manner in which criminal justice is administered."[94] Though speaking of the gallery's right to a "public" trial within the meaning of the Sixth Amendment, Justice Blackmun's insight would seem to apply even more to the jury's right, for every trial in which a jury sits is to that extent a public trial, of and by the people, and not just for them.

Nevertheless, in 1930 the Supreme Court held that the criminal jury trial right was the defendant's alone, to waive if he pleased. The Court explicitly framed the question as whether jury trial was "only [a] guaranty to the accused" instead of a component of the structure of "a tribunal as a part of the frame of government."[95] If the latter, the Court seemed to concede, a judge acting without a jury was simply not a court capable of trying a defendant, just as the Senate acting without the House is not a legislature capable of passing laws.

But the bicameral analogy is historically apt; it is anachronistic to see jury trial as an issue of individual right rather than (also, and more fundamentally) a question of government structure. None of the arguments in *Patton v. United States* survives close scrutiny. Predictably, the Court stressed the words of the Sixth Amendment guaranteeing to *"the accused"* the right of jury trial. But this ignores the clear words of Article III mandating that "the trial of *all* Crimes . . . *shall* be by Jury," a command no less mandatory and structural than its companion commands that the judicial power of the United States "*shall* be vested in" federal courts, whose judges "*shall*" have life tenure and undiminished salaries, and whose jurisdiction "*shall* extend to *all*" cases in certain categories.[96] The words in the Article III jury clause were plainly understood during the ratification period as words of obligation.[97] Nothing in the Sixth Amendment repeals those words—as would have been the case, for example, had the amendment explicitly conferred upon "the accused" a right to a nonjury trial. (Indeed, the Court has refused to recognize any constitutional "right" of a defendant to insist on a bench trial over the objection of the prosecutor.)[98] Before *Patton*, the Supreme Court was on record in *Callan v. Wilson* as affirming that the amendment was not "intended to supplant" Article III's jury clause.[99] In *Callan*, decided in 1888, the Court held that the undiminished words of Article III required jury trials in the District of Columbia, even though the Sixth Amendment speaks only of "State[s]." Nor have any other parts of Article III's jury clause—such as its impeachment exception—been deemed repealed by implication. *Patton*'s reading was thus at odds with precedent as well as with the plain words of the Ninth Amendment that the expression of some rights (such as "the accused's" right to jury trial) must never "be construed" by sheer implication to "deny or disparage" other rights guaranteed by the preexisting Constitution (such as the people's right to jury trial).[100]

But why, then, was the jury trial language of the amendment necessary? If Article III is as clear as I have suggested, and was so understood in 1789, why did the First Congress add the jury clause of the Sixth Amendment? The historical answer is unequivocal: to guarantee, among other things, a right to a trial by a jury from the "district" of the crime. Article III had not specified jury trial of "the vicinage," as did the prevailing common law,[101] and many Anti-Federalists wanted an explicit guarantee that juries would be organized around local rather than statewide communities.[102] Once again, we see the local communitarian spirit of the Bill of Rights. Note that, strictly speaking, Article III regulates venue—where the jurors will sit at trial—rather than vicinage—

where the jurors will come from. The Sixth Amendment thus speaks precisely to the issue of which moral community will sit in judgment over a crime.[103] Given the amendment's wording and the wording of Article III, perhaps the special Sixth Amendment right to a jury from the "district" is solely the accused's, waivable at will—but the underlying mandate of jury trial itself cannot be waived.

Even if a defendant may waive his right to a jury drawn from the crime district, the amendment does not give him an absolute right to demand a jury drawn from some other district. Moreover, the specification of a jury from the district of the place of the crime as the presumptively appropriate one will not always please defendants, as British soldiers tried by Boston juries for the Boston Massacre knew all too well. But when Parliament responded to the Boston Massacre trials with the so-called Administration of Justice Act allowing customs officers to be tried in England for murders committed in America, Americans denounced the act in no uncertain terms. Indeed, this Intolerable Act was condemned as a "mock Trial" regime in the Declaration of Independence.[104] All this shows again how jury trial was not simply and always an individual right but also an institution of localism and popular sovereignty.

The Sixth Amendment's legislative history overwhelmingly confirms the foregoing analysis. Until the mysterious House-Senate conference that we noted in conjunction with the First Congress's original First Amendment, the jury clause used language identical to that of Article III ("the trial of all crimes shall be . . . ").[105] When House and Senate failed to agree about whether explicitly to introduce the word *vicinage*, the compromise language of *district* was chosen,[106] and the clause was dropped into a catch-all criminal procedure amendment that spoke of the right of "the accused" to various benefits, including speedy trial, assistance of counsel, confrontation, and compulsory process. Beyond its explicit emphasis on local juries, the Sixth Amendment thus guarantees various incidents and attributes—"appendages," in Story's phrase—of traditional jury trial, appendages that might benefit the accused without compromising the mandate and vision of Article III. Article III does not in so many words, for example, guarantee a defendant's right to challenge a prospective juror for obvious bias or conflict of interest; but the amendment's explicit accent on the right of the accused to an *impartial* jury obviously protects the right to such challenges. Yet unlike waiver, challenges for cause would in no way undercut or repeal the mandate of Article III, or the people's right to serve as jurors; a would-be juror barred from sitting in case A (say, because of a prior relationship with, and hostility to, the defendant) could simply serve instead in case B, and the overall representativeness of each jury would be preserved.

Thus the amendment can indeed be read as adding something new to Article III without taking anything away from the original mandate that "the trial of *all* crimes *shall* be by jury." To put the historical point in its strongest light, it would be perverse to take a clause in the Bill of Rights designed to strengthen jury trial as evincing a desire to weaken it. Had this been the intended or even a plausible reading in 1789, there would have been howls of protest from Anti-Federalists like the Federal Farmer. Instead, there is not a scrap of evidence that anyone thought that the Article III mandate could be slyly undone by the Sixth Amendment.

Ignorance is indeed a great law reformer, but surely there are limits. *Patton* claimed that no one at the Founding viewed jury trial as going beyond the protection of the accused—a statement that ignores the writings of the Federal Farmer, the Maryland Farmer, Jefferson, and many others, not to mention the complexities of the denunciation in the Declaration of Independence of prodefendant "mock Trials."[107] Thus *Patton*'s claim that no third-party rights were at stake simply begs the question of jurors' rights and community rights. Also question-begging is reliance on the fact that various other Sixth Amendment rights (such as the rights to confrontation, compulsory process, and counsel) are waivable, for these concededly do not go to the structure, status, and jurisdiction of the court as a properly constituted tribunal and do not implicate any Article III mandate. Nor can reliance be placed on the greater power of a defendant to waive trial altogether by pleading guilty; for surely that would not allow the alleged lesser power of permitting a criminal defendant who pleaded not guilty to be tried by a federal "judge" who lacked Article III status—say, the Speaker of the House, in clear violation of the bill of attainder clause. Equally unavailing is the argument that civil jury trial is waivable. Indeed, the clear language of the Supreme

Court's earliest treatment of the waiver issue cuts exactly the opposite way. In 1819, the Court wrote: "Had the terms been, that 'the *trial* by jury shall be preserved,' it might have been contended, that they were imperative, and could not be dispensed with. But the words [of the Seventh Amendment] are, that the *right* of trial by jury shall be preserved, which places it on the foot of [waivable rights]."[108] As we have seen, the language of Article III is imperative in just the way the Court appeared willing to acknowledge. Indeed, as late as 1898, the Supreme Court, per Justice Harlan, was squarely on record as declaring that a criminal defendant could not waive jury trial.[109] *Patton* breezily dismissed the 1898 discussion as "dictum" (it wasn't) and failed even to mention an 1874 Supreme Court case whose unambiguous language squarely addressed the precise issue in *Patton:* "In a criminal case, [a defendant] cannot . . . be tried in any other manner than by a jury of twelve men, although he consent in open court to be tried by a jury of eleven men."[110]

Nevertheless, it would be a mistake to put all the blame for the vanishing significance of the jury on the shoulders of the *Patton* Court. The issue in *Patton* was a rather narrow one: could a defendant who pleaded not guilty be tried without a (twelve-person) jury? Even had *Patton* said no, backdoor evasion of jury trial was possible through the device of the guilty plea. Historically, the petit jury had a role only at trial; a guilty plea occurred prior to, and precluded, any trial (although even a guilty plea could occur only after a different jury—the grand jury—had authorized the charge).[111] As a practical matter, the back door opened by guilty pleas was of little significance two hundred years ago, for as Professor Alschuler has shown, such pleas were then highly atypical, and plea bargaining was generally viewed with suspicion, if not hostility.[112] Today, by contrast, roughly 90 percent of criminal defendants convicted in American courts plead guilty, and plea bargaining has the blessing of the Supreme Court.[113]

The Jury as Symbol

The issues of jury review and jury waiver exemplify the vast erosion of jury power along any number of doctrinal and practical dimensions. Juries stood at the center of the original Bill of Rights but sit on the periphery today. Indeed, to some extent, the centrality of the jury as late as 1789 may have reflected a mild ideological time lag. Each generation seeks lessons from the past, and for many well-educated eighteenth-century Americans, abiding lessons of liberty lay in the history of seventeenth-century England. Judges acting without juries could do outrageous deeds—this, for Americans, was the lesson of the Star Chamber. Craven and ambitious judges currying executive favor could become tools of tyranny—this, for Americans, was the lesson of the Bloody Assizes and the martyrdom of Algernon Sidney. (Even the great lawyer Sir Edward Coke had not escaped temptation, as his ruthless conduct as the prosecutor of Sir Walter Raleigh had shown.)[114]

To be sure, the Glorious Revolution of 1688, the English Bill of Rights of 1689, the Treason Act of 1696, and the Act of Settlement of 1701 reformed many of the worst features of Tudor and Stuart justice. The Act of Settlement, granting English judges independence from the crown, is especially important to note here. But distrust of judges lingered on in America—especially because the Act of Settlement did not extend extraterritorially to colonial judges, who continued to be subject to royal influence, and who at times proved too willing to dance the king's tune (especially when acting without juries in prerogative vice-admiralty courts).[115] Thus the Declaration of Independence thundered against the king for making "Judges dependent on his Will alone, for the tenure of their offices, and the amount and payment of their salaries."[116] The Glorious Revolution had also ushered in an era of Parliamentary supremacy, but once again, Americans did not really benefit. They could not vote for Parliament, and that body could trump the acts adopted by the colonial legislatures they *could* vote for. This was another large theme of the Declaration of Independence, which denounced Parliament's "pretended legislation" and assertions of "unwarrantable jurisdiction."[117] Lacking tight control over English Parliaments and royal judges, Americans in the pre-Revolution period instinctively turned to one institution they could and did control: the good old jury of the vicinage. (This emphasis on juries made all the more sense in a world where few American judges were deeply and distinctively learned in law, where common law was relatively simple rather than intricately regulatory, and where ordinary yeomen were remarkably literate and rights conscious—Blackstone's *Commentaries* was a runaway best-seller in the colonies.) The British well understood the nullifying possibilities of colonial juries and tried to channel as much judicial business as possible into juryless vice-admiralty courts.[118] Americans resisted, and the battle lines of liberty were clearly drawn.

In theory, the success of the American Revolution itself, and the adoption of the federal Constitution, could have triggered a complete rethinking of the role of the jury. Once American legislatures had wrested control from Parliament and federal judges had won life tenure and other attributes of independence, perhaps juries would not need to carry all the load they had borne before, from Zenger to Independence. But could Americans in 1789 be sure that a small and newfangled Congress would never become as aloof and distant as Parliament had been, or that federal judges seeking power and promotions would never abet a grasping executive?[119] Abiding ideologies of liberty and ingrained patterns of thought and action do not die overnight. Thus when Federalists proposed to summon up a new and awesome imperial government to stand in the shoes of the ousted British king, many suspicious Americans instinctively reached for their trusty ideological weapons, without asking whether these weapons had been crafted to win the last war, rather than the next one.

Today's generation of Americans must also ponder the lessons of the past—a past that includes not just the Creation but also the Reconstruction. The jury, as a local body, beautifully fit the localism of the Revolutionary era; but some fourscore years later the Civil War brought the surrender of the banner of extreme localism to the freedom flag of Union. Thus in Part Two we shall consider how the original jury idea must be Reconstructed by those who look to our constitutional past to help guide us toward our constitutional future.

Beyond Juries

The jury was the dominant motif of Amendments V–VIII, but not the only motif. Before we turn away from these judicial-process amendments let us examine a secondary, interrelated motif at work, a motif of criminal justice.

Consider, for example, the Sixth Amendment guarantee that "the accused shall enjoy the right to . . . a . . . public trial." At first glance, this might seem an obvious right of the defendant, and thus waivable by him. But as with the analytically and textually intertwined Sixth Amendment right of "the accused" to a jury trial, things may not be quite what they seem at first glance. Perhaps the public trial was also a right of, well, the public, and was as such not waivable.

Begin with the text. Although the amendment says that "the accused" shall enjoy the right to a public trial, it nowhere says that he has the right to a secret trial. Here, too, the Ninth Amendment explicitly cautions against a too-quick inference that the expression of one right (here, the accused's) implicitly negates another "right[] . . . retained by the people." And this explicit reminder seems especially apt when we deal with what are, quite literally, rights of "the people"—rights, that is, of the public and populace at large.

Historically, virtually all criminal trials in England and America have been trials open to the public.[120] Indeed, in his influential *Institutes,* Sir Edward Coke declared that the very word *court* implied public access: "[A]ll Causes ought to be heard, ordered, and determined before the judges of the kings courts openly in the kings courts, *wither all persons may resort;* and in no chambers, or other private places: for judges are not judges of *chambers,* but of *courts,* and therefore *in open court* . . . . "[121] Coke's contrast of *courts* with *chambers* had special meaning for eighteenth-century Americans; one of the defining characteristics of the Star Chamber that they had been taught to despise was that this (juryless) body interrogated suspects in private, not in public.[122] Joseph Story echoed Coke's ode to openness in his *Commentaries on the Constitution,* where he wrote that the Sixth Amendment "does but follow out the established course of the common law in all trials for crimes. *The trial is always public.*"[123]

To cast these historical points into a textual argument, the right of public trial is indeed a right of the "accused" and only the "accused," in the sense that he may waive trial altogether by pleading guilty. (If the accused pleads guilty, there is, legally speaking, nothing to try and thus no trial.) But if he pleads not guilty and thus demands a trial, he must get a public trial, whether he will or no; for a trial from which the people are excluded is not a "trial" at all within the meaning of the Constitution.

Structural analysis helps to identify some of the special purposes served by public trials in America. The phrase *the people* appears in no fewer than five of the ten amendments that make up our Bill of Rights;[124] and so we would do well to take seriously the republican and populist overtones of its etymological cousin,[125] *public,* in a sixth—*the* Sixth—Amendment. The framers crafted a system of re*public*an governments, state and federal—governments of, by, and for the people.[126] Here, the people would rule—not day to day, but ultimately, in the long run. All governmental policy and governmental policymakers could, in time, be lawfully replaced by the sovereign people via constitutional conventions and ordinary elections. This ultimate right of the public to change policy and policymakers called for a strong presumption that courts would be open.[127] If citizens did not like what they saw their government agents doing in open court, the people could throw the rascals out at the next election, or could petition and agitate to change the law.

The people, however, would not need to wait until election day to make a difference; their very presence in the courtroom could discourage judicial misbehavior. In the words of Sir Matthew Hale's widely influential treatise, "if the judge be PARTIAL, his partiality and injustice will be evident to all by-standers."[128] Sir William Blackstone concurred in his even more widely influential treatise: "[Objections to evidence] are publicly stated, and by the judge are openly and publicly allowed or disallowed, in the face of the country; which must curb any secret bias or partiality, that might arise in his own breast."[129] The ability of the public to judge the judge would tend to protect innocent defendants from judicial corruption or oppression, but public scrutiny was bad news for many a guilty defendant, who might prefer an incompetent judge or one "partial" to the defendant's cause—an old political friend, perhaps, or a new financial one.

So too, the public right to monitor witnesses at trial was designed to help the truth come out, and truth would as a rule help innocent defendants more than guilty ones. If, at trial, a bystander happened to have relevant information bearing on a key point, he could bring the matter to the attention of court and counsel. In part because of this, witnesses who testified would be less likely to perjure themselves in front of a public gallery—or at least this was the theory underlying the common law's commitment to public trials. In 1685, Solicitor General John Hawles put the point as follows: "[T]he reason that all trials are public, is, that any person may inform in point of fact, though not subpoena'd, that truth may be discovered in civil as well as criminal matters. There is an invitation to all persons, who can inform the court concerning the matter to be tried, to come into the court, and they shall be heard."[130] Truth was also Blackstone's theme: "This open examination of witnesses *viva voce*, in the presence of all mankind, is much more conducive to the clearing up of truth, than [a] private and secret examination . . . . [A] witness may frequently depose that in private, which he will be ashamed to testify in a public and solemn tribunal."[131]

In short, the public trial was designed to infuse public knowledge into the trial itself, and, in turn, to satisfy the public that truth had prevailed at trial. A public trial would protect innocence while making life more difficult for the guilty. When government officials or friends of judges misbehaved, only a public trial could assure the people that judges were not on the take or playing favorites. Thus, even if a defendant might prefer a closed proceeding (consider, for example, the British officers tried for their role in the Boston Massacre), the republican ideology underlying the public-trial clause overrode that preference in the name of democratic openness and education, public confidence, anticorruption, and truth seeking.

The Sixth Amendment vision of the gallery box blended nicely with its vision of the jury box. The people sitting in both boxes would be educated in their rights and duties and in the workings of the criminal justice system that operated in their name. The many heads in the gallery box could improve fact-finding by bringing information to light, and the twelve heads in a jury box would be more reliable and less idiosyncratic fact finders than a single judge. Also, the very presence of the people in both boxes could deter judicial corruption. A guilty defendant or a malicious prosecutor would have a harder time bribing a judge whose every move was monitored by the gallery; likewise, even Alexander Hamilton—hardly a jury worshiper—emphasized in *The Federalist* that juries made bribery more difficult. "As there is always more time and better opportunity to tamper with a standing body of magistrates than with a jury summoned for the occasion," judges acting alone would face more "temptations to prostitution" and offer less "security against corruption."[132]

Other clauses of the Sixth Amendment summoned up a somewhat different vision, less collective and more individualistic. Consider the clustered rights of confrontation, compulsory process, and counsel. Admittedly, here too the amendment does not explicitly confer upon the accused a constitutional right of waiver, or an explicit right to the opposite thing—the right not to cross-examine, or subpoena, or use a lawyer. But the counsel clause does say that counsel's job is to "assist[ ]" the accused in making "his"—the accused's—defense, and it is hard to see how the accused would still own his defense if some government-imposed agent took it over against his will; the assistant would be usurping the place of the master. More generally, in practice it would be exceedingly hard to force a lawyer upon a defendant of sound mind who said no; or to oblige an unwilling defendant to subpoena witness X, or to cross-examine witness Y. And so, with this cluster at least, we see a genuine affirmation of rights of the accused and only the accused, rights of a single person standing alone against the world. What ideas underlay this cluster?

One idea was autonomy. The accused, after all, was the one on trial, with his embodied "person" being "held," his "life or limb" on the line, in the graphic words of the Fifth Amendment (words that follow two graphic references in the Fourth Amendment to embodied "persons" whom the government seeks to "seiz[e]"). And so the Sixth Amendment gave the accused some freedom, some autonomy, in controlling the shape of "his defence": whom to cross-examine, whom to subpoena, whom (if anyone) to hire as a lawyer. The Founding vision of defendant autonomy, however, was hardly a robust one by modern standards. In seeking to make "his defence" an innocent accused might well wish to testify under oath and tell his story to the jury and the public; but the Sixth Amendment nowhere explicitly guaranteed this (to us) basic right.[133] On the contrary, throughout the Founding and antebellum eras, no American court, state or federal, allowed defendants to take the stand.[134] Not until the Civil War era did the rule begin to change, a change that, as we shall see in Part Two, fits well with the increased emphasis on individual autonomy and freedom represented by that era's Fourteenth Amendment.

Truth seeking was another theme of our clustered Sixth Amendment clauses. (Indeed, this idea also helps explain the common-law ban on defendant testimony: a man with so much at stake, the theory went, would be tempted to lie and was thus disqualified as an "interested party.")[135] As with a public trial, confrontation would deter perjury and promote the truth. Blackstone discussed these ideas together (in a chapter on trial by jury):

> The oath administered to the witness is not only that what he deposes shall be true, but that he shall also depose the *whole* truth . . . . And all this evidence is to be given in open court, in the presence of the parties, their attorneys, the counsel, and all by-standers; and before the judge and jury . . . .
>
> This open examination of witnesses *viva voce*, in the presence of all mankind, is . . . conducive to the clearing up of truth . . . . Besides[,] the occasional questions of the judge, the jury, and the counsel, propounded to the witnesses on a sudden, will sift out the truth much better than a formal set of interrogatories previously penned and settled: and the confronting of adverse witnesses is also another opportunity of obtaining a clear discovery, which can never be had upon any other method of trial.[136]

Similarly, the compulsory-process clause—a fraternal twin of the confrontation clause—would allow the whole truth to out by enabling the defendant to present his own witnesses to tell the jury and the gallery what the prosecutor's witnesses had left out. Since even an intelligent and knowledgeable defendant might not be particularly skilled at courtroom procedure and rules of evidence, he could seek the "assistance" of a legally trained "counsel" to help him present the whole truth in the courtroom. (The landmark English Treason Act of 1696, which first affirmed a right of counsel, explicitly spoke of "[c]ounsel learned in the law.")[137]

Notions of basic fairness and symmetry were also at work in the Sixth Amendment. If the prosecuting government could have a lawyer, why not the defendant? If the government could put witness X on the stand and ask him questions, why shouldn't the defendant be allowed to ask questions? If the government could use subpoenas to force unwilling witnesses to testify, why couldn't the defendant? The English Treason Act of 1696 explicitly invoked the symmetry principle in the compulsory-process context, giving defendants "the *like* Processe . . . to compell their Witnesses . . . as is usually granted to compell Witnesses to appeare against them."[138] In formulating the precise wording of the compulsory-process clause, Madison seems to have borrowed from Blackstone's *Commentaries,* which also explicitly embraced the symmetry principle: the accused must enjoy "the *same* compulsive process to bring in his witnesses for him, as was usual to compel their appearance against him."[139] One year after it proposed the confrontation clause, the First Congress drafted a statute defining rights of capital defendants, and here too the symmetry principle was explicit.[140]

Symmetry also helps make sense of two of the criminal-process clauses of the Fifth Amendment. If the government won a fair and suitably error-free criminal trial, it would not give the defendant a right to ignore the verdict and demand a new trial on a clean slate. Why should a defendant be placed in a lesser position if *he* won? Hence the double-jeopardy clause banning any government effort to say "heads we win, tails let's play again until you lose." If a defendant was not able to take the stand to testify in favor of himself, why should the government be able to oblige him to testify against himself? Hence the rule of the self-incrimination clause—a clause that also protected the innocent but inarticulate defendant, who might be made to look guilty if subject to crafty questioning from a trained inquisitor.[141]

In championing the ideas of basic fairness and symmetry, the framing generation had in mind notorious historical examples of unfairness that they wished to avoid. Sir Walter Raleigh, for instance, had been convicted of treason in a 1603 trial where the government procured an ex parte affidavit from a witness of dubious reliability but refused to let Raleigh meet his alleged accuser face to face, or cross-examine him, or subpoena him. Raleigh objected vigorously: "The Proof of the Common Law is by witness and jury; let Cobham be here, let him speak it. Call my accuser before my face . . . ."[142]

As Raleigh's and countless other cases made clear to late eighteenth-century Americans, treason law was an area where the danger of government self-dealing was especially acute. English history was littered with examples of officials seeking to entrench themselves by criminalizing political opposition, and imprisoning (or worse) political rivals.[143] England began to reform the worst features of its criminal justice system in a 1696 statute specially focused on treason trials. A century later and an ocean away, the men of the 1787 Philadelphia convention also devoted special care to the treason issue in a pair of clauses in Article III. Substantively, Article III declared that "Treason against the United States, shall consist only in levying War against them, or in adhering to their Enemies, giving them Aid and Comfort." Mere political opposition to the government or the executive—"constructive treason"—was thus shielded from criminal prosecution. (Here Article III foreshadowed the later speech, press, assembly, and petition clauses of our First Amendment.)[144] Procedurally, Article III specified that "No Person shall be convicted of Treason unless on the Testimony of two Witnesses to the same overt Act, or on Confession in open Court." The requirement of a confession in *open* court was generalized by the subsequent Sixth Amendment public-trial clause—no Star Chamber nonsense in America!—and the "witness" clauses of Article III and the Sixth Amendment also intermeshed. Lest government seek to evade the two-witness rule of Article III by fabricating some trumped-up affidavit, à la Raleigh, the Sixth Amendment confrontation clause forbade such ex parte affidavits, and the compulsory-process clause empowered a future Raleigh

to subpoena his alleged accuser on his own. Here again, in three clauses featuring the word *witness*, we see linkages between the original Constitution and the Bill of Rights.

The last two amendments of the Bill also featured an important
textual linkage to the original Constitution. This brings us to our final
Creation story.

Six

The Popular-Sovereignty Amendments

In light of the strongly populist cast of the preceding amendments, it is wholly fitting that the Bill of Rights ends with back-to-back invocations of "the people":

IX.
The enumeration in the Constitution, of certain rights, shall not be construed to deny or disparage others retained by the people.

X.
The powers not delegated to the United States by the Constitution, nor prohibited by it to the States, are reserved to the States respectively, or to the people.

Taking the People Seriously

The popular-sovereignty motif of the Tenth Amendment could not be more obvious. We the People, acting collectively, have delegated some powers to the federal government, have allowed others to be exercised by state governments, and have withheld some things from all governments. The Preamble and the Tenth Amendment are perfect bookends, fittingly the alpha and omega of the Founders' (revised) Constitution.*

The conspicuously collective meaning of "the people" in the Tenth Amendment (and elsewhere) should alert us that its core meaning in the Ninth is similarly collective. Indeed, the most obvious and inalienable right underlying the Ninth Amendment is the collective right of We the People to alter or abolish government, through the distinctly American device of the constitutional convention. We have already seen that this clarifying gloss—with antecedents in virtually every state constitution—was initially proposed as a prefix to the Preamble, only to be dropped for stylistic reasons and resurrected in the First Amendment's explicit right of "the people" to assemble in convention.[1] So too with both the Ninth and Tenth Amendments' use of that phrase. Indeed, Hamilton in *The Federalist* No. 84 explicated the Preamble in language that perfectly foreshadowed the later amendments' wording: "[Our Constitution is] professedly founded upon the power of *the people* . . . . Here, in strictness, *the people* surrender nothing; and as they *retain* everything they have no need of particular *reservations.* 'WE, THE PEOPLE of the United States, to secure the blessings of liberty to ourselves and our posterity, do ordain and establish this Constitution for the United States of America.' Here is a [clear] recognition of *popular rights* . . . ."[2] To see the Ninth Amendment, as originally written, as a palladium of countermajoritarian individual rights—like privacy—is to engage in anachronism.[3]

In words that anticipated Hamilton's *Federalist* No. 84, the great Federalist leader James Wilson reminded the Pennsylvania ratifying convention that "supreme . . . power *remains* in the people"—a point that he formulated a bit later as follows: The people "never part with the whole" of their "original power" and "they *retain* the right of recalling what they part with. . . . [T]he citizens of the United States may always say, WE *reserve* the right to do what we please."[4] Note how Wilson's emphatic

---

*For a very similar approach, *see* Alexander Meiklejohn, *The First Amendment Is an Absolute,* 1961 SUP. CT. REV. 245, 253–54.

WE tied back to the Preamble, while his other language foreshadowed the Ninth and Tenth Amendments. The linkage to the Preamble also appeared vividly in the remarks of South Carolina Representative Thomas Tudor Tucker in the First Congress, when an early version of the Tenth Amendment was under discussion: "Mr. Tucker proposed to amend the proposition, by prefixing to it 'all powers being derived from the people.' He thought this a better place to make this assertion than the introductory clause [the Preamble, that is] of the constitution, where a similar sentiment was proposed by the committee."[5] Eventually, of course, the same point was made by the amendment's last three words.

In short, conventional wisdom today misses the close triangular interrelation among the Preamble and the Ninth and Tenth Amendments. The Ninth is said to be about unenumerated individual rights, like personal privacy; the Tenth about federalism; and the Preamble about something else entirely. But look again at these texts. All are at their core about popular sovereignty. All, indeed, explicitly invoke "the people." In the Preamble, "We the people . . . *do*" exercise our right and power of popular sovereignty, and in the Ninth and Tenth "the people" expressly "retain" and "reserve" our "right" and "power" to do it again. If the Ninth is mainly about individual rights, why does it not speak of individual "persons" rather than the collective "the people"? If the Tenth is only about states' rights, why does it stand back-to-back with the Ninth, and what are its last three words doing there, mirroring the Preamble's first three?

The legislative history of these amendments confirms their close interrelations with each other and with the Preamble, and their obvious implications for the people's right to alter or abolish. Consider, for example, the initial formulations of these principles in the Virginia and New York ratifying conventions. First, Virginia:

[T]he powers granted under the Constitution, being derived from the people of the United States, may be resumed by them, whensoever the same shall be perverted to their injury or oppression, and that every power not granted thereby remains with them, and at their will; that, therefore, no right . . . can be cancelled, abridged, restrained, or mod-

ified, by [the U.S. government] except in those instances in which
power is given by the Constitution for those purposes . . . . [6]

Next, New York:

> That all power is originally vested in, and consequently derived from,
> the people, and that government is instituted by them for their com-
> mon interest, protection and security.
>
> . . . .
>
> That the powers of government may be reassumed by the people
> whensoever it shall become necessary to their happiness; that every
> power, jurisdiction, and right, which is not by the said Constitution
> clearly delegated to the Congress of the United States, or the depart-
> ments of the government thereof, remains to the people of the several
> states, or to their respective state governments, to whom they may
> have granted the same; and that those clauses in the said Constitu-
> tion, which declare that Congress shall not have or exercise certain
> powers, do not imply that Congress is entitled to any powers not giv-
> en by the said Constitution; but such clauses are to be construed ei-
> ther as exceptions to certain specified powers, or as inserted merely for
> greater caution.[7]

Both the Virginia and New York prototypes, of course, built on the
language of the Declaration of Independence, which featured the phrase
"the Right of the People" in its most famous passage: "[W]henever any
Form of Government becomes destructive of [its] ends, it is the *Right of
the People* to alter or to abolish it, and to institute new Government."[8]
Alexander Hamilton did not always agree with Thomas Jefferson, but
he agreed with him on this, as his own use of the phrase "the right of the
people" in *The Federalist* No. 78 made clear: "I trust the friends of the
proposed Constitution will never concur with its enemies in questioning that fundamental principle of republican government which admits
the right of the people to alter or abolish the established Constitution
whenever they find it inconsistent with their happiness . . . ."[9] The rights
of "the people" affirmed in the Ninth and Tenth Amendments may well
mean more than the right to alter or abolish, but surely they mean at
least this much at their core.

Taking the States Seriously

Finally, let us consider how the Ninth and Tenth Amendments elegantly integrate popular sovereignty with federalism.[10] All government power derives from the people, but these grants of power are limited. In the language of the Tenth Amendment, the federal government has only powers "delegated" to it, expressly or by implication, and certain "prohibit[ions]" are imposed on state governments. How are these government agents to be kept within these limits? In part by mutual jealousy and monitoring, as we have seen throughout. State legislatures could alert the people to any perceived usurpations by central agents (consider the "sirens" sounded by the Virginia and Kentucky legislatures in 1798, or the Hartford convention in 1814–15); state militias could thwart and thus deter a tyrannical standing army; state common law of trespass could help vindicate persons' Fourth Amendment rights and Fifth Amendment takings-clause rights; and so on. Once again, populism and federalism—liberty and localism—work together; We the People conquer government power by dividing it between the two rival governments, state and federal, a structural scheme textually reaffirmed by the Tenth Amendment. In this sense, the Tenth Amendment beautifully sums up many of the themes of prior amendments—and it is wholly unsurprising that, alone among the successful amendments, the Tenth was the only one proposed by every one of the state ratifying conventions that proposed amendments.[11]

The Ninth Amendment also sounds in part in federalism, but many constitutional scholars today have missed the beat. As with our First and Tenth Amendments, the Ninth explicitly sought to protect liberty by preventing Congress from going beyond its enumerated powers in Article I, section 8 and elsewhere in the Constitution. As Professor McAffee has shown, the amendment's legislative history strongly supports an enumerated-powers, federalism-based reading.[12] The obvious counterargument—chanted like a mantra by most mainstream scholars—is that this reading renders the Ninth Amendment wholly redundant of the Tenth. But this obvious counterargument is obviously wrong, and no amount of chanting can save it. To be sure, on a federalism-based reading, the Ninth and Tenth fit together snugly, as their words and their legislative history make clear; but each amendment complements the other without duplicating it. The Tenth says that Congress must point to some explicit or implicit enumerated power before it can act; and the Ninth addresses the closely related but distinct question of whether such express or implied enumerated power in fact exists. In particular, the Ninth warns readers not to infer from the mere enumeration of a right in the Bill of Rights that implicit federal power in fact exists in a given domain. Thus, for example, we must not infer from our First Amendment that Congress was ever given legislative power in the first place to regulate religion in the states, or to censor speech. (Sadly, some high Federalists in the late 1790s drew precisely this inference to support the federal Sedition Act of 1798.)[13]

Of course, both the Ninth and the Tenth go beyond pure federalism in their ringing affirmations of popular sovereignty. But the federalism roots of the Ninth Amendment, and its links to the unique enumerated-power strategy of Article I, help explain why no previous state constitution featured language precisely like the Ninth's—a fact conveniently ignored by most mainstream accounts. As we shall see in Part Two, however, by the 1860s the federalism reading of the Ninth Amendment had faded considerably, as many post-1791 state constitutions did echo the wording of the Ninth Amendment, but not the Tenth. And so clauses that originally dovetailed later came unglued; thus we now tell ourselves that the Tenth Amendment is about states' rights while the Ninth is about individual rights. In the end, this reading may well make sense today—but only (as we shall see in Part Two) after and because of the Reconstruction of the Bill of Rights.

The Bill of Rights as a Constitution

Before we turn to that Reconstruction,* let us step back and see what larger lessons may be pieced together from the story thus far.

In the preceding pages, I have tried to suggest how much is lost by the

---

*Between the Tenth Amendment and the Reconstruction Amendments, of course, came the intervening Eleventh and Twelfth Amendments. These fit rather well into our general story. The Eleventh, adopted in the mid 1790s, cut back on federal jurisdiction by amending Article III. The amendment reflected an Anti-Federalist suspicion of federal judges in diversity cases not implicating federal law. The Twelfth, adopted in the

clausebound approach that now dominates constitutional discourse. The clausebound approach misses the ways in which structure and rights mutually reinforce. It misses interesting questions within amendments, like "why are the press and religion clauses yoked together in a single amendment?" and "why is an obviously substantive takings clause bundled into an otherwise procedural Fifth Amendment?" It misses thematic continuities across different amendments, like the popular-sovereignty motif sounded by repeated invocations of "the people," and the ways in which jury trial issues inflected the thinking behind the First, Fourth, and Eighth Amendments, and the Fifth Amendment double-jeopardy clause. It misses the many linkages between the original Constitution and the Bill—the importance of earlier invocations of "the people" in the Preamble and Article I; the connection between the First Amendment free-speech clause and the Article I speech-and-debate clause; the relevance of the enumerated-power philosophy of Article I to First Amendment absolutism, and to the Ninth Amendment; the subtle interplay between the militia and army clauses of Article I and the Second and Third Amendments; the implications of the Article III jury-trial command for the Sixth Amendment; the nexus between the Article III diversity clause and the Seventh Amendment; the interconnections between the Article III treason clause and the First and Sixth Amendments; the nonexclusivity of Article V signaled by the First, Ninth, and Tenth Amendments; and so on.

How could we forget that our Constitution is a single document, and not a jumble of disconnected clauses—that it is *a* Constitution we are expounding?

Today, the very phrase *Bill of Rights* is virtually synonymous with a compilation of countermajoritarian personal rights. Cause and effect are hard to disentangle; does the definition drive, or is it driven by, the stan-

---

wake of the "Revolution of 1800," modified Article II in ways that facilitated a plebiscitarian presidency. Both amendments sounded in structure more than individual rights; one stressed states' rights, the other sought to strengthen majoritarian linkages between the people and the president. For more discussion and analysis, *see* Akhil Reed Amar, *Of Sovereignty and Federalism*, 96 YALE L. J. 1425, 1466–92 (1987) (Eleventh Amendment); Akhil Reed Amar and Vik Amar, *President Quayle?*, 78 VA. L. REV. 913, 918–24 (1992) (Twelfth Amendment).

dard reading of our Bill of Rights? Either way, we should recognize how different standard usage was two hundred years ago.* The virulent Anti-Federalist Luther Martin, for example, argued during 1788 for "a bill of rights" that would encompass "a stipulation in favour of the rights both of states and of men."[14] George Mason, the leading proponent of a bill of rights at the Philadelphia convention, also linked the project to an express reservation of states' rights.[15] Another leading Anti-Federalist urged a "declaration in favour of the rights of states and of citizens";[16] and we have already encountered a 1791 Georgia grand jury demanding "a Bill of rights clearly defining the reserved rights of the several States." In the New York ratifying convention, Thomas Tredwell lamented: "Here we find no security for the rights of individuals, no security for the existence of our state governments; here is no bill of rights . . . . "[17] In proposing provisions to be included in such a Bill, Tredwell emphasized populist provisions: "freedom of election, a sufficient and responsible representation, the freedom of the press, and the trial by jury both in civil and criminal cases."[18] In a similar populist spirit, Thomas Jefferson wrote that "a bill of rights is what *the people* are entitled to against every *government* on earth."[19]

Gordon Wood sums up this Anti-Federalist spirit well:

> [T]he Antifederalists' lack of faith was not in the people themselves, but only in the [regular government] organizations and institutions that presumed to speak for the people . . . . [E]nhancing the people out-of-doors as it correspondingly disparaged their elected officials, [Antifederalist thought] can never be considered undemocratic. [Antifederalists] were "localists," fearful of distant governmental, even representational, authority for very significant political and social reasons that in the final analysis must be called democratic.[20]†

---

*An excellent analysis appears in Arthur E. Wilmarth, Jr., *The Original Purpose of the Bill of Rights: James Madison and the Founders' Search for a Workable Balance Between Federal and State Power*, 26 AM. CRIM. L. REV. 1261 (1989).

†*Compare* HERBERT J. STORING, WHAT THE ANTI-FEDERALISTS WERE FOR 70 (1981) ("The fundamental case for a bill of rights is that it can be a prime agency of that political and moral education of the people on which free republican government depends.") *with* Herbert J. Storing, *The Constitution and the Bill of Rights, in* HOW DOES

The Federalists also understood that calls for a bill of rights were largely driven by populist and localist concerns. In 1788, Madison wrote Jefferson that proponents of a bill of rights sought "further guards to *public liberty* & individual rights."[21] In *The Federalist* No. 38, he noted that some critics "concur[red] in the absolute necessity of a bill of rights, but contend[ed] that it ought to be declaratory, not of the personal rights of individuals, but of the rights reserved to the States in their political capacity."[22] And in *The Federalist* No. 84, Hamilton stressed that "one object of a bill of rights [is] to declare and specify the *political* privileges of the citizens in the *structure* and *administration* of the government."[23]

Hamilton's answer to the drumbeat for a bill of rights was to stress the ways in which the original Constitution fit the bill, so to speak. For Hamilton and many others, the Philadelphia Constitution was "itself, in every rational sense, and to every useful purpose, A BILL OF RIGHTS."[24] But this point can be flipped around. As I have tried to show throughout, the Bill of Rights can itself be seen as a *Constitution* of sorts—that is, as a document attentive to structure, focused on the agency problem of government, and rooted in the sovereignty of We the People of the United States.

THE CONSTITUTION SECURE RIGHTS? 15, 27 (Robert A. Goldwin and William A. Schambra eds., 1985) ("Protecting individuals and minorities against unjust action by the majority, or the government reflecting the wishes of the majority, is a major benefit of a bill of rights in the Antifederalist view."). Although this last statement is, I believe, a bit too sweeping, I do not deny that individual rights made up one strand of the original tapestry of the Bill of Rights. For evidence of this strand in the Anti-Federalist literature, *see Letters of Agrippa* (XVI), 4 THE COMPLETE ANTI-FEDERALIST 109, 111 (Herbert J. Storing ed., 1981) (explicit argument for protections of "the minority against the usurpation and tyranny of the majority"); *The Address and Reasons of Dissent of the Minority of the Convention of Pennsylvania to Their Constituents, reprinted in 3 id.* at 145, 157 (Bill of Rights necessary to protect "those unalienable and personal rights of men") (authored by Samuel Bryan); *Letters of Centinel* (II), *reprinted in 2 id.* at 143, 144 (similar) (authored by Samuel Bryan); *Essays by a Farmer* (I), *reprinted in 5 id.* at 9, 15 (celebrating freedom of the press as an "inestimable right of the individual" and calling for a "bill of rights" to protect "the rights of individuals" against "the apparent interests of the majority"); 5 *id.* at 116–18 (Letter from Richard Henry Lee to Edmund Randolph, Oct. 16, 1787) (discussing both rulers-versus-ruled and majority-versus-minority concerns).

Seeing the Importance of Structure and the Problem of Agency Like the original Constitution, the original Bill of Rights was webbed with structural ideas. Federalism, separation of powers, bicameralism, representation, republican government, amendment—these issues were understood as central to the preservation of liberty. My point is not that substantive rights are unimportant, but that these rights were intimately intertwined with structural considerations. The most obvious prototype for an American Bill of Rights in the late eighteenth century was the English Bill of Rights of the late seventeenth century; and that Bill, too, dovetailed individual rights with structural issues—reining in executive authority, shielding legislative speech and debate, endorsing frequent Parliaments, limiting standing armies, and so on. Surely it would not be stretching things to call the English Bill of Rights a Constitution of sorts. The same is true, I suggest, of the original American Bill of Rights.

Consider, in this regard, Dean Choper's thesis that courts should treat "structural" issues such as federalism and separation of powers as nonjusticiable, and save their prestige for the protection of "individual rights."[25] For Choper, the only items that fall within the second category are those things that no government, state or federal, may do. Issues of federalism, Choper assures us, lie beyond the judicial ken because true liberty is not involved—the issue is simply *which* government can intrude.[26]

But two hundred years ago, the issue of which government often made all the difference. The original Constitution specified only three things that neither federal nor state government could do: pass bills of attainder, enforce ex post facto laws, and grant titles of nobility. To make matters even worse for Choper, the first two of these prohibitions obviously have structural overtones sounding in separation of powers notions about legislative generality and prospectivity.[27] When we look at the original Bill of Rights, an even starker pattern emerges: none of its provisions bound state governments. This regime, epitomized by *Barron v. Baltimore*[28]—a case Choper never even mentions in more than four hundred pages of text—was the de jure constitutional framework for almost a century. De facto, *Barron* survived well into this century, and was not decisively dethroned until the Warren Court. Only after the near-total incorporation of the Bill of Rights against states and the "reverse-incorporation" of equal-protection principles against the federal government, both of which occurred after World War II, did it become conventional to define individual rights as Choper does. Yet he nowhere signals his awareness of just how odd his ideas might have sounded to some members of earlier generations. When Choper does purport to do history, his claims become even more outlandish: "[T]he assertion that federalism was meant to protect . . . individual constitutional freedoms . . . has no solid historical or logical basis."[29]

I have singled out Dean Choper for special criticism because his work is particularly clear in its effort to distill and defend widely held but distinctly modern ideas about the Constitution. The work of Alexander Bickel also epitomizes much modern thinking about the Constitution. "The root difficulty," Bickel wrote in one of his most quoted sentences, "is that judicial review is a countermajoritarian force in our system."[30] By focusing so single-mindedly on one of the two main issues flagged by Madison in *The Federalist* No. 51—the problem of minority rights—Bickel's work has unfortunately diverted our attention from Madison's other chief concern, namely, the agency problem of government. As we have seen, only by taking seriously the agency issue can we fully understand the original Bill of Rights.

Putting the People Back into the Constitution Attention to the agency problem should remind us that all permanent government officials, even Article III judges, may at times pursue self-interested policies that fail to reflect the views and protect the liberties of ordinary Americans. As the Fourth Amendment warrant clause and the Eighth Amendment make clear, professional judges acting without citizen juries can sometimes be part of the problem rather than the solution.

Today it is commonplace to stress judicial review as the most natural enforcement mechanism of the Bill of Rights. But consider again the two historical quotations typically invoked for this idea. First, there is Madison's speech before the First Congress: "If [rights] are incorporated into the constitution, independent tribunals of justice will consider themselves in a peculiar manner the guardians of those rights; they will be an impenetrable bulwark against every assumption of power in the legislative or executive [department] . . . ."[31]

Madison surely had Article III judicial review in mind here, but he may also have been thinking of juries. He speaks not of judges but "tribunals," which from one perspective can be seen as encompassing both the upper house of the judge and the lower house of the jury. If "inde-penden[ce]" be the key to Madison's remarks, we must remember that juries were arguably even less dependent on executive and legislature, since jurors had never been appointed by these branches and did not draw any permanent salary from them. Emphasis on the populist and localist jury would fit perfectly with other things Madison said in this speech. In the sentence immediately after his mention of "independent tribunals," for example, he stressed federalism as an enforcement device: "Besides this security, there is a great probability that such a declaration in the federal system would be enforced; because the State Legislatures will jealously and closely watch the operations of this Government, and be able to resist with more effect every assumption of power, than any other power on earth can do; and the greatest opponents to a Federal Government admit the State Legislatures to be sure guardians of the people's liberty."[32] Moments earlier, Madison had pointed to the importance of "public opinion" in making the Bill of Rights more than a mere "paper barrier."[33]

Now turn to Jefferson's comment that a bill of rights would put a "legal check . . . into the hands of the judiciary. This is a body, which if rendered independent, and kept strictly to their own department merits great confidence for their learning and integrity."[34] Here, too, Jefferson plainly has in mind judicial review by judges. But elsewhere he made clear that he viewed juries as part of the "judiciary." Indeed, only three months after his approving comments about judges and judicial review, and a full decade before *Callender,* Jefferson argued that ordinary citizen jurors, where they suspected self-dealing or other agency bias on the bench, could constitute themselves as judges of both fact and law: "But we all know that permanent judges acquire an Esprit de corps, that being known they are liable to be tempted by bribery, that they are misled by favor, by relationship, by a spirit of party, by a devotion to the Executive or Legislative . . . . It is left therefore to the juries, if they think the permanent judges are under any biass whatever in any cause, to take upon themselves to judge the law as well as the fact. They never exercise this power but when they suspect partiality in the judges . . . ."[35]

Beyond juries, both Madison and Jefferson emphasized public education as the remedy for, and deterrent to, unconstitutional conduct. Wrote Jefferson, "Written constitutions may be violated in moments of passion or delusion, yet they furnish a text to which those who are watchful may again rally and recall *the people;* they fix too for *the people* the principles of their political creed."[36] The words of the Bill of Rights would themselves educate Americans; hence the appropriateness of such didactic, nonlegalistic phrases as "a well regulated Militia [is] necessary to the security of a free State."[37]* Such maxims were the heart and soul of early state constitutions.[38] Virginia's famous 1776 Declaration of Rights even featured a maxim about the need for maxims: "[N]o free government, or the blessings of liberty, can be preserved to any people, but by . . . virtue, and by frequent recurrence to fundamental principles."[39] A bill of rights would crystallize these principles so that they could be memorized and internalized—much like Scripture—by ordinary citizens.[40] In the words of one 1788 commentator, a bill of rights "will be the first lesson of the young citizens."[41] Patrick Henry and John Marshall agreed on very little in the Virginia ratifying convention, but when Henry declared that "[t]here are certain maxims by which every wise and

---

*This also helps explain why some Anti-Federalists did not pay much attention to the drafting intricacies raised by a civil-jury amendment, *see supra* Chapter 5. What they sought was an ode to the civil jury, a declaration of principle. *See* Charles W. Wolfram, *The Constitutional History of the Seventh Amendment,* 57 MINN. L. REV. 639, 663 n.67 (1973). Recall Daniel Webster's language, noted earlier: "[My constituents and I] live under a [state] constitution which *teaches us*" certain maxims of democratic self-governance. *See supra* Chapter 3. Also recall the obviously didactic language of the Massachusetts constitutional provisions concerning Harvard, and of sundry state constitutions regarding civilian supremacy over the military, *see supra* Chapters 2 and 3. Finally, recall Madison's proto–Seventh Amendment, featuring an ode to civil juries as "one of the best securities to the rights of the people," *see supra* Chapter 5.

enlightened people will regulate their conduct, [and] our [Virginia] bill of rights contains those admirable maxims," Marshall went out of his way to agree that such maxims "are necessary in any government, but more essential to a democracy than to any other."[42]

Madison, too, stressed popular education and popular enforcement: "What use then it may be asked can a bill of rights serve in popular Governments? . . . 1. The political truths declared in that solemn manner acquire by degrees the character of fundamental maxims of free Government, and as they become incorporated with the national sentiment, counteract the impulses of interest and passion. 2. [Whenever] usurped acts of the Government [occur], a bill of rights will be a good ground for an appeal to the sense of the community."[43] In 1792, Madison—the great champion of internal checks and balances—noted that such checks "are neither the sole nor the chief palladium of constitutional liberty. *The people* who are the authors of this blessing, must also be its guardians."[44]

The emphasis on popular enforcement would of course prove prescient. Less than a decade after the Bill of Rights became law, federal judges cheerfully sent men to jail for criticizing the government, but opponents of the Sedition Act—led by Jefferson and Madison—ultimately prevailed by "appeal[ing] to the sense of the community."[45] First, they attempted to "appeal" from judges to juries, who embodied this community sense. When blocked by judges, they used the media of state legislatures to transform the election of 1800 into a national public seminar on constitutional principles. Thus educated, ordinary citizens on election day registered the "community sense" that the act was a usurpation.

Although their personal labors in founding the University of Virginia signaled the special depth of their commitment, Madison and Jefferson were hardly unique in seeing the centrality of public education. In 1775, for example, Moses Mather declared that "[t]he strength and spring of every free government is the virtue of the people; virtue grows on knowledge, and knowledge on education."[46] After quoting Mather, Gordon Wood sums up the ethos of the era in his own words: "And education, it was believed, was the responsibility and agency of a republican government. So the circle went."[47] As Wood later observes, "The most obvious republican instrument for . . . inculcating virtue in a people was education."[48] We should not be surprised, then, that each of the first six presidents of the United States urged the formation of a national university. In the didactic language of the Massachusetts Constitution of 1780: "Wisdom and knowledge, as well as virtue, diffused generally among the body of the people, being necessary for the preservation of their rights and liberties; and as these depend on spreading the opportunities and advantages of education . . . it shall be the duty of legislatures and magistrates . . . to encourage [these ends]."[49]

The idea of popular education resurfaces over and over in the Bill of Rights. As we have seen, each of the three intermediate associations it safeguards—church, militia, and jury—was understood as a device for educating ordinary citizens about their rights and duties. An uneducated populace cannot be a truly sovereign populace.

Yet it is exactly such a sovereign people who constitute the rock on which our Constitution is built. The opening words of the Preamble, of course, dramatize this truth; but so do the words of the Bill of Rights. For I hope it has not escaped our notice that no phrase appears in more of the first ten amendments than "the people."

It remains, of course, to see what happens when the grand idea of the original Bill of Rights—the rights of the people—meets the grand idea of the Fourteenth Amendment: the privileges and immunities of citizens of the United States. The phrases are similar, yet different. The first was centrally directed at the federal government; the second, at the states. The first arose mainly to address the agency problem of government, whereas the second arose to address as well the distinct problem of minority rights. The first seems largely republican and collective, sounding mainly in political rights, in the public liberty of the ancients. The second seems more liberal and individualistic, sounding mainly in civil rights, in the private liberty of the moderns. How are these two grand ideas to be synthesized? How, in other words, is the Creation-era Bill of Rights to be Reconstructed? These are the questions of Part Two.

Part II

Reconstruction

Overleaf, *The Freedman's Bureau*
Harper's Weekly, July 25, 1868

Seven

Antebellum Ideas

Over the next six chapters, we must tackle questions like these: What is the relation between the Bill of Rights and the Fourteenth Amendment? Does the amendment "incorporate" the Bill, making the Bill's restrictions on federal power applicable against states? If so, which words in the Fourteenth Amendment work this change? Are all, or only some, of the provisions of the first ten amendments incorporated or absorbed into the Fourteenth? If only some, which ones, and why? Once incorporated or absorbed, does a right or freedom declared in the Bill necessarily constrain state and federal governments absolutely equally in every jot and tittle? Or, on the other hand, can a guarantee in the Bill ever lose something in the translation, so that only a part of the guarantee—perhaps only its "core"—applies against state governments by dint of the Fourteenth Amendment?

These questions have framed a debate that, in the words of Judge Henry Friendly, "go[es] to the very nature of our Constitution" with "profound effects for all of us."[1] Professor Van Alstyne has written that "it is difficult to imagine a more consequential subject,"[2] an assessment confirmed by the extraordinary number of twentieth-century legal giants who have locked horns in the debate—Hugo Black, Felix Frankfurter, William Brennan, Henry Friendly, William Crosskey, Louis Henkin, Erwin Griswold, and John Ely, to name only a few. Perhaps even more extraordinary has been the willingness of Supreme Court justices to reinforce their judicial pronouncements on the issue with extrajudicial elaborations. After his retirement from the bench and shortly before his death, Justice Frankfurter, for example, published as his parting words to the legal community an elaborate "memorandum" on "incorporation" in the *Harvard Law Review,* piling up case citations and other material to support his own preferred solution to the issue.[3] Three years later, Frankfurter's great sparring partner, Justice Black, publicly responded in his Carpentier Lectures, brushing aside the objection that judges should speak only within the confines of cases.[4] And in two James Madison Lectures delivered twenty-five years apart—each aptly titled "The Bill of Rights and the States"—Justice Brennan expanded upon his own proposed solution to the incorporation conundrum.[5]

When we shift our attention from lectures and law reviews to *United States Reports,* we see much more evidence of the centrality of the incorporation debate to twentieth-century constitutional law. Consider, for example, the lead paragraph of the most famous footnote in Supreme Court history: "There may be narrower scope for operation of the presumption of constitutionality when legislation appears on its face to be within a specific prohibition of the Constitution, such as those of the first ten amendments, which are deemed equally specific when held to be embraced within the Fourteenth."[6] In the half-century since *Caro-lene Products,* the Court has taken the hint of footnote four. A list of cases applying various parts of the Bill of Rights against states reads like the "greatest hits"[7] of the modern era: *New York Times v. Sullivan,*[8] *Abington School District v. Schempp,*[9] *Mapp v. Ohio,*[10] *Miranda v. Arizona,*[11] *Gideon v. Wainwright,*[12] *Duncan v. Louisiana,*[13] and on and on. Some cases, like *Sullivan,* merely applied provisions of the Bill of Rights that had long before been deemed "embraced within" the Fourteenth Amendment; others, like *Duncan,* achieved notoriety precisely because they decided to incorporate previously "unabsorbed" clauses. Speaking only of the latter set, Justice Brennan ranked the incorporation opinions ahead of reapportionment and desegregation cases as "the most important [series of decisions] of the Warren era."[14] In remarks sharply critical of Brennan and his brethren, Solicitor General Erwin Griswold offered an even more sweeping assessment of the stakes involved: "I can think of nothing in the history of our constitutional law which has gone so far since John Marshall and the Supreme Court decided *Marbury v. Madison* in 1803."[15]

And yet, despite the importance of the topic and all the attention devoted to it, we still lack a fully satisfying account of the relation between the first ten amendments and the Fourteenth. Minor variations aside, three main approaches have dominated the twentieth-century debate. The first, represented by Justice Frankfurter, insists that, strictly speaking, the Fourteenth Amendment never incorporated any of the provisions of the Bill of Rights.[16] The Fourteenth requires only that states honor basic principles of fundamental fairness and ordered liberty—principles that might indeed happen to overlap wholly or in part with some of the rules of the Bill of Rights but that bear no logical relation to those rules. The second approach, championed by Justice Black, insists on "total incorporation" of the Bill of Rights.[17] The Fourteenth Amendment, claimed Black, made applicable against the states each and every provision of the Bill, lock, stock, and barrel—at least if we define the Bill to include only the first eight amendments. Faced with these diametric views, Justice Brennan tried to steer a middle course of "selective incorporation."[18] Under this third approach, the Court's analysis could proceed clause by clause and right by right, fully incorporating every provision of the Bill deemed fundamental without deciding in advance whether each and every right would necessarily pass the test. Methodologically, Brennan's approach seemed to avoid a radical break with existing case law, which rejected total incorporation, and it even paid lip service to Frankfurter's insistence on fundamental fairness as the touchstone of the Fourteenth Amendment. In practice, though, Brennan's approach held out the possibility of total incorporation through the back door. For him, once a clause in the Bill was deemed fundamental it must be incorporated against the states in every aspect, just as Black insisted. And nothing in the logic of selective incorporation precluded the possibility that, when all was said and done, virtually every clause of the Bill would be deemed fundamental.

In the end, there is something to be said for each of these positions, but each is also fatally flawed. An alloy of the three seemingly incompatible elements—an alloy that I shall call "refined incorporation"—will prove far more attractive and durable than each unalloyed component. But before such an alloy can be fashioned, we need to do a considerable amount of preparatory work. The best place to begin is *Barron v. Baltimore*.[19]

Barron

In 1833, the Supreme Court confronted for the first time the argument that a state government had violated one of the provisions of the Bill of Rights. Narrowly framed, the issue raised by *Barron* was whether the Fifth Amendment's takings clause limited not just the federal government but states and municipalities as well. But the Court saw that the reasoning behind John Barron's contention radiated much further. Perhaps the Court could have ruled for Barron without necessarily implying that each and every prohibition of the Bill of Rights would thenceforth bind states. Unlike the takings clause the words of the First Amendment explicitly spoke of "Congress" as the target of limitation; and the logic underlying other particular provisions may also have made it peculiarly awkward to apply them against states. But the reasoning behind Barron's contention clearly would have required state compliance with a vast number of Bill of Rights prohibitions whose general language and logic made them indistinguishable from the takings clause. If the Fifth Amendment phrase "nor shall private property be taken for public use without just compensation" limited states, so, too, it would seem, did the Fourth Amendment phrase "no warrants shall issue, but upon probable cause," the Eighth Amendment phrase "excessive bail shall not be required," and so on. *Barron* thus presented a question "of great importance," as Chief Justice Marshall acknowledged at the outset of his opinion for the Court.[20] But Marshall immediately added that the ques-

tion was "not of much difficulty," and went on to dismiss Barron's argument in less than five pages.

One can quibble around the edges,* but the core of Marshall's argument is compelling. To be sure, the takings clause nowhere explicitly says
that it ties the hands of only the federal government and not the states.
But as Marshall explained, because state governments were already in
place in the 1780s, the dominant purpose of the Constitution was to create, yet limit, a new central government. "[L]imitations on power, if expressed in general terms, are naturally, and, we think, necessarily applicable to the government created by the instrument"—that is, the federal
government.[21] Though he did not cite it by name, Marshall seems to
have had in mind here the sweeping dictum of Hamilton's *Federalist* No.
83: "The United States, in their united or collective capacity, are the OB-
JECT to which all general provisions in the Constitution must necessarily be construed to refer."[22]

Close inspection of the original Constitution confirms the soundness
of the Hamilton-Marshall rule of construction. In Article I, section 9,
for example, we find a purely general prohibition akin to the takings
clause in its language and logic: "No Bill of Attainder or ex post facto
Law shall be passed." Yet as Marshall forcefully noted,[23] this general
prohibition limits only the federal government; hence the framers' inclusion of a separate clause explicitly limiting states, in Article I, section

---

*For example, the Court suggested that the limits imposed on states by Article I, sec-
tion 10 were "generally" to protect citizens of *other* states, 32 U.S. (7 Pet.) 243, 249 (1833).
This characterization obscures the Federalist framers' view of the centrality of the attainder, ex post facto, and contracts clauses as protections against one's own state. *See,
e.g.*, Akhil Reed Amar, *Of Sovereignty and Federalism*, 96 YALE L.J. 1425, 1440–41 (1987),
and sources cited therein. Marshall, of course, knew better. *See* Fletcher v. Peck, 10 U.S.
(6 Cranch) 87, 138–39 (1810) (Marshall, C.J.) (Article I, section 10 "may be deemed a bill
of rights for the people of each state"). Marshall's *Fletcher* opinion went unmentioned in
his *Barron* opinion. *Fletcher* and Marshall's later opinion in *Dartmouth College v. Woodward*, 17 U.S. (4 Wheat.) 518 (1819), construed contract-clause limitations on states
broadly. But read broadly, *Barron* threatened to undo these holdings—the only thing
stopping Georgia from simply confiscating the Yazoo lands, or New Hampshire from
simply appropriating Dartmouth College, was some version of a just-compensation
norm. Marshall in *Barron* did not give careful attention to the obvious tension here.

10: *"No State shall . . .* pass any Bill of Attainder [or] ex post facto Law." The absence of any similarly explicit language limiting states in the takings clause cut strongly against Barron's claim. Had the framers of the clause meant to limit states, wrote Marshall, "they would have declared this purpose in plain and intelligible language,"[24] like the "No State shall" phrasing of Article I, section 10.

But does not the language of the First Amendment cut exactly the other way, suggesting that where the Bill of Rights aimed to limit only the federal government, it used an explicit word like "Congress" to signal that intent? Once again, Marshall offered a careful parsing of Article I, section 9 to drive home his point: "Some of [the clauses in this section] use language applicable only to congress: others are expressed in general terms."[25] If the word "Congress" in the First Amendment could justify applying the takings clause and other general wording in the Bill of Rights to the states, then the same should hold true for Article I, section 9: the words "the United States" in the section 9 clause—"No Title of Nobility shall be granted by the United States"—should logically imply that the general wording of the attainder and ex post facto clause of section 9 applied against the states. Yet the Constitution plainly suggests otherwise. Marshall saw the language of section 9 as especially relevant because it was "in the nature of a bill of rights,"[26] as various Federalists had pointed out during the ratification period to counter Anti-Federalist concerns about the apparent absence of such a bill in the original Constitution.[27]

Purely as a matter of textual exegesis and application of lawyerly rules of construction, Marshall's argument is hard to beat. Why weren't the framers and ratifiers of the Bill of Rights entitled to rely on a natural and sensible rule of construction implicit in the Constitution itself and made explicit by Publius in his influential defense of the document?[28]

The legislative history of the Bill of Rights confirms that its framers and ratifiers did so rely. Various state conventions endorsed amendments limiting the new central government, some phrased in general language, others using words explicitly targeting the central government—"Congress," the "United States," and so on.[29] Yet no one ever suggested that the general language, simply because of its juxtaposition with other clauses worded differently, would limit state governments as well. When Madison distilled these endorsements into his own list of proposed limitations, he suggested that most of these limitations be inserted in Article I, section 9. Following the rule of construction implicit in that Article, he used general language and explicit references to Congress indiscriminately.[30] The proposed location of these clauses made it clear that, however worded, they applied only against the federal government. But the First Congress eventually decided to put these amendments at the end of the original Constitution. There is no evidence that this change was anything but aesthetic. Nevertheless, the change had the unhappy effect of blurring the implicit rule of construction at work, creating an interpretive trap for the unwary, which Marshall gracefully avoided by keeping his eyes on section 9.

Unlike state ratifying conventions, Madison believed that additional restrictions in favor of liberty should also be placed on state governments and said so on the floor of the House.[31] Even more important for our purposes, he proposed a constitutional amendment that used explicit language to communicate this idea—the very same explicit language that John Marshall seemed to be asking for in *Barron:* "No State shall violate the equal rights of conscience, or the freedom of the press, or the trial by jury in criminal cases."[32] Moments earlier, Madison had proposed that the following general language be inserted into section 9: "[N]or shall the full and equal rights of conscience be in any manner, or on any pretext, infringed" and "the freedom of the press . . . shall be inviolable."[33] Had this general wording, taken alone or in juxtaposition with references to Congress in nearby clauses, been understood to apply to states, Madison's "No state shall" proposal would have been horribly repetitive, eligible for inclusion in the department of redundancy department.[34] What's more, in limiting its list of rights that "No State shall" abridge to press, conscience, and juries, Madison's wording clearly suggested by negative implication that states could do other things prohibited (to the federal government) by the general language of his proposed section 9 insert. Still further corroboration comes from Madison's speeches on the House floor. Whereas he candidly admitted that his proto–Tenth Amendment "may be considered as superfluous" and "unnecessary," he described his "No State shall" proposal in very different language: "[T]his [is] the most valuable amendment in the whole list"[35]—valuable because it added something not implicit (or explicit) elsewhere in general language. Yet he also noted that even this most valuable amendment would bind states only to "those particular rights"[36] listed in the "No State shall" clause, once again making clear that merely general language would not limit states.[37]

So far, so good for Marshall's opinion. But what makes *Barron's* holding compelling is neither its technical parsing of Article I nor its use of lawyerly rules of construction nor even the narrow legislative history of the Bill of Rights in Congress. Rather, it is what Marshall near the end of his opinion called the "universally understood" historical background of the Bill of Rights.[38] In state convention after state convention in 1787–88, Anti-Federalists voiced loud concerns about a new, distant, aristocratic, central government that was being called into existence.[39] Many ultimately voted for the Constitution only because Federalists like Madison promised to consider a bill of rights soon after ratification. Madison kept his word; he knew that if he did not, states' rightists might call a second constitutional convention to repudiate the basic structure of the Constitution that he had worked so hard to build.[40] In short, without the goodwill of many moderate Anti-Federalists, prospects for the new Constitution looked bleak in 1787–88; and a bill of rights was the explicit price of that goodwill. But as we have seen, the bill of rights that Anti-Federalists sought was a bill to limit the *federal* government— not just for the sake of individual liberty but also to serve the cause of states' rights. Madison and his fellow Federalists could hardly have placated critics or won over skeptics by sneaking massive new restrictions on states into apparently innocuous general language. Nor would Anti-Federalists in Congress or in states have knowingly allowed such a Trojan horse through the gates. Madison did openly advocate a small number of additional restrictions on states—clearly labeled as such in a package wrapped in the words "No State shall"—but even that modest proposal was too much for a Senate jealously guarding states' rights.

Barron's holding thus kept faith with both the letter and the spirit of the original Bill of Rights. We should not be surprised, then, that the decision in *Barron* was unanimous, or that the Court repeatedly and unanimously reaffirmed *Barron*'s rule over the next thirty-three years in cases involving the First, Fourth, Fifth, Seventh, and Eighth Amendments.[41]

The *Barron* Contrarians

Having worked hard to understand *Barron*, we now must work equally hard to understand the contrary view, especially if we are to make full sense of the language and logic of the Fourteenth Amendment. In the fifteen years before *Barron*, a considerable number of considerable lawyers implied in passing or stated explicitly that various provisions in the Bill did limit states. Writing for the Court in 1819, Justice William Johnson obliquely suggested that the Seventh Amendment's guarantee of civil juries applied to states;[42] and the following year he stated even more explicitly in a separate concurrence that the double-jeopardy clause "operates equally upon both [state and federal] governments,"[43] although even here his statement was not free from ambiguity. He may simply have meant that the clause applied whenever either of two prosecutions for the same underlying offense was federal, even if the other was by state officials in state court for a state-law crime.[44] That same year, though, the New York Supreme Court stated in dictum that the double-jeopardy clause "operates upon state courts" even where both prosecutions were for state-law crime, and in 1823 the Mississippi Supreme Court appeared to agree.[45] In 1824, this view of the double-jeopardy clause was pressed in the Massachusetts Supreme Court, yet neither the government's attorney nor the judges appeared to challenge it—perhaps because even without the clause, the Commonwealth recognized a common-law double-jeopardy right at least as broad.[46] The following year William Rawle published a widely read treatise on the Constitution in which he argued at length that virtually all the general provisions of the Bill of Rights bound states.[47] And as late as 1833, the year *Barron* came down, we find Justice Baldwin on circuit implying that the Second and Fourth Amendments applied against states,[48] and Justice Story in his own treatise on the Constitution taking an uncharacteristically agnostic, even nonchalant, position on the whole matter: "It has been held in the state courts, (and the point does not seem ever to have arisen in the courts of the United States,) that [the Eighth Amendment] does not apply to punishments inflicted in a state court for a crime against such state; but that the prohibition is addressed solely to the national government, and operates, as a restriction upon its powers."[49]

The General-Wording/Negative-Implication Theory What were these lawyers and judges thinking? Some simply may not have given much thought to the *Barron* issue, especially where the case at hand was disposed of on other grounds. And a merely casual look at, say, the double-jeopardy clause might lead a judge to assume it applied to states as well; for as New York Chief Justice Ambrose Spencer noted, the language of the clause was "general in its nature, and unrestricted in its terms."[50] Rawle gave more attention to the matter and added a negative-implication argument that the contrast between the First Amendment's specific reference to Congress and the general language of various later amendments confirmed that they, unlike the First, applied to states.[51] Marshall refuted both of these arguments by his careful attention to Article I, section 9. (What's more, as we saw in Chapter 2, the framers' reference to "Congress" in the First Amendment had nothing to do with the *Barron* issue; rather, it was probably an expression of the strong states'-rights view that, unlike the areas addressed by later amendments, the First encompassed domains where Congress simply lacked enumerated power under Article I, section 8.) When forced to focus on this issue and only this issue in *Barron,* and when confronted by Marshall's textual analysis and historical narrative, Johnson and Baldwin reversed course,[52] and Story fell into line.

Barron, however, was hardly the last word, and the contrary view persisted over the next thirty-three years. At times it appears that lawyers who had simply never heard of *Barron* and its progeny casually assumed, along with Spencer or Rawle, that the general language of various provisions made application to states obvious. Thus in 1845, the Illinois Supreme Court noted in passing that the Fifth Amendment's due-process clause limited state action,[53] and two years later Ohio Attorney General Henry Stanbery glibly conceded in oral argument before the

U.S. Supreme Court that double jeopardy was "forbidden, as well to the States as to the general government, by the fifth . . . amendment[]."[54] Like Justice Johnson thirty years earlier, however, Stanbery may have meant to limit his concession to situations where one of the two prosecutions was federal, and the other state. Most important for our purposes, we must note that several capable lawyers in the Thirty-ninth Congress—the Congress that drafted the Fourteenth Amendment—seemed unaware of *Barron* until the case was brought to their attention by name by John Bingham, the principal draftsman of section 1 of the amendment.[55]

The Declaratory Theory It is tempting to dismiss all these folks as dolts, but we must resist. Modern academic law schools did not exist. Supreme Court reports were not as widely available as nowadays. And constitutional law took a back seat to common law in its importance to everyday legal practice. (Thus one of the biggest constitutional issues of the antebellum era was whether the vast domain of common law was state law or federal law.) Would-be lawyers began their training with Blackstone's *Commentaries,* not *United States Reports.*

Once we remember the centrality of Blackstone and the common law, we can see the *Barron* issue in a new light. For the common-law method in mid-nineteenth-century America involved careful examination of codes, charters, statutes, and the like in an effort to distill their animating principles—the spirit of the common law. Judges did not simply make up common law; they found it in authoritative legal sources like Magna Charta, the Petition of Right, the Habeas Corpus Act, the English Bill of Rights of 1689, and so on. Thus, even if the federal Bill of Rights did not, strictly speaking, bind the states of its own legislative force, was it not at least declaratory of certain fundamental common-law rights? And should not these declarations by We the People inform a state judge's analysis?

Thus we find Rawle in 1825 going beyond his narrow First Amendment negative-implication argument by claiming that certain amendments "form parts of the *declared* rights of the *people.*"[56] Tellingly, he stressed the preamble of the Second Amendment as "a *declaration* that a well regulated militia is necessary to the security of a free state."[57] Only after discussing the preamble alone did he quote its "corollary" that "the right of the people to keep and bear arms shall not be infringed," whose language, Rawle noted, was perfectly general.[58] Rawle then immediately invoked the English Bill of Rights of 1689 and Blackstone's analysis of the English common-law right to have arms.[59] For Rawle, all this suggested that the Second Amendment bound states. Nor did the Tenth Amendment stand in the way, for Rawle read its final clauses as acknowledging that "the people" had certain reserved rights in contradistinction to—and against—"the states."[60]

Rawle's analysis and language here were perhaps no more than suggestive, but they sketched out lines of argument that later *Barron* contrarians would develop more fully. Narrowly understood, the declaratory view of the Bill of Rights could provide even state courts with principled rules of decision, both procedural and substantive, when no state statute spoke directly to a given issue. Such, for example, was the situation in the New York and Massachusetts double-jeopardy cases in the 1820s. More broadly, the Bill could serve as a source of maxims, both political and judicial. Politically, a maxim like the preamble to the Second Amendment could warn the people of any state to be wary of any legislature, even a state legislature, that sought to disarm them.[61] Judicially, maxims drawn from the Bill of Rights could generate a set of rules of construction—what we would today call "clear-statement rules"— obliging a state legislature to speak with unmistakable clarity before trenching on a right "declared" in the U.S. Constitution. Indeed, in the hands of a strong believer in fundamental or natural rights, the declaratory view of the Bill could have even more far-reaching consequences.

As modern-day legal positivists, we tend to view the Bill as creating or conferring legal rights. But the congressional resolution accompanying the Bill explicitly described some of its provisions as "declaratory."[62] To a nineteenth-century believer in natural rights, the Bill was not simply an enactment of We the People as the Sovereign Legislature bringing new legal rights into existence, but rather a declaratory judgment by We the People as the Sovereign High Court that certain natural or fundamental rights already existed.[63] Under this view, the First Amendment was not merely an interpretation of the positive-law code of the original Constitution, declaring that Congress lacked Article I, section 8–enumerated power to regulate religion in the states or to suppress speech. The amendment was also a declaration that certain fundamental "rights" and "freedoms"—of assembly, petition, speech, press, and religious exercise—preexisted the Constitution. Why else, it might be asked, did the amendment speak of *the* freedom of speech, implying a preexisting entitlement?[64] The Ninth and Tenth Amendments did more than make explicit rules of construction for interpreting the Constitution as a positive-law code; they also declared that certain "rights" and "powers" were retained by "the people" and reserved to them in contradistinction to "states."

Technically speaking, perhaps the Bill did not bind state governments of its own legislative force. But under the strong declaratory view, the result was virtually the same. An honest state court would be bound (though the precise nature of the obligation, legal or moral, was somewhat fuzzy) to respect declarations of the High Court of We the People that certain rights and freedoms existed.* Unlike Rawle's negative-implication argu-

---

*Consider, for example, Massachusetts Chief Justice Lemuel Shaw's remarks in a prominent mid-nineteenth-century case involving a claim of right against the state: "[T]he amendments of the Constitution of the United States, in the nature of a bill of rights, [should be regarded] as the annunciation of great and fundamental principles, to be always held in regard, both morally and legally, by those who make and those who administer the law [rather than as mere] precise and positive directions and rules of action . . . ." Jones v. Robbins, 74 Mass. (8 Gray) 329, 340 (1857); *see also* Bradshaw v. Rogers, 20 Johns. 103, 106 (N.Y. Sup. Ct. 1822). In *Bradshaw,* Chief Justice Spencer invoked the Fifth Amendment just-compensation clause—the same clause later at issue in *Barron*— against a state law. Though conceding that the clause might lack "binding constitutional force upon the act under consideration" because the clause "related to the powers of the national government, and was intended as a restriction on that government," Spencer went on to argue that the clause was "*declaratory* of a great and fundamental principle of government; and *any law* violating that principle must be a nullity" (emphasis added). For similar views, see Bonaparte v. Camden & A.R. Co., 3 F. Cas. 821, 828 (C.C.D.N.J. 1830) (No. 1,617) (Baldwin, Circuit J.) ("Though it may well be doubted whether as a constitutional provision, [the Fifth Amendment takings clause] applies to the state governments, yet it is *the declaration* of what in its nature is the power of all governments, and the right of its citizens . . . .") (emphasis added); Magill v. Brown, 16 F. Cas. 408, 419, 427 (C.C.E.D. Pa. 1833) (No. 8,952) (Baldwin, Circuit J.) (using federal religion-

ment, demolished by *Barron*, this was an argument that states might be constrained even by the First Amendment—at least, by those clauses of the First Amendment that spoke of "rights" or "freedoms." (The establishment clause most distinctly did not.)

The obligation here would seem at least as strong as the duty of the honest common-law judge to consider well-reasoned precedents from well-respected sister courts in other jurisdictions. Or to take an example from modern-day Supreme Court case law, the obligation roughly mirrored the later rule that federal judges should consult state constitutions and state statutes to determine which punitive practices are violations of contemporary morality and thus "cruel and unusual" within the meaning of the Eighth Amendment.* More expansively, it could be argued that the ratification of the Bill by the collective state legislatures

---

clause principles as glosses on state-law rights); Johnson v. Tompkins, 13 F. Cas. 840, 852 (C.C.E.D. Pa. 1833) (No. 7,416) (Baldwin, Circuit J.) (certain "inherent and unalienable" rights predate state constitutions that protect but "do not create" these rights); Sinnickson v. Johnsons, 17 N.J.L. 129, 145–46 (1839) (dictum) (citing *Barron* yet embracing declaratory theory of just-compensation clause); Larthet v. Forgay, 2 La. Ann. 524, 525 (1847) (state-law case invoking federal Fourth Amendment as "an affirmance of a great constitutional doctrine of the common law").

See, e.g., Stanford v. Kentucky, 492 U.S. 361, 369–72 (1989). Compare, for example, Chancellor James Kent's opinion in *Gardner v. Trustees of Newburgh*, 2 Johns. Ch. 162, 165–68 (N.Y. Ch. 1816), where the great jurist applied the just-compensation requirement to a state statute despite the absence of any express language in the state constitution. After canvassing the "soundest authorities" of Grotius, Puffendorf, and Blackstone, and the express language of the Pennsylvania, Delaware, and Ohio state constitutions, Kent proclaimed: "But what is of higher authority, and is absolutely decisive of the sense of the people of this country, [the principle] is made a part of the Constitution of the United States, 'that private property shall not be taken for public use without just compensation' . . . ." *See also* Crenshaw v. Slate River Co., 27 Va. (6 Rand.) 245, 265 (1828) (opinion of Judge Carr) (requiring state payment of just compensation, despite absence of an explicit compensation clause in the state constitution; and invalidating state statute after invoking Blackstone, "the writers on Natural Law, Civil Law, Common Law, and the Law of every civilized country [and] the principle of the . . . Federal Constitution"); The Proprietors of the Piscataqua Bridge v. The New Hampshire Bridge, 7 N.H. 35, 66 (1834) (citing and following *Newburgh* and requiring just compensation even though those words did not appear in state constitution); State v. Dawson, 21 S.C.L. (3 Hill) 100,

estopped these bodies from denying that certain rights and freedoms existed. How, for example, could a state legislature disarm its people after it had ratified a document declaring that "A well regulated Militia [is] necessary to the security of a free State"?

But how does all this fancy theorizing deal with the obvious objection that even if the Bill "declared" rights and freedoms, it declared them only against the federal government? How could these declarations become transmogrified into limitations on states? There are really two objections here, one jurisprudential and one constitutional. The jurisprudential objection is best framed by the work of the early twentieth-century legal analyst Wesley Hohfeld, who insisted that rights logically implied correlative duties imposed on discrete persons or entities.[65] The nature of a right is thus defined every bit as much by the party against whom

---

106–23 (1836) (Richardson, J., dissenting) (invoking Blackstone, Rawle, Kent, Story, "magna charta and other fundamental Acts of the British Parliament," and explicit language of federal Fifth Amendment as declaratory glosses on the true meaning of the South Carolina Constitution; just compensation should thus be required even though these words did not appear in the South Carolina document); State v. Glen, 52 N.C. (7 Jones) 321, 331–32 (1859) (citing and correctly describing *Barron,* but requiring just compensation in the absence of an explicit state constitutional counterpart to the federal Fifth Amendment, following cases decided by "our sister States"); Henry v. Dubuque & Pacific Railroad Co., 10 Iowa 540, 543–44 (1860) (declaratory view of eminent-domain clause of state constitution); Johnston v. Rankin, 70 N.C. 550, 555 (1874) (noting that federal Fifth Amendment applies only to acts by the United States and not to the government of the state, but treating its underlying principle as "so grounded in natural equity" so as to be binding on the North Carolina government, despite the absence of clear language in the state constitution).

When combined with the cases cited *supra* page 149, note, and *infra* page 155, note, these cases suggest that *Barron* meant considerably less than many have thought on the precise issue of just compensation. Many state constitutions featured explicit just-compensation requirements, and in the other states, judges often invoked the federal clause as declaratory. *See generally* J. A. C. Grant, *The "Higher Law" Background of the Law of Eminent Domain,* 6 WIS. L. REV. 67 (1931). In Maryland itself—the state from which *Barron* sprang—see Harness v. Chesapeake & Ohio Canal Co., 1 Md. Ch. 248 (1848) (requiring just compensation on basis of broad "law of the land" clause of state constitution, invoking Kent, Magna Charta, the federal Fifth Amendment, *Newburgh,* and the *Dawson* dissent).

the right runs as by its substantive sweep. The analytic truth of Hohfeld's insight is hard to dispute, but it would be anachronistic to read this insight back into all rights rhetoric, especially natural-rights rhetoric, in mid- to late-nineteenth-century America. Hohfeld, after all, was responding to nineteenth-century judges and lawyers who were using the word *right* more loosely—sloppily, Hohfeld argued.

This emphasis on the word *right* also helps answer the constitutional objection rooted in *Barron*. Marshall insisted on reading the Bill of Rights with the same rules of construction implicit in the original Constitution, especially Article I, section 9. This is a view deeply supportive of the vision of the Bill sketched out in Part One, a view of the Bill as fundamentally analogous to the original Constitution, intertwining structure (especially federalism) and rights. But the declaratory view insisted that rights were different from structure. Here was a powerful wedge to break the linkage that Marshall sought to forge between Article I, section 9 and the Bill of Rights. For section 9 never invoked the word *rights* in either its general or specific language. (Indeed, the only spot where the word *right* appeared in the original Constitution was— of all places—the Article I, section 8 copyright clause.)[66] The closest thing section 9 offered to a declaration of right was its affirmation of "the Privilege of the Writ of Habeas Corpus"—and we should note that Rawle insisted that this and only this provision of section 9 bound states.[67] The *Barron* contrarians, then, denied that section 9 was, as a general matter, truly "in the nature of a bill of rights."[68] The first ten amendments, by contrast, were commonly described as such, and used the words *rights* and *freedoms* over and over—in no fewer than six different amendments.[69] Unlike section 9, then, the Bill truly declared rights that, according to contrarian ideology, bound all governments.

This way of thinking would have been foreign to many of the men who had clamored for a bill of rights in the 1780s. The word *right* had no talismanic natural-law significance; many sought a bill to confer—or declare—*states'* rights, once again revealing the original intertwining of rights and structure. Indeed, a feudal inheritance made it quite easy for many in the 1780s to intuit the idea Hohfeld would resurrect and refine after the heyday of natural-rights talk in the mid-nineteenth century.

Particularistic customs, charters, and the like gave distinct persons or entities distinct rights or privileges against distinct entities, but not others.[70] Indeed, much of the Declaration of Independence and its predecessor petitions can be seen as backward-looking invocations of particularistic rules and customs.

The *Barron* contrarians, by contrast, emphasized the Declaration's more sweeping and universalizing Enlightenment rhetoric of "self-evident truths" and the "inalienable rights" of "all men."[71] Contrarians self-consciously sought to distill the pure essence of rights—citizen rights, not state rights—that had been blended with structural issues in the Bill.[72] As an interpretation of the original Bill, their view had huge problems, but as a vision of the future Bill, it deserves our careful consideration, for it was a view that would ultimately prevail in the language and logic of the Fourteenth Amendment.[73]

The clearest contrarian articulations occurred in conscious reaction to *Barron* itself. In the 1840 case of *Holmes v. Jennison,* former New Hampshire Governor C. P. Van Ness politely but boldly attacked *Barron* in his oral argument before the Supreme Court: "With the utmost deference I beg leave to observe, that in my humble judgment, an error was committed by the Court . . . ."[74] After going out of his way to remind the justices that the original amendments to the Constitution were "commonly called the bill of rights," he distinguished between certain provisions that were merely "limitations of power" and others that "are to be understood as declarations of rights."[75] This latter category, argued Van Ness, encompassed "absolute rights, inherent in the people, and of which no power can legally deprive them," "principles which lie at the very foundation of civil liberty, and are most intimately connected with the dearest rights of the people[,] . . . . [p]rinciples which . . . deserve to be diligently taught to our children, and to be written upon the posts of the houses, and upon the gates."[76]* Though not clearly developed, here lay

---

*The last reference is of course biblical, *see* Deuteronomy 6:6–9, and is only one of countless examples of the strong religious emphasis among contrarians and, later, Reconstructors. It is also a reminder that, like Scripture, a bill of rights was written to be memorized and internalized by ordinary citizens. *See supra* Chapter 6.

seeds for a kind of selective incorporation based on whether a particular clause of the Bill was a mere "limitation of power" or alternatively a "declaration of right."

Far more elaborate were various opinions of the Supreme Court of Georgia in the late 1840s and early 1850s, two of which were authored by Chief Justice Joseph Henry Lumpkin. In the first, *Nunn v. Georgia*, Lumpkin wrote that he was "aware" of contrary rulings (presumably including *Barron*) but nevertheless invoked the Second Amendment to void a state statute.[77] Lumpkin began by emphasizing English common-law rights that preexisted state and federal constitutions. For him, state constitutions "confer no *new rights* on the people which did not belong to them before."[78] The federal Bill of Rights, "in declaring that the right of the people to keep and bear arms, should not be infringed, only reiterated a truth announced a century before, in the [English Bill of Rights] of 1689."[79] Like Rawle and Van Ness before him, Lumpkin stressed the federal Bill's declaratory and didactic nature. The people, wrote Lumpkin, adopted the Bill "as beacon-lights to guide and control the action of [state] legislatures, as well as that of Congress. If a well-regulated militia is necessary to the security of the State of Georgia and of the United States, is it competent for the [Georgia] General Assembly to take away this security, by disarming the People?"[80] Like Rawle, Lumpkin seemed to deny that the Tenth Amendment was a purely states'-rights provision, for he read it to imply that "the people" had certain rights in contradistinction to the "states." And in asking the question whether arms bearing was "a right reserved to the *States* or to *themselves* [that is, the people],"[81] Lumpkin found dispositive the language of the Second Amendment declaring a "right of the people."

Lumpkin reiterated and elaborated these themes in the 1852 case of *Campbell v. Georgia*, in which he explicitly cited *Barron* but once again held that the Bill's provisions generally bound states.[82] Though he did not "stop to examine" *Barron* in detail,[83] Lumpkin wisely avoided the narrow negative-implication argument that Marshall had demolished and tried to outflank Marshall's historical narrative by widening the time frame. Once again, he began not with the framing of the federal Bill of Rights but with the ancient landmarks of the common law: "Magna

Charta—the Petition of Right—the [English] Bill of Rights [of 1689]—and more especially, . . . the Act of Settlement, in Britain."[84] By emphasizing the common-law background, Lumpkin could plausibly portray the federal Bill of Rights as added "out of abundant caution" to clarify preexisting legal rights.[85] This declaratory purpose, Lumpkin argued, clearly justified application of the Bill to states, as emphasized by his own italics: The Bill of Rights' purpose "was to *declare* to the world the fixed and unalterable determination of our people, that these invaluable rights . . . should never be disturbed by *any* government." The Bill was *"our American Magna Charta."*[86]

Lumpkin then began a discussion about whether unenumerated "natural rights of man" "independently of [rights specified] in written constitutions" could ever limit American legislatures; and here he quoted and paraphrased broad natural law passages from various U.S. Supreme Court cases.[87] For reasons of institutional competence, Lumpkin did not "intend to put our opinion . . . upon this foundation, however solid it may be."[88] Given that "our ideas of natural justice are vague and uncertain," perhaps a wide-open hunt for natural law would allow judges too much discretion—freedom to make, rather than find, natural law.[89] "But," Lumpkin argued, "as to questions arising under these amendments, there is nothing indefinite. The people of the several States, by adopting these amendments, have defined accurately and recorded permanently *their* opinion, as to the great principles which they embrace . . . . "[90]* If this last argument looks vaguely familiar, it should. A

---

*Beyond *Nunn* and *Campbell,* the most important Georgia Supreme Court decisions in a contrarian vein involved application of the Fifth Amendment just-compensation clause—the same clause at issue in *Barron*—against various Georgia laws. In *Young v. McKenzie,* 3 Ga. 31 (1847), the court, per Justice Hiram Warner, stated that the clause did no "more than *declare* a great common law principle, applicable to all governments, both State and Federal, which has existed from the time of Magna Charta." *Id.* at 41 (emphasis altered); *see also id.* at 44 (explicitly noting congressional preamble to federal Bill of Rights describing its provisions as *"declaratory* and restrictive clauses" (emphasis added by the court)). In *Parham v. The Justices,* 9 Ga. 341 (1851), Justice Eugenius Nisbet, on behalf of the court, invoked Magna Charta, the common law, Blackstone, the "ablest" academic commentators, opinions from several sister state courts, the language of several

century later another southern judge—one Hugo LaFayette Black—
would make a strikingly similar argument on behalf of his crusade to incorporate the Bill of Rights against the states.

The Contrarian Context

In their belief that *Barron* had been wrongly decided, men like Van Ness
and Lumpkin found themselves in a distinct minority among antebellum lawyers, but time was on their side. As the years wore on, changes
were occurring in America that made major premises of the original Bill
of Rights—premises faithfully followed in *Barron*—more and more
problematic. Regardless of whether the original Bill was intended to apply against states, it became increasingly plausible to think that the Constitution should be amended to overrule *Barron*.

Technology, Geography, Biography, and Ideology Consider first the broad
technological changes in the first half of the nineteenth century. In the
1780s, Anti-Federalists had feared that national lawmakers would be literally too far removed from their constituents for mutual confidence to
develop; congressmen would lack current information about constituent
desires, and citizens would find it difficult to monitor their federal representatives. Hence, special constitutional restrictions on Congress
made sense. But over the next eighty years, improved roads, new canals,
and the invention of the railroad and the telegraph revolutionized trans-
portation and communication, diminishing the feeling that national
lawmakers were qualitatively more distant than state ones. The emergence of national political parties also helped link the District of Columbia to the hinterlands. Nor was the Congress of the mid-nineteenth

---

sister state constitutions, and, finally, the language of the federal Fifth Amendment. *Id.*
at 349–51. In support of the last item, Nisbet wrote: "The Constitution of the United
States upon this point, I know, has been held to be a restraint upon federal legislation
alone, and not to apply to the States. If that be admitted, yet it is still authority, most
significant, for the application of the rule in the States. . . . It is the *declaration* of the [judi-
cial] *opinion* of the *American people* . . . [and] a solemn avowal, by the people, that a power to take private property, without compensation, does not belong to any government."
Id. at 351 (emphasis added).

century drastically smaller, and thus more subject to cabal and intrigue, than its state counterparts. The specter of a thirteen-man House of Representatives that Patrick Henry had conjured up in 1788[91] seemed rather fanciful in 1859, when the size of the lower House had swelled to more than two hundred members, a number that made several state lower houses look rather small by comparison.

Geographic expansion also worked ideological inversions. In the 1780s, state governments had distinguished pedigrees dating back to their respective colonial foundings, while the national government proposed by Madison and his fellow Federalists was something altogether novel.[92] Prudence, if nothing else, dictated special skepticism about the new government, and special restrictions on it. By contrast, in the antebellum era, the federal government was well established, while various new states were springing to life as the nation pushed inexorably westward (an expansion spurred on, of course, by the technological advances we have just noted). But these new states gave rise to a puzzle: why should a territorial legislature, as an agent of Congress, be bound by all the restrictions of the federal Bill of Rights when state governments were not?* Indeed, did it make any sense that immediately upon admission to statehood, a territory could ignore all sorts of salutary restraints in the Bill that had previously applied to it? Congressman John Bingham apparently thought not, for in considering Oregon's proposed admission to the Union in 1859, he declared:

> In my judgment, sir, this constitution, framed by the people of Oregon, is repugnant to the Federal Constitution, and violative of the rights of citizens of the United States. I know, sir, that some gentlemen have a short and easy method of disposing of such objections as these, by assuming that the people of the State, after admission, may, by changing their constitution, insert therein every objectionable feature which, before admission, they were constrained to omit . . . .
>
> [But I deny] that the States are not limited by the Constitution of

---

*As we shall see in Chapter 8, Congress often extended the benefit of the federal Bill to territorial inhabitants in verbal formulas strikingly akin to the later Fourteenth Amendment language of "privileges" and "immunities" of "citizens of the United States."

the United States, in respect of the personal or political rights of citizens of the United States . . . .

. . . .

. . . [W]henever the Constitution guaranties to its citizens a right, either natural or conventional, such guarantee is in itself a limitation upon the States . . . . [93]

As we shall see in Chapters 8 and 9, Bingham would later write this philosophy into section 1 of the Fourteenth Amendment.

To see the geographic point biographically, contrast the lived experiences of James Madison, Thomas Jefferson, and Patrick Henry—whose combined travails helped birth the Bill of Rights—with the life experience of John Bingham, the father of the Bill's rebirth in section 1 of the Fourteenth Amendment. As white, male, propertied Virginians, Madison, Jefferson, and Henry belonged to an ongoing republic that had been practicing self-government for 150 years before the Constitution came along. Thus the Virginia House of Burgesses was already older for them than the Fourteenth Amendment is for us today. In a deep sense, the Virginia Declaration of Rights was for them prior to the federal Bill of Rights. Chronologically and perhaps emotionally, Virginia came first, before the Union. But not for Bingham, or for an entire generation of later Americans growing up in places like Ohio. Before Ohio was even a state, it was a federal territory, governed by the federal Constitution and the Union's Northwest Ordinance. For Bingham, *these* documents came first, framing the state and constraining its lawful powers.

Consider next the libertarian track record of central versus local government. The American Revolution had featured local colonies fighting an imperial center in the name of both freedom and federalism. In light of their experience with imperial arrogance and oppression on the one hand, and the heroic roles played by local governments in resisting oppression on the other, many Americans in the 1780s associated a strong central government with tyranny and a strong state government with freedom. This association was of course strengthened by the events in the following decade, with the Virginia and Kentucky legislatures leading the charge against the federal Sedition Act. But in the ensuing decades, it would be hard to argue that the central government acted qualitatively more repressively than local ones. Why, then, the *Barron* double standard?

In some situations, the very line separating state and federal government began to blur. We have already noted in passing the tricky double-jeopardy questions raised when both state and federal governments prosecuted a defendant for the same underlying offense; but the free-press clause posed an analogous puzzle that received far more public attention. In the 1830s, various states sought to ban "incendiary" publications and wanted federal officials to cooperate by closing the mails to such publications. Would such censorship constitute federal action violative of the First Amendment or state action beyond the amendment's scope?[94]

To an increasing number of friends of free speech, this knotty question, even if answerable, seemed to miss the point. Why should the right of citizens to publish controversial views turn on fine legal distinctions about which government's hand had really wielded the censor's red pen? If "incendiary" publications dealt with national political issues, why was a state tax on national speech any more constitutional than a state tax on the national bank?[95] And even if publications addressed only local matters, didn't the Constitution's requirement of republican government[96] and its overarching principle of popular sovereignty oblige state governments to allow citizens the greatest latitude in the expression of political opinions?[97] As to speech and press, then, a growing number of Americans were coming to appreciate the wisdom of Madison's failed "No State shall" amendment, which had tried to make clear that state officials should be no more free to censor than their federal counterparts.[98]

Madison, of course, in both *The Federalist* No. 10 and in the First Congress had argued that state governments were more likely to tyrannize minorities,[99] but as we have seen, the Senate rejected his original "No State shall" amendment. Part of the reason was that in the 1780s, liberty was still centrally understood as public liberty of democratic self-government—majoritarian liberty rather than liberty against popular majorities.[100] Madison thought otherwise but was a man ahead of his time. By the Civil War era, the general intellectual tide was shifting, as reflected in the publication in 1859 of John Stuart Mill's classic tract, *On Liberty*—on individual liberty.

Slavery But surely, to say all this about antebellum America is to rehearse *Hamlet* without the prince, for we have yet to confront the issue that shattered the Founders' Union: slavery. As important as canals, railroads, and telegraph lines were, none of these innovations was more significant than the cotton gin, which killed any chance that slavery might prove so unprofitable that it could be abolished without great economic dislocation. And no issues of geographic expansion posed by the new territories were as explosive as slavery and race—the subjects, indeed, of Bingham's specific objections to the Oregon Constitution. Nor did any issue place the libertarian track record of federal versus state governments in stronger light than did slavery. And on this question, states did not shine. Slavery was almost exclusively a creature of state law. Granted, the federal government had supported the slave system with fugitive slave laws and other policies, including a postal system that helped exclude abolitionist mailings from distribution in the South. (These mailings, of course, were the main targets of the 1830s bans on "incendiary" literature.) Yet a major platform of the Free Soil and Republican Parties in the 1840s and 1850s was that the Constitution frowned on federal involvement with slavery. Freedom was national, slavery local—hence the popular slogan "Freedom National," a slogan that would have sounded quite odd in the 1780s and 1790s.[101] Finally, of course, the abject plight of blacks dramatized the danger to liberty posed by even majoritarian government.

The structural imperatives of the peculiar institution led slave states to violate virtually every right and freedom declared in the Bill—not just the rights and freedoms of slaves, but of free men and women too.[102] Slavery bred repression.[103] Speech and writing critical of slavery, even if plainly religious or political in inspiration, was incendiary and had to be suppressed in southern states, lest slaves overhear and get ideas.[104] In 1859 a Virginia postmaster even banned the *New York Tribune*, a leading Republican newspaper, under a sweeping state censorship statute;

twenty years earlier, the state had tried to prosecute citizens for circulating an antislavery petition to Congress.[105] Teaching slaves to read
(even the Bible) was a criminal offense punished severely in some
states;[106] and in at least one state, writing, printing, publishing, or dis-
tributing abolitionist literature was punishable by death.[107] In a society
that saw itself under siege after Nat Turner's rebellion,[108] access to
firearms had to be carefully restricted, especially for free blacks.[109] The
problem of fugitive slaves put further pressure on civil liberties, triggering rules that made life treacherous indeed for free blacks. Typically, all
southern blacks were legally presumed to be slaves, subject to arbitrary
"seizures" of their "persons," triable as fugitives without juries in proceedings lacking basic rudiments of due process and, if adjudged to be
escaped slaves, subject to great cruelty as a warning to others.[110] To prevent the dissemination of abolitionist literature, slave states allowed
sweeping searches of mail and of suspicious travelers, and even issued
search warrants for books in clear contravention of Lord Camden's famous rulings in the 1760s.[111]

To counter this regime of repression, abolitionist and antislavery
lawyers could not simply rely on positive law, for slavery itself was deeply
embedded in positive law. Beginning in the 1830s, abolitionist lawyers
developed increasingly elaborate theories of natural rights, individual
liberty, and higher law, theories far more compatible with a declaratory
reading of the federal Bill than with *Barron*'s technical legalism.[112]*

*In light of the deep resonance between the declaratory view of the federal Bill and
abolitionism, it is of course ironic that perhaps the leading judicial exponent of the declaratory theory in the 1840s and 1850s was the emphatically proslavery Georgia Supreme
Court. For a concrete illustration of this irony, *see* State *ex rel*. Tucker v. Lavinia, 25 Ga.
311, 313–14 (1858) (Lumpkin, C.J.) (extending benefit of "great principle of the common
law" against double jeopardy to "slaves and free persons of color as well as to white
persons"). If free persons of color were entitled to the great common-law principle of
double jeopardy, why not also to *Nunn*'s great common-law principle of the right to keep
and bear arms? *Cf.* Cooper v. Mayor and Aldermen of Savannah, 4 Ga. 68, 72 (1848)
("Free persons of color have never been recognized here as citizens; they are not entitled
to bear arms, vote for members of the legislature or hold any civil office . . . . They have
no *political* rights, but they have *personal* rights, one of which is personal liberty.") (emphasis in original).

These theories are nicely visible in Ohioan Salmon P. Chase's famous oral argument in the 1847 fugitive slave case of *Jones v. Van Zandt:* "The provisions of the constitution, contained in the amendments . . . rather *announce* restrictions upon legislative power, imposed by the very nature of society and of government, than *create* restrictions, which, were they erased from the constitution, the Legislature would be at liberty to disregard. No Legislature is . . . at liberty to disregard the fundamental principles of rectitude and justice."[113]

The fabric of the original Bill of Rights, interweaving freedom and federalism, was unraveling under the strain of slavery. And once the Civil War came, *Barron* seemed plainly anachronistic. For if the years curving up to the Revolutionary War had dramatized the special danger of central tyranny, leading to *Barron's* Bill, the Civil War era demonstrated that states required constitutional restraints as well.

The abolition of slavery in the Thirteenth Amendment—the first federal constitutional amendment to restrict state law—was obviously the place to start. But was it enough? When the Thirty-ninth Congress convened in December 1865, various unrepentant southern governments were in the process of resurrecting de facto slavery through the infamous Black Codes. As with the slavery system itself, the new codes would invariably require systematic state abridgments of the core rights and freedoms in the Bill of Rights. These abridgments would hit blacks the hardest, but the resurrection of a caste system would also require repression of any whites who might question the codes or harbor sympathy for blacks.[114] In response, the Thirty-ninth Congress drafted the Civil Rights Act of 1866, and section 1 of the Fourteenth Amendment.

Its association with a proslavery court made the *Nunn/Campbell* line of cases a far less likely source of direct influence on Republicans in the Thirty-ninth Congress than the abolitionist sources discussed by Professor Michael Kent Curtis in his important book NO STATE SHALL ABRIDGE: THE FOURTEENTH AMENDMENT AND THE BILL OF RIGHTS (1986). Nevertheless, this line of cases is extremely important in proving that the declaratory reading of the federal Bill was not merely a fringe theory of a small group of abolitionist extremists but rather was attractive to many thoughtful lawyers steeped in the common-law method—and in particular, to judges attentive to issues of judicial role and self-conscious about the need to guide and constrain judicial discretion.

Eight

The Reconstruction Amendment: Text

No State shall make or enforce any law which shall abridge the privileges or immunities of citizens of the United States; nor shall any State deprive any person of life, liberty, or property, without due process of law; nor deny to any person within its jurisdiction the equal protection of the laws.

So reads the second sentence of the Fourteenth Amendment, a sentence around which the entire incorporation debate has swirled. For however much they disagree about everything else, all the participants in the incorporation debate agree that the answer to the debate lies in these words. In light of the stakes involved, and the brevity of the text, we would do well to weigh each word with care. And when we do, we shall see that the textual argument for (a certain sort of) incorporation is remarkably straightforward.

"No State shall . . ."

For those in the incorporation camp, the key sentence gets off to a great start. Anyone paying the slightest attention to constitutional text would find the same phrase in Article I, section 10, imposing various limitations on states, including several key rights designed principally for the benefit of in-state residents: "*No State shall . . .* pass any Bill of Attainder, ex post facto Law, or Law impairing the Obligation of Contracts, or grant any Title of Nobility." In 1810, Chief Justice Marshall's opinion for the Court in *Fletcher v. Peck* declared that the language of Article I, section 10 "may be deemed a bill of rights for the people of each state,"[1] a phrase repeated by the Supreme Court in 1853 and again in 1866, the same year in which the Fourteenth Amendment was drafted.[2] Of course, the Court did not mean to suggest that the catalogue of section 10 rights was identical to the list laid out in the first ten amendments—otherwise the entire *Barron* and incorporation debates would be moot. But the language of *Fletcher* and its progeny does confirm the rhetorical resonance between the phrase "No State shall" and the idea of a federally enforceable "bill of rights" against state governments. Madison had intuited this resonance a dozen years before *Fletcher* when he proposed to include in his "bill of rights" an amendment that "No State shall" abridge various rights of religion, expression, and jury trial.

Far more dramatic evidence of this resonance comes from *Barron,* where a unanimous Supreme Court stated that, had the framers of the original Bill of Rights meant to impose its rules on states, they would have used the Article I, section 10 phrase "No State shall" or some reasonable facsimile. But if the framers of the original Bill were entitled to rely on rules of construction implicit in the Philadelphia Constitution and made explicit by Publius in *The Federalist* No. 83, surely the framers of the Fourteenth Amendment were entitled to rely on the authoritative language of *Barron* itself. The Supreme Court Justices in *Barron* asked for "Simon Says" language, and that's exactly what the Fourteenth Amendment gave them.

Earlier drafts of the key sentence had omitted the words "No State shall" in favor of other formulations, but as Congressman John Bingham explained several years after the amendment's adoption, he rewrote section 1 in response to and in reliance upon *Barron:*

In reexamining that case of Barron, Mr. Speaker, after my struggle in the House in February 1866, . . . I noted and apprehended as I never did before, certain words in that opinion of Marshall. Referring to the first eight articles of amendments to the Constitution of the United States, the Chief Justice said: "Had the framers of these amendments intended them to be limitations on the powers of the State governments they would have imitated the framers of the original Constitution, and have expressed that intention." Barron *vs.* The Mayor, &c., 7 Peters, 250.

Acting upon this suggestion I did imitate the framers of the original Constitution. As they had said "no State shall emit bills of credit, pass any bill of attainder, ex post facto law, or law impairing the obligations of contracts;" imitating their example and imitating it to the letter, I prepared the provision of the first section of the fourteenth amendment as it stands in the Constitution . . . . [3]

" . . . make or enforce any law which shall abridge . . . "

As the key sentence rolls on, the incorporation reading gains steam. Various critical words of the next phrase—*make, any, law,* and *abridge*—call to mind the precisely parallel language in parallel sequence of the First Amendment—*make, no, law,* and *abridging.*[4] There are only three significant differences here.

First, the Fourteenth Amendment imposes a prohibition on states, whereas the First explicitly limits Congress. But this is of course exactly the point of incorporation. And what better way to make clear that even rights and freedoms in the original Bill of Rights that explicitly limited Congress should hereafter apply against states than by cloning the language of the First Amendment? (The word *abridge* in the Fourteenth Amendment is especially revealing, for nowhere outside the First Amendment had this word appeared in the Constitution before 1866.) Thus the Fourteenth Amendment announced its intention to go beyond the narrow negative-implication arguments of William Rawle and John Barron, as had Lumpkin in *Campbell,* where the Georgia chief justice explicitly included First Amendment freedoms in his catalogue of rights that bind states.[5]

Second, the Fourteenth Amendment uses the word *any* where the First uses *no,* but here again, there is an obvious reason. Following the

"Simon Says" rules of *Barron* "to the letter," the Fourteenth uses negative phrasing ("No State shall . . . ") where the First used affirmative ("Congress shall . . . "). The substitution of *any* for *no* simply balances the initial inversion.

Finally, the Fourteenth Amendment speaks of law "enforce[ment]" as well as lawmaking. Once again, this makes perfect sense if its purpose was to incorporate the rights and freedoms of the original Bill. Many of the Bill's provisions, especially those in Amendments V–VIII, dealt centrally with the enforcement of laws by executive and judicial officers. However suggestive the tracking of the First Amendment may be, there is no suggestion thus far that only the First Amendment is to be incorporated.

" . . . the privileges or immunities . . . "

Of course, my last sentence was a bit of a cheat; there is no suggestion "thus far" that only the First Amendment is to be incorporated because it is not yet clear what rights shall not be "abridge[d]" by states. The words that we have considered so far are wonderfully suggestive—exactly what one would expect if incorporation were a goal of the Fourteenth Amendment—but hardly definitive. If the Fourteenth Amendment had stated that "No State shall make any law abridging the right to spit on sidewalks," no one could argue with a straight face for incorporation of the federal Bill of Rights.

Happily, the final words of the first clause are very different, and once again exactly what one would expect if incorporation of a certain sort— which I shall soon elaborate—were intended. Consider first the words *privileges* and *immunities.* Now, these exact words do not appear in the Bill of Rights, but the words *right[s]* and *freedom[s]* speckle the Bill.[6] The plain meanings of these four words are roughly synonymous; indeed, the *Oxford English Dictionary* definition of *privilege* includes the word *right;* and of *immunity, freedom.*[7] What could be more common today than to speak of the "privilege" against compelled self-incrimination, or "immunity" from double prosecution? Nor is modern usage here any different from that of the eighteenth and nineteenth centuries. As Michael Kent Curtis observes in his illuminating and powerfully researched book on incorporation, the "words *rights, liberties, privileges*, and *immunities*, seem to have been used interchangeably."[8] To pick only one pre-Revolutionary example with obvious implications for the incorporation debate, the entitlements to civil and criminal juries, labeled in the Sixth and Seventh Amendments as "right[s]," were described by the 1775 Declaration of the Causes and Necessity of Taking Up Arms as the "inestimable privilege of trial by jury"; and in *The Federalist*'s most extended discussion of a possible bill of rights, Alexander Hamilton explained that "bills of rights are, in their origin, stipulations between kings and their subjects, abridgments of prerogative in favor of privilege, reservations of rights not surrendered to the prince."[9] A couple of generations later, Circuit Justice William Johnson described a congressional bill of 1822 as "in nature of a bill of rights, and of privileges, and immunities" of inhabitants of the Florida territory.[10] Among the rights listed in the bill were "freedom of religious opinions," "the benefit of the writ of habeas corpus," and protections against "excessive bail," "cruel and unusual punishments," and confiscation without "just compensation"—protections phrased almost identically with their federal Bill of Rights counterparts.[11]

Justice Johnson's phrasing was far from idiosyncratic: throughout the nineteenth century, Congress entered into various treaties of territorial accession guaranteeing to territorial inhabitants "all the privileges, rights, and immunities of the citizens of the United States," all the "rights, advantages, and immunities of citizens of the United States," and so on.* Though the precise verbal formulas varied, they all were un-

---

*See, e.g., Treaty Between the United States of America and the French Republic, April 30, 1803, 8 Stat. 200, 202 (treaty acquiring Louisiana providing, in Article III, that "The inhabitants of the ceded territory shall . . . be admitted as soon as possible . . . to the enjoyment of all the rights, advantages and immunities of citizens of the United States"); Treaty of Amity, Settlement and Limits, Between the United States of America and his Catholic Majesty, February 22, 1819, 8 Stat. 252, 258 (treaty acquiring Florida with similar promise, in Article 6, of "all the privileges, rights, and immunities of the citizens of the United States"); Act of March 3, 1843, ch. 101, 5 Stat. 645, 647 (extending to Stockbridge Tribe, in section 7, "all the rights, privileges, and immunities" of "citizens of the United States"); unperfected Treaty of April 12, 1844 *in* 1 CHRISTIAN L. WIKTOR,

derstood to encompass, among other things, the protections of the federal Bill of Rights. As Attorney General Benjamin Butler noted in an 1835 opinion on whether inhabitants of the Arkansas Territory could lawfully take steps toward forming a state government in the absence of congressional authorization: "[Territorial inhabitants] undoubtedly possess the ordinary privileges and immunities of citizens of the United States. Among those is the right of the people 'peaceably to assemble and to petition government for the redress of grievances.'"*

Such treaties continued to be promulgated throughout the 1860s. In 1862 and 1867, Congress extended the Bill of Rights to the Ottawa Indians and Alaskans, respectively, using the language of "rights" and "immunities" of "citizens of the United States"; and in 1868 Congress guaranteed the Sioux "all the privileges and immunities of such citizens."[12] The words *privileges* and *immunities* in the 1860s clearly embraced the closely related concept of *freedom* as used in the First Amendment. Only

---

UNPERFECTED TREATIES OF THE UNITED STATES OF AMERICA 1776–1976, at 187–90 (1976) (providing in Article II that the citizens of Texas shall enjoy "all the rights, privileges and immunities of citizens of the United States"); Treaty of Peace, Friendship, Limits, and Settlement with the Republic of Mexico, February 2, 1848, 9 Stat. 922, 930 (Treaty of Guadalupe Hidalgo providing in Article IX that Mexicans in ceded territory shall be admitted to "all the rights of citizens of the United States"); Treaty with the Wyandotts, January 31, 1855, 10 Stat. 1159 (treaty with Wyandott Indians containing, in Article I, language similar to that of Stockbridge Tribe Act). *See generally* Arnold T. Guminski, *The Rights, Privileges, and Immunities of the American People: A Disjunctive Theory of Selective Incorporation of the Bill of Rights*, 7 WHITTIER L. REV. 765, 783–90 (1985). In debates over the Civil Rights Act of 1866—a precursor of section 1—Senator Lyman Trumbull quoted the language of the Stockbridge Tribe Act to his colleagues. *See* CONG. GLOBE, 39th Cong., 1st Sess. 600 (1866).

*2 Op. Att'y Gen. 726, 732–33 (1852) (opinion of September 21, 1835). Butler was of course glossing the language of the Louisiana Purchase Treaty, quoted *supra* page 167, note.

We should also note here the continuing linkage between the textual formulation of the "right of the people to assemble" and the popular-sovereignty right of the people to alter, abolish, or create government in conventions. *See supra* Chapter 2. Indeed, in the sentence immediately following the passage quoted in the text, Butler wrote: "In the exercise of this [assembly] right, the inhabitants of Arkansas may peaceably meet together in . . . conventions . . . ."

weeks before adopting the Fourteenth Amendment, Congress passed the Civil Rights Act of 1866, widely seen as the statutory precursor of section 1. In draft, the act spoke of "civil rights and immunities," leading its sponsor to play the role of law dictionary: "What is an immunity? Simply 'freedom or exemption from obligation . . . .'"[13] Similarly, both the Maryland Constitution of 1867 and the Texas Constitution of 1866 referred to "liberty of the press" as a "privilege"; and an 1866 Supreme Court case described jury trial interchangeably as a "right," "freedom," and "privilege."[14]

We have already noted that most American lawyers began their legal education with Blackstone and the common law. When we turn to Blackstone, we find the words *privileges* and *immunities* used to describe various entitlements embodied in the landmark English charters of liberty of Magna Charta, the Petition of Right, the Habeas Corpus Act, the English Bill of Rights of 1689, and the Act of Settlement of 1701.[15] These English documents were the fountainhead of the common law and the acknowledged forebears of many particular rights that later appeared in the federal Bill, sometimes in identical language.[16] After invoking Blackstone and these landmarks, Chief Justice Lumpkin's opinion in *Campbell* unsurprisingly described various rights in the federal Bill as "privileges," including the right at issue in *Campbell* itself, the right to be confronted with witnesses.[17] Lumpkin's ideas about *Barron* may have been unorthodox in 1852, but his language was utterly conventional; that same decade, the Supreme Court in *Dred Scott* labeled the entitlements in the federal Bill "rights and privileges of the citizen" and described "liberty of speech," the right "to hold public meetings upon political affairs," and the freedom "to keep and carry arms" as "privileges and immunities of citizens."[18]

" . . . of citizens of the United States . . ."

But even once we recognize that various "rights" and "freedoms" in the Bill are in every respect and for every purpose "privileges" and "immunities," there remains one final textual stumbling block. Can we really say that the Bill's "rights" and "freedoms" are truly privileges and immunities of "citizens of the United States"?

Of course we can. In ordinary, everyday language we often speak of the United States Constitution and Bill of Rights as declaring and defining rights of Americans as Americans. Surely our Constitution is not centrally about declaring, say, the rights of Germans qua Germans, or the Chinese qua Chinese. This ordinary, everyday understanding of the Constitution is emblazoned in the Preamble in words familiar to every generation of Americans since the Founding: "*We the People of the United States,* in Order to . . . secure the Blessings of Liberty to *ourselves and our Posterity,* do ordain and establish this Constitution *for* the United States."

This ordinary understanding is not in the least bit damaged by the technical objection to incorporation that Professor Louis Henkin has raised: "[T]he provisions of the Bill of Rights are not rights of citizens only but are enjoyed by non-citizens as well."[19] Surely the fact that Americans may often extend many benefits of our Bill to, say, resident aliens—for reasons of prudence, principle, or both—does not alter the basic fact that these rights are paradigmatically rights of and for American citizens. Indeed, others may enjoy certain benefits only insofar as they interact with American citizens, typically because they either live on soil governed by American citizens or do things with important effects on American citizens. Peripheral applications of the Bill should not obscure its core.

In any event, Henkin's technical objection collapses under the weight of its own anachronism. At the time of the Fourteenth Amendment, the best-known case on the scope of the Bill of Rights was none other than *Dred Scott,* which involved, among other issues, questions arising under the due-process clause of the Fifth Amendment. *Dred Scott* declared the rights in the Bill to be not simply privileges, but "privileges *of the citizen.*"[20] This passage must be read in combination with the rest of the opinion, holding that because Dred Scott was not a citizen of the United States, he could not enjoy the privilege of diversity jurisdiction—or indeed, any of the "rights, and privileges, and immunities, guarantied by [the Constitution] to the citizen."[21] The central meaning and logic of the opinion, which took pains to stress the words of the Preamble,[22] was that the Constitution and the Bill of Rights were ordained and established by citizens of the United States, and for their benefit only.

Surely the framers of the Fourteenth Amendment were entitled to rely on Supreme Court interpretations in *Dred Scott* no less than in *Barron*, even as they sought to overrule them by using the "Simon Says" language suggested by the Court itself.* And once again, it is clear that they did so rely. John Bingham, the main author of section 1, not only cited *Dred Scott* in a speech before the House in early 1866 but quoted the following key language: "The words 'people of the United States' and 'citizens' are synonymous terms."[23] In the Senate debates on the Fourteenth Amendment, Senator John Henderson also quoted this language verbatim;[24] and in the most extended and authoritative discussion of section 1, Senator Jacob Howard likewise made plain that the language chosen was in response to *Dred Scott:* "[I]t is a fact well worthy of attention that the course of decision in our courts and the present settled doctrine is, that all these immunities, privileges, rights thus guarantied . . . or recognized by [the first eight amendments to the Constitution] are secured to the citizen solely as a citizen of the United States . . . . "[25]

Though many aspects of *Dred Scott* were highly offensive to members of the Thirty-ninth Congress, there was widespread support for the idea that the Bill of Rights was paradigmatically, even if not exclusively, a catalogue of privileges and immunities of "citizens."[26] Nor was this locution anything new or startling. In both *Nunn* and *Campbell,* for example, Chief Justice Lumpkin had described the Bill of Rights as protecting "citizens."[27]

" . . . nor shall any State deprive any person of life, liberty, or property, without due process of law . . . "

Henkin's technical objection to incorporation does not merely dissolve, it boomerangs. By focusing our attention on *Dred Scott* and citizenship,

---

*See U.S. Const. amend XIV, §1, cl. 1 ("All persons born or naturalized in the United States, and subject to the jurisdiction thereof, are citizens of the United States and of the State wherein they reside."). This first sentence of the Fourteenth Amendment consciously overruled *Dred Scott*'s holding that blacks could never be "citizens."

Henkin unwittingly destroys another more familiar technical argument against incorporation. Many commentators (Raoul Berger most stridently) have claimed that if the privileges-or-immunities clause was designed to incorporate the rights and freedoms of the Bill, the clause would incorporate the Fifth Amendment's due-process requirement and thereby render the Fourteenth Amendment's due-process clause redundant.[28] Berger's claim has loomed especially large because Justice Black, the leading judicial proponent of total incorporation, repeatedly ducked technical questions about the relation between section 1's privileges-or-immunities and due-process clauses. Instead, Black clung to the simple but vague formulation that the Fourteenth Amendment "as a whole" effected incorporation.[29] Professor John Hart Ely, while generally supportive of incorporation, went even further in legitimizing Berger's technical objection by frankly conceding the redundancy point.[30]

But we can now see why Berger's technical objection collapses, like Henkin's, and for the same reason. By incorporating the rights of the Fifth Amendment, the privileges-or-immunities clause, under the precedent of *Dred Scott*, would have prevented states from depriving "citizens" of due process. Bingham, Howard, and their colleagues wanted to go even further by extending the benefits of state due process to aliens. But for this, a special clause—speaking not of "citizens" but of "persons"—was needed. As Bingham explained his amendment on the floor of the House: "Is it not essential to the unity of the people that the citizens of each State shall be entitled to all the privileges and immunities of citizens [of the United States]? Is it not essential . . . that all persons, whether citizens or strangers, within this land, shall have equal protection in every State in this Union in the rights of life and liberty and property?"[31] A few weeks later, Bingham reiterated the point in debates over the Civil Rights Act of 1866 when he proposed to substitute the word *inhabitant* for *citizen:* "[A]re we not committing the terrible enormity of distinguishing here in the laws in respect to life, liberty, and property between the citizen and stranger within your gates . . . . Your Constitution says 'no person,' not 'no citizen,' 'shall be deprived of life, liberty, or property,' without due process of law."[32]

Howard's explanation to the Senate was identical. After emphasizing that the privileges and immunities of citizens of the United States included "the personal rights guarantied and secured by the first eight amendments of the Constitution"—a passage we shall return to later—he patiently elaborated that the subsequent clauses of section 1 were needed to "disable a State from depriving not merely a citizen of the United States, but any person, whoever he may be, of life, liberty, or property without due process of law, or from denying to him the equal protection of the laws of the State."[33] On this issue as well, the views of Bingham and Howard were widely shared by their Reconstruction colleagues.[34] Indeed, section 1's distinction between the rights of citizens and those of aliens stretches back to its earliest draft in committee: "Congress shall have power to . . . secure to all citizens . . . the same political rights and privileges; and to all persons in every State equal protection in the enjoyment of life, liberty, and property."[35]

But we have yet to feel the full zing of the anti-incorporation boomerangs, for just as Henkin's objection destroys Berger's, so Berger's emphasis on due process undermines Henkin. It would be odd to think that the words *due process* in the Fourteenth Amendment were intended to mean something very different than they did in the Fifth. Thus, when Andrew Jackson Rogers asked section 1's main architect, John Bingham, what he meant by "due process of law," Bingham tartly replied, "courts have settled that long ago, and the gentleman can go and read their decisions."[36] In 1866, the definitive statement of the meaning of the Fifth Amendment's due-process clause was the decade-old case of *Murray's Lessee v. Hoboken Land & Improvement Co.* In that case, a unanimous Supreme Court said that procedural due process embodied—incorporated, if you will—all the other procedural rules laid down in "the constitution itself."[37] Rawle had said much the same thing in his treatise thirty years earlier.[38] If, here too, the framers of the Fourteenth Amendment were entitled to rely on authoritative Supreme Court pronouncements (and it is hard to see why not), then the due-process clause of the Fourteenth Amendment *by itself* embodied—incorporated—various procedural safeguards specified in Amendments V–VIII. That leaves only six amendments in the Bill—the first four and the last two—where the privileges-or-immunities clause has independent bite.[39] Of these six, five explicitly speak of the rights of "the people,"[40] a phrase that *Dred Scott*, John Bingham, and many other commentators understood as for many purposes synonymous with "citizens." Thus Senate rules circa 1866 did not permit foreigners to petition that body[41] because petition was a right "of the people." The fit between the explicit rights of "the people" in the original Bill and those provisions where the privileges-or-immunities clause has independent bite may not be perfect, but surely it is close enough to explain why so many in 1866 would have naturally thought of the nonprocedural provisions of the original Bill as rights of citizens.[42]

Beyond Mechanical Incorporation

We have now come slowly, but I hope surely, to the deep truth at the core of Hugo Black's observation that "the words 'No State shall make or enforce any law which shall abridge the privileges or immunities of citizens of the United States' seem . . . an eminently reasonable way of expressing the idea that henceforth the Bill of Rights shall apply to the States."[43]

The best objection to Black's claim is that other language could have been used that would have expressed the purpose more clearly.[44] This objection does seem devastating to the particular brand of mechanical incorporation that Black's rhetoric at times appeared to suggest: that the privileges-or-immunities and due-process clauses were simply terms of art referring to the first eight amendments in every jot and tittle, and to nothing else. If the key clauses of the Fourteenth Amendment meant Amendments I–VIII—no more, no less—why were the amendments not invoked by name? Why, indeed, use words like *privileges* and *immunities* that are only roughly synonymous with, rather than identical to, the words of the first eight amendments themselves?

Black never offered satisfying answers to these questions, perhaps because the best answers require abandonment of mechanical incorporation. But for Black, part of the appeal of incorporation lay in its mechanical quality, its apparent ability to reduce judicial discretion by establishing an exact identity between the broad language of the Fourteenth Amendment and the seemingly more specific rules of Amendments I–VIII.[45]

The framers of the Fourteenth Amendment did not share Black's preoccupation with mechanical rules* and wrote an amendment whose faithful interpretation and implementation, alas, cannot be mechanical.[46] The best reading of the amendment suggests that it incorporates the Bill of Rights in a far more subtle way than Black admitted, including both more and less than the first eight amendments.

Clearly, the privileges-or-immunities clause encompasses more than the federal Bill as such. Article I, section 9, for example, declares that "The Privilege of the Writ of Habeas Corpus shall not be suspended," except in certain limited circumstances. Though Rawle had claimed otherwise in 1825, *Barron* squarely held that this clause, like all the other provisions in section 9, bound only the federal government.[47] By withholding habeas from blacks claiming to be kidnapped, antebellum southern states had facilitated the capture of dark-skinned men and women alleged to be fugitive slaves.[48] Although the Thirteenth Amendment had formally abolished slavery, states attempting to resurrect slavery de facto through Black Codes would predictably manipulate habeas to implement their scheme. Protecting the self-described "privilege" of habeas corpus against wayward states was thus of central concern to the framers of the Fourteenth Amendment.[49] In their initial pronouncements on the Fourteenth Amendment in the *Slaughter-House Cases,* the justices on the Supreme Court disagreed sharply about quite a lot, but none denied the Great Writ was indeed a "privilege of citizens of the United States" protected against state infringement by the new amendment. Indeed, Justice Miller's majority opinion, generally thought today to have rendered the privileges-or-immunities clause utterly meaningless, explicitly listed "the privilege of the writ of habeas corpus" in its catalogue of Fourteenth Amendment rights.[50]

So far, Justice Black may not have been troubled, for like Amendments I–VIII, the habeas clause is textually specified in the pre-1866 Constitu-

---

*One partial explanation is that many congressional architects of Reconstruction envisioned not only judicial enforcement of section 1 but also—and perhaps more centrally—congressional enforcement. Section 1 was thus in part a grant of power to themselves, and they drafted it broadly.

tion, and thus its incorporation, too, is relatively mechanical.[51] Indeed, Black might have used Miller's concession to undermine the rest of Miller's argument, which seemed to resist, if not reject, total incorporation of the first eight amendments. Under what theory does the privileges-or-immunities clause incorporate the Great Writ specified in Article I but not all the Great Rights specified after Article VII? It would be silly to argue that the difference is that the habeas clause used the magic word *privilege* whereas later clauses in the Bill used only synonyms like *right* or *freedom*. (Interestingly, Justice Bradley's dissent in *Slaughter-House* not only argued for incorporation of all the "personal privileges and immunities . . . specified in the original Constitution, or in the early amendments of it"; it also included in the catalogue "the *right* of habeas corpus.")[52]

But the habeas clause presents hidden problems for Black as well, for its use of the word *privilege* calls attention to the word and naturally directs our gaze to the most salient clause of the pre-1866 Constitution to use the word—the so-called comity clause of Article IV: "The Citizens of each State shall be entitled to all Privileges and Immunities of Citizens in the several States." These words clearly have some sort of connection to those of the Fourteenth Amendment—the pattern of the words *citizens, privileges,* and *immunities* in tight formation in both places calls for explanation. Black gave none. In the abstract, these words may not seem devastating to his mechanical view, especially in light of the widely held Republican view that these words in Article IV incorporated by reference the rights, freedoms, privileges, and immunities later specified in the federal Bill.[53*] But in 1866, those Article IV words also came packaged with an influential judicial gloss. Just as we cannot fully understand the words "No State shall" without reading *Barron;* or the words "citizens of the United States" without reckoning with *Dred Scott;* or the meaning of "due process" without confronting *Murray's Lessee;* so here, we must consider the leading comity clause case on the books in 1866: Justice Bushrod Washington's 1823 Circuit Court opinion in *Corfield v. Coryell.*

---

*The precise historical context that gave rise to this Republican linkage of the comity clause and the Bill of Rights will become more clear in Chapter 11.

In *Corfield,* Washington identified Article IV "privileges and immunities" as things that "are, in their nature, fundamental; which belong, of right, to the citizens of all free governments; and which have, at all times, been enjoyed by the citizens of the several states which compose this Union . . . [including] the following general heads: Protection by the government; the enjoyment of life and liberty, with the right to acquire and possess property of every kind, and to pursue and obtain happiness and safety."[54] Justice Washington went on to add to his nonexhaustive list "the benefit of the writ of habeas corpus" and the rights to "maintain actions of any kind in the courts" and to "take, hold and dispose of property, either real or personal."[55] Though he did not cite Blackstone by name, Washington seemed to be following a quintessentially common-law approach in deducing "fundamental" rights.

We have seen this kind of thinking before in the common-law approach of such *Barron* contrarians as Rawle and Lumpkin: fundamental rights deriving from a variety of sources (typically, nature and history) preexisted their textual specification in legislative codes. Where We the People had given Our judicial imprimatur to a right by including it in the federal Bill, such a right was virtually by definition "fundamental." Indeed, Lumpkin described the Bill as "a legal decalogue for every civilized society, in all time to come," declaring "vital truths . . . at the foundation of our free, republican institutions" and encompassing rights "at the bottom of every free government"[56]—formulations strikingly reminiscent of *Corfield*'s ode to "fundamental" rights belonging to "the citizens of all free governments; and which have, at all times, been enjoyed by the citizens" of America.

Lumpkin also suggested that for institutional reasons, rooted in fear of judicial discretion, perhaps judges should not invalidate statutes in the name of fundamental rights that had not yet received the People's imprimatur. But when read through the lens of the Article IV comity clause, as glossed by *Corfield*'s ode, the language of section 1 opens up broader possibilities. *Corfield*'s nonexhaustive list of fundamental rights radiated well beyond those enumerated in the federal Bill; and this open-ended list received considerable attention in the Thirty-ninth Congress. Thus, Senator Lyman Trumbull and Representative James Wilson both quoted Washington's ode, Blackstone, and other broad common-law and natural-rights language in support of their 1866 Civil Rights Act, whose provisions were generally understood to be subsumed within the privileges-or-immunities clause of the subsequent Fourteenth Amendment.[57] *Corfield* was again read broadly by Jacob Howard in his influential speech on section 1, which invoked both Washington's ode and the Bill of Rights as exemplifying "privileges and immunities of citizens of the United States."[58] Justice Black, though, stressed the Bill and shunned the ode.[59] For Black, Justice Washington's words conjured up the specter of judges invalidating statutes by invoking nontextually specified fundamental rights and by giving constitutional status to common-law rights like freedom of contract. The specter haunting Justice Black has a name. Its name is *Lochner*.[60]

But understanding that the privileges-or-immunities clause applied to various common-law rights may not necessarily lead us to *Lochner*. John Harrison has suggested, for example, that where a privilege or immunity derives not from the federal Constitution or Bill of Rights but from common law or state law, the privileges-or-immunities clause prohibits only irrational discrimination in defining and enforcing these rights.[61] Detailed analysis of his intricate arguments would take us rather far afield; for our purposes it is enough to note that section 1 is not limited to privileges and immunities specified in the pre-1866 Constitution. Other common-law rights were also included, though there remain questions about the precise kind of protection intended. For these nonconstitutional rights, perhaps only antidiscrimination ("equal") protection should be accorded, rather than fundamental rights ("full") protection.* Questions also remain about judicial competence to find un-

---

*The language of the 1866 Civil Rights Act speaks of the "full *and* equal benefit of all laws and proceedings for the security of person and property." Act of Apr. 9, 1866, ch. 31, §1, 14 Stat. 27 (emphasis added). For a reading of this act as encompassing a fundamental-rights core and an equal-rights outer layer, *see* JACOBUS TENBROEK, EQUAL UNDER LAW 189–90 (Collier, 1965) (1951). *See also* Earl M. Maltz, *Fourteenth Amendment Concepts in the Antebellum Era*, 32 AM. J. LEGAL HIST. 305, 323 (1988) (similar analysis of two-tiered full-and-equal-protection philosophy in antebellum jurisprudence). The language of the privileges-or-immunities clause can be understood as similarly two tiered. Harri-

specified rights;[62] but those fundamental rights that had already been specified and "declared" by We the People were easy cases for full judicial protection, and thus at the core of the Fourteenth Amendment.

So much, then, for section 1's penumbral radiations beyond the first eight amendments, for this is only half the story. Section 1 means not just more than mechanical incorporation but also less.[63] Once again, the habeas clause of Article I, section 9 helps illustrate the point. Why does the Fourteenth Amendment incorporate this self-proclaimed privilege, but not, for example, its section 9 companion clause, "No Capitation, or other direct, Tax shall be laid, unless in Proportion to the Census or Enumeration herein before directed to be taken"? The answer goes beyond

---

son's central textual argument is that the word *abridge* can be read to prohibit mere discrimination in the allocation of state-created rights—as in the Fourteenth Amendment, section 2 rules on "abridge[ment]" of the (state-law-created) "right to vote." Where only state-law-created rights are at stake, this is a plausible—perhaps the most plausible—reading of the word *abridge.* But where rights specified and declared by We the People in Our Constitution are at stake, the best understanding of *abridge* in section 1 surely comes from its fundamental-rights counterpart in the First Amendment, whose language section 1 so carefully tracks. *See supra* text accompanying notes 4–5; *see also* Live-Stock Dealers' & Butchers' Ass'n v. Crescent City Live-stock Landing & Slaughter-House Co., 15 F. Cas. 649, 652–53 (C.C.D. La. 1870) (No. 8,408) (Bradley, Circuit J.) (Fourteenth Amendment "not merely requires equality of privileges; but it demands that the privileges and immunities of all citizens shall be absolutely unabridged, unimpaired" and protects "privileges and immunities of an absolute and not merely of a relative character"). Plainly, the amendment's framers meant to prevent a state from abridging speech critical of the Black Codes, even where the state "evenhandedly" abridged the rights of all speakers, white and black, southern and northern.

To reach this result via a different path, consider how a judge is to determine whether a given right truly is fundamental in a particular time and place. If the right is inscribed in an enduring bill of rights, that inscription is itself decisive evidence of fundamentality. If not, a judge could see which rights the present government chose to extend to its most-favored citizens, and treat this extension as similar evidence of fundamentality. But if the government then chose to withdraw this right from its most-favored class rather than extend it to all citizens, that withdrawal would dissolve the basis on which our judge deemed the right fundamental in the first place. As a practical matter, this second category of mere state-law-created rights would enjoy a kind of antidiscrimination ("equal") protection rather than fundamental rights ("full") protection.

the fact that the capitation clause does not talk like a privilege; it doesn't walk or act like a private right either. Rather, it sounds in federalism, guaranteeing a fair distribution of the federal tax burden among states. As a state right of sorts, the capitation clause resists easy incorporation against states.

Yet the same holds true for various provisions of the original Bill of Rights. Justice Black himself saw the obvious difficulties of incorporating the Ninth and Tenth Amendments, which he read as pure federalism provisions. Thus Black argued only for incorporation of the first eight amendments. But federalism insinuated itself throughout the original Bill of Rights: separating citizen rights and state rights calls for a scalpel, not a meat cleaver. Is the establishment clause, for example, more like the habeas and free-speech clauses (and thus an easy candidate for incorporation) or more like the capitation clause and the Tenth Amendment (and thus rather awkward to incorporate)? Or is it, perhaps, some sort of hybrid that calls for "partial" incorporation?

Mechanical incorporation, then, rests on an optical illusion that the Constitution defines government structure, and the Bill declares citizen rights (redefining "the Bill" of course, as the first eight, or perhaps nine, amendments). The reality is, alas, more complicated.[64] The original Constitution also declares rights (witness the habeas clause); the Bill also embodies structure (witness the Tenth Amendment); and both the Constitution and the Bill intertwine rights and structure.

The wording of the Fourteenth Amendment is remarkably sensitive to this more complicated reality. Section 1 requires us to ask whether a given provision of the Constitution or Bill really does declare a privilege or immunity *of citizens* rather than, for example, a right of states. The answer will often be anything but mechanical, requiring considerable judgment and hard choices. But this is exactly what the words of section 1 demand. They avoid using the words "first eight amendments" or "Bill of Rights" not just because these words would have meant too little, but also because they would have meant too much. If refined incorporation of the sort I shall elaborate in Chapter 10 was indeed intended, it would have been hard to draft better language than the words of section 1.

Nine

The Reconstruction
Amendment: History

The easy case for (nonmechanical) incorporation, then, rests on the plain meaning of the words of section 1 circa 1866. Is there anything in the legislative history of these words that contradicts this straightforward reading? On the contrary.

The Thirty-Ninth Congress

Begin with section 1's principal draftsman, John Bingham. As we have seen, Bingham had argued before the House as early as 1859 that "whenever the Constitution guaranties to its citizens a right, either natural or conventional, such guarantee is in itself a limitation upon the States."[1] Over the next few minutes, he made clear that such "guarantees" that "no State may rightfully . . . impair" included the due-process and just-compensation mandates of the "fifth article of amendments," the "trial by jury," and the "right to know; to argue and to utter, according to conscience"—guarantees he described as "privileges and immunities of citizens of the United States."[2] *Citizens* here meant just that, as Bingham illustrated by quoting *Dred Scott* and other commentary.[3] But Bingham also said that *Dred Scott* had gone too far, limiting certain rights, such as due process, that under both natural law and constitutional text extended to all persons, whether citizens or not.[4] In a nutshell, Bingham's position was that no state could violate the Constitution's "wise and beneficent guarantees of political rights to the citizens of the United States, as such, and of natural rights to all persons, whether citizens or strangers."[5]

These views, expressed in 1859, track almost perfectly the natural meaning of the words Bingham drafted in 1866 as section 1 of the Fourteenth Amendment. Thus we find Bingham in 1866 repeating in speeches before the House arguments he had made seven years earlier. As we have already noted, Bingham once again quoted from *Dred Scott* on constitutional rights of "citizens" as "citizens," yet repeated his claim that *Dred Scott* was too stingy in refusing certain due-process protections to "persons, whether citizens or strangers."[6] In another nutshell, no state should be allowed to violate "the privileges and immunities of all the citizens of the Republic and the inborn rights of every person within its jurisdiction."[7] The privileges-or-immunities clause would protect citizen rights, and the due-process and equal-protection principles (which Bingham saw as paired, if not synonymous)[8] would protect the wider category of persons.

But what, precisely, were the "privileges or immunities of citizens of the United States"? In 1859, Bingham offered no comprehensive summary but strongly implied that all rights and freedoms guaranteed by the Constitution were included. Though he did not use the magic words *Bill of Rights,* he either quoted or paraphrased the rights to speech, press, religion, due process, just compensation, and jury trial. In 1866, Bingham spoke to the issue at much greater length and made himself abundantly clear. Over and over he described the privileges-or-immunities clause as encompassing "the bill of rights"—a phrase he used more than a dozen times in a key speech on February 28.[9] In that speech he also explained why a constitutional amendment was necessary, citing by name and quoting from the Supreme Court's opinions in *Barron* and one of its progeny, *Livingston v. Moore.*[10] The day before, a colleague of Bingham's, Robert Hale, had suggested that states were already bound by the Bill,[11] but Bingham set Hale and others straight with the following quotation from *Livingston:* "As to the amendments of the Constitution of the United States, they must be put out of the case, since it is now settled that those amendments do not extend to the States . . . . "[12] Six weeks later Bingham again held forth on the need for his amendment, invoking "the bill of rights" six times in a single speech and again reminding his colleagues that it "has been solemnly ruled by the Supreme Court of the United States" that "the bill of rights . . . does not limit the powers of States."[13] In a speech in January 1867, while the amendment was pending in the states, Bingham again reminded his audience that his amendment would overrule *Barron*.[14] In 1871, several years after the Fourteenth Amendment was ratified, Bingham was once more called upon to parse its words. He yet again cited by name and quoted from *Barron*,[15] and here, too, he immediately linked "the privileges and immunities of citizens of the United States" with the Bill of Rights:

> [T]he privileges and immunities of citizens of the United States, as contradistinguished from citizens of a State, are chiefly defined in the first eight amendments to the Constitution of the United States. Those eight amendments are as follows. [Bingham then proceeded to read the first eight amendments word for word.] These eight articles I have shown never were limitations upon the power of the States, until made so by the fourteenth amendment.[16]

In light of all this, it is astonishing that some scholars, most notably Charles Fairman and Raoul Berger, have suggested that when Bingham invoked "the bill of rights," he didn't mean what he said.[17*]

*If the issue is whether references to the "bill of rights" in 1866 naturally called to mind the first nine or ten rather than eight amendments—a point to which we shall return later—the observation about the ambiguity of the phrase is fair enough. But Fairman and Berger meant something quite different: that when Bingham said the "bill of rights" in 1866, perhaps he did not even mean the first eight amendments. Yet as we have seen, Bingham painstakingly cited *Barron,* quoted the language from *Livingston* on *"the amendments* to the Constitution of the United States," and later paraphrased these cases as holdings on *"the bill of rights."* Indeed, in the very same breath in which he first invoked *Barron,* Bingham spoke of "the bill of rights *under the articles of amendment."* CONG. GLOBE, 39th Cong., 1st Sess. 1089 (1866) (emphasis added). Over the course of 1866, Bingham had occasion to refer specifically to "freedom of speech," the right to

Two years before Bingham introduced his amendment, Representative James Wilson had made clear that he too understood the "privileges and immunities of citizens of the United States" to include the guarantees of the amendments. His words also show that he deemed all rights and freedoms in the Bill—even those declared only against Congress—to be binding on state governments:

> Freedom of religious opinion, freedom of speech and press, and the right of assemblage for the purpose of petition belong to every American citizen . . . . With these rights no State may interfere . . . .

"teach" religion, "freedom of conscience," "due process," the right to "just compensation" and protection against "confiscation," and the right against "cruel and unusual punishments." *Id.* at 158, 1065, 1094, 2542; BENJAMIN B. KENDRICK, THE JOURNAL OF THE JOINT COMMITTEE OF FIFTEEN ON RECONSTRUCTION 85 (1914); Charles Fairman, *Does the Fourteenth Amendment Incorporate the Bill of Rights?* 2 STAN. L. REV. 5, 76 (1949) (quoting CINCINNATI COM., Aug. 27, 1866, at 1). If all that weren't enough to make clear Bingham was using the words "the bill of rights" in their ordinary sense, his speeches both before and after 1866 offer powerful confirmation. For example, in January 1867, while the Fourteenth Amendment was being considered by the states, Bingham linked section 1 to "personal rights" under "the first ten articles of amendments" and specifically invoked "the eighth . . . amendment[]" protection against "the infliction of cruel punishments"; and the right to "just compensation" when "private property shall . . . be taken for public use" affirmed by "the fifth of the amendments." CONG. GLOBE, 39th Cong., 2d. Sess. 811 (1867). In a later speech, Bingham declared: "Jefferson well said of the first eight articles of amendments to the Constitution of the United States, they constitute the American Bill of Rights." CONG. GLOBE, 42d Cong., 1st Sess. 84 app. (1871); *see also* CONG. GLOBE, 37th Cong., 2d Sess. 1638 (1862) (remarks of John Bingham) (discussing due-process and just-compensation clauses of "the bill of rights").

More important, of course, everyone else in the Thirty-ninth Congress understood Bingham's references to "the bill of rights" as meaning just that. On February 27, the day after Bingham first introduced his amendment in the House as a proposal to enforce "this immortal bill of rights," CONG. GLOBE, 39th Cong., 1st Sess. 1034 (1866), Robert Hale responded with his own ode to "the bill of rights," which he unambiguously defined in passing as "these amendments to the Constitution, numbered from one to ten." *Id.* at 1064. Immediately following yet another Bingham paean to "the bill of rights," *id.* at 1291–93, James Wilson invoked the due-process clause of the Fifth Amendment, which "I find in the bill of rights which [Mr. Bingham] desires to have enforced by an amendment." *Id.* at 1294.

Sir, I might enumerate many other constitutional rights of the citizen which slavery has disregarded and practically destroyed, but I have [said] enough to illustrate my proposition: that slavery . . . denies to the citizens of each State the privileges and immunities of citizens . . . .

. . . The people of the free States should insist on ample protection to their rights, privileges and immunities, which are none other than those which the Constitution was designed to secure to all citizens alike . . . . [18]

Plainly, then, Wilson and Bingham both read the Bill through contrarian lenses, though Bingham was far more conscious that the Supreme Court had rejected this reading. And both leaders understood that the plain meaning of section 1 was that henceforth the federal government would have explicit power to compel state compliance with all the "privileges" and "immunities" of "citizens" set out in the Bill. Shortly before the amendment came before the House for final approval, the political leader Thaddeus Stevens delivered a speech describing its provisions. Here are his opening words on section 1: "I can hardly believe that any person can be found who will not admit that every one of these provisions is just. They are all asserted, in some form or other, in our DECLARATION or [of?] organic law. But the Constitution limits only the action of Congress, and is not a limitation on the States. This amendment supplies that defect . . . . "[19]

In the Senate, Jacob Howard offered the most comprehensive analysis of section 1:

[I]ts first clause, [which] I regard as very important . . . relates to the privileges and immunities of citizens of the United States as such, and as distinguished from all other persons . . . . [Here is what a] very learned and excellent judge says about these privileges and immunities of the citizens of each State in the several States [in] the case of Corfield vs. Coryell. [Howard then quoted Corfield at length.]

Such is the character of the privileges and immunities spoken of in [Article IV]. To these privileges and immunities, whatever they may be—for they are not and cannot be fully defined in their entire extent and precise nature—to these should be added the personal rights guarantied and secured by the first eight amendments of the Constitution; such as the freedom of speech and of the press; the right of the people peaceably to assemble and petition the Government for a redress of grievances, a right appertaining to each and all of the people; the right to keep and bear arms; the right to be exempted from the quartering of soldiers in a house without the consent of the owner; the right to be exempt from unreasonable searches and seizures, and from any search or seizure except by virtue of a warrant issued upon a formal oath or affidavit; the right of an accused person to be informed of the nature of the accusation against him, and his right to be tried by an impartial jury of the vicinage; and also the right to be secure against excessive bail and against cruel and unusual punishments.

. . . [T]he course of decision of our courts and the present settled doctrine is, that all these immunities, privileges, rights, thus guarantied by the Constitution or recognized by it . . . do not operate in the slightest degree as a restraint or prohibition upon State legislation. . . . [I]t has been repeatedly held that the restriction contained in the Constitution against the taking of private property for public use without just compensation is not a restriction upon State legislation, but applies only to the legislation of Congress.

. . . [T]hese guarantees . . . stand simply as a bill of rights in the Constitution . . . [and] States are not restrained from violating the principles embraced in them . . . . The great object of the first section of this amendment is, therefore, to restrain the power of the States and compel them at all times to respect these great fundamental guarantees.[20]

There is much more legislative history to confirm the material that we have canvassed so far—the leading scholarly work counts no fewer than thirty Republican statements in the Thirty-eighth and Thirty-ninth Congresses voicing contrarian sentiments, and not one supporting *Barron*.[21] As a lover of mercy, however, I shall resist the temptation to present all the evidence that anti-incorporationists have overlooked or distorted. For what we have seen thus far clinches the case for some sort of incorporation.

Consider first the sources. John Bingham was the author of section 1.

Thaddeus Stevens was not only the political leader of the House but also head of the House delegation of the all-important Committee on Reconstruction that officially reported the Fourteenth Amendment. Jacob Howard was Stevens's acting Joint Committee counterpart in the Senate. James Wilson was chairman of the House Judiciary Committee and sponsor of the Civil Rights Act of 1866, whose provisions section 1 was consciously designed and widely understood to embrace.

Consider next the context. Bingham's audience knew he was the author and thus paid particular attention to his expositions.[22] The *New York Times* covered his major speeches, summarizing one as "a proposition to arm the Congress . . . with power to enforce the Bill of Rights as it stood"; and Bingham published this speech in 1866 as a popular pamphlet subtitled "in support of the proposed amendment to enforce the bill of rights."[23] Stevens delivered a written speech (a rarity for him, as the *New York Herald* noted the next day)[24] in his formal capacity as House chairman of the Joint Committee. Howard, too, purported to speak on behalf of the committee, addressing a packed gallery in a speech whose passage on the Bill of Rights was reprinted in full on the front page of both the *New York Times* and the *Herald*.[25] (The latter ranked as the nation's best-selling newspaper at the time.)[26] And not a single person in either house spoke up to deny these men's interpretation of section 1. Surely, if the words of section 1 meant something different, this was the time to stand up and say so.

Consider, finally, that all these men offered glosses that mesh perfectly with each other and, most importantly, with the plain meaning of the words of section 1.

Incorporating Anti-Incorporation Insights

If the key sentence of section 1 does not in some way or another incorporate the Bill of Rights, then just what does it do? The two most prominent critics of incorporation, Charles Fairman and Raoul Berger, have suggested two radically different alternatives. Each has something going for it, something that does tend to undermine Black's brand of mechanical incorporation, but something that in fact supports a refined model of incorporation.

Fairman Professor Charles Fairman spent so much energy attacking Justice Black that he failed to offer any sustained narrative in support of an alternative reading of the Fourteenth Amendment. After about 130 pages of Black-bashing, Fairman concluded that "pretty clearly there never was any such clear conception" of precisely what would be included in and excluded from section 1's commands.* Nevertheless, Fairman cast his lot with Frankfurter, suggesting that principles of fundamental fairness and ordered liberty were probably better touchstones than anything else. And "surely," Fairman emphasized, "the federal requirements as to juries were not included."[27]

Fairman was half-right. Nothing in the words or history of section 1 yields a precise principle of *exclusion*. Had its framers intended to limit its scope to privileges, rights, and freedoms declared in the pre-1866 Constitution, better words could have been found. But nothing in Fairman's account of the legislative history of the Thirty-ninth Congress shows that jury-trial rights, or any other provisions of the federal Bill, were not seen as fundamental. Howard, for example, plainly said that all the privileges and immunities of Amendments I–VIII were included, but he also simultaneously described them as "these great fundamental guarantees."[28] Wilson's words in the Thirty-ninth Congress were almost identical, referring to "the great fundamental rights embraced in the bill of rights," which he had moments earlier described as "the great fundamental rights belonging to the citizen."[29] Wilson's Senate cosponsor of the Civil Rights Act was Lyman Trumbull, and he, too, equated constitutional rights with fundamental rights: "Each State, so [long as] it does not abridge the great fundamental rights belonging, under the Constitution, to all citizens, may grant or withhold such civil rights as it pleases . . . ."[30]

Thus we find repeated claims that all privileges and immunities guaranteed in the Bill are indeed fundamental and worthy of Fourteenth

---

*Fairman, *supra* page 183, note, at 138. I use the word *bashing* advisedly. Though his work has drawn much praise, in my view Professor Fairman was unfair to Justice Black, and his unfair substance and tone put almost an entire generation of lawyers, judges, and law professors off track.

Amendment protection. In light of these emphatic claims, did anyone argue that jury provisions—or any other rights—in the Bill were *not* fundamental, and should *not* be imposed on states? Fairman presents no one. He instead tries to make hay out of speeches about fundamental rights that did not explicitly mention the Bill of Rights. Typical of this dubious strategy is his treatment of Senator John B. Henderson, who, several days after Howard's speech, said, "[I]t will be a loss of time to discuss the remaining provisions of the section, for they merely secure the rights that attach to citizenship in all free Governments."[31] Fairman commented: "Unless the first eight Amendments enumerate 'rights that attach to citizenship in all free governments,' Henderson's understanding is to be counted as opposed to that of Howard."[32] But Fairman's "unless" swallows up the rest. Howard not only said plainly and at length that the rights in Amendments I–VIII were encompassed by section 1 (which Henderson nowhere denied); and Howard not only simultaneously defined these rights as "fundamental" (again, not a peep from Henderson); but moments later Howard appeared to equate, rather than distinguish between, "the privileges and immunities . . . secured by the first eight amendments of the Constitution" and "those fundamental rights lying at the basis of all society and without which a people cannot exist except as slaves."[33] Henderson's passing comment seems more an echo than a refutation of Howard's elaborate remarks.

We have seen rhetoric like Howard's before. Governor C. P. Van Ness, in his oral argument in *Holmes v. Jennison,* had described the rights in the Bill as "principles which lie at the very foundation of civil liberty"; and in two cases decided years apart, Georgia's Chief Justice Lumpkin had variously described the Bill—explicitly including jury-trial provisions—as declaring "vital truths . . . at the foundation of our free, republican institutions" and rights "at the bottom of every free government."[34] As we have already noted, the idea that rights declared in the Bill were ipso facto fundamental had deep jurisprudential roots in the methodology of the common law and in the fear of unfettered judicial discretion.

The Civil War experience provided powerful ideological, almost religious, reinforcement. The war had of course taken a terrible toll in lives and limbs, and even victory tasted bittersweet. Republicans in 1866 needed to convince their constituents that all had not been in vain, that the noble goals of the Union—preservation of nation and (later) freedom—had been worth the fight and had been won.[35] The Bill was a perfect symbol of both goals, even better in some ways than the Declaration of Independence and the original Constitution. The Declaration had arguably preceded nationhood and featured language of "free and independent states," a phrase repeatedly invoked on behalf of secession.[36] The original Constitution had been tainted by its open compromises with slavery, and it, too, could be seen as the product of independent state conventions, none of which could bind any other (again, points repeatedly emphasized by secessionists).[37] The Bill, by contrast, clearly derived from America as a nation and proclaimed freedom, not slavery. What better embodiment of the slogan, "Freedom National"—especially once the Bill's states'-rights features were filtered out by the phrase "privileges or immunities of *citizens* of the *United States*"?[38]

It has become commonplace to remark upon Lincoln's blending of religious and constitutional rhetoric—in his inaugural and Gettysburg addresses, for example—but Bingham's imagery also bears notice. For him the Bill was not simply "immortal,"[39] as he preached in his maiden sermon in support of his amendment, but "sacred," a word that punctuates his most extended meditation on the Bill:

> As a further security for the enforcement of the Constitution, and especially of this sacred bill of rights, to all the citizens and all the people of the United States, it is further provided that the members of the several State Legislatures and all executive and judicial officers, both of the United States and of the several States, shall be bound by oath or affirmation to support this Constitution. The oath, the most solemn compact which man can make with his Maker, was to bind the State Legislatures, executive officers, and judges to sacredly respect the Constitution and all the rights secured by it. . . .
>
> [The Bill of Rights encompasses] all the sacred rights of person—those rights dear to freemen and formidable only to tyrants—and of

which the fathers of the Republic spoke, after God had given them the victory . . . . [40]

Bingham waxed on at length, proclaiming the need for "fidelity to the sacred cause of the Constitution," describing the Founders' Bill as "essential provisions of your Constitution, divine in their justice, sublime in their humanity," invoking "God" countless times, and in fact closing with a reference to "the imperishable attribute of the God of nations."[41] Given all this iconography, the suggestion that some provisions of the Founders' Decalogue were dispensable would be as jarring (*heretical* is le mot juste) as the claim that some of the Ten Commandments really were not, well, fundamental.

Fairman was remarkably insensitive to all of this and indeed, quite anachronistic. Because he, in 1949, deemed various parts of the Bill to be optional or outdated, he tended to attribute similar views to the 1866 Congress: when Bingham said "bill of rights" he couldn't have meant it; his rhetoric showed sloppy thinking rather than a worldview to be taken seriously; silence on the other side must have meant that Bingham and company had not been understood; for surely some sane lawyer would otherwise have clearly spoken out against such silliness; and so on. Hugo Black, not Charles Fairman, proved the more faithful historian, for he understood—because he shared—the almost mystical attachment to the Bill of Rights exemplified by John Bingham. The title of Black's Carpentier Lectures on incorporation (among other things) says it all, and quite self-consciously: "A Constitutional Faith."[42]

Bingham's constitutional faith was not simply a private affair, for he wove it into the very fabric of the key sentence of section 1. How else to account for the sentence's pious blending of phraseology from no fewer than four sections of the pre-1866 Constitution (Article I, section 10; Article IV; and Amendments I and V) and its paraphrase of a fifth (substituting "citizens" for the Preamble's "We the People")?

Not all of Bingham's colleagues shared his faith, but they, too, had reasons to value virtually every privilege and immunity in the Bill. Even if not sacred because given from above (from the Fathers, the People, or the Almighty), the Bill had proved its secular value—if only by its unavailability—in the trenches of the antebellum crusade against slavery. As we have seen, slavery led to state repudiation of virtually every one of the Bill's rights and freedoms, most definitely including the Bill's "inestimable privilege" of juries—grand, petit, and civil—in cases involving liberty.[43] As it had for Anti-Federalists in the 1780s, the Bill encompassed for Republicans in the 1860s an armory of indispensable weapons against a tyranny that people had seen with their own eyes. The difference, of course, was that unlike the tyranny of George III, the tyranny of slavery could not be blamed on a distant and dictatorial center but instead had been perpetrated by local democracies. Just as the price of peace and union in 1789 was a bill of rights against the center, so the price of peace and (re)union in 1866 was a bill of rights against the periphery.

The Bill thus stood as a handy pledge of the good faith of the South, enforceable by congressional refusal to readmit states that continued to violate its provisions. On the very day that Bingham preached his most extended sermon on the Bill in the House, Senator James Nye proclaimed that Congress had "no power to invade" such privileges of the Bill as "freedom of speech," "freedom of the press," "freedom in the exercise of religion," and the "security of person," but that Congress did have power to "restrain the respective States from infracting them" by continuing to exclude as unrepublican any state violating these "personal rights."[44] Representative Roswell Hart agreed several weeks later, defining a "republican" government as one where: "citizens shall be entitled to all privileges and immunities of other citizens"; where "no law shall be made prohibiting the free exercise of religion"; where "the right of the people to keep and bear arms shall not be infringed"; where "the right of the people to be secure in their persons, houses, papers and effects, against unreasonable searches and seizures, shall not be violated"; and where "no person shall be deprived of life, liberty, or property without due process of law."[45] In a similar vein, Congressman Samuel Moulton argued against readmittance of various southern states because "there is neither freedom of speech, of the press, or protection to life, liberty, or property"; Representative Sidney Clarke opposed restoration of Mississippi to Congress because the state's policies disarming blacks violated the Second Amendment command that "the right of the people to keep and bear arms shall not be infringed"; and Representative Leonard Myers sought to exclude Alabama because of its "anti-republican laws" that banned firearms.[46]

In all of these roles—as a declaratory landmark for judges trying to find higher law, as a postwar symbol of "Freedom National," as a sacred gift from above, as a time-tested arsenal against tyranny, as a ready-made pledge of states' good faith, as a justiciable definition of republican government, and as a prudent bar against hasty readmission of the South—the Bill as a whole was more than the sum of its parts. Thus Fairman failed to find Republicans in the Thirty-ninth Congress picking the Bill apart, saying this right is fundamental but that right is not.

In spite of its flaws, Fairman's analysis does yield two important insights that any sensitive theory of incorporation must accommodate. First, Fairman rightly saw that the Bill of Rights was invoked in 1866 at a rather high level of generality. Virtually no one in Congress or in the states carefully considered clause by clause and right by right exactly how the Bill could be sensibly incorporated. Second, Fairman understood the Bill of 1789 as a creature of its time and intuited that some of its features might not fit well with the basic purposes of the Fourteenth Amendment, had these features been carefully considered in 1866. Fairman's precise formulation of this intuition—that "surely the federal requirements as to juries were not" part of section 1[47]—is dubious; but we shall see that various aspects of the original Bill, including its jury centerpieces, do not mechanically incorporate jot for jot. Perhaps we should recast Fairman's formulation as follows: "surely the federal[ism-based] requirements" in the original Bill should not be unthinkingly imposed on states.

Berger Whereas Fairman argued for a more open-ended alternative to mechanical incorporation, Raoul Berger followed Hugo Black by suggesting that section 1 had a precisely determinate meaning. But while Black read section 1 as a term of art meaning "No State shall abridge the Bill of Rights," Berger read the section as a very different term of art. Berger's argument proceeded in two steps. First, he insisted that section 1's commands were identical in meaning to those of the Civil Rights Act of 1866.[48] Second, he read that act narrowly, denying that the act itself

in any way incorporated the Bill of Rights.[49] Although each step in isolation is problematic enough, the biggest question is how Berger can
conjoin them, for each step in fact undoes the other.

The Civil Rights Act presents a great many interpretive riddles of its
own, which would take us far afield; but it is enough to note here that its
intricate phrasings have almost no textual overlap with the wording of
the key sentence of section 1.* If the two were supposed to be not merely complementary but identical, why did the same Congress use radically different words? At the very least, why did section 1 not explicitly refer to the act? Does Berger believe that the key sentence applied in the
territories, as the Civil Rights Act plainly did? Does he believe that the
Civil Rights Act—which pointedly speaks only of "citizens"—protects
aliens, too, as the due-process and equal-protection clauses clearly do?[50]

Of course, section 1 did not explicitly refer to "the Bill of Rights"
either, but as we saw earlier, any such simplistic reference would have been
both over- and underinclusive. Berger, by contrast, claims that the act and
section 1 were mathematically identical, despite the lack of textual overlap or cross-reference. Nothing in the text of the key sentence would lead
an ordinary reader to understand it to exactly mirror the rather obscure
and highly intricate words of a recent congressional statute, however important the statute might be. By contrast, ordinary Americans familiar
since childhood with the Bill of Rights were well positioned to understand its "rights" and "freedoms" as paradigmatic, even if not exhaustive,
of their "privileges" and "immunities" as "citizens of the United States."

*In relevant part, the act provided:

[C]itizens of the United States . . . of every race and color, without regard to any previous condition of slavery or involuntary servitude, except as a punishment for crime
whereof the party shall have been duly convicted, shall have the same right, in every
State and Territory in the United States, to make and enforce contracts, to sue, be
parties, and give evidence, to inherit, purchase, lease, sell, hold, and convey real and
personal property, and to full and equal benefit of all laws and proceedings for the
security of person and property, as is enjoyed by white citizens, and shall be subject to
like punishment, pains, and penalties, and to none other, any law, statute, ordinance,
regulation, or custom, to the contrary notwithstanding.

Act of Apr. 9, 1866, ch. 31, §1, 14 Stat. 27 (1866).

(Recall that the Bill was in fact worded so that, like Scripture, it might be easily memorized and internalized by ordinary Americans.)[51] Moreover, section 1's self-conscious blending of phrases from the pre-1866 Constitution would cue a careful reader to look to the Constitution first for (nonexhaustive) definitions of the rights and privileges of Americans.

In any event, the legislative history fails to establish the precise identity that Berger claims, but rather illustrates only that the broad language of section 1 was consciously designed and widely understood to encompass—that is, to be at least as broad as—the commands of the Civil Rights Act in the states. As its language and its proponents made clear, and no one denied, section 1 was also consciously designed to encompass the guarantees of the Bill of Rights. This is actually less confusing than it might sound; for the Civil Rights Act itself could plausibly be understood to incorporate the citizen rights and freedoms of the Bill of Rights. Berger tries to argue that the act prohibited only racial discrimination, but if so, the first step of his argument collapses. For if section 1 and the act were indeed identical in their substantive scope, as he insists, then the act must go beyond nondiscrimination to require states to provide all persons with due process. The act does contain language that can be read to incorporate due-process requirements; but as Michael Kent Curtis has shown, that very same language must also then be read to incorporate all the other rights and privileges of the Bill of Rights.*

---

*See MICHAEL KENT CURTIS, NO STATE SHALL ABRIDGE: THE FOURTEENTH AMENDMENT AND THE BILL OF RIGHTS 71–83 (1986); Michael Kent Curtis, *Further Adventures of the Nine-Lived Cat: A Response to Mr. Berger on Incorporation of the Bill of Rights*, 43 Ohio St. L.J. 90, 105–6 (1982). Though clumsily drafted, the act's last clause speaks of the "full . . . benefit of all laws and proceedings for the security of person and property." The rights and freedoms of the federal Bill had long been understood as fitting this description. Blackstone, for example, catalogued various common law antecedents of the Bill of Rights as encompassing "the right of personal security, the right of personal liberty, and the right of private property"; and Lumpkin in *Campbell* had described the federal Bill as providing "security for personal liberty and private property." 1 WILLIAM BLACKSTONE, COMMENTARIES *127–45; Campbell v. State, 11 Ga. 353, 372 (1853); *see also* JOEL TIFFANY, A TREATISE ON THE UNCONSTITUTIONALITY OF AMERICAN SLAVERY 97 (Cleveland: J. Calyer, 1849) (leading antebellum antislavery tract describing Bill of Rights as "guarantys . . . for personal security, personal liberty and pri-

Berger's argument thus self-destructs. To save his first step, we must read the act to go beyond nondiscrimination (for due process has bite against even nondiscriminatory laws); but in so doing, we undermine Berger's second step, which tries to neuter the incorporationist language of the act. To put the point another way, the more we insist on the link-

---

vate property"); *Ex parte* Milligan, 71 U.S. (4 Wall.) 2, 119–20 (1866) (contemporary Supreme Court case labeling Amendments Four, Five, and Six "securities for personal liberty"); CONG. GLOBE, 39th Cong., 1st Sess. 1833 (1866) (remarks of Rep. William Lawrence) (linking language of civil rights bill with due-process clause of "the bill of rights to the national Constitution"); *id.* at 1152–53 (similar remarks of Rep. M. Russell Thayer). In the Thirty-ninth Congress, Senator Lyman Trumbull introduced the Civil Rights Act by saying that it would protect the rights to teach, preach, and possess firearms—rights declared in the first two federal amendments. *Id.* at 474–75; *see also id.* at 478, 1266, 3210 (remarks of Sen. Willard Saulsbury and Reps. Henry Raymond and George Julian) (noting that act encompassed right to carry arms). Trumbull's House counterpart, James Wilson, declared that the act would protect "the great fundamental rights embraced in the bill of rights" and Bingham linked the act to the "bill of rights" six times. *Id.* at 1291–94. Consider also the Civil Rights Act's fraternal twin, the Freedman's Bureau Act. Initially introduced by the same sponsor on the same day, and featuring key provisions worded in almost the same language, the bills were understood as *in pari materia.* As finally adopted, the Freedman's Bureau Act spoke of the "full . . . benefit of all laws and proceedings concerning personal liberty, personal security, and [property,] *including the constitutional right to bear arms.*" 14 Stat. 173, 176 (1866) (emphasis added). This last clause was understood as declaratory, simply clarifying what was already implicit. HORACE EDGAR FLACK, THE ADOPTION OF THE FOURTEENTH AMENDMENT 17 (1908); CONG. GLOBE, 39th Cong., 1st Sess. 743 (1866) (remarks of Sen. Lyman Trumbull). All of this thus suggests that the right to bear arms—and presumably all other rights and freedoms in the Bill of Rights—were encompassed by both the Freedman's Bureau Act and its companion Civil Rights Act. (Of course, adoption of both acts presupposed congressional power to impose the general requirements of the Bill of Rights on states. Bingham, relying on *Barron,* denied that Congress had such power and argued that a constitutional amendment was thus required to validate the Civil Rights Act. CONG. GLOBE, 39th Cong., 1st Sess. 1291–93 (1866).)

It should also be noted that the first sentence of the Civil Rights Act proclaimed blacks to be citizens; and under a strong declaratory vision this proclamation itself carried with it all the privileges and immunities of national citizenship. *See id.* at 1088, 1153, 1266, 1757, 1832–33 (remarks of Reps. Frederick E. Woodbridge, M. Russell Thayer and Henry Raymond, Sen. Lyman Trumbull and Rep. William Lawrence); *see also infra* page 281, note.

age between the act and section 1, the more relevant the language and legislative history of the amendment become in clarifying the intricate wording of the act. And the amendment's language and legislative history do indeed cross-reference the rights and freedoms of the Bill of Rights.*

Berger's emphasis on the Civil Rights Act is nevertheless instructive. Much of the language and legislative history of the act stressed the importance of fundamental, Blackstonian common-law rights. As we shall see, Blackstone and the common-law tradition may help us separate those aspects of the pre-1866 Constitution that are indeed privileges or immunities of citizens from other aspects that may not sensibly incorporate.

Ratification: The Sounds of Silence

The Thirty-ninth Congress, of course, had only the power to propose. Yet both the text of section 1 and the public gloss Congress placed on that text made clear that Congress was proposing nothing less than a transformation of the original Bill of Rights. Fairman argues that virtually no one during the ratification debates explicitly reaffirmed incorporation, but Michael Kent Curtis has shown that here, too, Fairman overlooks a great deal of affirmative evidence for incorporation.[52] Moreover, the evidence that we have canvassed thus far warrants shifting the burden, at least of production, onto those who would claim that section 1 somehow changed its meaning during the ratification process. Yet Fairman presents not a single soul who explicitly denied that the text meant what it said: that no state shall abridge the rights and freedoms of Americans, most obviously those declared in the Bill of Rights.

*Berger's misstatements, distortions, and non sequiturs are legion, but two especially egregious claims merit special response: (1) "No reference to the Bill of Rights is to be found in the history of the Civil Rights Bill . . . ." and (2) "The [Civil Rights] Bill made no provision for a right to 'assemble or bear arms' nor did any spokesman for it read these terms into the bill." RAOUL BERGER, THE FOURTEENTH AMENDMENT AND THE BILL OF RIGHTS 24 n.21, 73 (1989). The speeches quoted or cited in the preceding footnote alone suffice to establish the gross error of such claims.

Fairman argues that if we listen carefully, we can hear a roaring silence that overwhelms incorporation. Rather than stuffing words into Fairman's mouth, I shall let him speak for himself, with my italics added:

> If it was understood, in the legislatures that considered the proposed Amendment, that its adoption would impose upon the state governments the provisions of the federal Bill of Rights, then *almost certainly* each legislature would take note of what the effect would be upon the constitutional law and practice of its own state. If, for instance, the state permitted one charged with "a capital or otherwise infamous crime" to be tried upon information rather than "on a presentment or indictment of a Grand Jury" (Amend. V) . . . *presumably* its legislature would not knowingly ratify such an Amendment without giving some thought to the implications. . . . [W]here the imposition of Amendments I to VIII would put a stop to some established practice, such as the mode of trial in civil or criminal cases, then *surely*—if the Amendment was really supposed to incorporate the Bill of Rights—one would *expect* to find a *marked* reaction. . . . Conversely, if we found disparity coupled with complete inaction, it would be *very hard* to believe the Fourteenth Amendment was understood to have that effect.[53]

As I hope my italics indicate, Fairman builds his argument on the assumption that the implications of section 1's key sentence were carefully considered during the ratification period. To twentieth-century readers, this seems an obviously sensible assumption. Isn't the key sentence the centerpiece of the Fourteenth Amendment? Yet as Fairman's own evidence shows, his assumption is false. His argument built on silence is an argument built on sand.

Fairman's most dramatic evidence concerns the grand jury. In nine or ten states, state constitutional provisions already on the books in 1866 or state constitutional amendments seriously considered shortly before or after had less stringent grand-jury rules than those prescribed by the Fifth Amendment. Yet these gaps were never discussed, leading Fairman to argue that incorporation could not have been intended.[54] Once again, I shall give the man some rope:

[A]n episode [from the Illinois constitutional convention of 1869–70] argues very persuasively that there was no contemporary understanding that the Fourteenth Amendment had incorporated the Bill of Rights. . . . [R]esolutions were offered looking to the abolition of the grand jury, . . . [leading Orville H. Browning] to urge the retention of the grand jury, "to which our ancestors had been accustomed" even before the foundation of our nation. Evidently he put all his strength into the speech. But he never so much as suggested that the Fourteenth Amendment incorporated the federal Bill of Rights and thus had fastened the grand jury upon the several states.

Another delegate, James McCoy, spoke with deep feeling of this "bulwark," this "wall of defense," this "sheet-anchor of our liberties" [yet failed to argue explicitly that the Fourteenth Amendment incorporated the Fifth] . . . .

. . . .

. . . If there was any idea among informed men in Michigan that the Fourteenth Amendment incorporated the Fifth, surely counsel would raise the point in appealing some conviction. . . . [T]his is even more significant than a strong decision, since in criminal cases even the most forlorn hope would have been pursued.[55]

All this seems to be very impressive anti-incorporation evidence indeed—until, that is, one gives the matter the slightest thought. If Fairman's claim was that section 1 was utterly meaningless, imposing no obligations whatsoever on states, these data points would indeed fit the hypothesis. Fairman wisely avoided this outlandish claim, arguing instead that section 1 simply required fundamental fairness and ordered liberty. But if the debate is between incorporation and fundamental fairness—between Black and Frankfurter—the silence that Fairman trumpets becomes background noise with no resolving power whatsoever. If Orville Browning and James McCoy failed to argue that the Fourteenth Amendment "incorporated" the Fifth, they equally failed to argue that it required ordered liberty and fundamental fairness. Yet such an argument would have buttressed their claims that the grand jury should be retained because the institution was fundamental—"a wall of defense" to which "our ancestors had been accustomed," a "bulwark," a "sheet-anchor of our liberties." Clearly an institution as venerable and wide-spread as the grand jury, with roots in the mythic "ancient constitution" of England and in force in 1866 in all but a handful of states, could be plausibly claimed to be implicit in ordered liberty. Even if such an argument was not a knockdown winner, it was more than a "forlorn hope." Yet Fairman's vaunted "informed men in Michigan" did not raise this particular argument either. They simply did not speak to the Fourteenth Amendment at all, and thus their silence, interesting as it may be, has no legal resolving power between Black and Frankfurter.

Fairman's anachronistic hostility to grand juries[56] led him to dismiss the possibility that these bodies might have been seen as "fundamental" in the mid-nineteenth century; but consider the words of Massachusetts Chief Justice Lemuel Shaw in a leading state court opinion authored less than a decade before the Fourteenth Amendment. The grand jury, said Shaw, was a "*fundamental* principle[] of free government," one of the "ancient *immunities* and *privileges* of English liberty."[57] Shaw also argued that the placement of a given right in "a bill of rights," state or federal, was itself evidence of its "fundamental" nature[58]—an argument which, if taken seriously, causes Fairman's approach to collapse into incorporation.

But Fairman's problems are only beginning. Forget about the privileges-or-immunities clause for a moment. Whatever else it does or does not require, section 1 undeniably mandates that states follow "due process of law." Now this phrase had a rich tradition, going back to Sir Edward Coke's famous commentaries on Magna Charta, where the great lord chief justice defined the core meaning of the phrase as "indictment or presentment of good and lawfull men"—that is, a grand jury.[59] American lawyers were intimately familiar with Coke's definition. Many citations could be drawn from seventeenth- and eighteenth-century sources, including Penn, Adams, and Hamilton,[60] but for our purposes the major nineteenth-century legal authorities are even more significant. Here is what Joseph Story wrote in his influential *Commentaries on the Constitution:* "Lord Coke says, that [the words *by the law of the land*] mean by due process of law, [which in turn means] due presentment or indictment, and being brought in to answer thereto by due process of the common law. So that this clause [that is, the due-process clause of the Fifth Amendment] in effect affirms the right of trial according to the process and proceedings of the common law."[61] Early editions of Chancellor Kent's *Commentaries on American Law* are even more emphatic: "The words by the *law of the land,* as used in *magna charta . . .* are understood to mean due process of law, that is, by indictment or presentment of good and lawful men; and this, says Lord Coke, is the true sense and exposition of those words."[62]

In perhaps the most famous abolitionist opinion of the antebellum era, the 1854 case of *In re Booth,*[63] the Wisconsin Supreme Court quoted this excerpt from Kent verbatim in a key passage holding Congress's Fugitive Slave Act unconstitutional (a holding decisively reversed by the Taney Court when the case finally reached it under the name of *Ableman v. Booth*).[64] Similarly, in the 1857 case of *Jones v. Robbins,* Chief Justice Shaw not only cited Kent and Story but went on to hold that the words of the Massachusetts Constitution, echoing Magna Charta, required grand juries in all cases involving infamous punishment: "Lord Coke himself explains his own meaning by saying, 'the law of the land,' as expressed in *Magna Charta,* was intended due process of law, that is, by indictment or presentment of good and lawful men."[65] Consider also the language of Alvan Stewart in one of the leading antislavery tracts of the antebellum era, an 1837 essay that Professor tenBroek has identified as a major source of Republican thought in the 1860s: "[N]o lawyer in this country or England, who is worthy of the appellation, will deny that the true and only meaning of the phrase, 'due process of law,' is an indictment or presentment by a grand jury, of not less than twelve, nor more than twenty-three men; a trial by a petit jury of twelve men, and a judgment pronounced on the finding of the jury, by a court."[66]

We need not say that due process in 1866 meant nothing more than grand juries—Story and Stewart seemed to read the clause more sweepingly; later editions of Kent followed suit; and, of course, *Murray's Lessee* also suggested a broader understanding, even as the Court unanimously reiterated that "due process" was "undoubtedly intended to convey the same meaning as the words, 'by the law of the land,' in *Magna Charta*."[67] (There are also questions about redundancy if we assume that the Fifth Amendment's due-process clause merely replicated its grand-jury clause.) We need not even say definitively that due process in 1866 necessarily included a grand-jury requirement;[68] it is enough to say that the argument was a very strong one indeed, supported by eminent legal authorities on both sides of the Atlantic.[69] Yet Fairman's "informed men in Michigan," Illinois, and elsewhere apparently did not even pause to consider this eminently plausible reading of the due-process clause of the Fourteenth Amendment.

What does this prove? Not that the words *due process* never meant grand juries; for we have seen far too much contrary evidence. Not even that the meaning of *due process* miraculously changed in 1866, for it would take more than uninformed and unreflective silence to prove this. Rather, Fairman's own data clearly show that, contrary to his workhorse assumptions, many informed men simply were not thinking carefully about the words of section 1 at all.[70] The upshot is that silence alone is a dubious key to unlocking the meaning of section 1.[71]

Nor can it be argued that silence in fact demonstrates that section 1 meant nothing (the outlandish position that Fairman wisely eschewed). Much of the silence that Fairman finds crucial came not from state legislatures ratifying the amendment but from subsequent state conventions and the like. Even during the ratification process, silence about a provision did not magically erase it from the text. If it did, we would have to blot out many key provisions of the original Constitution, not to mention the original Bill of Rights.

But even if the silence that Fairman trumpeted has little power to resolve the incorporation debate, we should stop to consider what this silence does tell us about both the Fourteenth Amendment and the Bill of Rights. Let us begin by taking seriously the analogy between the original Constitution and the Fourteenth Amendment. Many key provisions of the original document received relatively little attention during ratification simply because there were so many other important things to talk about. The same was true of the Fourteenth Amendment. The point is not simply quantitative—the five sections of the Fourteenth Amendment contain about as many words as the first ten amendments put together—but qualitative. The Fourteenth Amendment proposed nothing less than a comprehensive blueprint for the Reconstruction—the Re-Constitution—of a nation torn asunder by the Civil War.[72] (Hence the amendment's gestation in the Joint Committee on Reconstruction.)

Although twentieth-century readers rarely look past the key sentence of section 1, politicians of the day who did the proposing and ratifying saw other provisions as more important. Section 2 laid down new rules for representation in Congress, and section 3 determined which southern leaders would be eligible to hold state or federal office. Taken together, these two provisions could profoundly shape the configuration of political power in America. Thus, even in the Fourteenth Amendment, structural issues predominated. Although Thaddeus Stevens opened his formal exposition of the amendment by briefly noting that section 1 would reverse the *Barron* rule,[73] he devoted far more attention to later sections that sought to determine who would control the country in the critical years ahead: "The second section I consider the most important in the article."[74] A few days later when a draft of section 3 came under fire, Stevens responded: "Without that, [the amendment] amounts to nothing. I do not care the snap of my finger whether it be passed or not if that be stricken out. Before another Congress shall have assembled here, and before [the rest of the amendment] can be carried into full effect, there will be no friends of the Union left on this side of the House to carry it out . . . . [T]he House will be filled with yelling secessionists and hissing copperheads. Give us the third section or give us nothing."[75] The ratification debates confirm Stevens's views about the importance of sections 2 and 3, though of course Americans disagreed sharply about whether these provisions commended or condemned the amendment.[76]

In addition, the amendment gave rise to fierce debates over issues not presented on the face of the document but inextricably intertwined with it: the legitimacy of the rump Congress that had proposed the amendment, the legality of various efforts to condition southern readmission to Congress on the amendment's ratification, the exclusion of Democrats from key caucuses discussing the amendment, and Congress's failure to "present" the amendment to President Andrew Johnson.[77]

All this brings us to a second similarity between the original Constitution and the Fourteenth Amendment: partisan feeling ran high in both ratification periods. In 1787 and 1788, partisanship led Federalists to vote quickly and quietly in those state conventions where they had the votes, leaving relatively little record of their formal deliberations. But in the state conventions of Virginia, Massachusetts, New York, and North Carolina, Anti-Federalists and fence-sitters constituted an initial majority of the delegates, obliging Federalists to do much more explaining. In 1866 the Thirty-ninth Congress followed the Philadelphia convention model by shrouding early deliberations in the secrecy of the Joint Committee on Reconstruction. Just as Americans in 1787 had waited with increasing apprehension for the word from Philadelphia, people in 1866 impatiently looked for white smoke to emerge from the mysterious Joint Committee conclave. When official proposals did finally issue, their public exposition by leading architects like Bingham, Howard, and Stevens received special attention. But as in the 1780s, partisanship impoverished deliberation. Many of the key discussions in Washington "were carried on not in the legal Senate of the United States, but in a party meeting"[78] from which Democrats were excluded. And during the ratification debates, many Republicans again kept silent in public deliberations, content that they had the votes to pass the amendment and fearful that any statement might give Democrats political ammunition.[79]

So much, then, for what Fairman's silence tells us about the Fourteenth Amendment. What does it say about the Bill of Rights? Mainly that the Bill was relatively uncontroversial in 1866. As Michael Kent Curtis and William Winslow Crosskey have painstakingly proved, the vast majority of Republican leaders in 1866 were contrarians.[80] Some, like Bingham, were highly conscious of *Barron*, while others had apparently never heard of the case. Yet all could agree that Bingham's section 1 was simply declaratory of preexisting rights and freedoms of citizens, many of which had already been declared by the Fathers.[81] The biggest section 1 debate among Republicans was not what the words meant, but whether the words were necessary, given that the rights they protected already existed. Thus a committee of the Massachusetts legislature opposed the Fourteenth Amendment because existing amendments, including the First (which of course spoke explicitly of Congress), already "cover[ed] the whole ground" of section 1.[82] Given that most Republicans viewed section 1 as declaratory, it received considerably less attention during ratification than the more radical changes proposed by later sections.

Democratic critics of the amendment also had much easier targets than section 1. Who wants to campaign against the Bill of Rights? With a few exceptions, most notably the grand-jury rules we have already considered, the substance of the federal Bill's rights and freedoms did not greatly diverge from rights already formally protected under state laws and state constitutions. True, the slavery experience led many states to betray their own constitutional safeguards of speech, press, personal security, and the like, but the principles themselves were deeply etched in both the popular and the legal mind. Given this, one would expect that opposition to section 1 would find expression in the idiom of federalism: responsibility for preservation of citizen rights, freedoms, privileges, and immunities should not be handed over to Congress and federal courts but should remain with the states. And this is exactly the kind of rhetoric that one does find during ratification.[83]

Finally, we must remember that the Bill of Rights had yet to prove itself in the courtroom as a powerful brake on runaway government. The antebellum crusaders against slavery had sorely felt the lack of a federally enforceable bill of rights against states, but no one had seen exactly how much protection such a bill would in fact afford. Judicial review of Congress, though trumpeted in *Marbury v. Madison,*[84] had little bite before 1866: the only successful invocation of the Bill of Rights against Congress in the Supreme Court was *Dred Scott*'s malodorous dictum that exclusion of slavery from the territories violated due process.[85] The truly important exercises of judicial review in the antebellum era had come at the expense of state governments, not Congress[86]—and *Barron* had made clear that the Founders' Bill of Rights was inapplicable in state cases. Though the transformative possibilities of incorporation should have been obvious to anyone who had seen what the Marshall Court had done with the sparse words of Article I, section 10 in cases like *Fletcher v. Peck* and *Dartmouth College,* a well-developed Supreme Court jurisprudence of the Bill of Rights had yet to emerge. Indeed, as I hope to show in Chapter 12, the eventual emergence of this jurisprudence in the twentieth century owes far more to the Fourteenth Amendment than to anything in the original Bill.

Early Interpretation: In Search of Reasons

Postratification discussions of the Fourteenth Amendment cannot change its original meaning but can cast light backward. In examining early interpretations, we must not simply count noses but also weigh reasons: do any of the early interpretations of the amendment deepen our understanding of the evidence that we have seen thus far?

Here, too, silence alone will prove relatively unhelpful. Consider, for example, the 1869 case of *Twitchell v. Pennsylvania,* where the Supreme Court brusquely dismissed claims that the state had violated various provisions of the Fifth and Sixth Amendments.[87] Though neither counsel nor the Court even mentioned the newly ratified Fourteenth Amendment, various critics of Justice Black have argued that the silence alone is devastating to the incorporation thesis. Thus Felix Frankfurter wrote as follows in his parting memorandum in the *Harvard Law Review:* "*Twitchell* [indicates that no one] even thought of proposing that these amendments had been newly brought to bear on the States by the Fourteenth. Yet the Fourteenth's formulation and adoption had been a subject of great interest, especially to lawyers and judges, only months prior to the decision of these cases. The significance of this contemporaneous understanding need not be labored."[88] Raoul Berger agreed: "Oversight will not account for the omission; the Amendment had been widely discussed; bench and bar are alert to every new and relevant enactment; they would not be oblivious to the revolution worked by the alleged incorporation of the Bill of Rights."[89] Fairman, too, thought *Twitchell* quite impressive evidence: "[I]t did not occur to counsel for the petitioner to suggest that the Fourteenth Amendment, adopted less than a year before, had worked any change in the law applicable to the case. . . . Even though counsel for the petitioner had failed to invoke the *Fourteenth* Amendment, one supposes that the Court, had it been stirred by the least uncertainty, would have suggested the question and heard argument before disposing of the petition of one sentenced to death."[90]

But had Fairman, Frankfurter, or Berger paused to examine their supposed trump card before playing it with such flourish, they might have realized that *Twitchell* is in fact an embarrassing joker. Counsel explicitly argued, among other things, that Pennsylvania had violated "due process of law" but invoked only the Fifth Amendment—a (literally) fatal mistake, for the Court simply rejected the claim with a quick citation to *Barron*.[91] But again, what does this prove? If *Twitchell*'s silence is evidence that the Fourteenth Amendment does not incorporate earlier amendments, it is equally strong evidence that the Fourteenth does not require state due process. But in light of the plain words of the Fourteenth Amendment, this latter claim is absurd. *Twitchell*'s silence thus proves too much—and therefore nothing at all. Or more precisely, it, proves that, contrary to Berger and Fairman's glib assumptions, only "oversight will [] account for the omission"; "bench and bar are [not] alert to every new and relevant enactment"; and the Court did not pay careful attention "before disposing of the petition of one sentenced to death."* Frankfurter notwithstanding, *Twitchell*'s embarrassing silence shows no "contemporaneous understanding" and has no "significance" in the incorporation debate.

When we turn instead to what important decisionmakers actually did

---

Twitchell is perhaps explicable as an unthinking reflection of the notion that section I would have its main application in southern states. *See* Fairman, *supra* page 183, note, at 112; RAOUL BERGER, GOVERNMENT BY JUDICIARY 150–55 (1977); R. BERGER, FOURTEENTH AMENDMENT, *supra* page 197, note, at 38–39; HAROLD M. HYMAN AND WILLIAM M. WIECEK, EQUAL JUSTICE UNDER LAW 414 (1982). But surely the amendment as written applies to all states, North and South, as later (more self-conscious) courts have made undeniably clear. Thus to understand and explain *Twitchell* is not to justify it, much less use it as a springboard for serious Fourteenth Amendment analysis, as Frankfurter and company appear to. *Cf.* CONG. GLOBE, 39th Cong. 1st Sess. 158 (1866) (remarks of Rep. John Bingham noting that "in some sense, all the States of the Union" had flouted "the absolute guarantees of the Constitution").

say when they focused on the relation between the Fourteenth Amendment and the Bill, we find powerful confirmation of incorporation. Over and over in the years between 1868 and 1873, various members of Congress, both Democrats and Republicans, suggested that the Bill of Rights defined paradigmatic privileges and immunities of Americans that no state could abridge and that Congress could protect by legislation under section 5 of the Fourteenth Amendment. This was no idle chatter, for Congress in fact legislated on the basis of this understanding.[92]

From left to right, the dominant congressional ideology of the time came from the declaratory theory that we first glimpsed in Chapter 7. Thus in 1872 Republican Senator John Sherman declared that the "privileges, immunities, and rights, (because I do not distinguish between them, and cannot do it,) of citizens of the United States" may be found in "the common law," "the great charters of England," "the Constitution of the United States," "the constitutions of the different States," the "Declaration of Independence," and other authoritative declarations.[93] Or as Democratic Senator Reverdy Johnson, who had represented the slavemaster in *Dred Scott*, put the point in an 1866 oral argument in the Supreme Court: "The Constitution of the United States, to be sure, so far as the article which proclaims that there shall be no interference with religion is concerned, is not obligatory upon the State of Missouri; but it announces a great principle of American liberty, a principle deeply seated in the American mind [that no legislature, even a state legislature, should violate]."[94]

In light of this reigning ideology, consider the now-familiar words of section 1983 of Title 42, first adopted as section 1 of the act of April 20, 1871, known as "An Act to Enforce the Provisions of the Fourteenth Amendment to the Constitution of the United States, and for other Purposes."[95] The clear words of this section prohibited state officers from depriving persons of "any rights, privileges, or immunities secured by the Constitution." Given declaratory theory, this Enforcement Act section plainly obliged states to honor rights proclaimed in the federal Bill. Even congressional conservatives and Democrats recognized congressional power to go this far[96]—they simply challenged Congress's right to go further: states should be bound by the Bill of Rights, but Congress should not enjoy free-floating power to bind states to new rights or to regulate private persons at will. (Other sections of the Enforcement Act were thus hotly contested, for they did seek to regulate "private" conspiracies against federal rights.)

Perhaps the most illuminating case arising under Reconstruction-era legislation was the 1871 circuit court case *United States v. Hall.* In the course of deciding whether Congress had power to legislate under section 5 of the Fourteenth Amendment, Judge (later Justice) William Woods had to confront the words of the amendment's section 1. His conclusion plainly supported incorporation: "We think, therefore, that the . . . rights enumerated in the first eight articles of amendment to the constitution of the United States are the privileges and immunities of citizens of the United States."[97] But it is his reasoning that is most illuminating. Like Rawle, Lumpkin, Shaw, Howard, Wilson, and many others, Woods treated rights declared in the Constitution as ipso facto fundamental, following the classic methodology of finding the common law: "What are the privileges and immunities of citizens of the United States here referred to [in section 1]? They are undoubtedly those which may be denominated fundamental; which belong of right to the citizens of all free states, and which have at all times been enjoyed by citizens of the several states which compose this Union . . . . Corfield v. Coryell. Among these we are safe in including those which in the constitution are expressly secured to the people, either as against the action of the federal or state governments."[98]

Several months before *Hall,* Woods had held circuit court with Justice Joseph Bradley in New Orleans, where they heard the *Crescent City Live-stock Case.* In this case, the two judges had avoided a comprehensive definition of "the essential privileges which belong to a citizen of the United States, as such," but had equated them with "fundamental principles of free government."[99] No specific mention was made of the Bill of Rights, but Bradley's 1871 correspondence with Woods showed that the justice endorsed *Hall*'s methodology and result. Indeed, the passage from Woods that we have just seen was lifted almost verbatim from a letter that Bradley had written to Woods.[100] In a still earlier letter to

Woods, Bradley wrote as follows: "The right of the people to assemble together and discuss political questions . . . is one of the most sacred rights of citizenship, and cannot be abridged by any state. . . . [This right is protected] against a state . . . as one of the privileges and immunities belonging to all citizens . . . [b]y the 14th amendment . . . ."[101]

Members of the executive branch and other legal commentators shared the views expressed in Bradley's letter. In another 1871 case, U.S. Attorney Daniel Corbin invoked *Barron* and then declared that "the fourteenth amendment changes all that theory, and lays the same restriction upon the States that before lay upon the Congress of the United States—that, as Congress heretofore could not interfere with the right of the citizen to keep and bear arms, now, after the adoption of the fourteenth amendment, the State cannot interfere with the right of the citizen to keep and bear arms. The right to keep and bear arms is included in the fourteenth amendment, under 'privileges and immunities.'"[102]

As Dean Richard Aynes has painstakingly proved, similar views marked all three of the major constitutional treatises that were published after proposal but before ratification of the Fourteenth Amendment and that addressed the amendment.[103] John Norton Pomeroy viewed section 1 as "a remedy" for *Barron's* rule concerning "the immunities and privileges guarded by the Bill of Rights"; similarly, Timothy Farrar carefully elaborated the declaratory theory of the federal Bill—indeed, in a later, 1872 edition of his treatise, Farrar noted that the amendment had "swept away" *Barron* and its progeny.[104] Finally, in an 1868 treatise, George Paschal noted in passing—as if the issue were obvious—that "the general principles which had been construed to apply only to the national government, are thus imposed [by the Fourteenth] upon the States. Most of the States, in general terms, had adopted the same bill of rights in their own constitutions."[105]

Justice Bradley's position became public in 1873, when he got a second crack at the *Crescent City* case, then on appeal as one of the famous *Slaughter-House Cases*.[106] The cases provided the Supreme Court its first opportunity to carefully reflect and opine on the Fourteenth Amendment, and Bradley in dissent offered the most comprehensive analysis of the issue that most concerns us: the relation between the new amendment and the rights recognized in the pre-1866 Constitution. Wrote Bradley:

> The people of this country brought with them to its shores the rights of Englishmen . . . . [Bradley then cited and discussed "fundamental rights" found in, among other places, Magna Charta, Blackstone's *Commentaries*, and Justice Washington's catalogue of common-law rights in *Corfield*.] But we are not bound to resort to implication, or to the constitutional history of England, to find an *authoritative declaration* of some of the most important privileges and immunities of citizens of the United States. It is in the Constitution itself.[107]

Bradley proceeded to offer a representative sample of the "privileges and immunities of citizens of the United States" declared in the pre-1866 Constitution, including the ban against bills of attainder and ex post facto laws, and the rights to habeas corpus, trial by jury, free exercise, free speech, free press, free assembly, and security against unreasonable searches.[108] Bradley then resumed his analysis of unwritten fundamental law but later returned to the Constitution, concluding as follows:

> Admitting . . . that formerly the States were not prohibited from infringing any of the fundamental privileges and immunities of citizens of the United States, except in a few specified cases, that cannot be said now, since the adoption of the fourteenth amendment. In my judgment, it was the intention of the people of this country in adopting the amendment to provide National security against violation by the States of the fundamental rights of the citizen.[109]

Like Woods, Bradley apparently understood all rights and privileges in the Bill of Rights as ipso facto fundamental, but Bradley went beyond Woods by adding to the list various privileges and immunities declared in the original Constitution. In the process, Bradley hinted at a more refined version of incorporation, apparently based on whether a given provision of the pre-1866 Constitution had roots as a common-law privilege or immunity. Thus Bradley included both the habeas clause from Article I and the jury rights in Article III on his list yet appeared pointedly to exclude nonestablishment when listing First Amendment rights. We shall return to this hint later.

Justice Bradley's opinion was joined by Justice Swayne, who went on to add some rather confusing remarks of his own. Justices Field and Miller also wrote opinions in *Slaughter-House,* but neither provided a careful analysis of incorporation. Field's discussion of privileges and immunities simply stressed *Corfield,* the common law, and fundamental rights without mentioning the Bill, probably because none of its provisions was directly implicated by the facts at hand.[110] Bradley at least saw no contradiction between Field's approach and his own, for he joined Field's opinion. Justice Miller's opinion for the Court did not squarely address Bradley's incorporation analysis, offering only the following cryptic remark: "The right to peaceably assemble and petition for redress of grievances, the privilege of the writ of habeas corpus, are rights of the citizen guaranteed by the Federal Constitution."[111] Read for all it might be worth, this passage could imply that all the rights and freedoms declared in the pre-1866 Constitution were "privileges and immunities of citizens of the United States" that no state could thereafter abridge.[112] The conventional reading, however, is far more narrow: Miller had in mind only state interference with efforts to assemble and petition the *federal* government, and to secure habeas relief on the basis of *federal* laws in *federal* courts.[113]

The conventional reading falls far short of incorporation, but if we are looking for reasons rather than counting noses, Miller's opinion has nothing to offer. Miller's one-liner never explains why other rights and freedoms of the pre-1866 Constitution are somehow not privileges and immunities of citizens of the United States at the center of section 1's letter and spirit. Moreover, the conventional reading has the effect of rendering the privileges-or-immunities clause wholly unnecessary—"a vain and idle enactment,"[114] in the famous words of Justice Field. Clearly the supremacy clause standing alone, or as glossed by *McCulloch,*[115] would have sufficed to prohibit state interference with federal petitions and federal writs. Like *Twitchell,* then, *Slaughter-House* is no trump card for anti-incorporationists. If read conventionally, the majority opinion rejects not just Black's incorporation but Frankfurter's and Fairman's ordered liberty, Berger's terms of art, and indeed every theory of section 1 that gives Bingham's key clause any independent bite.*

We must nevertheless keep Miller's opinion in mind, for it helps to explain the impoverishment of Fourteenth Amendment discourse in the Supreme Court over the next several generations. By strangling the privileges-or-immunities clause in its crib, *Slaughter-House* forced contrarian-minded litigants to argue that the original Bill applied against states either directly of its own force or via the Fourteenth Amendment's due-process clause. The Court continued to dismiss the former argument with a quick invocation of *Barron* and also regularly rebuffed the latter. If we are simply counting noses, there are lots of justices involved,[116] though a fair count would require toting up the probably larger number of incorporation-minded congressmen in the years immediately after ratification. But once again, if we are looking for reasons, for analysis of the letter and spirit of the privileges-or-immunities clause, we find next to nothing in the High Court between *Slaughter-House* and Hugo Black's heroic reexamination and resurrection of the clause in his famous 1947 dissent in *Adamson v. California*. In the vast wasteland between Bradley and Black, only three Supreme Court landmarks stand out: John Randolph Tucker's celebrated oral argument in *Spies v. Illinois* in 1887; Justice Field's eventual decision (joined by the first Justice Harlan and Justice Brewer) to embrace Tucker's analysis in the 1892 case, *O'Neil v.*

---

*The obvious inadequacy of Miller's opinion—on virtually any reading of the Fourteenth Amendment—powerfully reminds us that interpretations offered in 1873 can be highly unreliable evidence of what was in fact agreed to in 1866–68. What began as a war for union in 1861 became a contest for freedom in 1863 and a crusade for universal civil rights in 1866. By 1870 the Fifteenth Amendment could affirm black suffrage rights in ways that were politically impossible only three years earlier. Revolutions can thus explode outward, but at some point the forces of contraction and counterrevolution take over. By 1873 some of the justices were ignoring some of the core commitments of the Fourteenth Amendment, ratified only five years earlier. (Similarly, as we witnessed in Chapter 2, the Sedition Act of 1798 slighted some of the core commitments of the original Constitution and Bill of Rights.)

For two superb accounts of the shifting political tides in the Reconstruction era, see ERIC FONER, RECONSTRUCTION (1988), and MICHAEL LES BENEDICT, A COMPROMISE OF PRINCIPLE (1974).

Vermont; and Justice Harlan's subsequent reaffirmations of this approach in a series of cases in the early 1900s.[117]

Justice Black in *Adamson* relied on each of these landmarks, apparently believing that they supported his brand of mechanical incorporation.[118] Yet the words of Bradley, Tucker, Field, and Harlan in fact support a considerably more refined version of incorporation, a version that synthesizes the strengths of the three modern positions on incorporation that have dominated legal discourse since *Adamson:* Hugo Black's total incorporation model, William Brennan's selective incorporation approach, and Felix Frankfurter's anti-incorporationist emphasis on fundamental fairness.

It is now time, with the help of Bradley, Tucker, Field, and Harlan, to elaborate this synthesis.

Ten

Refining Incorporation

The easy case for incorporation cannot be easily rebutted as a matter of either text or legislative history. Nevertheless, incorporation raises many more difficulties than Black admitted. The major problem is structural: the original Bill of Rights and the Fourteenth Amendment feature very different constitutional architectures. Sensibly fitting the two together requires far more judicial artisanship—far more judgment—than Black's rhetoric suggested.

The Problem: Fitting Creation Pegs into Reconstruction Holes

As we saw in Part One, the 1789 Bill tightly knit together citizens' rights and states' rights; but the 1866 amendment unraveled this fabric, vesting citizens with rights *against* states. The original Bill also focused centrally on empowering the people collectively against government agents following their own agenda. The Fourteenth Amendment, by contrast, focused on protecting minorities against even responsive, representative, majoritarian government. Over and over, the 1789 Bill proclaimed "the right[s]" and "the powers" of "the people"—phrases conjuring up civic republicanism, collective political action, public rights, and positive liberty. The complementary phrase in the 1866 amendment—"privileges or immunities of citizens"—indicates a subtle but real shift of emphasis, reflecting a vision more liberal than republican, more individualistic than collectivist, more private than public, more negative than positive.

Or, at least, so I shall argue in detail in Chapters 11 and 12. For now, a single example suffices to illustrate the analytic difficulties posed by incorporation: the right to keep and bear arms. The 1789 instantiation of this right was intimately connected with federalism concerns about a federally controlled standing army that might seek to overawe state-organized militias. By contrast, in 1866, John Bingham, Jacob Howard, Thaddeus Stevens, and company were hardly in the mood to rail against a federal standing army; these men, after all, wanted to use precisely such an army to reconstruct recalcitrant southern states. How, then, to square their understanding of "the right . . . to keep and bear arms" with the rather different vision of the Second Amendment's Anti-Federalist architects, George Mason and Elbridge Gerry?

Another problem: the Second Amendment focused on arms bearing as a political right akin to voting. Thus, a strong argument could be made that the original amendment protected only adult male citizens. These men, of course, constituted the "militia" of the amendment's preamble, and we can sensibly read the phrase *the people* in the amendment's main clause as synonymous with *the militia,* thereby eliminating the grammatical and analytic tension that would otherwise exist between the two clauses.[1] Such a reading also draws support from the original Constitution's use of the phrase *the people* to connote voters—the same adult male citizens who, roughly speaking, constituted the militia.[2] By contrast, the privileges-or-immunities clause spoke of all citizens, pointedly including women and children, as made clear by the words immediately preceding Bingham's key sentence defining citizens to include "[a]ll persons born or naturalized in the United States." Time and again Reconstructors in 1866 declared that section 1 and its companion Civil Rights Act focused on "civil rights," not "political rights" like voting and militia service.* But how to fit that vision together with the original Second Amendment?

Put another way, the Second Amendment fused together arms bearing, militia service, and (implicitly) political participation, yet the overall architecture of the Fourteenth Amendment seems to pull them apart,

---

*See, e.g., Report of the Joint Committee on Reconstruction, 39th Cong., 1st Sess. 7, 12, 15 (1866) (distinguishing between "civil" and "political" rights, and linking section 1 with "*civil* rights and privileges") (emphasis added); CONG. GLOBE, 39th Cong., 1st Sess. 476, 599, 606, 1117, 1151, 1159, 1162, 1263, 1293, 1757, 1832, 1836, 3035 (1866) (remarks of Sen. Lyman Trumbull, Reps. James Wilson, M. Russell Thayer, William Windom, John Broomall, Samuel Shellabarger, and William Lawrence, and Sen. John Henderson) (Civil Rights Bill does not encompass political rights like voting); *id.* at 2542, 2766 (remarks of John Bingham and Jacob Howard) (clearly stating that section 1 did not encompass right of suffrage); *id.* at 2462, 2469, 2508, 2530, 2539, 3038 (similar observations from Reps. James Garfield, William Kelley, George Boutwell, Samuel Randall, and John Farnsworth, and Sen. Richard Yates); JOSEPH B. JAMES, THE FRAMING OF THE FOURTEENTH AMENDMENT 163 (1956) (quoting 1866 campaign speech of Thaddeus Stevens conceding that section 1 "does not touch . . . political rights"); PHILADELPHIA N. AM. AND U.S. GAZETTE, Sept. 28, 1866, at 2, *quoted in* CHESTER JAMES ANTIEAU, THE ORIGINAL UNDERSTANDING OF THE FOURTEENTH AMENDMENT 50–51 (1981) ("In making all native born and naturalized persons citizens, this section does not make them voters, for if it did, then would all women and minors have the right of suffrage, since they are just as much persons . . . . The fact that this section does not give the colored man the right of suffrage constitutes the main reason why the extreme advocates of Negro suffrage oppose the Amendment."); *see also* Minor v. Happersett, 88 U.S. (21 Wall.) 162 (1875) (right of suffrage not a section 1 privilege or immunity); H.R. Rep. No. 22, 41st Cong., 3d Sess. 1–4 (1871), *reprinted in* THE RECONSTRUCTION AMENDMENTS' DEBATES 466–67 (Alfred Avins ed., 1967) (Victoria Woodhull petition report authored by John Bingham) (similar); MICHAEL KENT CURTIS, NO STATE SHALL ABRIDGE: THE FOURTEENTH AMENDMENT AND THE BILL OF RIGHTS 149 (1986); EARL M. MALTZ, CIVIL RIGHTS, THE CONSTITUTION, AND CONGRESS, 1863–1869, at 118–20 (1990).

To see the same point textually rather than historically, recall that women and children were paradigmatic citizens—enjoying many rights that Dred Scott, as a free black, could not, according to the Supreme Court—but not voters. Citizenship did not entail suffrage. Nor did the common nineteenth-century phrase *civil rights,* which was often invoked in contradistinction to four clustered "political rights" (the rights to vote, hold office, serve on juries, and serve in militias). Gender helped to crystallize this civil/political distinction—men enjoyed "political rights," but not women—and so did the

with civil rights at the core of section 1 and political rights featured separately in section 2. (We should note that section 2 appeared to preserve the linkage between the militia and voting. Though the word *militia* went unspoken, the section defined a state's presumptive electorate as "male citizens twenty-one years of age" or older.)* What changes, if any, must "the right . . . to keep and bear arms" undergo if it is to be redefined as an essentially "civil" right?

The Solution: Refined Incorporation

Thus far, the Supreme Court has avoided these puzzles by refusing to review cases involving the possible incorporation of the Second Amendment,[3] but analogous questions can be raised about other provisions of the original Bill. Finding sensible answers will require nothing less than

---

language of the Article IV comity clause. Under this clause, a Massachusetts man would enjoy many equal "civil" rights in South Carolina—the right to own real property for example, a right often denied to aliens. But a Massachusetts man could not vote in a South Carolina election, serve in a South Carolina legislature, sit in a South Carolina jury box, or participate in a South Carolina militia. The Article IV comity clause did not extend to these political rights, *see* Bank of Augusta vs. Earle, 38 U.S. (13 Pet.) 519, 552 (1839) (oral argument of Daniel Webster), and neither did the similar language of section 1, which also spoke of "privileges" and "immunities" of "citizens." *See* CONG. GLOBE, 39th Cong., 1st Sess. 1836, 3035 (1866) (remarks of Rep. William Lawrence and Sen. John Henderson); *id.* 40th Cong., 3d Sess. 1003 (1869) (remarks of Sen. Jacob Howard); *Minor,* 88 U.S. at 174; THE RECONSTRUCTION DEBATES, *supra,* at 466 (Woodhull petition report). For more discussion, see Chapter 11. In viewing the Fourteenth Amendment as a source of equal voting rights, modern courts have stressed the language not of privileges or immunities but of equal protection. *See, e.g.,* Reynolds v. Sims, 377 U.S. 533 (1964). Textually, the equal-protection clause embraces all persons—paradigmatically nonvoting aliens—making the clause a most unsturdy foundation for political rights.

*See, e.g., CONG. GLOBE, 39th Cong., 1st Sess. 406 (1866) (remarks of Rep. Samuel Shellabarger, describing an early prototype of section 2) ("[This proposal] approximates more nearly than any other plan to the attainment of that eminent justice of counting every man as part of the foundation of your Government whom you may compel to fight for your Government; and it invites the States to adjudge every one whom the law deems fit to bear arms for his country also fit to be counted as an elector of his country. This is done by making the basis of representation nearly the same relatively as that part of society which is capable of bearing arms.").

a new model of incorporation. To see why, we need only briefly review the two self-proclaimed incorporation models that have emerged on the modern Court.

Total and Selective Incorporation Revisited Begin with Hugo Black's insight that *all* the "privileges" and "immunities" of "citizens" in the original Bill should be protected against state action. Yet the words of section 1 are not limited to the Bill; they must also encompass all the privileges and immunities of the original Constitution, most obviously the privilege of habeas corpus. Of course, not all of the original Constitution's restrictions on federal power are pure citizen rights; some—like the habeas clause's next-door neighbor, the capitation clause—are more concerned with states' rights and thus awkward to incorporate against states. The original Bill of Rights mirrored the Constitution in this respect, including both states' rights and citizens' rights. And states' rights are not obviously limited to the Ninth and Tenth Amendments—consider, for example, the establishment clause[4]—so Black's quick redefinition of the Bill of Rights as meaning only Amendments I–VIII will not do the trick.

More promising here is Justice Brennan's invitation to consider incorporation clause by clause and right by right, an invitation that needs to be extended beyond the Bill to encompass the original Constitution as well. After individualized consideration we may well decide that virtually every provision of the first eight amendments is appropriately incorporated, but Black's approach simply prejudges the issue by deciding wholesale tough questions that are best handled one by one. Thus even if we decide that it does make sense to incorporate the rights underlying the establishment clause, we must honestly confront the special problems here rather than sweeping them under the rug of total incorporation.

Black's total approach, though, had an obvious advantage over Brennan's selective model. Black kept faith with section 1's text and history, embracing all the Bill's privileges and immunities. In contrast, Brennan's approach seemed to countenance refusal to incorporate a right or privilege if the justices did not deem that right "fundamental"—notwithstanding We the People's declaratory judgment that the right was so fundamental as to warrant inclusion in the Bill. While admiring the pragmatic flexibility Brennan's approach allowed,[5] critics condemned selective incorporation as unprincipled. Thus Louis Henkin wrote that "[s]elective incorporation finds no support in the language of the amendment, or in the history of its adoption," and Judge Friendly went so far as to remark that "[w]hatever one's views about the historical support for Mr. Justice Black's wholesale incorporation theory, it appears undisputed that the selective incorporation theory has none."[6]

To the extent that selective incorporation was simply Brennan's polite way of achieving total incorporation by indirection, clause by clause, without having to overrule pre–Warren Court precedent repudiating Black, the practical difference between the two models of incorporation shrinks. And in the cases that they decided, Justice Brennan and his brethren never met a right in the Bill they didn't like or deem fundamental enough to warrant incorporation. But four rights in Amendments I–VIII have remained outside the selective fold: the right to keep and bear arms, the right against quartering soldiers, and the rights to grand and civil juries. For the Third Amendment, a plausible explanation for failure to incorporate is that a proper case never materialized: the right rarely arises in modern litigation. Yet as to the other three rights, the modern Court has let stand lower-court decisions rejecting incorporation.[7] By refusing to discuss openly why these three rights somehow were not fundamental enough to justify incorporation, the justices have seemed to plead no contest to the critics' charge that selective incorporation was unprincipled. Indeed, as to grand juries, it does seem hard to see why this "ancient immunity and privilege" of English liberty is not embraced—doubly—by the privileges-or-immunities and due-process clauses.

The Second Amendment poses somewhat different complications. Perhaps the Supreme Court has assumed that the Second is a purely federalism-based right of organized state militias and thus inappropriate for incorporation against states. If so, the Court's assumption rests on a dubious reading of the word *militia* and inattention to the grammar and syntax of the Amendment, which speaks of a right of "the people," not "the states."[8] Even more embarrassing, whatever the reasons for reading the Second Amendment as a states'-rights provision analogous to the Tenth Amendment, there are more powerful reasons for so reading the establishment clause,[9] which has already been incorporated.[10]

A New Synthesis But the focus on the Second Amendment suggests a different filter that leads to a new, refined model of incorporation. Instead of asking whether a given provision is fundamental, as Brennan suggests, we must ask whether it is a personal privilege—that is, a private right—of individual citizens, rather than a right of states or the public at large.

This question responds to the structural difficulty of incorporation yet keeps faith with section 1's letter and spirit. This question, or something like it, is obviously the refinement we need once we remember that section 1 incorporates "the privileges or immunities of citizens" declared in the original Constitution as well as the Bill of Rights. For how else could we separate those Article I limitations that should be incorporated, like habeas, from those that should not, like capitation (a state right) or even bicameralism (a right of the public at large)? The same filter works for the Bill of Rights, and for the same reasons. Indeed, the filter nicely combines the respective strengths of Black's and Brennan's models of incorporation. With this filter, we can preserve the textual and historical support for Black's insistence that all the Bill's privileges or immunities are indeed incorporated while accommodating Brennan's intuition that perhaps not every provision of the first eight amendments sensibly incorporates. This synthesis offers a principled substitute to the seeming ad hockery of selective incorporation as now practiced.

To view an entitlement as a private right is not to deny that it may have public or political significance but only to recognize that it is a right vested in discrete individuals. Thus a publisher has a private right—a privilege—to print newspaper editorials even (indeed, especially) if the editorials take a stand on public or political matters. (Seen from another angle, the publisher's privilege is rooted in, even if not exhausted by, her private rights to her bodily liberty and her property, rights that would be violated by jails or fines.)

But the Second Amendment illustrates that states' rights and individual rights, "private" rights of discrete citizens and "public" rights of the citizenry generally, were sometimes marbled together into a single clause. A truly sensible and sensitive incorporation must go beyond a binary "all in" or "all out" approach to individual clauses. At times, judges must mine and refine citizen rights from the mixed ore in which they are embedded in the 1789 Bill. It is exactly at this point that elements of Frankfurter's analysis enter our new synthesis, for he recognized the distortions introduced by mechanical jot-for-jot incorporation.

Black's insistence on jot-for-jot state compliance followed naturally from his commitment to total incorporation (but only of Amendments I–VIII), his disdain for judicial discretion, and his belief in enforcing absolute rights in all their strictness. Harder to understand was Brennan's insistence "that once a provision of the Federal Bill was deemed incorporated, it applied identically in state and federal proceedings."[11] If judges had discretion to decide which clauses were "fundamental" and which were not, why didn't they have equal discretion to decide which doctrinal subrules of a given clause were fundamental?[12]

The right question is not whether a clause is fundamental but whether it is truly a private right of the citizen rather than a right of the states or the public generally. So, too, Frankfurter's instinct must be analogously recast. Various rules and subdoctrines associated with the original Bill may not incorporate jot for jot—indeed, the very metaphor of incorporation may mislead. But the reason is not that these rules and subdoctrines are not fundamental; rather, it is that they may reflect federalism and other structural concerns unique to the central government. For example, to the extent that the First Amendment freedom of speech is read as an absolute, not as a matter of free-speech doctrine but for reasons of federalism rooted in a lack of enumerated congressional power in Article I, section 8—to *that* extent, the clause does not sensibly incorporate jot for jot. Likewise, an argument can be made that the Seventh Amendment is rooted in federalism concerns that should not be imposed on states. If so, refined incorporation can offer a more principled basis for retaining one of the widely hailed[13] pragmatic virtues of Brennan's approach: namely, the refusal to require state courts in the late twentieth century to follow English civil-jury rules circa 1791.

Indeed, as the Second Amendment illustrates, the very same words "the right . . . to keep and bear arms" take on a different coloration and nuance when they are relabeled "privileges or immunities of citizens" rather than "the right of the people," and when they are severed from their association with a well-regulated militia. To recast the textual point as a historical one, the core applications and central meanings of the right to keep and bear arms and other key rights were very different in 1866 than in 1789. Mechanical incorporation obscured all this and, indeed, made it easy to forget that when we "apply" the Bill of Rights against the states today, we must first and foremost reflect on the meaning and the spirit of the amendment of 1866, not the Bill of 1789.

A Creation Analogy Thus in the very process of being absorbed into the Fourteenth Amendment, various rights and freedoms of the original Bill may be subtly but importantly transformed in much the same way the Bill of Rights transformed language that it had absorbed from still earlier sources. Consider, for example, the freedom of the press. Historian Leonard Levy has piled up mounds of evidence that the phrase "freedom of the press" at common law in England and in the colonies meant only freedom from prior restraint. Since the framers of the First Amendment used the same phrase with little extended discussion, Levy at times suggests they probably meant to incorporate the common-law doctrine jot for jot.[14]

The argument shows more historical doggedness than legal sensitivity. In England, Parliament was sovereign. Legal rights in such a system sensibly ran only against executive and judicial officials, like licensers appointed by the Crown, rather than against Parliament itself. But in a document self-consciously based on popular sovereignty, as proudly proclaimed in the opening words of the Preamble, is it sensible to mechanically incorporate rules based on an utterly contrary premise? Don't We the Sovereign People of America necessarily have the same inherent rights of free political expression enjoyed by members of the Sovereign

Parliament in England? If so, "freedom of the press" in the First Amendment necessarily means more than mere freedom from prior restraint. The prior-restraint ban may indeed be part of our First Amendment, but surely that ban does not exhaust the constitutional meaning of "freedom of the press."

To put the structural point textually, the old phrase "freedom of the press" takes on new meaning when conjoined—as it never had been in England or the colonies—with "the freedom of speech."[15] Surely the two rights in the federal Bill are *in pari materia*;[16] each must be construed in relation to the other, and it would be curious if freedom of the printed word were drastically more truncated than freedom of oral expression.[17] Yet the idea that "freedom of speech" means only freedom from prior restraint is utterly outlandish—wholly lacking in historical support and difficult even to imagine in practice. (Licensing the few printing presses that existed in the seventeenth and eighteenth centuries is one thing; but what would it *mean* to purport to license speakers and require official preclearance before one could open one's mouth?)[18] Rather, "freedom of speech" had a rich tradition, in England and in the states, of guaranteeing absolute freedom of speech and debate within the sovereign legislature. And thus, the extension of this right to ordinary citizens in the First Amendment is indeed simply a textual recognition of the structural truth of American popular sovereignty.

Not all of this was spelled out in elaborate detail in 1789, though Madison did briefly remark on the differences between the British system and the American theory of popular sovereignty on the very day he introduced the Bill of Rights.[19] Nevertheless, most twentieth-century lawyers would have little trouble admitting that various common-law principles may have changed shape in subtle but important ways when absorbed into the Constitution and Bill of Rights.[20] The common law, after all, is famous for its ability to adapt itself to new situations, remolding its contours to accommodate a new legal landscape.[21]

Most lawyers today, though, have failed to reflect seriously on the analogous dynamic raised by Reconstruction's absorption of the Bill of Rights. Disciples of Black and Brennan posit an essentially mechanical process that denies the need to reshape 1789 doctrines to fit the 1866 vision, and followers of Frankfurter insist that, strictly speaking, there is no logical relationship at all between the Bill and Fourteenth Amendment. What is called for, then, is a new way of thinking about this relationship that is neither mechanical (like Black and Brennan) nor autistic (like Frankfurter)—an approach that tries to remold the provisions of the original Bill into "privileges" and "immunities" of "citizens" to fit the spirit and the architecture of the Fourteenth Amendment.

Ironically, English common law may be of great help here, for it featured expositions of many privileges and immunities with counterparts in the Bill of Rights, but without the Bill's federalism, majoritarian, and public-rights glosses. To be sure, we must be wary of Blackstonian rules to the extent that they are inconsistent with popular-sovereignty theory—for *this* feature of the American Constitution was not repudiated by the Fourteenth Amendment. Nevertheless, English common law offers a crude but helpful test to sort out which aspects of the pre-1866 Constitution were indeed privileges of individuals (for example, habeas) and which were instead structural provisions unique to the federal government and inappropriate for imposition on states (for example, capitation and bicameralism).

The Old Roots of the New Synthesis Although the model of refined incorporation will no doubt strike most twentieth-century lawyers as novel, it has deep historical roots. Recall, for example, that even before the Fourteenth Amendment, the *Barron* contrarian C. P. Van Ness argued in 1840 that certain aspects of the Founders' Bill should apply to states.[22] Van Ness pointedly eschewed total incorporation: "Each article, therefore, if not each clause, should be construed simply according to its own nature, and the terms in which it may be expressed."[23] In considering the "nature" of each clause, Van Ness proposed that courts distinguish between mere "limitations of governmental power," the prototype of which, he thought, was the Tenth Amendment, and "declarations of rights" inherent in the individual, like the right to due process.[24] The former did not sensibly apply against the states, but the latter did, argued Van Ness. Though Van Ness did not elaborate this distinction in great detail, later commentators did.

Consider, for example, John Bingham's remarks in 1859: "'privileges and immunities of *citizens* in the several States' [do not include] rights and immunities *of* the several States."[25] When Bingham later framed his proposed amendment, he used words that spoke of rights of citizens in contradistinction to rights of the several states; of private rights (for that is what the word *privileges* quite literally means) like habeas in contradistinction to public rules of government structure like bicameralism. Although it would be a mistake to read too much into the subtle vagaries of expression in the Thirty-ninth Congress, virtually no one spoke of mechanically incorporating the Bill of Rights as such. Typical were formulations speaking of "the great fundamental rights" possessed "by the *citizen*" and "*embraced in* the bill of rights," and of "natural and personal rights."[26] Indeed, both Bingham and Howard seemed to redefine "the Bill of Rights" as encompassing only the first eight rather than ten amendments, presumably because they saw the Ninth and Tenth Amendments as federalism provisions.[27] But even after slicing off Amendments IX and X, Bingham and Howard, unlike Black, avoided the language of jot-for-jot incorporation, speaking instead of "the privileges and immunities of *citizens* . . . *defined in*" and "the *personal* rights guarantied and secured by" the "first eight amendments."[28] Even more significant, members of the Thirty-ninth Congress regularly linked the Bill of Rights with the classic common-law rights of individuals exemplified in Blackstone,* *Corfield,* and the Civil Rights Act of 1866.

Bradley's *Slaughter-House* opinion also invoked Blackstone, *Corfield,* and the common law alongside the Bill of Rights. Let us examine more carefully his nonexhaustive catalogue of "privileges or immunities of citizens" derived from the pre-1866 Constitution: "the right of habeas corpus, the right of trial by jury, of free exercise of religious worship, the

---

*Blackstone's *Commentaries* from the 1760s may have loomed larger a century later in the framing of the Fourteenth Amendment than in the framing of the Bill of Rights in the 1790s. Sir William Blackstone himself had championed Parliamentary sovereignty and opposed the colonial cause, and this obviously did not endear him to men who risked their lives in the Revolution. By the mid-nineteenth century, however, the American Revolution was secure. Americans could now forgive Blackstone his allegiance, and many lawyers of this era began their legal training with the *Commentaries.*

right of free speech and a free press, the right peaceably to assemble for the discussion of public measures, the right to be secure against unreasonable searches and seizures, and above all, and including almost all the rest, the right of not being deprived of life, liberty, or property, without due process of law."[29]

The order of this list shows that Bradley is tracking the order in which various privileges and immunities are mentioned in the pre-1866 Constitution. Habeas comes first (from Article I, section 9), and then jury trial—not from the Sixth Amendment, but from Article III—followed by a paraphrase of the First Amendment absent the establishment clause. Though Bradley does not elaborate his implicit filter, it seems that he is influenced by common-law categories of personal liberty and security. Such a filter would explain why, for example, jury trial is taken from Article III but bicameralism is not taken from Article I. This implicit filter might also explain the omission of the establishment clause, which, unlike its First Amendment companions, does not so obviously resonate with common-law rights of personal property, personal security, and bodily liberty.

Further support for this reading of Bradley comes from an adjoining passage where he summarizes "the *personal* privileges and immunities of citizens" that were explicitly protected against state action by the original Constitution: "The States were merely prohibited from passing bills of attainder, ex post facto laws, laws impairing the obligation of contracts, and perhaps *one or two more*."[30] Left out of Bradley's filtered version of Article I, section 10 are the prohibitions that "No state shall enter into any Treaty, Alliance, or Confederation; grant Letters of Marque and Reprisal; coin Money; emit Bills of Credit; make any Thing but gold and silver Coin a Tender in Payment of Debts; . . . or grant any Title of Nobility." Once again, the items that Bradley explicitly includes seem much more closely connected with classic common-law rights of the individual to liberty and property than do the items he excludes. What common-law right would be violated by a state's granting of a title of nobility?

Far more direct was John Randolph Tucker's famous oral argument in the 1887 Chicago anarchist case *Spies v. Illinois*. Here for the first time an attorney before the Court clearly argued for incorporation on the basis of the privileges-or-immunities clause. But Tucker's brand of incorporation was distinctly more refined than Black's. Like Bradley, Tucker included in his catalogue of privileges and immunities those rights "declare[d]" in the original Constitution, as well as the Bill, including "the security for habeas corpus [and] the limits imposed on Federal power in the Amendments and in the original Constitution as to trial by jury, &c."[31] When he turned his eye to the Bill proper (which he labeled "the Declaration of Rights"), he made explicit the common-law filter that Bradley had only implied:

> Though originally the first ten Amendments were adopted as limitations on Federal power, yet *in so far as* they secure and recognize fundamental rights—*common law rights*—of the man, they make them privileges and immunities of the man as citizen of the United States, and [those privileges] cannot now be abridged by a State under the Fourteenth Amendment. In other words, while the ten Amendments, as limitations on power, only apply to the Federal government, and not to the States, yet *in so far as they declare* or recognize rights of *persons*, these rights are theirs, as citizens of the United States, and the Fourteenth Amendment as to such rights limits state power . . . . [32]

Tucker strained, rather unconvincingly, to introduce further modifications of his basic model to accommodate post-*Slaughter-House* precedent,[33] but his general approach was both revealing and helpful.

The Court disposed of *Spies* without reaching the issues raised by Tucker. Five years later, Justice Field, joined by Justices Harlan and Brewer, ranged far beyond the narrow pleadings in the case before him to embrace Tucker's argument: "[A]fter much reflection I think the definition given at one time before this court by a distinguished advocate— Mr. John Randolph Tucker, of Virginia—is correct."[34] Field went on to distinguish between those aspects of the Bill that were mere "limitations on power" and those that instead "declare or recognize the rights of persons."[35] Some of Field's hinted applications of this distinction appear doubtful—once again, it seems, the result of an awkward effort to accommodate post-*Slaughter-House* precedents on grand and civil juries.[36]

But we are concerned here not with individual applications, but with a basic model for incorporation; and the Van Ness–Tucker–Field distinction, or something like it, is what we need to distill those aspects of the pre-1866 Constitution that sensibly incorporate from those that do not.

By 1900, Justice Field had left the Court, but Justice Harlan continued to carry forward the crusade to breathe life back into the privileges-or-immunities clause. His first extended analysis of the clause came in *Maxwell v. Dow*, where he vigorously argued that all the personal rights, freedoms, privileges, and immunities in the "National Bill of Rights" applied against states by dint of the Fourteenth Amendment.[37] Yet once again, if we examine the evidence closely, we see a more refined approach than Black would later offer. Thus in canvassing the rights and freedoms of the First Amendment, Harlan quoted or paraphrased each of its clauses except establishment.[38] Moments later, he offered the following hypothetical:

> Suppose the State of Utah should amend its constitution and make the Mormon religion the established religion of the State, to be supported by taxation on all the people of Utah. . . . If such an amendment were alleged to be invalid under the National Constitution, could not [today's opinion] be cited as showing that the right to the *free exercise of religion* was not a privilege of a "citizen of the United States" within the meaning of the Fourteenth Amendment?[39]

Harlan's decision to characterize this hypothetical fact pattern as violating free exercise rather than nonestablishment principles is subtle but significant. To infringe upon the free exercise of religion is necessarily to invade individual rights of property and bodily liberty, but perhaps not all establishments would do so. Would a simple legislative declaration that "Utah is a Mormon state" infringe classic common-law rights of liberty and property any more than a granting of a title of nobility? Harlan instead pointedly chose a hypothetical involving state taxation depriving individual taxpayers of their property and indirectly compelling them to affirm religious beliefs contrary to their own. Though he offered less elaboration than Tucker, he too seemed to be using an implicit common-law filter. Indeed, without some such filter, Harlan's approach would be hard to fathom, for like Tucker and Field, but unlike Black, Harlan spoke again and again of "the first ten" rather than eight amendments.[40]

Harlan returned to the privileges-or-immunities clause eight years later in his celebrated dissent in *Twining v. New Jersey*, a case raising the question of whether a state could compel a citizen to incriminate himself. Though tipping his hat to *Barron*, Harlan described the privilege against compelled self-incrimination as an English common-law privilege preexisting the federal Constitution.[41] In language reminiscent of *Corfield*'s ode, Harlan wrote that "real, genuine freedom could not exist in any country" that abridged this freedom, which ranked "among the essential, fundamental principles of English law."[42] For Harlan, rights declared in "the name of the People of the United States" by the original Bill of Rights became applicable against the states via the Fourteenth Amendment; but once again, Harlan filtered the Bill through the common law, stressing "privileges and immunities mentioned in the original Amendments, and universally regarded as our heritage of liberty from the common law."[43]

Nineteenth-century lawyers and judges who took incorporation seriously thus point us toward a considerably more refined brand of incorporation than Justice Black (or any other twentieth-century figure, for that matter) served up. It remains to see what the Bill of Rights would look like—first clause by clause, then as a whole—if reread through the lens of refined incorporation.

Eleven

Reconstructing Rights

What would acceptance of the refined incorporation model mean in practice? What follows are suggestive but not exhaustive applications, which seek to illustrate the analytic virtues of the refined model and the kinds of insights it makes possible. As with any general framework, though, my model might yield different results if worked by another hand. Thus some readers may reject some of my applications while accepting my basic framework of refined incorporation. Even this limited agreement would be real progress: lawyers, judges, and scholars would be asking the same (and the right) questions even if they reached different answers.

Freedom of Expression

"Congress shall make no law . . . abridging the freedom of speech, or of the press; or the right of the people peaceably to assemble, and to petition the Government for a redress of grievances." Textually, the argument for applying these rights against states via the Fourteenth Amendment is wonderfully straightforward. The First Amendment explicitly speaks of "right[s]" and "freedom[s]" (entitlements also known as "privileges" and "immunities"); and after the Civil War and Emancipation, it would be extraordinarily perverse to refuse to incorporate (in a refined way) clauses whose explicit battle cry is "freedom." What's more, the First Amendment's words that these freedoms and rights "shall" not be "abridg[ed]" by "law" perfectly harmonize with their echoes in the key sentence of section 1.[1] That harmony is no accident; the key sentence was drafted to resonate with the nonabridgment clause of the First Amendment. Nor can it be argued that First Amendment "rights" and "freedoms" are somehow not private rights of individual citizens. Though narrower in scope than their American counterparts, the freedoms of press, petition, and peaceable assembly were, according to Blackstone, core common-law rights "of persons" and of "every freeman."[2] As we have seen, these rights were broadened in the 1780s by American popular-sovereignty theory, which also extended to ordinary citizens the freedom of speech previously enjoyed only by legislators.

Of course, federalism played an important role in the unreconstructed First Amendment, but not in a way that impedes incorporation of its explicit rights and freedoms. Even if we assume that freedom of speech in state legislatures enjoyed special First Amendment status above and beyond the freedom extended to ordinary citizens,[3] nothing about incorporation takes away state legislatures' freedom of speech; incorporation simply limits their freedom to use state law to silence ordinary citizens, and *that* freedom is not in any way protected by the First Amendment. Thus the amendment nowhere forbids Congress to "make any law *protecting* freedom of speech" and so on against repressive state action. On the contrary, a strong argument can be made that Congress was empowered and perhaps required to pass precisely these sorts of laws to vindicate the Article IV guarantee that each state would have a republican government. Could such a government ever punish citizens for speaking, writing, peaceably assembling, or petitioning against it?[4]

Many *Barron* contrarians in the antebellum era thought not. Today we might at first wonder how faithful interpreters of the First Amendment could earnestly argue, even before 1866, that its Congress-limiting protections of free expression could bind states; but few moderns have any problems seeing a presidential censorship edict, or a judicial contempt order imprisoning a reporter critical of the court, as raising "First Amendment" concerns.[5] To be sure, the amendment speaks only of "Congress"; but any automatic negative inference that citizens therefore lack analogous rights against the president or federal judges—or states—flies in the face of the Ninth Amendment. When supporters of the Fourteenth Amendment described its provisions as "declaratory" of the existing Constitution, properly construed, we must not assume that they necessarily meant to include only those generally worded provisions of the Bill of Rights and to exclude those clauses explicitly linked to Congress.

Thus neither the First Amendment's arguably special protection of state legislative speech nor its use of the word *Congress* presents any stumbling block to incorporation. But a third federalism component of the original amendment does raise an interesting incorporation question. As suggested in Chapter 2, the particularly absolutist phrasing of the First Amendment—"Congress shall make no law"—may well have reflected a widespread understanding in 1789 that Congress simply lacked enumerated power to suppress speech and press. To this extent, the First Amendment resembled the Tenth, specifying not a private right of citizens based on personal liberty but a state right rooted in federalism. Under the model of refined incorporation, the federalism aspect of First Amendment absolutism does not sensibly incorporate against states. But then we are left with a seeming paradox: the First Amendment might constrain Congress more strictly than the Fourteenth constrains states even though both amendments seem to speak with one voice, that the freedom of expression "shall" not be "abridg[ed]" by "law."

The paradox is more apparent than real. As a practical matter, we must remember that the federalism-based argument for First Amendment absolutism has never been taken seriously by federal courts and is unlikely to be revived in the modern era. But if the theory ever were taken seriously, it could indeed permit differential treatment of state and federal governments.[6] Even if couched as an interpretation of the First Amendment, federalism-based absolutism is, in large part, rooted elsewhere—in a strict interpretation of Article I, section 8, claiming that Congress lacks enumerated power to censor. But nothing in the text, history, or logic of the Fourteenth Amendment suggests that the federal system of enumerated powers should be overlaid on—incorporated against—states. Put another way, if we take federalism seriously, even before we reach the question whether federal power is trumped by the First Amendment in a given area, we must ask an analytically prior question: does the Constitution in fact grant the federal government power here? And if the answer is no, we must not assume that state governments also necessarily lack power, for perhaps Congress is denied a particular power precisely because the Constitution meant to leave it to the states.

At first, the federalism-based reading of the First Amendment might seem tailor-made for Hugo Black, who championed First Amendment absolutism, preached fidelity to the Founders' "original intent," and also proved willing to invalidate acts of Congress on grounds of federalism.[7] Yet Black never relied on federalism to bolster his First Amendment absolutism, and with good reason. Such a move would have driven an analytic wedge between the First and Fourteenth Amendments, thereby destroying Black's own theory of mechanical incorporation. This wedge would not necessarily require abandonment of absolutism in free-speech cases involving states: Black could well have defended First Amendment absolutism on grounds of both federalism and freedom, and the latter set of arguments clearly would apply equally against states. But if Black had ever admitted that any of the provisions of Amendments I–VIII had any federalism component whatsoever, he would have been forced to admit the analytical possibility that perhaps not all of his (redefined) Bill of Rights sensibly incorporated jot for jot. The analytic structure of total incorporation would have crumbled.

But even if Black's precise analytic path to incorporation of speech, press, petition, and assembly cut a few corners, he ended up in the right place: as a matter of constitutional text and structure, these freedoms and rights are indeed easy cases for full application against states via the Fourteenth Amendment. An ounce of history here provides powerful confirmation. From the 1830s on, abolitionist crusaders had understood that freedom of speech for all men and women went hand in hand with freedom of bodily liberty for slaves. The Slave Power posed a threat to Freedom—of all kinds—and could maintain control only through suppression of opposition speech, with gag rules on antislavery petitions, bans on "incendiary" publications, censorship of the mails, exclusions of outside agitators, banishments of dissenters, intrusions on the right of peaceable assembly, and so on.[8] This global theory of freedom was not limited to a few lawyers or theorists spearheading the crusade but was truly the popular platform of the antislavery movement, perhaps best exemplified by an 1856 Republican Party campaign slogan: "Free Speech, Free Press, Free Men, Free Labor, Free Territory, and Frémont."[9]

During the Thirty-eighth and Thirty-ninth Congresses, Republicans invoked speech, press, petition, and assembly rights over and over—more frequently than any other right, with the possible exception of due process.[10] These invocations occurred in a variety of overlapping contexts: as glosses on the "civil rights" to be protected by the Civil Rights and Freedman's Bureau Acts, as part of the definition of republican government (whose violation justified continued southern exclusion from the national legislature), as "fundamental rights" of all citizens, and as paradigmatic "privileges or immunities" of national citizenship and/or interstate comity.

Once again, the centrality of these rights was not an idea limited to a few leading lawyers or theorists but was widely understood by the polity. Various petitions from ordinary constituents to Congress in 1866 stressed the importance of the rights of "speech," "press," and "assembly" (while of course embodying the interrelated right of petition);[11] the *New York Evening Post* noted that the freedoms of speech and of the press were guaranteed by the Civil Rights Act (even though the act did not explicitly speak of those freedoms) and later read section 1 of the proposed amendment as covering the same ground;[12] the *Philadelphia North American and United States Gazette* in September 1866 listed freedoms of speech, press, and assembly as paradigmatic "privileges and immunities" of citizenship within the meaning of the then-pending amendment;[13] various prominent Congressmen on the campaign trail in 1866 (including Bingham, Wilson, and Speaker of the House Schuyler

Colfax) emphasized the amendment's protection of freedom of speech;[14] state politicians in leading northern states—Wisconsin, Pennsylvania, Ohio, Massachusetts, New York, and so on—linked the amendment to freedom of discussion;[15] and various popular 1865 and 1866 conventions, both northern and southern, not only embodied the right to peaceably assemble but used these occasions to reaffirm the importance of speech, press, petition, and assembly rights.[16]

Thus far, the refined incorporation model and Black's total incorporation approach appear to converge. But refined incorporation can help us to see what Black's approach obscured: how the very meaning of freedom of speech, press, petition, and assembly was subtly redefined in the process of being incorporated. In the eighteenth century the paradigmatic speaker was someone like John Peter Zenger or James Callender,[17] a relatively popular publisher saying relatively popular things critical of less popular government officials. In the mid-nineteenth century the paradigm shifted to the Unionist, the abolitionist, and the freedman, to speakers like Samuel Hoar, Harriet Beecher Stowe, and Frederick Douglass. Hoar was a Massachusetts lawyer (and, coincidentally, the son-in-law of founder Roger Sherman), who in 1844 went to South Carolina with his daughter to defend the rights of free blacks—only to be ridden out of town on a rail by an enraged populace after the South Carolina legislature passed an act of attainder and banishment.[18] A generation later, Hoar's case still burned bright in the memories of members of Congress, who repeatedly cited the incident.[19] Stowe penned the "incendiary" best-seller *Uncle Tom's Cabin*—a novel that outraged the proslavery South and inspired the antislavery North in the 1850s, leading Lincoln to describe her as "the little woman who wrote the book that made this great war."[20] Frederick Douglass escaped from slavery in Maryland in 1838, published a daring autobiography in 1845, founded a leading abolitionist newspaper, which he edited over the next two decades, and became a preeminent orator on behalf of civil rights and suffrage for both women and freedmen.

The shift from Zenger and Callender to Hoar, Stowe, and Douglass was subtle but significant. All can be seen as outsiders, but with an important difference. As representatives of the Fourth Estate, Zenger and

Callender were outside the government that sought to censor them, but Hoar, Stowe, and Douglass were outsiders in a much deeper sense. Vis-à-vis the southern society that tried to suppress their speech, Hoar, Stowe, and Douglass were geographic, cultural, and ethnic outsiders who were critical of dominant social institutions and opinions.[21] Put another way, this shift directs us away from Madison's first concern in *The Federalist* No. 51 (the agency problem of protecting the people against unrepresentative government), and toward his second concern (protecting minorities from "factional" majority tyranny). The new First-Fourteenth Amendment tradition is less majoritarian and more libertarian.[22] To recast this point in a temporal frame, the abolitionist experience dramatized why even majoritarians should logically support strong First Amendment protections for offensive and provocative speech of fringe groups. For if allowed to preach its gospel freely, a zealous fringe group in one era (like proponents of abolition, equality, and black suffrage in 1830) could conceivably convert enough souls to the crusade to become a respectable or even dominant political force over the next generation (like the Republican Party of the 1860s).

My language here—*preach, gospel, zealous, convert, souls,* and *crusade*—reflects the religious inspiration of many abolitionists.[23] Stowe's husband, father, and many brothers, for example, were famous New England clergymen. The well-publicized martyrdom of Elijah Lovejoy also dramatized the centrality of religious speech. Lovejoy, a Presbyterian minister, used his church weekly to condemn slavery. His writings cost him his life in 1837 when he was murdered by an angry mob bent on silencing his press.[24]

Republicans naturally understood the religious roots of abolitionism and often stressed the need to protect religious speech. We have already noted Bingham's 1859 speech proclaiming the centrality of the right to "utter, according to conscience";[25] on the campaign trail in 1866 he reminded his audience that men had been imprisoned in Georgia for teaching the Bible and made clear that the Fourteenth Amendment would put an end to such state action, a theme to which he returned in a key speech on the amendment before the House in 1871.[26] In early 1866 Lyman Trumbull introduced his Civil Rights Bill by stressing the need to protect the freedom "to teach" and "to preach," citing a Mississippi Black Code punishing any "free negroes and mulattoes" who dared to "exercis[e] the functions of a minister of the Gospel."[27] A few weeks later, Senator Henry Wilson painted in more vivid colors, accusing the Slave Power of "murder[ing] editors" and hanging "ministers of the living God for questioning the divinity of slavery."[28] Similarly, in 1865 Representative James M. Ashley linked religion to freedom of speech—"[the Slave Power] has silenced every free pulpit within its control . . . and made free speech and a free press impossible within its domain"—and in 1864 Representative Ebon Ingersoll stressed the role of antislavery speech of "minister[s] of the gospel."[29] On this point, the voices of northern white Republicans harmonized with those of southern black freedmen. Thus we find an 1865 convention of South Carolina blacks linking "the school, the pulpit, [and] the press."[30]

These sentiments had been maturing for forty years, as the American antislavery movement wandered in the political wilderness in search of the promised land of freedom. As early as 1819 Maryland had arrested and prosecuted a Methodist minister, the Reverend Jacob Gruber, for preaching a sermon that the authorities feared might incite slaves to revolt.[31] The tame sermon had condemned slavery but nonetheless exhorted slaves to obey their masters, and Gruber eventually won acquittal (defended by a Maryland lawyer and state senator named Roger B. Taney). Maryland was hardly unique. An antebellum Louisiana law made it a capital offense to use "language in any public discourse, from the bar, the bench, the stage, *the pulpit,* or in any place whatsoever" that might incite "insubordination among the slaves."[32] In 1849 Virginia convicted a minister, Jarvis Bacon, for an ambiguous antislavery allusion in a sermon; relying on both the free-speech and religious guarantees of the Virginia Constitution, Bacon's lawyers eventually persuaded the state supreme court to construe the ambiguity in Bacon's favor and set aside his conviction.[33] North Carolina preachers were less lucky. Jesse McBride, an antislavery preacher from Ohio, was sentenced to imprisonment for a year, to an hour in a pillory, and to twenty lashes but was ultimately released as part of an agreement that he leave the state.[34] In 1859, in a national cause célèbre, North Carolina sentenced the elderly

Reverend Daniel Worth to a year in prison for circulating an antislavery tract. Like McBride, Worth eventually slipped out of the jurisdiction; and the state, in turn, rewrote its laws to make "incendiary" antislavery expression punishable by death for the first offense.[35]

In response, the forces of freedom increasingly stressed the linkage between expressive freedom and religious freedom.[36] On the campaign trail in 1860, Abraham Lincoln condemned sedition laws "suppressing all declarations that slavery is wrong, whether made in politics, in presses, in pulpits, or in private."[37] The religion-speech nexus was also prominent in congressional debates on the eve of the Civil War; Ohio Representative Cydnor Tomkins, for example, attacked southern laws that tried "to seal every man's lips, and stop every man's mouth," laws that made a felon of "the man who dares proclaim the precepts of our holy religion."[38] Similarly, Congressman Owen Lovejoy, brother of the martyred Elijah, railed against southern laws that "imprison or exile preachers of the Gospel," and proclaimed the right of discussing slavery as one of "the privileges and immunities of the Constitution . . . which guaranties to me free speech."[39]

In 1789 the freedoms of speech and press had been yoked with religious freedoms largely for reasons of federalism; both religious regulation in the states and press censorship were seen as beyond the enumerated powers of Congress. This federalism-based reading of the original First Amendment draws support from the dramatic fact that no previous state constitution had linked these two sets of rights in a single provision. But once yoked together in the federal Bill, these clauses helped reinforce a libertarian theory of freedom of all expression—political, religious, and even artistic (*Uncle Tom's Cabin* was all three). By the 1860s libertarianism had displaced federalism and majoritarianism as the dominant, unifying theme of the First Amendment's freedoms.[40]

The centrality of religious speech in the 1860s proved especially significant for women. Though excluded from exercising the formal political rights of voting, holding public office, and serving on juries or militias, women played leading roles in religious organizations.[41] These organizations engaged in moral crusades with obvious political overtones: antigambling, antiprostitution, temperance, abolition, and (eventually) suffrage. As a result, the voices of women were much harder to ignore in the 1860s than they had been in the 1790s.[42] In the debates over the Constitution and Bill of Rights, only one woman, Mercy Otis Warren, participated prominently, and even then under a pseudonym. (Indeed, her important pamphlet during the ratification debates was long ascribed to Elbridge Gerry and was not credited to her until 1932.)[43] But in 1866 the most widely read condemnation of slavery had been written by a woman under her own name, and in a campaign orchestrated by Susan B. Anthony and Elizabeth Cady Stanton, thousands and thousands of women flooded the Thirty-ninth Congress with petitions for women's suffrage, which had been a nonissue for the Founding Fathers.[44] At least five petitions from women on the suffrage issue were presented on the floor of Congress in the first two months of 1866 alone.[45] Two years earlier, on February 9, 1864, the Women's National Loyal League had presented Congress with a mammoth emancipation petition bearing exactly one hundred thousand signatures, nearly two-thirds of them women's signatures; eventually, the league gathered about four hundred thousand names.[46] Women were central exercisers of First Amendment freedoms in the Reconstruction era in a way they had not been at the Founding—yet another example of the rising importance of outsider speech. Interestingly, in discussing the Hoar affair before the Thirty-eighth Congress, Representative William D. Kelley pointedly spoke not only of Samuel Hoar but also of Hoar's "beautiful and accomplished daughter"[47]—the granddaughter of founder Roger Sherman. In the same spirit, Representative John Kasson noted that "innocent ladies, cultivated, intelligent, Christian women, have been driven from the cities and States of the South . . . because they had dared to say something offensive to this intolerant spirit of slavery," and Representative Morris reminded his audience that southern states had "incarcerated Christian men and women for teaching the alphabet."[48] In his vivid speech in the Thirty-ninth Congress, Senator Henry Wilson likewise denounced the Slave Power for having "imprisoned women for teaching little children to read God's holy Word."[49]

Northern states had also sinned in the antebellum era, at times abridging expression and association, and violating the Article IV privileges and immunities of out-of-state citizens. Here, too, one of the most famous antebellum cases involved women and religion. Prudence Crandall was a Quaker who ran a school for girls in Canterbury, Connecticut. When she began admitting black girls in the early 1830s, the state passed a law restricting the right of various "school[s]," "academ[ies]" and "literary institution[s]" to teach nonresident blacks.[50] In 1833 the state prosecuted Crandall for teaching students like Ann Eliza Hammond, a black seventeen-year-old from Rhode Island.[51] Ultimately the state's highest court ruled for Crandall on a technicality, thus avoiding serious analysis of her expressive rights and the Article IV privileges and immunities of free blacks like Hammond.[52] Crandall's case grabbed nationwide attention and galvanized the early abolitionist movement. Indeed, one distinguished scholar has described Crandall's arguments as "the first comprehensive crystallization of abolitionist constitutional theory."[53] More than thirty years after Crandall's case, Representative William Lawrence of Ohio reminded the Thirty-ninth Congress of the need to protect "a white woman" who kept a "colored school."[54] Though not directly referring to Crandall, Lawrence's passing remark reflects the increasing visibility in the mid-nineteenth century of speech and association rights of women, especially religious women.[55]

Just as the centrality of religious speech helped bring women into the core of the First Amendment, it also helped blacks win inclusion. As with women, the exclusion of blacks from formal political rights like voting underscored the importance of their participation in other organizations, like churches, that could help gather the voice of the community.[56] Southern governments, of course, were all too aware of the "incendiary" dangers posed by any assembly of blacks, even (or perhaps especially) an assembly of God. After all, Nat Turner, who led a famous slave revolt in the 1830s, had been a black preacher—hence the Mississippi Black Code cited by Trumbull, prescribing thirty-nine lashes for any black exercising the functions of a minister.[57] But Republicans like Trumbull strongly affirmed the "civil" rights of blacks to assemble and preach, even as these same Republicans disclaimed any intent to confer upon blacks "political" rights like the franchise.[58] Charles Sumner provided the Joint Committee on Reconstruction yet another dramatic example of black speech, laying before the committee a petition "from the colored citizens of South Carolina," claiming to represent "four hundred and two thousand citizens of that State, being a very large majority of the population." Unsurprisingly, the petition prayed for "constitutional protection in keeping arms, in holding public assemblies, and in complete liberty of speech and of the press."[59] As W. E. B. Du Bois later explained, "For the first time in history the people of the United States listened not only to the voices of the Negroes' friends, but to the Negro himself."[60]

The gloss of the Fourteenth Amendment experience on the First Amendment text has important doctrinal implications. As the paradigmatic speaker in need of constitutional protection shifted from a localist criticizing the central government to a Unionist defending its Reconstruction policies, carpetbagging federal judges appointed in Washington became more trustworthy guardians of First Amendment freedoms than localist juries. When the core of the amendment was protection of the people collectively from unrepresentative government, perhaps an unelected federal judge on the federal payroll was a suspect sentry; but when the central mission of free speech shifted to protection of currently unpopular ideas from a current majority, an Article III officer with life tenure, sheltered from current political winds and sensitive to the long-term value of free speech, enjoyed certain advantages over a jury structured to reflect the dominant community sentiment of the hour. If women and blacks were central speakers in the Reconstruction paradigm, would a jury of twelve white men be in every sense a jury of their "peers"? And if not, there was less reason to expect that such a jury would represent their interests and rights any better than would a federal judge.

Thus it is the Fourteenth Amendment experience, I submit, that best justifies the emphasis in modern First Amendment doctrine on federal judges, rather than juries, as guardians of free speech. Yet the reigning doctrinal approach of jot-for-jot incorporation has obscured the significance of the Fourteenth Amendment, which all but drops out of the free-speech picture. Advocates and scholars focus all their analytic and narrative attention on the Creation, not the Reconstruction. In championing the rights of Communists and Jehovah's Witnesses in the twentieth century, the American Civil Liberties Union has analogized to

Zenger more than to the abolitionists—who are the truer forebears of modern political and religious speakers perceived as "nuts" and "cranks" by the dominant culture. Similarly, in the landmark First Amendment case of our era, *New York Times v. Sullivan,* Justice Brennan quoted Madison and thoughtfully reflected on the lessons of the Alien and Sedition Act controversy but said virtually nothing about the Reconstruction Amendment except that it incorporated the First Amendment against states (presumably jot for jot).[61] Yet the facts before the Court in *Sullivan* cried out for comparison with the Reconstruction era. Southern followers of the Reverend Martin Luther King, many of them black and many of them religious, had used a northern newspaper to criticize southern officials, and a southern jury composed of good old boys had socked the speakers with massive punitive damages. Many of the doctrinal rules crafted by *Sullivan* and its progeny reflect obvious suspicion of juries—resulting, for example, in various issues being classified as legal questions or mixed questions of law and fact inappropriate for unconstrained jury determination[62]—yet that suspicion is better justified by the Reconstruction experience than by the Creation.

But if various jury-restricting doctrines are indeed products of the interaction between the First and Fourteenth Amendments, how to justify the Court's application of these doctrines in pure First Amendment cases involving only the federal government? Can it be argued that the Fourteenth Amendment has a doctrinal "feedback effect" against the federal government, despite the amendment's clear textual limitation to state action?

Yes, it can. To begin with, consider Professor Monaghan's reminder that constitutional text does not specify precisely which institutional, procedural, and doctrinal rules best implement the First Amendment's substantive values.[63] In Monaghan's elegant phrase, the text does not supply a complete theory of "First Amendment due process," specifying, for example, the precise respective roles of judge and jury. In crafting such a theory, interpreters must obviously consider the First Amendment's primary purpose—but this, too, is not textually specified, so structural inferences may loom larger. The failure of the First Amendment to explicitly restrict state legislation, for example, combined with

Madison's structural observation in *The Federalist* No. 10 that state governments were more majoritarian than Congress, plausibly implies that the core purpose of the unreconstructed First Amendment was to prevent not majority tyranny, but self-dealing by unrepresentative government agents.[64] Given an agency-cost theory of free speech, a jury may well be the best guardian of the First Amendment's core—a conclusion buttressed by the efforts of eighteenth-century speakers like Zenger and Callender to appeal from judge to jury.[65] But if the original "First Amendment due process" theory is built in part on structural inferences from *Barron,* then the Fourteenth Amendment's repudiation of *Barron* requires us to rethink the original assumptions that led us to juries. Once the Fourteenth Amendment is on the books, the agency theory of free speech is less explanatory than the minority-protection theory, for the latter better accounts for speech limitations on majoritarian state legislatures. And the minority-protection theory suggests a different optimal allocation between judge and jury. To put the structural point textually, the parallel language between the First Amendment and the Fourteenth should strongly incline us toward a unitary theory of freedom of speech against both state and federal governments.

It might at first seem as if we have once again simply reached the same result as Hugo Black—identical treatment of First and Fourteenth Amendment speech cases—but by a much more tortuous route. On the contrary, refined incorporation reaches a conclusion different from Black's: that "freedom of speech" was subtly redefined in 1866, just as "freedom of the press" was subtly redefined in 1789. The 1866 redefinition changed the central purpose and optimal "due process" implementation of freedom of speech, making central certain types of speech that had previously been far more peripheral: religious speech, artistic speech, and, most important, minority speech.

We can chart a similar expansion of the core in "the right of the people peaceably to assemble, and to petition." These words, as originally written, linked tightly to popular-sovereignty theory. In its strictest sense, "the people" encompassed voters—the same adult male citizens who, roughly speaking, constituted "the militia" that was equated with "the people" in the next sentence of the Bill of Rights. And the paradigmatic exercise of (We) "the [P]eople's" right to assemble was a constitutional convention called by political rights holders (adult male citizens) to alter or abolish government. Other meanings of *the people* and *assembly* were also encompassed, but as we saw in Chapter 2, popular-sovereignty theory colored the amendment's core. By 1866 all this had subtly changed. The phrase *the people* was still read relatively strictly— we have seen, for example, that the Senate refused to allow foreigners to petition[66]—but clearly encompassed those who were not political rights holders. American women deluged the 1866 Congress with petitions precisely because they were *not* voters. Sumner's petition from the South Carolina "convention" of "colored citizens" came from a group excluded from the vote, the militia, and the jury—excluded from the polity, strictly defined.[67] Likewise, while the debate on the Fourteenth Amendment was drawing to a close in the Thirty-ninth Congress, another prominent convention of nonvoters—the Eleventh Woman's Rights Convention—was meeting in New York City.[68]

In introducing a women's suffrage petition in 1866 (from Mrs. Gerrit Smith, wife of a leading antebellum abolitionist), Senator John B. Henderson sharply distinguished between the rights of suffrage and petition: "The right of petition is a sacred right, and whatever may be thought of giving the ballot to women, the right to ask it of the Government [by petition] cannot be denied them."[69] Though skeptical about granting the American woman the political right to vote, Henderson declared that "no civil right," presumably including the right to petition, "can be denied her."[70] In a similar vein, the Republican *New York Evening Post* rejected the notion that the Civil Rights Act embraced political rights like jury service and office holding but cheerfully conceded that the rights of speech, press, petition, and assembly, though unenumerated, were clearly covered by the act.[71] So, too, in Professor tenBroek's rich account of abolitionist theory in the antebellum era, the core right of assembly at issue seems to be the right of blacks "to assemble peaceably on the Sabbath for the worship of [the] Creator."[72] This was, of course, a core right that southern states had violated; the framers of the Fourteenth Amendment thus took direct aim at laws like the one Virginia had passed in 1833 proclaiming that "[e]very *assemblage* of negroes for the purpose of religious worship, when such worship is conducted by a negro, . . . shall be an unlawful *assembly*."[73]

In a nutshell, the hybrid rights of assembly and petition were increasingly being characterized as civil, not political rights—a shift reflected in and perhaps caused by the exercise of these rights by women and blacks. Assemblies and petitions by the disenfranchised were no longer seen as peripheral to, or derivative of, a popular-sovereignty core celebrating the right of the (political) people to (re)assemble, through specially elected representatives, in constitutional conventions. Whereas the lived experience of 1787–89, with precisely such conventions of "the people" actually assembling, glossed the text with popular-sovereignty theory, a different lived experience in the 1860s offered a different, civil-rights gloss on the very same words.

Freedom of Religion

We have seen how, in the cases of speech, press, assembly, and petition, the same words meant slightly different things when first inscribed in the 1790s and when later reglossed in the 1860s. Could the same thing be true of the establishment and free-exercise clauses?

Begin with the establishment clause text prohibiting Congress from making any law "respecting an establishment of religion." We have seen that these words, as originally written, stood as a pure federalism provision. Congress could make "no law respecting [state] establishment [policy]"—that is, no law either establishing a national church or disestablishing a state church. On this reading, the clause was utterly agnostic on the substantive issue of establishment; it simply mandated that the issue be decided state by state and that Congress keep its hands off, that Congress make no law "respecting" the vexed question. In short, the original establishment clause was a home rule–local option provision mandating imperial neutrality.

Agnosticism, home rule, and imperial neutrality made a good deal of political sense in 1789, when some states gave specified sects privileged status and other states didn't. Proestablishment New Hampshiremen and antiestablishment Virginians might sharply disagree on the substantive issue of church-state relations but could agree on the jurisdictional idea that Congress should keep out: this was the lowest common denominator.

The precise wording of the clause, though, gave rise to a critical ambiguity: what about federal territories? Public debates over the Constitution and Bill of Rights in the 1780s and 1790s paid remarkably little heed to the territories. These debates took place within existing states—ratification of the Constitution under Article VII and of the Bill of Rights under Article V occurred state by state, and Americans living outside a state had no formal role. Furthermore, these debates focused overwhelmingly on the ways in which an upstart Congress might displace the powers of existing state governments, governments that had century-deep roots.

Had New Hampshire's original proposed religion clause—"Congress shall make no laws touching religion"[74]—been adopted, a powerful textual argument could have been made that Congress could not make proreligion law even in the territories. But as finally worded, perhaps the First Amendment barred only congressional laws interfering with *state* religious policies, laws "respecting" state "establishment" policy. Such a reading would resonate with Federalist arguments that the establishment clause was purely declaratory because Article I had given Congress no enumerated power in the first place to intermeddle with religion in the states. Article IV, however, had given Congress plenary power over federal territories—and perhaps the establishment clause was not meant to modify this. As we saw in Chapter 2, the precise wording of the "Congress shall make no law" amendment derived from and inverted the language of the Article I necessary-and-proper clause; and had the amendment been tucked into the original Constitution rather than tacked onto the end, its most natural niche would have been in Article I, section 8. Little attention seems to have been paid to how this "no law respecting" language would apply to territorial governance under Article IV.

On the very day it debated an early version of the establishment clause, the First Congress pushed forward an ordinance to govern the western territory by extending the Confederation Congress's Northwest Ordinance of 1787, a regime that one leading scholar has described as "suffused with aid, encouragement, and support for religion."[75] Over the next two decades, Congress applied this regime to other territories, and various territorial governments aided and sponsored religion in sundry ways.[76] Some modern scholars have read all this as a record of sheer hypocrisy—"no law" apparently did not mean "no law."[77] Others have claimed that early congressional practice shows that only strict and totalizing sectarian establishments were banned by the First Amendment, and that generalized support for religion was not covered by the clause.[78] But a federalism-based reading can offer a third possibility: the clause merely barred Congress from interfering with *state* establishment policy. Putting the textual point functionally, perhaps Congress, when legislating in a plenary way for a territory, stood in the shoes of a state government and could adopt the same kinds of proreligion laws that states could.[79] (This federalism reading might also explain otherwise "anomalous" congressional activity like providing religious chaplains for Congress and the federal military; perhaps these, too, were distinctive federal "enclaves" in which congressional policy did not intrude between a state and its own citizens.)[80]

On this reading, it is tempting to say that, like the Tenth Amendment, the establishment clause simply does not apply to federal territories. But this is technically incorrect. The clause does apply—formally, the Constitution always applies. But (on one reading) the clause simply has no bite, just as the presence of the Article IV clause giving Congress plenary power to "make all needful Rules and Regulations respecting the Territory . . . belonging to the United States" means that the Tenth Amendment formally applies to the territories but has little bite there (at least insofar as the amendment affirms certain principles of federalism as opposed to popular sovereignty). Note also how the use of the word *respecting* in the Article IV clause reminds us that this same word in the original establishment clause can indeed be read agnostically (no law "concerning" an establishment) rather than in an antiestablishment way (no law "tending toward" an establishment).

As the nineteenth century wore on, the technically correct notion that the establishment clause applied to the territories began to mutate, giving way in some places to a different—substantive—interpretation. A territorial legislature derived all its powers from Congress; thus, what

Congress could not do, its territorial agent could not do. When, say, Fourth Amendment rights were at stake, it made little difference whether its ban on general warrants—"no Warrants shall issue, but . . ." —was phrased as a limit on Congress or on its territorial agent. But to say that, for example, the Iowa territorial legislature "shall make no law respecting an establishment of religion" was rhetorically to say some-thing rather different than that Congress should make no such law. Un-like Congress, the Iowa territorial legislature obviously had no power to legislate over other states; thus to say that *this* legislature should make no law obviously implied no law *in the territory*. The agnostic federalism reading—hard enough for some to see when the establishment clause addressed "Congress"—faded from view, replaced by a substantive anti-establishment interpretation.

As various territorial legislatures matured into state legislatures, it seemed only natural to bind them to the same (substantive) nonestab-lishment rule, using language borrowed from the federal template. When Iowa gained statehood in 1846, its first state constitution proclaimed in its Bill of Rights that "[t]he general assembly shall make no law respect-ing an establishment of religion or prohibiting the free exercise thereof," words repeated verbatim in its Constitution of 1857.[81] Virtually identical phrases appeared in the territorial Constitution of Deseret in 1849, and its successor Utah Territory draft constitution of 1860.[82] Similarly, in the 1859 Constitution of the Jefferson Territory (today known as Colorado), we find the following clause: "The General Assembly shall make no laws respecting an establishment of religion, nor shall any religious test be re-quired of any citizen."[83] In his influential constitutional treatise of 1868, the respected Michigan jurist Thomas Cooley likewise wrote that, under prevailing state constitutions, state legislatures were barred from creating "[a]ny law respecting an establishment of religion."[84]

This antiestablishment interpretation gaining steam in the West was also winning friends in the East. Surely the First Amendment's five other clauses—protecting free exercise, free speech, free press, assembly, and petition—had bite in the territories vis-à-vis both Congress and territorial legislatures; why not the establishment clause, too? The lawyerly and technical counterarguments were that these five other clauses explicitly affirmed "freedoms" whereas the establishment clause did not; and that these other clauses asymmetrically guarded against federal action *restricting*—"prohibit[ing] and abridg[ing]"—rights, whereas the bland word *respecting* affirmed a wholly symmetric and agnostic federalism rule that had no bite outside states. (The First Amendment did not bar Congress from *promoting* speech, press, assembly, and petition, but it forbade all federal action *concerning* establishment in the states.) But these lawyerly and technical counterarguments were, well, lawyerly and technical, requiring exquisite attention to textual detail and fine analytic distinctions. Thus we find Chief Justice Taney lumping together all the First Amendment clauses in *Dred Scott:*

> [N]o one, we presume, will contend that Congress can make any law in a Territory respecting the establishment of religion, or the free exercise thereof, or abridging the freedom of speech or of the press, or the right of the people of the Territory peaceably to assemble, and to petition the Government for the redress of grievances.
>
> . . . .
>
> . . . [These and other prohibitions of the Bill of Rights are] not confined to the States, but the words are general, and extend to the whole territory over which the Constitution gives [Congress] power to legislate, including those portions of it remaining under Territorial Government, as well as that covered by States. It is a total absence of power everywhere within the dominion of the United States, and places the citizens of a Territory, so far as these rights are concerned, on the same footing with citizens of the States . . . . [85]

Of course, Taney had an agenda of his own in *Dred Scott:* to minimize congressional power in the territories. If Congress could make a law promoting religion and morality in the territories, why couldn't it make a law prohibiting the irreligious and immoral institution of slavery in the territories? (The famous Northwest Ordinance of 1787, blessed by the First Congress, had of course done both.) Taney's ruling in *Dred Scott* that, under the Fifth Amendment due-process clause, Congress could not bar slavery from federal territory came right in the middle of the above-quoted passage (as indicated by the first ellipsis).[86]

Writing five years earlier, another southern judge, Georgia Chief Justice Joseph Henry Lumpkin, had explicitly grouped together all six First Amendment clauses and opined that states as well as Congress should be bound by all six.[87] He, too, read the word *respecting* as antiestablishment rather than agnostic:

> Our revolutionary sires wisely resolved that religion should be purely voluntary in this country; that it should subsist by its own omnipotence, or come to nothing. Hence, they solemnly determined that there should be no church established by law, and maintained by the secular power. Now, the doctrine is, that Congress may not exercise this power, but that each State Legislature may do so for itself. As if a National religion and State religion, a National press and State press, were quite separate and distinct from each other; and that the one might be subject to control, but the other not!
>
> Such logic, I must confess, fails to commend itself to my judgment.[88]

Having considered antebellum interpretations from the West and the South, let us now turn to the Northeast. As early as 1820, shortly before the Massachusetts constitutional convention, a proposal surfaced to clone the words of the First Amendment religion clauses into the state constitution, substituting the Massachusetts legislature for Congress.[89] Though not adopted by the convention, this proposal obviously read the word *respecting* as antiestablishment rather than agnostic. In 1833 a more momentous event occurred, as Massachusetts became the last state to abolish state financial support for a legally privileged sect.

In the 1780s several states featured sectarian establishments; by the 1860s none did. Virtually all states in the mid-nineteenth century favored religion generally, and some privileged Christianity or Protestantism above other religions, but none singled out one Christian sect for special favor. The common denominator among states had thus shifted dramatically, and popular understandings of the establishment clause may have reflected this shift. What began as an agnostic but strict federalism rule—*no law* intermeddling with religion in the states—was gradually mutating into a soft substantive rule: religion in general could be promoted, but not one sect at the expense of others.* Whereas the founding spotlight shone bright on congressional power in the states—this was the key concern in 1788–91—by the 1850s Americans were fighting out many of the most intense constitutional issues of the day in and over the territories. Whereas the original Bill of Rights had in many cases borrowed language from older state constitutions, newer states were now returning the compliment by borrowing from (and in the process redefining) the words of the federal Bill. By 1866 half the states had begun as federal territories; the modal and model state was no longer Madison's Virginia, but Bingham's Ohio.

But even if by 1866 the establishment clause was no longer a state right, pure and simple, can we really say that it was a private right of discrete individuals, as opposed to a right of the public at large? To the extent a state created a coercive establishment, decreeing that individuals profess a state creed or attend a state service or pay money directly to a state church, such coercion would implicate bodily liberty and property of discrete individuals and would thus intrude upon paradigmatic privileges and immunities of citizens. (Put another way, all these examples also seem like textbook violations of religious "free exercise.") But what of a noncoercive establishment—say, a simple state declaration on a state seal proclaiming Utah "the Mormon State"?

If we look to Blackstone, we will not find this kind of nonestablish-

---

*Joseph Story's influential treatise of 1833 nicely straddled the issue, featuring both the older federalism-based, agnostic-absolutist reading and the more modern soft-substantive reading of the establishment clause. See 3 JOSEPH STORY, COMMENTARIES ON THE CONSTITUTION OF THE UNITED STATES §1873, at 731 (Boston: Hilliard, Gray, 1833) ("The whole power over the subject of religion is left exclusively to the state governments"); id. §1871, at 728 ("The real object of the amendment was, not to countenance, much less to advance Mahometanism, or Judaism, or infidelity, by prostrating Christianity; but to exclude all rivalry among Christian sects").

We should also note here that in 1864, federal coins began to bear the nonsectarian motto "In God We Trust." In 1865 Congress endorsed this coin motto, an action arguably defensible under either the older "special federal enclave not interfering with state religious policy" theory or the newer "no preference among sects" ideology. See Act of March 3, 1865, ch. 100, 13 Stat. 517, 518. For discussion, see 3 ANSON PHELPS STOKES, CHURCH AND STATE IN THE UNITED STATES 601–3 (1950).

ment right classified as a common-law "privilege" or "immunity." Of course, this is neither surprising nor particularly dispositive, given that England never had a strict rule of nonestablishment in the first place but only a more narrow regime of "toleration."[90] Consider also the Article IV privileges-and-immunities clause. In important ways this clause prefigured the similarly yet differently worded Fourteenth Amendment, and southern violations of Article IV helped to define paradigmatic privileges of national citizenship to be protected by Bingham and company. Flagrant southern denials of speech, press, assembly, and petition rights of antebellum Yankees had dramatized the need to protect these paradigmatic "privileges" of geographic and demographic outsiders. But no comparable noncoercive establishment targeting out-of-staters seems to have burned itself into the minds of Reconstruction Republicans; indeed, it is rather hard to imagine how a noncoercive state religious endorsement could have implicated Article IV.

The historical evidence from the 1860s and early 1870s is somewhat sparse and rather mixed. On the one hand, a variety of congressmen catalogued the "personal rights" protected by the First Amendment as encompassing speech, press, petition, and assembly, but not nonestablishment: rather, they spoke only of "free exercise" or of "freedom of conscience."[91] On the other hand, as noted in Chapter 9, silence alone does not prove much, and even this seemingly selective silence went unelaborated. At one point, Senator Trumbull declared that "our laws are to be enacted with a view to educate, improve, enlighten, *and Christianize* the Negro";[92] on the other hand, perhaps he intended no governmental endorsement of or preference toward Christianity but merely the abolition of long-standing state restraints on black churches, thus freeing blacks to choose Christ on their own. Several Congressmen and commentators in the late 1860s and early 1870s did treat nonestablishment as an individual right,[93] but here, too, we find little elaboration.

Perhaps the greatest elaboration came from Thomas Cooley's influential 1868 treatise. Under prevailing state constitutions, wrote Cooley, states generally could not enact "[a]ny law respecting an establishment of religion. . . . There is not religious *liberty* where any one sect is favored by the State . . . . It is not toleration which is established in our system, but religious *equality.*"[94] Even a noncoercive establishment, Cooley suggested, violated principles of religious liberty and religious equality—violated norms of equal rights and privileges. And once we see this, it turns out that the question—should we incorporate the establishment clause?—may not matter all that much, because even if we did not, principles of religious liberty and equality could be vindicated via the free-exercise clause (whose text, history, and logic make it a paradigmatic case for incorporation) and the equal-protection clause (which frowns on state laws that unjustifiably single out some folks for special privileges and relegate others to second-class status).[95] Surely Alabama could not adopt a state motto proclaiming itself "the White Supremacy State"; such a motto would offend basic principles of equal citizenship and equal protection.[96] And so a law that proclaimed Utah a Mormon state should be suspect whether we call this a violation of establishment principles, free-exercise principles, equal-protection principles, equal-citizenship principles, or religious-liberty principles. Once we remember that we are not incorporating clauses mechanically but reconstructing rights, we reach the unsurprising conclusion that our basic touchstones should be the animating Fourteenth Amendment ideals of liberty and equality.

Let us now turn to the free-exercise principle and trace how it, too, was reconstructed by the Fourteenth Amendment. Outraged by decades of religious persecution in the antebellum South, leading Republicans in the Thirty-eighth and Thirty-ninth Congresses repeatedly stressed the need to protect "freedom of religious opinion," "a free exercise of religion," "freedom of conscience," "freedom in the exercise of religion," and "the free exercise of religion."[97] In some form or other, they insisted that henceforth this basic First Amendment freedom apply against states.*

---

*In 1875 Representative James G. Blaine proposed a constitutional amendment which, among other things, provided that "No state shall make any law respecting an establishment of religion or prohibiting the free exercise thereof." Some scholars have argued that this amendment, which passed the House but died in the Senate in 1876, strongly cuts against Fourteenth Amendment incorporation (of the religion clauses, or more generally). It's hard to see why. The argument assumes that, had the Fourteenth Amendment already incorporated the religion clauses, the Blaine Amendment would have been redundant. But (1) The general premise about nonredundancy is deeply flawed. As we have

But in what form, exactly? The original free-exercise clause merely barred laws targeted at religious exercise as such; its letter and spirit allowed Congress to make genuinely secular laws, even though those laws might obstruct particular religious practices. Perhaps the Fourteenth Amendment sweeps more broadly. The unreconstructed First Amendment text speaks of the moment when "Congress" "make[s]" a "law," a moment when the religious practice may not even exist. By contrast, the Fourteenth Amendment text squarely regulates all branches of "State" government and explicitly addresses the moment when a law is "enforce[d]"—when the conflict between the law and the religious practice is visible to all. We have seen that the First Amendment has no textual tools for distinguishing among various possible claims of religious exemption from general secular laws.[98] The Fourteenth Amendment, by contrast, hints at a possible distinction in its language of *privileges:* where only coreligionists are involved in a religious practice—with no direct

---

seen, many of the provisions of the original Bill were seen as "declaratory" of existing law, rightly understood—and thus in some sense redundant—and this declaratory theory was one of the driving forces behind the Fourteenth Amendment. (2) In fact, the Blaine Amendment as a whole was hardly redundant. Its other provisions sought to add new (rather dubious) rules to the Constitution; in short, it seems that Blaine and others were cleverly trying to bundle their dubious new rules alongside a far more acceptable clause. (3) The events of 1875 and 1876 are of limited value in determining what the Fourteenth Amendment meant when proposed and adopted in 1866–68. *Slaughter-House* had strangled the privileges-or-immunities clause in its crib in 1873, and later cases in early 1876 refused to revive the clause; Congress thereafter had to take account of these (mis)interpretations. But for what it's worth, even Democratic spokesmen in 1874 admitted that states were already bound by the First Amendment's religious guarantees by dint of the Fourteenth Amendment. *See, e.g.,* 2 CONG. REC. 384–85 (1874) (remarks of Rep. Roger Mills); *id.* at 242 app. (remarks of Sen. Thomas Norwood). (4) The wording of the Blaine Amendment reaffirms that by 1875, at least, *respecting* had come to be widely understood as antiestablishment rather than agnostic.

For an illuminating discussion of what the Blaine Amendment was in fact all about and more analysis of why it poses no real obstacle to refined incorporation, see Kurt T. Lash, *The Second Adoption of the Establishment Clause: The Rise of the Nonestablishment Principle,* 27 Ariz. St. L.J. 1085, 1145–50 (1995). *See also* MICHAEL KENT CURTIS, NO STATE SHALL ABRIDGE: THE FOURTEENTH AMENDMENT AND THE BILL OF RIGHTS 169–70 (1986).

invasions of the lives, limbs, or property of nonbelievers—a religious practice could be deemed suitably "priv[ate]" and hence "privilege[d]" from intruding legislation.[99] On this libertarian reading, a general secular murder law would trump the religious claims of a cult that demanded human sacrifice of nonbelievers, but the Catholic Church would be "privileged" to employ only male priests regardless of general laws outlawing sex discrimination in employment.[100]

Professor Lash has argued that this textually possible reconstruction of free exercise is also historically plausible.[101] Reconstruction Republicans, Lash argues, at times sought to shield religion even from secular laws. Southern laws making it a crime to teach blacks to read were secular enough, but these laws outraged Republicans because of their devastating effect on (Protestant) religion; they outlawed teaching blacks to read the Holy Bible, the word of God.[102] In the years immediately after the ratification of the Fourteenth Amendment, Congress considered civil rights legislation banning segregation in various public places. Early drafts applied this antisegregation rule not only to innkeepers and cemetery associations but also to church organizations. Here, too, the law was suitably secular in purpose, but Reconstruction Republicans ultimately exempted churches from its scope out of respect for the autonomy and institutional privacy—the religious "privileges" and "immunities"—of religious organizations.[103]

If, as Lash claims, "freedom of religion" in the 1860s meant libertarian autonomy from governmental intrusion in ways that it did not in the 1790s, this shift fits snugly into our overall story of rights reconstruction. Under the Creation vision of free exercise in 1791, Congress might, but need not, choose to exempt a given religious practice from a general secular law. In this world, large, politically powerful religions could win exemptions more easily than could fringe minority sects; Creation free exercise was, to this extent, a majoritarian right. But the Reconstruction Amendment accentuated minority liberty, and this accent perhaps invites special judicial accommodation of minority sects that the legislature does not know or care about.

With this account of expressive and religious rights in place, we can now see how the entire First Amendment was, in profound ways, reconstructed by the Fourteenth. Today nothing is more common than for distinguished jurists to speak of the firstness of our First Amendment. In 1989 Justice Blackmun emphasized the point as follows: "If numbers are important, this is the *First* Amendment, not the Second or the Sixteenth, but the *First*."[104] And from the pen of no less a man than Robert Jackson, we find the following in *United States Reports:* "This freedom was first in the Bill of Rights because it was first in the forefathers' minds."[105] When we recall that in 1789 our First Amendment was technically *third* in our Founding forefathers' minds, we may start to smirk, and think of Archie Bunker's declaration that "If English was good enough for Jesus Christ, it's good enough for me." But if we smirk here, the joke in the end is on us; like Hugo Black, Justices Blackmun and Jackson have ended up in the right place, even if they cut a few corners getting there. For the men and women who reglossed our Bill of Rights in the 1860s, *our* First Amendment was *their* First Amendment—first in the text, and first in their hearts. The antebellum experience had indeed dramatized for them the substantive firstness of the First Amendment; in the minds of *these* forefathers—and foremothers, too*—religion and expression stood as the nation's first freedoms, the paradigmatic "privileges" and "immunities" of "citizens of the United States."

Guns and Homes

The right to keep and bear arms was also a paradigmatic "privilege" of "citizens of the United States." But the right in 1789 and the right in 1866 meant different things.

In the Creation era, republicans like Patrick Henry, George Mason, and Elbridge Gerry proclaimed that freedom ultimately rested on the

---

*A nice illustration of the visibility of women's expressive activity in this era appears in the fourteenth (!) plank of the Republican platform of 1872: "The Republican party is mindful of its obligations to the loyal women of America for their noble devotion to the cause of freedom. Their admission to wider fields of usefulness is viewed with satisfaction, and the honest demand of any class of citizens for additional rights should be treated with respectful consideration." NATIONAL PARTY PLATFORMS 1840–1964, at 47 (Kirk H. Porter and Donald Bruce Johnson eds., 3d ed., 1966). For discussion, see THE CONCISE HISTORY OF WOMAN SUFFRAGE 23–24 (Mari Jo Buhle and Paul Buhle eds., 1978).

bedrock of an arms-bearing citizenry. Some fourscore years later, Reconstruction Republicans like Lyman Trumbull, Jacob Howard, Charles Sumner, James Nye, Samuel Pomeroy, Sidney Clarke, Josiah Grinnell, Roswell Hart, Henry Raymond, Nathaniel Banks, Thomas Eliot, George Julian, and Leonard Myers echoed their forebears' odes to arms in speeches in the Thirty-ninth Congress.[106]

But sometimes the same sounds mean different things.[107] We should not confuse the small-r republicans of the 1780s with the capital-R Republicans of the 1860s; when these two sets of men spoke of the need to protect the right to arms, they had rather different pictures in mind.[108]

At the Founding, the Second Amendment sounded in federalism; state-organized militias were to keep central tyranny at bay and discourage easy resort to that bane of classical republicanism, a central standing army. The world looked different to Reconstruction Republicans. Massachusetts militiamen may have fought for freedom at Lexington and Concord in 1775, but Mississippi militiamen had killed for slavery at Vicksburg in 1863. In 1866 various southern white militias, often "composed of Confederate veterans still wearing their gray uniforms, . . . frequently terrorized the black population, ransacking their homes to seize shotguns and other property and abusing those who refused to sign plantation labor contracts."[109] A federal standing army was less a republican (small r) bane than a Republican (capital R) boon: a freedom-loving Union government in the uneasy years ahead might need to use a central army to reconstruct the South, making it safe for all true republicans and especially for all true Republicans.[110]

At the Founding, the right of the people to keep and bear arms stood shoulder to shoulder with the right to vote; arms bearing in militias embodied a paradigmatic *political* right flanking the other main political rights of voting, office holding, and jury service. Thus "the people" and the "militia" at the heart of the Second Amendment were quintessential voters and jurymen, the same "people" in the Preamble, in Article I, section 2, and in the First, Fourth, Ninth, and Tenth Amendments. But Reconstruction Republicans recast arms bearing as a core *civil* right, utterly divorced from the militia and other political rights and responsibilities. Arms were needed not as part of political and politicized militia service but to protect one's individual homestead. Everyone—even nonvoting, nonmilitia-serving women—had a right to a gun for self-protection.

Creation-era arms bearing was collective, exercised in a well-regulated militia embodying a republican right of the people, collectively understood. Reconstruction gun-toting was individualistic, accentuating not group rights of the citizenry but self-regarding "privileges" of discrete "citizens" to individual self-protection. The Creation vision was public, with the militia muster on the town square. The Reconstruction vision was private, with individual freedmen keeping guns at home to ward off Klansmen and other ruffians.

Time and again Founding republicans in 1789 spoke of "the militia"; Reconstruction Republicans in 1866 almost never did. If blacks had a right to be in militias, why not in juries, or voting booths, or legislative assemblies? The basic analytic framework holding together the Fourteenth Amendment—the distinction between civil rights like worship, speech, property, and guns on the one hand and political rights like voting and jury service on the other—would have come unglued.[111]

But how, exactly, did Reconstruction Republicans accomplish their remarkable rereading of the arms right? And where, precisely, does the Fourteenth Amendment work its noteworthy rewriting of the arms right and the inscription of the civil rights–political rights distinction? Finally, what, ultimately, was the new vision of arms offered by the Reconstruction Republicans, and why did they deem it so fundamental?

Once we remember that, strictly speaking, 1860s Republicans sought not to incorporate clauses but to apply (refined) rights against states, it seems rather natural textually that Reconstructors like Jacob Howard, James Nye, Samuel Pomeroy, Sidney Clarke, Nathaniel Banks, Thomas Eliot, Roswell Hart, and Henry Raymond invoked the operative rights clause of the Second Amendment while utterly ignoring its preambulatory ode to the militia.[112] (And as noted, Reconstructors obviously had good functional and ideological reasons for downplaying militias.) Moreover, when Reconstructors paraphrased or quoted the Second Amendment's second clause, they often subtly recast it. It was now less a right of the people, and more an individualistic privilege of persons.

Many examples could be adduced here, but perhaps the most vivid came from Congress as a whole. In Chapter 9 we noted the connections (but not identity) between section 1 of the Fourteenth Amendment and the Civil Rights Act of 1866. Alongside that act, Congress passed the Freedman's Bureau Act, a sister statute introduced the same day by the same sponsor and featuring key clauses in *pari materia.* As finally adopted, the Freedman's Bureau Act affirmed that "laws . . . concerning *personal* liberty, *personal* security, and the acquisition, enjoyment, and disposition of estate, real and *personal, including the constitutional right to bear arms,* shall be secured to and enjoyed by all the citizens."[113]

All the citizens here—and in the Fourteenth Amendment—meant women, too, as Reconstructors were at pains to explain. Indeed, the case of the unmarried white woman in many ways defined the basic legal category of civil as opposed to political rights. Although these women could not vote, hold office, sit on juries, or serve in militias, they could worship, speak, print, assemble, petition, sue, contract, own property, and bring diversity cases in federal courts. In short, antebellum single white women enjoyed civil but not political rights, and Republican Reconstructors in 1866 made clear that henceforth all blacks should enjoy all of these basic rights, too.* Thus, the Reconstruction Congress expressly

---

*For clear examples of the white woman being used as the paradigmatic civil rights holder, see CONG. GLOBE, 38th Cong., 1st Sess. 840 (1864) (remarks of Sen. James Harlan); CONG. GLOBE, 39th Cong., 1st Sess. 1255, 1263, 1757, 122 app. (1866) (remarks of Sen. Henry Wilson, Rep. John Broomall, and Sens. Lyman Trumbull and John Henderson); Bradwell v. Illinois, 83 U.S. (16 Wall.) 130, 137 (1872) (oral argument of Sen. Matthew Carpenter). Women agreed that the rights of blacks and women were now linked. In 1866 the Eleventh National Woman's Rights Convention unanimously adopted Susan B. Anthony's resolution declaring that "[b]y the act of Emancipation and the Civil Rights bill, the negro and woman now hold the same civil and political *status,* alike needing only the ballot; and . . . the same arguments apply equally to both classes, proving all partial legislation fatal to republican institutions." 2 HISTORY OF WOMAN SUFFRAGE 171–72 (Elizabeth Cady Stanton, Susan B. Anthony, and Matilda Joslyn Gage eds., AYER Co. reprint, 1985) (1882).

To be sure, the Fourteenth Amendment divided the women's movement, with some women supporting it and others opposing ratification. But the opposition had nothing to do with the inclusive language of section 1, which women rightly read as protecting

repudiated *Dred Scott*'s claim that because free blacks could never be citizens, they lacked many of these basic rights of white women.

Further support for the existence and importance of a basic legal distinction between civil and political rights came from the Article IV comity clause. As a Massachusetts man temporarily visiting South Carolina, Samuel Hoar was entitled to worship, speak, print, assemble, petition, sue, contract, own real property, and bring diversity cases (civil rights all), but he was not entitled to exercise the political rights of voting in a South Carolina election or serving in a South Carolina militia, jury, or legislature. Thus when the architects of the Fourteenth Amendment reconfigured the words of the comity clause—*privileges, immunities,* and *citizens*—they obviously did so with the basic civil-political distinction in mind.[114]

The tripartite phraseology of the 1866 Freedman's Bureau statute—affirming rights of "personal liberty," "personal security," and property—derived directly from Blackstone's influential chapter on the "Absolute Rights of Individuals."[115] (Indeed, the sponsors of the sibling Civil Rights Bill in both House and Senate, James Wilson and Lyman Trumbull, explicitly quoted from Blackstone's chapter in support of their bill.)[116] When we consult that chapter, we find Blackstone affirming an individual right of the subject to "hav[e] arms" to protect his "three great

---

all citizens and persons. Unlike the later Fifteenth Amendment, section 1 pointedly spoke not of race but of more general liberty and equality. Indeed, the key language of section 1 closely tracked the language of a December 1865 essay by Elizabeth Cady Stanton calling for an amendment in which "the women as well as the men shall be secured in all the rights, privileges, and immunities of citizens." *Id.* at 94 n.*. This essay in turn echoed Stanton's famous 1848 Seneca Falls Declaration demanding for women "all the rights and privileges which belong to them as citizens of the United States." 1 *id.* at 70–71.

Many women, though, were outraged by section 2 of the Fourteenth Amendment, which excluded women from the presumptive electorate and, for the first time, put the word *male* into the Constitution. But section 2 cast no shadow on section 1, which dealt with civil rights, not political rights. For more discussion, see Akhil Reed Amar, *Women and the Constitution,* 18 HARV. J.L. & PUB. POL'Y 465, 467–70 (1995); Nina Morais, Note, *Sex Discrimination and the Fourteenth Amendment: Lost History,* 97 YALE L. J. 1153 (1988); Sandra L. Rierson, *Race and Gender Discrimination: A Historical Case for Equal Treatment Under the Fourteenth Amendment,* 1 DUKE J. GENDER L. & POL'Y 89 (1994).

and primary rights, of personal security, personal liberty, and private property" and his ultimate individual right of "self-preservation."[117] The accent here is distinctly individualistic, private, and nonmilitary. Note that Blackstone uses the phrase *having arms* rather than the more military-sounding phrase, *bearing arms*. In 1840 the Tennessee Supreme Court went so far as to say that the phrase *bear arms* had "a military sense, and no other. . . . A man in the pursuit of deer, elk and buffaloes, might carry his rifle every day, for forty years, and, yet, it would never be said of him, that he had *borne arms* . . . ."[118] Although some Americans at the Founding did use the phrase more broadly—Pennsylvania Anti-Federalists, for example, linked the "right to bear arms" with "killing game"[119]—the paradigmatic image of arms in the unreconstructed Second Amendment was surely military. The musketed Minutemen stood at center stage, pushing Blackstone to the wings.

But events over the next eighty years in America conspired to move Blackstone to the center. Southern states, ever fearful of slave insurrections, enacted sweeping antebellum laws prohibiting not just slaves but free blacks from owning guns.[120] In response, antislavery theorists emphasized the personal right of all free citizens—white and black, male and female, northern and southern, visitor and resident—to own guns for self-protection. Here is what Joel Tiffany, in a highly influential antislavery treatise, had to say about the Second Amendment in 1849:

> Here is another of the immunities of a citizen of the United States, which is guaranteed by the supreme, organic law of the land. This is one of the subordinate rights, mentioned by Blackstone, as belonging to every Englishman. It . . . is accorded to every subject for the purpose of protecting and defending himself, if need be, in the enjoyment of his absolute rights of life, liberty and property. . . . The colored citizen, under our [federal] constitution, has now as full and perfect a right to keep and bear arms as any other; and no State law, or State regulation has authority to deprive him of that right.[121]

Tiffany's paragraph is studded with gems. If we read carefully we can see the declaratory theory of *Barron* contrarianism; the language of "immunities" of national "citizens"; and a highly refined, Blackstone-tinged, individualistic rereading of the Second Amendment.

Tiffany's treatise became a basic handbook for many Republicans who later served in the Thirty-ninth Congress,[122] but even antiabolitionists were coming under the Blackstonian spell. In the 1846 case *Nunn v. Georgia*, the proslavery contrarian Chief Justice Joseph Henry Lumpkin proclaimed not only that the Second Amendment bound the states but also that "The right [is guaranteed to] the whole people, old and young, men, women and boys, and not militia only, to keep and bear arms of every description, and not such merely as are used by the militia."[123] A couple of years later, however, the Georgia court pulled back, suggesting that maybe arms bearing wasn't quite the global civil right that *Nunn*'s dicta made it seem: "Free persons of color have never been recognized here as citizens; they are not entitled to bear arms, vote for members of the legislature, or to hold any civil office. . . . They have no *political* rights, but they have *personal* rights, one of which is personal liberty."[124]

Roger Taney and Joel Tiffany hardly saw eye to eye in the 1850s, but they both agreed on this: *if* free blacks were citizens, it would necessarily follow that they had a right of *private* arms bearing. According to *Dred Scott*, the "privileges and immunities" of "citizens" included "full liberty of speech in public and in private upon all subjects upon which its own citizens might speak; to hold public meeting upon political affairs, and to keep and carry arms wherever they went."[125] Of course, for Taney all this wrongly meant that black citizenship could never be; but we must not miss his privatizing of liberty with the words "privileges and immunities," with his accent on "private" as well as "public" speech, and with his emphasis on nonmilitia gun-toting in his substitution of "carry" for "bear" and his addition of the phrase "wherever they went."

Taney's invocation of "privileges and immunities" of "citizens" "wherever they went" obviously calls to mind the rights of out-of-staters under the Article IV comity clause. When we recall the plight of Samuel Hoar and his daughter in South Carolina, we can see again how a right to a gun for self-protection, even for someone who had no right to be part of the state militia, was viewed by the antislavery movement as the most basic of liberties, rooted in real ways in the right to life itself.

To be sure, arms bearing for blacks also had huge symbolic significance. A gun was an emblem of freedom. In an appendix to his edition of Blackstone's *Commentaries,* St. George Tucker reminded his readers of the ancient law of William the Conqueror, under which English villeins were emancipated as follows: "If any person is willing to enfranchise [that is, free] his slave, let him . . . deliver him free arms, to wit, a lance and a sword; thereupon he is a free man."[126]

But a gun was far more than a badge. Even free blacks (to say nothing of slaves) had suffered unspeakable violence at the hands of white governments, white mobs, and white thugs; and in the wake of Emancipation, many southern governments forbade gun ownership among blacks but not whites.[127] Blacks immediately sensed the grave threat posed by this aspect of the Black Codes and took quick action. In November 1865 South Carolina blacks assembled in convention to take stock of their situation. Led by men like Jonathan C. Gibbs, Richard H. Cain, Francis L. Cardozo, Alonzo Ransier, Robert C. De Large, and Jonathan B. Wright—several of whom would later rank among the first black congressmen in American history—these blacks petitioned Congress in bold contrarian words: "We, the colored people of the State of South Carolina, in Convention assembled, . . . ask that, inasmuch as the Constitution of the United States explicitly declares that the right to keep and bear arms shall not be infringed . . . that the late efforts of the Legislature of this State to pass an act to deprive us [of] arms be forbidden, as a plain violation of the Constitution."[128]

One of the core purposes of the Civil Rights Act of 1866 and of the Fourteenth Amendment was to redress the grievances of this and other petitions, outlaw the infamous Black Codes, and affirm the full and equal right of every citizen to self-defense. Thus in introducing his Civil Rights Bill, whose first draft proclaimed blacks "citizens of the United States" and affirmed their "civil rights," Lyman Trumbull explicitly took aim at a Mississippi law that prohibited "any negro or mulatto from having fire-arms."[129] Moments later, he read to his colleagues ex-

cerpts from Blackstone's famous chapter on the "Absolute Rights of Individuals."[130] We should also note how Trumbull's small shift from
"arms" to "fire-arms" helped ease his emphasis on private gun-toting. A
similar shift appeared in the speech of Representative Josiah Grinnell,
who attacked a Kentucky Black Code that forbade blacks to "keep" or
"buy[]" a "gun"—even "a musket which he has carried through the
war."[131] Senator James Nye was more explicit, noting the role of black
men in the Union army, and then immediately accenting *private* gun
ownership: "As citizens of the United States they have equal right to protection, and to keep and bear arms *for self-defense*."[132]

Note how Senator Samuel Pomeroy's speech likewise linked guns with
the private rather than the political: "Every man should have a homestead, that is, the right to acquire and hold one, and the right to be safe
and protected in that citadel of his love. . . . He should [also] have the
right to bear arms for the defense of himself and family and his homestead. And if the cabin door of the freedman is broken open and the in-
truder enters for purposes as vile as were known to slavery, then should a
well-loaded musket be in the hand of the occupant . . . ."[133] A couple of
days later, Representative Henry Raymond opined on the nature of civil
rights owing to all citizens and conjured up a similar home-centered vision, affirming that the freedman "has a country and a home; a right to
defend himself and his wife and children; a right to bear arms; a right to
testify in the Federal courts."[134] Raymond was a founder and editor of
the *New York Times,* but even the rival *New York Evening Post* shared his
views on the meaning of the Civil Rights Bill. The *Post* advised its readers that though the Bill did not enfranchise blacks or grant them other
political rights, it did affirm their civil rights to own firearms.[135]

Southern blacks sang in the same key as did these northern whites.
Consider, for example, an editorial that appeared in the *Loyal Georgian,*
a prominent black newspaper, one month before the congressional
speeches of Nye, Pomeroy, and Raymond:

Have colored persons a right to own and carry fire arms? . . . [Blacks]
are not only free but citizens of the United States and as such entitled

to the same privileges granted to other citizens by the Constitution. . . .

Article II, of the amendments to the Constitution of the United States, gives the people the right to bear arms and states that this right shall not be infringed. Any person, white or black, may be disarmed if convicted of making an improper or dangerous use of weapons, but no military or civil officer has the right or authority to disarm a class of people, thereby placing them at the mercy of others. All men, without distinction of color, have the right to keep arms to defend their homes, families or themselves.[136]

In these words, we hear the unmistakable accent of the *Barron* contrarians—with the Second Amendment being invoked to limit state government and heavy stress placed on the "privileges" of national "citizens." And if we listen closely, we can also hear in these words the subtle privatization of the Second Amendment—the shift from "keep" to "own," from "bear" to "carry," from "arms" to "fire arms," from "militia" to "persons," and from collective self-defense ("the security of a free state") to individualized self-defense (of persons' "homes, families or []selves").

In short, between 1775 and 1866 the poster boy of arms morphed from the Concord minuteman to the Carolina freedman. The Creation motto, in effect, was that if arms were outlawed, only the central government would have arms. In Reconstruction a new vision was aborning: when guns were outlawed, only the Klan would have guns. This idea, focusing on private violence and the lapses of local government rather than on the public violence orchestrated by central soldiers, is far closer to the unofficial motto of today's National Rifle Association: "When guns are outlawed, only outlaws will have guns." Yet just as Justice Brennan in *New York Times v. Sullivan*[137] tried to spin a Creation story starring Madison rather than tell a Reconstruction tale touting Hoar, Douglass, and Stowe, today's NRA pays far too much attention to 1775–91 and far too little to 1830–68. In the case of the NRA, the ironies here are rich indeed, given that the organization was itself founded after the Civil War by a group of ex-Union officers.[138]

With this account of the Second Amendment's reconstruction in mind, let us briefly ponder related issues concerning the Third and Fourth Amendments. The Third was originally understood as a military Amendment, reflecting classic republican skepticism of peacetime armies. It also stood as a separation-of-powers provision, requiring legislative authorization of troop quartering in wartime. These basic features make the Third a poor candidate for unrefined, mechanical incorporation: 1860s Republicans did not share their small-r forbears' disdain for central armies, and surely Reconstructors did not mean to impose every aspect of federal separation of powers onto states. The modern Supreme Court has never squarely confronted these issues—a proper Third Amendment incorporation case has yet to materialize—but the Court has, in passing dicta, reconstructed the amendment in an unreflective but highly plausible way. In landmark cases like *Griswold v. Connecticut*, the Court has viewed the Third Amendment as an embodiment of a right of "privacy" in the home.[139] Thus the justices have privatized and domesticated the Third Amendment in a way rather precisely analogous to the way that Reconstruction Republicans privatized and domesticated the Second. The Founding linkage between Second and Third is rather neatly preserved by treating both as centrally protecting the privacy "privilege" in one's homestead.

Indeed, the Third Amendment, on this reconstructed account, now bridges together a home-centric Second Amendment and a Fourth Amendment that was from the beginning protective of the private domain—of private "persons" and their private "papers" in their private "houses." The Slave Power had grossly offended this privacy—of slaves, of free blacks, of resident southern antislavery whites, and of visiting northern abolitionist whites—in countless ways, from dragnet sweeps of those suspected of harboring fugitive slaves, to intrusions upon the mails and suspicious sojourners, to unprecedented search warrants directed at political pamphlets.[140] In response, Reconstruction Congressmen and commentators affirmed Fourth Amendment rights as basic "privileges" and "immunities" that henceforth should never be abridged by any American government.[141]

The Fourth Amendment thus offers a rather easy case for incorporation, all the more so because its words banning unreasonable intrusions and overbroad warrants track those of so many state constitutions already in place in 1866. But, as with virtually every other clause thus far, we must ponder the ways in which the Reconstruction experience refracted the Founders' words, and perhaps deepened and extended their meaning. In particular, we must recall that the Reconstruction Congress meant to stamp out antebellum laws and Black Codes that had designated blacks as special targets for various searches and seizures. The biggest point here is that in the Fourteenth Amendment, unlike the Fourth, the privacy privilege of the citizen sits next to an explicit guarantee of equal protection. As our society gives meaning to the notion that searches and seizures must not be "unreasonable," the Fourteenth Amendment reminds us that equality values must supplement privacy values. A relatively unintrusive search might not be "unreasonable" in terms of privacy alone; but if, say, blacks are being singled out without good cause, such a search may well offend reconstructed reasonableness.[142]

Property and Procedure

Having considered the first four amendments, let us now turn to the next four. We need not tarry long over the Fifth Amendment's just-compensation clause; this one's easy. Textually, the clause represents a paradigmatic American privilege and immunity. Historically, the author of the Fourteenth Amendment specifically and repeatedly stated his intent to overturn *Barron's* rule about the Bill of Rights generally and the takings clause in particular. On the floor of the House, Bingham proudly proclaimed that his amendment would protect the thousands of loyal "citizens of the United States whose property, by State legislation, has been wrested from them under confiscation."[143] On the Senate side, Jacob Howard likewise explicitly discussed *Barron* and just compensation.[144] Structurally, just compensation stood as one of the most individualistic and libertarian rights of the original Bill. In 1789, Madison cleverly packaged this clause and thus slipped it past a Congress that was considerably less libertarian than he; but in 1866 the dominant mood of Congress had become far more sensitive to individual rights. Doctrinally, virtually all mid-nineteenth-century jurists deemed just compensation a fundamental principle of justice;[145] as noted in Chapter 7, *Barron* in fact had rather little effect in the just-compensation context. Judges in virtually every state either enforced an explicit just-compensation rule in their state constitution or inferred such a rule, often following a declaratory methodology. Thus we should not be surprised that, decades before most other rights came to be applied against states, the U.S. Supreme Court applied just-compensation principles to states as early as 1897.[146]

Jury rights have fared less well in the Supreme Court; apart from the Second Amendment, the only rights in the first eight amendments that the modern Court has refused to incorporate are the rights to grand juries and civil juries. As we shall see, in the end, various aspects of the Founders' jury clauses do not mechanically incorporate jot for jot, and at times the Court may well have ended up in the right place for the wrong reason. But the story is far more complicated than has been understood by courts and commentators thus far.

In 1866 juries—grand, petit, and civil—had long been recognized as "inestimable privilege[s]" of Americans[147] and as basic components of due process of law, with roots in a mythic ancient constitution and Magna Charta.[148] According to Blackstone's influential *Commentaries*, "The trial by jury, . . . as the grand bulwark of [every Englishman's] liberties, is secured to him by the great charter [in its 'law of the land' precursor of 'due process']."[149] The textual argument for some sort of incorporation of jury rights against states thus draws upon both the privileges-or-immunities clause and the due-process clause of section 1.

In the forty years that led up to section 1, abolitionists had repeatedly stressed the fundamentality of jury trials. At a theoretical level, they attacked slavery as a legal system that deprived human beings of their lives, liberty, and property with no semblance of due process, no individualized adjudication of wrongdoing in jury trials.[150] Thus we should note here that the Thirteenth Amendment abolished slavery and involuntary servitude "except as a punishment for crime whereof the party shall have been duly convicted." We should also note the subtle textual link between the "*duly* convicted" clause of the Thirteenth Amendment and its "*due* process" cousin in the Fourteenth.

This emphasis on jury trial was not merely high theory. It shaped the battle lines of perhaps the biggest politico-legal clash of the antebellum era: the fugitive-slave controversy. Surely a free black woman in, say, Ohio was entitled to a jury before her liberty could be snatched away if ever some greedy white man called her his slave. So argued the abolitionist lawyer (and later chief justice) Salmon P. Chase in the famous 1837 case of Matilda Lawrence.[151] Though Chase lost the case—and Lawrence lost her freedom—various northern states responded by adopting personal-liberty laws guaranteeing alleged fugitive slaves the benefit of a jury trial.[152] But in 1842 the Supreme Court struck down a state personal-liberty law on preemption grounds in *Prigg v. Pennsylvania*.[153] With the issue thus nationalized, the main battle shifted from state capitals to Washington, D.C., where in 1850 Congress adopted its infamous Fugitive Slave Act, placing an alleged fugitive's freedom entirely in the hands of a commissioner rather than a jury. In response Congressman Horace Mann complained that the act's lack of jury trial violated the Fifth Amendment due-process clause,[154] and Senator Charles Sumner thundered that

> In denying the Trial by Jury [this act] is three times unconstitutional; first as the Constitution declares "the right of the people to be secure in their persons against unreasonable seizures;" secondly as it further declares, that "No person shall be deprived of life, liberty, or property, without due process of law;" and thirdly, because it expressly declares, that "in suits at common law . . . the right of jury trial shall be preserved." By this triple cord did the framers of the Constitution secure the Trial by Jury in every question of Human Freedom.[155]*

---

*In the famous *Booth* litigation discussed in Chapter 9, the Wisconsin state-trial judge held that the Fugitive Slave Act of 1850 violated the Seventh Amendment, and the Wisconsin Supreme Court held that the act violated jury-trial rights affirmed by the Fifth Amendment due-process clause. *In re* Booth, 3 Wis. 1, 39–41, 64–70 (1854). The United States Supreme Court reversed, in a Taney opinion that slapped down the state judges on jurisdictional grounds, and then asserted—in a sweeping sentence utterly devoid of argument or analysis—that the Fugitive Slave Act was "in all its provisions, fully authorized by the Constitution of the United States." Ableman v. Booth, 62 U.S. (21 How.) 506, 526 (1859). It is perhaps worth noting that the federal act that Taney and his colleagues found so unproblematic permitted summary and ex parte proceedings, forbade

In linking Seventh Amendment jury rights to Fourth Amendment rights against unreasonable seizures, Sumner carried forward the Founders' vision, but with a twist; here the defendant (alleged fugitive) sought the benefit of the jury rather than the plaintiff, as in the Founders' model.

Sixteen years later the Thirty-ninth Congress likewise invoked the Founders' model of juries while at the same time inverting it. Whereas the Founders emphasized Americans' rights to participate in government by serving in juries, Reconstructors at first emphasized the right to be tried by juries.[156] Yet again, we see a Founding "political" right mutating (at least initially) into a Reconstruction "civil" right. In debates over the Civil Rights Act of 1866, the leading Republican sponsors and supporters of the act took pains to deny opponents' claims that it would confer on blacks the right to serve on juries; jury service, supporters claimed, was a political right beyond the scope of the statute, not a civil right within the meaning of the act.[157]

Here, too, the text of the original Constitution eased the transition: the Fifth, Sixth, and Seventh Amendments speak of the parties' rights more than the jurors' rights; and the Article IV comity clause likewise protected Samuel Hoar's right to be tried by a South Carolina jury but not to sit on one. As notorious cases like Matilda Lawrence's demonstrated, even women—who had no right to sit on juries—deserved a right to be tried by juries.

But Republicans soon saw the practical problems of putting asunder what the Founders had joined together. Exactly how much would blacks in the South benefit if all-white grand juries refused to indict whites who terrorized blacks, or if all-white petit jurors acquitted these thugs? Formally, blacks were not even parties to these criminal prosecutions; and so if the jury was a right only of litigants rather than of jurors, it would not seem to give blacks much protection. Now consider cases where a black was indeed a party—say, a criminal defendant.

---

the alleged fugitive from testifying, and went on to create a biased fact finder: in a case of possibly mistaken identity, a commissioner would receive ten dollars if he ruled for the slave catcher but only five dollars if he ruled for the alleged slave. 9 Stat. 462, 463–64.

Under a pure civil rights model, how much would he benefit merely from the "civil" right to be tried by a jury from which all blacks were excluded?

These questions were hardly theoretical—they arose urgently, graphically, and repeatedly in the Reconstruction era.[158] Eventually, Reconstruction Republicans came to realize that—for blacks at least—civil jury rights without political jury rights were rather empty. When the British Empire had run into American jury nullification one hundred years earlier, the Empire had little choice but to sidestep juries with vice-admiralty and other juryless tribunals. But Reconstruction Republicans facing southern jury nullification had another option at hand: Republicans could reconstruct juries by repopulating them with blacks alongside whites.[159]

In the 1880 case of *Strauder v. West Virginia,* the Supreme Court invalidated a conviction of a black defendant in a state where blacks were prevented from serving on grand and petit juries.[160] *Strauder* straddled the question of whose rights this scheme violated. At a couple of points, the Court seemed to focus on the rights of excluded black jurors denied "the privilege of participating equally in the administration of justice" and the "right to participate in the administration of the law."[161] But where exactly did this political right come from? And if it did exist, why was it limited to cases involving black defendants, as the Court elsewhere seemed to suggest?

Indeed, most of *Strauder*'s language stressed the violation of the civil rights of the black defendant.[162] But this civil rights account left the Court vulnerable to Justice Field, whose dissent punched huge holes in the majority's opinion.[163] If being tried by a jury that excluded members of one's race was a Thirteenth Amendment badge of servitude, how to account for the widespread antebellum practice of most free states, where blacks could not serve as jurors? If West Virginia's all-white jury violated Strauder's right to due process, did this mean that a similarly all-white jury that came about randomly, in a process that did not exclude blacks, would likewise violate due process? And what precisely was the inequality at issue? Didn't Strauder get the same kind of jury that white defendants did—namely, twelve white men? Indeed, a single all-white grand jury might indict many defendants, white and black, male and female. Where was the inequality when all literally got the same grand jury? Put another way, if black men were entitled to be tried by a jury that did not exclude black men, did this mean that women were entitled to juries that did not exclude women? Children to juries that did not exclude children? So too with aliens? If, when trying blacks, West Virginia could not bar blacks from the jury box, could it bar them from the bench? From the legislature that enacted the underlying criminal law at issue? As all these questions made clear, the civil rights account in *Strauder* ultimately traded on a political rights vision that black men—but not, say, women or children or aliens—were entitled to be represented on juries and elsewhere.

Congress had been wrestling with similar questions, and in 1875 it adopted a statute barring state and federal courts from excluding blacks from juries in any case, regardless of the race of the parties.[164] The facts of *Strauder* had arisen before the act took effect, and thus the *Strauder* Court paid the act little heed. But the act's language gives us a key clue to solve all of *Strauder*'s riddles. The key right, proclaimed the act, was not the defendant's civil right but the juror's political right. And the source of that right was neither the Thirteenth Amendment, nor the Fourteenth Amendment's due-process clause, nor the Fourteenth Amendment's privileges-or-immunities clause, nor the Fourteenth Amendment's equal-protection clause. It was the Fifteenth Amendment whose language the 1875 act obviously borrowed and built upon: neither the federal nor the state government could deny the right of "citizens" to serve and vote on juries "on account of race, color, or previous condition of servitude."[165]

On this account, the Fifteenth Amendment, rightly read, affirms blacks' political rights—to vote, serve on juries, and hold office—just as the Fourteenth Amendment had affirmed blacks' civil rights to do virtually everything but. To put the point more textually, blacks had a right to *vote*, but not just for representatives. They had a right to vote in juries, and in legislatures, too—a right to be voted for as well as to vote.

Jurors vote—that is what they do*—and in America, ordinary voters had always served as jurors, as Tocqueville made clear.[166] Thus the Fifteenth Amendment helped restore much of the original political vision underlying juries that the Fourteenth Amendment had warped. Through the voting amendment, black men won political rights—to vote, to serve on juries, to hold office—that white women lacked. (On this account, we should view the subsequent Nineteenth Amendment as conferring comparable jury and office-holding rights on women.[167] Shockingly, the Supreme Court failed to affirm women's equal right to vote in juries until 1975, more than a half-century after the suffrage amendment's adoption, and even then failed to mention the Nineteenth Amendment.)[168]

Having seen one way that the Fourteenth Amendment (initially) reconstructed the Founders' jury, let us now turn to a second. The Founders' jury right was not merely political and collective; it was also localist. The Reconstructors' jury right was not just (initially) civil and individualistic; it was also nationalist. Various aspects of the original Sixth and Seventh Amendments sounded in federalism, and, where

---

*This is not to say that voting is the only thing jurors do. They also deliberate (as should voters in ordinary elections). See Douglas Gary Lichtman, The Deliberative Lottery: A Thought Experiment in Jury Reform, 34 AM. CRIM. L. REV. 133, 145, 153 n.76 (1996).

Above and beyond the simple textual argument that the Fifteenth Amendment right to vote encompasses a right to vote on juries (and in legislatures), three additional arguments are at work here. First, if the Fourteenth Amendment is best understood as protecting all civil rights (though it does not use this phrase), the Fifteenth is best understood as protecting all political rights, of which the right to vote was emblematic. Second, even if the Fifteenth Amendment did not ipso facto make blacks jurors, it did redefine the electorate in each state, and many state laws and state constitutions themselves made voters ipso facto jurors. Finally, the Fifteenth Amendment worked a kind of estoppel argument. States were estopped from claiming that blacks as such lacked what it took to be voters—and if blacks had the right stuff for the ballot box, why not the jury box, too? Any jury exclusion of black voters would seem very hard to defend rationally. For much more elaboration and historical documentation, see Vikram David Amar, Jury Service as Political Participation Akin to Voting, 80 CORNELL L. REV. 203 (1995).

states are involved, these aspects should be filtered out by a suitably refined model of incorporation.

Consider, for example, the Sixth Amendment rule that the accused be tried by an impartial jury "of the State . . . wherein the crime shall have been committed." At the federal level, this rule did not quite mean what it said. Suppose a crime was committed outside any state—say, in the territories, or on the high seas. Article III had earlier dealt with precisely these scenarios: "[B]ut when [the crime was] not committed within any State, the Trial shall be at such Place or Places as the Congress may by Law have directed." Nothing in the Sixth Amendment, rightly read, repealed this part of Article III; and so Congress could indeed punish criminals in the territories or on the high seas. The Sixth Amendment thus operated as a federalism provision of sorts, specifying jury vicinage when a crime happened to be committed within a given state.

But mechanical incorporation of this federalism clause against states would make little sense. Suppose a state wants to prosecute a resident for a crime committed in federal territory or on the high seas. To mechanically incorporate the seeming Sixth Amendment ban without also incorporating the Article III exception/gloss would prevent state prosecution altogether. Or suppose State A wants to prosecute a resident for a crime committed in State B. The Sixth Amendment, if incorporated literally, would pose almost insurmountable obstacles: State A would somehow have to summon a jury from State B. Congress, under Article III, can punish American residents who commit crimes in other countries; why can't a state likewise punish its residents who commit crimes in other states?

Consider also the district clause of the Sixth Amendment, calling for a criminal jury from the "district" as well as the state of the crime. Should congressionally drawn district lines be imposed on state trials? Even William Rawle, an early *Barron* contrarian, thought not. The clause, claimed Rawle, "has more immediate reference to the judicial proceedings of the United States, and may therefore be considered as restraints only on the legislation of the United States."[169]

Next, consider the Seventh Amendment. As we saw in Chapter 5, under the best reading of the original amendment, federal courts were obliged to provide a civil jury whenever the state court across the street would do so. But to incorporate this amendment against states would be to redundantly insist that state courts provide civil juries whenever state law said so. In the 1850 contrarian case of *Campbell v. Georgia*, Chief Justice Lumpkin quoted or paraphrased, in order, every clause of first eight amendments, except the Seventh, and insisted that all the quoted or paraphrased clauses bound the states.[170] Was his omission intentional? We should also note that when Congress in 1864 repealed the (juryless) Fugitive Slave Act of 1850, a Republican Congressman proclaimed the repeal to be "in accordance with the Constitution of the United States *and the laws of the state where such person is found.*"[171] Was this, too, rooted in a states'-rights reading of the Seventh Amendment?

If so, perhaps the Supreme Court's strong disinclination to incorporate the Seventh Amendment against states might be defensible— though some fancy doctrinal footwork might be needed to explain why the states'-rights reading of the Seventh Amendment makes sense in the incorporation context even though the Supreme Court does not embrace it in Seventh Amendment doctrine proper. But even here a plausible argument might run as follows: Where federal courts are concerned, Seventh Amendment doctrine should be uniform across all states—this uniformity facilitates venue transfers, consolidation of cases, and other time-saving mechanisms within the federal judiciary. But given that the ultimate reasons for rejecting the highly plausible states'-rights reading of the Seventh Amendment sound in terms of administrative convenience within a federal judiciary, those reasons are logically inapplicable to state courts, and should not be incorporated against them.

Given that so much of the hostility to incorporation has been driven by doubts about the fundamentality of juries, we would do well to trace the roots of these doubts. In a series of turn-of-the-century cases involving far-flung American territories like Puerto Rico, Hawaii, and the Philippines, the Court proclaimed that truly fundamental aspects of the American Constitution applied to such territories but that trial by jury wasn't, well, fundamental.[172] The ironies here are delicious. In the late eighteenth century, colonial Americans grasped local institutions like the jury to assert some small measure of self-governance against royal judges whom they did not pick and a Parliament for which they did not vote. Those colonists also understood how jury service made men into first-class citizens, worthy of republican self-government. One century later, Americans stood in the shoes of the old British Empire, seeking to exploit various colonies for imperial advantage. Now jury service somehow looked less fundamental to Americans. With the same disdain the British had once reserved for Americans, Americans now wondered whether backward colonists were really capable and worthy of self-government and whether jury trial was truly appropriate.

The first Justice Harlan dissented in these cases, using language that nicely paralleled his dissent in *Hurtado v. California* on the role of jury trials within states.[173] According to Harlan, grand and petit juries were fundamental guarantees "for the benefit of all, of whatever race or nativity, in the states compassing the Union, or in any territory."[174] Two generations later, Justice Hugo Black would sound similar themes, insisting in *Reid v. Covert* that the entire Constitution and Bill of Rights applied extraterritorially.[175]

These great opinions make clear the little-noted link between two long-standing debates about the Bill of Rights. First, did it apply in the territories (and if so, how)? Second, did it apply against states (and if so, how)?[176] Interestingly, both debates have featured rhetoric of "incorporation"—of "incorporated" versus "unincorporated" territories, and of "incorporation" of the Bill of Rights against states. Most fundamentally, the territorial debate reminds us that issues of geographic expansion helped to remold the Bill of Rights. The idea of a national bill of rights locked arms with the idea of a national citizenship above and beyond state citizenship. The territories powerfully reinforced this sense of national citizenship; Americans residing in these territories were not citizens of any state but were most definitely citizens of the United States (a point that Justice Bradley emphasized in his *Slaughter-House* dissent).[177] Thus the first sentence of the Fourteenth Amendment affirmed the importance of national citizenship, and its second sentence modified the words of Article IV by stressing nationalistic citizenship in the *"United* States" rather than federalistic citizenship in "the *several* states." In short, the territorial experience had helped make clear by 1866 what was less visible in 1789: the United States government was not a purely federal affair but also, in part, a national system that could sometimes operate directly on national citizens, unmediated by states. Indeed, as we saw in the context of both the establishment clause and the Sixth Amendment state-of-crime clause, the territories nicely previewed what I have called refined incorporation. In order to decide whether a given aspect of the Bill of Rights, or the original Constitution, sensibly has bite in the territories, we must ask a kind of "refined" question: is the clause at hand a national-rights clause that should have bite, or a pure federalism clause that should have none?*

Turning from juries to the remaining provisions of Amendments V–VIII, we find that these are rather easy candidates for incorporation. Protections against double jeopardy and compelled self-incrimination, as well as the rights of confrontation, compulsory process, counsel, bail, and the like, were in 1866 seen not only as fundamental "privileges" and "immunities" but also as components of "due process." (As noted in Chapter 8, in the 1856 case of *Murray's Lessee,* the Court declared that the general notion of due process incorporated all the specific procedural guarantees set out elsewhere in the Bill of Rights.) Moreover, the controversy over fugitive-slave rendition had heightened abolitionists' sensitivity to fair procedure. The infamous federal Fugitive Slave Act of 1850 deprived blacks of some of the most basic fair-trial rights: confrontation, cross-examination, and an unbiased decisionmaker, to name

---

*Thus the 1856 Republican Party platform implicitly argued that the Second Amendment was not purely a states'-rights provision when it criticized violations of "[t]he right of the people to keep and bear arms" in the Kansas Territory. NATIONAL PARTY PLATFORMS, *supra* page 257, note, at 27.

just three.[178] In sharp contrast, various northern personal liberty laws had gone so far as to vest alleged fugitives with rights of appointed counsel.[179]

The Slave Power had also filled law books with outrageous punishments. An 1854 North Carolina statute provided that antislavery agitation should be punished by whipping for the first offense and by death for the second.[180] In 1860 the state legislature decided that this was too soft on crime and decreed death for first offenders.[181] On the eve of the Civil War, Republican Congressman Cydnor Tompkins attacked the "barbarity and cruelty" of the Slave Power, whose laws "strip naked and cut gashes into the back of the man who utters opinions" against slavery.[182] In the Thirty-ninth Congress, John Bingham on at least two occasions specifically stated that section 1 would ban cruel and unusual punishment; and other leading Republicans also condemned "the lash and the scourge," "laceration of the body," and other savagely "cruel or unusual punishment."[183]

But yet again we must note a subtle reconstruction at work. In 1789 the right as written had relatively little judicially enforceable bite against Congress; a congressionally authorized penalty might be "cruel," but would it be both cruel "and unusual"? At most, the clause seemed to disfavor the oddball statute, wholly out of sync with other congressional criminal laws. This strong majoritarian bias is hardly surprising when we recall that the clause was lifted almost verbatim from the English Bill of Rights of 1689. That Bill was not designed to create judicially enforceable rights against the legislature; on the contrary, as suggested in Chapter 5, that 1689 clause was written to restrain lawless and bloody judges like George Jeffreys. Thus we should not be surprised that in the antebellum era leading figures such as Rawle claimed that the original Eighth Amendment could never be used by judges to invalidate congressionally approved punishments.[184]

Once applied against states, though, the clause might have more judicially enforceable bite against state legislatures. When judged against a national baseline, perhaps a single state legislature, or the legislatures of an entire region, might indeed be "unusual" and out of sync with general national sentiment and national morality. (To many northerners, this was precisely the case of the antebellum southern legislatures in the grip of the Slave Power.) Once again, the same words seemed to mean slightly different things in 1789 and 1866.

Odds and Ends

Finally, let us consider the last two amendments of the Founders' Bill. Do these amendments sensibly incorporate? As it turns out, the question does not much matter.

Consider the Tenth Amendment first. To the extent that the amendment affirms principles of federalism and enumerated federal power, it obviously makes little sense to apply these principles against states. And to the extent that the amendment affirms basic ideas of popular sovereignty, it adds little to the Article IV republican-government clause, which has always applied against states.

A similar story can be told about the Ninth Amendment. Viewed merely as a federalism-based companion to the Tenth, the Ninth does not sensibly incorporate in any refined way. And to the extent that the Ninth affirms unenumerated rights other than federalism, these rights, as refracted through the prism of "privileges" and "immunities," add little to the privileges-or-immunities clause itself, because (as we saw in Chapter 8) that clause is itself obviously open-ended.

But as Professor Yoo has shown, the story of the Ninth Amendment is worth considering in more detail.[185] Originally, the amendment largely sounded in federalism; thus no original state constitution featured a similarly worded counterpart. But by 1867 fifteen states—the overwhelming majority of which had begun as federal territories—had borrowed from the federal template and adopted "baby Ninth Amendments."[186] None of these states adopted baby Tenth Amendments; and so, as with the establishment clause, we see again how words had begun to mutate in meaning. What began as a federalism clause intertwined with the Tenth Amendment soon took on a substantive life of its own, as a free-floating affirmation of unenumerated rights. Similarly, what began as a republican affirmation of collective rights of the people had begun to mutate—especially when seen through the prism of the Fourteenth Amendment—into a celebration of liberal civil rights of persons. Thus we find Senator James Nye in the Thirty-ninth Congress describing the Ninth as a kind of gap filler among the first eight amendments, lest something essential in the specification of "natural *and personal* rights" in earlier amendments "should have been overlooked."[187] Six years later, Senator John Sherman offered a similarly Blackstone-tinged reading of the Ninth Amendment, as affirming "unenumerated rights . . . as innumerable as the sands of the sea" and defined in "the common law."[188]

If we seek to give meaning to the Ninth Amendment's affirmation of unenumerated rights vis-à-vis the *federal* government, taking seriously the "feedback" effect of incorporation against federal action, the most sensible place to start would be with a kind of "reverse incorporation" of equal-protection principles against federal actors. The first sentence of the Fourteenth Amendment proclaimed all Americans, black and white alike, citizens of the United States. And what it meant to be a citizen was to have certain privileges and immunities—against all government, state and federal. Under this declaratory reading, the "No state shall" sentence declared privileges and immunities but did not create them. *The* privileges and immunities of citizens, rightly understood, bound Congress in just the same way that *the* freedom of speech, rightly understood, had always bound states (under the declaratory theory).* The

---

**See, e.g.*, The Slaughter-House Cases, 83 U.S. (16 Wall.) 36, 119 (1873) (Bradley, J., dissenting) ("But even if the Constitution were silent, the fundamental privileges and immunities of citizens, as such, would be no less real and no less inviolable than they now are. It was not necessary to say in words that the citizens of the United States should have and exercise all the privileges of citizens. . . . Their very citizenship conferred these privileges, if they did not possess them before."); *see also supra* page 195, note.

It remains possible that in certain domains—say, affirmative action—judges should give special deference to Congress where Congress invokes its section 5 powers to help implement the spirit of the Fourteenth Amendment. But the justification for such judicial deference would not be that Congress is free from the constraints imposed by equal-protection principles. Rather, the notion here might be that section 5 gives Congress a special role in *protecting* vulnerable racial minorities and in *vindicating* their equal citizenship in an oft-unequal society. *See generally* Eric Schnapper, *Affirmative Action and the Legislative History of the Fourteenth Amendment*, 71 VA. L. REV. 753 (1985).

entire spirit of the Fourteenth Amendment was to affirm rights against all governments and insist that state and federal governments be held to the same standard. Thus we should not be surprised by the first Justice Harlan's linkage of incorporation and reverse incorporation in a couple of his greatest dissents. In *Plessy v. Ferguson,* for example, Harlan affirmed "the clear, distinct, unconditional recognition by our governments, *National and State,* of every right that inheres in civil freedom [that is, incorporation], and of the equality before the law of all citizens of the United States without regard to race [that is, reverse incorporation]."[189] Similarly, in his great dissent in the *Civil Rights Cases,* Harlan proclaimed that citizenship itself entailed various "rights, privileges, or immunities," one of which was "exemption from race discrimination in respect of any civil right belonging to citizens of the white race."[190] In 1896 he put the point even more simply: "All citizens are equal before the law."[191]

To see the point one final way, consider the Fifth Amendment due-process clause, which, according to the modern Court, contains an "equal protection" component. A quick look at the Fourteenth Amendment may make us skeptical. Doesn't its phraseology obviously contradistinguish between equal protection and due process? But on a declaratory view, these two clauses were not so much separate ideas as connected ones, two sides of the same coin. Both affirmed the rights of persons as contradistinguished from the rights of citizens. And due process *of law* connoted a suitably general, evenhanded law. According to Cooley's landmark treatise, perhaps "[n]o definition [of due process] is more often quoted" than Daniel Webster's in his famous *Dartmouth College* oral argument: "due process" meant "law of the land" by which "is most clearly intended the general law . . . . The meaning is, that every citizen shall hold his life, liberty, property, and immunities under the protection of general rules . . . ."[192] Various state constitutions spoke of "protection" of "life, liberty, and property,"[193] and Bingham's first draft of section 1 went a step further, proclaiming "*equal protection* in the rights of life, liberty, and property."[194] When he declared to his colleagues that "every word of this proposed Amendment is today in the Constitution of our

RECONSTRUCTING RIGHTS 283

country" no one challenged him; his colleagues understood that, even if literally wrong he was legally right.*

And so we see yet again how words inserted into the Constitution in 1791 must be read afresh after 1866.

---

*See CONG. GLOBE, 39th Cong., 1st Sess. 1034 (1866); *see also id.* at 1094, 1292 (remarks of Rep. John Bingham) (extolling "due process of law—law in its highest sense . . . which is impartial, equal, exact justice" and proclaiming that "in respect to life and liberty and property, the people by their Constitution declared the equality of all men, and by express limitation forbade the Government of the United States from making any discrimination"). For more discussion of Bingham's linkage of due process and equal protection, *see supra* Chapter 9, note 8. We should also recall that Justice Harlan, the great dissenter in *Plessy*, built that dissent in part upon an earlier opinion, where he had proclaimed that the "guarantees of life, liberty, and property are for all persons, within the jurisdiction . . . without discrimination against any because of their race." Gibson v. Mississippi, 162 U.S. 565, 591 (1896). Note how this formulation marries due-process language ("life, liberty, and property") with equal-protection language ("all persons within the jurisdiction"—a phrase found only in the equal-protection clause) and equal-protection norms against race discrimination. Taken seriously, this marriage supports the reading of the Fifth Amendment's due-process clause as a ban on invidious race discrimination, as Harlan's very next sentence in *Gibson* made clear: "Those guarantees . . . must be enforced in the courts, *both of the Nation and* of the State, without reference to considerations based upon race." *Id.* (emphasis added). For much more discussion and documentation of the arguments for "reverse incorporation," see Akhil Reed Amar, *Constitutional Rights in a Federal System: Rethinking Incorporation and Reverse Incorporation, in* BENCH-MARKS: GREAT CONSTITUTIONAL CONTROVERSIES IN THE SUPREME COURT 71 (Terry Eastland ed., 1995). *See also* Mark A. Graber, *A Constitutional Conspiracy Unmasked: Why "No State" Does Not Mean "No State,"* 10 CONST. COMMENTARY 87 (1993).

Twelve

A New Birth of Freedom

Clause by clause, amendment by amendment, the Bill of Rights was refined and strengthened in the crucible of the 1860s. Indeed, the very phrase *bill of rights* as a description of the first ten (or nine, or eight) amendments was forged anew in these years.

A Bill by Any Other Name

Here, then, is a remarkable fact: before the adoption of the Fourteenth Amendment, the Supreme Court never—not once—referred to the 1791 decalogue as "the" or "a" "bill of rights." Yet within a few years of John Bingham's odes to the Bill, the Court began to adopt Bingham's terminology. Contrarians like Bingham helped change the vocabulary of legal discourse—and ultimately changed its substance and structure.

The 1807 Supreme Court case of *Ex parte Burford* epitomized High Court terminology in the *Barron* era. Note the obvious contrast of language as Chief Justice Marshall quoted warrant-limiting clauses from the Virginia and federal Constitutions, respectively: "By the 10th article of the *bill of rights* of Virginia it is declared [quotation]. . . . By the [original] 6th [that is, our 4th] *article of amendments to the Constitution of the United States,* it is declared [quotation]."[1] In the 1833 case of *Livingston v. Moore,* which applied *Barron's* rule to the Fourth and Seventh Amendments, the Supreme Court likewise referred to the "ninth article of the amendments of the Constitution of the United States and the sixth section of the Pennsylvania bill of rights."[2] Antebellum state court usage often followed a similar pattern: when in 1841 the Massachusetts Supreme Judicial Court unselfconsciously referred to "the bill of rights," it obviously meant the *state's* bill.*

When the antebellum Supreme Court discussed the first ten amendments as a set, it often did so in ways that emphasized their protections of states' rights. Consider, for example, two cases reaffirming *Barron: Fox v. Ohio* and *Withers v. Buckley.* In *Fox,* decided in 1847, the Court reaffirmed that the initial "*amendments* to the constitution . . . were not designed as limits on the State governments . . . . They are exclusively restrictions upon *federal* power, intended to prevent interference with *the rights of the States,* and of their citizens."[3] *Withers,* decided a decade later, echoed all this, stylistically and substantively: "The *amendments* thus adopted were designed to be modifications of the powers vested in the *Federal* Government [only. . . . The Fifth Amendment] was applicable to the Federal Government alone, and not to the States, *except so far as it was designed for their security against Federal power.*"[4] In 1841, an attor-

---

*Commonwealth v. Dana, 43 Mass. (2 Mel.) 329, 334, 336 (1841); *see also* Johnson v. Tompkins, 13 F. Cas. 840, 849 (1833) (C.C.E.D. Pa. 1833) (No. 7,416) (Baldwin, Circuit J.) (juxtaposing a part of "the ninth article of the bill of rights in the constitution of Pennsylvania" with the strikingly similar language of the "fourth amendment to the constitution of the United States"). *But see* United States v. Gibert, 25 F. Cas. 1287, 1294, 1297 (C.C.D. Mass. 1834) (No. 15,204) (Story, Circuit J.) (referring to "certain amendments of the [U.S.] constitution, in the nature of a bill of rights" and to the double-jeopardy clause as "an article of a bill of rights"). Note, even here, the slightly self-conscious words *in the nature of* and *a* (rather than *the*). *Cf.* Jones vs. Robbins, 74 Mass. (8 Gray) 329, 343–44 (1857) (noting that federal amendments were "in the nature of a bill of rights" and thus declaratory of principles that could limit states). The *Jones* case is discussed *supra* page 149, note, and page 200.

ney before the Court did use the phrase *bill of rights*, but he, too, linked the early amendments to states' rights: "[Antifederalists criticized the] want of a bill of rights, similar to that subsequently adopted by the ten amendments to the constitution, and *especially the tenth* . . . . "[5]

Thus the only clear modern-sounding description of the federal "bill of rights" in all of *United States Reports* in the antebellum era came from the oral argument of contrariarian C. P. Van Ness in the 1840 *Holmes v. Jennison* case, an argument we first encountered in Chapter 7. In the course of attacking *Barron*, Van Ness spoke of "the amendments to the Constitution of the United States, commonly called the bill of rights."[6]

Rhetoric and substance mutually reinforced. If one saw Amendments I–X as largely sounding in federalism, deeply protective of states' rights, and thus inapplicable against state governments, these amendments really weren't like state bills of rights protecting citizens. Conversely, to a contrarian, the amendments declared fundamental freedoms of all Americans, and the set thus *was* like a state bill of rights, and thus *did* apply (in a suitably refined way) against states.

These are precisely the rhetorical battle lines that shaped debate over the anti-*Barron* amendment in the Thirty-ninth Congress. Contrarians repeatedly appealed to "the bill of rights"—a phrase that John Bingham invoked more than a dozen times in a single day.[7] And here are the words of Bingham's fellow Republican Robert Hale: "Now, what are these amendments to the Constitution, numbered from one to ten, one of which is the fifth article in question? . . . They constitute the bill of rights, a bill of rights for the protection of the citizen, and defining and limiting the power of Federal and State legislation."[8] In a similar vein, leading contrarians like Representatives James Wilson and William Lawrence and Senator Jacob Howard all spoke of "the" or "a" "bill of rights."[9]

Opponents spoke a very different language. Democrat Michael Kerr cited both *Barron* and *Fox* and twice referred to "the first eleven amendments," which he defined as "limitations upon the power of Congress and not upon the powers of the States. They are not guarantees at all, except to protect the States against the usurpations of Congress and the General Government. They simply say that Congress shall not invade the rights of the States .... "[10] Likewise, Democratic Representative Andrew Jackson Rogers, after paraphrasing *Barron* and its progeny, refrained from calling the amendments a bill of rights and instead labeled them "clauses of the Constitution of the United States."[11]

When we move outside Congress, we see a similar rhetorical pattern among Reconstruction commentators. Contrarian commentator Timothy Farrar described the initial amendments as "in the nature of a bill of rights," and his fellow contrarian and treatise writer John Norton Pomeroy referred even less self-consciously to "our national bill of rights."[12]

Apparently all this Republican "bill of rights" talk in the air in 1866–68 began to waft in the direction of the Supreme Court. In the 1871 *Legal Tender Cases*, an attorney invoked the "great bill of rights contained in the amendments"—and for the first time in history, a Supreme Court Justice (albeit in dissent) linked the original amendments to the phrase *bill of rights*.[13] Within a decade, the Supreme Court was beginning to slip into contrarian vocabulary even as it clung to *Barron;* in the 1880 case of *Ex parte Siebold,* Justice Bradley's opinion for the Court analogized state and federal constitutions, proclaiming that both were "restrained by a sufficiently rigid bill of rights for the protection of its citizens from oppression."[14] Three years later, the Court provided still further elaboration of the nature of the initial federal amendments: criticism of the lack of a "formal Bill of Rights" in the original Constitution led to "the adoption of the first ten amendments . . . most of them [designed] for the protection of private rights of persons and property."[15] By the 1890s, this rhetorical trickle had swelled into a steady stream of references to the "first ten amendments . . . in the nature of a bill of rights" to protect "persons and property" and "unalienable rights";[16] to "provisions in the nature of a Bill of Rights" "securing to every individual" "rights of the citizen," some of which traced back to "the days of Magna Charta";[17] to "the first ten amendments to the Constitution, commonly known as the Bill of Rights," which "embod[ied] certain guaranties and immunities which we had inherited from our English ancestors";[18] to "the earliest amendments to the Constitution of the United States, in the nature of a Bill of Rights";[19] and so on. In 1900, we find the phrase, "the National

Bill of Rights," appearing no fewer than four times in a single opinion—
Justice Harlan's great dissent in *Maxwell v. Dow*.[20] Gone was the view,
publicly expressed by Supreme Court Justice Samuel F. Miller as late
as 1880, that "our Constitution, unlike most modern ones, does not contain any formal declaration or bill of rights."*

The Rebirth of the Bill

It is time to sum up. In the preceding pages, I have tried to trace the deep
roots of American thinking about the Bill of Rights. With these roots
exposed to view, perhaps we today may better understand where we are,
where we came from, and how we got here. Perhaps we can now better
understand, and in places improve upon, the conventional wisdom about
the Bill of Rights described in this book's Introduction.

I began by noting that "the Bill of Rights stands as the high temple
of our constitutional order." Whence this view of the Bill? The conventional narrative focuses on those present at the Creation—on the hasty
oversights and omissions in the last days of a hot summer in Philadelphia; on the centrality of the (absence of a) Bill of Rights in ratification
debates; and on the quick repair worked by the First Congress, fixing in
place the keystone of the arch of liberty. And we all lived happily ever
after.

There is some truth in this stock story so far as it goes, but it
doesn't go far enough. Most dramatically, it ignores all the ways in which
the Reconstruction generation—not their Founding fathers or grandfa-
thers—took a crumbling and somewhat obscure edifice, placed it on
new, high ground, and remade it so that it truly would stand as a temple of liberty and justice for all.

We would do well to remember that a separate Bill of Rights was no

---

*SAMUEL F. MILLER, THE CONSTITUTION OF THE UNITED STATES: THREE LEC-
TURES DELIVERED BEFORE THE UNIVERSITY LAW SCHOOL OF WASHINGTON, D.C. 59
(Washington, D.C.: W. H. and O. H. Morrison, 1880). Samuel Miller, of course, was
also the author of the Court's odd opinion in the *Slaughter-House Cases*. Note also John
Randolph Tucker's famous oral argument in 1887 referring to the early amendments as
"the Declaration of Rights." *See supra* page 228.

part of Madison's carefully conceived original plan at Philadelphia. To some extent, his ultimate sponsorship of the Bill must be seen as a sop—a peace offering—to Anti-Federalists;[21] and many in the First Congress were relatively uninterested in the Bill, finding it a "nauseous" distraction.[22] John Bingham, by contrast, placed the Bill of Rights at the center of his thinking about constitutionalism; his speeches in the Thirtyninth Congress are far more inspired, and perhaps more inspiring, than Madison's in the First.

Mid-twentieth-century skeptics worried aloud that incorporation would ultimately weaken the Bill of Rights.[23] If the Bill were to be applied against the states, the argument went, it would need to be watered down to take account of the considerable diversity of state practice; and then in turn, the federal government would be held to only this watereddown version. In a couple of doctrinal corners, this fear has been borne out. For example, in a series of preincorporation dissents, Justices Black and Douglas insisted that federal criminal contempt, as then defined, could not be deemed a "petty" offense unprotected by the Constitution's twin jury commands (in Article III and the Sixth Amendment).[24] But the very day the Sixth Amendment was incorporated against states in *Duncan v. Louisiana*, Black and Douglas seemed to pull their punches in a companion case, arising out of a *state* criminal contempt prosecution; they now joined a Court opinion that recognized a sizable "petty crime" exception to jury trial.* *Duncan* itself explicitly signaled the possible causal link between incorporation and watering-down with the following ominous observation: "It seems very unlikely to us that our decision today will require widespread changes in state criminal processes. First, our decisions interpreting the Sixth Amendment are always sub-

---

*See Bloom v. Illinois, 391 U.S. 194 (1968). In *Bloom*, as in *Duncan*, the Court did award the defendant a jury; and had Black and Douglas forced the issue, no majority opinion might have been possible in *Duncan*, for Justices Stewart and Harlan dissented, and Justice Fortas concurred, explicitly rejecting the notion of jot-for-jot incorporation. But on the same day, Black and Douglas did write separately in yet another case, reiterating their objection to any but the most trivial of "petty crime" exceptions and dismissing the language of *Bloom* (and implicitly *Duncan*) as "dictum." Dyke v. Taylor Implement Mfg. Co., 391 U.S. 216, 223 (1968) (Black, J., dissenting, joined by Douglas, J.).

ject to reconsideration."[25] The upshot of all this became clear over the next decade when the Court, responding to the variety of state jury practice, implausibly held that the Sixth Amendment did not really require twelve-person juries[26]—a view that cut against a near-universal assumption of every justice who had addressed the issue prior to *Duncan.*

But to dwell on the few doctrinal corners where the anti-incorporation Cassandras proved right is to miss the much larger story on the other side: extension of the Bill of Rights against the states has, in general, dramatically strengthened the Bill, not weakened it, in both legal doctrine and popular consciousness. Unused muscles atrophy, while those that are regularly put to use grow strong. In the first century of our nation's existence, the Bill of Rights played a surprisingly trivial role: only once before 1866 was it used by the Supreme Court to invalidate federal action, and that one use was *Dred Scott's* highly implausible and strikingly casual claim that the Fifth Amendment due-process clause invalidated free-soil territory laws like the Northwest Ordinance and the Missouri Compromise.[27] In a review of newspapers published in 1841, Dean Robert Reinstein could find not a single fiftieth anniversary celebration of the Bill of Rights.[28]

In area after area, incorporation enabled judges first to invalidate state and local laws—and then, with this doctrinal base thus built up, to begin to keep Congress in check.[29] Countless examples could be offered, but our First Amendment is perhaps the best. Before 1925, when the Court began in earnest the process of First Amendment incorporation,[30] free speech had never prevailed against a repressive statute in the United States Supreme Court. (And although no case ever reached the Supreme Court, we should recall that no federal judge in the 1790s ever invalidated the infamous Sedition Act of 1798.) Within a few years of incorporation, however, freedom of expression and religion began to win in cases involving states like Kansas (*Fiske,* 1927), California (*Stromberg,* 1931), Minnesota (*Near,* 1931), and Connecticut (*Cantwell,* 1940).[31] These and other cases began to build up a First Amendment tradition,[32] in and out of court, and that tradition could then be used against even federal officials. Not until 1965 did the Supreme Court strike down an act of Congress on First Amendment grounds, and when it did so, it relied squarely on doctrine built up in earlier cases involving states.[33] Consider also the more recent flag-burning cases. The Supreme Court laid down the requisite doctrine in a 1989 case involving a Texas statute and then, in 1990, stood its ground on precisely that doctrine to strike down an act of Congress.[34]

This swelling body of legal doctrine has spilled out of courtrooms and soaked into the vocabulary and worldview of law students, journalists, activists, and ultimately the citizenry at large. But without incorporation, and the steady flow of cases created by state and local laws, the Supreme Court would have had far fewer opportunities to be part of the ongoing American conversation about liberty. Here, too, we see that the central role of the Bill of Rights today owes at least as much to the Reconstruction as to the Creation.

In both legal and popular culture, notions of individual and minority rights loom large today. Conventional wisdom attributes these themes to the Founders' Bill; but as we have seen, this conventional story misreads the Creation and misses the Reconstruction. James Madison did believe in strong individual rights; in many ways, however, he was ahead of his time, and the First Congress did not always share his vision. Bingham and the Thirty-ninth Congress did embrace individualism, but the conventional narrative uses Madison as an anachronistic trope in lieu of Bingham. Congressman Madison first proposed a "No State shall" Fourteenth Amendment, so we tend to slight the later Congressman who actually got his own "No State shall" Fourteenth Amendment enacted. Madison was antiestablishment, so the original First Amendment was too, we tell ourselves. Madison thought that property rights were central, so the takings clause was paradigmatic of the Founding era, we think. Madison stressed federal protection of minority rights in *The Federalist* No. 10, so this now-classic text must always have been canonical, we suppose. Madison spoke of the role of judges, so the original Bill of Rights was judge-centric, we assume. On all these points, and many others, we might do well to study John Bingham more, and lift some of the load from James Madison's stooped shoulders.

A further point: modern academic discourse about the Bill of Rights is unreflectively clausebound. Yet this discourse ignores the ways in which the Bill is, well, a *bill*—a set of interconnected provisions. There is some irony here. Madison stressed the didactic role that a bill of rights could play, yet his original planned amendments would have scattered various provisions throughout the original document. Only late in the process—and over Madison's objections—were his proposed amendments recast into a single set to be placed together at the end of the original Constitution. When, providentially, only ten amendments were ratified in the 1790s, the ultimate effect was to create a kind of decalogue— ten commandments—whose whole was greater than the sum of its parts.* In real estate, the three most important things are location, location, and location; a nice house gains value when it sits next to other nice houses. So, too, each clause of the early amendments gains by its proximity to the others.[35] No one understood this better than John Bingham and his fellow contrarians. Whereas others spoke of discrete "articles of amendment," he and they holistically insisted on the centrality of the "*Bill* of Rights," exemplifying a unified theory of liberty.

The modern notion of a self-contained federal bill of rights thus derives at least as much from Bingham as from Madison. The federal Constitution contains no explicit caption introducing a "bill of rights"— unlike many early state constitutions, which feature a self-styled "declaration of rights" preceding an explicit "frame of government." And because the first ten federal amendments ultimately came in as appendixes rather than as a preface, still later amendments had the effect of pushing the

---

*By adding amendments to the end of the original Constitution rather than interweaving them into, and rewriting, the original text, the Founders also bequeathed subsequent generations of interpreters a unique problem: deducing exactly how much of the earlier text must be reinterpreted in light of a new amendment at the end. This is, of course, a question at the heart of the incorporation debate.

The practice of adding new words to the end rather than interweaving them into the original also gives constitutional interpretation an archaeological feel, as we encounter different historical layers of text, with each generation adding atop its predecessor. This feature of our constitutional practice calls attention to generational issues, as Bruce Ackerman has emphasized in much of his important work. *See generally* 1 WE THE PEOPLE: FOUNDATIONS (1991). This generational emphasis has heavily influenced the preceding pages.

early amendments to the middle—ten early postscripts before later post-postscripts. It was Bingham's generation that in effect added a closing parenthesis after the first eight (or nine, or ten) amendments, distinguishing *these* amendments from all others. As a result, Americans today can lay claim to a federal "*Bill* of Rights" set apart from everything else, and symbolically first even if textually middling.

This brings us to our last point; for Bingham and others also insisted that the early amendments were largely a "Bill of *Rights*"—of persons, not states. Today's conventional wisdom sharply distinguishes between structural issues and rights issues. Here, too, this distinction is attributed to the Founders—their Constitution delineated structure; their Bill, rights. But once again this conventional account misreads the Founding and misses the Reconstruction. Structure and rights tightly intertwined in the original Constitution and in the original Bill, which themselves tightly intertwined. The basic need to separate rights from structure comes from the Fourteenth Amendment itself—from the need for a suitable filter that enables incorporation to mine and refine rights from the mixed ore in which these rights were initially embedded in the Founders' quarry. Although incorporation does require us to separate rights from structure for some purposes, it does not require us to ignore the subtle interplay between them for other purposes; indeed, a suitably refined model should highlight this interplay.

What, in the end, are we to make of the pervasive ways in which our stock stories have exaggerated the Creation and diminished the Reconstruction? If this book is right, then many of us are guilty of a kind of curiously selective ancestor worship—one that gives too much credit to James Madison and not enough to John Bingham, that celebrates Thomas Jefferson and Patrick Henry but slights Harriet Beecher Stowe and Frederick Douglass.* Great as men like Madison and Jefferson were, they lived and died as slaveholders, and their Bill of Rights was tainted by its quiet complicity with the original sin of slavery.[36] Even as we celebrate the Founders, we must ponder the sobering words of Charles

---

*With these names, I mean to juxtapose the emblematic drafters, poets, and orators, respectively, of the Creation and the Reconstruction.

Cotesworth Pinckney in the 1788 South Carolina ratifying debates: "Another reason weighed particularly, with the members from this state, against the insertion of a bill of rights. Such bills generally begin with declaring that all men are by nature born free. Now, we should make that declaration with a very bad grace, when a large part of our property consists in men who are actually born slaves."[37]

But the Reconstruction Amendment did begin with an affirmation of the freedom, and citizenship, of all. Those who birthed it renounced the Slave Power and all its works. These midwives were women alongside men, blacks alongside whites. After their mighty labors, more work did remain to be done—more work always remains to be done, if all are to be free and equal. But because of these men and women, our Bill of Rights was reborn.

Afterword

In the preceding twelve chapters I have tried to tell a tale of the Bill of Rights. I have narrated this story from a certain perspective, animated by certain premises, and constrained by certain parameters. With the tale now told, I propose to step outside my narrative and reflect on its method and scope. In the course of these reflections, I hope to note some of the debts that I owe to scholars who have come before and to flag some of the opportunities that I foresee for scholars who will come after.

A Note on Text and Textualism

The tale I have tried to tell in this book is, in some important ways, textual. It takes as its subject the set of words—the text—that we call the Bill of Rights, namely, the first ten amendments and the interlocking Fourteenth Amendment designed to apply the Bill to the states. The text of the Bill has shaped both this book's basic architecture and much of its internal analysis. Thus the order of the chapters basically tracks the textual order of the amendments themselves (I–X, and then XIV); and within each chapter, the specific words of the Bill oft loom large.

This textual emphasis surely limits my tale, but it also helps empower it. (The foul lines in baseball limit the field of play but also make the game possible.) As we consider various possible accounts of this amendment or that one, or of the Bill of Rights as a whole, we should be willing to measure these accounts against the text itself in order to see which ones best fit the precise words that eventually became the Supreme Law of the Land. The status of the Bill as law reinforces the importance of textualism. Granted, lawyers and judges must often go beyond the letter of the law, but the text itself is an obvious starting point of legal analysis. Is it even possible to deduce the spirit of a law without looking at its letter?

A textual analysis of the Bill of Rights can also illuminate patterns and thus cast light on the true spirit of the law as a whole. Throughout my tale I have tried to show how various words in the original Constitution repeat themselves in the Bill of Rights; how various textual motifs recur within the first ten amendments; and how the Fourteenth Amendment's key sentence features remarkable and revealing textual cross-references to the original Constitution and Bill. An important aspect of our Constitution, I suggest, is its intratextuality.

Another feature of our Bill of Rights might be termed its intertextuality—the illuminating ways in which it both builds on and deviates from the precise texts of such earlier landmarks of liberty as the English Bill of Rights, the Declaration of Independence, and various state constitutional declarations of rights. This, too, has been part of my story.

Thus far I have offered a few points on behalf of textualism that might appeal to lawyers. But this is a book written not just for lawyers and judges but for ordinary citizens who care about our Constitution and our rights. And here, I think, lies perhaps the strongest reason for offering an account of the Bill of Rights that takes text seriously. The American people—outside courtrooms, outside law offices—confront, and lay claim to, the Bill of Rights as a text. Its grand phrases—"the freedom of speech," "the right to keep and bear arms," "due process of law," and so on—define a basic vocabulary of liberty for ordinary citizens. "We the

People of the United States," in whose name the Bill speaks and to whom it speaks, speak in the words of the Bill. James Madison and John Bingham would no doubt be pleased by this fact of modern life; both understood that a Bill that did not live in the hearts and minds of ordinary Americans would probably, in the long run, fail.

Had I set out to write a less textual, less constrained book about "liberty in America"—"these are a few of my favorite rights"—I must confess that I might have been tempted to avoid all mention of the right to keep and bear arms. (Today's justices and most of today's constitutional scholars have apparently yielded to a similar temptation to keep mum about arms.) But in a textualist book about the first ten amendments, I was obliged to confront the stubborn text that stands between the words of Amendments I and III; and in a textualist book about the core privileges and immunities of national citizenship affirmed by the Fourteenth Amendment, I was constrained to consider how the Second Amendment's text was reglossed by a later constitutional text. In the process, I was forced to confront the Second Amendment, a text that—in part because it *is* a text appearing in every American's copy of the Bill of Rights—abides in the hearts of millions of ordinary citizens.

Textualism has helped shape not only what this book includes but also what it excludes. Perhaps the most troubling exclusion is this: this book gestures toward, but fails to offer a systematic account of, many of the liberty-bearing provisions of our Constitution that lie outside the Bill of Rights. The protection of habeas corpus and the bans on bills of attainder, ex post facto laws, and titles of nobility in Article I, sections 9 and 10; the narrow definition of treason in Article III; the grand guarantee of republican government in Article IV; the prohibition of religious tests for public office in Article VI; the toweringly important abolition of slavery in the Thirteenth Amendment; the sweepingly inclusive voting amendments (the Fifteenth, Nineteenth, Twenty-fourth, and Twenty-sixth)—all these and other important provisions receive little attention here. In both ordinary language and legal doctrine, these provisions lie outside the text of the Bill of Rights and so I have pushed them off stage. My narrow spotlight on the first ten amendments and section 1 of the Fourteenth Amendment has the practical virtues of (1) constraining authorial selectivity; (2) easing exposition and making the overall project less vast and more tractable; and (3) taking seriously both legal and ordinary understandings of the Bill as a coherent and self-contained entity. But my narrow focus has the theoretical vices of (1) obscuring the centrality of other liberty-bearing provisions; (2) unintentionally undercutting a central thesis of this work—the interconnections between the Bill and many of these other clauses and among these other clauses themselves; and (3) encouraging readers to think of words more than things—to organize their understandings around the Bill rather than around, say, the concept of "liberty."

These are substantial vices, and they point the way for future scholars to press ahead on at least two fronts where I have fallen short. First, a great book remains to be written on what might be called the diaspora of rights—those scattered provisions before and after the Bill of Rights that could be viewed as a companion Bill of Rights in exile. Such a book could well (though it need not) be textualist in ways similar to this one, but it would take different constitutional texts as its subject. Second, there is still room for a great book on rights organized around concepts rather than words—"liberty," "equality," "democracy," "privacy," and so forth. Such a book could well (though it need not) be textualist in its ultimate aspiration—to account for the words that are actually in our Constitution—but not necessarily in its organizational structure. The exposition, in other words, might be structured around concepts rather than clauses.

A conceptual book on "liberty" might well devote more space than I have here to the idea of unenumerated rights. In both the Ninth Amendment and the privileges-or-immunities clause, the written Constitution seems to gesture beyond itself, toward rights not textually specified in the document itself. But what, exactly, are those rights, and how to find them? In this book, I have used (among other things) a couple of textual techniques—of intra- and intertextuality—to (partially) answer these questions. Surely, I have suggested, the rights of the people in the Ninth Amendment should be read in connection with the Preamble's proclamation (and enactment) of the right of "the People" to "ordain and establish . . . Constitution[s]," and in tandem with the Declaration of

Independence's affirmation (and enactment) of "the Right of the People to alter or abolish . . . Government." Surely, I have suggested, judges confronting the open-ended language of the Fourteenth Amendment should consider the legal texts of other charters of liberty—Magna Charta, Petition of Right, the English Bill of Rights, state constitutions, and the like—as helpful sources. I do not mean to suggest that, methodologically, these intra- and intertextual techniques exhaust the repertoire of legitimate interpretive approaches to unenumerated rights or that, substantively, other kinds of unenumerated rights should be ruled out. But to have pursued fully all possible nontextual approaches to nontextual rights would be to have written a very different kind of book. My strategy, instead, has been to focus tightly on the enumerated rights; we need a good account of these rights before we can use open-ended language to interpolate between and extrapolate beyond these textual rights. Even if the unenumerated rights are not merely gap fillers and handmaidens of enumerated rights, at times they may play these roles;[1] hence the need for a close examination of the letter of enumerated rights so that we may properly vindicate their spirit with the open-ended clauses.

If rights can be unenumerated, is it possible to imagine entire constitutional amendments that are unwritten? Bruce Ackerman has powerfully argued that our Constitution today is largely the product of the interaction of three great constitutional moments—the Founding, the Reconstruction, and the New Deal.[2] Thus the need, on Ackerman's account, for constitutional interpretation that "synthesizes" the meanings of all three moments. For Ackerman, the incorporation of the Bill of Rights raises paradigmatic questions of "one-two" (that is, Founding-Reconstruction) synthesis; and much of my book is an effort to try to do the kind of detailed interpretive work that Ackerman at a more abstract level has called for. But what about Ackerman's third moment (the New Deal)? How is it to be integrated into the analysis?

In this book, I have not even tried to answer this question; I have merely set the scene. Given that Ackerman's third moment left no textual trace in the Constitution, its proper interpretation and synthesis might call for interpretive techniques rather different from the ones I have featured here. And, I confess, I have not studied the history of the New Deal carefully enough to take a final position on Ackerman's arresting thesis about a third constitutional moment in the 1930s.

There is another, more textualist, account of twentieth-century constitutionalism that perhaps warrants consideration as a possible alternative to Ackerman's. One great strength of Ackerman's account is its recognition that Americans in the early twentieth century transformed the eighteenth- and nineteenth-century document that they inherited. One obvious weakness is that Ackerman's New Deal Amendment does not appear in the text of the Constitution in the same way that, say, the Bill of Rights and the Fourteenth Amendment do. Because of this, ordinary citizens and lawyers alike may have trouble accepting Ackerman's bold theory. But early-twentieth-century Americans did amend the Constitution in a variety of "progressive" ways in the 1910s, with a series of textual amendments. All these amendments drained power from state governments—the Sixteenth by authorizing a national income tax, the Seventeenth by eliminating state legislative election of U.S. senators, and the Nineteenth by mandating a federal rule for women's suffrage even in state elections.[3] The Sixteenth Amendment was also profoundly redistributive, authorizing a "progressive" income tax that would take more proportionately from the rich than the poor. Given that two of the central themes of Ackerman's nontextual New Deal Amendment—increased national power and the increased permissibility of economic redistribution—are also central themes of the textual Progressive-era amendments, is it truly necessary to postulate an unwritten amendment in the 1930s to account for a more nationalist and redistributive constitutional regime in the twentieth century?

I repeat that I do not seek to answer such questions in this book; I aim only to set the scene for future scholarship to pick up where I have left off. And on the main topic of my book—"one-two" synthesis—my conclusions generally reinforce Ackerman's. Modern scholars and citizens attribute too much of modern constitutionalism to the Founding ("one"), and not enough to the Reconstruction ("two").

A final note on my particular brand of textualism. In pondering the words of our Bill of Rights, I have been powerfully influenced by certain theoretical claims advanced by my colleagues Bruce Ackerman, Jed Rubenfeld, and Jack Balkin. Beneath the words of a constitutional clause, Ackerman reminds us, there often lie years of embodied struggle by public-minded citizens working to transform their ideals into enduring higher law. In parsing the texts of Amendments I–X and XIV, I have tried to locate these texts in the context of the broader struggles of the Revolutionary and Reconstruction generations, respectively. The story of the original Bill of Rights must flash back to critical events in the 1760s and 1770s, and the story of the Fourteenth Amendment cannot ignore the decades of bitter toil that ultimately bore much fruit in the harvest. Next, consider Rubenfeld's elegant insight that at the core of many a constitutional text lies a paradigm case—a specific, historical evil that the drafting generation lived through and sought to destroy with a text that in effect proclaimed "never again!"[4] Throughout this book, I have been on the lookout for possible paradigm cases at work—the prosecution of Zenger, the imperial assault on Massachusetts minutemen, the Boston Quartering Act, the searches and seizures in *Wilkes v. Wood,* the vice-admiralty courts, the Hoar affair, the suppression of abolitionist speech, the disarming of freedmen, the dragnet searches of black homes, the Black Codes, and so on. Finally, Balkin has used semiotic theory to show that a text—like any other sign—can mean different things in different contexts.[5*] Thus, the same set of words could mean one thing when proclaimed in 1789 and something slightly different when reglossed in 1866. In his work Balkin has tried to show how this fascinating phenomenon is possible in theory; in this book, I have tried to show how such a thing happened in fact.

A Note on History, Historians, and Historiography

If my tale in this book has, in some important ways, been framed by text and textualism, it has also, in some important ways, been shaped by his-

---

*The theoretical work of Larry Lessig is also quite important here, illuminating the ways in which meaning is produced by an interaction of text and context. *See, e.g.,* Lawrence Lessig, Note, *Plastics: Unger and Ackerman on Transformation,* 98 YALE L.J. 1173 (1989); Lawrence Lessig, *Fidelity in Translation,* 71 TEX. L. REV. 1165 (1993).

tory and historians. At the most basic level, this is a law book (written about law by a law professor) that seeks to realign the dominant legal narrative about the Creation and Reconstruction with the dominant historical narrative (as evidenced in history books written about history by history professors). In a nutshell: lawyers' accounts of the Creation cannot ignore the lessons of the "republican revival," and our narrations of Reconstruction must be informed by generations of revisionist historians.

Consider first the Creation. Early in the century, Charles Beard proclaimed the Constitution an undemocratic coup, perpetrated by moneymen and centrally designed to entrench private property.[6] By the middle of this century, Louis Hartz and others saw the document as fundamentally individualist, libertarian, and (once again) property focused.[7] But more recently, Douglass Adair, J. G. A. Pocock, Bernard Bailyn, Gordon Wood, Pauline Maier, Garry Wills, and other historians have explored the strong republican strands of the Founding, offering up accounts that highlight themes of popular sovereignty and civic virtue.[8] These are themes, I have suggested, that powerfully illuminate the text of the original Bill of Rights.

In the mid 1960s Cecelia Kenyon published a pathbreaking one-volume compilation of Anti-Federalist material, and in the early 1980s, Herbert Storing's comprehensive seven-volume collection of Anti-Federalist literature came to print.[9] The Bill of Rights, of course, was initially an Anti-Federalist idea that moderate Federalists ultimately accepted and adjusted; but until Kenyon and Storing, lawyers lacked easy access to the rich body of Anti-Federalist literature that helped frame the overall debate. As a result, the conventional narrative among lawyers has tended to slight one of the main sources of our Bill of Rights, and lawyers have underestimated the importance of Anti-Federalist themes of citizen participation and states' rights in the public discourse leading up to the Bill.

Now turn to the Reconstruction. Early in this century, the reigning historical narrative, exemplified by the work of William Dunning and his disciples, viewed Reconstruction as a tragic era in American history.[10] Republican Reconstructors on this account were knaves and fools. The work of Charles Fairman and Raoul Berger was very much in the grip of this view: John Bingham, for example, was depicted as a pompous airhead rather than as one of the most high-minded and impressive lawyers of his generation, the James Madison of Reconstruction. In legal circles, the work of Fairman and Berger continues to enjoy a wide circulation and a high reputation. In this book I have been sharply (perhaps too sharply) critical of the work of these two men. I have taken this tone precisely because their work continues to exert such influence in legal circles long after many of its intellectual foundations have been undermined by decades of serious and sustained scholarship of professional historians.

Beginning with the work of the great W. E. B. Du Bois in the 1930s,[11] American historians have largely demolished the claims of the Dunning school. In Part Two of this book, I have tried to bring the legal narrative back into sync with the insights of such lawyers and historians as Howard Jay Graham, Jacobus tenBroek, William Winslow Crosskey, Kenneth Stampp, Harold Hyman, William Wiecek, Les Benedict, Eric Foner, Bob Cottrol, and Lea VanderVelde.[12] I owe an especially deep debt to the work of Michael Kent Curtis and Richard Aynes.[13] In my view, serious lawyers should begin with the works of these scholars and not with the work of Fairman and Berger.

An immense amount of work on Reconstruction remains to be done. Most important, lawyers today still lack easy access to many of the most important primary sources from the 1830s through the 1860s. Consider, for a moment, the library of Creation material at hand for the armchair lawyer or judge. Publius's *Federalist* has always been around; Madison's notes of the Philadelphia convention and Jonathan Elliot's compilations of various ratification convention material came to print a century and a half ago; more than a hundred years ago, Paul Leicester Ford published handy collections of ratification pamphlets; Max Farrand published his superb edition of the records of the Philadelphia convention early this century; and the last three decades have witnessed an explosion of helpful collections, editions, and compilations. This is not the place to list them all, but a few deserve special mention: Bernard Bailyn's 1965 *Pamphlets of the American Revolution* and his later two-volume Library of

America compilation of material on *The Debate on the Constitution;* the multivolume *Documentary History of the Ratification of the Constitution* project being carried on at the University of Wisconsin; Kenyon's and Storing's above-noted collections of Anti-Federalist literature; the First Federal Congress project being edited by Charlene Bangs Bickford, Kenneth R. Bowling, and Helen E. Veit; Philip Kurland's and Ralph Lerner's wide-ranging five-volume compilation, *The Founders' Constitution;* Maeva Marcus's multivolume *Documentary History of the Supreme Court;* Bernard Schwartz's handy two-volume documentary history, *The Bill of Rights;* and most recently, Neil Cogan's superb one-volume compilation, *The Complete Bill of Rights.**

By comparison, the antislavery and Reconstruction primary sources are not nearly so accessible. If, as this book has argued, much of our modern Constitution comes not from the Creators but from the Reconstructors, there is, I repeat, much work to be done by would-be Kenyons, Storings, Farrands, Bailyns, and Cogans. (Cogan himself is already at work on such a Reconstruction-era compilation, but as with the Founding materials, the enormous task at hand will require the best efforts of many dedicated scholars.)

Before concluding these remarks about history, historians, and historiography, perhaps I should address one final topic: my own historical situatedness. In telling a tale of the Bill of Rights, I cannot pretend to a God's-eye view, even as I have aspired to narrate a history that is, in some old-fashioned sense, objectively true. No doubt, in ways I cannot fully understand, I have been influenced by the history of my own times, even as I try to tell the story of an earlier era. I grew up during the Cold War, and the second Reconstruction of the 1960s; and more recently I have witnessed a resurgent wave of American feminism and the collapse of

---

*To make things easier for lawyers and layfolk who may lack access to a major research library, I have tried where possible to cite various eighteenth-century materials as reprinted in later, more accessible compilations. For debates in the First Congress I generally cite the handy Schwartz collection, which faithfully reprints materials from the harder-to-find and harder-to-use *Annals of Congress;* for the Virginia and Kentucky Resolutions, I often cite the convenient Kurland and Lerner set, which reprints various less accessible versions of these legislative documents; and so on.

the Soviet empire in Eastern Europe. The Cold War heightened my interest in political ideas—of liberty, democracy, and equality—and sensitized me to the ways in which a repressive regime built on unfreedom would try to keep outside agitators out and inside agitators down. When John Kennedy proclaimed (in words that I memorized in elementary school) that in the long run the world could not exist "half slave and half free," he was of course recalling the earlier American experience I have tried to describe in Part Two. Likewise, the second Reconstruction that took flight as I was maturing has surely influenced my ideas about the importance of the first Reconstruction. And as I saw the Wall come down in Europe and observed Eastern European countries trying to fashion new, democratic constitutions, I became more aware of the agency problem of government above and beyond the problem of minority rights. In many of these places, the mass of people arrayed themselves against a small clique of entrenched, self-serving party officials, and the first problem of government was to break the stronghold of arrogant officialdom. Finally, the renaissance of feminism over the past three decades has, I hope, encouraged me to listen for the voices of women, as I have tried to do, however inadequately, in my account of Reconstruction. (I have tried to listen for, but, alas, have heard much less from, women in the public discourse about the Bill in the Founding era.)[14]

A Note on Judges and Precedent

If this book has a set of heroes and heroines, it is the American People—or more precisely, the generations of Revolutionaries and Reconstructors who birthed and rebirthed the Bill of Rights. It might be asked, what about judges?

The careful reader will no doubt notice that judges are not exactly the heroes and heroines of my tale. Federal judges, after all, enthusiastically enforced the infamous Sedition Act of 1798, cheerfully sending men to prison for their antigovernmental speech and neutering juries along the way. It is hard to imagine a bigger betrayal of the original Bill of Rights, whether we look at the First, or the Sixth, or the Tenth Amendment. A century later, the Supreme Court strangled the privileges-or-immunities clause in its crib in the *Slaughter-House Cases;* blessed Jim

Crow in *Plesy;* and blithely allowed judges to fine a newspaper publisher (in a juryless proceeding lacking specific statutory authorization) simply because the publisher had the audacity to criticize the very judges in question.[15] (Thus a single court acted as legislature, prosecutor, complaining witness, judge, and jury—quite a trick if you can get away with it.) Due process of law, according to the Taney Court, was satisfied by fugitive-slave hearings presided over by a financially biased adjudicator, but violated by free-soil laws like the Northwest Ordinance.[16] And although Roger Taney himself (rightly) had doubts about the federal government's power to draft citizens outside of the Constitution's careful militia system, the Supreme Court, in the *Selective Draft Law Cases,* gave this argument the back of its hand.[17]*

The foregoing summary of the role of judges is a trifle one-sided, of course, and in at least three important ways, my story has tried to include the judiciary. First, I have argued that in order to understand the text of the Bill and the Fourteenth Amendment, we must understand the extant legal doctrine against which these texts were adopted. We cannot fully understand the Fourth Amendment without understanding *Wilkes,* or the Fourteenth without understanding *Barron, Corfield, Dred Scott,* and *Murray's Lessee.*

Second, I have highlighted a common-law method of law finding evident in (among other things) judicial cases, and responsive to the distinct problems facing a judge who must interpret a seemingly open-ended legal text. More generally, I have tried to consider how various texts in the Bill of Rights might be translated into workable legal doctrine suitable for judicial implementation.

Finally, although my narrative has not traveled through all the modern case law on the Bill of Rights, in important ways it has traded upon these cases. In a book that tries to explain to fellow citizens what the Bill of Rights and the Fourteenth Amendment texts "really" meant to those who birthed them, I need not write at length about what judges later had

---

*More abstractly, the methodology of textualism, and the concept of original intent, always create the theoretical possibility of critiquing case law from perspectives outside of case law itself.

to say about original intent. To the extent that a later judge got it right, his or her exposition might be illuminating; but so would a similar exposition by a later scholar. (Or to put it a different way, the judge who later got it right might well have been in dissent—like the elder Justice Harlan, and Justice Black in *Adamson*—yet the judge's exposition might nonetheless illuminate.) But in a book that also seeks to explain the text to lawyers and judges, this strategy of ignoring judges qua judges will not do. As Philip Bobbitt and Richard Fallon have observed, textual arguments count in court—and so do arguments from history and original intent—but precedent counts, too.[18] Judges must consider all these factors, and others as well, when deciding cases. And here is where my account in this book trades on precedent. I have told a tale that, at the end of the day, ends up supporting most of today's precedent about the Bill of Rights.

To be sure, my exposition does not travel through all the modern cases. I do not, for example, try to show why judges were right in refusing to incorporate First Amendment freedoms before 1925, or why they were right in waiting until 1964 to repudiate the odious Sedition Act of 1798. Rather, I have tried to show why, in general, courts today have ended up in pretty much the right place, even if they have not always offered the best textual and historical reasons.* *New York Times v. Sullivan* was right in its result and its instincts, even if its narrative paid too little tribute to the Reconstruction. Selective incorporation is largely right in result and instinct—and we can even explain why perhaps the Seventh Amendment should not be incorporated (although the failure to incorporate the right to keep and bear arms and the grand jury are hard to justify). From start to finish this book has aimed to explain how today's judges and lawyers have often gotten it right without quite realizing why.

---

*One important exception to this generalization is the field of constitutional criminal procedure, a field where, in a previous work, I have sharply criticized modern judicial doctrine. *See* AKHIL REED AMAR, THE CONSTITUTION AND CRIMINAL PROCEDURE: FIRST PRINCIPLES (1997). Although my critique in that work implicates an important quadrant of the Bill of Rights, my critique there is tangential to the main issues of Creation-Reconstruction synthesis at the core of the present book.

Appendix

Amendments I–X and XIV

Amendment I Congress shall make no law respecting an establishment of religion, or prohibiting the free exercise thereof; or abridging the freedom of speech, or of the press, or the right of the people peaceably to assemble, and to petition the Government for a redress of grievances.

Amendment II A well regulated Militia, being necessary to the security of a free State, the right of the people to keep and bear Arms, shall not be infringed.

Amendment III No Soldier shall, in time of peace be quartered in any house, without the consent of the Owner, nor in time of war, but in a manner to be prescribed by law.

Amendment IV The right of the people to be secure in their persons, houses, papers, and effects, against unreasonable searches and seizures, shall not be violated, and no Warrants shall issue, but upon probable cause, supported by Oath or affirmation, and particularly describing the place to be searched, and the persons or things to be seized.

Amendment V No person shall be held to answer for a capital, or otherwise infamous crime, unless on a presentment or indictment of a Grand Jury, except in cases arising in the land or naval forces, or in the Militia, when in actual service in time of War or public danger; nor shall any person be subject for the same offence to be twice put in jeopardy of life or limb, nor shall be compelled in any criminal case to be a witness against himself, nor be deprived of life, liberty, or property, without due process of law; nor shall private property be taken for public use without just compensation.

Amendment VI In all criminal prosecutions, the accused shall enjoy the right to a speedy and public trial, by an impartial jury of the State and district wherein the crime shall have been committed, which district shall have been previously ascertained by law, and to be informed of the nature and cause of the accusation; to be confronted with the witnesses against him; to have compulsory process for obtaining witnesses in his favor, and to have the assistance of counsel for his defence.

Amendment VII In Suits at common law, where the value in controversy shall exceed twenty dollars, the right of trial by jury shall be preserved, and no fact tried by a jury shall be otherwise re-examined in any Court of the United States, than according to the rules of the common law.

Amendment VIII Excessive bail shall not be required, nor excessive fines imposed, nor cruel and unusual punishments inflicted.

Amendment IX The enumeration in the Constitution, of certain rights, shall not be construed to deny or disparage others retained by the people.

Amendment X The powers not delegated to the United States by the Constitution, nor prohibited by it to the States, are reserved to the States respectively, or to the people.

Amendment XIV Section 1. All persons born or naturalized in the United States and subject to the jurisdiction thereof, are citizens of the United States and of the State wherein they reside. No State shall make or enforce any law which shall abridge the privileges or immunities of citizens of the United States; nor shall any State deprive any person of life, liberty, or property, without due process of law; nor deny to any person within its jurisdiction the equal protection of the laws.

Section 2. Representatives shall be apportioned among the several States according to their respective numbers, counting the whole number of persons in each State, excluding Indians not taxed. But when the right to vote at any election for the choice of electors for President and Vice President of the United States, Representatives in Congress, the Executive and Judicial officers of a State, or the members of the Legislature thereof, is denied to any of the male inhabitants of such State, being twenty-one years of age, and citizens of the United States, or in any way abridged, except for participation in rebellion, or other crime, the basis of representation therein shall be reduced in the proportion which the number of such male citizens shall bear to the whole number of male citizens twenty-one years of age in such State.

Section 3. No person shall be a Senator or Representative in Congress, or elector of President and Vice President, or hold any office, civil or military, under the United States, or under any State, who, having previously taken an oath, as a member of Congress, or as an officer of the United States, or as a member of any State legislature, or as an executive or judicial officer of any State, to support the Constitution of the United States, shall have engaged in insurrection or rebellion against the same, or given aid or comfort to the enemies thereof. But Congress may by a vote of two-thirds of each House, remove such disability.

Section 4. The validity of the public debt of the United States, authorized by law, including debts incurred for payment of pensions and bounties for services in suppressing insurrection or rebellion, shall not be questioned. But neither the United States nor any State shall assume or pay any debt or obligation incurred in aid of insurrection or rebellion against the United States, or any claim for the loss or emancipation of any slave; but all such debts, obligations and claims shall be held illegal and void.

Section 5. The Congress shall have power to enforce, by appropriate legislation, the provisions of this article.

Notes

Note: For a general discussion of this book's sources and citation practice, see *supra* pages 302–4 and note.

Introduction

1. For a more detailed discussion of how law school teachers have carved up the Bill of Rights *see* Howard W. Gutman, *Academic Determinism: The Division of the Bill of Rights,* 54 S. CAL. L. REV. 295, 328–31 (1981). Gutman closes his essay with a suggestion that legal discourse about rights be severed from analysis of constitutional structure, *id.* at 379–81. Although this plea stands directly opposed to my own approach, Gutman's little-known essay is the font of many important insights. It deserves a place on the "must read" list of all serious students of the Bill of Rights.

2. Professor Levinson has powerfully documented the general lack of interest in the Second Amendment among mainstream constitutional theorists. *See* Sanford Levinson, *The Embarrassing Second Amendment,* 99 YALE L. J. 637, 637–42 (1989). Levinson criticizes this lack of interest, but even one so catholic as he is willing to allow the Third Amendment to languish in obscurity. *See id.* at 641.

Since the publication of Levinson's essay, a few mainstream theorists have entered the Second Amendment debate—*see, e.g.,* William Van Alstyne, *The Second Amend-*

ment and the Personal Right to Bear Arms, 43 DUKE L. J. 1236 (1994); David C. Williams, *Civic Republicanism and the Citizen Militia: The Terrifying Second Amendment*, 101 YALE L. J. 551 (1991)—but only a few.

3. *Accord* Gutman, *supra* note 1, at 328 and n.146 ("No work since [the 1890s] has provided an integrated analysis of the Bill of Rights.").

The best modern account of the Bill is a book by a practitioner: EDWARD DUM-BAULD, THE BILL OF RIGHTS AND WHAT IT MEANS TODAY (1957). The book contains a wealth of historical material about the Bill and its antecedents, but offers little in the way of comprehensive constitutional theory.

4. *See, e.g.*, GERALD GUNTHER, CONSTITUTIONAL LAW 65–393 (12th ed. 1991) (Part 2, "The Structure of Government"); *id.* at 394–1675 (Part 3, "Individual Rights"). Professor Gunther's casebook is far from unique in this respect. *See* Gutman, *supra* note 1, at 372 and n.424.

5. *See, e.g.*, William J. Brennan, Jr., *Why Have a Bill of Rights?*, 26 VAL. U. L. REV. 1, 12 (1991) (suggesting that the "salient purpose" of a bill of rights is to "protect minorities . . . from the passions or fears of political majorities").

6. THE FEDERALIST No. 51, at 323 (James Madison) (Clinton Rossiter ed., 1961).

One. First Things First

1. 347 U.S. 483 (1954).

2. *See, e.g.*, JESSE H. CHOPER, JUDICIAL REVIEW AND THE POLITICAL PROCESS 252–54 (1980). I, too, am guilty. *See, e.g.*, Akhil Reed Amar, *A Neo-Federalist View of Article III: Separating the Two Tiers of Federal Jurisdiction*, 65 B. U. L. REV. 205 (1985).

3. For an elegant discussion of the differences between judicial invalidations of congressional statutes and other forms of judicial review, *see* CHARLES L. BLACK, JR., STRUCTURE AND RELATIONSHIP IN CONSTITUTIONAL LAW 67–93 (1969).

4. OLIVER WENDELL HOLMES, COLLECTED LEGAL PAPERS 295–96 (1920).

5. James B. Thayer, *The Origin and Scope of the American Doctrine of Constitutional Law*, 7 HARV. L. REV. 129 (1893).

6. *See, e.g.*, Akhil Reed Amar, *Of Sovereignty and Federalism*, 96 YALE L. J. 1425, 1440–41 (1987) [hereinafter *Sovereignty*], and sources cited therein.

7. *See generally* GORDON S. WOOD, THE CREATION OF THE AMERICAN REPUBLIC, 1776–1787, at 463–67 (1969) ("The Abandonment of the States").

8. *See generally* Amar, *Sovereignty*, *supra* note 6, at 1492–1520.

9. *Id.* at 1500–1503.

10. *See also* Andrew C. McLaughlin, *The Background of American Federalism*, 12 AM. POL. SCI. REV. 215, 222 (1918) (noting overlap between "states rights" and "individual rights" rhetoric in colonial arguments against Parliament); ALEXANDER H. PEKELIS, LAW AND SOCIAL ACTION 94–95 (1950) (similar).

11. *See, e.g.*, 5 THE FOUNDERS' CONSTITUTION 132 (Philip B. Kurland and Ralph Ler-

ner eds., 1987) (Kentucky Resolution No. 3) (intertwining First and Tenth Amendment arguments). For more discussion, *see infra* Chapter 2.

12. *See* Amar, *Sovereignty, supra* note 6, at 1451–66, 1492–1520.

13. *See id.* at 1451–66.

14. *See, e.g., id.* at 1425–29, 1488 n.252; A. PEKELIS, *supra* note 10, at 127.

15. Though I shall disagree with him a great deal in Part Two, I note that Dean Griswold agreed with me on at least this much. *See* Erwin N. Griswold, *Due Process Problems Today in the United States, in* THE FOURTEENTH AMENDMENT 161, 162–63, 165 (Bernard Schwartz ed., 1970).

16. U.S. CONST. art. V.

17. 2 DOCUMENTARY HISTORY OF THE CONSTITUTION OF THE UNITED STATES OF AMERICA 321–22 (Washington: Department of State, 1894) [hereinafter DOCUMENTARY HISTORY OF THE CONSTITUTION] (ellipsis in original).

18. Under this formula, each slave was counted as three-fifths of a free person. U.S. CONST. art. I, §2, cl. 3.

19. The best known exponent of this view, of course, was Montesquieu. This view resounds throughout Anti-Federalist speeches and writings. For a smattering, *see* CECELIA M. KENYON, THE ANTIFEDERALISTS 24, 39, 101–2, 132–33, 208, 302, 324 (1966) (reprinting work of "Centinel," "The Pennsylvania Minority," "John De Witt," "Agrippa," " The Federal Farmer," "Cato," and "Brutus").

20. For more discussion, *see* Akhil Reed Amar, Marbury, *Section 13, and the Original Jurisdiction of the Supreme Court,* 56 U. CHI. L. REV. 443, 469–71 and n.128 (1989); Akhil Reed Amar, *Some New World Lessons for the Old World,* 58 U. CHI. L. REV. 483, 485–97 (1991).

21. THE FEDERALIST No. 14, at 100 (James Madison) (Clinton Rossiter ed., 1961) [hereinafter all citations are to this edition].

22. *Cf.* THE FEDERALIST No. 63, at 387 (James Madison) ("true distinction . . . [of] the American governments lies *in the total exclusion of the people in their collective capacity,* from any share" in day-to-day governance).

23. THE FEDERALIST No. 10, at 82 (James Madison).

24. For a more elaborate discussion of Madison's precise imagery of "refinement," *see* GARRY WILLS, EXPLAINING AMERICA 223–47 (1981).

25. *See, e.g.,* THE FEDERALIST No. 10, at 82 (James Madison); *id.* No. 55, at 342 (James Madison); *id.* No. 58, at 360 (James Madison); *id.* No. 62, at 379 (James Madison). *See also infra* text accompanying notes 50–54.

26. THE FEDERALIST No. 10, at 83 (James Madison).

27. This was, of course, part of the Federalists' design. *See* G. WOOD, *supra* note 7, at 471–518 ("The Worthy Against the Licentious"); G. WILLS, *supra* note 24, at 216–47.

28. *See generally* Amar, *Sovereignty, supra* note 6; Akhil Reed Amar, *Philadelphia Revisited: Amending the Constitution Outside Article V,* 55 U. CHI. L. REV. 1043 (1988); Akhil

Reed Amar, *The Consent of the Governed: Constitutional Amendment Outside Article V*, 94 COLUM. L. REV. 457 (1994); Akhil Reed Amar, *The Central Meaning of Republican Government: Popular Sovereignty, Majority Rule, and the Denominator Problem*, 65 U. COLO. L. REV. 749 (1994).

29. *See* HERBERT J. STORING, WHAT THE ANTI-FEDERALISTS WERE FOR 16-18, 41, 51-52 (1981); Carol M. Rose, *The Ancient Constitution vs. The Federalist Empire: Anti-Federalism from the Attack on "Monarchism" to Modern Localism*, 84 NW. U. L. REV. 74, 90-91 (1989), and sources cited therein; C. KENYON, *supra* note 19, at xl; *Essays of Brutus* (IV), *reprinted in* 2 THE COMPLETE ANTI-FEDERALIST 382-86 (Herbert J. Storing ed., 1981); *Letters from the Federal Farmer* (II), *reprinted in id.* at 233-34; *Letters from the Federal Farmer* (VII), *reprinted in id.* at 268-69; 2 BERNARD SCHWARTZ, THE BILL OF RIGHTS: A DOCUMENTARY HISTORY 1187 (1971) (Letter from Richard Henry Lee and William Grayson to Virginia Speaker of the House of Representatives (Sept. 28, 1789)).

30. Rose, *supra* note 29, at 91; *Essays by a Farmer* (IV), *reprinted in* 5 THE COMPLETE ANTI-FEDERALIST, *supra* note 29, at 38.

31. 2 DEBATES ON THE ADOPTION OF THE FEDERAL CONSTITUTION 287 (Jonathan Elliot ed., AYER Co. reprint ed. 1987) (1836) [hereinafter ELLIOT'S DEBATES].

32. 3 *id.* at 46.

33. *See supra* text accompanying note 26; *cf.* 2 ELLIOT'S DEBATES, *supra* note 31, at 474 (remarks of James Wilson at Pennsylvania ratifying convention).

34. 1 RECORDS OF THE FEDERAL CONVENTION OF 1787, at 568 (Max Farrand rev. ed., 1937) [hereinafter M. FARRAND].

35. 2 *id.* 553-54.

36. On the details of engrossing and signing, *see* Akhil Reed Amar, *Our Forgotten Constitution: A Bicentennial Comment*, 97 YALE L. J. 281, 282-83 (1987); S. Doc. No. 49, 87th Cong., 1st Sess. 51 (1961) (historical notes authored by Denys P. Myers).

37. 2 M. FARRAND, *supra* note 34, at 643-44.

38. *Id.* at 644.

39. THE FEDERALIST No. 23, at 156 (Alexander Hamilton).

40. *Id.* No. 32, at 196 (Alexander Hamilton).

41. EDWARD DUMBAULD, THE BILL OF RIGHTS AND WHAT IT MEANS TODAY 161, 175-76, 181, 185-86, 193, 202 (1957).

42. *Id.* at 163, 175, 180, 181, 185, 189, 201-2. *See also* David A. Anderson, *The Origins of the Press Clause*, 30 U.C.L.A. L. REV. 455, 482 (1983) ("In fact, freedom of press or speech was never first on anyone's list.").

43. 2 ELLIOT'S DEBATES, *supra* note 31, at 249 (emphasis added). For a sample of similar concerns about congressional size voiced by other Anti-Federalists, *see* C. KENYON, *supra* note 19, at lii (Kenyon's introductory essay), 12 ("Centinel"), 37, 49 ("Pennsylvania Minority"), 79-80, 86 ("Philadelphiensis"), 107-9 ("John De Witt"), 192

(George Mason), 209, 213, 216, 222–30 ("The Federal Farmer"), 242, 263 (Patrick Henry), 307, 310–11 ("Cato"), 361 ("Albany Manifesto"), 375–89 (Melancton Smith), 396 (Thomas Tredwell). On the size of state legislatures during the Revolutionary era, *see* G. WOOD, *supra* note 7, at 167.

44. *See* 2 DOCUMENTARY HISTORY OF THE CONSTITUTION, *supra* note 17, at 385–90.

45. *See id.* at 321–90. The ratification tally in this official document corresponds with that in HERMAN AMES, THE PROPOSED AMENDMENTS TO THE CONSTITUTION OF THE UNITED STATES DURING THE FIRST CENTURY OF ITS HISTORY 320 (New York: Burt Franklin, 1896), and suggests that the tallies in 2 B. SCHWARTZ, *supra* note 29, at 1203, and 1 ELLIOT'S DEBATES, *supra* note 31, at 339–40, *reprinted in* 5 THE FOUNDERS' CONSTITUTION, *supra* note 11, at 41, are in error. Elliot omits both Vermont's ratification of all twelve amendments and Pennsylvania's eventual decision to ratify the (original) First Amendment on September 21, 1791. Elliot also erroneously states that Rhode Island ratified Congress's Second Amendment. Schwartz ignores Pennsylvania's ratification of the original First Amendment, and mistakenly implies that both Rhode Island and Pennsylvania ratified the original Second Amendment. (Apparently they did not.) *Compare* B. SCHWARTZ at 1203, *with id.* at 1197, 1200, 1201. The Holmes Devise account of ratification is also faulty. *See* JULIUS GOEBEL, JR., 1 HISTORY OF THE SUPREME COURT OF THE UNITED STATES: ANTECEDENTS AND BEGINNINGS TO 1801, at 456 (1971).

46. E. DUMBAULD, *supra* note 41, at 213 (emphasis added); *see also* 2 B. SCHWARTZ, *supra* note 29, at 1132–33 (Aug. 21, 1789).

47. 2 B. SCHWARTZ, *supra* note 29, at 1162 (Sept. 21, 1789).

48. *Id.* at 1162 (Sept. 24, 1789).

49. E. DUMBAULD, *supra* note 41, at 175–76, 181, 185–86, 193, 202.

50. *See supra* text accompanying note 25.

51. THE FEDERALIST No. 55, at 342 (James Madison).

52. 2 B. SCHWARTZ, *supra* note 29, at 1026 (June 8, 1789).

53. *Id.* at 1132–33 (Aug. 21, 1789).

54. *Id.* at 1084 (Aug. 14, 1789). *See also* 2 M. FARRAND, *supra* note 34, at 553 (noting Sherman's opposition to motion to increase size of House).

55. *See supra* note 45.

56. *See supra* text accompanying note 32.

57. *See, e.g.,* 1 M. FARRAND, *supra* note 34, at 37, 490–92, 500–502.

58. *Id.* at 4, 37; 3 *id.* at 574–75 and n.6.

59. 2 B. SCHWARTZ, *supra* note 29, at 1078 (Aug. 14, 1789).

60. Maryland, North Carolina, South Carolina, Delaware, Vermont, and Virginia. *See* 2 DOCUMENTARY HISTORY OF THE CONSTITUTION, *supra* note 17, at 321–90; H. AMES, *supra* note 45, at 317; *see also supra* note 45.

61. 2 DOCUMENTARY HISTORY OF THE CONSTITUTION, *supra* note 17, at 322 (ellipsis in original).

62. For Anti-Federalist efforts to link the small size of Congress to its corruptibility, *see* sources cited *supra* note 29. For a Federalist response addressing these linked fears and explicitly invoking the emoluments clause, *see* 2 ELLIOT'S DEBATES, *supra* note 31, at 474-75 (remarks of James Wilson at Pennsylvania ratifying convention).

63. E. DUMBAULD, *supra* note 41, at 161, 188, 195, 204-5.

64. *See* 4 JOHN BACH MCMASTER, A HISTORY OF THE PEOPLE OF THE UNITED STATES 357-62 (1927). At least two state legislatures also denounced the congressional act. *Id.* at 361; 3 HENRY ADAMS, HISTORY OF THE UNITED STATES OF AMERICA DURING THE SECOND ADMINISTRATION OF JAMES MADISON 134-38 (New York: Charles Scribner's Sons, 1891). After the electoral tidal wave, a duly chastened lame duck Congress repealed (prospectively) the pay increase. *See id.* at 144-46; J. MCMASTER at 371.

Half a century later, Congress enacted a (retroactive) 40 percent pay increase for itself in an 1873 bill that critics quickly dubbed the Salary Grab Act. Once again, voters responded by tossing out record numbers of incumbents in the next election. There were of course many other factors at play in the election of 1874, which helped pull down the curtain on the era of Reconstruction. For a brief discussion of the role of this 1873 act in "the greatest reversal of partisan alignments in the entire nineteenth century," *see* ERIC FONER, RECONSTRUCTION 523 (1988).

Two. *Our* First Amendment

1. *See, e.g.,* ALEXANDER MEIKLEJOHN, POLITICAL FREEDOM: THE CONSTITUTIONAL POWERS OF THE PEOPLE (1960); CHARLES L. BLACK, JR., STRUCTURE AND RELATIONSHIP IN CONSTITUTIONAL LAW 33-50 (1969).

2. *See, e.g.,* Ronald K. L. Collins and David M. Skover, *The Future of Liberal Legal Scholarship*, 87 MICH. L. REV. 189, 214 (1988). The authors' identification of the First Amendment with minority rights is especially revealing in light of their view, to which I subscribe, that the Bill of Rights was less centrally focused on minority rights than on protecting "the entire citizenry from governmental abuses of power." *Id.; see also* William T. Mayton, *Seditious Libel and the Lost Guarantee of a Freedom of Expression*, 84 COLUM. L. REV. 91, 127 n.189 (1984) (presenting First Amendment as in large part a federalism provision; but nevertheless implying that its core concern was to prevent majority tyranny).

3. Abrams v. United States, 250 U.S. 616, 624-31 (1919) (Holmes, J., dissenting); Gitlow v. New York, 268 U.S. 652, 672-73 (1925) (Holmes and Brandeis, JJ., dissenting); *see also* Whitney v. California, 274 U.S. 357, 372-80 (1927) (Brandeis and Holmes, JJ., concurring).

4. *See, e.g.,* Kingsley Pictures Corp. v. Regents, 360 U.S. 684, 688-89 (1959) (amendment's "guarantee is not confined to the expression of ideas that are conventional or shared by a majority").

5. *See supra* Introduction.

6. *Cf.* Michael W. McConnell, *Contract Rights and Property Rights: A Case Study in the Relationship Between Individual Liberties and Constitutional Structure,* 76 CALIF. L. REV. 267, 288–93 (1988) (similar structural analysis of contracts and takings clauses based on framework of Federalist Nos. 10 and 51). For emphasis on agency costs and self-dealing in the general First Amendment literature, *see, e.g.,* A. MEIKLEJOHN, *supra* note 1, at 6–7, 35–36; FREDERICK SCHAUER, FREE SPEECH: A PHILOSOPHICAL ENQUIRY 38–39, 43–44 (1982); Cass R. Sunstein, *Government Control of Information,* 74 CAL. L. REV. 889, 892 (1986); Ronald A. Cass, *The Perils of Positive Thinking: Constitutional Interpretation and Negative First Amendment Theory,* 34 U.C.L.A. L. REV. 1405, 1449 (1987); Ronald A. Cass, *Commercial Speech, Constitutionalism, Collective Choice,* 56 U. CIN. L. REV. 1317, 1354–56 (1988).

7. 2 BERNARD SCHWARTZ, THE BILL OF RIGHTS: A DOCUMENTARY HISTORY 1027 (1971) (June 8, 1789); EDWARD DUMBAULD, THE BILL OF RIGHTS AND WHAT IT MEANS TODAY 208 (1957).

8. 2 B. SCHWARTZ, *supra* note 7, at 1029 (June 8, 1789). Madison had previously expressed the same view in a letter to Jefferson on the subject of a possible bill of rights: "In our Governments the real power lies in the majority of the Community, and the invasion of private rights is *cheifly* [*sic*] to be apprehended, not from acts of Government contrary to the sense of its constituents, but from acts in which the Government is the mere instrument of the major number of the constituents." Letter from James Madison to Thomas Jefferson (Oct. 17, 1788), *in* 11 THE PAPERS OF JAMES MADISON 298 (Robert A. Rutland et al. eds., 1977). Yet Madison's views were atypical, as his next sentence reveals: "This is a truth of great importance, but not yet sufficiently attended to . . . ." Madison went on to say that a Bill of Rights would probably be most effective where unpopular and unrepresentative government action was at issue. "[T]here may be occasions on which the evil may spring from [government self-interest]; and on such, a bill of rights will be a good ground for an appeal to the sense of the community." *Id.* at 299.

9. E. DUMBAULD, *supra* note 7, at 208, 211.

10. 2 B. SCHWARTZ, *supra* note 7, at 1113 (Aug. 17, 1789).

11. E. DUMBAULD, *supra* note 7, at 215.

12. *Id.* at 217–19.

13. *See, e.g.,* U.S. CONST. art IV, §4 (guaranteeing republican government at state level); *see generally* Akhil Reed Amar, *The Central Meaning of Republican Government: Popular Sovereignty, Majority Rule, and the Denominator Problem,* 65 U. COLO. L. REV. 749, 755–56, 761–66 (1994) [hereinafter *Republican Government*].

14. *See generally* C. BLACK, *supra* note 1, at 33–50. Interestingly, when antislavery Congressmen sought to codify this rule in the 36th Congress, they were voted down 36–20 by a straight party-line vote. Their bill was worded as follows: "But the free

discussion of the morality and expediency of slavery should never be interfered with by the laws *of any State,* or of the United States; and the freedom of speech and of the press, on this and every other subject of domestic *and national* policy, should be maintained inviolate in all the States." CONG. GLOBE, 36th Cong., 1st Sess. 2321 (1860) (emphasis added). For a discussion, *see* ALAN P. GRIMES, DEMOCRACY AND THE AMENDMENTS TO THE CONSTITUTION 40 (1978).

15. 376 U.S. 254, 270 (1964).

16. 376 U.S. at 276.

17. Contemporary critics of the act highlighted its self-dealing features. *See, e.g.,* James Madison, *Report on the Virginia Resolutions* (Jan. 1800), *reprinted in* 5 THE FOUNDERS' CONSTITUTION 141, 144-45 (Philip B. Kurland and Ralph Lerner eds., 1987); *see also* 8 ANNALS OF CONG. 2153 (July 1798) (remarks of Edward Livingston stressing "majorit[arian]" thrust of speech and press clauses).

For more discussion of the act's self-dealing features, *see* Mayton, *supra* note 2, at 112 and n.120, 123-24; Akhil Reed Amar, *The Case of the Missing Amendments: R. A. V. v. City of St. Paul,* 106 HARV. L. REV. 124, 143 (1992).

18. *See supra* Chapter 1.

19. *See* 4 WILLIAM BLACKSTONE, COMMENTARIES ON THE LAWS OF ENGLAND 150-53 (Oxford: Clarendon, 1765); 2 DEBATES ON THE ADOPTION OF THE FEDERAL CONSTITUTION 449-50 (Jonathan Elliot ed., AYER Co. reprint ed. 1987) (1836) [hereinafter ELLIOT'S DEBATES] (remarks of James Wilson at Pennsylvania ratifying convention); 3 JOSEPH STORY, COMMENTARIES ON THE CONSTITUTION OF THE UNITED STATES §1879 (Boston: Hilliard, Gray, 1833).

20. Prior to Bloom v. Illinois, 391 U.S. 194 (1968), it appears that American judges, following English authorities, claimed a right to enforce injunctions through contempt proceedings from which juries were excluded, even in cases resulting in serious punishment of the contemner. *See* Vincent Blasi, *Toward a Theory of Prior Restraint: The Central Linkage,* 66 MINN. L. REV. 11, 23, 44-45 (1981).

21. *See, e.g., Letters of Centinel* (I), *reprinted in* 2 THE COMPLETE ANTI-FEDERALIST 136 (Herbert J. Storing ed., 1981) ("[I]f I use my pen with the boldness of a freeman, it is because I know that *the liberty of the press yet remains unviolated,* and *juries yet are judges.*") (emphasis in original); *Essays by Cincinnatus* (I), *reprinted in* 6 *id.* at 9 (invoking "Peter Zenger's case" to link the "freedom of the press, the sacred palladium of public liberty" to "trial by jury"). For early state constitutions linking press freedom and jury trial, *see, e.g.,* GA. CONST. OF 1777, art. LXI; PA. CONST. OF 1790, art. IX, §7; DEL. CONST. OF 1792, art. I, §5; KY. CONST. OF 1792, art. XII, §8; TENN. CONST. OF 1796, art. XI, §19.

22. Professors Monaghan and Schauer have both noted this shift, but neither points to the Fourteenth Amendment to justify or explain it—yet another illustration, perhaps, of the invisibility of the incorporation doctrine. *See* Henry P. Monaghan,

First Amendment "Due Process," 83 HARV. L. REV. 518, 526–32 (1970); Frederick Schauer, *The Role of the People in First Amendment Theory,* 74 CALIF. L. REV. 761, 765 (1986). As Professor Michael Kent Curtis has noted to me, in many contexts, doctrine might be crafted so that press freedom would prevail if *either* judge *or* jury sides with the press.

23. For evidence that any publisher who attacked the act might have feared prosecution under it, see LEONARD W. LEVY, JEFFERSON AND CIVIL LIBERTIES: THE DARKER SIDE 52–53 (1963).

24. *Cf.* A. MEIKLEJOHN, *supra* note 1, at 34–35 (discussing absolute right of free political speech and debate in Congress); ZECHARIAH CHAFEE, JR., THREE HUMAN RIGHTS IN THE CONSTITUTION OF 1787, at 4–89 (1956) (offering similar analysis, with rich historical detail).

25. An act for declaring the rights and liberties of the subject and settling the succession of the crown (Bill of Rights), 1689, 1 W. & M., ch. 2, §9. *See also* MD. CONST. OF 1776 (Declaration of Rights), art. VIII; MASS. CONST. OF 1780, pt. I, art. XXI; N.H. CONST. OF 1784, pt. I, art. I, §XXX; 1 W. BLACKSTONE, *supra* note 19, at 159–60; LEONARD W. LEVY, EMERGENCE OF A FREE PRESS 102–3 (1985). Indeed, of the original thirteen colonies, only Pennsylvania's 1776 constitution extended "freedom of speech" beyond the legislature, *id.* at 5. And as Gordon Wood has shown, the unusual unicameral legislative system in Pennsylvania can be understood as constituting the citizens themselves as the implicit lower house. *See* GORDON S. WOOD, THE CREATION OF THE AMERICAN REPUBLIC, 1776–1787, at 231–32, 249–51 (1969).

Note also that, in early free-speech formulations, freedom of speech in Parliament could be punished by Parliament itself; in its origins, the free-speech right was majoritarian, shielding popular Parliamentary speakers, while exposing minority speakers to possible majoritarian sanction within Parliament itself.

26. Articles of Confederation, 1781, art. V, cl. 5.

27. *See supra* Chapter 1; *infra* text accompanying notes 87–92.

28. 3 JEAN-JACQUES ROUSSEAU, DU CONTRAT SOCIAL ch. XII (1762) (emphasis added) (my translation; in original, "le Souverain ne sauroit agir que quand le peuple est assemblé").

29. 3 ELLIOT'S DEBATES, *supra* note 19, at 37 (emphasis added).

30. *See* Akhil Reed Amar, *Philadelphia Revisited: Amending the Constitution Outside Article V,* 55 U. CHI. L. REV. 1043, 1065–66 (1988) [hereinafter *Philadelphia Revisited*]; 1 JAMES BURGH, POLITICAL DISQUISITIONS 6 (1774), *quoted in* James Gray Pope, *Republican Moments: The Role of Direct Popular Power in the American Constitutional Order,* 139 U. PA. L. REV. 287, 325–26 (1990).

31. *See, e.g.,* 2 B. SCHWARTZ, *supra* note 7, at 1021–22 (remarks of John Page) (June 8, 1789); JULIUS GOEBEL, JR., HISTORY OF THE SUPREME COURT OF THE UNITED STATES: ANTECEDENTS AND BEGINNINGS TO 1801, at 413–30 (1971); Paul Finkelman,

James Madison and the Bill of Rights: A Reluctant Paternity, 1990 SUP. CT. REV. 301, 336–37.

32. *See* Akhil Reed Amar, *Of Sovereignty and Federalism,* 96 YALE L. J. 1425, 1439 (1987).

33. I have elsewhere attempted to develop this argument in much greater detail; my seemingly counterintuitive but increasingly confident view is that Article V does not specify the exclusive mode of lawful constitutional alteration. *See* Amar, *Philadelphia Revisited, supra* note 30; Akhil Reed Amar, *The Consent of the Governed: Constitutional Amendment Outside Article V,* 94 COLUM. L. REV. 457 (1994) [hereinafter *Consent*]; Amar, *Republican Government, supra* note 13. For especially clear linkages between the people's power to ordain and their power to alter, *see, e.g.,* Amar, *Consent,* at 474, 476, 486, 490, and sources quoted therein.

34. 2 B. SCHWARTZ, *supra* note 7, at 1026 (June 8, 1789) (emphasis added).

35. *Id.* at 1072 (Aug. 13, 1789).

36. *Id.* at 1077 (Aug. 14, 1789).

37. *See, e.g., id.* at 1022 (remarks of John Page referring to "assembling of a convention") (June 8, 1789); *see also* Amar, *Philadelphia Revisited, supra* note 30, at 1058 and sources cited therein (linking ideas of convention and assembly); Pope, *supra* note 30 (connecting people's right to assemble to conventions and other forms of popular sovereignty and mass mobilization).

38. G. WOOD, *supra* note 25, at 312.

39. 1 W. BLACKSTONE, *supra* note 19, at 147–48.

40. *See, e.g.,* VA. CONST. OF 1776 (Declaration of Rights), pmbl.; MASS. CONST. OF 1780, pt. II, ch. VI, art. X.

41. *See, e.g.,* Kamper v. Hawkins, 3 Va. 20, 69 (1793) (opinion of Justice Tucker); McCulloch v. Maryland, 17 U.S. (4 Wheat.) 316, 403 (1819); Barron v. Baltimore, 32 U.S. (7 Pet.) 243, 249–50 (1833). *See also* JAMES M. VARNUM, THE CASE OF TREVETT V. WEEDEN 30 (1787).

42. *See* 1 RECORDS OF THE FEDERAL CONVENTION OF 1787, at 22 (Max Farrand rev. ed., 1937) [hereinafter M. FARRAND]; 2 *id.* at 133.

43. *See* 3 ELLIOT'S DEBATES, *supra* note 19, at 37, quoted *supra* text accompanying note 29 (remarks of Edmund Pendleton at Virginia ratifying convention); *id.* at 51 (remarks of Patrick Henry at Virginia ratifying convention); Amar, *Consent, supra* note 33, at 494 (quoting remarks of John Smilie in Pennsylvania ratifying convention). *See also* 2 THE WORKS OF JAMES WILSON 762 (Robert Green McCloskey ed., 1967).

44. Indeed, the congressional resolution accompanying the Bill explicitly described it as containing "declaratory" as well as "restrictive" provisions. 2 DOCUMENTARY HISTORY OF THE CONSTITUTION OF THE UNITED STATES OF AMERICA 321 (Washington: Department of State, 1894). Our Tenth Amendment is of course an obvious example, and was so understood from the outset. *See* 2 B. SCHWARTZ, *supra* note 7, at 1033 (re-

marks of James Madison admitting that his proto–Tenth Amendment "may be considered as superfluous") (June 8, 1789). *Cf. Letters from the Federal Farmer* (XVI), *reprinted in* 2 THE COMPLETE ANTI-FEDERALIST, *supra* note 21, at 324 ("We do not by declarations change the nature of things, or create new truths . . . .").

45. 3 ELLIOT'S DEBATES, *supra* note 19, at 658–59.

46. PA. CONST. OF 1776 (Declaration of Rights), art. XVI; N.C. CONST. OF 1776 (Declaration of Rights), art. XVIII; VT. CONST. OF 1777, ch. I, §XVIII; MASS. CONST. OF 1780, pt. I, art. XIX; N.H. CONST. OF 1784, pt. I, art. I, §XXXII; VT. CONST. OF 1786, ch. I, §XXII; I ELLIOT'S DEBATES, *supra* note 19, at 328 (New York); *id.* at 335 (Rhode Island); 4 *id.* at 244 (North Carolina).

47. 2 B. SCHWARTZ, *supra* note 7, at 1091 (Aug. 15, 1789).

48. *See, e.g., id.* at 1097 (remarks of Michael Jenifer Stone) (instruction "would change the Government entirely" from one "founded upon representation" into a "democracy of singular properties") (Aug. 15, 1789). Stone's formulation tracks Madison's *Federalist* No. 10 distinction between representative republics and direct democracies.

49. GARRY WILLS, EXPLAINING AMERICA 216–30 (1981); *see also* THE FEDERALIST No. 63, at 387 (James Madison), *quoted supra* Chapter 1, n.22.

Only after the instruction debate in the First Congress did state constitutions begin to sever the rights of instruction and assembly. *See, e.g.,* KY. CONST. OF 1792, art. XII, §22.

50. I borrow here the phrasing of my colleague Bruce Ackerman. *See* Bruce A. Ackerman, *The Storrs Lectures: Discovering the Constitution,* 93 YALE L. J. 1013 (1984); 1 BRUCE ACKERMAN, WE THE PEOPLE: FOUNDATIONS (1991). Elsewhere I have explained more precisely the extent of my agreements and disagreements with his theory of constitutional amendment. Amar, *Philadelphia Revisited, supra* note 30; Amar, *Consent, supra* note 33. For a basic statement of the two-track model in *The Federalist,* see THE FEDERALIST No. 53, at 331 (James Madison) (Clinton Rossiter ed., 1961) [hereinafter all citations are to this edition].

51. Amar, *Philadelphia Revisited, supra* note 30, at 1065–66.

52. G. WOOD, *supra* note 25, at 312; *see also* EDWARD DUMBAULD, THE DECLARATION OF INDEPENDENCE AND WHAT IT MEANS TODAY 103–5 (1950) (linking assembly, petition, conventions, and rights "of the people"); Norman B. Smith, *"Shall Make No Law Abridging . . . ": An Analysis of the Neglected, But Nearly Absolute, Right of Petition,* 54 U. CIN. L. REV. 1153, 1179 (1986) (petition right "inextricably linked to the emergence of popular sovereignty").

53. *See* DECLARATION OF RIGHTS art. 8 (1774); sources cited *supra* note 46. The converse was not true: two states explicitly protected petition without mentioning assembly. *See* DEL. DECLARATION OF RIGHTS OF 1776, §9; MD. CONST. OF 1776 (Declaration of Rights), art. XI. In an otherwise superb essay on the right of petition, Professor Schnapper appears to overlook these two counterexamples. *See* Eric Schnapper, *"Li-*

belous" Petitions for Redress of Grievances—Bad Historiography Makes Worse Law, 74
Iowa L. Rev. 303, 347 n.249 (1989).

54. 1 Elliot's Debates, *supra* note 19, at 328 (New York); 2 *id.* at 553 (proposals of Maryland convention committee minority); 3 *id.* at 658–59 (Virginia); 4 *id.* at 244 (North Carolina); *see also* 1 *id.* at 335 (1790 Rhode Island convention).

55. On the political rights/civil rights distinction, *see infra* Chapter 3.

56. *See* Stephen A. Higginson, Note, *A Short History of the Right to Petition Government for the Redress of Grievances,* 96 Yale L. J. 142, 155–58 (1986). So too, a single individual can, merely by drafting and filing a complaint, compel both a defendant to answer upon pain of default and a judge to provide a judicial opinion applying the law to a set of facts. Less dramatically, a mere fifth of a single house may compel the recording of any vote in the house journal. U.S. Const. art. I, §5, cl. 3.

57. Higginson, *supra* note 56, at 153–55; *accord* Smith, *supra* note 52, at 1178–79.

58. Raymond C. Bailey, Popular Influence upon Public Policy: Petitioning in Eighteenth-Century Virginia 64 (1979).

59. *See* Jack N. Rakove, Original Meanings 311 (1996).

60. 1 W. Blackstone, *supra* note 19, at 139 (emphasis added). Early editions of Blackstone contained a mistranscription—"two" rather than "ten"—that later editions (beginning with the fourth, in 1770) corrected. One scholar has questioned whether these restrictions were rigorously enforced after the Glorious Revolution. Smith, *supra* note 52, at 1162. *But see id.* at 1166 (noting 1781 ruling by Lord Mansfield that restrictions were still in effect).

Note also that Blackstone's reading of the true meaning of the 1689 Bill on this point is hardly self-evident; I take no position here on its ultimate correctness as a reading of the 1689 Bill.

61. 1 Blackstone's Commentaries 299–300 app. (St. George Tucker ed., Philadelphia: Burch and Small, 1803).

62. For more support and elaboration, *see* E. Dumbauld, *supra* note 7, at 104 and n.5; 2 William Winslow Crosskey, Politics and the Constitution in the History of the United States 1057, 1060, 1072–74 (1953); Wilbur Katz, Religion and American Constitutions 8–10 (1964); Gerard V. Bradley, Church-State Relationships in America 76, 92–95 (1987); Stephen D. Smith, Foreordained Failure: The Quest for a Constitutional Principle of Religious Freedom 17–34 (1995); Edward S. Corwin, *The Supreme Court as National School Board,* 14 Law & Contemp. Probs. 3, 11–12 (1949); Joseph M. Snee, *Religious Disestablishment and the Fourteenth Amendment,* 1954 Wash. U. L. Q. 371; Michael A. Paulsen, *Religion, Equality, and the Constitution: An Equal Protection Approach to Establishment Clause Adjudication,* 61 Notre Dame L. Rev. 311, 321–23 (1986); William C. Porth and Robert P. George, *Trimming the Ivy: A Bicentennial Re-Examination of the Establishment Clause,* 90 W. Va. L. Rev. 109, 136–39 (1987); Daniel O. Conkle,

Toward a General Theory of the Establishment Clause, 82 Nw. U. L. Rev. 1113, 1132–35 (1988); William K. Lietzau, *Rediscovering the Establishment Clause: Federalism and the Rollback of Incorporation,* 39 DePaul L. Rev. 1191 (1990); Kurt T. Lash, *The Second Adoption of the Establishment Clause: The Rise of the Nonestablishment Principle,* 27 Ariz. St. L. J. 1085, 1089–99 (1995); Jed Rubenfeld, *Antidisestablishmentarianism: Why RFRA Really* Was *Unconstitutional,* 95 Mich. L. Rev. 2347 (1997).

63. *See* L. Levy, *supra* note 23, at 5; Michael W. McConnell, *The Origins and Historical Understanding of Free Exercise of Religion,* 103 Harv. L. Rev. 1409, 1437 (1990). *Cf.* G. Bradley, *supra* note 62, at 13 ("each of the thirteen original states generously aided and promoted religion and should therefore, according to Levy's methodology, be called establishment regimes").

64. *See* Pa. Const. of 1776, §10; Del. Const. of 1776, art. 22; N.C. Const. of 1776, art. XXXII; N.J. Const. of 1776, art. XIX. In Rhode Island, Jews and Catholics were apparently ineligible for citizenship, *see* G. Bradley, *supra* note 62, at 29.

65. Thomas J. Curry, The First Freedoms: Church and State in America to the Passage of the First Amendment 162–63, 221 (1986).

66. 1 Elliot's Debates, *supra* note 19, at 326 (emphasis added); *see generally* 2 W. Crosskey, *supra* note 62, at 1068, 1073–74; G. Bradley, *supra* note 62, at 76, 79; David A. Anderson, *The Origins of the Press Clause,* 30 U.C.L.A. L. Rev. 455, 481 n.164 (1983).

67. E. Dumbauld, *supra* note 7, at 39, 43 n.37 (discussing events of August 15 and 20, 1789).

68. 3 J. Story, *supra* note 19, at §1873.

69. 32 U.S. (7 Pet.) 243 (1833).

70. *See supra* text accompanying notes 23–27.

71. *See* G. Bradley, *supra* note 62, at 95; Conkle, *supra* note 62, at 1141; Porth and George, *supra* note 62, at 136–39.

72. *Compare* Proclamation Appointing a Day of Thanksgiving and Prayer (Nov. 11, 1779), *reprinted in* 3 The Papers of Thomas Jefferson 177 (Julian P. Boyd ed., 1951) *with* Letter from Thomas Jefferson to Attorney General Levi Lincoln (Jan. 1, 1802), *in* 8 The Writings of Thomas Jefferson 129 (Paul Leicester Ford ed., New York: G. P. Putnam's Sons, 1897); *see also* Second Inaugural Address (Mar. 4, 1805), *reprinted in id.* at 341, 344 (suggesting that states have power over religion where federal government has none).

73. Letter of Thomas Jefferson to Reverend Samuel Miller (January 23, 1808), *in* 5 The Founders' Constitution, *supra* note 17, at 98–99.

74. 1 Annals of Cong. 949–50 (Joseph Gales ed., 1789) (1st ed. pagination).

75. *See* Anderson, *supra* note 66, at 484; *but see id.* at 488 (noting anachronism of this reading). *See also* Murray Dry, *Flag Burning and the Constitution,* 1990 Sup. Ct. Rev. 69, 72.

76. *See generally* Mayton, *supra* note 2, at 117–19.

77. 2 M. FARRAND, *supra* note 42, at 617–18.

78. *See a Citizen of New Haven (II)*, *reprinted in* ESSAYS ON THE CONSTITUTION OF THE UNITED STATES 237, 239 (Paul Leicester Ford ed., New York: Burt Franklin, 1892) (Sherman); *The Landholder (VI)*, *reprinted in id.* at 161, 164 (Ellsworth); *Remarks on the New Plan of Government, reprinted in id.* at 395, 398 (Williamson); 4 ELLIOT'S DE-BATES, *supra* note 19, at 208–9 (Spaight); 3 *id.* at 203–4, 469 (Randolph); THE FED-ERALIST No. 84, at 513–14 (Hamilton); *Answers to Mr. Mason's Objections, reprinted in* PAMPHLETS ON THE CONSTITUTION OF THE UNITED STATES 360–61 (Paul Leices-ter Ford ed., New York: Burt Franklin, 1888) (Iredell); 4 ELLIOT'S DEBATES, *supra* note 19, at 259–60 (Charles Pinckney); *id.* at 315 (Charles Cotesworth Pinckney); *An Examination into the Leading Principles of the Federal Constitution . . . reprinted in* PAMPHLETS, *supra*, at 25, 48 (Webster); 2 ELLIOT'S DEBATES, *supra* note 19, at 449, 468 (Wilson); *Substance of an Address . . . reprinted in* PAMPHLETS, *supra*, at 156–57 (Wilson). At least one leading Anti-Federalist agreed with the Federalists on this point, *see Letters from the Federal Farmer (IV)*, *reprinted in* 2 THE COMPLETE ANTI-FEDERALIST, *supra* note 21, at 250. For a similar statement in the First Congress, *see* 2 B. SCHWARTZ, *supra* note 7, at 1034–35 (remarks of James Jackson) (June 8, 1789).

79. *See, e.g.*, 3 ELLIOT'S DEBATES, *supra* note 19, at 93, 330 (Madison); 2 *id.* at 455 (Wil-son); 4 *id.* at 194–95 (Iredell); 3 *id.* at 203–4, 469 (Randolph); 4 *id.* at 208 (Spaight); *The Landholder (VI)*, *reprinted in* ESSAYS ON THE CONSTITUTION OF THE UNITED STATES, *supra* note 78, at 164 (Ellsworth); 2 B. SCHWARTZ, *supra* note 7, at 1088 (Au-gust 15, 1789) (Sherman).

80. *See* U.S. CONST. art. I, §8, cls. 11–16 (war, army, and militia powers); *id.* cls. 1, 3, 11 (customs, commerce, and capture powers); *id.* cl. 9 (power to constitute tribunals).

81. 17 U.S. (4 Wheat.) 316 (1819).

82. 17 U.S. (4 Wheat.) at 423.

83. E. DUMBAULD, *supra* note 7, at 213–14.

84. *Id.* at 47 and n.14.

85. 1 ELLIOT'S DEBATES, *supra* note 19, at 327.

86. *See* Anderson, *supra* note 66, at 481.

87. 7 THE WRITINGS OF THOMAS JEFFERSON, *supra* note 72, at 288–89 (facsimile in-sert).

88. 8 *id.* at 311 (Letter of Thomas Jefferson to Abigail Adams, September 11, 1804).

89. 4 ELLIOT'S DEBATES, *supra* note 19, at 571.

90. *Id.* at 576.

91. 2 B. SCHWARTZ, *supra* note 7, at 1088 (August 15, 1789).

92. *Id.* Madison's language here sharply contrasts with his discussion of our Fourth Amendment, which Madison saw as cutting across, rather than marking the bound-ary of, Article I–enumerated power. *See id.* at 1030–31 (June 8, 1789).

93. 2 ANNALS OF CONG. 1951 (1834) (February 2, 1791).

94. *See* A. MEIKLEJOHN, *supra* note 1, at 19; 2 W. CROSSKEY, *supra* note 62, at 1057.

95. *See* United States v. Cruikshank, 92 U.S. 542, 552–53 (1876) ("The very idea of a government, republican in form, implies a right on the part of its citizens to meet peaceably for consultation in respect to public affairs and to petition for a redress of grievances."); Amar, *Republican Government, supra* note 13, at 755 and n.25.

96. In an intriguing article, Professor McConnell advances several arguments on behalf of the view that the original free-exercise clause created a right to an exemption from general, secular, nonpretextual congressional laws. In my view, these arguments fail. The argument from the logical priority of God—*see, e.g.,* McConnell, *supra* note 63, at 1446, 1453, 1497, 1509, 1512, 1516—proves too much, for a bona fide religious claim must always prevail on this logic. Once any kind of limited state trump is allowed, the demands of God are no longer prior but are being judged by an ultimately secular standard, even if a strict one (e.g., a "compelling interest"). Even worse, the *text* of the First Amendment nowhere suggests that kind of compelling interest or any other balancing test—in sharp contrast to the text of several state constitutions that McConnell invokes, *id.* at 1456–57. None of these states used a "shall make no law" formulation and none linked religion and press, thus suggesting that the First Amendment importantly *differed* from state antecedents. (And for an argument that Professor McConnell may have misread these state provisions, *see* Philip A. Hamburger, *A Constitutional Right of Religious Exemption: An Historical Perspective,* 60 GEO. WASH. L. REV. 915 (1992).) In addition to lacking textual and structural support, the exemption thesis also finds next to no support in the legislative history of First Amendment in Congress and in state ratifying conventions; and very little support in early expositions.

97. 494 U.S. 872 (1990).

98. 494 U.S. at 878.

99. 330 U.S. 1 (1947).

100. *See* G. WOOD, *supra* note 25, at 427 ("Religion was the strongest promoter of virtue, the most important ally of a well-constituted republic."). On the importance of virtue for self-governing republics, *see* THE FEDERALIST No. 55, at 346 (James Madison); Amar, *Republican Government, supra* note 13, at 759–60.

101. PA. CONST. OF 1776, §§44–45 (emphasis added).

102. MASS. CONST. OF 1780, pt. I, art. III.

103. *Id.* pt. II, ch. V, §1, art. I.

104. The linkage between education and religion was so obvious that when Madison proposed giving Congress explicit textual authority to establish a national university, he felt compelled to explicitly deny power to make that university sectarian. The proposal failed. 2 M. FARRAND, *supra* note 42, at 616. *See also* 1 W. BLACK-

STONE, *supra* note 19, at 97 (linking together the "establish[ment]" of "the church of Scotland, and also the four universities of that kingdom").

105. *See* 3 J. STORY, *supra* note 19, at §1873; HERBERT J. STORING, WHAT THE AN-TIFEDERALISTS WERE FOR 22–23 (1981); *Letters of Agrippa (XII), reprinted in* 4 THE COMPLETE ANTI-FEDERALIST, *supra* note 21, at 94.

106. MASS. CONST. OF 1780, pt. I, art. III.

107. 1 ALEXIS DE TOCQUEVILLE, DEMOCRACY IN AMERICA 320 n.4 (Phillips Bradley ed., Vintage, 1945).

108. *Id.* at 320.

Three. The Military Amendments

1. 3 DEBATES ON THE ADOPTION OF THE FEDERAL CONSTITUTION 37 (Jonathan Elliot ed., AYER Co. reprint ed., 1987) (1836) [hereinafter ELLIOT's DEBATES].

2. EDWARD DUMBAULD, THE BILL OF RIGHTS AND WHAT IT MEANS TODAY 174 (1957) (emphasis added).

3. Apparently, the violent nature of revolution induced Locke to strictly limit the legitimate occasions for the exercise of the people's right to revolt. The people, said Locke, could reclaim their sovereignty only when government action approached true and systematic tyranny. JOHN LOCKE, THE SECOND TREATISE OF GOVERN-MENT §§221–43 (Thomas P. Peardon ed., 1952). Between 1776 and 1789, Americans domesticated and defused the idea of violent revolution by channeling it into the newly renovated legal instrument of the peaceful convention. Through the idea of conventions, Americans *legalized* revolution, substituting ballots for bullets. As a result, by 1789 Americans could expand the Lockean right to "revolt"—to alter or abolish government—into a right the people could invoke (by convention) at any time and for any reason. *See, e.g.,* GORDON S. WOOD, THE CREATION OF THE AMERICAN REPUBLIC, 1776–1787, at 342–43 (1969); 1 THE WORKS OF JAMES WILSON 77–79 (Robert Green McCloskey ed., 1967); 2 ELLIOT's DEBATES, *supra* note 1, at 432–33 (remarks of James Wilson at Pennsylvania ratifying convention); Akhil Reed Amar, *The Consent of the Governed: Constitutional Amendment Outside Article V,* 94 COLUM. L. REV. 457, 458, 463–64, 475–76 (1994). Yet as the Second Amendment reminds us, even the new legal institutions ultimately rested on force—force that ideally would never need to be invoked, yet whose latent existence would nevertheless deter.

4. 3 ELLIOT's DEBATES, *supra* note 1, at 51.

5. For arguments supporting a broad reading of the amendment as protecting arms bearing outside of military service, *see generally* Stephen P. Halbrook, *What the Framers Intended: A Linguistic Analysis of the Right to Bear Arms,* LAW & CONTEMP. PROBS., Winter 1986, at 151; *see, e.g., id.* at 155 (discussing essay by Tench Coxe, written ten days after Madison proposed his Bill of Rights, construing his proto-Second

Amendment to protect the people "in their right to keep and bear their *private arms*") (emphasis added); *see also supra* text at note 2 (quoting Pennsylvania Anti-Federalists linking "right to bear arms" with "killing game"). *But see, e.g.,* Aymette v. State, 21 Tenn. (2 Hum.) 154, 161 (1840) ("The phrase *'bear arms,'* . . . has a military sense, and no other . . . . A man in the pursuit of deer, elk and buffaloes, might carry his rifle every day, for forty years, and, yet, it would never be said of him, that he had *borne arms* . . . ."); Don B. Kates, *Handgun Prohibition and the Original Meaning of the Second Amendment,* 82 MICH. L. REV. 204, 219-20, 267 (1983) [hereinafter *Original Meaning*] (similar). Kates has subsequently modified his position in response to Halbrook's evidence. Don B. Kates, *The Second Amendment: A Dialogue,* LAW & CONTEMP. PROBS., Winter 1986, at 143, 149. For a vigorous (if vicious) argument that Kates was more right the first time—that the phrase "keep and bear arms" is exclusively military—*see* Garry Wills, *To Keep and Bear Arms,* N.Y. REV. OF BOOKS, Sept. 21, 1995, at 62.

6. I have been importantly influenced here by the pioneering work of Elaine Scarry. *See, e.g.,* Elaine Scarry, *War and the Social Contract: Nuclear Policy, Distribution, and the Right to Bear Arms,* 139 U. PA. L. REV. 1257 (1991).

7. THE FEDERALIST No. 28, at 180 (Alexander Hamilton) (Clinton Rossiter ed., 1961) [hereinafter all citations are to this edition].

8. *Id.* No. 46, at 299 (James Madison).

9. *See generally* Akhil Reed Amar, *Of Sovereignty and Federalism,* 96 YALE L. J. 1425, 1494-1500 (1987).

10. *See, e.g.,* 3 ELLIOT'S DEBATES, *supra* note 1, at 48, 52, 169, 386 (remarks of Patrick Henry at Virginia ratifying convention); *id.* at 379-80 (remarks of George Mason at Virginia ratifying convention); 2 *id.* at 545-46 (Proceedings of the Meeting at Harrisburg, Pennsylvania, September 3, 1788); 3 THE RECORDS OF THE FEDERAL CONVENTION OF 1787, at 208-9 (Max Farrand rev. ed., 1937) [hereinafter M. FARRAND] (Luther Martin's *Genuine Information*); 2 DOCUMENTARY HISTORY OF THE RATIFICATION OF THE CONSTITUTION 509 (Merrill Jensen ed. 1976) (remarks of John Smilie at Pennsylvania ratifying convention) [hereinafter DOCUMENTARY HISTORY].

11. *See, e.g.,* JOHN HART ELY, DEMOCRACY AND DISTRUST 94-95, 227 n.76 (1980); LAURENCE H. TRIBE, AMERICAN CONSTITUTIONAL LAW §5-2, at 299 n.6 (2d ed. 1988). For a more detailed catalogue of Second Amendment scholarship, *see* Kates, *Original Meanings, supra* note 5, at 206-7.

12. *See* L. TRIBE, *supra* note 11, at 299 n.6.

13. *See* U.S. CONST. amend. X (distinguishing between "States respectively" and "the people").

14. 2 BERNARD SCHWARTZ, THE BILL OF RIGHTS: A DOCUMENTARY HISTORY 1107 (1971) (August 17, 1789) (emphasis added).

15. *See, e.g.,* Kates, *Original Meaning, supra* note 5, at 214-18; David T. Hardy, *Armed Cit-*

izens, Citizen Armies: Toward a Jurisprudence of the Second Amendment, 9 HARV. J. L. & PUB. POL'Y 559, 623–28 (1986); *Letters from the Federal Farmer* (III, XVIII), *reprinted in* 2 THE COMPLETE ANTI-FEDERALIST 242, 341–42 (Herbert J. Storing, ed. 1981); *Letters of Centinel* (IX), *reprinted in* 2 *id,* at 179, 182; 2 DOCUMENTARY HISTORY, *supra* note 10, at 509 (remarks of John Smilie in Pennsylvania ratifying convention).

16. In addition to sources cited *supra* note 15, *see* STEPHEN P. HALBROOK, THAT EVERY MAN BE ARMED: THE EVOLUTION OF A CONSTITUTIONAL RIGHT (1984); William E. Nelson, *The Eighteenth-Century Background of John Marshall's Constitutional Jurisprudence,* 76 MICH. L. REV. 893, 920 (1978).

17. E. DUMBAULD, *supra* note 2, at 214.

18. *See, e.g.,* THE FEDERALIST No. 25, at 166 (Alexander Hamilton); *id.* No. 29, at 184 (Alexander Hamilton); *id.* No. 46, at 299 (James Madison).

19. *See, e.g.,* 3 ELLIOT'S DEBATES, *supra* note 1, at 425 (remarks of George Mason at Virginia ratifying convention) ("Who are the militia? They consist now of the whole people . . . . "); *id.* at 112 (remarks of Francis Corbin at Virginia ratifying convention) ("Who are the militia? Are we not militia?"); *Letters from the Federal Farmer* (XVIII), *reprinted in* 2 THE COMPLETE ANTI-FEDERALIST, *supra* note 15, at 341 ("A militia, when properly formed, are in fact the people themselves . . . and include . . . all men capable of bearing arms . . . . ").

20. 2 DOCUMENTARY HISTORY, *supra* note 10, at 1778–80 (Microfilm supp.).

21. *See, e.g.,* J. ELY, *supra* note 11, at 227 n.76; L. TRIBE, *supra* note 11, at 299 n.6.

22. 188 U.S. 321 (1903).

23. *See, e.g.,* VA. CONST. OF 1776 (Declaration of Rights), §13; DEL. DECLARATION OF RIGHTS OF 1776, §18; MD. CONST. OF 1776 (Declaration of Rights), art. XXV; N.H. CONST. OF 1784, pt. I, art. I, §XXIV; *see also* Hardy, *supra* note 15, at 626 n.328.

24. *Cf.* State v. Reid, 1 Ala. 612, 616–17 (1840) (distinguishing between arms regulation and arms prohibition).

25. *See infra* Chapter 11, text at notes 106–38.

26. *See infra* page 278, note.

27. U.S. CONST. art. I, §8, cls. 1, 9. *See* 4 ELLIOT'S DEBATES, *supra* note 1, at 210 (remarks of Richard Spaight in North Carolina ratifying convention: "Men are to be *raised* by bounty.") (emphasis added).

28. British impressment in the 1770s was one of the major grievances triggering the American Revolution and was explicitly denounced by the Declaration of Independence. In the later impressment debate leading to the War of 1812, Secretary of State Monroe declared that impressment "is not an American practice, but is utterly repugnant to our Constitution" 28 ANNALS OF CONG. 81 (1814) (remarks of Senator Jeremiah Mason). Yet even if naval impressment were deemed permissible, army conscription power would not necessarily follow. Historically the two were distinct issues—the British government before the Revolution "did attempt to exercise in this

country the supposed right of impressment for the Navy, which it never did for the Army." *Id.* As explained below, the word *army*, in contradistinction to *militia*, connoted a volunteer force. The word *navy* was more ambiguous, as illustrated by the British-American tussles over impressment. These textual and historical points can be recast into a structural argument: impressing "private" sailors who had already voluntarily agreed to abandon ordinary civilian life and submit to the harsh discipline and command on a merchant ship involved a smaller marginal deprivation of liberty than wrenching citizen farmers from their families and land through an army draft.

29. *See, e.g.,* THE FEDERALIST No. 24, at 161 (Alexander Hamilton) (defining *army* as "permanent corps in the pay of government"); WEBSTER'S AMERICAN DICTIONARY (1828). In addition to the sources cited *supra* notes 16–17, see JOHN REMINGTON GRAHAM, A CONSTITUTIONAL HISTORY OF THE MILITARY DRAFT (1971); Harrop A. Freeman, *The Constitutionality of Direct Federal Military Conscription*, 46 IND. L. J. 333, 337 n.14 (1971); Leon Friedman, *Conscription and the Constitution: The Original Understanding*, 67 MICH. L. REV. 1493 (1969); Alan Hirsch, *The Militia Clauses of the Constitution and the National Guard*, 56 U. CIN. L. REV. 919, 958–59 (1988); 3 JOSEPH STORY, COMMENTARIES ON THE CONSTITUTION OF THE UNITED STATES, §1179 (Boston: Hilliard, Gray, 1833).

30. *But see* Michael J. Malbin, *Conscription, the Constitution, and the Framers: An Historical Analysis*, 40 FORDHAM L. REV. 805, 824 (1972). Malbin claims that although Congress can conscript under the army clause, the militia clause is not thereby rendered trivial. According to him, had Congress not been able to rely on the militia as a back-up military force, Congress would have been tempted to keep a large (and thus dangerous) standing army at all times. The militia clause removes this temptation, and thus adds something valuable, he claims. Malbin's argument fails miserably. If Congress did have army conscription power, as he claims, surely it would have the lesser power under the army clause to draft back-up army "reserves," obviating the need for large standing armies—but once again, this contingent draft violates the cooperative federalism safeguards imposed by the militia clause.

31. *See, e.g.,* Stephen P. Halbrook, *The Right of the People or the Power of the State: Bearing Arms, Arming Militias, and the Second Amendment*, 26 VAL. U. L. REV. 131, 195 (1991) (quoting 1791 essay contradistinguishing "a well regulated militia" and "a regular, standing army, composed of mercenaries"). The idea of a national army based on a national draft is a distinctly modern one, born in Napoleonic France in 1798—a decade after ratification of our Constitution. *See* Harrop A. Freeman, *The Constitutionality of Peacetime Conscription*, 31 VA. L. REV. 40, 68 (1944); Friedman, *supra* note 29, at 1498–99 and n.20; Malbin, *supra* note 30, at 811. Tellingly, although many leading Anti-Federalists voiced loud fears about the federal government's power to mistreat conscripted militiamen, virtually nothing was said about possible mistreatment of conscripted army soldiers—the very idea bordered on oxymoron. Put another way, even the most suspicious Anti-Fed-

eralists generally seemed to assume that the federal government could not use the army clause to justify conscription, and no Federalists, of course, ever supported such a reading. *See* Friedman, *supra* note 29, at 1525–33; *see also Essay by Deliberator, reprinted in* 3 THE COMPLETE ANTI-FEDERALIST, *supra* note 15, at 178–79. *But see Essays of Brutus* (VIII), *reprinted in* 2 *id.* at 406 (questioning whether Congress might have impressment power under the army clause but referring to this as a draft "from the militia"). Elsewhere, Brutus took the extreme position that the Article I enumeration of powers imposed no meaningful or sincere limits on congressional authority.

32. *See* Friedman, *supra* note 29, at 1508. States' rights advocates viewed the state appointment of officers as vital. When Madison proposed to limit states to appointments "under the rank of General," the Philadelphia convention voted overwhelmingly against him. Roger Sherman called the modification "absolutely inadmissible," and Elbridge Gerry sarcastically suggested that the convention might as well abolish state governments altogether, create a king, and be done with it. 2 M. FARRAND, *supra* note 10, at 388.

33. At least seven Revolution-era constitutions or bills of rights echoed—almost *in haec verba*—the language of the Virginia Bill of Rights of 1776, §13: "[I]n all cases the military should be under strict subordination to, and gove. ned by, the civil power." These provisions were invariably placed alongside paeans to "the militia" and/or guarantees of the right of "the people" to keep and bear arms. *See* PA. CONST. OF 1776 (Declaration of Rights), art. XIII; DEL. DECLARATION OF RIGHTS OF 1776, §20; MD. CONST. OF 1776 (Declaration of Rights), art. XXVII; N.C. CONST. OF 1776 (Declaration of Rights), art. XVII; VT. CONST. OF 1777, ch. 1, §XV; MASS. CONST. OF 1780, pt. I, art. XVII; N.H. CONST. OF 1784, pt. I, art. I, §XXVI. *See generally* 2 ALEXIS DE TOCQUEVILLE, DEMOCRACY IN AMERICA, 279–302 (Phillips Bradley ed., Vintage, 1945). Although not explicitly analyzing the allocation of military power under the U.S. Constitution, Tocqueville's account of civilian versus professional armies strongly supports my analysis.

34. United States v. Miller, 307 U.S. 174, 179 (1939) (quoting ADAM SMITH, THE WEALTH OF NATIONS, Book V, Chapter 1).

35. *See, e.g.,* THE FEDERALIST Nos. 25, 29 (Alexander Hamilton).

36. *See supra* text accompanying notes 9–10; *see also supra* note 32.

37. *See* 2 B. SCHWARTZ, *supra* note 14, at 1107 (remarks of Elbridge Gerry) ("What, sir, is the use of a militia? It is to prevent the establishment of a standing army, the bane of liberty.") (August 17, 1789); *cf.* Malbin, *supra* note 30, at 824 n.69 (criticizing overreliance on republican ideology in interpreting militia and army clauses of Article I). Interestingly, at the Philadelphia convention George Mason proposed an anti-standing army preamble to the Article I militia clause, but the proposal failed. 2 M. FARRAND, *supra* note 10, at 617.

38. 17 U.S. (4 Wheat.) 316, 419–21 (1819).

39. 1 PAPERS OF DANIEL WEBSTER: SPEECHES AND FORMAL WRITINGS 21 (Charles M. Wiltse ed., 1986).

40. *Id.* at 25–29.

41. *Id.* at 30.

42. *Report and Resolutions of the Hartford Convention, reprinted in* 1 GREAT ISSUES IN AMERICAN HISTORY 237, 240 (Richard Hofstadter ed., 1958).

43. The precise degree to which constitutional scruples contributed to the bills' defeat is the subject of some dispute. *Compare* Malbin, *supra* note 30, at 820–21 and n.56, *with* Friedman, *supra* note 29, at 1541–44, *and* Freeman, *supra* note 29, at 341–42. *See generally* JACK FRANKLIN LEACH, CONSCRIPTION IN THE UNITED STATES: HISTORICAL BACKGROUND 30–126 (1952).

44. 245 U.S. 366 (1918).

45. Debs v. United States, 249 U.S. 211 (1919).

46. Abrams v. United States, 250 U.S. 616 (1919).

47. 376 U.S. 254, 273–76 (1964).

48. E. DUMBAULD, *supra* note 2, at 166.

49. THE DECLARATION OF INDEPENDENCE paras. 13–16 (U.S. 1776).

50. DEL. DECLARATION OF RIGHTS OF 1776, §§18–21; MD. CONST. OF 1776 (Declaration of Rights), arts. XXV–XXVIII; N.H. CONST. OF 1784, pt. I, arts. XXIV–XXVII.

51. MD. CONST. OF 1776 (Declaration of Rights), arts. XXVIII–XXIX; MASS. CONST. OF 1780, pt. I, arts, XXVII–XXVIII.

52. E. DUMBAULD, *supra* note 2, at 178, 182, 185, 190, 201; 1 ELLIOT'S DEBATES, *supra* note 1, at 335. See also 2 M. FARRAND, *supra* note 10, at 341 (Pinckney's report).

53. 3 ELLIOT'S DEBATES, *supra* note 1, at 410–11. *See also* Morton J. Horwitz, *Is the Third Amendment Obsolete?*, 26 VAL. U. L. REV. 209, 210 (1991) (noting linkages between opposition to standing armies and opposition to quartering troops).

54. The national government may call out the militia only to "execute the Laws of the Union, suppress Insurrections and repel Invasions." U.S. CONST. art. I, §8, cl. 15.

55. *See also* SECOND CONTINENTAL CONGRESS, DECLARATION OF THE CAUSES AND NECESSITY OF TAKING UP ARMS para. 3 (1775) (condemning "quartering soldiers upon the colonists in time of profound peace"), *supra* note 52 (citing Pinckney's report).

56. Youngstown Sheet & Tube Co. v. Sawyer, 343 U.S. 579, 587–88 (1952).

57. 343 U.S. at 644 (Jackson, J., concurring).

58. 381 U.S. 479, 484 (1965).

59. *See* Laird v. Tatum, 408 U.S. 1, 15 (1972), *id.* at 22 (Douglas, J., dissenting) (Army surveillance case).

Four. Searches, Seizures, and Takings

1. Lawrence Delbert Cress, *An Armed Community: The Origins and Meaning of the Right to Bear Arms,* 71 J. AM. HIST. 22, 31 (1984).

2. EDWARD DUMBAULD, THE BILL OF RIGHTS AND WHAT IT MEANS TODAY 182–85 (1957).

3. *Id.* at 184 (emphasis added).

4. MASS. CONST. OF 1780, pt. I, art. XIV; N.H. CONST. OF 1784, pt. I, art. I, §XIX; E. DUMBAULD, *supra* note 2, at 191 (New York); *id.* at 200 (North Carolina).

5. E. DUMBAULD, *supra* note 2, at 207.

6. PA. CONST. OF 1776 (Declaration of Rights), art. X. Vermonters copied Pennsylvania's language, VT. CONST. OF 1777, ch. 1, §XI; VT. CONST. OF 1786, ch. 1, §XII, but the legal status of Vermont's statehood had not been definitively resolved in 1789.

7. *See, e.g., infra* text at notes 11, 20, 24.

8. 98 Eng. Rep. 489 (C.P. 1763), 19 Howell's State Trials 1153.

9. On Wilkes *see* RAYMOND WILLIAM POSTGATE, THAT DEVIL WILKES (1929); GEORGE F. E. RUDÉ, WILKES AND LIBERTY (1962); PAULINE MAIER, FROM RESISTANCE TO REVOLUTION 162–69 (1972); Powell v. McCormack, 395 U.S. 486, 527–31 (1969). On Camden *see* TELFORD TAYLOR, TWO STUDIES IN CONSTITUTIONAL INTERPRETATION 184 n.35 (1969). (I am also grateful for helpful information furnished by Donald Grove, tour coordinator of the Baltimore Orioles, and by my resourceful research assistant Teena-Ann Sankoorikal.) On *Wood* and its companion cases *see* T. TAYLOR at 29–35 and accompanying endnotes; NELSON B. LASSON, THE HISTORY AND DEVELOPMENT OF THE FOURTH AMENDMENT TO THE UNITED STATES CONSTITUTION 43–49 (1937).

10. Rex v. Wilkes, 95 Eng. Rep. 737 (C. P. 1763), 19 Howell's State Trials 981.

11. MASS. CONST. OF 1780, pt. I, art. XIV (emphasis added).

12. *See, e.g.,* Johnson v. United States, 333 U.S. 10, 14–15 (1948).

13. *See generally* Akhil Reed Amar, *Of Sovereignty and Federalism,* 96 YALE L. J. 1425, 1486–87, 1506–7 (1987) [hereinafter *Sovereignty*]; Akhil Reed Amar, *Fourth Amendment First Principles,* 107 HARV. L. REV. 757, 812–13 (1994) [hereinafter *Fourth Amendment*]; WILLIAM E. NELSON, AMERICANIZATION OF THE COMMON LAW 17 (1975).

14. *See, e.g.,* W. NELSON, *supra* note 13, at 190 n.57 (citing Massachusetts case with jury verdict that officer not guilty "If this Warrant be Lawfull in This Case," but guilty otherwise); *id.* 92 ("due issuance of a [judicial] warrant was an absolute defense to an officer who was sued for an unlawful search or arrest"). In *Wood* and *Entick,* had the warrants been lawful, each surely would have been a good defense. *See* 4 WILLIAM BLACKSTONE, COMMENTARIES ON THE LAWS OF ENGLAND 288 (Oxford: Clarendon, 1765) (general warrant "is therefore in fact no warrant at all: for it will not justify the officer who acts under it; whereas a lawful warrant will at all events indemnify the officer, who executes the same ministerially"); Amar, *Fourth Amendment, supra* note 13, at 778–79.

15. See Amar, *Fourth Amendment, supra* note 13, at 818 n.228; *cf.* Antonin Scalia, *The Rule of Law as a Law of Rules,* 56 U. CHI. L. REV. 1175, 1180–86 (1989).

16. *Accord* T. TAYLOR, *supra* note 9, at 21–50. Professor Taylor offers a wealth of historical evidence against collapsing the Fourth Amendment's distinct requirements, but nowhere suggests the possible relevance of jury-trial issues. Although Professor Nelson suggests that arrests and searchers always required warrants in colonial Massachusetts, W. NELSON, *supra* note 13, at 17–18, he elsewhere cites two early-nineteenth-century cases holding that no arrest warrant was needed "in cases of treason and felony, and . . . to preserve the peace and to prevent outrage." *Id.* at 226 n.126. The later cases accord with Professor Taylor's extensive evidence, and with Blackstone. *See* 4 W. BLACKSTONE, *supra* note 14, at 286–92; *see generally* Amar, *Fourth Amendment, supra* note 13, at 764 and n.13.

17. *See supra* Chapter 2.

18. *See* STEPHEN A. SALTZBURG, AMERICAN CRIMINAL PROCEDURE 56 (4th. ed. 1992); N. LASSON, *supra* note 9, at 24–50; 3 JOSEPH STORY, COMMENTARIES ON THE CONSTITUTION OF THE UNITED STATES §1895 (Boston: Hilliard, Gray, 1833); *see also* 2 DEBATES ON THE ADOPTION OF THE FEDERAL CONSTITUTION 551 (Jonathan Elliot ed., AYER Co. reprint ed. 1987) (1836) [hereinafter ELLIOT'S DEBATES] (Maryland convention recognition that general warrants were "the great engine by which power may destroy those individuals who resist usurpation").

19. E. DUMBAULD, *supra* note 2, at 209.

20. *Essay of a Democratic Federalist, reprinted in* 3 THE COMPLETE ANTI-FEDERALIST 61 (Herbert J. Storing ed., 1981).

21. 2 DOCUMENTARY HISTORY OF THE RATIFICATION OF THE CONSTITUTION 526 (Merrill Jensen ed., 1976).

22. *Essays by Hampden, reprinted in* 4 THE COMPLETE ANTI-FEDERALIST, *supra* note 20, at 198, 200.

23. *Notes on* Erving v. Cradock, *reprinted in* JOSIAH QUINCY, JR., REPORTS OF CASES ARGUED AND ADJUDGED IN THE SUPERIOR COURT OF JUDICATURE OF THE PROVINCE OF MASSACHUSETTS BAY BETWEEN 1761 AND 1772, at 553, 557 (Boston: Little, Brown, 1865).

24. *Essays by a Farmer* (I), *reprinted in* 5 THE COMPLETE ANTI-FEDERALIST, *supra* note 20, at 5, 14.

25. *Genuine Information of Luther Martin, reprinted in* 2 *id.* at 70–71 (emphasis deleted).

26. *Notes of Samuel Chase* (IIB), *reprinted in* 5 *id.* at 82.

27. 2 ELLIOT'S DEBATES, *supra* note 18, at 550.

28. *Id.* at 551–52. For further linkages between the Fourth and Seventh Amendments, *see* Amar, *Fourth Amendment, supra* note 13, at 778 n.79.

29. 95 Eng. Rep. 807 (C. P. 1765), 19 Howell's State Trials 1029, 1073.

30. *See* William J. Stuntz, *The Substantive Origins of Criminal Procedure,* 105 YALE L. J. 393 (1995); Eric Schnapper, *Unreasonable Searches and Seizures of Papers,* 71 VA. L. REV. 869 (1985).

31. Stuntz, *supra* note 30, at 403.

32. Zurcher v. Stanford Daily, 436 U.S. 547, 564 (1978) (citations omitted) (quoting Stanford v. Texas, 379 U.S. 476, 485 (1965) and Roaden v. Kentucky, 413 U.S. 496, 501 (1973)). For my criticism of *Zurcher*'s failure to apply this framework properly, *see* Amar, *Fourth Amendment, supra* note 13, at 805–6.

33. *See* Amar, *Sovereignty, supra* note 13, at 1504–10; Akhil Reed Amar, *Foreword: Lord Camden Meets Federalism: Using State Law to Counter Federal Abuses*, 27 RUTGERS L. J. 845 (1996).

34. *See* Amar, *Sovereignty, supra* note 13, at 1510–12.

35. *See* 1 W. BLACKSTONE, *supra* note 14, at 117, 135 (capitalization altered).

36. *See supra* Chapter 2.

37. *See* E. DUMBAULD, *supra* note 2, at 53, 162 (item 14).

38. *Id.* at 162 (item 23).

39. *See* MASS. CONST. OF 1780, pt. I, art. X; *see also* VT. CONST. OF 1777, ch. I, §II; *see generally* William Michael Treanor, Note, *The Origins and Original Significance of the Just Compensation Clause of the Fifth Amendment*, 94 YALE L. J. 694 (1985).

40. Michael W. McConnell, *Contract Rights and Property Rights: A Case Study in the Relationship Between Individual Liberties and Constitutional Structure*, 76 CAL. L. REV. 267, 288–93 (1988).

41. 1 BLACKSTONE'S COMMENTARIES 305–6 app. (St. George Tucker ed., Philadelphia: Burch and Small, 1803).

42. *See* Jed Rubenfeld, *Usings*, 102 YALE L. J. 1077, 1122–23 (1993); John Jay (A Freeholder), *A Hint to the Legislature of the State of New York* (1778), *reprinted in* 5 THE FOUNDERS' CONSTITUTION 312, 312 (Philip B. Kurland and Ralph Lerner eds., 1987) (emphasis deleted).

Five. Juries

1. Hugo L. Black, *The Bill of Rights*, 35 N.Y. U. L. REV. 865, 870 (1960); *see also* Adamson v. California, 332 U.S. 46, 70–71 (1947) (Black, J., dissenting) (noting connection between First Amendment and limitations on "arbitrary court action" imposed by Fifth, Sixth, and Eighth Amendments); Feldman v. United States, 322 U.S. 487, 500–502 (1944) (Black, J., dissenting) (similar).

2. John H. Baker, *Criminal Courts and Procedure at Common Law 1550–1800, in* CRIME IN ENGLAND 1550–1800, at 15, 42 (J. S. Cockburn ed., 1977).

3. LEONARD W. LEVY, ORIGINS OF THE FIFTH AMENDMENT 332 (2d ed. 1986). *See also* William J. Stuntz, *The Substantive Origins of Criminal Procedure*, 105 YALE L. J. 393, 411–19 (1995).

4. 8 WILLIAM HOLDSWORTH, A HISTORY OF ENGLISH LAW 408 (2d ed. 1937).

5. *See* 2 THE RECORDS OF THE FEDERAL CONVENTION OF 1787, at 587–88 (Max Farrand rev. ed., 1937) [hereinafter M. FARRAND].

6. *See* EDWARD DUMBAULD, THE BILL OF RIGHTS AND WHAT IT MEANS TODAY 176, 181–82, 183–84, 188, 190–92, 200, 204 (1957).

7. LEONARD W. LEVY, THE EMERGENCE OF A FREE PRESS 227 (1985). For a superb overview of the central role of juries in the Founding era, *see* Alan Howard Scheiner, Note, *Judicial Assessment of Punitive Damages, The Seventh Amendment, and the Politics of Jury Power,* 91 COLUM. L. REV. 142 (1991).

8. THE DECLARATION OF INDEPENDENCE para. 20 (U.S. 1776); DECLARATION OF RIGHTS OF THE CONTINENTAL CONGRESS, art. 5 (1774); DECLARATION OF THE CAUSES AND NECESSITY OF TAKING UP ARMS para. 3 (1775).

9. *An Old Whig* (VIII), *reprinted in* 3 THE COMPLETE ANTI-FEDERALIST 46, 49 (Herbert J. Storing ed., 1981). *See also Letters of Cato* (VII), *reprinted in* 2 *id.* at 123, 125 ("rulers in all governments will erect an interest separate from the ruled, which will have a tendency to enslave them").

10. E. DUMBAULD, *supra* note 6, at 209; *Letters from the Federal Farmer* (IV), *quoted infra* text accompanying note 44.

11. *See* Ronald F. Wright, *Why Not Administrative Grand Juries?,* 44 ADMIN. L. REV. 465, 469 (1992).

12. *See* Charles W. Wolfram, *The Constitutional History of the Seventh Amendment,* 57 MINN. L. REV. 639, 655 (1973).

13. *See* Wright, *supra* note 11, at 469; David A. Anderson, *The Origins of the Press Clause,* 30 U.C.L.A. L. REV. 455, 511–12 (1983).

14. 2 THE WORKS OF JAMES WILSON 537 (Robert Green McCloskey ed., 1967).

15. For further discussion and more modern examples, *see* Renée B. Lettow, Note, *Reviving Federal Grand Jury Presentments,* 103 YALE L. J. 1333 (1994).

16. *See* United States v. Cox, 342 F. 2d 167, 185–96 (1965) (Wisdom, J., concurring). Judge Wisdom's approach was anticipated by Chief Justice John Marshall on circuit in United States v. Hill, 26 F. Cas. 315, 316 (C. C. D. Va. 1809) (No. 15,364) ("The usage of this country has been, to pass over, unnoticed, presentments on which the [district] attorney does not think it proper to institute proceedings."). *But see* 1 Op. Att'y Gen. 42 (1794) (opinion by Attorney General Bradford suggesting that district attorney should follow grand jury's lead).

17. *See* Lettow, *supra* note 15, at 1359 n.131.

18. 2 THE DOCUMENTARY HISTORY OF THE SUPREME COURT OF THE UNITED STATES, 1789–1800, at 224 (Maeva Marcus ed., 1988). For similar language, *see id.* at 333, 472. On the special protections enjoyed by petitions, *see* Eric Schnapper, *"Libelous" Petitions for Redress of Grievances—Bad Historiography Makes Worse Law,* 74 IOWA L. REV. 303 (1989).

19. *See* Adamson v. California, 332 U.S. 46, 70–71 (1947) (Black, J., dissenting); Green v. United States, 356 U.S. 165, 209 (1958) (Black, J., dissenting); *Cf. Essays by a Farmer* (IV), *reprinted in* 5 THE COMPLETE ANTI-FEDERALIST, *supra* note 9, at 39 ("When-

ever therefore the trial by juries has been abolished, . . . [t]he judiciary power is immediately absorbed, or placed under the direction of the executive . . . . ").

20. *See* GEORGE LEE HASKINS AND HERBERT A. JOHNSON, 2 HISTORY OF THE SUPREME COURT OF THE UNITED STATES: FOUNDATIONS OF POWER: JOHN MARSHALL, 1801–15, at 140, 159 (1981); JAMES MORTON SMITH, FREEDOM'S FETTERS 139–417 (1956).

21. MASS. CONST. OF 1780 pt. I, art. XXVI; N.H. CONST. OF 1784, pt. I, art. XXXIII (emphasis added). On the special judge-limiting nature of the Eighth Amendment, *cf.* WILLIAM RAWLE, A VIEW OF THE CONSTITUTION OF THE UNITED STATES OF AMERICA 131 (Philadelphia: Nicklin 2d. ed., 1829).

22. *See* 4 WILLIAM BLACKSTONE, COMMENTARIES ON THE LAWS OF ENGLAND 372 (Oxford: Clarendon, 1765).

23. 1 ALEXIS DE TOCQUEVILLE, DEMOCRACY IN AMERICA 293–94 (Phillips Bradley ed., Vintage 1945).

24. 1 M. FARRAND, *supra* note 5, at 490.

25. On state variation, *see, e.g.,* THE FEDERALIST No. 83 (Alexander Hamilton); Wolfram, *supra* note 12, at 665 and sources cited therein.

26. Judiciary Act of September 24, 1789, §34, 1 Stat. 73, 88.

27. THE FEDERALIST No. 83, at 504 (Alexander Hamilton) (Clinton Rossiter ed., 1961) [hereinafter all citations are to this edition].

28. *See* Dimick v. Schiedt, 293 U.S. 474, 476–77 (1935); Wolfram, *supra* note 12, at 639–42. As Professor Wolfram notes, this historical test traces back to Justice Story's circuit court opinion in United States v. Wonson, 28 F. Cas. 745 (C. C. D. Mass. 1812) (No. 16,750).

29. *See* 13 THE OXFORD ENGLISH DICTIONARY 701 (2d. ed. 1989).

30. Wolfram, *supra* note 12, at 733.

31. *See, e.g.,* Dice v. Akron, Canton and Youngstown R.R., 342 U.S. 359 (1952).

32. *See* Wolfram, *supra* note 12, at 670–71; *supra* Chapter 4. *See also* E. DUMBAULD, *supra* note 6, at 176, 182 (reprinting proposed amendments from Massachusetts and New Hampshire ratifying conventions linking civil juries and diversity cases).

33. *See, e.g.,* VA. CONST. OF 1776 (Declaration of Rights), §11 ("ancient trial by jury . . . ought to be held sacred"); N.C. CONST. OF 1776 (Declaration of Rights), art. XIV (similar); PA. CONST. OF 1776 (Declaration of Rights), art. XI ("trial by jury . . . ought to be held sacred"); VT. CONST. OF 1777 (Declaration of Rights), art. XIII (similar); MASS. CONST. OF 1780, pt. I, art. XV ("trial by jury . . . shall be held sacred" except in cases "in which it has heretofore been otherways . . . practised"); N.H. CONST. OF 1784, pt. I, art. XX (similar); N.Y. CONST. OF 1777, art. XLI ("in all cases in which it hath heretofore been used" jury trial shall "remain inviolate forever"); N.J. CONST. OF 1776, art. XXII ("inestimable right of trial by jury shall remain"); MD. CONST. OF 1776 (Declaration of Rights), art. III (protecting "trial by jury, according to the course

of" the "common law of England"); Del. Declaration of Rights of 1776, §13 (general ode to jury); Ga. Const. of 1777, arts. XL–XLIII (various jury protections); S.C. Const. of 1778, art. XLI ("law of the land" clause).

34. E. Dumbauld, *supra* note 6, at 184, 200.

35. *See* Ralph Lerner, *The Supreme Court as Republican Schoolmaster,* 1967 Sup. Ct. Rev. 127.

36. *Letters from the Federal Farmer* (XV), *reprinted in* 2 The Complete Anti-Federalist, *supra* note 9, at 315, 320.

37. 1 A. de Tocqueville, *supra* note 23, at 295–96 (emphasis added). Francis Lieber, one of the leading constitutional commentators of the mid-nineteenth century, shared Tocqueville's assessment. *See* Francis Lieber, On Civil Liberty and Self-Government 250 (Philadelphia: Lippincott, Grambo, 1853).

38. 1 A. De Tocqueville, *supra* note 23, at 297.

39. *Essays by a Farmer* (IV), *reprinted in* 5 The Complete Anti-Federalist, *supra* note 9, at 39.

40. *Letters from the Federal Farmer* (IV), *reprinted in* 2 *id.* at 249; *cf. Letters of Cato* (V), *reprinted in id.* at 119 ("the opportunity you will have to participate in government [is] one of the principal securities of a free people").

41. *Letters from the Federal Farmer* (XV), *reprinted in id.* at 320.

42. *Quoted in* Wythe Holt, *"The Federal Courts Have Enemies in All Who Fear Their Influence on State Objects": The Failure to Abolish Supreme Court Circuit-Riding in the Judiciary Acts of 1792 and 1793,* 36 Buff. L. Rev. 301, 325 (1987).

43. Herbert J. Storing, What the Anti-Federalists Were For 19 (1981) (footnote omitted). Storing's language here closely tracks that of various Anti-Federalist essayists who in turn borrowed from Blackstone. *See Letters of Centinel* (II), *reprinted in* 2 The Complete Anti-Federalist, *supra* note 9, at 149 (jury trial "preserves in the hands of the people, that share which they ought to have in the administration of justice"); *Essays by a Farmer* (II), *reprinted in* 4 *id.* at 212, 214 (similar); *The Impartial Examiner* (I), *reprinted in* 5 *id.* at 173, 183 (similar); 3 W. Blackstone, *supra* note 22, at 379–80. *See also* 2 Bernard Schwartz, The Bill of Rights: A Documentary History 1174 (1971) (quoting speech of Governor John Hancock to Massachusetts legislature) (jury trial provisions "appear to me to be of great consequence. In all free governments, a share in the administration of the laws ought to be vested in, or reserved to the people . . . . "). The centrality of the jury is nowhere more evident than in Hancock's speech on Congress's proposed Bill of Rights. No clauses are mentioned other than the three dealing with juries.

44. *Letters from the Federal Farmer* (IV), *reprinted in* 2 The Complete Anti-Federalist, *supra* note 9, at 249–50; *see also id.* at 320 (XV).

45. Letter from Thomas Jefferson to L'Abbé Arnoux (July 19, 1789), *in* 15 The Papers of Thomas Jefferson 282, 283 (Julian P. Boyd ed., 1958) [hereinafter J. Boyd]; *see*

also 2 THE WORKS OF JOHN ADAMS 253 (Charles Francis Adams ed., Boston: Little, Brown, 1850) (diary entry, Feb. 12, 1771) ("the common people, should have as complete a control" over judiciary as over legislature; the "rights of juries and of elections" stand or fall together).

46. 1 A. DE TOCQUEVILLE, *supra* note 23, at 293–94. For similar emphasis on the political nature of the jury as an institution, *see Letters from the Federal Farmer* (XV), *reprinted in* 2 THE COMPLETE ANTI-FEDERALIST, *supra* note 9, at 315, 320 ("jury trial, especially politically considered, is by far the most important feature in the judicial department in a free country"). Professor Nelson writes that jurors were typically selected "by lot from a list of freeholders, elected by the voters of a jurisdiction, or summoned by the sheriff from among the bystanders at court." William E. Nelson, *The Eighteenth-Century Background of John Marshall's Constitutional Jurisprudence,* 76 MICH. L. REV. 893, 918 n.140 (1978). Thomas Jefferson was harshly critical of this last method, which he believed vested too much discretion in permanent executive officials. *See* Petition on Election of Jurors (Oct. 1798), *reprinted in* 7 THE WRITINGS OF THOMAS JEFFERSON 284, 285 (Paul Leicester Ford ed., New York: G. P. Putnam's Sons, 1896) [hereinafter P. Ford]; First Annual Message (Dec. 8, 1801), *reprinted in* 8 *id.* at 108, 123–24 (1897); Letter from Thomas Jefferson to Sarah Mease (March 26, 1801), *in id.* at 34, 35; Letter from Thomas Jefferson to Samuel Kercheval (July 12, 1816), *in* 10 *id.* at 37, 39 (1899).

47. JOHN TAYLOR, AN INQUIRY INTO THE PRINCIPLES AND POLICY OF THE GOVERNMENT OF THE UNITED STATES 209 (W. Stark ed., 1950) (1814).

48. *Essays by a Farmer* (IV), *reprinted in* 5 THE COMPLETE ANTI-FEDERALIST, *supra* note 9, at 36, 38; *see also id.* at 37 (referring to jury as a "distinct branch" within the judiciary).

49. *Essays by Hampden, reprinted in* 4 *id.* at 198, 200; THE FEDERALIST No. 9, at 72 (Alexander Hamilton). On Publius's use of "checks and balances" language, *see* GARRY WILLS, EXPLAINING AMERICA 117–25 (1981).

50. 1 A. DE TOCQUEVILLE, *supra* note 23, at 293.

51. *See supra* text at note 44; *see also Essays by a Farmer* (I), *reprinted in* 4 THE COMPLETE ANTI-FEDERALIST, *supra* note 9, at 205, 206 (proposing rotating jurors to be sent from each state to U.S. Supreme Court).

52. *See, e.g.,* GORDON S. WOOD, THE CREATION OF THE AMERICAN REPUBLIC, 1776–1787, at 521–22 (1969); H. STORING, *supra* note 43, at 17, 84 n.15; *Essays of Brutus* (XVI), *reprinted in* 2 THE COMPLETE ANTI-FEDERALIST, *supra* note 9, at 444–45; 2 DEBATES ON THE ADOPTION OF THE FEDERAL CONSTITUTION 309–11 (Jonathan Elliot ed., AYER Co. reprint ed., 1987) (1836) [hereinafter ELLIOT'S DEBATES] (remarks of Melancton Smith at New York ratifying convention). On the possible use of lotteries to achieve legislative rotation, *see* Akhil Reed Amar, Note, *Choosing Representatives by Lottery Voting,* 93 YALE L. J. 1283 (1984).

53. Letter from Thomas Jefferson to George Washington (May 2, 1788), *in* 13 J. Boyd, *supra* note 45, at 124, 128 (1956); Letter from Thomas Jefferson to James Madison (July 31, 1788), *in id.* at 440, 442–43; Letter from Thomas Jefferson to James Madison (Dec. 20, 1787), *in* 12 *id.* at 438, 440–41 (1955); Letter from Thomas Jefferson to Francis Hopkinson (Mar. 13, 1789), *in* 14 *id.* at 649, 650.

54. 2 ELLIOT'S DEBATES, *supra* note 52, at 288.

55. 4 W. BLACKSTONE, *supra* note 22, at 355. *See also* United States v. Haskell, 26 F. Cas. 207, 212 (C. C. E. D. Pa. 1823) (No. 15,321) (Washington, Circuit J.) ("jeopardy" means "nothing short of the acquittal or conviction of the prisoner, and the judgment of the court thereupon"). *Compare* JOHN BOUVIER, A LAW DICTIONARY 67 (10th ed., Philadelphia: 1865) ("jeopardy" triggered by "verdict of a jury") *with id.* at 752 (11th ed., 1868) ("jeopardy" triggered when "jury has been charged with [defendant's] deliverance"). For a similar shift in Joseph Story's language, *compare* 3 JOSEPH STORY, COMMENTARIES ON THE CONSTITUTION OF THE UNITED STATES §1781 (Boston: Hillard, Gray, 1833), *with* United States v. Gibert, 25 F. Cas. 1287, 1295–96 (C. C. D. Mass. 1834) (No. 15,204) (Story, Circuit J).

56. *See, e.g.,* Crist v. Bretz, 437 U.S. 28, 32–36 (1978). Since the double-jeopardy clause subsumes the pleas of autrefois acquit and autrefois convict, it would seem most sensible to require a prior verdict. This is, indeed, the English rule, *see* JAY A. SIGLER, DOUBLE JEOPARDY 15–16, 32 n.138, 126–28 (1969); and seems to make good sense, *id.* at 42, 127, 223. For more discussion, *see* Akhil Reed Amar, *Double Jeopardy Law Made Simple,* 106 YALE L. J. 1807 (1997) (suggesting that "jeopardy" is a process that begins with an indictment and ends with a final and suitably error-free verdict).

57. *See* Peter Westen and Richard Drubel, *Toward a General Theory of Double Jeopardy,* 1978 SUP. CT. REV. 81, 124–32; *see also* Gregg v. Georgia, 428 U.S. 153, 200 n.50 (1976) (plurality opinion). Whether juries should be told by judges that they have this right is an analytically distinct issue.

58. N.H. CONST. OF 1784 pt. I, art. I §XVI. A century earlier, the colony of Pennsylvania had anticipated the double-jeopardy principle by providing that the jury "shall have final judgment." PA. CONST. OF 1682, art. VIII ("Laws Agreed Upon In England &c").

59. E. DUMBAULD, *supra* note 6, at 177.

60. *Id.* For further evidence of linkages between the Sixth and Seventh Amendments and the double-jeopardy clause, see *Essays of Brutus* (XIV), *reprinted in* 2 THE COMPLETE ANTI-FEDERALIST, *supra* note 9, at 431, 432; Luther Martin, *Genuine Information, reprinted in id.* at 19, 70; United States v. Gibert, 25 F. Cas. 1287, 1294, 1302 (C. C. D. Mass. 1834) (No. 15,204) (Story, Circuit J.); *Ex. Parte* Lange, 85 U.S. (18 Wall.) 163, 170 (1873).

61. 3 J. STORY, *supra* note 55, at §1785.

62. *See, e.g.,* 3 THE PAPERS OF ALEXANDER HAMILTON 485 (Harold C. Syrett and Jacob

E. Cooke eds., 1962) (1784 "Letter of Phocion" defining "due process of law" as "*indictment or presentment of good and lawful men* and trial and conviction in consequence") (quoting Coke in italicized language); 2 JAMES KENT, COMMENTARIES ON AMERICAN LAW 13 (2d ed., 1832) (parroting Coke's definition of due process of law, quoted *supra*); 3 J. STORY, *supra* note 55, at §1783 (similar). Here, as elsewhere, I do not argue that the clause cannot be applied beyond what I have called its "core" meaning. Indeed, refusal to do so here would render the provision wholly redundant, as the Supreme Court has noted. *See* Murray's Lessee v. Hoboken Land and Improvement Co., 59 U.S. (18 How.) 272, 276 (1856).

63. Most current immunity doctrines are of a distinctly modern vintage. *See* Akhil Reed Amar, *Of Sovereignty and Federalism,* 96 YALE L. J. 1425, 1487 (1987). I sharply criticize both judge-created immunity doctrine and the judge-created exclusionary rule in Akhil Reed Amar, *Fourth Amendment First Principles,* 107 HARV. L. REV. 757 (1994).

64. These issues are unhelpfully conflated in Alan W. Scheflin, *Jury Nullification: The Right to Say No,* 45 S. CAL. L. REV. 168 (1972). *See, e.g., id.* at 169 n.2 (equating jury decision that statute is "unconstitutional" with judgment that statute is "wrong"). *But see* 2 THE WORKS OF JAMES WILSON, *supra* note 14, at 542 (jury, in deciding legal questions, is bound by rules of legal reasoning); Henfield's Case, 11 F. Cas. 1099, 1121 (C. C. D. Pa. 1793) (No. 6,360) (Wilson, Circuit J.) (similar). For other careful distinctions between jury review and jury nullification, *see* United States v. Smith and Ogden, 27 F. Cas. 1186, 1242 (C. C. D. N.Y. 1806) (No. 16,342a); United States v. Wilson 28 F. Cas. 699, 700, 708–9 (C. C. D. Pa. 1830) (No. 16,730) (Baldwin, Circuit J.).

65. *See* Virginia v. Zimmerman, 28 F. Cas. 1227, 1227 (C. C. D. D. C. 1802) (No. 16,968) (opinion of Cranch, J.) (jury's right to decide law implies counsel's right to argue law to jury); United States v. Morris, 26 F. Cas. 1323, 1331–36 (C. C. D. Mass. 1851) (No. 15,815) (Curtis, Circuit J.) (preventing counsel from arguing constitutionality of statute to jury on ground that jury had no right to decide law).

66. 25 F. Cas. 239 (C. C. D. Va. 1800) (No. 14,709).

67. *See* materials in STEPHEN B. PRESSER AND JAMIL S. ZAINALDIN, LAW AND JURISPRUDENCE IN AMERICAN HISTORY 228–47 (2d ed., 1989).

68. *Proceedings in Commemoration of the 200th Anniversary of the First Session of the Supreme Court of the United States,* 493 U.S. v, x (1990) (remarks of Rex Lee).

69. 25 F. Cas. at 253.

70. *See* Marbury v. Madison, 5 U.S. (1 Cranch) 137 (1803); *see generally* Akhil Reed Amar, Marbury, *Section 13, and the Original Jurisdiction of the Supreme Court,* 56 U. CHI. L. REV. 443, 445–46 (1989).

71. 1 THE WORKS OF JAMES WILSON, *supra* note 14, at 186.

72. 2 ELLIOT'S DEBATES, *supra* note 52, at 94.

73. 5 U.S. (1 Cranch) at 177.

74. J. TAYLOR, *supra* note 47, at 200–201.

75. *Letters from the Federal Farmer* (XV), *reprinted in* 2 THE COMPLETE ANTI-FEDER-
ALIST, *supra* note 9, at 315, 320.

76. *See* Mark DeWolfe Howe, *Juries as Judges of Criminal Law,* 52 HARV. L. REV. 582
(1939); Nelson, *supra* note 46, at 904–17; Note, *The Changing Role of the Jury in the
Nineteenth Century,* 74 YALE L. J. 170 (1964).

77. Georgia v. Brailsford, 3 U.S. (3 Dall.) 1, 4 (1794).

78. *See, e.g.,* THOMAS JEFFERSON, *Notes on the State of Virginia, in* THE PORTABLE
THOMAS JEFFERSON 23, 177 (Merrill D. Peterson ed., 1980) (Query XIV); Letter from
Thomas Jefferson to L'Abbé Arnoux (July 19, 1789), *in* 15 J. Boyd, *supra* note 45, at
282–83; Petition on Election of Jurors (Oct. 1798), *reprinted in* 7 P. Ford, *supra* note
46, at 284; Letter from Thomas Jefferson to Samuel Kercheval (July 12, 1816), *in* 10
id. at 37, 39 (1899); 2 THE WORKS OF JOHN ADAMS, *supra* note 45, at 254–55 (diary
entry, Feb. 12, 1771); 2 THE WORKS OF JAMES WILSON, *supra* note 14, at 540; Henfield's Case, 11 F. Cas. 1099, 1121 (C. C. D. Pa. 1793) (No. 6,360) (Wilson, Circuit J.);
Bingham v. Cabot, 3 U.S. (3 Dall.) 19, 33 (1795) (Iredell, J.); People v. Croswell, 3
Johns. Cas. 337, 375–77 (1804) (Kent, J.). For an even more expansive view from a leading Anti-Federalist, *see Letters from the Federal Farmer* (XV), *reprinted in* 2 THE
COMPLETE ANTI-FEDERALIST, *supra* note 9, at 315, 319–20. This view of the power
of American juries was articulated as early as 1692. L. LEVY, *supra* note 7, at 24–25.
Even Alexander Hamilton seems to have believed that juries in criminal cases could
decide both law and fact, and disregard the bench's instructions on law—or so he argued as defense counsel in 1804. *See Croswell,* 3 Johns. Cas. at 345–47, 353–63; Sparf
and Hansen v. United States, 156 U.S. 51, 147–48 (1895) (Gray and Shiras, JJ., dissenting). *But cf.* Edith Guild Henderson, *The Background of the Seventh Amendment,*
80 HARV. L. REV. 289 (1966) (distinguishing between civil and criminal juries, and
dismissing *Georgia v. Brailsford* as anomalous).

   For more documentation and discussion, see LLOYD E. MOORE, THE JURY: TOOL
OF KINGS, PALLADIUM OF LIBERTY 104–10 (2d ed., 1988); JOSIAH QUINCY, JR., RE-
PORT OF CASES ARGUED AND ADJUDGED IN THE SUPREME COURT OF JUDICATURE
OF THE PROVINCE OF MASSACHUSETTS BAY BETWEEN 1761 AND 1772, at 553–72
(Boston: Little, Brown, 1865); Ronald J. Bacigal, *A Case for Jury Determination of
Search and Seizure Law,* 15 U. RICH. L. REV. 791 (1981).

79. *See supra* text accompanying note 69. In the retrial of the famous *Fries Case,* Chase
made a similar concession. *See* Fries Case, 9 F. Cas. 924, 930 (C. C. D. Pa. 1800) (No.
5,127) ("the Jury are to decide on the present, and in all criminal cases, both the law
and the facts").

80. *See generally* Antonin Scalia, *The Rule of Law as a Law of Rules,* 56 U. CHI. L. REV.
1175, 1180–86 (1989).

81. Professor Scheflin apparently fails to understand this. *See* Scheflin, *supra* note 64, at 169 n.2; Alan Scheflin and Jon Van Dyke, *Jury Nullification: The Contours of a Controversy*, LAW & CONTEMP. PROBS., Autumn 1980, at 51, 56.

82. *See generally* Akhil Reed Amar, *A Neo-Federalist View of Article III: Separating the Two Tiers of Federal Jurisdiction*, 65 B. U. L. REV. 205 (1985) [hereinafter *A Neo-Federalist View*].

83. *See* Akhil Reed Amar, *The Two-Tiered Structure of the Judiciary Act of 1789*, 138 U. PA. L. REV. 1499 (1990) [hereinafter *Judiciary Act*].

84. *See* WILLIAM E. NELSON, AMERICANIZATION OF THE COMMON LAW 19, 26, 28, 166 (1975); Note, *supra* note 76, at 174 n.27.

85. *See* United States v. Hudson & Goodwin, 11 U.S. (7 Cranch) 32 (1812). The *Hudson* case raises many complications, but I would distill its central insight as follows: In the absence of express congressional authorization, federal courts may not fashion general criminal rules—especially where Congress's constitutional authority to enact identical rules is in question. I would defend this insight by invoking the structure of the original Constitution (i.e., separation of powers, federalism, and their intersection through "the political safeguards of federalism"), the Constitution's own heightened procedural rules governing criminal sanctions, and general rules requiring strict construction where penal policy is involved. Thus, various earlier federal judicial decisions in tension with *Hudson* were dubious precedents indeed, defensible only if Congress in the First Judiciary Act meant to delegate its own (limited) criminal authority to federal courts, and such a sweeping statutory grant somehow did not violate constitutional norms of nondelegation. *See* Judiciary Act of 1789, ch. 20, §11, 1 Stat. 73, 78–79 (giving Circuit Courts "exclusive cognizance of all crimes and offences cognizable under the authority of the United States" subject to certain exceptions). For more discussion, see Gary D. Rowe, Note, *The Sound of Silence: United States v. Hudson & Goodwin, The Jeffersonian Ascendancy, and the Abolition of Federal Common Law Crimes*, 101 YALE L. J. 919 (1992).

86. Letter to David Humphreys (Mar. 18, 1789), *in* 5 P. Ford, *supra* note 46, at 90 (1895); 2 THE WORKS OF JOHN ADAMS, *supra* note 45, at 253 (diary entry, Feb. 12, 1771). *See also* State v. Wilkinson, 2 Vt. 480, 488–89 (1829) (defending jury law finding as a "power the people exercise in criminal cases, in the persons of jurors, selected from among themselves from time to time").

87. 2 THE WORKS OF JAMES WILSON, *supra* note 14, at 541.

88. *Letters from the Federal Farmer* (XV), *reprinted in* 2 THE COMPLETE ANTI-FEDERALIST *supra* note 9, at 315, 320.

89. 2 THE WORKS OF JOHN ADAMS, *supra* note 45, at 254 (diary entry, Feb. 12, 1771).

90. 156 U.S. 51 (1895). *Sparf* was anticipated by a key circuit court decision by Joseph Story attacking the notion of jury as law finder, *see* United States v. Battiste, 24 F. Cas. 1042 (C. C. D. Mass. 1835) (No. 14,545).

91. *See, e.g.,* Blyew v. United States, 80 U.S. (13 Wall.) 581 (1872); The Slaughter-House Cases, 83 U.S. (16 Wall.) 36 (1873); United States v. Reese, 92 U.S. 214 (1876); United States v. Cruikshank, 92 U.S. 542 (1876); The Civil Rights Cases, 109 U.S. 3 (1883).

92. *See* Westen and Drubel, *supra* note 57, at 131-32; Peter Westen, *The Three Faces of Double Jeopardy: Reflections on Government Appeals of Criminal Sentences,* 78 MICH. L. REV. 1001, 1012-18 (1980).

93. 1 A. DE TOCQUEVILLE, *supra* note 23, at 296.

94. Gannett Co. v. DePasquale, 443 U.S. 368, 428-29 (1979) (Blackmun, J., concurring in part and dissenting in part).

95. Patton v. United States, 281 U.S. 276, 293 (1930).

96. On the mandatory character of these other words of Article III, see Amar, *A Neo-Federalist View, supra* note 82; Amar, *Judiciary Act, supra* note 83. Joseph Story, whose opinion of the Court in *Martin v. Hunter's Lessee,* 14 U.S. (1 Wheat.) 304 (1816), emphasized the plain meaning of "shall" and "all" in Article III's jurisdictional and tenure provisions, also deemed these words mandatory in the criminal jury context. *See* United States v. Gibert, 25 F. Cas. 1287, 1305 (C. C. D. Mass. 1834) (No. 15,204) (Story, Circuit J.).

97. *See, e.g.,* THE FEDERALIST No. 83, at 496 (Alexander Hamilton); 3 ELLIOT'S DEBATES, *supra* note 52, at 520-21 (remarks of Edmund Pendleton at Virginia ratifying convention); 4 *id.* at 145, 171 (remarks of James Iredell in North Carolina ratifying convention); *id.* at 290 (remarks of Rawlins Lowndes at South Carolina ratifying convention); CECELIA M. KENYON, THE ANTIFEDERALISTS 51 (1985) (report of Pennsylvania convention minority).

98. *See* Singer v. United States, 380 U.S. 24 (1965).

99. 127 U.S. 540, 549 (1888) (Harlan, J.).

100. One of the core purposes of the Ninth Amendment was to prevent this sort of misconstruction. *See* Thomas B. McAffee, *The Original Meaning of the Ninth Amendment,* 90 COLUM. L. REV. 1215 (1990). For other applications, *see infra* Chapter 6.

101. *Cf.* DECLARATION OF RIGHTS OF THE CONTINENTAL CONGRESS, art. 5 (1774) ("the respective colonies are entitled to . . . the great and inestimable privilege of being tried by their peers of the vicinage, according to the course of [common] law").

102. *See, e.g., Letters from the Federal Farmer* (II–IV), *reprinted in* 2 THE COMPLETE ANTI-FEDERALIST, *supra* note 9, at 230-31, 244, 245, 249; *Letters of Agrippa* (V), in 4 *id.* at 77, 78-79; C. KENYON, *supra* note 97, at 36, 51 (report of Pennsylvania convention minority); 3 ELLIOT'S DEBATES, *supra* note 52, at 545, 568-69, 578-79 (remarks of Patrick Henry and William Grayson in Virginia ratification debates); 4 *id.* at 150, 154 (remarks of Joseph McDowall and Samuel Spencer in North Carolina ratifying convention); 2 *id.* at 400 (remarks of Thomas Tredwell in New York ratifying convention); *id.* at 109-10 (remarks of Mr. Holmes in Massachusetts rat-

ifying convention); E. DUMBAULD, *supra* note 6, at 183, 190, 200 (declarations of rights of Virginia, New York, and North Carolina ratifying conventions).

103. *See generally* Drew L. Kershen, *Vicinage,* 29 OKLA. L. REV. 801 (1976); Drew L. Kershen, *Vicinage,* 30 OKLA. L. REV. 1 (1977).

104. THE DECLARATION OF INDEPENDENCE para. 17 (U.S. 1776).

105. E. DUMBAULD, *supra* note 6, at 208, 212, 215.

106. *Id.* at 49 and n.22, 54; for background, *see* JULIUS GOEBEL, JR., 1 HISTORY OF THE SUPREME COURT OF THE UNITED STATES: ANTECEDENTS AND BEGINNINGS TO 1801, at 449, 454–55; 2 B. SCHWARTZ, *supra* note 43, at 1157, 1166–67 (Letters from James Madison to Edmund Pendleton, Sept. 14 and 23, 1789).

107. *Compare Patton,* 281 U.S. at 296–97, *with* material quoted *supra* text accompanying notes 40–54, 103. *Patton* suggested that the colonies allowed bench trials in criminal cases, 281 U.S. at 306, but more recent historical studies have called into question the evidence underlying *Patton's* claims. *See* Susan C. Towne, *The Historical Origins of Bench Trial for Serious Crime,* 26 AM. J. LEGAL HIST. 123 (1982). In any event, this history is of only tangential relevance to the meaning of Article III and the Sixth Amendment, whose wording differed considerably from various colonial and state constitutional antecedents.

108. Bank of Columbia v. Okely, 17 U.S. (4 Wheat.) 235, 244 (1819). In dramatic contrast to the universal view during the ratification debates that Article III did mandate jury trial in all criminal cases—and properly so—various proposals for civil jury were expressly limited to situations where "the parties, or either of them request it." E. DUMBAULD, *supra* note 6, at 176, 182 (proposed amendments of Massachusetts and New Hampshire ratifying conventions); *id.* at 177 (proposal of committee of Maryland ratifying convention).

109. Thompson v. Utah, 170 U.S. 343, 353–54 (1898). Unanimity on this point is evident as late as 1904, even as the Court split on the analytically distinct issue of the degree to which petty crimes fell within the scope of the Article III mandate. Schick v. United States, 195 U.S. 65 (1904).

110. Insurance Co. v. Morse, 87 U.S. (20 Wall.) 445, 451 (1874) (dictum).

111. *See, e.g.,* United States v. Gibert, 25 F. Cas. 1287, 1304 (C. C. D. Mass. 1834) (No. 15,204) (Story, Circuit J.); *Schick,* 195 U.S. at 81–82 (Harlan, J., dissenting); FRANCIS H. HELLER, THE SIXTH AMENDMENT 71 (1951).

112. Albert W. Alschuler, *Plea Bargaining and Its History,* 79 COLUM. L. REV. 1, 1–24 (1979); *see also* W. NELSON, *supra* note 84, at 100 (noting judicial discouragement of guilty pleas in capital cases).

113. *See* Alschuler, *supra* note 112, at 1, 40 (citing statistics and Supreme Court cases).

114. *See* IRVING BRANT, THE BILL OF RIGHTS: ITS ORIGIN AND MEANING 82 (1965).

115. *See* BERNARD BAILYN, THE ORIGINS OF AMERICAN POLITICS 68–70, 111 (Vintage

1970) (1967); BERNARD BAILYN, THE IDEOLOGICAL ORIGINS OF THE AMERICAN REVOLUTION 105-8 (1967) [hereinafter IDEOLOGICAL].

116. THE DECLARATION OF INDEPENDENCE para. 11 (U.S. 1776).

117. *Id.* paras. 15, 31.

118. B. BAILYN, IDEOLOGICAL, *supra* note 115, at 108.

119. *See* JACK N. RAKOVE, ORIGINAL MEANINGS 148 (1996) (describing Anti-Federalists' "intense suspicion" of the national judiciary, drawing "upon an older tradition that treated the judiciary itself as an agent of arbitrary power").

120. *See in re* Oliver, 333 U.S. 257, 266 (1948).

121. EDWARD COKE, THE SECOND PART OF THE INSTITUTES OF THE LAWS OF ENGLAND 103 (London: E. and R. Brooke, 5th ed., 1797) (emphasis added).

122. *See in re* Oliver, 333 U.S. at 268-69 and n.22.

123. 3 J. STORY, *supra* note 55, §1785 at 662 (emphasis added).

124. *See* U.S. CONST. amends. I, II, IV, IX, X.

125. *See* 12 THE OXFORD ENGLISH DICTIONARY 778 (2d. ed., 1989).

126. *See generally* Akhil Reed Amar, *The Central Meaning of Republican Government: Popular Sovereignty, Majority Rule, and the Denominator Problem,* 65 U. COLO. L. REV. 749 (1994).

127. *See* Gannett Co. v. DePasquale, 443 U.S. 368, 428-29 (1979) (Blackmun, J., concurring in part and dissenting in part) (quoting Cox Broadcasting Corp. v. Cohn, 420 U.S. 469, 495 (1975)).

128. MATTHEW HALE, THE HISTORY OF THE COMMON LAW OF ENGLAND 344 (London: Henry Butterworth, 6th ed., 1820).

129. 3 W. BLACKSTONE, *supra* note 22, at 372. Though this passage occurs in the context of a discussion of evidence law in civil cases, Blackstone elsewhere makes clear that the same principles apply to criminal cases. *See* 4 *id.* at 350.

130. Sir John Hawles, Remarks upon Mr. Cornish's Trial, *in* 11 Howell's State Trials 455, 460.

131. 3 W. BLACKSTONE, *supra* note 22, at 373. For very similar language, see M. HALE, *supra* note 128, at 345 (quoted *infra* note 136).

132. THE FEDERALIST No. 83, at 500-501 (Alexander Hamilton).

133. *Cf.* Rock v. Arkansas, 483 U.S. 44, 51-53 (1987) (affirming a criminal defendant's constitutional right to testify).

134. *See generally* Joel N. Bodansky, *The Abolition of the Party-Witness Disqualification: An Historical Survey,* 70 KY. L. J. 91 (1982); Ferguson v. Georgia, 365 U.S. 570, 573-77 (1961).

135. *See* Bodansky, *supra* note 134, at 92.

136. 3 W. BLACKSTONE, *supra* note 22, at 372-73. *See also* 4 *id.* at 350. Blackstone borrowed heavily, it seems, from Hale: "[O]ftentimes witnesses will deliver [in private]

that, which they will be shamed to testify publicly. . . . [M]any times the very MANNER of delivering testimony, will give a probable indication, whether the witness speaks truly or falsely. . . . [Cross-examination] beats and boults out the truth much better . . . and [is] the best method of searching and sifting out the truth. . . . " M. HALE, *supra* note 128, at 345.

137. 7 and 8 Will. 3, ch. 3, §1.

138. *Id.* §7 (emphasis added). On the more general symmetry principle underlying this act, *see* John H. Langbein, *The Historical Origins of the Privilege Against Self-Incrimination at Common Law,* 92 MICH. L. REV. 1047, 1056, 1067–68 (1994).

139. 4 W. BLACKSTONE, *supra* note 22, at 345 (emphasis altered).

140. Federal Crimes Act of 1790, ch. 9, 1 Stat. 112, 118–19.

141. *See* Wilson v. United States, 149 U.S. 60, 66 (1893); Akhil Reed Amar and Renée B. Lettow, *Fifth Amendment First Principles: The Self-Incrimination Clause,* 93 MICH. L. REV. 857, 922–24 (1995); Stephen J. Schulhofer, *Some Kind Words for the Privilege Against Self-Incrimination,* 26 VAL. U. L. REV. 311 (1991).

142. The Trial of Sir Walter Raleigh, 2 Howell's State Trials 15–16 (Oyer and Terminer 1603).

143. *See, e.g.,* ZECHARIAH CHAFEE, JR., THREE HUMAN RIGHTS IN THE CONSTITUTION OF 1787, at 127 (1956).

144. *See* William T. Mayton, *Seditious Libel and the Lost Guarantee of a Freedom of Expression,* 84 COLUM. L. REV. 91, 115–17 (1984).

Six. The Popular-Sovereignty Amendments

1. *See supra* Chapter 2.

2. THE FEDERALIST No. 84, at 513 (Alexander Hamilton) (emphasis altered) (Clinton Rossiter ed., 1961) [hereinafter all citations are to this edition].

3. *Accord* Thomas B. McAffee, *The Original Meaning of the Ninth Amendment,* 90 COLUM. L. REV. 1215 (1990). Although a source of many insights, Professor McAffee's essay seems to glide a bit too quickly past the phrase "retained by the people" and the popular-sovereignty theory underlying that phrase. For an equally insightful corrective, *see* Jeff Rosen, Note, *Was the Flag Burning Amendment Unconstitutional?* 100 YALE L. J. 1073 (1991).

4. 2 DEBATES ON THE ADOPTION OF THE FEDERAL CONSTITUTION 432, 437 (Jonathan Elliot ed., AYER Co. reprint ed., 1987) (1836) (emphasis added) [hereinafter ELLIOT'S DEBATES].

5. 2 BERNARD SCHWARTZ, THE BILL OF RIGHTS: A DOCUMENTARY HISTORY 1118 (1971) (August 18, 1789).

6. 1 ELLIOT'S DEBATES, *supra* note 4, at 327.

7. *Id.*

8. THE DECLARATION OF INDEPENDENCE para. 2 (U.S. 1776) (emphasis added).

9. THE FEDERALIST No. 78, at 469 (Alexander Hamilton) (emphasis added; footnote omitted).

10. For further elaboration, see Akhil Reed Amar, *Of Sovereignty and Federalism*, 96 YALE L. J. 1425, 1492–1519 (1987).

11. *See* EDWARD DUMBAULD, THE BILL OF RIGHTS AND WHAT IT MEANS TODAY 163 (1957).

12. *See generally* McAfee, *supra* note 3.

13. *See, e.g.*, 5 THE FOUNDERS' CONSTITUTION 136, 137 (Philip B. Kurland and Ralph Lerner eds., 1987) (reprinting Report of the Minority on the Virginia Resolutions, Jan. 22, 1799) (attributed to John Marshall). *But see* Stewart Jay, *Origins of Federal Common Law: Part Two*, 133 U. PA. L. REV. 1231, app. B at 1329–30 and n.8 (1985) (raising questions about this attribution).

14. 3 THE RECORDS OF THE FEDERAL CONVENTION OF 1787, at 290 (Max Farrand rev. ed., 1937) [hereinafter M. FARRAND] (Luther Martin's Reply to the Landholder).

15. 2 *id.* at 640 (George Mason's objections to Constitution); 3 ELLIOT'S DEBATES, *supra* note 4, at 444 (remarks of Mason in Virginia ratifying convention).

16. *Letters of Agrippa* (XVI), *reprinted in* 4 THE COMPLETE ANTI-FEDERALIST III (Herbert J. Storing ed., 1981).

17. 2 ELLIOT'S DEBATES, *supra* note 4, at 401; *see also* 3 *id.* at 445–46 (similar remarks of Patrick Henry at Virginia ratifying convention); McAffee, *supra* note 3, at 1241–44 (discussing and quoting other Anti-Federalists linking Bill of Rights with states' rights).

18. 2 ELLIOT'S DEBATES, *supra* note 4, at 399.

19. Letter from Thomas Jefferson to James Madison (Dec. 20, 1787), *in* 1 B. SCHWARTZ, *supra* note 5, at 607 (emphasis added).

20. GORDON S. WOOD, THE CREATION OF THE AMERICAN REPUBLIC, 1776–1787, at 520 (1969); *see also id.* at 516 (describing Anti-Federalists as populists who emphasized widespread participation in government).

21. 1 B. SCHWARTZ, *supra* note 5, at 615 (letter of Oct. 17, 1788) (emphasis added).

22. THE FEDERALIST No. 38, at 235 (James Madison).

23. *Id.* No. 84, at 515 (Alexander Hamilton) (emphasis added).

24. *Id.; see also* PENNSYLVANIA AND THE FEDERAL CONSTITUTION, 1787–1788, at 252 (John Bach McMaster and Frederick D. Stone eds., Lancaster: Inquirer, 1888) (remarks of Thomas McKean in Pennsylvania ratifying convention) ("[T]he whole plan of government is nothing more than a bill of rights—a declaration of the people in what manner they choose to be governed.").

25. *See* JESSE H. CHOPER, JUDICIAL REVIEW AND THE POLITICAL PROCESS (1980).

26. *Id.* at 174–75.

27. *See* JOHN HART ELY, DEMOCRACY AND DISTRUST 90 (1980). (Both "[c]lauses prove on analysis to be separation of powers provisions, enjoining the legislature to act

prospectively and by general rule (just as the judiciary is implicitly enjoined by Article III to act retrospectively and by specific decree)."); Akhil Reed Amar, *Attainder and Amendment* 2: Romer's *Rightness*, 95 MICH. L. REV. 203, 209–11 (1996).

28. 32 U.S. (7 Pet.) 243 (1833).

29. J. CHOPER, *supra* note 25, at 244.

30. ALEXANDER M. BICKEL, THE LEAST DANGEROUS BRANCH 16 (1962).

31. 2 B. SCHWARTZ, *supra* note 5, at 1031 (June 8, 1789).

32. *Id.* at 1031–32.

33. *Id.* at 1030.

34. Letter from Thomas Jefferson to James Madison (Mar. 15, 1789), *in* 14 THE PAPERS OF THOMAS JEFFERSON 659 (Julian P. Boyd ed., 1958).

35. Letter from Thomas Jefferson to L'Abbé Arnoux (July 19, 1789), *in* 15 *id.* at 282 (citing book "Jurors judges both of law and fact by Jones"); for further evidence of Jefferson's views, see sources cited *supra* Chapter 5, note 78.

36. Letter from Thomas Jefferson to Joseph Priestley (June 19, 1802), *in* 8 THE WRITINGS OF THOMAS JEFFERSON 158, 159–60 (Paul Leicester Ford ed., New York: G. P. Putnam's Sons, 1897).

37. *See, e.g.,* 3 JOSEPH STORY, COMMENTARIES ON THE CONSTITUTION OF THE UNITED STATES §1859 (Boston: Hilliard, Gray, 1833) (Bill of Rights "serves to guide, and enlighten public opinion"); *Letters from the Federal Farmer* (XVI), *reprinted in* 2 THE COMPLETE ANTI-FEDERALIST, *supra* note 16, at 324–25 (A declaration of rights "establish[es] in the minds of the people truths and principles which they might never otherwise have thought of, or soon forgot. If a nation means its systems, religious or political, shall have duration, it ought to recognize the leading principles of them in the front page of every family book. What is the usefulness of a truth in theory, unless it exists constantly in the minds of the people, and has their assent . . . . [E]ducation [consists of] a series of notions impressed upon the minds of the people by examples, precepts and declarations."); 1 BLACKSTONE'S COMMENTARIES 308 app. (St. George Tucker ed., Philadelphia: Burch and Small, 1803) ("A bill of rights may be considered, not only as intended to give law, and assign limits to a government . . . , but as giving *information to the people* [so that] every man of the meanest capacity and understanding may *learn* his own rights . . . .") (emphasis added).

38. *See* Robert C. Palmer, *Liberties, in* CONSTITUTION AND RIGHTS IN THE EARLY AMERICAN REPUBLIC 55 (William E. Nelson and Robert C. Palmer eds., 1987); IRVING BRANT, THE BILL OF RIGHTS 37–42 (1965).

39. VA. CONST. OF 1776 (Declaration of Rights), §15.

40. Madison well understood the mnemonic benefits of maxims for ordinary citizens. *See* THE FEDERALIST NO. 53, at 330–32 (James Madison); 2 M. FARRAND, *supra* note 14, at 616–17 (Madison endorsing anti–standing army maxim for inclusion in Article I, §8); *see also supra* page 84, text accompanying note (discussing Madison's

proposed didactic maxim about jury trial); E. DUMBAULD, *supra* note 11, at 207 (Madison proposing an amendment that described freedom of the press as "one of the great bulwarks of liberty"). Hamilton, less of a true populist, was more critical. *See* THE FEDERALIST No. 84, at 513 (Alexander Hamilton) (didactic "aphorisms which make the principal figure in several of our State bills of rights . . . would sound much better in a treatise of ethics than in a constitution of government"). Hamilton was of course also less enthusiastic about militias and juries. *See id.* Nos. 26, 29, 83 (Alexander Hamilton).

41. *Letter from a Delegate Who Has Catched Cold, reprinted in* 5 THE COMPLETE ANTI-FEDERALIST, *supra* note 16, at 268, 273; *see also* 1 WILLIAM BLACKSTONE, COMMEN-TARIES ON THE LAWS OF ENGLAND 6 (Oxford: Clarendon, 1765) (in ancient Rome, "boys were obliged to learn the twelve tables by heart").

42. 3 ELLIOT'S DEBATES, *supra* note 4, at 137, 223.

43. 1 B. SCHWARTZ, *supra* note 5, at 616–17. (Letter of James Madison to Thomas Jefferson Oct. 17, 1788). Madison here prefigured the words of Edmund Randolph concerning the Virginia Bill of Rights, quoted in *id.* at 249.

44. 14 THE PAPERS OF JAMES MADISON 218 (Robert A. Rutland et al. eds., 1983) (*National Gazette* essay on U.S. government, Feb. 4, 1792); *accord* G. WOOD, *supra* note 20, at 33–35 (Constitution "ultimately sustained" by "the very spirit of the people"); *id.* at 377 ("genius" and "habits" of people prevail over "paper . . . form[s]" in constitutions and bills of rights) (quoting Noah Webster).

45. *See supra* text accompanying note 43.

46. *Quoted in* G. WOOD, *supra* note 20, at 120.

47. *Id.*

48. *Id.* at 426.

49. MASS. CONST. OF 1780, pt. II, ch. V, §II.

Seven. Antebellum Ideas

1. Henry J. Friendly, *The Bill of Rights as a Code of Criminal Procedure,* 53 CAL. L. REV. 929, 934 (1965).

2. William W. Van Alstyne, *Foreword* to MICHAEL KENT CURTIS, NO STATE SHALL ABRIDGE: THE FOURTEENTH AMENDMENT AND THE BILL OF RIGHTS at ix (1986).

3. Felix Frankfurter, *Memorandum on "Incorporation" of the Bill of Rights into the Due Process Clause of the Fourteenth Amendment,* 78 HARV. L. REV. 746 (1965). Judge Friendly notes that this memorandum was Frankfurter's "last published work." Friendly, *supra* note 1, at 934 n.27.

4. *See* William C. Warren, *Foreword* to HUGO LAFAYETTE BLACK, A CONSTITUTIONAL FAITH at x–xi (1968); HUGO LAFAYETTE BLACK, A CONSTITUTIONAL FAITH at xvi–vii, 34–42 (1968).

5. William J. Brennan, Jr., *The Bill of Rights and the States,* 36 N.Y.U. L. REV. 761 (1961)

[hereinafter Brennan I]; William J. Brennan, Jr., *The Bill of Rights and the States: The Revival of State Constitutions as Guardians of Individual Rights*, 61 N.Y.U. L. REV. 535 (1986) [hereinafter Brennan II].

6. United States v. Carolene Products Co., 304 U.S. 144, 152 n.4 (1938).

7. This phrase is meant to suggest the importance of the cases and not necessarily their correctness.

8. 376 U.S. 254 (1964) (freedom of speech and press).

9. 374 U.S. 203 (1963) (nonestablishment of religion).

10. 367 U.S. 643 (1961) (exclusion of evidence obtained by unreasonable search and seizure); *see also id.* at 661–66 (Black, J., concurring) (relying in part on right against compelled self-incrimination).

11. 384 U.S. 436 (1966) (privilege against compelled self-incrimination and right to counsel).

12. 372 U.S. 335 (1963) (right to counsel).

13. 391 U.S. 145 (1968) (right to criminal jury).

14. Brennan II, *supra* note 5, at 535–36; *see also* William J. Brennan, Jr., *State Constitutions and the Protection of Individual Rights*, 90 HARV. L. REV. 489, 492–93 (1977).

15. Erwin N. Griswold, *Due Process Problems Today in the United States, in* THE FOURTEENTH AMENDMENT 161, 164 (Bernard Schwartz ed., 1970) (citation omitted).

16. *See* Adamson v. California, 332 U.S. 46, 59–68 (1947) (Frankfurter, J., concurring); Frankfurter, *supra* note 3.

17. *See* Betts v. Brady, 316 U.S. 455, 474–75 and n.1 (1942) (Black, J., dissenting); *Adamson,* 332 U.S. at 68–123 (Black, J., dissenting); *Duncan,* 391 U.S. at 162–71 (Black, J., concurring); H. BLACK, *supra* note 4, at 34–42. For an early hint of Black's maturing views, *see* Chambers v. Florida, 309 U.S. 227, 235 n.8 (1940) (Black, J.).

18. *See* Ohio *ex rel.* Eaton v. Price, 364 U.S. 263, 274–76 (1960) (separate opinion of Brennan, J.); Cohen v. Hurley, 366 U.S. 117, 154–60 (1961) (Brennan, J., dissenting); Malloy v. Hogan, 378 U.S. 1 (1964) (Brennan, J.); Brennan I, *supra* note 5; Brennan II, *supra* note 5.

19. 32 U.S. (7 Pet.) 243 (1833).

20. *Id.* at 247.

21. *Id.*

22. THE FEDERALIST No. 83, at 503 (Alexander Hamilton) (Clinton Rossiter ed., 1961) [hereinafter all citations to THE FEDERALIST are to this edition].

23. 32 U.S. (7 Pet.) at 248.

24. *Id.* at 250.

25. *Id.* at 248.

26. *Id.*

27. *See, e.g.,* THE FEDERALIST No. 84, at 510–12 (Alexander Hamilton).

28. Professor Crosskey flails mightily against this rule of construction, but without much

success. *See* 2 WILLIAM WINSLOW CROSSKEY, POLITICS AND THE CONSTITUTION IN THE HISTORY OF THE UNITED STATES 1049–82 (1953). Crosskey offers two constitutional counterexamples that, he claims, disprove the rule that generally worded constitutional limitations never apply against states. *Id.* at 1079–80. The first claimed counterexample, the full-faith-and-credit clause of Article IV, explicitly uses the word *State* twice. U.S. CONST. art. IV, §1. Crosskey's attempt to argue that the phrase "in each State" does not include action *by* states makes a hash of the obvious interstate comity logic of the clause, confirmed by its placement in Article IV immediately preceding other obvious comity clauses—clauses that clearly use the phrases "in the several States," "in any State," and "in another State" to encompass action *by* states. U.S. CONST. art. IV, §2, cls. 1–2; *see also id.* art. VI (judges "in every State" in context clearly encompass judges *of* states).

Crosskey's only other example—the appellate jurisdiction of the Supreme Court—rests on a highly strained textual analogy to a set of words that looks very different from those of the takings clause. Unlike the takings clause, the appellate jurisdiction clause is not a limitation on, but an empowerment of, federal authority. *Id.* art. III, §2. To the extent that the clause does implicitly limit federal authority—for example, by denying federal courts jurisdiction over nondiverse cases arising wholly under state law—these limitations apply only against federal courts and not state courts, in perfect keeping with *Barron*. Furthermore, the appellate jurisdiction clause must be read in the context of the language of Article III as a whole, which does make plain that state courts are to be reviewed by federal tribunals. *See* Akhil Reed Amar, *A Neo-Federalist View of Article III: Separating the Two Tiers of Federal Jurisdiction,* 65 B. U. L. REV. 205 (1985). In the words of Publius, "The objects of appeal, not the tribunals from which it is to be made, are alone contemplated." THE FEDERALIST NO. 82, at 494 (Alexander Hamilton). Such was the near universal understanding in 1787–89. Crosskey, by contrast, fails to identify even a single eighteenth-century figure who thought that the Bill of Rights applied directly against states.

29. *See, e.g.,* 1 DEBATES ON THE ADOPTION OF THE FEDERAL CONSTITUTION 322–23, 326–27 (Jonathan Elliot ed., AYER Co. reprint ed., 1987) (1836) [hereinafter ELLIOT'S DEBATES] (ratifying conventions of Massachusetts and New Hampshire); 3 *id.* at 659–61 (Virginia ratifying convention).

30. 2 BERNARD SCHWARTZ, THE BILL OF RIGHTS: A DOCUMENTARY HISTORY 1026–28 (1971) (June 8, 1789) (speaking of "national" government and "*the* Legislature" in some provisions, yet using global language elsewhere (emphasis added)).

31. *Id.* at 1032–33 (June 8, 1789); *id.* at 1113 (Aug. 17, 1789). *See supra* Chapter 2.

32. 2 B. SCHWARTZ, *supra* note 30, at 1027 (June 8, 1789) (emphasis added).

33. *Id.* at 1026.

34. The redundancy here is of a different order than that embodied in Madison's pro-

posed prototype of the Tenth Amendment, which used words very different from anything in the original Constitution to make textually explicit a structural idea only implicit earlier—the idea of limited federal power. And Madison was at pains to point out that whereas his proto–Tenth Amendment added nothing new, his proto–Fourteenth did. *See infra* text accompanying notes 35–37.

35. 2 B. SCHWARTZ, *supra* note 30, at 1033 (June 8, 1789); *id.* at 1113 (Aug. 17, 1789).

36. *Id.* at 1033 (June 8, 1789).

37. Even the most vociferous twentieth-century critic of the *Barron* rule, William Winslow Crosskey, concedes that the language of Madison's "No State shall" proposal makes it tough to argue that the other generally worded amendments limited states. But, he argues, when the Senate voted down Madison's pet proposal, the general amendments were automatically transformed into limitations on states. 2 W. CROSSKEY, *supra* note 28, at 1066–76. It is a clever argument, but there is no evidence to support it. Crosskey fails to identify a single person—in the Senate, in the House, in the states, or in the newspapers—who claimed that the general words would bind states. Nor is it plausible prima facie to presume that the Senate—the federal branch specially structured to safeguard state governments from federal encroachment—actually sought to *increase* the number of "particular rights" binding states by rejecting Madison's pet proposal. Yet this is exactly what Crosskey claims the Senate must have intended. Crosskey does point to other actions simultaneously taken by the Senate behind closed doors, but these actually appear to cut just the other way, suggesting a states'-rights explanation for the difference in wording between the First Amendment and the next seven see Chapter 2. As we saw in that chapter, the action of the Senate and the precise language of the First Amendment's unique reference to Congress reflect a surprisingly widely held view that—unlike the domains addressed in Amendments II–VIII—the areas covered by the First Amendment simply lay beyond Congress's enumerated Article I, section 8 powers.

38. 32 U.S. (7 Pet.) 243, 250 (1833).

39. *See generally* Part One.

40. *See* Paul Finkelman, *James Madison and the Bill of Rights: A Reluctant Paternity*, 1990 SUP. CT. REV. 301, 335.

41. *See* Livingston v. Moore, 32 U.S. (7 Pet.) 469, 482, 539, 551–52 (1833) (Fourth and Seventh Amendments); Holmes v. Jennison, 39 U.S. (14 Pet.) 540, 555, 582, 587 (1840) (opinions of Thompson and Barbour, J J.) (Fifth Amendment due process); Permoli v. New Orleans, 44 U.S. (3 How.) 589, 609 (1845) (First Amendment free exercise); Fox v. Ohio, 46 U.S. (5 How.) 410, 434–35 (1847) (Fifth Amendment double jeopardy); Town of East Hartford v. Hartford Bridge Co., 51 U.S. (10 How.) 511, 539 (1850) (Fifth Amendment just compensation); Smith v. Maryland, 59 U.S. (18 How.) 71, 72, 76 (1855) (Fourth Amendment); Withers v. Buckley, 61 U.S. (20 How.) 84, 89–91

(1858) (Fifth Amendment just compensation); Pervear v. Massachusetts, 72 U.S. (5 Wall.) 475, 476, 479–80 (1866) (Eighth Amendment).

The only troubled note in this unanimous chorus was sounded by Justice McLean in a pair of double-jeopardy dissents. *See* Fox, 46 U.S. (5 How.) at 438–40 (McLean, J., dissenting); Moore v. Illinois, 55 U.S. (14 How.) 13, 21–22 (1852) (McLean, J., dissenting). McLean never claimed that the Fifth Amendment barred a state from punishing the same person twice for the same offense; but he did think that the amendment, in tandem with its counterpart double-jeopardy clauses in the state constitutions, prevented the federal and state governments from each punishing the same person once for the same conduct. *See infra* text accompanying notes 43–44, 54.

42. Bank of Columbia v. Okely, 17 U.S. (4 Wheat.) 235, 240–42 (1819). For a parsing of Johnson's language as inconsistent with the later *Barron* opinion, *see* William Winslow Crosskey, *Charles Fairman, "Legislative History," and the Constitutional Limitations on State Authority*, 22 U. CHI. L. REV. 1, 127–29 (1954).

43. Houston v. Moore, 18 U.S. (5 Wheat.) 1, 33–34 (1820) (separate opinion of Johnson, J.).

44. For a similar view, *see* State v. Antonio, 3 S.C. (3 Brev.) 562, 565 (1816).

45. People v. Goodwin, 18 Johns. 187, 200–201 (N.Y. Sup. Ct. 1820); State v. Moor, 1 Miss. 134, 138 (1823) (citing and following *Goodwin*).

46. Commonwealth v. Purchase, 19 Mass. (2 Pick.) 521, 522 (1824).

47. WILLIAM RAWLE, A VIEW OF THE CONSTITUTION OF THE UNITED STATES OF AMERICA 120–30 (Philadelphia: H. C. Carey and I. Lea, 1825).

48. Johnson v. Tompkins, 13 F. Cas. 840, 849–52 (C. C. E. D. Pa. 1833) (No. 7,416); *see also* Magill v. Brown, 16 F. Cas. 408, 419, 427 (C. C. E. D. Pa. 1833) (No. 8,952) (Baldwin, Circuit J.) (invoking federal religion clauses to gloss Pennsylvania state law).

49. 3 JOSEPH STORY, COMMENTARIES ON THE CONSTITUTION OF THE UNITED STATES §1897 (Boston: Hilliard, Gray, 1833). This language—the sum total of the *Commentaries'* analysis of the *Barron* issue—appears to have been written before *Barron*, though Story did manage to include in the published edition a footnote citation to *Barron. See* Crosskey, *supra* note 42, at 138–39 and n.251.

50. People v. Goodwin, 18 Johns. 187, 200 (N.Y. Sup. Ct. 1820).

51. W. RAWLE, *supra* note 47, at 120.

52. Baldwin did not participate in the Supreme Court's 1833 term and thus was not present for *Barron* or its kindred *Livingston v. Moore*, 32 U.S. (7 Pet.) 469, 482, 539, 551–52 (1833). *See* G. EDWARD WHITE, 3–4 HISTORY OF THE SUPREME COURT OF THE UNITED STATES: THE MARSHALL COURT AND CULTURAL CHANGE, 1815–35, at 299 (1988). After 1833, however, he does not appear to have challenged *Barron's* rule—indeed, as we shall see, even his earlier invocations of the Bill of Rights in cases involving states can be technically reconciled with *Barron*.

53. Rhinehart v. Schuyler, 7 Ill. (2 Gilm.) 473, 522 (1845); *see also* Cockrum v. State, 24

Tex. 394, 401-2 (1859) (invoking counsel's claim that state law violated federal Second Amendment, and discussing principles of that amendment without adverting to *Barron*).

54. Fox v. Ohio, 46 U.S. (5 How.) 410, 420 (1847).

55. *See infra* Chapter 9.

56. W. RAWLE, *supra* note 47, at 120 (emphasis added).

57. *Id.* at 121 (emphasis altered).

58. *Id.* at 122.

59. *Id.* at 122-23.

60. *Id.* at 120-21.

61. On the general role of maxims in Bill of Rights, *see supra* Chapter 6.

62. 2 DOCUMENTARY HISTORY OF THE CONSTITUTION OF THE UNITED STATES OF AMERICA 321 (Washington: Dept. of State, 1894). *See supra* Chapter 2, note 44.

63. For a nice elaboration of this concept, *see* Jeff Rosen, Note, *Was the Flag Burning Amendment Unconstitutional?*, 100 YALE L. J. 1073, 1074-83 (1991); *see also* JACOBUS tenBROEK, EQUAL UNDER LAW 90-91, 128 (Collier, 1965) (1951) (early amendments seen by contrarians as "declaratory constitutional safeguards of natural rights" and "a meeting ground of constitutional and natural rights"); Howard Jay Graham, *Our "Declaratory" Fourteenth Amendment*, 7 STAN. L. REV. 3, 3-4 (1954) (noting centrality of eighteenth- and nineteenth-century conception of various constitutional provisions as "declaratory"); *cf.* 2 ELLIOT'S DEBATES, *supra* note 29, at 433 (remarks of James Wilson at Pennsylvania ratifying convention) (describing People as the Ultimate Supreme Court: "from their power, . . . there is no appeal"); WILLIAM E. NELSON, THE FOURTEENTH AMENDMENT 59 (1988) (quoting 1867 Pennsylvania legislator who described constitutional amendments as submitted to the people "sitting as a jury"—that is, a judicial body); Akhil Reed Amar, *The People as Supreme Court: Some Incomplete Notes on Sager*, 88 Nw. U. L. REV. 457 (1993) (explaining implications of this view).

For more general background, see 1 WILLIAM BLACKSTONE, COMMENTARIES* 42, 53-55, 57-58, 86; BERNARD BAILYN, THE IDEOLOGICAL ORIGINS OF THE AMERICAN REVOLUTION 69 n.13, 78, 187-98 (1967); GORDON S. WOOD, THE CREATION OF THE AMERICAN REPUBLIC, 1776-1787, at 294 (1969); Suzanna Sherry, *The Founders' Unwritten Constitution*, 54 U. CHI. L. REV. 1127, 1132-33 (1987); Suzanna Sherry, *Natural Law in the States*, 61 U. CIN. L. REV. 171 (1992). *See also supra* Chapter 2, note 44.

64. *Cf.* United States v. Given, 25 F. Cas. 1324, 1325 (C. C. D. Del. 1873) (No. 15,210) (Strong, Circuit J.).

65. Wesley N. Hohfeld, *Some Fundamental Legal Conceptions as Applied in Judicial Reasoning*, 23 YALE L. J. 16 (1913).

66. U.S. CONST. art. I, §8, cl. 8 (empowering Congress to secure to "Authors and Inventors the exclusive Right to their respective Writings and Discoveries").

67. W. RAWLE, *supra* note 47, at 113.
68. *Cf. supra* text accompanying notes 26–27.
69. U.S. CONST. amend. I ("freedom" of speech and of the press; "right" to assemble and petition; "free" exercise of religion): *id.* amend. II ("right" to keep and bear arms); *id.* amend. IV ("right" against unreasonable searches and seizures); *id.* amend. VI ("right" to various procedural protections in criminal prosecutions); *id.* amend. VII ("right" to civil jury); *id.* amend. IX ("rights" retained by the people).
70. *See* Carol M. Rose, *The Ancient Constitution vs. The Federalist Empire: Anti-Federalism from the Attack on "Monarchism" to Modern Localism,* 84 Nw. U. L. REV. 74, 75–84 (1989).
71. For a superb treatment of the issue, *see* Robert J. Reinstein, *Completing the Constitution: The Declaration of Independence, Bill of Rights, and Fourteenth Amendment,* 66 TEMPLE L. REV. 361 (1993).
72. *See* J. TENBROEK, *supra* note 63, at 90–91 (contrarians "disregard[ed]" federalism in parsing the Constitution: "Once a mention of *the rights* [to be protected] was found, the rest was easy." (emphasis added)).
73. *Cf.* Strauder v. West Virginia, 100 U.S. 303, 307–8, 310 (1880) (self-consciously inferring "rights" and "immunities" from constitutional provisions worded as "prohibitions"); *Ex parte* Virginia, 100 U.S. 339, 345 (1880) (similar).
74. 39 U.S. (14 Pet.) 540, 555 (1840).
75. *Id.* at 555–56.
76. *Id.* at 556–57.
77. Nunn v. Georgia, 1 Ga. 243, 250 (1846).
78. *Id.* at 249.
79. *Id.*
80. *Id.* at 250–51 (emphasis omitted).
81. *Id.* at 250.
82. Campbell v. State, 11 Ga. 353 (1852).
83. *Id.* at 369.
84. *Id.* at 365. This catalogue appears to be taken directly from Blackstone. *See infra* Chapter Eight, text accompanying note 15.
85. Campbell v. State, 11 Ga. at 365.
86. *Id.* at 367–68.
87. *Id.* at 369–70 (citing, inter alia, Fletcher v. Peck, 10 U.S. (6 Cranch) 87 (1810); Terrett v. Taylor, 13 U.S. (9 Cranch) 43 (1815); Green v. Biddle, 21 U.S. (8 Wheat.) 1 (1823)).
88. 11 Ga. at 371.
89. *Id.*
90. *Id.* at 372 (emphasis added).
91. *See* 3 ELLIOT'S DEBATES, *supra* note 29, at 46; *supra* Chapter 1.

92. *See, e.g.,* 1 THE RECORDS OF THE FEDERAL CONVENTION OF 1787, at 250, 338, 439 (Max Farrand rev. ed., 1937) (remarks of John Lansing and Luther Martin); CECELIA M. KENYON, THE ANTI-FEDERALISTS 93, 124, 133, 171, 185, 240–41, 251, 254 (1966) (collecting objections to novelty of proposed Constitution from various Anti-Federalists). For Publius's attempt to blunt this critique, see THE FEDERALIST No. 14, at 104–5 (James Madison).

93. CONG. GLOBE, 35th Cong., 2d Sess. 982 (1859); *see also* CONG. GLOBE, 37th Cong., 2d Sess. 1640 (1862) (remarks of John Bingham, invoking the congressional "act for the admission of [Bingham's home state of] Ohio on the condition of perpetual freedom to all law-abiding men within her limits"); CONG. GLOBE, 40th Cong., 2d Sess. 2463 (1868) (remarks of John Bingham discussing condition imposed upon admission of Missouri safeguarding privileges and immunities of citizens); Howard Jay Graham, *The "Conspiracy Theory" of the Fourteenth Amendment,* 47 YALE L. J. 371, 395 n.84 (1938) (discussing this aspect of Bingham's thought as possibly influenced by congressional statutes conditioning admission of new states on compliance with due process and other guarantees).

94. *See* WILLIAM M. WIECEK, THE SOURCES OF ANTISLAVERY CONSTITUTIONALISM IN AMERICA 1760–1848, at 172–82 (1977); David Yassky, *Eras of the First Amendment,* 91 COLUM. L. REV. 1699, 1713–17 (1991). At almost the same time, a similar blurring of the state-federal line was at work in various slave rendition cases under Congress's Fugitive Slave Act of 1793, which involved state magistrates enforcing federal laws and raised intricate questions of state incorporation of federal law. *See, e.g.,* SALMON P. CHASE, SPEECH OF SALMON P. CHASE IN THE CASE OF THE COLORED WOMAN MATILDA 23–25, 32–36 (Cincinnati: Pugh and Dodd, 1837).

95. *Cf.* McCulloch v. Maryland, 17 U.S. (4 Wheat.) 316 (1819); CHARLES L. BLACK, JR., STRUCTURE AND RELATIONSHIP IN CONSTITUTIONAL LAW 33–50 (1969). *See also supra* Chapter 2, note 14.

96. U.S. CONST. art. IV, §4 (guaranteeing "a Republican Form of Government" to "every State in this Union"); *see also* Akhil Reed Amar, *The Central Meaning of Republican Government: Popular Sovereignty, Majority Rule, and the Denominator Problem,* 65 COLO. L. REV. 749, 755–56 (1994); *supra* Chapter 2, note 95.

97. *See generally* ALEXANDER MEIKLEJOHN, POLITICAL FREEDOM: THE CONSTITUTIONAL POWERS OF THE PEOPLE (1960); Alexander Meiklejohn, *The First Amendment Is an Absolute,* 1961 SUP. CT. REV. 245; Michael Kent Curtis, *The 1859 Crisis Over Hinton Helper's Book,* The Impending Crisis: *Free Speech, Slavery, and Some Light on the Meaning of the First Section of the Fourteenth Amendment,* 68 CHI.-KENT L. REV. 1113, 1127, 1132 (1993) [hereinafter *1859 Crisis*].

98. In 1836, William Plumer, a former New Hampshire senator, published a pamphlet declaring that freedom of speech and of the press were reserved to the people from both state and federal interference; and the Vermont legislature resolved that "nei-

ther Congress nor the state Governments have any constitutional right to abridge the free expression of opinions, or the transmission of them through the public mail." W. WIECEK, *supra* note 94, at 177, 181-82 (quoting "CINCINNATUS" [WILLIAM PLUMER], FREEDOM'S DEFENCE; OR, A CANDID EXAMINATION OF MR. CALHOUN'S REPORT ON THE FREEDOM OF THE PRESS . . . 11, 19 (Worcester: Dorr, Howland, 1836) and Vermont's resolution of Nov. 16). So too, in that year, the Massachusetts Anti-Slavery Society argued that "The power of restricting freedom of speech and of the press was withheld from the Legislature of MASSACHUSETTS, *for the same reason* that it was withheld from the GENERAL GOVERNMENT, and to *the same extent."* Michael Kent Curtis, *The Curious History of Attempts to Suppress Antislavery Speech, Press, and Petition in 1835-37,* 89 Nw. U. L. REV. 785, 862 (1995) (quoting A FULL STATEMENT OF THE REASONS . . . 17 (Boston, 1836) (emphasis in original)) [hereinafter *Curious History*].

99. *See supra* Chapter 2.

100. *See* G. WOOD, *supra* note 63, at 24-25, 60-61, 362 (1969); GORDON S. WOOD, THE RADICALISM OF THE AMERICAN REVOLUTION 104 (1991); *see also* DEL. DECLARATION OF RIGHTS OF 1776, art. 6 ("the right of the people to participate in the Legislature, is the foundation of liberty and of all free government"); MD. CONST. OF 1776 (Declaration of Rights), art. V (similar).

101. *See* NATIONAL PARTY PLATFORMS, 1840-1968, at 5 (Kirk H. Porter and Donald Bruce Johnson eds., 3rd ed., 1966) (Liberty Platform of 1844, §§10, 11); *id.* at 13-14 (Free Soil Platform of 1848, *passim*); *id.* at 18 (Free Democratic Platform of 1852, §§IV, VII); *id.* at 27 (Republican Platform of 1856, para. 3); *id.* at 32 (Republican Platform of 1860, §§5, 8); *see generally* ERIC FONER, FREE SOIL, FREE LABOR, FREE MEN 73-102 (1970); HAROLD M. HYMAN AND WILLIAM M. WIECEK, EQUAL JUSTICE UNDER LAW 17-18, 92-93 170 (1982).

102. *See, e.g.,* M. CURTIS, *supra* note 2, 36; WILLIAM GOODELL, THE AMERICAN SLAVE CODE IN THEORY AND PRACTICE 372-84 (Negro Universities Press, 1968) (1853); H. HYMAN AND W. WIECEK, *supra* note 101, at 15, 401-2; J. TENBROEK, *supra* note 63, at 38-39, 125-26; W. WIECEK, *supra* note 94, at 182-83, 280-81.

103. *See* CONG. GLOBE, 36th Cong., 1st sess. 2595-2601 (1860) (remarks of Sen. Charles Sumner); Curtis, *1859 Crisis, supra* note 97, at 1129.

104. *See* M. CURTIS, *supra* note 2, at 23, 30-38; KENNETH M. STAMPP, THE PECULIAR INSTITUTION 211-12 (1956); Alfred Avins, *Incorporation of the Bill of Rights: The Crosskey-Fairman Debates Revisited,* 6 HARV. J. ON LEGIS. 1, 17-26 (1968); *see generally* CLEMENT EATON, THE FREEDOM OF THOUGHT STRUGGLE IN THE OLD SOUTH (1964); RUSSELL B. NYE, FETTERED FREEDOM (1963); Curtis, *Curious History, supra* note 98; Curtis, *1859 Crisis, supra* note 97.

105. *See* Curtis, *1859 Crisis, supra* note 97, at 1134-35.

106. *See* CONG. GLOBE, 39th Cong., 1st Sess. 1013 (1866) (remarks of Rep. Tobias Plants);

K. STAMPP, *supra* note 104, at 208, 211; J. TENBROEK, *supra* note 63, at 124–25; Avins, *supra* note 104, at 17; Curtis, *1859 Crisis, supra* note 97, at 1123.

107. *See* Kurt T. Lash, *The Second Adoption of the Free Exercise Clause: Religious Exemptions Under the Fourteenth Amendment*, 88 NW. U. L. REV. 1106, 1134 and n.127 (1994).

108. *See* K. STAMPP, *supra* note 104, at 132–40. For earlier fears, *see* W. WIECEK, *supra* note 94, at 123–24, 128–49.

109. *See* STEPHEN P. HALBROOK, THAT EVERY MAN BE ARMED 96–106 (1984); Robert J. Cottrol and Raymond T. Diamond, *The Second Amendment: Towards an Afro-Americanist Reconsideration*, 80 GEO. L. J. 309, 333–38 (1991).

110. *See* K. STAMPP, *supra* note 104, at 153, 188–91, 193–94, 212, 215–17; M. CURTIS, *supra* note 2, at 40, 50; THOMAS D. MORRIS, FREE MEN ALL (1974).

111. *See* Curtis, *1859 Crisis, supra* note 97, at 1162, 1171. On the clear impermissibility of warrants for books, *see* Entick v. Carrington, 95 Eng. Rep. 807 (C. P. 1765), 19 Howell's State Trials 1029 (Camden, C. J.); Eric Schnapper, *Unreasonable Searches and Seizures of Papers*, 71 VA. L. REV. 869 (1985).

112. For a nice discussion of the influence of this abolitionist theory on the Reconstruction Republicans of the Thirty-ninth Congress, *see* M. CURTIS, *supra* note 2, at 26–56; *see also* Curtis, *Curious History, supra* note 98, at 860 (outlining declaratory theory of anti-slavery leader Gerrit Smith); *see generally* William E. Nelson, *The Impact of the Anti-Slavery Movement upon Styles of Judicial Reasoning in Nineteenth Century America*, 87 HARV. L. REV. 513 (1974); Earl M. Maltz, *Fourteenth Amendment Concepts in the Antebellum Era*, 32 AM. J. LEGAL HIST. 305, 309 (1988).

113. THE ANTISLAVERY ARGUMENT 391–92 (William H. Pease and Jane H. Pease eds., 1965) (emphasis added).

114. *See, e.g.,* CONG. GLOBE, 39th Cong., 1st Sess. 1065 (1866) (remarks of Rep. John Bingham) (stressing need to protect "thousands of loyal white citizens" in the South from property confiscations and other repressive measures); Charles Fairman, *Does the Fourteenth Amendment Incorporate the Bill of Rights?*, 2 STAN. L. REV. 5, 90 (1949) (quoting October 1866 speech of Vermont Governor Paul Dillingham on need to ratify Fourteenth Amendment to "secure to the original Union men of the South equal rights and impartial liberty"); The Slaughter-House Cases, 83 U.S. (16 WALL.) 36, 123 (1873) (Bradley, J., dissenting) ("The mischief to be remedied was not merely slavery . . . [but also] that intolerance of free speech and free discussion which often rendered life and property insecure, and led to much unequal legislation."); *Ex parte* Virginia, 100 U.S. 339, 364–65 (1880) (Field, J., dissenting) (discussing importance of protecting various Northerners and Unionists in South); *see generally* S. EXEC. DOC. No. 2, 39th Cong., 1st Sess. (1865) (report of Carl Schurz) (detailing need to protect white Unionists and Yankees in the South); CHESTER JAMES ANTIEAU, THE ORIGINAL UNDERSTANDING OF THE FOURTEENTH AMENDMENT 24–25 (1981) (collecting similar quotations).

Eight. The Reconstruction Amendment: Text

1. 10 U.S. (6 Cranch) 87, 138 (1810).
2. *See* Piqua Branch of the State Bank v. Knoop, 57 U.S. (16 How.) 369, 385, 392 (1853); Cummings v. Missouri, 71 U.S. (4 Wall.) 277, 322, 325 (1866).
3. CONG. GLOBE, 42d Cong., 1st Sess. 84 app. (1871) (emphasis altered).
4. U.S. CONST. amend. I ("Congress shall make no law . . . abridging . . . .").
5. Campbell v. State, 11 Ga. 353, 366, 373 (1852).
6. U.S. Const. amend. I ("freedom" of speech and of the press; "right" to assemble and petition; "free" exercise of religion); *id.* amend. II ("right" to keep and bear arms); *id.* amend. IV ("right" against unreasonable searches and seizures); *id.* amend. VI ("right" to various procedural protections in criminal prosecutions); *id.* amend. VII ("right" to civil jury); *id.* amend. IX ("rights" retained by the people).
7. 12 OXFORD ENGLISH DICTIONARY 522 (2d ed. 1989) (defining "privilege" as, among other things, a "right, advantage, or immunity"); 7 *id.* at 691 (defining "immunity" as, among other things, "freedom from liability to taxation, jurisdiction, etc.").
8. MICHAEL KENT CURTIS, NO STATE SHALL ABRIDGE: THE FOURTEENTH AMENDMENT AND THE BILL OF RIGHTS 64–65 (1986); *see also* CHESTER JAMES ANTIEAU, THE ORIGINAL UNDERSTANDING OF THE FOURTEENTH AMENDMENT 38 (1981) ("The American generations that ratified the Constitution and, later, the Fourteenth Amendment used the terms, 'rights,' 'liberties,' 'privileges,' and 'immunities' as virtual synonyms.").
9. SECOND CONTINENTAL CONGRESS, DECLARATION OF THE CAUSES AND NECESSITY OF TAKING UP ARMS, para. 3 (1775), *reprinted in* 1 GREAT ISSUES IN AMERICAN HISTORY 46, 49 (Richard B. Hofstadter ed., 1958); THE FEDERALIST No. 84, at 513–14 (Alexander Hamilton) (Clinton Rossiter ed., 1961). For more eighteenth-century examples, *see* Robert J. Reinstein, *Completing the Constitution: The Declaration of Independence, Bill of Rights and Fourteenth Amendment*, 66 TEMPLE L. REV. 361, 401 and n.212 (1993).
10. American Ins. Co. v. Canter, 26 U.S. (1 Pet.) 511, 515, 517 (1828) (reprinting circuit opinion of Justice Johnson).
11. An Act for the Establishment of a Territorial Government in Florida, ch. 10, 3 Stat. 654, 658 (1822).
12. Treaty Between the United States of America and the Ottawa Indians of Blanchard's Fork and Roche De Boef, June 24, 1862, 12 Stat. 1237; Treaty Concerning the Cession of Russian Possession in North America by His Majesty the Emperor of all the Russias to the United States of America, March 30, 1867, 15 Stat. 539, 542; Treaty Between the United States of America and Different Tribes of Sioux Indians, April 29, 1868, 15 Stat. 635, 637; *see generally* Arnold T. Guminski, *The Rights, Privileges, and Immunities of the American People: A Disjunctive Theory of Selective Incorporation of the Bill of Rights*, 7 WHITTIER L. REV. 765, 789–90 (1985).

13. CONG. GLOBE, 39th Cong., 1st Sess. 1117 (1866) (remarks of Rep. James Wilson).

14. MD. CONST. OF 1867 (Declaration of Rights), art. 40; TEX. CONST. OF 1866, art. I, §5; *Ex Parte* Milligan, 71 U.S. (4 Wall.) 2, 122–23 (1866).

15. 1 WILLIAM BLACKSTONE, COMMENTARIES *127–45; *see also id.* at *164–65 (discussing "privilege of speech" and "freedom of speech" interchangeably and referring to "privilege" against "seizures"). These passages from Blackstone, and their implications for the Fourteenth Amendment, are thoughtfully analyzed in M. CURTIS, *supra* note 8, at 64, 74–76.

16. *See, e.g.,* Act for Declaring the Rights and Liberties of the Subject, and Settling the Succession of the Crown (Bill of Rights), 1689, 1 W. & M., ch. 2, §10 (Eng.) ("excessive bail ought not to be required, nor excessive fines imposed; nor cruel and unusual punishments inflicted"). The language of the Eighth Amendment substitutes "shall not be" for "ought not to be" but is otherwise identical.

17. Campbell v. State, 11 Ga. 353, 373, 374 (1852).

18. Dred Scott v. Sandford, 60 U.S. (19 How.) 393, 449–50, 416–17 (1857); *see also* Strauder v. West Virginia, 100 U.S. 303, 307–8, 310 (1880) (self-consciously equating "rights" and "immunities" in Fourteenth Amendment analysis); *Ex parte* Virginia, 100 U.S. 337, 345 (1880) (same); Boyd v. United States, 116 U.S. 616, 618 (1886) (invoking "privileges and immunities of the citizen" such as Fourth and Fifth Amendment rights); Downes v. Bidwell, 182 U.S. 244, 282 (1901) (referring to "immunities from unreasonable searches and seizures, as well as cruel and unusual punishments").

19. Louis Henkin, *"Selective Incorporation" in the Fourteenth Amendment,* 73 YALE L. J. 74, 78 n.16 (1963). For an earlier version of this argument, *see* Maxwell v. Dow, 176 U.S. 581, 595–96 (1900). For a powerful answer, *see id.* at 608 (Harlan, J., dissenting) (invoking the Preamble).

20. 60 U.S. at 449 (emphasis added).

21. *Id.* at 403.

22. *Id.* at 404, 410–11.

23. CONG. GLOBE, 39th Cong., 1st Sess. 430 (1866) (quoting *Dred Scott,* 60 U.S. at 404).

24. *Id.* at 3032 (quoting *Dred Scott,* 60 U.S. at 404).

25. *Id.* at 2765.

26. *See e.g., id.* at 1072 (remarks of Sen. James Nye, describing Bill of Rights as "the natural and personal rights of the citizen"); *id.* at 1153 (remarks of Rep. M. Russell Thayer) (describing due-process clause as one of "those guarantees of the Constitution of the United States which are intended for the protection of all citizens"); *id.* at 1263 (remarks of Rep. John Broomall) (describing "the right of speech," "the writ of *habeas corpus,* and the right of petition" as "the rights and immunities of citizens"); *id.* at 1118, 1294 (remarks of Rep. James Wilson) (describing "fundamental civil rights" belonging to "citizens of the United States, as such" and rights of "the citizen" "embraced in the bill of rights"); *id.* at 1832–33 (remarks of Rep. William Lawrence) (de-

scribing "bill of rights to the national Constitution" as "rights which pertain to every citizen"); *see generally* M. CURTIS, *supra* note 8, at 54, 103.

27. Nunn v. Georgia, 1 Ga. 243, 250–51 (1846); Campbell v. State, 11 Ga. 353, 365 (1852).

28. Raoul Berger, *Incorporation of the Bill of Rights in the Fourteenth Amendment: A Nine-Lived Cat,* 42 OHIO ST. L. J. 435, 462 (1981) [hereinafter *Incorporation*]; RAOUL BERGER, THE FOURTEENTH AMENDMENT AND THE BILL OF RIGHTS 91–92 (1989); *see also* D. O. McGovney, *Privileges or Immunities Clause Fourteenth Amendment,* 4 IOWA L. BULL. 219, 233 (1918); Stanley Morrison, *Does the Fourteenth Amendment Incorporate the Bill of Rights?,* 2 STAN. L. REV. 140, 159 (1949); Daniel O. Conkle, *Toward a General Theory of the Establishment Clause,* 82 NW. U. L. REV. 1113, 1137 n.119 (1983); *cf.* 1 DAVID P. CURRIE, THE CONSTITUTION IN THE SUPREME COURT 346 n.129 (1985) (due-process clause "provides another argument against incorporation; it suggests that when the drafters of the amendment meant to make bill of rights provisions apply to the states, they said so").

29. *See* Adamson v. California, 332 U.S. 46, 71–72, 74 (1947) (Black, J., dissenting); Duncan v. Louisiana, 391 U.S. 145, 166 n.1 (1968) (Black, J., concurring); *see also* Betts v. Brady, 316 U.S. 455, 474–75 and n.1 (1942) (Black, J., dissenting). Even before Black publicly announced his incorporation theory in *Betts* and *Adamson,* Justice Frankfurter, dissenting from an earlier Black opinion, anticipated and exploited Black's weak spot: "To say that the protection of freedom of speech of the First Amendment is absorbed by the Fourteenth does not say enough. Which one of the various limitations upon state power introduced by the Fourteenth Amendment absorbs the First?" Bridges v. California, 314 U.S. 252, 280–81 (1941) (Frankfurter, J., dissenting).

30. JOHN HART ELY, DEMOCRACY AND DISTRUST 27 (1980). A similar concession from a sophisticated textualist appears in Douglas Laycock, *Taking Constitutions Seriously: A Theory of Judicial Review,* 59 TEX. L. REV. 343, 348 (1981).

31. CONG. GLOBE, 39th Cong., 1st Sess. 1090 (1866).

32. *Id.* at 1292.

33. *Id.* at 2765–66.

34. On the salience of the citizen-person distinction, *see, e.g., id.* at 505, 1115, 2560, 2768–69, 2890 (remarks of Sen. Reverdy Johnson, Rep. James Wilson, and Sens. William Morris Stewart, Benjamin Wade, and Edgar Cowan); Ho Ah Kow v. Nunan, 12 F. Cas. 252, 256 (C. C. D. Cal. 1879) (No. 6,546) (Field, Circuit J.); EARL M. MALTZ, CIVIL RIGHTS, THE CONSTITUTION, AND CONGRESS, 1863–1869, at 62–64, 97 (1990); HAROLD M. HYMAN AND WILLIAM M. WIECEK, EQUAL JUSTICE UNDER LAW 411 (1982); ALAN P. GRIMES, DEMOCRACY AND THE AMENDMENTS TO THE CONSTITUTION 49 (1978); 2 WILLIAM WINSLOW CROSSKEY, POLITICS AND THE CONSTITUTION IN THE HISTORY OF THE UNITED STATES 1100–1103, 1109–10 (1953); M. CURTIS, *supra* note 8, at 107; John Harrison, *Reconstructing the Privileges or Immunities Clause,* 101 YALE L. J. 1385 (1992). On the entitlement of aliens to the "pro-

tection" of the laws, *see* CONG. GLOBE, 39TH CONG., 1st. Sess. 1757, 2890 (1866) (remarks of Sens. Lyman Trumbull and Edgar Cowan).

35. BENJAMIN B. KENDRICK, THE JOURNAL OF THE JOINT COMMITTEE OF FIFTEEN ON RECONSTRUCTION 51 (1914). On the care taken by the committee to distinguish between the rights of persons and those of citizens, *see* HORACE EDGAR FLACK, THE ADOPTION OF THE FOURTEENTH AMENDMENT 63–64 (1908).

36. CONG. GLOBE, 39TH Cong., 1st Sess. 1089 (1866).

37. 59 U.S. (18 How.) 272, 276–77 (1856); *accord* The Slaughter-House Cases, 83 U.S. (16 Wall.) 36, 118 (1873) (Bradley, J., dissenting).

38. WILLIAM RAWLE, A VIEW OF THE CONSTITUTION OF THE UNITED STATES OF AMERICA 129 (Philadelphia: H. C. Carey and I. Lea, 1825).

39. Thus, by dint of *Murray's Lessee,* aliens are entitled under the Fourteenth Amendment to all the procedural safeguards specified in the original Bill. In an otherwise thoughtful analysis of the incorporation debate, Professor Israel overlooks this, leading him to ask "why the framers of the Fourteenth Amendment would have desired to grant such privileges as jury trial and grand jury indictment only to citizens." Jerold H. Israel, *Selective Incorporation: Revisited,* 71 GEO. L. J. 253, 260 (1982). The short answer is that the framers of the Fourteenth Amendment intended exactly the opposite. The point is an especially important one because it was the only real "deficienc[y] in the textual support" for incorporation that Israel identified. *Id.; see also* Henkin, *supra* note 19, at 78 (overlooking *Murray's Lessee* in claiming that it is "clear" that "Court has not read 'due process of law' as a short-hand way of referring to specifics of the Bill of Rights").

40. U.S. CONST. amends. I, II, IV, IX, X.

41. *See, e.g.,* CONG. GLOBE, 41st Cong., 2d Sess. 1536 (1870) (remarks of Sen. Samuel Pomeroy); *see also* CONG. GLOBE, 39th Cong., 1st. Sess. 1293 (1866) (remarks of Rep. Samuel Shellabarger) (noting that petition was a right of the citizen qua citizen—as "a member of the body-politic" in contradistinction to "aliens and slaves") (quoting Sen. John C. Calhoun).

42. Some modern scholars have resisted the notion that the words of the privileges-or-immunities clause mean what they say in limiting their protection to "citizens." No less eminent a figure than John Hart Ely has suggested that the clause could instead be read as meaning that no state shall deny to any person the rights of citizens. Under this reading, the phrase "privileges or immunities of citizens" would "define the class of rights rather than limit the class of beneficiaries." J. ELY, *supra* note 30, at 25. Ely offers a false dichotomy, for the original phrase is best read as doing both, defining the rights *of* Americans *as* Americans. Ely's reading does more than stretch the phrase's text; it blurs the legislative history of the amendment and renders the due-process clause an embarrassing redundancy that incorporationists must somehow explain away. (Ely notes the redundancy, then proceeds to sidestep it. *Id.* at 27.)

Now John Ely, of all people, should know better—as a textualist, as a believer in attention to legislative purpose, and as a friend of incorporation. Something else must be going on, and it is not hard to figure out what: like Justice Black before him, Ely is obviously concerned about state mistreatment of aliens. But the concern is largely misplaced. To begin with, aliens do enjoy against states the full benefit of all procedural rights of the original Bill by dint of the Fourteenth Amendment due-process clause and *Murray's Lessee, see supra* note 39. As to other rights, equal-protection principles will require states to justify any discrimination between citizens and aliens. Finally, aliens may sometimes be able to present themselves as third-party beneficiaries of citizen rights. Just as a doctor can invoke a female patient's abortion right, so aliens addressing American citizens about national issues should be protected by the *citizens'* right to a free press and freedom of speech—rights which of course go beyond freedom to print and to speak. To me, at least, that much was decided by the judgment of the court of history against the Alien and Sedition Acts. "The essential point is not that the alien has a right to speak but that we citizens have a right to hear him." ALEXANDER MEIKLEJOHN, POLITICAL FREEDOM: THE CONSTITUTIONAL POWERS OF THE PEOPLE 53 (1960).

Gaps between citizen and alien rights against states will remain—as some must, unless the two-tiered language of section 1 is meaningless—but these are gaps that most of us (aliens included) can probably live with. An alternative approach would be to understand the intent of the Fourteenth Amendment at a slightly higher level of generality. Nothing in the two-tiered language or legislative history requires that states be more free than the federal government to abridge privileges of the Bill. These privileges were understood in 1866 to be privileges enjoyed only by citizens because of *Dred Scott*. But if this aspect of *Dred Scott* were later abolished vis-à-vis the federal government for any privilege, perhaps we should read the Fourteenth Amendment, in the spirit of dynamic conformity, to incorporate the broader under-standing of that privilege against states. As Ely rightly points out, the text can be read to include aliens; and the legislative history shows an intent to give aliens broad-er rights against states than they enjoyed against federal officials. Technical redun-dancy of the due-process clause is also avoided because the clause would have inde-pendent bite until judges repudiated *Dred Scott* on the question of alien rights vis-à-vis the federal government. Under this approach, because of subsequent legal developments, the best reading of the original privileges-or-immunities clause may have evolved into something rather similar to what Ely implies it meant all along.

43. Duncan v. Louisiana, 391 U.S. 145, 166 (1968) (Black, J., concurring).

44. *See* Berger, *Incorporation, supra* note 28, at 453; Morrison, *supra* note 28, at 159. For a far more sophisticated version of this critique, *see* J. ELY, *supra* note 30, at 28.

45. Black's critics were quick to claim that even the "ostensibly . . . 'specific'" rules laid down in the original Bill were "not very specific," Henkin, *supra* note 19, at 83–84,

86. As Professor Bobbitt has noted, however, incorporation did enable Black to substitute a longer set of words in the original Bill for the shorter set in the key sentence of section 1—no small thing to a textualist. PHILIP BOBBITT, CONSTITUTIONAL FATE 32, 246–47 (1982).

46. For a similar analysis, *see* J. ELY, *supra* note 30, at 28.

47. Various later contrarians sharply disagreed. *See* JACOBUS TENBROEK, EQUAL UNDER LAW 68, 72–73, 84 (Collier, 1965) (1951) (discussing centrality of universal habeas right in writings of Alvan Stewart, Lysander Spooner, Joel Tiffany, and James Birney).

48. Various northern states responded with personal liberty laws designed to assure alleged fugitives access to the habeas writ. *See* H. HYMAN AND W. WIECEK, *supra* note 34, at 110, 152–53; *see also id.* at 107, 150–52 (antebellum attacks on federal fugitive slave laws as violating habeas rights); M. CURTIS, *supra* note 8, at 43, 106 (importance of habeas to abolitionists).

49. *See* CONG. GLOBE, 38th Cong., 1st Sess. 1971–1972 (1864); (remarks of Rep. Glenni Scofield on need to protect habeas); *id.* 39th Cong., 1st Sess. 475, 499, 1117, 1263, 2765 (1866) (invocations of habeas by Sens. Lyman Trumbull and Edgar Cowan, Reps. James Wilson and John Broomall, and Sen. Jacob Howard); M. CURTIS, *supra* note 8, at 143–44 (noting remarks of Rep. William Lawrence in 1866 election that described habeas as paradigmatic of Fourteenth Amendment privileges or immunities); Michael Kent Curtis, *The 1859 Crisis over Hinton Helper's Book,* The Impending Crisis: *Free Speech, Slavery, and Some Light on the Meaning of the First Section of the Fourteenth Amendment,* 68 CHI.-KENT L. REV. 1113, 1172–73 (1993) (discussing federal Habeas Corpus Act of 1867 protecting against *state* deprivations of liberty); Richard L. Aynes, *On Misreading John Bingham and the Fourteenth Amendment,* 103 YALE L. J. 57, 84 (1993) (discussing 1867 treatise by Judge Timothy Farrar listing habeas as a privilege of citizens that states cannot infringe).

50. 83 U.S. (16 Wall.) 36, 79 (1873) (emphasis deleted). This concession was, however, ambiguous, *see infra* Chapter 9.

51. *See* Adamson v. California, 332 U.S. 46, 91 (1947) (Black, J., dissenting) (contrasting "particular standards enumerated in the Bill of Rights *and other parts of the Constitution*" with "'natural law' . . . *undefined by the Constitution*" (emphasis added)); *cf.* CONG. GLOBE, 39th Cong., 1st Sess. 813, 432 (1866) (Rep. John Bingham affirming need to protect "the written guarantees of the Constitution" and "all its guarantees").

52. 83 U.S. (16 Wall.) at 118 (Bradley, J., dissenting) (emphasis altered); *see also id.* at 115 ("Another of these *rights* was that of habeas corpus . . . . ") (emphasis altered).

53. On the Republican connection between the comity clause and the federal Bill, *see* William Winslow Crosskey, *Charles Fairman, "Legislative History," and the Constitutional Limitations on State Authority,* 22 U. CHI. L. REV. 1 (1954); M. CURTIS, *supra* note 8, at 43–44, 47–48, 62–91, 149–51; J. TENBROEK, *supra* note 47, at 96 n.3, 110; Aynes, *supra* note 49, at 69–85.

54. 6 F. Cas. 546, 551–51 (C. C. E. D. Pa. 1823) (No. 3,230) (Washington, Circuit J.).

55. *Id.* at 552. It is worthy of note that *Corfield*'s author, Justice Bushrod Washington, was the first president of the American Colonization Society. *See* Reinstein, *supra* note 9, at 388 n.154.

56. Campbell v. State, 11 Ga. 353, 372–73 (1852); Nunn v. Georgia, 1 Ga. 243, 250–51 (1846).

57. CONG. GLOBE, 39th Cong., 1st Sess. 474–75, 1117–19 (1866).

58. *Id.* at 2765–66.

59. Thus in his celebrated *Adamson* dissent, Black offered no account of or quotation to *Corfield*, editing out Howard's extended quotation of the case, and passing over in silence Bingham's later allusion to "that decision in the fourth of Washington's Circuit Court Reports." Adamson v. California, 332 U.S. 46, 105, 115 (1947) (Black, J., dissenting).

60. Lochner v. New York, 198 U.S. 45 (1905). *Lochner* was cited with disapproval in Black's *Adamson* dissent. 332 U.S. at 83 n.12.

61. Harrison, *supra* note 34. For similar views, *see* 1 D. CURRIE, *supra* note 28, at 347–50; WILLIAM E. NELSON, THE FOURTEENTH AMENDMENT 115–24 (1988).

62. *See supra* Chapter 7 text accompanying notes 87–90.

63. It is at this point that my conclusions differ most from those of commentators who, in effect, adopt a "Bill of Rights–plus" test for the Fourteenth Amendment, embracing both mechanical incorporation and fundamental fairness as independent principles of inclusion. *See, e.g.,* Adamson v. California, 332 U.S. 46, 123–25 (1947) (Murphy and Rutledge, JJ., dissenting); *cf.* Michael Kent Curtis, *Further Adventures of the Nine-Lived Cat: A Response to Mr. Berger on Incorporation of the Bill of Rights,* 43 OHIO ST. L. J. 89, 92, 101, 117, 118, 120 (1982) (arguing that the Fourteenth Amendment encompasses more than the Bill of Rights, and especially encompasses rights set out elsewhere in the Constitution).

64. *Cf.* J. TENBROEK, *supra* note 47, at 83.

Nine. The Reconstruction Amendment: History

1. CONG. GLOBE, 35th Cong., 2d Sess. 982 (1859).

2. *Id.* at 983–85.

3. *Id.* at 983.

4. Said Bingham: "[N]atural or inherent rights, which belong to all men irrespective of all conventional regulations, are by this constitution guarantied by the broad and comprehensive word 'person,' as contradistinguished from the limited term citizen— as in the fifth article of amendments . . . that 'no person shall be deprived of life, liberty, or property but by due process of law, nor shall private property be taken without just compensation.'" *Id.* at 983; *see also* CONG. GLOBE, 37th Cong., 2d Sess. 1638 (1862) (remarks of John Bingham) (similar). Bingham's inclusion of the takings clause in this category explains a passing proposal that he made seven years later in

the Joint Reconstruction Committee, a proposal that Charles Fairman and Raoul Berger tried to use against Bingham and incorporation. *See* Charles Fairman, *Does the Fourteenth Amendment Incorporate the Bill of Rights?*, 2 STAN. L. REV. 5, 41-42 (1949); RAOUL BERGER, GOVERNMENT BY JUDICIARY 142 (1977) [hereinafter JUDICIARY]. For other criticism of Fairman's and Berger's views on this point, *see* MICHAEL KENT CURTIS, NO STATE SHALL ABRIDGE: THE FOURTEENTH AMENDMENT AND THE BILL OF RIGHTS 83-84 (1986).

5. CONG. GLOBE, 35th Cong., 2d Sess. 983 (1859).
6. CONG. GLOBE, 39th Cong., 1st Sess. 430 (1866) (quoting *Dred Scott,* 60 U.S. at 404); *id.* at 1090.
7. CONG. GLOBE, 39th Cong., 1st Sess. 2542 (1866).
8. *See* CONG. GLOBE, 37th Cong., 2d Sess. 1638 (1862) (remarks of John Bingham); *id.* 39th Cong., 1st Sess. 1094, 1292 (1866) (remarks of John Bingham); William Winslow Crosskey, *Charles Fairman, "Legislative History," and the Constitutional Limitations on State Authority,* 22 U. CHI. L. REV. 1, 16, 25, 69 (1954); Howard Jay Graham, *The "Conspiracy Theory" of the Fourteenth Amendment,* 47 YALE L. J. 371, 396-97 and n.87 (1938); *see also infra* Chapter 11, text at notes 192-94.
9. CONG. GLOBE, 39th Cong., 1st Sess. 1088-94 (1866).
10. *Id.* at 1089-90.
11. *Id.* at 1064.
12. *Id.* at 1090 (quoting Livingston v. Moore, 32 U.S. (7 Pet.) 469, 551-52 (1833)).
13. *Id.* at 1291-93.
14. CONG. GLOBE, 39th Cong., 2d Sess. 811 (1867).
15. CONG. GLOBE, 42d Cong., 1st Sess. 84 app. (1871) (emphasis altered).
16. *Id.*
17. Fairman, *supra* note 4, at 26, 33-34, 134, 136; R. BERGER, JUDICIARY, *supra* note 4, at 141-42; Raoul Berger, *Incorporation of the Bill of Rights in the Fourteenth Amendment: A Nine-Lived Cat,* 42 OHIO ST. L. J. 435, 463 (1981) [hereinafter *Incorporation*]. For a powerful rebuttal to the general claims of Berger's article, *see* Michael Kent Curtis, *Further Adventures of the Nine-Lived Cat: A Response to Mr. Berger on Incorporation of the Bill of Rights,* 43 OHIO ST. L. J. 89 (1982).
18. CONG. GLOBE, 38th Cong., 1st Sess. 1202-3 (1864). I am especially indebted here to the work of Michael Kent Curtis, who, I believe, first brought this important Wilson passage to light. *See* M. CURTIS, *supra* note 4, at 37-38.

Hale echoed Wilson's and Bingham's sentiments on February 27, 1866:

[T]hese amendments to the Constitution, numbered from one to ten, . . . constitute the bill of rights, a bill of rights for the protection of the citizen, and defining and limiting the power of Federal and State legislation.

. . . .

... [There is much force in the reasoning that] there has been from first to last, a violation of the provisions in this bill of rights by the very existence of slavery itself ....

CONG. GLOBE, 39th Cong., 1st Sess. 1064-65 (1866).

19. *Id.* at 2459. If, as my bracketed question suggests, Stevens's statement may have been inaccurately transcribed and he in fact said "of" not "or," the word *declaration* refers not to Jefferson's document of July 4, 1776, but instead to a declaratory theory of the Constitution and Bill of Rights—whose wording does indeed match that of section 1 far more than does the wording of Jefferson's Declaration of Independence. *But see* Robert J. Reinstein, *Completing the Constitution: The Declaration of Independence, Bill of Rights, and Fourteenth Amendment,* 66 TEMPLE L. REV. 361, 389-90 (1993) (beautifully tracing analytic and historical linkages between the Declaration of Independence and section 1 of the Fourteenth Amendment).

20. CONG. GLOBE, 39th Cong., 1st Sess. 2765-66 (1866).

21. M. CURTIS, *supra* note 4, at 112.

22. Even Senators knew of Bingham's authorship and views. Senator James Doolittle, for example, reminded his colleagues that section 1 had been prepared by "Mr. Bingham," who, Doolittle recalled, had also argued that the Civil Rights Act was unconstitutional under extant case law and required a constitutional amendment (namely Bingham's) to validate it. Doolittle went on to praise Bingham's "very able speech" in the House which argued that only an amendment would suffice to "declare the civil rights of all persons" (Doolittle's paraphrase)—a speech in which Bingham invoked "the bill of rights" a half dozen times. CONG. GLOBE, 39th Cong., 1st Sess. 2896 (1866).

23. *See* Richard L. Aynes, *On Misreading John Bingham and the Fourteenth Amendment,* 103 YALE L. J. 57, 72 and n.84 (1993) (quoting N.Y. TIMES, Mar. 1, 1866, at 5, and JOHN A. BINGHAM, ONE COUNTRY, ONE CONSTITUTION, AND ONE PEOPLE: SPEECH OF HON. JOHN A. BINGHAM, OF OHIO, IN THE HOUSE OF REPRESENTATIVES, FEB. 28, 1866, IN SUPPORT OF THE PROPOSED AMENDMENT TO ENFORCE THE BILL OF RIGHTS (Washington: Cong. Globe Office, 1866)).

24. *See* JOSEPH B. JAMES, THE FRAMING OF THE FOURTEENTH AMENDMENT 125 (1956).

25. *See id.* at 135-36; Fairman, *supra* note 4, at 68-69; Crosskey, *supra* note 8, at 102-3.

26. ERIC FONER, RECONSTRUCTION 260-61 (1988).

27. *Id.* at 139.

28. Quoted *supra* text accompanying note 20.

29. CONG. GLOBE, 39th Cong., 1st Sess. 1294 (1866); *see also id.* at 1118 (remarks of Wilson) (referring to "the great fundamental civil rights" of "citizens of the United States, as such" protected by "the American Constitution").

30. *Id.* at 1760; *see also id.* at 1151-53 (remarks of Rep. Russell Thayer) (equating constitutional rights of the citizen with "fundamental" rights).

31. *Id.* at 3031.

32. Fairman, *supra* note 4, at 63.

33. CONG. GLOBE, 39th Cong., 1st Sess. 2765–66 (1866).

34. 39 U.S. (14 Pet.) 540, 556–57 (1840); Nunn v. Georgia, 1 Ga. 243, 250–51 (1846); Campbell v. State, 11 Ga. 353, 372–73 (1852); *see supra* Chapter 8, text accompanying note 56; *see also* Young v. McKenzie, 3 Ga. 31, 44 (1847) (just compensation norm "applicable to all republican governments").

35. On the importance of war rhetoric stressing the need for national protection as the counterpart to national allegiance, *see* Daniel A. Farber and John E. Muench, *The Ideological Origins of the Fourteenth Amendment,* 1 CONST. COMMENTARY 235, 266–69, 276–77 (1984).

36. THE DECLARATION OF INDEPENDENCE para. 32 (U.S. 1776); 1 JEFFERSON DAVIS, THE RISE AND FALL OF THE CONFEDERATE GOVERNMENT 86 (T. Yoseloff) (1958 1881). For a powerful exposition of the high place of honor nevertheless held by the Declaration among antebellum antislavery crusaders and Reconstruction Republicans, *see* Reinstein, *supra* note 19. And for a brilliant discussion of Lincoln's use of the Declaration, *see* GARRY WILLS, LINCOLN AT GETTYSBURG (1992).

37. *See* 1 J. DAVIS, *supra* note 36, at 99–120. *But see* Akhil Reed Amar, *Of Sovereignty and Federalism,* 96 YALE L. J. 1425, 1444–66 (1987) (rejecting secessionist interpretation of Founding).

38. *See* CONG. GLOBE, 39th Cong. 1st Sess. 1090 (1866) (remarks of Rep. John Bingham proclaiming that the Bill of Rights "more than any other provision of the Constitution, makes that unity of government which constitutes us one people").

39. *Id.* at 1034.

40. *Id.* at 1090.

41. *Id.* at 1090–94; *cf. id.* at 1034 (remarks of Bingham on "immortal" bill of rights).

42. HUGO LAFAYETTE BLACK, A CONSTITUTIONAL FAITH at xvi–xvii, 34–42 (1968).

43. Though technically civil, suits involving alleged fugitive slaves implicated bodily liberty more dramatically than most criminal cases.

44. CONG. GLOBE, 39th Cong., 1st Sess. 1072 (1866).

45. *Id.* at 1629.

46. *Id.* at 1617, 1838–39, 1621.

47. Fairman, *supra* note 4, at 139.

48. RAOUL BERGER, THE FOURTEENTH AMENDMENT AND THE BILL OF RIGHTS 22 (1989) [hereinafter FOURTEENTH AMENDMENT]; *cf.* Fairman, *supra* note 4, at 44 (suggesting "correspondence" and "essential[] identi[ty]" between act and section 1).

49. R. BERGER, FOURTEENTH AMENDMENT, *supra* note 48, at 115–19.

50. Plainly, the act was intended to protect only citizens, *see, e.g.,* CONG. GLOBE, 39th Cong., 1st Sess. 1115, 1294 (1866) (remarks of Rep. James Wilson). For much more documentation, *see supra* Chapter 8, note 34.

51. *See supra* Chapter 6.

52. *Compare* Fairman, *supra* note 4, at 81–132 *with* M. CURTIS, *supra* note 4, at 131–53.

53. Fairman, *supra* note 4, at 82–83.

54. *Id.* at 84–85 (Connecticut), 97 (Ohio), 98–100 (Illinois), 101 (Kansas), 103 (Missouri), 106 (Indiana), 110–11 (Wisconsin), 115–16 (Michigan), 123 (Nebraska), 125 (California).

55. *Id.* at 98–100, 116 (citation omitted).

56. *Id.* at 82–83, 111, 137.

57. Jones v. Robbins, 74 Mass. (8 Gray) 329, 343–44 (1857) (emphasis added).

58. *Id.* at 340.

59. EDWARD COKE, THE SECOND PART OF THE INSTITUTES OF THE LAWS OF ENGLAND *50–51.

60. *See supra* Chapter 5, note 62; A. E. DICK HOWARD, THE ROAD FROM RUNNYMEDE 158–59, 422 (1968); 2 THE LEGAL PAPERS OF JOHN ADAMS 200–201 (L. Kinvin Wroth and Hiller B. Zobel eds., 1965). *See generally* M. CURTIS, *supra* note 4, at 181–82.

61. 3 JOSEPH STORY, COMMENTARIES ON THE CONSTITUTION OF THE UNITED STATES §1783, at 661 (Boston: Hilliard, Gray, 1833) (citations omitted).

62. 2 JAMES KENT, COMMENTARIES ON AMERICAN LAW 13 (New York: Clayton and Van Norden, 2d ed., 1832) (citations omitted).

63. *In re* Booth, 3 Wis. 1, 66 (1854).

64. Ableman v. Booth, 62 U.S. (21 How.) 506, 526 (1859).

65. Jones v. Robbins, 74 Mass. (8 Gray) 329, 343, 346 (1857). For similar discussions linking due process with grand jury indictment, see State v. Keeran, 5 R.I. 497, 505–6 (1858); State v. Paul, 5 R.I. 185, 197 (1858); Greene v. Briggs, 10 F. Cas. 1135, 1140 (C. C. D. R. I. 1852) (No. 5,764) (Curtis, Circuit J.); Taylor v. Porter, 4 Hill 140, 146 (N.Y. Sup. Ct. 1843).

66. ALVAN STEWART, A CONSTITUTIONAL ARGUMENT ON THE SUBJECT OF SLAVERY (1837), *reprinted in* JACOBUS TENBROEK, EQUAL UNDER LAW 281, 283 (Collier, 1965) (1951).

67. Murray's Lessee v. Hoboken Land and Improvement Co., 59 U.S. (18 How.) 272, 276 (1856). *See also* Dred Scott v. Sandford, 60 U.S. (19 How.) 393, 626–27 (1857) (Curtis, J., dissenting) (similar).

68. *Cf.* Rowan v. State, 30 Wis. 129 (1872) (rejecting claim that "due process" requires grand juries in unique context of state constitutional amendment eliminating specific reference to grand jury while substituting general due-process language).

69. Justice Frankfurter once claimed that the due-process clause would be an "extraordinarily strange" way of requiring grand juries. Adamson v. California, 332 U.S. 46, 63 (1947) (Frankfurter, J., concurring). What seems even stranger, however, is Frankfurter's apparent ignorance of the history of the phrase, given all his breastbeating about Anglo-American legal traditions.

70. For a possible explanation, *see infra* page 207, note.

71. In light of Fairman's pointed emphasis on Orville Browning's failure to invoke the Fourteenth Amendment in 1869–70, perhaps some additional details that Fairman omitted should be noted. In 1866, while the amendment was still pending, Browning, as President Johnson's secretary of interior, led the administration's charge against ratification. In a widely influential document, Browning argued that the amendment's due-process clause would "subordinate the State judiciaries to Federal supervision" and "totally annihilate the independence and sovereignty of State judiciaries in the administration of State laws." M. CURTIS, *supra* note 4, at 151–52. These facts put Browning's later conduct in a rather different light from that offered by Professor Fairman.

72. *See, e.g.,* EARL M. MALTZ, CIVIL RIGHTS, THE CONSTITUTION, AND CONGRESS, 1863–1869, at 79–81 (1990). Various Democrats in Congress objected unsuccessfully to this Republican bundling of separable issues. *See* J. JAMES, *supra* note 24, at 148–49.

73. Quoted *supra* text accompanying note 19.

74. CONG. GLOBE, 39th Cong., 1st Sess. 2459 (1866).

75. *Id.* at 2544. Section 3 was later amended. *Id.* at 2869; J. JAMES, *supra* note 24, at 142.

76. *See* M. CURTIS, *supra* note 4, at 13–15, 131; HORACE EDGAR FLACK, THE ADOPTION OF THE FOURTEENTH AMENDMENT 208–9 (1908); E. FONER, *supra* note 26, at 257, 268–70; BENJAMIN B. KENDRICK, THE JOURNAL OF THE JOINT COMMITTEE OF FIFTEEN ON RECONSTRUCTION 348–52 (1914); E. MALTZ, *supra* note 72, at 93; Alfred Avins, *Incorporation of the Bill of Rights: The Crosskey-Fairman Debates Revisited,* 6 HARV. J. ON LEGIS. 1, 9 (1968); Crosskey, *supra* note 8, at 112; *see also* ALAN P. GRIMES, DEMOCRACY AND THE AMENDMENTS TO THE CONSTITUTION 44–47 (1987) (noting centrality of sections 2 and 3 in House and Senate debates). In retrospect, because of underenforcement, evasion, and amnesty, these provisions ended up playing a much smaller role than originally anticipated.

77. *See* WILLIAM E. NELSON, THE FOURTEENTH AMENDMENT 93–96 (1988); JOSEPH B. JAMES, THE RATIFICATION OF THE FOURTEENTH AMENDMENT (1984).

78. J. JAMES, *supra* note 24, at 150; *see also* H. FLACK, *supra* note 76, at 121.

79. M. CURTIS, *supra* note 4, at 6.

80. *See generally id., passim;* Crosskey, *supra* note 8.

81. In addition to the various sources quoted earlier, *see, e.g.,* CONG. GLOBE, 39th Cong., 1st Sess. 2468 (1866) (remarks of Rep. William Kelley) ("if [provisions of section 1] are not already" in the Constitution, they should be); *id.* at 2539 (remarks of Rep. John Farnsworth) (privileges-or-immunities and due-process clauses of section 1 are "reaffirmation" and "surplusage"); *id.* at 256 app. (remarks of Rep. Jehu Baker) (section 1 is "more valuable for clearing away bad interpretations . . . of the Constitution . . . than for any positive grant of new power"); *id.* at 340 (remarks of Sen. Edgar Cowan) (suggesting Fifth Amendment due process restricts states); *id.* at 1833 (re-

marks of Rep. William Lawrence) (similar); *id.* at 1151–52 (remarks of Rep. Russell Thayer) (similar); *id.* at 1294 and 157 app. (remarks of Rep. James Wilson) (similar).

82. H. R. Doc. No. 149, Mass. Gen. Ct. 1–4 (1867).

83. *See, e.g.*, CHESTER JAMES ANTIEAU, THE ORIGINAL UNDERSTANDING OF THE FOURTEENTH AMENDMENT 62–70 (1981); M. CURTIS, *supra* note 4, at 149–52; E. MALTZ, *supra* note 72, at 116; W. NELSON, *supra* note 77, at 104–9. On the possibly broad power of Congress to enforce section 1, see C. ANTIEAU, at 40–42, 55–56.

84. 5 U.S. (1 Cranch) 137 (1803).

85. Dred Scott v. Sandford, 60 U.S. (19 How.) 393, 450–52 (1857).

86. *See, e.g.*, Fletcher v. Peck, 10 U.S. (6 Cranch) 87 (1810); Martin v. Hunter's Lessee, 14 U.S. (1 Wheat.) 304 (1816); McCulloch v. Maryland, 17 U.S. (4 Wheat.) 316 (1819); Dartmouth College v. Woodward, 17 U.S. (4 Wheat.) 518 (1819); Gibbons v. Ogden, 22 U.S. (9 Wheat.) 1 (1824); Osborn v. Bank of the United States, 22 U.S. (9 Wheat.) 738 (1824); Prigg v. Pennsylvania, 41 U.S. (16 Pet.) 539 (1842).

87. Twitchell v. Pennsylvania, 74 U.S. (7 Wall.) 321 (1869).

88. Felix Frankfurter, *Memorandum on "Incorporation" of the Bill of Rights into the Due Process Clause of the Fourteenth Amendment*, 78 HARV. L. REV. 746, 750 (1965).

89. R. BERGER, JUDICIARY, *supra* note 4, at 153.

90. Fairman, *supra* note 4, at 132–33; *see also* Wallace Mendelson, *Mr. Justice Black's Fourteenth Amendment*, 53 MINN. L. REV. 711, 721 (1969).

91. 74 U.S. (7 Wall.) at 321, 323–26.

92. *See generally* M. CURTIS, *supra* note 4, at 154–70. Professor Fairman tried to point to various congressional decisions between 1866 and 1870 that he claimed were implicitly inconsistent with incorporation. Fairman, *supra* note 4, at 122–32. In admitting or readmitting states, Congress (claimed Fairman) appeared to approve without comment various state constitutions that did not perfectly comport with the federal Bill of Rights. Once again, Fairman's chief evidence focused on silence about grand juries. As we have already seen, this argument proves nothing more than the silliness of Fairman's method in drawing strong inference from mere silence. What's more, the alleged inconsistencies Fairman points to are truly de minimis in light of the basic facial consistency of these state constitutions with the privileges and immunities of the federal Bill of Rights. Given this basic consistency and the centrality of many other factors in the (re)admission process, it is unsurprising that little attention was paid to microscopic details about the precise incidents and triggers of grand juries. For similar responses to Fairman on this point see E. MALTZ, *supra* note 72, at 116–17; Crosskey, *supra* note 8, at 85–88.

93. CONG. GLOBE, 42d Cong., 2d. Sess. 844 (1872).

94. Cummings v. Missouri, 71 U.S. (4 Wall.) 277, 313 (1867).

95. 17 Stat. 13.

96. M. CURTIS, *supra* note 4, at 166–68.

97. United States v. Hall, 26 F. Cas. 79, 82 (C. C. S. D. Ala. 1871) (No. 15,282).

98. *Id.* at 81. Several early federal prosecutors seemed to follow Wood's approach. *See* ROBERT J. KACZOROWSKI, THE POLITICS OF JUDICIAL INTERPRETATION: THE FEDERAL COURTS, DEPARTMENT OF JUSTICE, AND CIVIL RIGHTS, 1866–1876, at 125–30 (1985); *see also* State *ex rel.* The St. Joseph & Denver City R. R. v. Commissioners of Nemaha County, 7 Kan. 542, 555 (1871) (Brewer, J., dissenting) (describing bill of rights as "those essential truths, those axioms of civil and political liberty upon which all free governments are founded"); State *ex rel.* Liversey v. Judge of Civil Dist. Ct., 34 La. Ann. 741, 743 (1882) (bill of rights "declaratory of the general principles of republican government, and of the fundamental rights of the citizen").

99. Live-stock Dealers & Butchers' Ass'n v. Crescent City Live-stock Landing & Slaughter-House Co., 15 F. Cas. 649, 652 (C. C. D. La. 1870) (No. 8,408).

100. R. KACZOROWSKI, *supra* note 98, at 16. I am grateful to Professor Kaczorowski for supplying me with a photocopy of this March 12, 1871, letter.

101. Letter of January 3, 1871 (photocopy on file with author).

102. PROCEEDINGS IN THE KU KLUX TRIALS AT COLUMBIA, S.C., IN THE UNITED STATES CIRCUIT COURT, NOVEMBER TERM, 1871, at 147 (Columbia: Republican Printing, 1872) (discussing United States v. Mitchell, 26 F. Cas. 1283 (C. C. D. S. C. 1871) (No. 15,790)).

103. Aynes, *supra* note 23, at 83–94.

104. JOHN NORTON POMEROY, AN INTRODUCTION TO THE CONSTITUTIONAL LAW OF THE UNITED STATES 151, 147 (New York: Hurd and Houghton, 1870) (1868); TIMOTHY FARRAR, MANUAL OF THE CONSTITUTION OF THE UNITED STATES OF AMERICA 58–59, 145, 395–97 (Boston: Little, Brown, 1867); *id.* at 546 (3d ed., Boston: Little, Brown, 1872).

105. GEORGE W. PASCHAL, THE CONSTITUTION OF THE UNITED STATES 290 (Washington: W. H. and O. H. Morrison, 1868). Also revealing is Paschal's cross-referencing of the Bill of Rights and the "privileges and immunities" language of Article IV.

106. 83 U.S. (16 Wall.) 36 (1873); *see also* Blyew v. United States, 80 U.S. (13 Wall.) 581, 596 (1872) (Bradley, J., dissenting) (Civil Rights Bill of 1866 designed to protect blacks in "having firearms, . . . exercising the functions of a minister of the gospel, . . . [in] being taught to read and write," and against "laws which subjected them to cruel and ignominious punishments not imposed upon white persons").

107. 83 U.S. (16 Wall.) at 114–18 (Bradley, J., dissenting) (emphasis added).

108. *Id.* at 118.

109. *Id.* at 121–22.

110. *Id.* at 96–111 (Field, J., dissenting).

111. *Id.* at 79 (Miller, J.) (emphasis deleted).

112. *Cf.* JOHN HART ELY, DEMOCRACY AND DISTRUST 196 n.59 (1980) (suggesting broad incorporationist reading of Miller's language).

113. *See* 2 WILLIAM WINSLOW CROSSKEY, POLITICS AND THE CONSTITUTION IN THE HISTORY OF THE UNITED STATES 1128–30 (1953); Richard L. Aynes, *Constricting*

the Law of Freedom: Justice Miller, the Fourteenth Amendment and the Slaughter-House Cases, 70 CHI.-KENT L. REV. 627, 653–55 (1994).

114. 83 U.S. (16 Wall.) at 96 (Field, J., dissenting).

115. McCulloch v. Maryland, 17 U.S. (4 Wheat.) 316 (1819) (striking down state interference with federal bank).

116. See, for example, the list of cases compiled in Frankfurter, *supra* note 88. Upon close inspection, the list is less impressive than it looks. Many of the cited passages simply reject the claim that a provision of the original Bill applied *of its own force* against states—technically, a quite different claim from one based on incorporation (or what have you) via the Fourteenth Amendment. This is no mere pedantic quibble, for the Court took this pleading technicality quite seriously for many years, as illustrated by both *Twitchell v. Pennsylvania*, 74 U.S. (7 Wall.) 321 (1869) (discussed *supra* text accompanying notes 87–91), and *Palmer v. Ohio*, 248 U.S. 32, 34 (1918) (dismissing Fifth Amendment just-compensation claim against state as "palpably groundless" even though the Court had earlier incorporated "just compensation" principle into Fourteenth Amendment in *Chicago, B. & Q. R. R. v. Chicago*, 166 U.S. 226 (1897)). Indeed, in the most important case Frankfurter himself cites, the Court, after quickly dismissing the *Barron* argument, treats the same basic claim, repackaged as a Fourteenth Amendment argument, with much greater attention. Spies v. Illinois, 123 U.S. 131, 165–67 (1887); *see also* Miller v. Texas, 153 U.S. 535, 538 (1894) (similar).

117. *Spies*, 123 U.S. at 150–52 (oral argument of John Randolph Tucker); O'Neil v. Vermont, 144 U.S. 323, 360–64 (1892) (Field, J., dissenting); Maxwell v. Dow, 176 U.S. 581, 605–17 (1900) (Harlan, J., dissenting); Patterson v. Colorado, 205 U.S. 454, 463–65 (1907) (Harlan, J., dissenting); Twining v. New Jersey, 211 U.S. 78, 114–27 (1908) (Harlan, J., dissenting). The foregoing passages are identified as "landmarks" not because they support my analysis (although they do), but because they constitute virtually the only extended discussion in the *United States Reports* between *Slaughter-House* and *Adamson* of the relationship (or lack thereof) between the federal bill and the privileges-or-immunities clause.

For a similar analysis under the due-process clause, *see* Hurtado v. California, 110 U.S. 516, 546 (1884) (Harlan, J., dissenting). For a beautifully clear exposition of the idea that "the several rights guaranteed by the first eight amendments" were protected by the Fourteenth, which thus overruled *Barron*, see the pre-*O'Neil* article, Charles R. Pence, *The Construction of the Fourteenth Amendment*, 25 AM. L. REV. 536, 537 (1891). "[T]he fourteenth amendment was designed to protect from State abridgment those fundamental rights which were esteemed so valuable as to be incorporated in the constitution of the United States." *Id.* at 550.

118. Adamson v. California, 332 U.S. 46, 120–23 (1947) (Black, J., dissenting). Justice Black omitted specific reference to Justice Harlan's dissent in *Patterson* but cited other similar Harlan opinions.

Ten. Refining Incorporation

1. Indeed, before undergoing stylistic surgery in the Senate, the amendment as passed by the House in 1789 read as follows: "A well regulated militia, composed of the body of the People, being the best security of a free state, the right of the People to keep and bear arms, shall not be infringed . . . . " EDWARD DUMBAULD, THE BILL OF RIGHTS AND WHAT IT MEANS TODAY 214 (1957).

2. See supra Chapter 3 (linking reference to "the people" in Second Amendment to references to "the people"—paradigmatically, voters—in Preamble and Article I, section 2).

3. See, e.g., Burton v. Sills, 248 A.2d 521 (N.J. 1968), appeal dismissed, 394 U.S. 812 (1969); Quilici v. Village of Morton Grove, 695 F.2d 261 (7th Cir. 1982), cert. denied, 464 U.S. 863 (1983).

4. See supra Chapter 2.

5. Louis Henkin, "Selective Incorporation" in the Fourteenth Amendment, 73 YALE L. J. 74, 76 (1963); LOUIS LUSKY, BY WHAT RIGHT? 163 (1975); see also Jerold H. Israel, Selective Incorporation: Revisited, 71 GEO. L. J. 253, 272 & n.138 (1982).

6. Henkin, supra note 5, at 77–78; Henry J. Friendly, The Bill of Rights as a Code of Criminal Procedure, 53 CAL. L. REV. 929, 934 (1965) (citation omitted); see also MICHAEL KENT CURTIS, NO STATE SHALL ABRIDGE: THE FOURTEENTH AMENDMENT AND THE BILL OF RIGHTS 112 (1986) ("[I]t is difficult to see a logical basis for eliminating some guarantees but not others."); L. LUSKY, supra note 5, at 163 (selective incorporation has "no conceivable historical basis").

7. In addition to the Second Amendment cases cited supra note 3, see, e.g., Gyuro v. Connecticut, 242 A.2d 734 (Conn.), cert. denied, 393 U.S. 937 (1968) (grand jury); Melancon v. McKeithen, 345 F. Supp. 1025 (E. D. La. 1972), aff'd, 409 U.S. 943 (1972) (over dissent of Douglas, J.) (civil jury); see also Beck v. Washington, 369 U.S. 541, 545 (1962) (opinion of the Court, including Justice Brennan, endorsing long-standing Supreme Court case law that states may "dispens[e] entirely" with grand juries).

8. See supra Chapter 3.

9. See supra Chapter 2.

10. No one recognized the special awkwardness of incorporating the establishment clause better than Brennan, as shown by his concurrence in Abington School Dist. v. Schempp, 374 U.S. 203, 254–58 (1963) (Brennan, J., concurring).

11. William J. Brennan, Jr., The Bill of Rights and the States: The Revival of State Constitutions as Guardians of Individual Rights, 61 N.Y.U. L. REV. 535, 545 (1986).

12. Friendly, supra note 6, at 936; Henkin, supra note 5, at 82.

13. See, e.g., L. LUSKY, supra note 5, at 162–63; Henkin, supra note 5, at 76; Israel, supra note 5, at 272 and n.138; see also HUGO LAFAYETTE BLACK, A CONSTITUTIONAL FAITH at xvi–xvii, 36 (1968) ("[m]ost of those who object to complete incorporation of the Bill of Rights point to the Seventh Amendment" as "objectionable"); Adam-

son v. California, 332 U.S. 46, 63–65 (1947) (Frankfurter, J., concurring) (jaundiced view of civil juries); Charles Fairman, *Does the Fourteenth Amendment Incorporate the Bill of Rights?*, 2 STAN. L. REV. 5, 82–83, 137 (1949) (similar); Erwin N. Griswold, *Due Process Problems Today in the United States, in* THE FOURTEENTH AMENDMENT 161, 166 (Bernard Schwartz ed., 1970) (similar).

14. LEONARD W. LEVY, EMERGENCE OF A FREE PRESS 281 (1985). At times Levy appears to hedge this suggestion, *see id.* at 268–73.

15. Of the original thirteen colonies, only Pennsylvania explicitly guaranteed "freedom of speech" for citizens in its constitution, in a provision also declaring that "freedom of the press ought not to be restrained." PA. CONST. OF 1776 (Declaration of Rights), art. XII; L. LEVY, *supra* note 14, at 5. The federal Bill, of course, changed "ought" to "shall." *See* IRVING BRANT, THE BILL OF RIGHTS 37–42 (1965).

16. This is hardly a novel claim. *See, e.g.,* 1 BLACKSTONE'S COMMENTARIES app. 17 (St. George Tucker ed., Philadelphia: Burch and Small, 1803).

17. Thus Madison's original proposed amendment read as follows: "The people shall not be deprived or abridged of their right to speak, to write, or to publish their sentiments; and the freedom of the press, as one of the great bulwarks of liberty, shall be inviolable." E. DUMBAULD, *supra* note 1, at 207.

18. For a similar analysis, *see* William T. Mayton, *Seditious Libel and the Lost Guarantee of a Freedom of Expression,* 84 COLUM. L. REV. 91, 120 n.154 (1984); Richard A. Posner, *Free Speech in an Economic Perspective,* 20 SUFFOLK U. L. REV. 1, 4 (1986).

19. 2 BERNARD SCHWARTZ, THE BILL OF RIGHTS: A DOCUMENTARY HISTORY 1028–29 (1971) (June 8, 1789). Madison returned to this theme in much greater detail a decade later in his careful exposition of the unconstitutionality of the Sedition Act. *See* James Madison, *Report on the Virginia Resolutions* (Jan. 1800), *reprinted in* 4 DEBATES ON THE ADOPTION OF THE FEDERAL CONSTITUTION 546, 569–71 (Jonathan Elliot ed., AYER Co. reprint ed., 1987) (1836); *see also* 4 ANNALS OF CONG. 934 (1794) (remarks of James Madison) ("If we advert to the nature of Republican Government, we shall find that the censorial power is in the people over the Government, and not in the Government over the people.").

20. For an elegant and persuasive exemplar of this approach in the context of speech and press rights, *see* David M. Rabban, *The Ahistorical Historian: Leonard Levy on Freedom of Expression in Early American History,* 37 STAN. L. REV. 795 (1985).

21. *See, e.g.,* 1 THE WORKS OF JAMES WILSON 335, 353–54 (Robert Green McCloskey ed., 1967).

22. *See supra* Chapter 7.

23. Holmes v. Jennison, 39 U.S. (14 Pet.) 540, 555 (1840) (oral argument).

24. *Id.* at 555–57.

25. CONG. GLOBE, 35th Cong., 2d Sess. 984 (1859) (emphasis added).

26. CONG. GLOBE, 39th Cong., 1st Sess. 1294, 1072–75 (1866) (remarks of Rep. James Wil-

son and Sen. James Nye) (emphasis added). For similar formulations, see M. CUR-
TIS, *supra* note 6, at 54.

27. Quoted *supra* Chapter 8, text at note 3; page 183, note; Chapter 9 text at notes
16, 20.

28. Quoted *supra* Chapter 9 text at notes 16, 20 (emphasis added).

29. The Slaughter-House Cases, 83 U.S. (16 Wall.) 36, 118 (1873) (Bradley, J., dissenting)
(emphasis omitted).

30. *Id.* (emphasis altered).

31. Spies v. Illinois, 123 U.S. 131, 151 (1887) (oral argument) (emphasis omitted).

32. *Id.* (emphasis added).

33. *Id.* at 152 (attempting to distinguish *Hurtado v. California,* 110 U.S. 516 (1884), and
Walker v. Sauvinet, 92 U.S. 90 (1875), which had rejected Fourteenth Amendment
incorporation of the Bill's grand jury and civil jury requirements against states).

34. O'Neil v. Vermont, 144 U.S. 323, 361 (1892) (Field, J., dissenting).

35. *Id.* at 363.

36. *Id.* at 362.

37. Maxwell v. Dow, 176 U.S. 581, 614-15 (1900) (Harlan, J., dissenting).

38. *Id.* at 615.

39. *Id.* at 615-16 (emphasis added).

40. *Id.* at 607, 608, 612, 617; *see also* Spies v. Illinois, 123 U.S. 131, 151 (1887) (Tucker's oral
argument); *O'Neil,* 144 U.S. at 361-63 (Field, J., dissenting).

41. Twining v. New Jersey, 211 U.S. 78, 117-18 (1908) (Harlan, J., dissenting).

42. *Id.* at 118.

43. *Id.* at 117, 122; *see also* Patterson v. Colorado, 205 U.S. 454, 463-65 (1907) (Harlan, J., dissenting), where Justice Harlan noted that the First Amendment, "although in form pro-
hibitory, is to be regarded as having a reflex [i.e., declaratory] character and as affirma-
tively recognizing freedom of speech and freedom of the press as rights belonging to
citizens of the United States." Because these rights were declared "attributes of national citizenship," they were, Harlan argued, clearly protected against state action by the
Fourteenth Amendment, which "prohibited the States from impairing or abridging the
privileges of citizens of the United States." *Id.* For a similar analysis under the due
process clause, *see* Hurtado v. California, 110 U.S. 516, 546 (1884) (Harlan, J., dissenting)
(inclusion of a right in the federal Bill is itself decisive evidence of its fundamental nature, reflecting the People's "judgment" that the right "was a fundamental principle in
liberty and justice" that lay "at the foundation of our civil and political institutions").

Eleven. Reconstructing Rights

1. *See supra* Chapter 8.

2. 1 WILLIAM BLACKSTONE, COMMENTARIES *143 (petition and assembly); 4 *id.* at *152
(press).

3. *See supra* Chapter 2.

4. *See supra* Chapter 2, note 95.

5. In discussing the "reflex character" of the First Amendment as declaratory of principles applicable against states, the first Justice Harlan also noted that the amendment's principles bound not just Congress but also federal courts. *See* Patterson v. Colorado, 205 U.S. 454, 464 (1907) (Harlan, J., dissenting).

6. *See* WILLIAM W. VAN ALSTYNE, INTERPRETATIONS OF THE FIRST AMENDMENT 43–46 (1984).

7. *See, e.g.,* Oregon v. Mitchell, 400 U.S. 112 (1970).

8. *See generally* CLEMENT EATON, THE FREEDOM-OF-THOUGHT STRUGGLE IN THE OLD SOUTH (rev. ed. 1964); RUSSELL B. NYE, FETTERED FREEDOM (1963); W. SHERMAN SAVAGE, THE CONTROVERSY OVER THE DISTRIBUTION OF ABOLITION LITERATURE, 1830–1860 (1938); ERIC FONER, FREE SOIL, FREE LABOR, FREE MEN 100–101, 122–23 (1970); HAROLD M. HYMAN AND WILLIAM M. WIECEK, EQUAL JUSTICE UNDER LAW 118–19 (1982); WILLIAM E. NELSON, THE FOURTEENTH AMENDMENT 42–43 (1988); WILLIAM M. WIECEK, THE SOURCES OF ANTISLAVERY CONSTITUTIONALISM IN AMERICA 1760–1848, at 172–88 (1977); Howard Jay Graham, *The Early Antislavery Backgrounds of the Fourteenth Amendment,* 1950 WIS. L. REV. 479, 610, 632–47; William E. Nelson, *The Impact of the Antislavery Movement upon Styles of Judicial Reasoning in Nineteenth Century America,* 87 HARV. L. REV. 513, 533–37 (1974); *see also* sources cited *supra* Chapter 7, notes 103–7.

Perhaps the most dramatic incident occurred in 1856 on the floor of the U.S. Senate, where South Carolina Congressman Preston Brooks attacked the defenseless Massachusetts Senator Charles Sumner with a cane and beat him into bloody unconsciousness in retaliation for an antislavery speech Sumner had made on the floor of the Senate a few days earlier. Many northerners were shocked, but many southern citizens and governments applauded Brooks's action, sending him complimentary canes and bullwhips.

9. MICHAEL KENT CURTIS, NO STATE SHALL ABRIDGE: THE FOURTEENTH AMENDMENT AND THE BILL OF RIGHTS 32 (1986); *see also* NATIONAL PARTY PLATFORMS 1840–1968, at 7 (Kirk H. Porter and Donald Bruce Johnson eds., 3rd ed., 1966) (Liberty Platform of 1844 condemning "all rules, regulations and laws, in derogation" of "freedom of speech and of the press, and the right of petition," rights labeled "sacred and inviolable").

In 1860 Senate Republicans unanimously supported a resolution that no state could abridge "freedom of speech and of the press, on [slavery] and every other subject of domestic and national policy." *See* Michael Kent Curtis, *The 1859 Crisis over Hinton Helper's Book,* The Impending Crisis: *Free Speech, Slavery, and Some Light on the Meaning of the First Section of the Fourteenth Amendment,* 68 CHI.-KENT L. REV. 1113, 1157–58 (1993) [hereinafter *1859 Crisis*].

10. *See, e.g.,* CONG. GLOBE, 38th Cong., 1st Sess. 114, 1202, 1313, 1369, 1439, 1971–72, 2615, 2979, 2990 (1864) (remarks of Reps. Isaac Arnold and James Wilson, Sens. Lyman Trumbull, Daniel Clark, and James Harlan, and Reps. Glenni Scofield, Daniel Morris, John Farnsworth, and Ebon Ingersoll); CONG. GLOBE 38th Cong., 2d Sess. 138, 193, 237 (1864) (remarks of Reps. James Ashley, John Kasson, and Green Smith); CONG. GLOBE, 39th Cong., 1st Sess. 167, 474–75, 783, 1013, 1066, 1072, 1263, 1293, 1617, 142 app., 2332 (1866) (remarks of Sens. Timothy Howe and Lyman Trumbull, Reps. Hamilton Ward, Tobias Plants, and Hiram Price, Sen. James Nye, Reps. John Broomall, Samuel Shellabarger, and Samuel Moulton, and Sens. Henry Wilson and James Dixon). As is true of much else in Part Two, this compilation owes a great debt to the work of Michael Kent Curtis.

11. *See, e.g.,* CONG. GLOBE, 39th Cong., 1st Sess. 337, 436, 494 (1866) (petitions presented by Sens. Charles Sumner, Lyman Trumbull, and Jacob Howard).

12. HORACE E. FLACK, THE ADOPTION OF THE FOURTEENTH AMENDMENT 42, 143 (1908).

13. CHESTER JAMES ANTIEAU, THE ORIGINAL UNDERSTANDING OF THE FOURTEENTH AMENDMENT 32 (1981).

14. *Id.* at 24 (Bingham and Rep. Columbus Delano); CURTIS, *supra* note 9, at 138–39, 144–45 (Bingham, Wilson, Delano, Reps. William D. Kelley and William Boyd Allison, and Sen. Richard Yates); FLACK, *supra* note 12, at 149 (Colfax).

15. C. ANTIEAU, *supra* note 13, at 24–25, 30–33; M. CURTIS, *supra* note 9, at 140, 145–53.

16. *See, e.g.,* M. CURTIS, *supra* note 9, at 135 (quoting appeal from convention of southern loyalists denouncing slave-state violations of "constitutional guarantees of the right to peaceably assemble and petition for redress of grievances" and of "constitutional guarantees of freedom and free speech and a free press"); ERIC FONER, RECONSTRUCTION 113 (1988) (discussing South Carolina colored convention of 1865, which affirmed the rights of speech, press, petition, and assembly, *see infra* text at note 59); W. E. BURGHARDT DU BOIS, BLACK RECONSTRUCTION IN AMERICA 230–35 (Russell and Russell, 1962) (1935) (discussing black conventions more generally).

17. On Zenger, see *supra* Chapter 2; on Callender, see *supra* Chapter 5.

18. For an account, *see* 1 HENRY WILSON, HISTORY OF THE RISE AND FALL OF THE SLAVE POWER IN AMERICA 578–82 (Boston: Houghton and Mifflin, 1872).

19. *See* CONG. GLOBE, 38th Cong., 1st Sess. 2984, 2990 (1864) (remarks of Reps. William Kelley and Ebon Ingersoll); CONG. GLOBE, 38th Cong., 2d Sess. 193, 237 (1865) (remarks of Reps. John Kasson and Green Smith); CONG. GLOBE, 39th Cong., 1st Sess. 41, 157–58, 474–75, 1263 (1865–66) (remarks of Sen. John Sherman, Rep. John Bingham, Sen. Lyman Trumbull, and Rep. John Broomall); *id.* at 142 app. (remarks of Sen. Henry Wilson); *see also* C. ANTIEAU, *supra* note 13, at 24 (quoting 1866 remarks of Rep. Columbus Delano); Charles Fairman, *Does the Fourteenth Amendment Incor-*

porate the Bill of Rights?, 2 STAN. L. REV. 5, 22 (1949) (Samuel Hoar episode was "stock example" in Reconstruction Congress).

20. CHARLES EDWARD STOWE AND LYMAN BEECHER STOWE, HARRIET BEECHER STOWE: THE STORY OF HER LIFE 202-3 (1911).

21. On the ways in which the Slave Power specially targeted "outside agitators," *see* Curtis, *1859 Crisis, supra* note 9, at 1134, 1161.

22. *See, e.g.,* CONG. GLOBE, 42d Cong., 1st Sess. 380 (1871) (remarks of Rep. John Hawley) (on need to protect "freedom of speech" contrary to "dominant" opinion).

23. *See generally* Graham, *supra* note 8; H. HYMAN AND W. WIECEK, *supra* note 8, at 140, 150; Nelson, *supra* note 8, at 525-28, 534-36; Daniel A. Farber and John E. Muench, *The Ideological Origins of the Fourteenth Amendment,* 1 CONST. COMMENTARY 235, 239, 248 (1984).

24. For a rich and gripping discussion, see Michael Kent Curtis, *The 1837 Killing of Elijah Lovejoy by an Anti-Abolition Mob: Free Speech, Mobs, Republican Government, and the Privileges of American Citizens,* 44 U.C.L.A. L. REV. 1109 (1997).

25. *See supra* Chapter 9, text accompanying note 2.

26. C. ANTIEAU, *supra* note 13, at 24; CONG. GLOBE, 42d Cong., 1st Sess. 84 app. (1871).

27. CONG. GLOBE, 39th Cong., 1st Sess. 474-75 (1866); *see also* JACOBUS tenBROEK, EQUAL UNDER LAW 124-25 (Collier, 1965) (1951) (discussing centrality in abolitionist theory of right to "teach or be taught the Gospel" to nourish the "immortal mind").

28. CONG. GLOBE, 39th Cong., 1st Sess. 142 app. (1866).

29. CONG. GLOBE, 38th Cong., 2d Sess. 138 (1865); CONG. GLOBE, 38th Cong., 1st Sess. 2990 (1864); *see also id.* at 2615 (1864) (remarks of Rep. Daniel Morris) (discussing incarceration of "*Christian* men and women for teaching the alphabet" (emphasis added)); *id.* at 2979 (remarks of Rep. John Farnsworth) (denouncing Slave Power assault on "churches" and censorship of those who spoke against "the evil and sin of slaveholding").

30. 2 PROCEEDINGS OF THE BLACK STATE CONVENTIONS, 1840-1865, at 302 (Philip S. Foner and George E. Walker eds., 1980) [hereinafter PROCEEDINGS].

31. *See* Kurt T. Lash, *The Second Adoption of the Free Exercise Clause: Religious Exemptions Under the Fourteenth Amendment,* 88 Nw. U. L. REV. 1106, 1133 n.125 (1994) [hereinafter *Free Exercise*].

32. *See* KENNETH M. STAMPP, THE PECULIAR INSTITUTION 211 (1956) (emphasis added).

33. *See* Curtis, *1859 Crisis, supra* note 9, at 1135.

34. *See id.* at 1136.

35. *See id.* at 1159-67.

36. For an early illustration, *see* Michael Kent Curtis, *The Curious History of Attempts to Suppress Antislavery Speech, Press, and Petition in 1835-37,* 89 Nw. U. L. REV. 785, 862-63 (1995) [hereinafter *Curious History*] (discussing efforts in 1830s of Massachu-

setts antislavery society to invoke Virginia statue of religious freedom on behalf of a general right of freedom of opinion and expression encompassing free speech and free press).

37. *See* Curtis, *1859 Crisis, supra* note 9, at 1157; ABRAHAM LINCOLN: SPEECHES AND WRITINGS 1859-1865, at 128, 149 (Don E. Fehrenbacher ed., 1989).

38. *See* Curtis, *1859 Crisis, supra* note 9, at 1156 (quoting 36th CONG. GLOBE, 1st Sess. 1857 (1860)).

39. *Id.* at 1159 (quoting 36th CONG. GLOBE, 1st Sess. 205 app. (1860)); *see also id.* at 1155 (quoting similar language of Rep. Sidney Edgerton).

40. St. George Tucker's 1803 edition of Blackstone's *Commentaries* provides an interesting illustration of transition. In key passages, Tucker embraced a Tenth Amendment–like reading of the First Amendment, in keeping with the Virginia and Kentucky Resolves. 2 BLACKSTONE'S COMMENTARIES 28-30 app. (St. George Tucker ed., Philadelphia: Burch and Small, 1803). But elsewhere Tucker wrote of "liberty of speech and discussion in all speculative matters . . . whether religious, philosophical, or political," *id.* at app. 11; and he also proclaimed that "[n]othing could more clearly evince the inestimable value that the American people have set upon the liberty of the press, than their uniting it in the same sentence, and even in the same member of a sentence, with the rights of conscience and the freedom of speech." *Id.* at app. 16-17.

41. *See generally* 1 ALEXIS DE TOCQUEVILLE, DEMOCRACY IN AMERICA 315 (Vintage ed., 1945); SARA M. EVANS, BORN FOR LIBERTY 67-92 (1989).

42. *See* W. WIECEK, *supra* note 8, at 152, 154, 167, 184, 195 (discussing Elizabeth Heyrick, Sarah Grimké, Lucretia Mott, and women's voices more generally in petitioning and in organizations like the Boston Female Anti-Slavery Society); Curtis, *Curious History, supra* note 6, at 863 (discussing women like the Grimké sisters who joined abolitionist crusades and were prominent speakers); S. EVANS, *supra* note 41, at 67-118 (describing women's increasingly visible political role); Lea S. VanderVelde, *Their Presence in the Gallery* (1997) (unpublished manuscript) (discussing visible and vocal presence of women in the gallery of the Reconstruction Congress).

43. *See* Charles Warren, *Elbridge Gerry, James Warren, Mercy Warren and the Ratification of the Federal Constitution in Massachusetts,* 64 MASS. HIST. SOC'Y PROC. 143 (1931). On Warren's stature generally, see LINDA K. KERBER, WOMEN OF THE REPUBLIC 80-84, 227, 256-57 (1980).

44. *See* Nina Morais, Note, *Sex Discrimination and the Fourteenth Amendment: Lost History,* 97 YALE L. J. 1153, 1155-56 (1988).

45. *See id.* at 1156.

46. 2 HISTORY OF WOMAN SUFFRAGE 78-79 (Elizabeth Cady Stanton, Susan B. Anthony, and Matilda Joslyn Gage eds., AYER Co. reprint, 1985) (1882); *see also* L. KERBER, *supra* note 43, at 112-13 (discussing "the women's abolitionist petitions that flooded Congress in the 1830s and forced confrontation of the slavery issue").

47. CONG. GLOBE, 38th Cong., 1st Sess. 2984 (1864). For an earlier reference, see CONG. GLOBE, 36th Cong., 1st Sess. 2598–99 (1860) (remarks of Sen. Charles Sumner).

48. CONG. GLOBE, 38th Cong., 2d Sess. 193 (1865); Cong. Globe, 38th Cong., 1st Sess. 2615 (1864); *see also* CONG. GLOBE, 36th Cong., 1st Sess. 205 app. (1860) (remarks of Rep. Owen Lovejoy) (Slave Power "drive[s] away young ladies that go to teach school").

49. CONG. GLOBE, 39th Cong., 1st Sess. 142 app. (1966).

50. Crandall v. State, 10 Conn. 339, 340–41 (1834).

51. For excellent accounts of the Crandall affair, *see* Graham, *supra* note 8, at 498–506; H. HYMAN AND W. WIECEK, *supra* note 8, at 94–95; W. WIECEK, *supra* note 8, at 162–67.

52. *Crandall*, 10 Conn. at 365–72.

53. Graham, *supra* note 8, at 505.

54. CONG. GLOBE, 39th Cong., 1st Sess. 1833 (1866).

55. On the centrality of women in teaching, see S. EVANS, *supra* note 41, at 70–72.

56. On the centrality of the black church, see generally E. FONER, *supra* note 16, at 88–95, 282.

57. *See* CONG. GLOBE, 39th Cong., 1st Sess. 474 (1866).

58. *See supra* page 217, note.

59. CONG. GLOBE, 39th Cong., 1st Sess. 337 (1866).

60. W. DU BOIS, *supra* note 16, at 230.

61. New York Times Co. v. Sullivan, 376 U.S. 254 (1964).

62. *See, e.g.*, William J. Brennan, Jr., *The Supreme Court and the Meiklejohn Interpretation of the First Amendment*, 79 HARV. L. REV. 1, 7–8 (1965).

63. Henry P. Monaghan, *First Amendment "Due Process,"* 83 HARV. L. REV. 518 (1970).

64. This, of course, was part of the argument of Chapter 2.

65. *See supra* Chapters 2 and 5.

66. *See supra* Chapter 8, text at note 41.

67. On the abundance of black petitions generally, *see* W. DU BOIS, *supra* note 16, at 230–35; E. FONER, *supra* note 16, at 115; *see also* KENNETH M. STAMPP, THE ERA OF RECONSTRUCTION, 1865–1877, at 165 (1965) (discussing how Tennessee blacks first petitioned their state legislature for suffrage and then asked Congress not to seat the state delegation till the petition was granted).

68. *See* JOSEPH B. JAMES, THE FRAMING OF THE FOURTEENTH AMENDMENT 130 (1956).

69. CONG. GLOBE, 39th Cong., 1st Sess. 951 (1866). In this petition, Mrs. Smith asked readers to "Remember, the right of petition is our only right in the Government . . . ." *Id.* The feminist leader Elizabeth Cady Stanton agreed that under extant law, petition was "the only right [woman] has in the Government." ELIZABETH CADY STANTON, EIGHTY YEARS AND MORE 244 (Schocken, 1971) (1898) (reprinting letter dated Jan. 2, 1866); *see also* SARAH GRIMKÉ, LETTERS ON THE EQUALITY OF THE SEXES

AND OTHER ESSAYS 71, 72 (Elizabeth Ann Bartlett ed., 1988) (reprinting September 6, 1837, letter on legal disabilities of women: "Woman has no political existence. With the single exception of presenting a petition to the legislative body, she is a cipher in the nation . . . . "); 2 HISTORY OF WOMAN SUFFRAGE, *supra* note 46, at 170 (reprinting May 10, 1866, address to Congress of the Eleventh National Woman's Rights Convention) ("As the only way disfranchised citizens can appear before you, we availed ourselves of the sacred right of petition.").

70. CONG. GLOBE, 39th Cong., 1st Sess. 952 (1866).

71. *See* H. FLACK, *supra* note 12, at 42.

72. J. TENBROEK, *supra* note 27, at 124–25.

73. *See* Lash, *Free Exercise, supra* note 31, at 1134 n.133 (quoting Virginia Code of 1833, §31) (emphasis added). For similar antebellum laws in South Carolina and the District of Columbia, *see id.*

74. *See supra* Chapter 2, text at note 66.

75. *See* GERARD V. BRADLEY, CHURCH-STATE RELATIONSHIPS IN AMERICA 98 (1987) (describing the events of July 21, 1789); 1 ANNALS OF CONG. 685; 1 Stat. 50, ch. 8.

76. For an overview, see G. BRADLEY, *supra* note 75, at 99–104.

77. For a discussion of such views, see STEVEN D. SMITH, FOREORDAINED FAILURE 8–11 (1995).

78. *See generally* G. BRADLEY, *supra* note 75.

79. *See* S. SMITH, *supra* note 77, at 28.

80. For a similar suggestion, *see* Jed Rubenfeld, *Antidisestablishmentarianism: Why RFRA Really Was Unconstitutional,* 95 MICH. L. REV. 2347 (1997).

81. IOWA CONST. of 1846, art. I, §3; IOWA CONST. OF 1857, art. I, §3.

82. *See* 9 SOURCES AND DOCUMENTS OF UNITED STATES CONSTITUTIONS 380 (William F. Swindler ed., 1979) (reprinting Constitution of the State of Deseret, art. VII, §3); *id.* at 388 (reprinting Utah Draft Constitution of 1860, art. II, §3).

83. 2 *id.* at 18 (reprinting Constitution of Jefferson Territory, art. I, §3).

84. THOMAS M. COOLEY, A TREATISE ON THE CONSTITUTIONAL LIMITATIONS WHICH REST UPON THE LEGISLATIVE POWER OF THE STATES OF THE AMERICAN UNION 469 (Boston: Little, Brown, 1868).

85. Dred Scott v. Sandford, 60 U.S. (19 How.) 393, 450–51 (1857). Note how Taney misparaphrases the words of the First Amendment here, omitting the word *prohibiting* and thus treating the word *respecting* as applicable to the free-exercise clause as well as the establishment clause.

86. *Id.* at 450 ("And an act of Congress which deprives a citizen of the United States of his liberty or property, merely because he came himself or brought his property into a particular Territory of the United States . . . could hardly be dignified with the name of due process of law.").

87. Campbell v. State, 11 Ga. 353, 366 (1852).

88. *Id.*

89. For the details, *see* 2 WILLIAM G. MCLOUGHLIN, NEW ENGLAND DISSENT, 1630-1833, at 1151 (1971). For discussion of an 1811 article that read the First Amendment as anti-establishment and proposed a state constitutional counterpart, *see id.* at 1097.

90. *See generally* 4 W. BLACKSTONE, *supra* note 2, at *41-65.

91. *See* CONG. GLOBE, 36th Cong., 1st Sess. 198 app. (1860) (remarks of Rep. W. E. Simms); CONG. GLOBE, 38th Cong., 1st Sess. 1202 (1864) (remarks of Rep. James Wilson); CONG. GLOBE, 39th Cong., 1st Sess. 105-58, 1072, 1629 (1866) (remarks of Rep. John Bingham, Sen. James Nye, and Rep. Roswell Hart); CONG. GLOBE, 42d Cong., 1st Sess. 84-85 app., 475 (1871) (remarks of Reps. John Bingham and Henry Dawes); *see also* M. CURTIS, *supra* note 9, at 135, 139-40 (quoting similar speeches outside of Congress by Judge Lorenzo Sherwood and Judge Preston Davis); United States v. Hall, 26 F. Cas. 79, 81 (C. C. S. D. Ala. 1871) (No. 15,282) (Woods, J.) (stressing speech, press, assembly, and free-exercise rights as Fourteenth Amendment privileges and immunities while omitting mention of establishment clause). *See generally* WILLIAM D. GUTHRIE, LECTURES ON THE FOURTEENTH ARTICLE OF AMENDMENT TO THE CONSTITUTION OF THE UNITED STATES 58-59 (Boston: Little, Brown, 1898) (defining as Fourteenth Amendment privileges and immunities each of the five rights and freedoms of the First Amendment, but omitting non-establishment).

92. CONG. GLOBE, 39th Cong., 1st Sess. 322 (1866) (emphasis added).

93. *See, e.g.,* 2 CONG. REC. 242 app. (1874) (remarks of Rep. Thomas Norwood); TIMOTHY FARRAR, MANUAL OF THE CONSTITUTION OF THE UNITED STATES OF AMERICA §442, at 396 (Boston: Little, Brown, 1867); GEORGE W. PASCHAL, LECTURE DELIVERED TO THE AMERICAN UNION ACADEMY OF LITERATURE, SCIENCE, AND ART, AT ITS SPECIAL MEETING CALLED FOR THE PURPOSE, MARCH 7, 1870, *reprinted in* GEORGE W. PASCHAL, THE CONSTITUTION OF THE UNITED STATES at xli (2d ed., Washington: W. H. and O. H. Morrison, 1876).

94. T. COOLEY, *supra* note 84, at 469 (emphasis added). Cooley went on to defend non-preferential, nonsectarian governmental endorsements of religion, such as government-sponsored fast days and thanksgivings, while warning that care must "be taken to avoid discrimination in favor of any one denomination or sect." *Id.* at 471.

95. For a nice discussion, *see* Ira C. Lupu, *Keeping the Faith: Religion, Equality, and Speech in the U.S. Constitution*, 18 CONN. L. REV. 739, 743 (1986).

96. *See generally* James Forman, Jr., Note, *Driving Dixie Down: Removing the Confederate Flag from Southern State Capitols*, 101 YALE L. J. 505 (1991).

97. *See, e.g.,* CONG. GLOBE, 38th Cong., 1st Sess. 1202 (1864) (remarks of Rep. James Wilson); CONG. GLOBE, 39th Cong., 1st Sess. 156-57, 1072, 1629 (1866) (remarks of Rep. John Bingham, Sen. James Nye, and Rep. Roswell Hart). *See generally* sources cited *supra* note 91.

98. This was clearly a concern of the *Smith* Court, which expressed evident distaste for ad hoc judicial balancing. *See* Employment Division v. Smith, 494 U.S. 872, 889 n.5 (1990).

99. For a somewhat similar suggestion, see Michael W. McConnell, *Free Exercise Revisionism and the* Smith *Decision*, 57 U. Chi. L. Rev. 1109, 1145–46 (1990).

100. What if a religious group indulged voluntary sacrifice of its own adult members? If we strictly applied the autonomy principle, these acts of religious "suicides" and "suicide assistance" could be criminalized only in the event that the volunteers were mentally incompetent. Otherwise, how could government bar an adult of sound mind from literally dedicating his life to God in an act of supreme sacrifice? This hypothetical may tempt us to bend the autonomy principle here, but before we do, we should remember that many churches were built by martyrs who gave up their earthly lives to win something they deemed even more precious.

101. *See* Lash, *Free Exercise, supra* note 31.

102. *See supra* text accompanying note 26; Cong. Globe, 39th Cong., 1st Sess. 783 (remarks of Rep. Hamilton Wood).

103. For discussion and analysis see Lash, *supra* note 31, at 1151 n.202, 1154–55.

104. Harry A. Blackmun, *The First Amendment and Its Religious Clauses: Where Are We? Where Are We Going?*, 14 Nova. L. Rev. 29, 31 (1989).

105. Everson v. Board of Education, 330 U.S. 1, 26 (1947) (Jackson, J., dissenting).

106. Cong. Globe, 39th Cong., 1st Sess. 337, 474, 585, 651, 654, 1073, 1182, 1266, 1621, 1629, 1838, 2765, 3210 (1866) (remarks of Sens. Charles Sumner and Lyman Trumbull, Reps. Nathaniel Banks, Josiah Grinnell, and Thomas Eliot, Sens. James Nye and Samuel Pomeroy, Reps. Henry Raymond, Leonard Myers, Roswell Hart, and Sidney Clarke, Sen. Jacob Howard, and Rep. George Julian); *see also id.* at 2774 (remarks of Rep. Thomas Eliot quoting General Fisk).

For a more general discussion of firearms and the Fourteenth Amendment, see Stephen P. Halbrook, That Every Man Be Armed 106–53 (1984); Robert J. Cottrol and Raymond T. Diamond, *The Second Amendment: Toward an Afro-Americanist Reconsideration*, 80 Geo. L. J. 309, 342–49 (1991); Stephen P. Halbrook, *Personal Security, Personal Liberty, and "The Constitutional Right to Bear Arms": Visions of the Framers of the Fourteenth Amendment*, 5 Seton Hall Const. L. J. 341 (1995) [hereinafter *Fourteenth Amendment*]; Sayoko Blodgett-Ford, *The Changing Meaning of the Right to Bear Arms*, 6 Seton Hall Const. L. J. 101 (1995); *see also* M. Curtis, *supra* note 9, at 138–41.

107. For a theoretical discussion of how this can occur, *see* J. M. Balkin, *Deconstructive Practice and Legal Theory*, 96 Yale L. J. 743 (1987).

108. To cast the point within the felicitous framework of Professor Rubenfeld, my claim here, and throughout this chapter, is that the Founding and Reconstruction visions

of various rights featured slightly different "paradigm cases." *See generally* Jed Rubenfeld, *Reading the Constitution as Spoken,* 104 YALE L. J. 1119, 1169–71 (1995).

109. E. FONER, *supra* note 16, at 203; *see also* CONG. GLOBE, 39th Cong., 1st Sess. 40 (1866) (remarks of Sen. Henry Wilson) ("In Mississippi rebel State forces, men who were in the rebel armies, are traversing the State, visiting the freedmen, disarming them, perpetrating murders and outrages upon them"); *id.* at 914, 941 (remarks of Sens. Henry Wilson and Lyman Trumbull, each quoting Dec. 13, 1865, letter from Colonel Samuel Thomas to Major General O. O. Howard) ("Nearly all the dissatisfaction that now exists among the freedmen is caused by the abusive conduct of [the ex-confederate Mississippi] militia."); HARPER'S WEEKLY, Jan. 13, 1866, at 3, col. 2 ("The militia of [Mississippi] have seized every gun and pistol found in the hands of the (so called) freedmen"); *see generally* Halbrook, *Fourteenth Amendment, supra* note 106.

110. For general discussions of congressional use of the military in Reconstruction, see E. FONER, *supra* note 16, at 271–77, 307–8, 438; MICHAEL LES BENEDICT, A COMPROMISE OF PRINCIPLE 223–43 (1974); K. STAMPP, *supra* note 67, at 144–47.

111. *See supra* page 217, note.

112. *See supra* note 106.

113. 14 Stat. 173, 176 (1866) (emphasis added).

114. *See supra* page 217, note.

115. *See supra* page 195, note.
    The link between Blackstone and the language of the Civil Rights Bill is nicely illuminated by Professor Curtis. *See* M. CURTIS, *supra* note 9, at 74–76.

116. *See* CONG. GLOBE, 39th Cong., 1st Sess. 474, 1118, 1757 (1866).

117. 1 W. BLACKSTONE, *supra* note 2, at *141–44.

118. Aymette v. State, 21 Tenn. (2 Hum.) 154, 161 (1840).

119. *See supra* Chapter 3, text at note 2.

120. *See* Cottrol and Diamond, *supra* note 106, at 333–38; S. HALBROOK, *supra* note 106, at 96–106.

121. JOEL TIFFANY, A TREATISE ON THE UNCONSTITUTIONALITY OF AMERICAN SLAVERY 117–118 (Cleveland: J. Calyer, 1849) (emphasis deleted).

122. On Tiffany's importance and influence, see J. TENBROEK, *supra* note 27, at 72–74, 108–13.

123. 1 Ga. 243, 251 (1846) (emphasis deleted).

124. Cooper v. Mayer and Alderman of Savannah, 4 Ga. 68, 72 (1848).

125. Dred Scott v. Sandford, 60 U.S. (19 How.) 393, 416–17 (1857).

126. 2 BLACKSTONE'S COMMENTARIES, *supra* note 40, at 65 app. (St. George Tucker ed., 1803).

127. *See* Cottrol and Diamond, *supra* note 106, at 333–49; E. FONER, *supra* note 16, at

119–23, 148; W. DuBois, *supra* note 16, at 166–67, 223. *See generally* Halbrook, *Fourteenth Amendment, supra* note 106.

128. 2 PROCEEDINGS, *supra* note 30, at 284, 302.

129. CONG. GLOBE, 39th Cong., 1st Sess. 474 (1866).

130. *Id.*

131. *Id.* at 651.

132. *Id.* at 1073 (emphasis added).

133. *Id.* at 1182. Pomeroy's next sentence made clear that he also supported political rights for blacks; but his rhetoric tended to privatize the arms right. *But cf. id.* at 1183 (discussing right to vote and right to bear arms in the same sentence; but not describing arms bearing as a political rather than a civil right). *See also id.* at 371 (remarks of Sen. Garrett Davis) (both parties "were for every man bearing his arms about him and keeping them in his house, his castle, for his own defense").

134. *Id.* at 1266. Similarly, Congressman Henry Dawes in 1871 declared that the privileges and immunities of the American citizen included "the right to keep and bear arms in his defense." CONG. GLOBE, 42nd Cong., 1st Sess. 475 (1871).

135. *See* H. FLACK, *supra* note 12, at 42.

136. LOYAL GEORGIAN, Feb. 3, 1866, at 3, col. 4, *quoted in* Halbrook, *Fourteenth Amendment, supra* note 106, at 380, n.198. This editorial borrowed language from a December 22, 1865, Freedman's Bureau circular. *See* Ex. Doc. No. 70, House of Representatives, 39th Cong., 1st Sess., at 65 (1866). For discussion, *see* Halbrook, *supra*, at 380–81, 396.

137. 376 U.S. 254 (1964).

138. *See* NATIONAL RIFLE ASSOCIATION OF AMERICA, AMERICANS AND THEIR GUNS 31–35 (James B. Trefethen compiler, James E. Serven ed., 1967).

139. 381 U.S. 479, 484 (1965).

140. *See, e.g.,* Cottrol and Diamond, *supra* note 106, at 337; E. FONER, *supra* note 16, at 203; Curtis, *1859 Crisis, supra* note 9, at 1162, 1171.

141. *See, e.g.,* CONG. GLOBE, 39th Cong., 1st Sess. 1629, 2765 (1866) (remarks of Rep. Roswell Hart and Sen. Jacob Howard); CONG. GLOBE, 42d Cong., 1st Sess. 84 app., 475 (1871) (remarks of Reps. John Bingham and Henry Dawes); M. CURTIS, *supra* note 9, at 139–40 (quoting remarks of Judge Noah Dawes at Republican Union State Convention, held in Syracuse on September 5, 1866); T. FARRAR, *supra* note 93, at 395–97.

142. Important discussions of this issue include RANDALL KENNEDY, RACE, CRIME, AND THE LAW 136–67 (1997), Sheri Lynn Johnson, *Race and the Decision to Detail a Suspect,* 93 YALE L. J. 214 (1983), and Tracey Maclin, *"Black and Blue Encounters"—Some Preliminary Thoughts About Fourth Amendment Seizures: Should Race Matter?,* 26 VAL. U. L. REV. 243 (1991). My own views are set out in AKHIL REED AMAR, THE CONSTITUTION AND CRIMINAL PROCEDURE: FIRST PRINCIPLES 37–38, 160 (1997).

143. CONG. GLOBE, 39th Cong., 1st Sess. 1065 (1866); *see also* CONG. GLOBE, 39th Cong., 2d Sess. 811 (1867) (remarks of Rep. John Bingham reaffirming that his pending amendment would ensure that states were held to the rule that "private property shall not be taken for public use without just compensation"). For further evidence of Bingham's views, *see supra* Chapter 9, note 4. *See also* CONG. GLOBE, 39th Cong., 1st Sess. 1833 (1866) (remarks of Rep. William Lawrence affirming fundamentality of just-compensation principle).

144. *Id.* at 2765-66.

145. *See, e.g,* 2 JAMES KENT, COMMENTARIES *339 (just compensation requirement "is founded in natural equity, and is laid down by jurists as an acknowledged principle of universal law"); 3 JOSEPH STORY, COMMENTARIES ON THE CONSTITUTION OF THE UNITED STATES §1784, at 661 (Boston: Hilliard, Gray, 1833) (same). For representative odes to just compensation in mid-nineteenth century case law, *see supra* page 149, note, and page 150, note.

146. Chicago B. & Q. R. R. v. Chicago, 166 U.S. 226, 236 (1897).

147. *See supra* Chapter 8, text at note 9.

148. *See supra* Chapter 5, text at note 62; Chapter 9, text at notes 59-69.

149. 4 W. BLACKSTONE, *supra* note 2, at *349. Modern scholars have questioned Blackstone's historical claims about Magna Charta's original meaning—but his views on the point were utterly orthodox in the eighteenth and nineteenth centuries. *See* A. E. DICK HOWARD, THE ROAD FROM RUNNYMEDE 340-41 (1968); ALVAN STEWART, A CONSTITUTIONAL ARGUMENT ON THE SUBJECT OF SLAVERY (1837) *reprinted in* J. TENBROEK, *supra* note 27, at 281-84; Murray's Lessee v. Hoboken Land & Improvement Co., 59 U.S. (18 How.) 272, 276 (1856);Strauder v. West Virginia, 100 U.S. 303, 308-09 (1880).

150. *See* J. TENBROEK, *supra* note 27, at 50, 64-69; M. CURTIS, *supra* note 9, at 106.

151. SALMON P. CHASE, SPEECH OF SALMON P. CHASE IN THE CASE OF THE COLORED WOMAN, MATILDA 31, 36 (Cincinnati: Pugh and Dodd, 1837). For a nice overview of the case, *see* H. HYMAN AND W. WIECEK, *supra* note 8, at 106-7.

152. *See id.* at 97, 107, 158-59; W. WIECEK, *supra* note 8, at 197-99. *See generally* THOMAS D. MORRIS, FREE MEN ALL (1974).

153. 41 U.S. (16 Pet.) 539 (1842).

154. *See* T. MORRIS, *supra* note 152, at 138.

155. EMANCIPATOR AND REPUBLICAN, Nov. 14, 1850 (emphasis deleted). Bingham agreed that the 1850 act violated rights of due process and jury trial. *See* CONG. GLOBE, 36th Cong., 2d Sess. 83 (1861).

156. *See, e.g.,* CONG. GLOBE, 35th Cong., 2d Sess. 985 (1859) (remarks of Rep. John Bingham) (acknowledging that states could deny blacks the vote but not the right to be tried by jury); CONG. GLOBE, 39th Cong., 1st Sess. 2765-66 (1866) (remarks of Sen. Jacob Howard) (similar).

157. *See id.* at 1117, 1294, 1832, 156 app. (remarks of Reps. James Wilson and William Lawrence). *See also id.* at 632 (remarks of Rep. Samuel Moulton). For representative statements in Reconstruction Congresses about the importance of jury trial, *see* CONG. GLOBE, 38th Cong. 1st Sess. 114, 1971–72 (1864) (remarks of Reps. Isaac Newton Arnold and Glenni Scofield); CONG. GLOBE, 38th Cong., 2d Sess. 215 (1865) (remarks of Rep. Chilton White); CONG. GLOBE, 41st Cong., 2d Sess. 515 (1870) (remarks of Sen. Joseph Fowler); CONG. GLOBE, 41st Cong. 3rd Sess. 1245 (1871) (remarks of Rep. William E. Lawrence); CONG. GLOBE, 42d Cong., 1st Sess. 475, 84–85 app. (1871) (remarks of Reps. Henry Dawes and John Bingham); CONG. GLOBE, 42d Cong., 2d Sess. 844 (1872) (remarks of Sen. John Sherman).

158. *See* E. FONER, *supra* note 16, at 204, 245; H. HYMAN AND W. WIECEK, *supra* note 8, at 322–24, 425; M. CURTIS, *supra* note 16, at 136–37; Ronald F. Wright, *Why Not Administrative Grand Juries?*, 44 ADMIN. L. REV. 465, 469 n.18 (1992); CONG. GLOBE, 42d Cong., 1st Sess. 158, 820, 220 app. (1871) (remarks of Sens. John Sherman and Allen Thurman).

159. *Cf.* CONG. GLOBE, 42d Cong., 1st Sess. 220 app. (1871) (remarks of Democratic Sen. Allen Thurman) (arguing that problem of white southern jury nullification in Klan trials was insoluble "unless you intend to transport these offenders [north], as our forefathers were transported to Great Britain for trial"; such a strategy would be "a plain violation of the Constitution"). For a prescient anticipation of the problem of white nullification and a plea for black representation on juries, *see* CONG. GLOBE, 38th Cong., 2d Sess. 289 (1865) (remarks of Rep. William Kelley).

160. 100 U.S. 303, 304–5 (1880).

161. *Id.* at 308.

162. *See, e.g., id.* at 305 (discussing "right to trial" of defendant and "the defendant['s] . . . right to have a jury"); *id.* at 309 (describing discrimination "against a colored man when he is put upon trial"); *id.* at 310 (condemning "denial of the equal protection of the laws to a colored man when he is put on trial"); *id.* at 312 (affirming "immunity from discrimination against [defendant] in the selection of jurors").

163. *See id.* at 312 (Field, J., dissenting); *Ex parte* Virginia, 100 U.S. 339, 349–70 (1880) (Field, J., dissenting); *see also* Virginia v. Rives, 100 U.S. 313, 335 (1880) (Field, J., concurring in judgment).

164. Act of March 1, 1875, ch. 114, 18 Stat. 335 (codified as amended at 18 U.S.C. §243 (1988)).

165. *Compare id.* ("no *citizen* . . . shall be disqualified for service as grand or petit jurors in any court of the *United States, or of any State, on account of race, color, or previous condition of servitude*") (emphasis added), *with* U.S. CONST. amend. XV ("The right of *citizens* of the United States to vote shall not be denied or abridged by the *United States, or by any State on account of race, color, or previous condition of servitude.*") (emphasis added).

For a discussion of the legislative history of this statute, and its connections to the Fifteenth Amendment, *see* Vikram David Amar, *Jury Service as Political Participation Akin to Voting*, 80 CORNELL L. REV. 203, 238-41 (1995).

166. *See supra* Chapter 5, text at note 46.

167. *See generally* Vikram David Amar, *supra* note 165, at 241-42; Barbara Allen Babcock, *A Place in the Palladium: Women's Rights and Jury Service*, 61 U. CIN. L. REV. 1139 (1993); Jennifer K. Brown, Note, *The Nineteenth Amendment and Women's Equality*, 102 YALE L. J. 2175 (1993); *see also* Palmer v. State, 150 N.E. 917, 918 (Ind. 1926) (post–Nineteenth Amendment case requiring that women be eligible to sit on state juries: "Where, by statute, jurors are to be selected from qualified electors, the adoption of a constitutional amendment making women electors qualifies them for jury duty." (citing cases)). Feminists in the early twentieth century appear to have clearly understood that women's capacity to serve on juries was intimately linked to the larger issue of women's suffrage. *See, e.g.,* Susan Glaspell, *A Jury of Her Peers, reprinted in* THE BEST SHORT STORIES OF 1917, at 256-82 (Edward J. O'Brien ed., 1918).

168. *See* Taylor v. Louisiana, 419 U.S. 522 (1975). Interestingly, the Nineteenth Amendment did get fleeting mention in one of the first postsuffrage Supreme Court cases involving sex discrimination on juries. *See* Fay v. New York, 332 U.S. 261, 290 (1947).

169. WILLIAM RAWLE, A VIEW OF THE CONSTITUTION OF THE UNITED STATES OF AMERICA 124-25 (Philadelphia: H. C. Carey and I. Lea, 1825). For discussion of similar views expressed by New York Chief Justice Ambrose Spencer, *see* William Winslow Crosskey, *Charles Fairman, "Legislative History," and the Constitutional Limitations on State Authority*, 22 U. CHI. L. REV. 1, 126-27 (1954).

170. 11 Ga. 353, 366-67 (1852).

171. CONG. GLOBE, 38th Cong., 1st Sess. 2919 (1864) (remarks of Rep. Daniel Morris) (emphasis added).

A states'-rights reading of the Seventh Amendment would mean that, like the Tenth Amendment, the Seventh had little bite in the territories. This result might be thought inconsistent with the reasoning and result in the antebellum case *Webster v. Reid*, 52 U.S. (11 How.) 437 (1850), where the Supreme Court invalidated a nonjury trial in the Iowa territory on Seventh Amendment grounds. But the Northwest Ordinance—prominently relied upon at oral argument, and in the opinion itself, *see id.* at 447-48, 453, 460—may have provided a special baseline right of jury trial that the Seventh Amendment "preserved." For a somewhat similar (and narrow) reading of *Webster*, see 1 DAVID P. CURRIE, THE CONSTITUTION IN THE SUPREME COURT 271-72 n.264 (1985).

172. *See, e.g.,* Downes v. Bidwell, 182 U.S. 244 (1901); Hawaii v. Mankichi, 190 U.S. 197 (1903); Dorr v. United States, 195 U.S. 138 (1904).

173. *See Downes,* 182 U.S. at 377-78 (Harlan J., dissenting); *Mankichi,* 190 U.S. at 244-45

(Harlan, J., dissenting); *Dorr,* 195 U.S. at 154 (Harlan J., dissenting); *see also* Trono v. United States, 199 U.S. 521, 537 (1905) (Harlan, J., dissenting).

174. *Dorr,* 195 U.S. at 154.

175. 354 U.S. 1, 5–14 (1957) (plurality opinion of Black, J.).

176. For a nice noting of the linkage between these questions, *see* Gerald L. Neuman, *Whose Constitution?,* 100 YALE L. J. 909, 963 and nn. 330–31, 967 (1991).

177. The Slaughter-House Cases, 83 U.S. (16 Wall.) 36, 119 (1873) (Bradley, J., dissenting) ("these privileges they would enjoy whether they were citizens of any State or not. Inhabitants of Federal territories and new citizens, made such by annexation of territory or naturalization, though without any status as citizens of a State, could, nevertheless, as citizens of the United States, lay claim to every one of the privileges and immunities which have been enumerated"). Cf. *id.* at 72–74 (Miller, J.).

178. 9 Stat. 462, 463–64. For discussion of the unfair procedures of this Act, see *supra* page 270, note; H. HYMAN AND W. WIECEK, *supra* note 8, at 151; T. MORRIS, *supra* note 152, at 130–47.

179. H. HYMAN AND W. WIECEK, *supra* note 8, at 110, 152.

180. *See* Curtis, *1859 Crisis, supra* note 9, at 1164 (citing N.C. REV. CODE ch. 34, §16 (1854)).

181. *See id.* at 1167 (citing 1860 N.C. Sess. Laws, ch. 23, at 39 (1860)).

182. CONG. GLOBE, 36th Cong., 1st Sess. 1857 (1860).

183. *See* CONG. GLOBE, 39th Cong., 1st Sess. 500, 2542 (1866) (remarks of Sen. Edgar Cowan and Rep. John Bingham); 39th Cong., 2d Sess. 811–12 (1867) (remarks of Reps. John Bingham and John Kasson); *see also* Ho Ah Kow v. Nunan, 12 F. Cas. 252 (C. C. D. Ca. 1879) (No. 6,546) (Field, Circuit J.) (voiding, under Fourteenth Amendment "cruel and unusual punishment" of Chinese prisoners subjected to a cutting of their hair in a manner designed to degrade them).

184. WILLIAM RAWLE, A VIEW OF THE CONSTITUTION OF THE UNITED STATES OF AMERICA 130–31 (Philadelphia: Nicklin, 2d ed., 1829).

185. *See generally* John Choon Yoo, *Our Declaratory Ninth Amendment,* 42 EMORY L. J. 967 (1993).

186. In chronological order of initial adoption, see ALA. CONST. OF 1819, art. I, §30; ME. CONST. OF 1819, art I, §24; ARK. CONST. OF 1836, art. II, §24; R.I. CONST. OF 1842, art. I, §23; N.J. CONST. OF 1844, art. I, §21; IOWA CONST. OF 1846, art. I, §24; CAL. CONST. OF 1849, art. I, §21; MD. CONST. OF 1851, art. 42 (Declaration of Rights); OHIO CONST. OF 1851, art. I, §20; MINN. CONST. OF 1857, art. I, §16; ORE. CONST. OF 1857, art. I, §34; KAN. CONST. OF 1859, §20 (Bill of Rights); NEV. CONST. OF 1864, art. I, §20; GA. CONST. OF 1865, art. I, §21; NEB. CONST. OF 1866–67, art. I, §20.

187. CONG. GLOBE, 39th Cong., 1st Sess. 1072 (1866) (emphasis added).

188. CONG. GLOBE, 42d Cong., 2d Sess. 843–44 (1872).

189. 163 U.S. 537, 560 (1896) (Harlan, J., dissenting) (emphasis added).

190. 109 U.S. 3, 48 (1883) (Harlan, J., dissenting).

191. Gibson v. Mississippi, 162 U.S. 565, 591 (1896). For evidence from the Fourteenth Amendment's ratification period supporting Harlan's reading, *see* C. ANTIEAU, *supra* note 13, at 14-16.

192. T. COOLEY, *supra* note 84, at 353-54 (quoting Dartmouth College v. Woodward, 17 U.S. (4 Wheat.) 518, 581 (1819)).

193. In the Founding era, *see, e.g.*, PA. CONST. OF 1776 (Declaration of Rights), art. VIII; DEL. DECLARATION OF RIGHTS OF 1776, §10; VT. CONST. OF 1777, ch. 1, art. IX; MASS CONST. OF 1780, pt. I, art X; N.H. CONST. OF 1784, pt. 1, art XII.

194. CONG. GLOBE, 39th Cong., 1st Sess. 1034 (1866) (emphasis added).

Twelve. A New Birth of Freedom

1. *Ex parte* Burford, 7 U.S. 13 (3 Cranch) 448, 451 (1807) (emphasis added).

2. 32 U.S. (7 Pet.) 469, 551 (1833).

3. Fox v. Ohio, 46 U.S. (5 How.) 410, 434 (1847) (emphasis added).

4. Withers v. Buckley, 61 U.S. (20 How.) 84, 90 (1858) (emphasis added).

5. Groves v. Slaughter, 40 (15 Pet.) U.S. 449, lxiii app. (1841) (oral argument of Robert Walker) (emphasis added).

6. Holmes v. Jennison, 39 U.S. (14 Pet.) 540, 555 (1840) (oral argument of C. P. Van Ness).

7. *See* CONG. GLOBE, 39th Cong., 1st Sess. 1088-93 (1866).

8. *Id.* at 1064.

9. *Id.* at 1294, 1832, 2266.

10. *Id.* at 1270.

11. *Id.* at 135 app.

12. TIMOTHY FARRAR, MANUAL OF THE CONSTITUTION OF THE UNITED STATES OF AMERICA §437, at 392 (Boston: Little, Brown, 1867); JOHN NORTON POMEROY, INTRODUCTION TO THE CONSTITUTIONAL LAW OF THE UNITED STATES §228, at 144 (New York: Hurd and Houghton, 1870) (1868).

13. 79 U.S. (12 Wall.) 457, 505-6 (1871) (oral argument of Clarkson Potter); *id.* at 666 (Field, J., dissenting).

14. 100 U.S. 371, 394 (1880).

15. Kring v. Missouri, 107 U.S. 221, 226-27 (1883).

16. Monongahela Navigation Co. v. United States, 148 U.S. 312, 324 (1893).

17. Mattox v. United States, 156 U.S. 237, 243 (1895).

18. Robertson v. Baldwin, 165 U.S. 275, 281 (1897).

19. Bauman v. Ross, 167 U.S. 548, 574 (1897).

20. 176 U.S. 581, 607, 614, 616, 617 (1900) (Harlan, J., dissenting).

21. *See generally* Kenneth R. Bowling, *"A Tub to the Whale": The Founding Fathers and Adoption of the Federal Bill of Rights*, 8 J. EARLY REPUBLIC 223 (1988); Paul Finkel-

man, *James Madison and the Bill of Rights: A Reluctant Paternity,* 1990 SUP. CT. REV. 301.

22. Letter from James Madison to Richard Peters (August 19, 1789), *in* 12 THE PAPERS OF JAMES MADISON 346 (R. Rutland et al. eds., 1979).

23. *See, e.g.,* Henry J. Friendly, *The Bill of Rights as a Code of Criminal Procedure,* 53 CAL. L. REV. 929, 937 n.42 (1965); Ker v. California, 374 U.S. 23, 45–46 (1963) (Harlan, J., concurring in the result); Duncan v. Louisiana, 391 U.S. 145, 182 n.21 (1968) (Harlan, J., dissenting).

24. *See* United States v. Green, 356 U.S. 165, 201 and n.11 (1958) (Black, J., dissenting, joined by Douglas, J.); United States v. Barnett, 376 U.S. 681, 759 and n.48 (1964) (Goldberg, J., dissenting, joined by Douglas, J.); *id.* at 747 (Black, J., dissenting, joined by Douglas, J.); Cheff v. Schnackenberg, 384 U.S. 373, 384–93 (1966) (Douglas, J., dissenting, joined by Black, J.).

25. Duncan v. Louisiana, 291 U.S. at 158 n.30; *see also id.* at 213 (Fortas, J., concurring) ("I see no reason whatever, for example, to assume that our decision today should require us to impose federal requirements such as unanimous verdicts or a jury of 12 upon the states.").

26. *See* Williams v. Florida, 299 U.S. 78 (1970); Ballew v. Georgia, 435 U.S. 223 (1978).

27. Dred Scott v. Sandford, 60 U.S. (19 How.) 393, 450 (1857). For discussion, *see supra* Chapter 11, text at note 86.

28. Robert J. Reinstein, *Completing the Constitution: The Declaration of Independence, Bill of Rights and Fourteenth Amendment,* 66 TEMPLE L. REV. 361, 365 n.25 (1993).

29. For general affirmations of this point, *see* William J. Brennan, Jr., *Why Have a Bill of Rights?,* 26 VAL. U. L. REV. 1, 7 (1991); John Paul Stevens, *The Bill of Rights: A Century of Progress,* 59 U. CHI. L. REV. 13, 19–21 (1992); Geoffrey R. Stone, Foreword, *The Bill of Rights in the Welfare State: A Bicentennial Symposium,* 59 U. CHI. L. REV. 5, 6 (1992). In specific doctrinal areas, *see, e.g.,* Mary Ann Glendon and Raul F. Yanes, *Structural Free Exercise,* 90 MICH. L. REV. 477, 479 (1991) (religion); Daniel Shaviro, *The Confrontation Clause Today in Light of its Common Law Background,* 26 VAL. U. L. REV. 337, 338 (1991) (confrontation clause).

30. Although the Court pretended to assume, for the sake of argument, that speech and press clause principles applied against states in *Patterson v. Colorado,* 205 U.S. 454, 462 (1907), in retrospect it is clear that its sustained drive for First Amendment incorporation began in *Gitlow v. New York,* 268 U.S. 652, 666 (1925).

31. *See* Fiske v. Kansas, 274 U.S. 380 (1927); Stromberg v. California, 283 U.S. 359 (1931); Near v. Minnesota, 283 U.S. 697 (1931); Cantwell v. Connecticut, 310 U.S. 296 (1940).

32. *See generally* HARRY KALVEN, JR., A WORTHY TRADITION: FREEDOM OF SPEECH IN AMERICA (1988).

33. *See* Lamont v. Postmaster General, 381 U.S. 301, 306 (1965).

34. *See* Texas v. Johnson, 491 U.S. 397 (1989); United States v. Eichman, 496 U.S. 310, 315 (1990).

35. *See* Edmond Cahn, *The Firstness of the First Amendment,* 65 YALE L. J. 464, 468-70 (1956).

36. *See generally* Thurgood Marshall, *Reflections on the Bicentennial of the United States Constitution,* 101 HARV. L. REV. 1 (1987).

37. See 4 DEBATES ON THE ADOPTION OF THE FEDERAL CONSTITUTION 316 (Jonathan Elliot ed., AYER Co. reprint ed., 1987) (1836). Major portions of this quotation appear in T. FARRAR, *supra* note 12, §439, at 394.

Afterword

1. *See generally* JOHN HART ELY, DEMOCRACY AND DISTRUST 87-88 (1980).

2. *See* 1 BRUCE ACKERMAN, WE THE PEOPLE: FOUNDATIONS (1991).

3. I omit here the Eighteenth Amendment, enacting Prohibition, as this amendment was of course later repealed by the Twenty-first Amendment. Note also that, technically, the Nineteenth Amendment was not ratified until 1920, though it was proposed by Congress in 1919.

4. *See* Jed Rubenfeld, *Reading the Constitution as Spoken,* 104 YALE L. J. 1119 (1995).

5. *See* J. M. Balkin, *Deconstructive Practice and Legal Theory,* 96 YALE L. J. 743 (1987); *see also* J. M. Balkin, *Ideological Drift and the Struggle over Meaning in Legal and Political Theory,* 25 CONN. L. REV. 869 (1993) (discussing related concept of "ideological drift").

6. *See* CHARLES A. BEARD, AN ECONOMIC INTERPRETATION OF THE CONSTITUTION OF THE UNITED STATES (1913).

7. *See, e.g.,* LOUIS HARTZ, THE LIBERAL TRADITION IN AMERICA: AN INTERPRETATION OF AMERICAN POLITICAL THOUGHT SINCE THE REVOLUTION (1955).

8. *See, e.g.,* DOUGLASS ADAIR, FAME AND THE FOUNDING FATHERS (1974); J. G. A. POCOCK, THE MACHIAVELLIAN MOMENT: FLORENTINE POLITICAL THOUGHT AND THE ATLANTIC REPUBLICAN TRADITION (1975); BERNARD BAILYN, THE IDEOLOGICAL ORIGINS OF THE AMERICAN REVOLUTION (1967); GORDON S. WOOD, THE CREATION OF THE AMERICAN REPUBLIC, 1776-1787 (1969); PAULINE MAIER, FROM RESISTANCE TO REVOLUTION (1972); GARRY WILLS, EXPLAINING AMERICA: THE FEDERALIST (1981). For an important plea for more specificity in defining, and less sloganeering in deploying, the concept of republicanism, *see* Daniel T. Rodgers, *Republicanism: The Career of a Concept,* 79 J. AM. HIST. 11 (1992).

9. *See* CECELIA M. KENYON, THE ANTIFEDERALISTS (1966); THE COMPLETE ANTIFEDERALIST (Herbert J. Storing ed., 1981).

10. For good general discussion, *see* KENNETH M. STAMPP, THE ERA OF RECONSTRUCTION, 1865-1877, at 3-23 (1965); ERIC FONER, RECONSTRUCTION at xix-xxvii (1988).

See also W. E. BURGHARDT DU BOIS, BLACK RECONSTRUCTION IN AMERICA 731 (1935) (setting out bibliography of "standard" "anti-negro" works).

11. *See generally* W. DU BOIS, *supra* note 10.

12. *See, e.g.,* HOWARD J. GRAHAM, EVERYMAN'S CONSTITUTION (1968); JACOBUS TEN-BROEK, EQUAL UNDER LAW (1965); William Winslow Crosskey, *Charles Fairman, "Legislative History," and the Constitutional Limitations on State Authority,* 22 U. CHI. L. REV. 1 (1954); K. STAMPP, *supra* note 10; HAROLD M. HYMAN AND WILLIAM M. WIECEK, EQUAL JUSTICE UNDER LAW (1982); WILLIAM M. WIECEK, THE SOURCES OF ANTISLAVERY CONSTITUTIONALISM IN AMERICA, 1760–1848 (1977); MICHAEL LES BENEDICT, A COMPROMISE OF PRINCIPLE (1974); E. FONER, *supra* note 10; Robert J. Cottrol and Raymond T. Diamond, *The Second Amendment: Towards an Afro-Americanist Reconsideration,* 80 GEO. L. J. 309 (1991); Lea S. VanderVelde, Their Presence in the Gallery (1997) (unpublished manuscript).

13. *See, e.g.,* MICHAEL KENT CURTIS, NO STATE SHALL ABRIDGE (1986); Richard L. Aynes, *On Misreading John Bingham and the Fourteenth Amendment,* 103 YALE L. J. 57 (1993); Richard L. Aynes, *Charles Fairman, Felix Frankfurter, and the Fourteenth Amendment,* 70 CHI.-KENT L. REV. 1197 (1995).

14. For an outstanding general discussion, see LINDA K. KERBER, WOMEN OF THE RE-PUBLIC (1980).

15. *See* The Slaughter-House Cases, 83 U.S. (16 Wall.) 36 (1873); Plessy v. Ferguson, 163 U.S. 537 (1896); Patterson v. Colorado, 205 U.S. 454 (1907).

16. *See* Abelman v. Booth, 62 U.S. (21 How.) 506, 526 (1859); Dred Scott v. Sandford, 60 U.S. (19 How.) 393, 450 (1857).

17. *See* The Selective Draft Law Cases, 245 U.S. 366 (1918).

18. *See generally* PHILIP BOBBITT, CONSTITUTIONAL FATE (1982); Richard H. Fallon, Jr., *A Constructivist Coherence Theory of Constitutional Interpretation,* 100 HARV. L. REV. 1189 (1987).

Index

Abington School District v. Schempp, 138
Ableman v. Booth, 201, 270n
Abolitionism: and declaratory theory, 161–62, 201; and jury trial, 269–71; and press and speech freedoms, 160–61, 234–35, 236, 243, 301; and religious freedom, 237–38
Accused, rights of, 104–6, 111–12, 114–18
Ackerman, Bruce, 292, 299–300, 301
Act of Settlement of *1701,* 109, 155
Adair, Douglass, 79n, 302
Adams, Abigail, 40
Adams, John, 66n, 100n, 101, 102–3, 200
Adamson v. California, 213, 214, 307
Administration of Justice Act, 106
African Americans. *See* Blacks; Slavery
Alien and Sedition Acts, 6, 23, 24, 25, 243. *See also* Sedition Act of 1798

Aliens, rights of, 48n, 170, 172–74, 182, 194, 218n, 245, 273, 364n.39, 364–65n.42
Alschuler, Albert W., 108
Amendment process. *See* Popular sovereignty
American Civil Liberties Union, 242–43
Anthony, Susan B., 240, 260n
Anti-Federalists: and arms bearing, 47, 50, 262; and compromises with Federalists, 14n, 92, 144, 302; and congressional size, 9–11, 13–14, 29; and jury trial, 93, 94–95, 105, 107; localism of, 19n, 126–27; and property protection, 79. *See also* States' rights
Arms bearing, 46, 297; for blacks, 48n, 161, 262–66; Blackstone on, 261–62; broad understanding of, 49–50; and citizenship, 52, 216, 257–58; as

Arms bearing (*continued*)
common-law right, 148, 154, 161n; and hunting, 47, 49, 262; as individual right, 265–66; in militias, 51–52, 216, 258; as political right, 48–49, 216–18, 258; and popular sovereignty, 47–48, 148, 154; Reconstruction, 258–62, 264–65; and suffrage, 48–49n, 216–18; for women, 48–49, 259, 262–63. *See also* Second Amendment

Army. *See* Military; Militia

Articles of Confederation, 11, 17, 25

Assembly clause: and arms bearing, 47–48; and blacks, 241–42, 245–46, 264, 301; incorporation of, 32, 210–12, 226–27, 234–36, 244–46; and instruction rights, 28–29; and majoritarianism, 26; and minority rights, 245–46; and petition rights, 30; and popular sovereignty, 26–30, 46–47, 125, 168n, 244–45; and Preamble, 26–28; and religion, 241, 245–46; and women, 239–41, 245–46. *See also* First Amendment

Aynes, Richard, 210, 303

Bacon, Jarvis, 238

Bailyn, Bernard, 302–4

Baldwin, Henry, 145, 146, 149–50n, 285n

Balkin, Jack, 301

Banks, Nathaniel, 258, 259

Barron v. Baltimore, 33, 128–29, 140–45, 147, 152, 153, 154, 156, 164–66, 175, 176, 204, 306

Beard, Charles, 78, 79n, 302

Benedict, Les, 213n, 303

Berger, Raoul, 172, 183, 187, 193–97, 206–7, 303

Bible, 131, 153n, 161, 237, 256

Bickel, Alexander, 129

Bickford, Charlene Bangs, 304

Bill of Rights: conventional understanding of, xii, xiii, 125; declaratory theory of, 28, 147–56, 161n, 208, 210; fundamental nature of, 149n, 188–93, 200, 211; and nationalist tradition, 3–4, 190; negative-implication theory of, 146–47; primary sources on, 303–4; and slavery, 160–62, 192; symbolism of, 189–91, 291–93; and technological change, 156–57; in territories, 157–58, 167–69, 247–51, 277–78, 391n.171; textual analysis of, 295–301. *See also* Incorporation; Refined incorporation model; *specific amendments*

Bill of Rights, English. *See* English Bill of Rights of 1689

Bill of Rights, original, 3, 7–8; congressional salaries in, 17–19; congressional size and representation in, 10–17; as Constitution, 124–33; First Amendment of, 8–17, 36, 106; and individual rights, 127n, 219; jury-related amendments of, 81–83; Madison's proposal for, 17, 22, 27–28, 37, 39; order of amendments, 37, 292–93; popular enforcement of, 129–33; popular sovereignty motif of, 64–65, 112, 119, 125–27, 215–16; Second Amendment of, 17–19, 36; and states' rights, 4–6, 144–45; structural provisions of, xii–xiii, 8–9, 128

Bingham, John, 171, 174, 186, 204, 268, 282–83, 291–93, 303; on alien rights, 172, 182; and *Barron* decision, 147, 164–65, 182–83, 204; on Bill of Rights, 182–83, 183–84n, 187, 190–91, 196n, 292–93; constitutional faith of, 191; incorporation philosophy of, 157–58, 181–82; on private rights, 226; on punishment, 279

Black, Hugo, 82, 138, 156, 188, 206, 236,

244, 289; in *Adamson v. California*, 213, 214, 307; and common-law rights, 178; constitutional faith of, 191; First Amendment absolutism of, 234; and *Lochner*, 178; and mechanical incorporation, 174–76, 222; and Ninth and Tenth Amendments, xv, 180; total incorporation approach of, xiv, 139, 172, 214, 219, 222

Black Codes, 162, 175, 241, 264, 265

Blackmun, Harry A., 104, 257

Blacks: arms bearing for, 148n, 61, 262–66; civil rights for, 260–61; and First Amendment rights, 161, 237–38, 241–42, 245–46, 253; and jury trial, 161, 269–74; and militias, 258–59; political rights for, 213n, 273–74. *See also* Slavery

Blackstone, William, 110, 147, 178, 211, 226; on arms bearing, 148, 261–62; on assembly, 28, 232; and common-law rights, 195n, 197; on double-jeopardy, 96; on establishment, 252–53; on freedom of the press, 232; on jury trial, 96, 115, 269; on just compensation, 77; on petition, 31–32, 232; on privileges and immunities, 169; on public trial, 112, 115; and symmetry principle, 116; on witness testimony, 113, 115

Blaine Amendment, 254–55n

Bloody Assizes, 87, 109

Bloom v. Illinois, 289n

Booth, In re, 201, 270n

Boston Massacre, 106, 113

Boston Quartering Act. *See* Quartering Act of 1774

Boudinot, Elias, 35

Bowling, Kenneth R., 304

Bradley, Joseph, 176, 209–12, 226–27, 278, 281n, 287

Brandeis, Louis, 21

Brennan, William, 138, 243, 266; selective incorporation approach of, xiv, 139–40, 214, 219–20, 222

Brewer, David, 213, 228

Browning, Orville H., 199, 372n.71

Brown v. Board of Education, 3–4

Bunker Hill, xvi, 1, 50. *See also* Lexington and Concord

Butler, Benjamin, 168

Cain, Richard H., 264

Calhoun, John C., 6

Callan v. Wilson, 105

Callender, James, 98, 100, 236–37, 244

Camden, Lord (Charles Pratt), 66–67, 74, 75–76, 161

Campbell v. Georgia, 154, 165, 169, 171, 276

Capitation clause, 180, 219

Cardozo, Francis L., 264

Champion v. Ames, 52

Chase, Salmon P., 162, 270

Chase, Samuel, 75, 98, 99, 101, 102

Choper, Jesse, 128–29

Citizenship: as birthright of all, including blacks and women, 171n, 196n, 216, 217–18n, 260, 281–82, 294; interstate, 176, 218n, 235, 253, 261, 271; national, 278; privileges and immunities related to, 169–71, 181–86, 196n, 281–82; relation to equality, 254, 281–82

Civil Rights Act of *1866*, 162, 169, 172, 178, 178–79n; and arms bearing, 260, 264–65; and Bill of Rights, 193–97; and common-law rights, 197, 226, 261; and free expression, 235; and jury trial, 245, 271; and political rights, 217n

Civil Rights Act of *1875*, 256, 273

Civil Rights Cases, 282

Civil rights–political rights distinction, 48–49, 216–18, 246, 258–61, 271–74

Civil War: and abolition, 162; draft in, 58n; relation to secession, 6, 103

Clarke, Sidney, 192, 258, 259

Cogan, Neil, 304

Coke, Edward, 109, 111, 200–201

Colfax, Schuyler, 236

Colonial period: judges in, 109; juries in, 24, 74, 84–85, 109–10, 277; press freedom in, 24; states'-rights roots in, 5, 158. *See also specific events, persons, places*

Colorado draft constitution, 249

Comity clause, 176–77, 218n, 253, 261, 271, 278

Common-law rights, 195n; adaptation of, 223–24; and declaratory theory, 147–48, 155; due process, 200–201; freedom of expression, 223–24, 232; and privileges and immunities, 169, 177–79, 197, 208, 211, 225; self-incrimination, 230; sources of, 147, 154–55, 169

Compulsory-process clause, 114–18, 278–79

Concord. *See* Lexington and Concord

Confrontation clause, 114–18, 278–79

Congress: enumerated powers of, 36–41, 42, 123–24, 125, 233–34; First, 8, 14–15, 16, 17, 18, 20, 28, 33, 35, 51, 129, 247; First Amendment limits on, 21–22, 140, 143, 146, 165, 232–34, 250; growth in membership, 156–57; military powers of, 36, 53–62; representation and size in, 10–17, 29, 36, 203; salaries in, 17–19, 36, 85; speech freedom in, 24–25. *See also* Federalism; Reconstruction Congress

Conscription. *See* Draft

Constitutional Convention, 17, 83, 88, 117; secrecy surrounding, 204; Washington's address to, 12–13

Constitutions, state. *See* State constitutions

Continental Congress, 30, 83

Contracts clause, 78–79, 141n, 164

Cooley, Thomas, 249, 253–54, 282

Corbin, Daniel, 210

Corfield v. Coryell, 176–78, 185, 209, 211, 212, 226, 306

"Cornelius," 19n

Cottrol, Bob, 303

Counsel, right of, 114–18, 278–79

Courts. *See* Fifth Amendment; Judges; Jury trial; Sixth Amendment; *specific cases*

Coxe, Tench, 52, 328–29n.5

Crandall, Prudence, 241

Crescent City Live-stock Case, 209, 210

Cress, Lawrence, 64–65

Crosskey, William Winslow, 138, 204, 303, 354n.37

Curtis, Michael Kent, 162, 166–67, 197, 204, 303

Dartmouth College v. Woodward, 141n, 206, 282

Davis, Jefferson, 6, 7

Declaration of Independence: and declaratory theory, 153; and judicial independence, 109; and jury trial, 83; and military, 60–61; and mock trial, 106–7; and parliamentary jurisdiction, 109; and property, 79; and right to alter or abolish government, 47, 122, 298–99; symbolism of, 153, 190, 370n.36; and writs of assistance, 66n

Declaration of Rights (First Continental Congress, 1774), 30, 83, 131–32

Declaration of the Causes and Necessity of Taking up Arms (Second Continental Congress, 1775), 83, 167, 333n.55

Declaratory theory, 147–56, 161n, 208, 210
De Large, Robert C., 264
Delaware: and congressional size, 16–17
Delaware Constitution, military issues in, 60
Deuteronomy. *See* Bible
Double-jeopardy clause, 96–97, 114, 116, 125, 145–47, 159, 166
Douglas, William O., 62, 289
Douglass, Frederick, 236, 237, 293
Draft, 53–59, 61
Dred Scott v. Sanford, 169, 170–72, 176, 182, 205, 250, 261, 263, 290, 306, 365n.42
Du Bois, W. E. B., 242, 303
Due-process clause, 146, 181; and *Dred Scott* decision, 170–71, 182, 205, 250, 290, 365n.42; and equal protection, 182, 282–83; and grand-jury rule, 97, 173–74, 200–202, 226–27, 269; and just compensation, 78; and *Murray's Lessee*, 173, 201–2, 278; and privileges-or-immunities clause, 172
Duncan v. Louisiana, 138–39, 289
Dunning, William, 302

Education: as guardian of rights, 131–33; and religious establishment, 44–45
Eighth Amendment, 140, 145; connection to First Amendment, 82–83; and jury trial, 82, 87, 96, 125; and punitive practices, 82, 87, 150, 161, 279–80
Elections: of *1800*, 23; of *1816*, 19, 23, 31; of *1874*, 318n.64
Eleventh Amendment, 124n
Eliot, Thomas, 258, 259
Ellsworth, Oliver, 36
Ely, John Hart, 138, 172, 364–65n.42
Enforcement Act, 208–9
English Bill of Rights of *1689*, 24–25, 31, 60, 61, 87, 109, 128, 147, 148, 154–55, 169

English law: and arms bearing, 264; and assembly rights, 28; and judges, 87, 109; and petition rights, 31–32; and public trial, 111; and punishment, 82; and quartering, 60, 61; and religion, 253; and search and seizure, 65–67, 70–71n, 75–76; and self-incrimination, 82–83; and speech freedom, 24–25; and treason, 117. *See also* Common-law rights
Entick v. Carrington, 66n, 75–76
Equal-protection clause, 23, 129, 163, 182, 254, 268, 281, 282–83
Establishment clause, 227; and education, 44–45; and federalism, 32–35, 40, 246–54; incorporation of, 41–42, 180, 219, 221, 246–54; and territorial expansion, 247–51. *See also* First Amendment
Exclusionary rule, xi, 98, 342n.63
Ex parte Burford, 284–85
Ex parte Siebold, 287

Fairman, Charles, 183, 187, 212, 303; anachronistic views of, 191, 200, 202; anti-incorporation evidence of, 193, 197–99; and fundamental rights, 188, 189; on *Twitchell* decision, 206–7; unfairness of, 188n
Farrar, Timothy, 210, 287
Federal Farmer, 93, 94–95, 103, 107
Federalism: and *Barron*, 128–29, 140, 144; and enumerated powers, 36–41, 42, 53–57, 123–24; and establishment clause, 32–35, 40, 246–54; and incorporation, 179–80, 193, 215–23; and juries, 88–93, 105–6, 110, 193, 274–76; and liberty, 4–7, 24–25, 45, 123, 129–29, 158–62; and militia organization, 50–59, 258; and press and speech freedoms, 36–41, 232–34; and search and seizure, 76; and

Federalism (*continued*)
    takings, 78–80. *See also* Comity clause;
    Congress; States' rights
Federalist, 12, 52; No. *1*, 10; No. *2*, 9; Nos.
    3–9, 9; No. *9*, 95; No. *10*, 4, 9, 11, 21, 29,
    78, 79n, 159, 244, 291; No. *14*, 9–10; No.
    23, 14; No. *28*, 50; No. *32*, 14; No. *38*,
    127; No. *46*, 4, 50; No. *51*, xii–xiii, 21,
    79, 129, 237; No. *55*, 16; No. *63*, 315n.22,
    323n.49; No. *78*, 122; No. *83*, 89–90, 141,
    164; No. *84*, 120, 127, 167
Federalists: and compromises with Anti-
    Federalists, 14n, 27, 92, 144, 302; and
    instruction rights, 29; and nationalist
    tradition, 4, 110; and national size,
    9–10; and press and religious freedoms,
    36; and property protection, 78–79; in
    state ratifying conventions, 204
Field, Stephen Johnson, 212, 213, 228, 229,
    272
Fifteenth Amendment, 48n, 213n, 273–74,
    297
Fifth Amendment: and symmetry princi-
    ple, 116. *See also specific clauses*
First Amendment: congress-limiting
    protections of, 21–22, 140, 143, 146, 165,
    232–34, 250; connection to Eighth
    Amendment, 82–83; declaratory theory
    of, 149, 150; expressive rights, 20–32,
    39–41, 231–46; and federalism, 6, 35–43,
    124, 125, 232–34; firstness of, 3, 8, 257;
    incorporation of, 23–25, 32, 33–34,
    41–42, 43–44, 180, 219, 221, 231–57,
    290–91; individual rights perspective
    on, 21, 24, 25–26, 236–37, 242–44, 246,
    256; libertarian reading of, 35, 239, 256;
    and majoritarianism, 21–23, 26, 29, 256;
    and paper searches, 76; and popular
    sovereignty, 25, 26–28, 30–32, 46–47,
    125, 168n, 223–24, 244–45; populist roots

of, 23; and religious rights, 32–45,
    246–57. *See also* Assembly clause; Es-
    tablishment clause; Free-exercise
    clause; Press, freedom of; Speech, free-
    dom of
First Amendment, original, 8–17, 36, 97,
    106
Fletcher v. Peck, 141n, 164, 206
Foner, Eric, 213n, 303
Fourteenth Amendment: analogy with
    Constitution, 202–4; approaches to in-
    corporation, xiii–xv, 139–40, 219–23;
    and birthright citizenship, 171n, 216,
    217–18n, 281–82, 294; and civil
    rights–political rights distinction,
    216–18, 246, 258–61, 271–74; critics of
    incorporation, 187–89, 191, 193–202;
    early interpretations of, 206–14; En-
    forcement Act, 208–9; incorporation
    reading of, 163–74; legislative history
    of, 181–87; and minority rights, xii, 7,
    23, 24, 32, 73, 124, 160, 215–16, 237,
    242–44, 256, 291; and national citizen-
    ship, 278; and privacy, 43–44, 62, 216,
    255–56, 259, 263, 265–68; ratification de-
    bates on, 197–206; structural provisions
    of, 203; and women's movement,
    260–61n. *See also* Incorporation; Re-
    fined incorporation model; *specific
    clauses*
Fourteenth Amendment, original (pro-
    posed by First House, failed in Sen-
    ate), 22, 38, 78, 79, 83, 143–44, 164, 291
Fourth Amendment: collective language
    in, 64–65, 73; connection to First
    Amendment, 75–76; connection to
    Seventh Amendment, 68–76, 80, 91,
    125; connection to takings clause, 80;
    connection to Third Amendment, 62;
    and federalism, 76, 123; incorporation

of, 267–68; and individual rights, 67–68, 114. *See also* Searches and seizures

Fox v. Ohio, 285

Frankfurter, Felix, 138; fundamental fairness doctrine of, xiv, 188, 199, 212–14, 222, 225; on grand-jury rule, 371n.69; on *Twitchell* decision, 206–7

Freedman's Bureau Act, 196n, 235, 260, 261

Free-exercise clause, 35, 39–40, 42–44, 229, 250, 254–56. *See also* First Amendment

Free-press clause. *See* Press, freedom of

Free-speech clause. *See* Speech, freedom of

Friendly, Henry, 137, 138

Fugitive Slave Act, 201, 270, 270–71n, 276, 278–79

Fugitive slaves, 160, 161, 162, 175, 201, 270, 270–71n

Fundamental fairness doctrine, xiv, 188, 199, 214, 222, 225

Georgia Constitution: and jury trial, 101–2; and religious establishment, 33

Georgia Supreme Court, 154–55, 161n. *See also* Lumpkin, Joseph Henry

Gerry, Elbridge, 51, 66n, 240, 257–58, 332nn.32,37

Gibbs, Jonathan C., 264

Gideon v. Wainwright, 138

Glorious Revolution of *1688*, 60, 109

Gorham, Nathaniel, 13

Graham, Howard J., 303

Grand jury, 84–86, 97, 198–202, 220, 269, 277, 307

Grinnell, Josiah, 258, 265

Griswold, Erwin, 138, 139

Griswold v. Connecticut, 62

Gruber, Jacob, 238

Guminski, Arnold, 168n

Guns. *See* Arms bearing

Habeas clause, 175–76, 179–80, 211, 212, 227, 297

Hale, Matthew, 112

Hale, Robert, 182, 286

Halifax, Lord, 72

Hamilton, Alexander, 4, 9, 36, 141; on congressional size, 12, 14; on jury trial, 89–90, 92, 343n.78; on militia, 56; on nonfederal regime, 50; on object of bill of rights, 127, 167; on popular sovereignty, 120, 122. See also *Federalist*

Hammond, Ann Eliza, 241

Hampden, 74, 95

Harlan, John Marshall (elder), 108, 213, 214, 228, 229–30, 277, 282, 283n, 288, 307

Harrison, John, 178

Hart, Roswell, 192, 258, 259

Hartford convention, 58, 123

Hartz, Louis, 302

Harvard College, 44

Hawles, John, 113

Henderson, John B., 171, 189, 245

Henkin, Louis, 138, 170, 171–72

Henry, Patrick: on arms bearing, 47–48, 257–58; on congressional size, 12, 16, 157; as orator, 66n, 293; on popular maxims, 131–32; on standing army, 60–61; as Virginian, 14, 158

Higginson, Stephen, 31

Hoar, Samuel, 236, 237, 240, 261, 263, 271, 301

Hohfeld, Wesley, 151–52

Holmes, Oliver Wendell, 4, 21

Holmes v. Jennison, 153, 189, 286

House of Burgesses, 5, 158

Howard, Jacob, 187, 204, 226, 258, 259, 268, 286; on privileges and immunities, 171, 172–73, 178, 185–86, 188, 189

Hurtado v. California, 277

Hyman, Harold, 303

Impressment, military, 53, 79–80, 330–31n.28

Incorporation, xiii–xiv, 7, 129; critics of, 187–89, 191, 193–202; debate over, 137–40; mechanical, 174–80; reverse, 281–83; selective model of, xiv, 139–40, 214, 219–20, 222–23; technical objections to, 170–74; total model of, xiv, 139, 172, 214, 219, 222; and watering down, 289–90. *See also* Fourteenth Amendment; Privileges-or-immunities clause; Refined incorporation model; *specific rights*

Instruction rights, 28–29

Iowa Constitution, religious freedom in, 249

Iredell, James, 36, 90n, 101

Jackson, James, 27

Jackson, Robert, 257

Jay, John, 9, 80. See also *Federalist*

Jefferson, Thomas, 79; and education, 132; and election of *1800*, 6, 23, 99, 132; and First Amendment federalism, 6, 34–35, 39–40; on juries, 101–3, 130–31; and legislative rotation, 95–96; and rights of the people, 102, 122, 126, 131; as slaveowner, 293; as Virginian, 158

Jeffreys, George, 87, 279

Johnson, Andrew, 204

Johnson, Reverdy, 208

Johnson, William, 145, 146, 167

Joint Committee on Reconstruction, 187, 204, 241

Jones v. Robbins, 201

Jones v. Van Zandt, 162

Judges, 305–6, 307; distrust of, 69–70, 74–75, 82, 84, 87, 100, 109–10, 112–14, 124n, 130–31, 347n.119; and exclusionary rule, xi, 97–98, 342n.63; as guardians and educators, 4, 24, 93, 97–98, 129–30, 205–6, 242–44, 290–91

Judicial review, 4, 98–102, 129–30, 205

Judiciary Act of *1789,* 89, 101

Julian, George, 258

Jury nullification, 98, 103–4, 110, 272

Jury trial: and abolitionism, 269–71; amendments guaranteeing, 81–83, 96–97, 167; and Article III mandate, 83, 104–8, 227; and blacks, 271–74; centrality of, 83, 96–98, 108–10; in colonial period, 24, 74, 84–85, 109–10, 277; and double-jeopardy clause, 96–97, 125; and due-process clause, 97, 173–74, 200–202, 220, 226–27, 269; and federalism, 69, 76, 88–93, 197, 103, 105–6, 110, 275–76; grand jury, 84–86, 97, 198–200, 202, 220, 269, 277, 307; as guardian of rights, 23–24, 70–71n, 74–75, 83–88, 100, 109–10, 130–31, 242–44, 270–74; incorporation of, 269–78; and judge's instructions, 93–94, 101–2; and minority protection, 23–24, 242–44, 271–74; as political participation, 11, 48–49, 94–96, 217–18n, 261, 271–74; and populism, 83–88; and press freedom, 23–24, 72n, 75, 84–85, 88, 242–44, 320n.21; as privilege, 167, 200, 226–28, 269; review, 87–88, 98–104; rotating service in, 95–96; in search-and-seizure cases, 68–76, 80, 87–88, 91, 125; security against corruption in, 113–14; state-law approach to, 89–93, 222, 275–76; waivability of, 104–8, 112; witness testimony in, 113, 115; and women, 48–49, 217–18n, 260, 271, 273–74. *See also* Seventh Amendment; Sixth Amendment

Just-compensation clause. *See* Takings clause

Kasson, John, 240

Kelley, William D., 240

Kent, James, 101, 201

Kentucky Resolutions, 5–6, 25, 39–40, 56, 58, 123, 158

Kenyon, Cecelia, 302

Kerr, Michael, 286

King, Martin Luther, Jr., 243

Kurland, Philip, 304

Lash, Kurt T., 254–55n, 256

Lasson, Nelson B., 66n

Lawrence, Matilda, 270, 271

Lawrence, William, 241, 286

Legal Tender Cases, 287

Lerner, Ralph, 93, 304

Levy, Leonard, 83, 223

Lexington and Concord, 50, 55n, 258, 262, 266, 301. *See also* Bunker Hill

Libel cases: juries in, 23–24, 72n, 75, 84–85, 88, 242–44, 320n.21

Lincoln, Abraham, 48n, 190, 239

Livermore, Samuel, 33

Livingston, Gilbert, 11–12, 96

Livingston v. Moore, 182–83

Lochner v. New York, 178

Locke, John, 47

Lovejoy, Elijah, 237

Lovejoy, Owen, 239

Loyal Georgian, 265

Lumpkin, Joseph Henry, 165, 276; on arms bearing, 154, 263; on citizen rights, 154–55, 169, 171; common-law and declaratory approach of, 154–55, 177, 189; on religious establishment, 251

McBride, Jesse, 238–39

McConnell, Michael W., 79, 327n.96

McCoy, James, 199

McCulloch v. Maryland, 37, 42, 57, 212

Madison, James: as ahead of his time, 22–23, 159, 268, 291; and collective rights, 65; and congressional representation, 10, 12, 16, 29, 244; and education, 131, 132, 350–51n.40; and enumerated power, 36, 40–41; and establishment clause, 31, 40, 291; and instruction rights, 29; and judicial review, 129–30; and militia organization, 50; and minority rights, xii–xiii, 21–22, 79n, 159–60, 237; and nationalist tradition, 4, 79n; and national size, 9–10; petition of, 31; on popular enforcement and popular sovereignty, 129–30, 132, 224; and press and speech freedom, 22, 40, 377n.19; proposed amendments of, 16, 17, 22, 27–28, 29, 37, 38, 39, 78, 79, 83, 143–44, 164, 291, 292; as slaveowner, 293; and states' rights, 4, 6, 88, 127; and takings clause, 77–78, 268; as Virginian, 14, 158. See also *Federalist*

Magna Charta, 147, 154–55, 169, 200, 201, 202, 211, 269, 287, 389n.149

Maier, Pauline, 302

Mann, Horace, 270

Mapp v. Ohio, 138

Marbury v. Madison, 99, 100, 139, 205

Marcus, Maeva, 304

Marshall, John, 139, 284; and *Barron* rule, 33, 140–44, 146, 152, 154, 165; *Fletcher v. Peck,* 141n, 164, 206; *McCulloch v. Maryland,* 37–38, 57; on popular maxims, 131–32

Martin, Luther, 75, 126

Maryland Constitution, 169; and military issues, 60; and religious establishment, 33

Maryland Farmer, 74–75, 94, 100

Maryland ratifying convention, 60, 74, 75, 97

Mason, George, 83, 126, 257–58

Massachusetts Constitution: and assembly rights, 28–29; and excessive fines, bails, and punishments, 87; and grand jury, 201; and military issues, 60; and popular enforcement and education, 44, 133; and property protection, 79; and religious establishment, 32, 44, 45, 251–52; and search and seizure, 65, 67

Massachusetts ratifying convention, 14, 100, 204

Mather, Moses, 132

Maxwell v. Dow, 229–30, 288

Memorial and Remonstrance Against Religious Assessments, 31

Military: civilian control over, 55, 60; and draft, 53–59, 61; impressment, 53, 79–80, 330–31n.28; as mercenary force, 53; national army, 331n.31; quartering of, 59–61, 267; standing army, 11, 51, 53–59, 60–61, 84, 123, 216, 258. *See also* Arms bearing; Militia

Militia: and draft, 53–59, 61; as akin to jury, 48–49, 84, 88–89, 97, 217–18n, 258–61; localism in, 5, 50–59, 88–89, 123, 216, 258; modern meaning of, 51; Reconstruction, 258, 259; in revolutionary period, xvi, 1, 5, 50–51, 55n, 258, 262, 266, 301; social aspects of, 55n; *vs.* standing army, xvi, 1, 50–60, 84, 97, 123, 216, 258; state regulation of, 50, 52–59, 151; suffrage for, 48n, 218n; "well-regulated", 52, 56. *See also* Second Amendment

Mill, John Stuart, 160

Miller, Samuel (Rev.), 35

Miller, Samuel F., 175, 176, 212, 213, 288

Minutemen. *See* Bunker Hill; Lexington and Concord

Miranda v. Arizona, 138

Monaghan, Henry P., 243

Moulton, Samuel, 192

Murray's Lessee v. Hoboken Land & Improvement Co., 173, 176, 201–2, 278, 306

Myers, Leonard, 193, 258

National Guard, 51

Nationalist tradition, 3–4

National Rifle Association, 266

Necessary-and-proper clause, 37, 39, 40, 42, 56–57

Negative-implication theory, 146–47, 149–50, 154, 165

New Deal Amendment, 300

New Hampshire Constitution: and assembly rights, 29; and excessive fines, bails, and punishments, 87; and military issues, 60; and religious establishment, 32, 33; and right of revolution, 58, 131n; and search and seizure, 65

New Hampshire ratifying convention, 14, 60

New York Evening Post, 245, 265

New York Herald, 187

New York ratifying convention, 11, 14, 18, 29, 60, 65, 96, 122, 126, 204

New York Times, 187, 265

New York Times v. Sullivan, 23, 59, 138, 243, 266, 307

Nineteenth Amendment, 274, 300

Ninth Amendment: declaratory reading, 149; and federalism, 123–24, 125, 180, 226; and nondisparagement, 105, 111; and popular sovereignty, 64, 111,

120–22, 124, 125, 149; unenumerated
rights of, 280–81, 298
Nisbet, Eugenius, 155–56n
North Carolina Constitution: and assem-
bly rights, 28
North Carolina ratifying convention, 14,
18, 29, 60, 65, 92, 204
Northwest Ordinance of *1787*, 44, 158,
247, 250
Nunn v. Georgia, 154, 171, 263
Nye, James, 192, 258, 259, 265, 281

Ohio: as former territory, 158; as modal
and model state, 252
O'Neil v. Vermont, 213–14
Ordered liberty. *See* Fundamental fairness
doctrine
Otis, James, 66n

Parham v. The Justices, 155n
Parsons, Theophilus, 100
Patton v. United States, 104–5, 107, 108
Peace of Augsburg, 34
Pendleton, Edmund, 26–27, 28, 47
Pennsylvania Constitution: and assembly
rights, 28; and search and seizure, 65;
and speech freedom, 321n.25
Pennsylvania ratifying convention, 74
Petition rights, 19, 30–32, 86, 161, 174, 212,
235, 241–42, 244–46. *See also* First
Amendment
Philadelphia convention. *See* Constitu-
tional Convention
*Philadelphia North American and United
States Gazette*, 235
Pinckney, Charles, 36
Pinckney, Charles Cotesworth, 36,
293–94
Plessy v. Ferguson, 282
Pocock, J. G. A., 302

Political rights. *See* Civil rights–political
rights distinction
Pomeroy, John Norton, 210, 287
Pomeroy, Samuel, 258, 259, 265
Popular sovereignty: in Declaration of
Independence, 47, 122, 298–99; and enforcement of rights, 23, 47–48, 73, 80,
83–88, 98–104, 129–33; in First Amendment, 25n, 26–28, 223–24; in Fourth
Amendment, 64–65, 73; and jury system, 11, 83–88, 130–31, 271–74, 277; in
Ninth and Tenth Amendments,
119–22, 124; in Preamble, 27–28, 47, 49,
64, 120, 121; in Second Amendment,
46–50; in state constitutions, 64–65
Pratt, Charles. *See* Camden, Lord
Preamble, and popular sovereignty,
27–28, 47, 49, 64, 120, 121
Press, freedom of, 20–21; common law
meaning of, 23–24, 223–24; and federalism, 39–41; and Federalists, 36; incorporation of, 22–23, 226–27, 231–44; and
juries, 23–24, 72n, 75, 84–85, 88, 242–44,
320n.21; Madison's proposal for, 22–23;
and religious freedom, 239; and slave
system, 159, 160–61, 234–42. *See also*
First Amendment
Prigg v. Pennsylvania, 270
Prior restraint: and First Amendment, 23,
24, 97, 223–24; and Fourth Amendment, 71–72
Privacy rights, 43–44, 62, 216, 255–56, 259,
263, 265–68
Privileges-or-immunities clause, xiv–xv,
23, 32; and alien rights, 170, 364n.39,
364–65n.42; Bingham's description of,
182–83; and citizenship, 169–71, 181–86,
196n, 281–82; and comity clause,
176–77, 217–18n, 235, 253, 261, 271, 278;
common-law approach to, 169, 177–79,

Privileges-or-immunities clause
(*continued*)
197, 208, 211, 225; and due process,
171–74; and habeas clause, 175–77,
179–80, 211, 212, 227; link to Bill of
Rights, 183–85; and *Maxwell v. Dow*,
229–30; and reverse incorporation,
281–82; and *Slaughter-House Cases*, 212,
213, 226–27; and *Spies v. Illinois*,
227–28; and *Twining v. New Jersey*,
230; wording of, 163–71, 180. *See also*
Fourteenth Amendment
Probable-cause, 68, 70, 71, 84
Property rights, 77–80, 268–69, 291
Prynne, William, 82, 87
Public trial, 104, 111–14, 117
Punishment, 82, 87, 150, 161, 279

Quartering, 59–61, 267
Quartering Act of *1774*, 59, 301

Raleigh, Walter, 109, 117
Randolph, Edmund, 36, 90n
Ransier, Alonzo, 264
Rawle, William, 145, 146, 147–48, 152, 165,
173, 175, 177, 275
Raymond, Henry, 258, 259, 265
Reasonableness requirement, 68, 76, 88,
101
Reconstruction Amendment. *See* Fourteenth Amendment; Privileges-or-immunities clause
Reconstruction Congress: and arms bearing, 258, 259–62, 264–65; Bill of Rights
terminology in, 286–87; Civil Rights
bill in, 162, 169, 172, 177–78, 193–97,
217n, 226, 235, 260–61, 264–65, 271–72;
and First Amendment rights, 235–36,
237–38, 240–42, 245, 254–56; Fourteenth
Amendment in, 181–97; and jury
rights, 217–18n, 271, 273; and women's

suffrage, 216–18, 240, 245, 260, 261–61n
Refined incorporation model, xiv–xv, 140,
180, 187; and arms bearing, 257–66;
common law filter for, 197, 211, 225,
227–30; and expressive freedoms,
231–46; historical roots of, 225–30; and
jury rights, 269–77; private rights filter
for, 221, 225; and religious freedom,
246–57; and search and seizure, 267–68;
in territorial debate, 277–78
Reid v. Covert, 277
Reinstein, Robert, 290, 357n.71, 361n.9,
369n.19
Religious freedom: and blacks, 161,
237–38, 241, 245–46, 253, 256; and
Blaine Amendment, 254–55n; and free-
exercise clause, 35, 39–40, 42–44, 226,
229, 250, 254–56; of speech, 237–39; and
women, 239–41. *See also* Establishment
clause; First Amendment
Report of 1800, 4, 40
Representation, congressional, 8–17, 29,
36, 203
Republican-government clause, 22, 41,
112, 159, 192–93, 232, 297, 327n.95
Reverse incorporation, 281–83
Rhode Island: and congressional representation, 10; ratifying convention, 29,
60
Rogers, Andrew Jackson, 173, 287
Rubenfeld, Jed, 80, 301
Rules of Decision Act, 89

Schnapper, Eric, 75–76
Schwartz, Bernard, 304
Scriptures. *See* Bible
Searches and seizures: of blacks, 161, 268,
301; in English law, 65–67, 70–71n;
jury's role in, 68–76, 80, 87–88, 91, 125;
paper searches, 75–76, 161; and probable cause, 68, 70, 71; reasonableness re-

quirement of, 68, 76, 88, 101; in state constitutions, 65; for stolen goods, 72, 74; and warrant clause, 68–73, 84, 129, 140; warrantless, 71, 73; writs of assistance case, 66n. *See also* Fourth Amendment

Second Amendment: and Federalism, 50–59, 258; incorporation of, 147–48, 216–18, 220–23; and populism, 46–50; preamble to, 47, 147–48. *See also* Arms bearing; Militia

Second Amendment, original, 17–19, 36, 97

Sedition Act of *1798*, 23, 98–103, 132, 158, 290, 305, 307. *See also* Alien and Sedition Acts

Seizures. *See* Searches and seizures

Selective Draft Law Cases, 58–59, 306

Selective incorporation model, xiv, 139–40, 222–23

Self-incrimination clause, 82–83, 116, 166, 230

Seneca Falls Declaration, 261n

Seventeenth Amendment, 300

Seventh Amendment: connection to First Amendment, 23–24, 75, 87–88, 242–44; connection to Fourth Amendment, 68–76, 80, 87–88, 91, 125; connection to takings clause, 80, 88; and incorporation, 92, 222, 275–76; and state-law approach, 89–93. *See also* Jury trial

Shaw, Lemuel, 149n, 200

Sherman, John, 208, 281

Sherman, Roger, 16, 27–28, 36, 90n, 236, 240, 332n.32

Sidney, Algernon, 109

Sixteenth Amendment, 300

Sixth Amendment: and autonomy principle, 114–15; connection to Fifth Amendment, 114, 116; connection to

treason clause, 117–18; and incorporation, 269–75, 278–79, 289–90; and symmetry principle, 116; and truth seeking, 115–16. *See also* Jury trial; *specific clauses*

Slaughter-House Cases, 175, 176, 210–13, 226–27, 278, 288n, 306

Slavery: and civil liberties, 160–62, 192, 205, 234–35, 236, 254, 256, 258, 262, 264, 267, 269–72, 278–79; in territories, 250, 252. *See also* Abolitionism; Blacks; Fugitive slaves

Smith, Adam, 55

Smith, Melancton, 14

Smith, Mrs. Gerrit, 245

South Carolina Constitution, and religious establishment, 33

South Carolina ratifying convention, 14

Spaight, Richard Dobbs, 36

Sparf and Hansen v. United States, 103

Speech, freedom of, 20–22, 149; of blacks, 237–38, 241–42; in common law, 224; incorporation of, 23, 222, 226–27, 231–44; for legislators, 24–25, 125, 224; religious, 237–39; of women, 239–41. *See also* First Amendment

Spencer, Ambrose, 146, 149n

Spies v. Illinois, 213, 227–28

Stampp, Kenneth, 303

Stanbery, Henry, 146–47

Stanton, Elizabeth Cady, 240, 261n

Star Chamber, 82, 109, 111

State constitutions: assembly rights in, 28–29, 30; baby Ninth Amendments of, 124, 280; general importance of, 29n; jury trial in, 83, 92; military issues in, 52, 60, 61; popular maxims in, 131–32, 133; and popular sovereignty, 64–65; and press freedom, 39, 239; and religious establishment, 32–33, 249, 251; search-and-seizure clauses of, 65. *See also specific states*

States' rights: foundations of, 4–6; and jury trial, 88–93, 276; Madison's limits on, 6, 143–44; and military power, 50–53, 54, 332n.32; and religious establishment, 34–35; in twentieth century, 6–7. *See also* Federalism

Stephens, Alexander, 6

Stevens, Thaddeus, 6, 185, 187, 203, 204

Stewart, Alvan, 201

Storing, Herbert J., 94, 302

Story, Joseph, 33, 97, 106, 111, 145–46, 200–201, 252n

Stowe, Harriet Beecher, 236, 237, 293

Strauder v. West Virginia, 272–73

Stuntz, William J., 75–76

Suffrage: and arms bearing, 48–49n, 218n; black, 213n, 273–74, 297; women's, 48n, 240, 245, 260–61n, 274, 297, 300. *See also* Civil rights–political rights distinction

Sumner, Charles, 241, 245, 258, 270–71, 379n.8

Supremacy clause, 22

Supreme Court, U.S. *See specific cases*

Swayne, Justice, 212

Takings clause, 77–80, 88, 123, 140–42, 149n, 150n, 155n, 181, 268–69

Taney, Roger B., 58n, 238, 250, 263, 306

Taylor, John, 95, 100

TenBroek, Jacobus, 201, 245, 303

Tenth Amendment, 9, 14, 51, 149; and federalism, 6, 123, 124; and incorporation, xiv, 34, 180, 219, 226, 280; and popular-sovereignty, 64, 119–22, 124, 125

Territories. *See* Bill of Rights, in territories

Texas Constitution, 169

Thayer, James B., 4

Third Amendment, 59–63, 220, 267

Thirteenth Amendment, 48n, 162, 175, 269, 297

Tiffany, Joel, 262–63

Tocqueville, Alexis de, 45; on jury trial, 88, 93–94, 95, 104, 274

Tompkins, Cydnor, 239, 279

Total incorporation model, xiv, 139, 172, 214, 219, 222

Treason Act of *1696*, 109, 116

Treason clause, 117, 125

Treaty of Westphalia, 34

Tredwell, Thomas, 126

Trumbull, Lyman, 253; on arms bearing, 258, 264–65; and Civil Rights Act, 177–78, 196n, 237–38, 261; on fundamental rights, 188

Tucker, John Randolph, 213–14, 227–28

Tucker, St. George, 32, 79, 264

Tucker, Thomas Tudor, 29, 35, 121

Turner, Nat, 241

Twelfth Amendment, 124–25n

Twenty-seventh Amendment, 17

Twining v. New Jersey, 230

Twitchell v. Pennsylvania, 206–7, 375n.116

Uncle Tom's Cabin (Stowe), 236, 239

Unenumerated rights, 280–81, 298–99

United States Reports, 138, 147, 257, 286

United States v. Callender, 98, 101, 103

United States v. Hall, 209

Utah Constitution, territorial, 249

Van Alstyne, William W., 137–38

VanderVelde, Lea, 303

Van Ness, C. P., 153, 189, 286

Veit, Helen E., 304

Vermont Constitution: assembly rights in, 28; speech freedom in, 25n

Vining, John, 16, 17

Virginia: Declaration of Rights, 131–32, 158; House of Burgesses, 5, 158; as modal and model state, 252; petitions in, 31; ratifying convention, 12, 14, 18, 26, 28, 39, 47–48, 60, 65, 92, 121–22, 204; Resolutions, 4, 5–6, 25, 40, 56, 57–58, 123, 158; states'-rights tradition in, 5, 158; supports original First Amendment, 14–15

Virginia Constitution, 284–85; speech freedom in, 238

Voting rights. *See* Suffrage

Warner, Hiram, 155n

War of *1812*, 57

Warrant clause, 68–73, 84, 129, 140

Warren, Charles, 66n

Warren, Mercy Otis, 66n, 240

Washington, Bushrod, 176–77, 178, 211

Washington, George, on congressional size and representation, 12–13

Webster, Daniel, 57, 131n, 282

Webster, Noah, 36

Whitehill, Robert, 74

Wiecek, William, 303

Wilkes, John, 66–67, 72, 74

Wilkes v. Wood, 65–67, 70–71n, 72, 76

Williamson, Hugh, 36

Wills, Garry, 29, 302

Wilson, Henry, 240

Wilson, James (Founder), 36, 90n; on grand jury, 85, 86; on jury review, 99–100, 101, 103; on popular sovereignty, 120–21

Wilson, James (Reconstructor), 187; on Bill of Rights, 183–84n, 196n, 286; and Civil Rights Act, 177–78, 196n, 261; on fundamental rights, 188; on privileges and immunities of citizens, 184–85

Wilson, Woodrow, 48n

Wirt, William, 98–99, 103

Withers v. Buckley, 285–86

Wolfram, Charles, 90n, 131n

Women: activism of, 239–41, 245–46, 257n, 260–61n, 293–94, 305; and arms bearing, 48–49, 259, 262–63; and expressive freedom, 239–41, 245–46; Fourteenth Amendment centrality of, 216–18, 239–41, 245–46, 260–61, 293–94; and religious freedom, 239–41; suffrage for, 48n, 240, 245, 260–61n, 274, 297, 300

Women's National Loyal League, 240

Wood, Gordon, 28, 29n, 30, 126, 132–33, 302, 321n.25

Woods, William, 209–10

Worth, Daniel, 239

Wright, Jonathan B., 264

Writs of assistance, 66n

Yoo, John Choon, 280

Youngstown Sheet & Tube Co. v. Sawyer, 62

Young v. McKenzie, 155n

Zenger, John Peter, 24, 84–85, 110, 236–37, 243, 244, 301

About the Author

Akhil Reed Amar received his B.A. from Yale College in 1980 and his J.D. from Yale Law School in 1984. After clerking for Judge Stephen Breyer, he joined the Yale Law School faculty in 1985, where he has served as Southmayd Professor of Law since 1993. In 1993 he received the Paul Bator award from the Federalist Society for Law and Public Policy, and in 1997 he was awarded an honorary doctorate of law by Suffolk University. He has delivered endowed lectures at more than a dozen universities and had written widely on constitutional issues for such publications as the *New York Times*, the *Washington Post*, the *Washington Monthly*, *Policy Review*, the *New Republic*, and *Slate*. He is the author of *The Consitution and Criminal Procedure: First Principles*, a coauthor (with Alan Hirsch) of *For the People*, and coeditor (with Paul Brest and Sanford Levinson) of *Processes of Constitutional Decisionmaking* (4th ed.).